Literature and
Its Times

VOLUME 1

Ancient Times to the
American and French Revolutions
(Prehistory–1790s)

Literature and Its Times

Profiles of 300 Notable Literary Works and the Historical Events that Influenced Them

Joyce Moss • George Wilson

DETROIT   NEW YORK   TORONTO   LONDON

Literature and Its Times

Profiles of 300 Notable Literary
Works and the Historical Events
that Influenced Them

VOLUME **1**

Ancient Times to the American and French Revolutions (prehistory-1790s)

JOYCE MOSS • GEORGE WILSON

STAFF

Jeff Hill and Lawrence J. Trudeau, *Production Editors*
Susan Trosky, *Permissions Manager*
Kimberly F. Smilay, *Permissions Specialist*

Mary Beth Trimper, *Production Director*
Evi Seoud, *Production Manager*
Shanna Heilveil, *Production Assistant*

Cynthia Baldwin, *Product Design Manager*
Mary Claire Krzewinski, *Senior Art Director*

Barbara J. Yarrow, *Graphic Services Supervisor*
Randy Bassett, *Image Database Supervisor*
Robert Duncan, *Scanner Operator*
Pamela Hayes, *Photography Coordinator*

ISBN 0-7876-0606-5 (Set)
ISBN 0-7876-0607-3 (Volume 1)

Printed in the United States of America
10 9 8 7 6 5 4 3 2

Library of Congress Cataloging-in-Publication Data

Literature and its times : profiles of 300 notable literary works and the historical events that influenced them / [edited by Joyce Moss and George Wilson].
      p.   cm.
  Includes bibliographical references and index.
  Contents: v. 1. Ancient times to the American and French Revolutions, (pre-history-1790s) -- v. 2. Civil wars to frontier societies (1800-1880s) -- v. 3. Growth of empires to the Great Depression (1890-1930s) -- v. 4. World War II to the affluent fifties (1940-1950s) -- v. 5. Civil rights movements to future times (1960-2000).
  ISBN 0-7876-0607-3 (vol. 1 : alk. paper). -- ISBN 0-7876-0608-1 (vol. 2 : alk. paper). -- ISBN 0-7876-0609-X (vol. 3 : alk. paper). -- ISBN 0-7876-0610-3 (vol. 4 : alk. paper). -- ISBN 0-7876-0611-1 (vol. 5 : alk. paper)
  1. Literature and history. 2. History in literature. 3. Literature--History and criticism.
I. Moss, Joyce, 1951- . II. Wilson, George, 1920- .
PN50.L574 1997
809'.93358--dc21

                            97-34339
                            CIP

Contents

Preface. . . . . *vii*

Acknowledgments . . . . *xi*

Introduction . . . . *xiii*

Chronology of Relevant Events . . . . *xv*

Contents by Title . . . . *xxiii*

Contents by Author. . . . . *xxv*

Photo Credits . . . . *xxvii*

Entries *1*

Index. 427

Preface

"Even a great writer can be bound by the prejudices of his time . . . we cannot place Shakespeare in a sealed container. He belonged to his time," notes Alexander Leggatt in his essay "*The Merchant of Venice*: A Modern Perspective" (William Shakespeare, *The Merchant of Venice* [New York: Washington Square Press, 1992], 217). This reasoning, applicable to any work and its author, explains why *Literature and Its Times* fixes a wide range of novels, short stories, biographies, speeches, poems, and plays in the context of their particular historical periods.

In the process, the relationship between fact and fantasy or invention becomes increasingly clear. The function of literature is not necessarily to represent history accurately. Many writers aim rather to spin a satisfying tale or perhaps to convey a certain vision or message. Nevertheless, the images created by a powerful literary work—be it the Greek poem *Iliad*, the Spanish novel *The Adventures of Don Quixote*, or the American play *The Crucible*—leave impressions that are commonly taken to be historical. This is true from works that depict earlier eras to ones that portray more modern occurrences, such as the world wars or race relations. The fourteenth-century poem *Inferno* from the *Divine Comedy* by Dante Alighieri is probably the most powerful example. So vividly does *Inferno* describe Hell that for more than two centuries people took its description as truth, going so far as to map Hell according to the details of the poem.

In taking literature as fact, then, one risks acquiring a mistaken or an unverified notion of history. Yet, by the same token, history can be very well informed by literary works. An author may portray events in a way that for the first time aptly captures the fears and challenges of a period, enabling readers to better understand it and their own place in the historical continuum. This is easily illustrated by tracing novels that feature women's issues, from Nathaniel Hawthorne's *The Scarlet Letter* (1640s setting) to Leo Tolstoy's *Anna Karenina* (1870s) to Alice Walker's *The Color Purple* (1920s–40s) and Amy Tan's *The Joy Luck Club* (1940s–80s).

Placing a given work in historical context involves pinpointing conditions in the society in which it was written as well as set. Stephen Crane's *Red Badge of Courage* is set in the early 1860s. Published three decades later, it was written in a different social context and, in this case, in response to a literary trend of Crane's own era. Only by gaining insight into this era as well as the one in which the work takes place can it be fully appreciated; *Literature and Its Times* therefore addresses the author's time frame too.

The task of reconstructing the historical contexts of a work can be problematic. There are stories—the tales of England's King Arthur, for example—that defy any attempt to fit them neatly into a particular time. Living in a later era, their authors, consciously or not, mixed events that actually belong to two or more different periods. In some cases, this is an innocent mistake by a writer who did not have the benefit of accurate sources. In other cases, fidelity to the actual events of the time is of little concern to the writer; his or her main interest is the fictional world to be portrayed. In still other cases, the mixture of times is intentional. Happily, present-day knowledge makes it possible for this series to begin unweaving the historical mixture in these types of works.

Literature and Its Times relates history to literature on a case-by-case basis, intending to help readers respond fully to a work and to assist them in distinguishing fact from invention in the work. The series engages in this mission with a warm appreciation for the beauty of literature independent of historical facts, but also with the belief that ultimate regard is shown for a literary work and its author by positioning it in the context of pertinent events.

Selection of Literary Works

Literature and Its Times includes novels, short stories, plays, poems, biographies, essays, speeches, and documents. The works chosen for inclusion have been carefully selected on the basis of how frequently they are studied and how closely they are tied to pivotal historical events. Reflected in the selection are works not only by classic and still widely read authors but also by noteworthy ethnic and female authors. To finalize the selection, the complete list of titles was submitted to a panel of librarians, secondary teachers, and college professors. Please see "Acknowledgments" for a specific listing of these reviewers.

Format and Arrangement of Entries

The five volumes of *Literature and Its Times* are arranged chronologically from ancient times to the present. The set of entries within each volume is arranged alphabetically by title. As the series progresses, the range of years covered in each successive volume grows narrower due to the increasing number of works published in more recent times.

Each entry is organized according to the following sections.

1. ***Introduction***—identifying information in three parts:

   The literary work—describes the genre, the time and place of the work, and the year(s) it was first performed or published;

   Synopsis—summarizes the storyline or contents;

   Introductory paragraph—introduces the literary work in relation to the author's life.

2. ***Events in History at the Time the Literary Work Takes Place***—describes social and political events that relate to the plot or contents of the literary work and that occurred during the period the story takes place. Subsections vary depending on the literary work. The section takes a deductive approach, starting with events in history and telescoping inward to events in the literary work.

3. ***The Literary Work in Focus***—describes in brief the plot or contents of the work. Generally this summary is followed by a subsection on one or more elements in the work that illuminate real events or attitudes of the period. The subsection takes an inductive approach, starting with the literary work and broadening outward to events in history. It is usually followed by a third subsection detailing the sources used by the author to create the work.

4. ***Events in History at the Time the Literary Work Was Written***—describes social, political, and/or literary events in the author's lifetime that relate to the plot or contents of the work. When relevant, the section includes events in the author's life. Also discussed in the section are the initial reviews or reception accorded to the literary work.

5. ***For More Information***—provides a list of all sources that have been cited in the entry as well as sources for further reading about the different issues or personalities featured in the entry.

If a literary work is set and written in the same time period, sections 2 and 4 of the entry on that work ("Events in History at the Time the Literary Work Takes Place" and "Events in History at the Time the Literary Work Was Written") are combined into the single section "Events in History at the Time of the Literary Work."

Additional Features

Whenever possible, primary source material is provided through quotations in the text and material in sidebars. There are also sidebars with historical details that amplify issues raised in the main text and with anecdotes that give readers a fuller understanding of the temporal context. Timelines appear in various entries to summarize intricate periods of history. To enrich and further clarify information, historically noteworthy illustrations have been included in the series. Maps as well as photographs provide visual images of potentially unfamiliar settings.

Comments and Suggestions

Your comments on this series and suggestions for future editions are welcome. Please write: Editors, *Literature and Its Times,* Gale Research, Inc., 835 Penobscot Building, Detroit, Michigan 48226-4094; or call toll-free: 1-800-877-4253.

Acknowledgments

For their careful review of entries in *Literature and Its Times*, the following professors and lecturers from the University of California at Los Angeles (UCLA) deserve the deepest appreciation:

English Department

Robert Aguirre
Martha Banta
Lynn Batten
A. R. Braunmuller
Daphne Brooks
King-Kok Cheung
Michael Colacurcio
Ed Condren
Jack Kolb
Jinqui Ling
Chris Mott
Michael North
Barbara Packer
David Rodes
Karen Rowe

Comparative Literature Department

Eric Gans
Kathryn King
Mary Kay Norseng
Ross Shideler

Slavic Languages and Literature Department

Micheal Heim
Peter Hodgson

Gratitude is also extended to professors from other institutions for their valuable review of selected entries, and to history department chairman Robert Sumpter for his guidance and reviews:

Rabbi Stanley Chyet, Hebrew Union College
Agnes Moreland Jackson, Pitzer College, English and Black Studies
Michael McGaha, Pomona College, Romance Languages and Literatures— Spanish Section
Robert Sumpter, Mira Costa High School, History Department

A host of contributers assisted in collecting and composing data for the entries in *Literature and Its Times*. Their painstaking hours of research and composition are deeply appreciated.

Diane R. Ahrens
Eric A. Besner
Suzanne C. Borghei
Luke Bresky
Anne Brooks
Corey Brettschneider
Thomas Cooper
Patricia Carroll
Terence Davis
Mark Druskoff
Shelby Fulmer
Betsy Hedberg-Keramidas

Acknowledgments

Ryan Hilbert
Lisa Gabbert
Anne Kim
Amy Merritt
Michael Le Sieur
Barbara A. Lozano
Michele Mednick
Michelle Miller
Larry Mowrey
Evan Porter
Edward R. O' Neill
David Riemer
Monica Riordan
Jane E. Roddy
George Ross
Rita Schepergerdes
Roberta Seid
Shira Tarrant
Benjamin Trefny
Pete Trujillo
Lorraine B. Valestuk
Colin Wells
Sandra Wade-Grusky
Allison Wiesz
Jeannie Wilkinson
Denise Wilson
Brandon Wilson
Antoine Wilson

A special thank you is extended to Lorraine B. Valestuk, Ph.D., for her refinement of data and to Cheryl Steets, Ph.D., for her deft copy editing. Anne Leach indexed the volumes with proficiency and literary sensitivity. The editors also thank Larry Trudeau and Jeff Hill of Gale Research for their careful editorial management.

Lastly the editors express gratitude to those who guided the final selection of literary works included in the series:

Neil Anstead, Director of Humanities,
  Los Angeles Unified School District

William Balcolm, Librarian,
  Villa Park Public Library, Villa Park, IL

Marth Banta, Professor,
  University of California at Los Angeles

Carol Clark, Head Librarian,
  Robert E. Lee High School, Springfield, VA

Chris García, Head Librarian,
  Beverly Hills Children's Library, Beverly Hills, CA

Nancy Guidry, Young Adult Librarian,
  Santa Monica Public Library, Santa Monica, CA

Kenneth M. Holmes, Ph.D.,
  Educational Consultant,
  Educational Concepts Unlimited, Bellville, IL

Carol Jago, Mentor Teacher,
  English Department, Santa Monica Public High School, Santa Monica, C A

Jim Merrill, Instructor,
  Oxnard Community College, Oxnard, CA

Mary Purucker, Head Librarian,
  Santa Monica High School, Santa Monica, CA

Karen Rowe, Professor,
  University of California at Los Angeles

Hilda K. Weisburg, Librarian,
  Sayreville War Memorial High School, Parlin, NJ

Dr. Brooke Workman, Teacher,
  West High School, Iowa City, IA

Richard Yarborough, Professor,
  University of California at Los Angeles

Introduction to Volume 1

Reaching back to the mythical past, Volume 1 of *Literature and Its Times* begins with literary works set in ancient times and advances forward chronologically to 1799. Its earliest works—for example, Sophocles' *Antigone,* Virgil's *Aeneid,* and Homer's *Iliad*—concern the customs of ancient peoples. Discussed in the volume are recent findings in anthropology and archaeology that help illuminate these customs and works.

Between the classical era and the medieval era, few literary works beyond the poem *Beowulf* have survived, though later authors (such as T. H. White in *The Once and Future King*) have composed works that aim to evoke this period. The 1300s saw a scattering of momentous literary works, such as Geoffrey Chaucer's *Canterbury Tales.* At the same time, a renewed hunger for learning began to surface in Italy's city-states, which would ultimately lead to an increase in literary activity. But not until the late 1400s, a few decades after the printing press first appeared (circa 1450), was there a vigorous outpouring of literature. It would be the first of many such outpourings in subsequent centuries.

The literature produced in these later centuries reflected the personalities, concerns, and phenomena of their times. It set out to achieve various goals: to move readers to action (Niccolò Machiavelli's *The Prince*), to entertain them (William Shakespeare's *A Midsummer Night's Dream* or Alexandre Dumas's *The Three Musketeers*), and/or to portray past events (the French

Revolution—Charles Dickens's *A Tale of Two Cities*). Some of these later works (for example, Mary Shelley's *Frankenstein*) made bold to criticize the "progress" of their particular society.

Coinciding with the literary works were a few major movements that gained a popular following over the centuries:

Humanism—(1300s to 1500s) involved a revival of interest in Greek and Roman literature, individualism, and a new regard for worldly as well as religious concerns;

Enlightenment—(1600s and 1700s) gave precedence to science, celebrating the power of reason and the ability of a person to understand the universe and improve human life;

Romanticism—(1700s to the mid-1800s) focused on the emotional, mysterious, and spontaneous in reaction to the Enlightenment's stress on reason, order, and balance.

Outside the field of literature but greatly affecting it was a religious movement of the early 1500s, the Reformation. The period between the ancient Greeks and the humanists had seen the birth of the Christian faith. The humanist era, in turn, saw a new individualism that led to a pivotal rift in that faith—the separation of the Protestant religions from the Catholic Church. This rift reflected a critical spirit, which became a hallmark of the humanist era and survived into the following centuries. The spirit manifested itself in literary works such as Jonathan Swift's *Gulliver's Travels,* which, along with novels like

Daniel Defoe's *Robinson Crusoe,* also added to a body of travel literature that mirrored empire building and the contact between cultures in the 1600s and 1700s.

Authors featured various ethnic, religious, and other social groups in their works. In the tradition of the humanists, some of these authors—Washington Irving ("Rip Van Winkle") and Nathaniel Hawthorne ("Young Goodman Brown"), for example—began examining American behavior with a critical eye, generating stories that laid the foundation for a new national literature. Other works focused on relationships between peoples of the Old World and the New (see Herman Melville's *Benito Cereno*). Still others, like Mary Wollstonecraft's *A Vindication of the Rights of Woman,* remained focused on the Old World, or Europe, attempting to change stubborn habits and prejudices in their own lands.

Chronology of Relevant Events

Prehistory–1790s

ANCIENT WORLD

The Minoan and Mycenaean cultures were the first advanced cultures to develop in Europe, leading to the Greek and then the Roman culture.

	Historical Events	Literary Works Set in the Period
3000 B.C.	c. 3000 b.c. Minoan civilization begins on Crete	
2500 B.C.		
2000 B.C.	c. 2000 b.c. Myceraean civilization appears on Greek mainland	
1500 B.C.		
		c. 1400 b.c. *Medea* by Euripides
		c. 1300 b.c. *The Bull from the Sea* by Mary Renault
		1200s b.c. *Antigone* by Sophocles
	c. 1200 b.c. Date ascribed to Trojan War	c. 1200 b.c. *Aeneid* by Virgil
		c. 1200 b.c. *Iliad* by Homer
		c. 1200 b.c. *Odyssey* by Homer
	c. 1100 b.c. Mycenaean civilization disappears	1100s b.c. *A Midsummer Night's Dream* by William Shakespeare

Historical Events	Literary Works Set in the Period
1000 B.C.	1000–1 b.c.? *King Lear* by William Shakespeare
c. 850–750 b.c. Homer composes epic poems	
800–701 b.c. Celts move into England	
c. 521 b.c. Siddhartha Gautama leaves home to travel in India and delivers first sermon, founding Buddhism	
500 B.C.	500–400 b.c. *Siddhartha* by Hermann Hesse
400s b.c. Tragedies by Aeschylus, Sophocles, and Euripides performed	
462–429 b.c. Greek classical culture reaches its height	
431–404 b.c. Peloponnesian War	
399 b.c. Socrates put to death	Late 400s b.c. *Republic* by Plato
335 b.c. Aristotle founds school known as the Lyceum	
c. 300 b.c. Greeks introduce Stoic ideals: human beings should resign themselves to fate and subordinate passion to reason	

ROMAN REPUBLIC AND EMPIRE

The Romans adapted achievements from the Greeks, also developing their own advanced codes of law. Eventually the Romans became dominant in Europe, North Africa, and the Near East. Their history covers a thousand years, including the birth and acceptance of Christianity.

Historical Events	Literary Works Set in the Period
500 B.C. 509 b.c. Roman Republic established	
100 B.C. 60 b.c. First triumvirate established with Pompey, Crassus, and Julius Caesar as rulers	
49–44 b.c. Caesar becomes dictator until he is assassinated	45 b.c. *Julius Caesar* by William Shakespeare
30 a.d. Jesus Christ is crucified	
43 Roman emperor Claudius conquers southeast England	
100 A.D.	
311 Christianity made legal in the Roman Empire	
395 Roman Empire separated into Eastern and Western divisions	
476 Roman Empire ends in the West	
500 A.D.	

Historical Events	Literary Works Set in the Period

EARLY MIDDLE AGES

After Rome's downfall came the rise of barbaric kingdoms that faded within a few centuries, except for two that endured: the Anglo-Saxons in Britain and the Franks in Gaul.

	Historical Events	Literary Works Set in the Period
500	c. 450 Anglo-Saxon invasion of England, conquest of native Britons 500–1000 Early Middle Ages, sometimes known as the Dark Ages	c. 400s? *The Hobbit* by J. R. R. Tolkien c. 500 *Beowulf* c. 500? *The Once and Future King* by T. H. White
	800 Charlemagne of France crowned "Emperor of the Romans"	Before 780 *Hamlet* by William Shakespeare
	800s Viking invasions in Europe give rise to feudal society	
	865 Danes establish large settlement in England	
	871 Alfred the Great becomes first King of England	
	962 Beginning of Holy Roman Empire with German ruler Otto I	
1000	1016–35 Danish leader Canute rules over England, Denmark, and Norway	

CENTRAL AND LATE MIDDLE AGES

At the height of the Middle Ages, the Catholic Church reached the apex of its power, with Christians going on military expeditions to recover the Holy Land from the Muslims. At the close of the Middle Ages (1300s to early 1500s, Europe was suffering intensely from death and destruction.

	Historical Events	Literary Works Set in the Period
1000	1000–1350 Central Middle Ages	1000s *Macbeth* by William Shakespeare
	1066 Norman Conquest of England	
	1095 First Crusade begins	
1100	1147 Second Crusade begins 1154 English King Henry II founds Plantagenet dynasty	1100s *Ivanhoe* by Sir Walter Scott 1154–1247? *The Merry Adventures of Robin Hood* by Howard Pyle
	1189 Third Crusade begins	
1200	1215 Magna Carta signed	
	1290 Jews expelled from England	
	1291 Crusades end	
1300	1300s–1500s Late Middle Ages	1300 *Inferno* by Dante Alighieri
	1337–1453 Hundred Years' War between England and France	
	1347–51 Black Death ravages Europe	
	1399 England's Henry IV takes crown from King Richard II	Late 1300s *Canterbury Tales* by Geoffrey Chaucer

	Historical Events	Literary Works Set in the Period
1400		1402 *Henry IV, Part I* by William Shakespeare
		1482 *The Hunchback of Notre Dame* by Victor Hugo
	1485 Henry VII begins Tudor dynasty in England	
1500		

RENAISSANCE

Beginning in Italy about a century before it spread through Europe, the Renaissance was a period of rebirth. It featured renewed interest in classical Greece and Rome along with a burst of creative efforts in the arts and sciences.

	Historical Events	Literary Works Set in the Period
1200		
	1277–1447 Visconti family rules Milan	
1300		
	1330s–40s Italian writer Petrarch begins humanism movement	c. 1348 *Romeo and Juliet* by William Shakespeare
		Late 1300s? *The Merchant of Venice* by William Shakespeare
1400		1400s–1600s? *The Tempest* by William Shakespeare
	1434 Medici family rises to power in Florence	
	1450–1535 Sforza family rules Milan	
	c. 1450 Printing press is developed	
	1469–92 Florentine culture flourishes under Lorenzo de' Medici	
	1490s–1520s High Renaissance	
	1494 French troops invade Italy	
	1498 Leonardo da Vinci completes fresco of Last Supper in Milan	
1500		
	1508–12 Michelangelo paints frescoes in Sistine Chapel	1513 *The Prince* by Niccolò Machiavelli
	1516 The humanist Thomas More writes Utopia	
	1529 Niccolò Machiavelli publishes *The Prince*	
		1571 *Othello* by William Shakespeare
1600		Early 1600s *The Adventures of Don Quixote* by Miguel de Cervantes Saavedra

REFORMATION

During the Renaissance, there was a religious movement known as the Reformation, which led to the division between Protestants and Catholics and to changes within the existing Catholic Church.

	Historical Events	Literary Works Set in the Period
1400	1480 Catholic Church in Spain begins Inquisition, torturing Jewish and Muslim converts that it suspects of heresy	
	1492 Jews expelled from Spain	
	1495 Jews expelled from Portugal	

Historical Events	Literary Works Set in the Period
1500	Early 1500s *A Man for All Seasons* by Robert Bolt
1517 Martin Luther posts ideas on church door in Wittenberg, Germany, which begins the Protestant Reformation	
1534 King Henry VIII of England breaks with Catholic Church of Rome in Act of Supremacy	
1535 England's Sir Thomas More tried for treason and executed	
1600	
1627 Uprising of French Protestants, or Huguenots	1625–28 *The Three Musketeers* by Alexandre Dumas
1667 John Milton publishes *Paradise Lost,* envisioning creation, the Crucifixion, and human corruption through Milton's day	Creation–1667 *Paradise Lost* by John Milton
1700	

AGE OF OVERSEAS EMPIRES

New monarchies arose in France, England, and Spain during the late 1400s to the early 1600s. Establishing strong central rule, they ventured out to build empires and establish colonies in the Americas. The colonies grew, struggling to form societies of their own. Meanwhile, the monarchies in France and England suffered war in Europe and challenges to their power at home. They weathered these struggles, then proceeded to vie with each other for control of their empires in America.

Historical Events	Literary Works Set in the Period
1400	
1492–1504 Christopher Columbus completes four voyages of discovery to the Americas	
1494–1559 Italian Wars	
1497 John Cabot lays English claim to North America	
1500	
1558–1603 Elizabeth I rules England	
1600 1603 English conquest of Ireland completed	1600s–1700s? *Beauty* by Robin McKinley
1609 Henry Hudson discovers Hudson River for Dutch	
1607 First permanent English colony founded at Jamestown, Virginia	
c. 1610 Founding of French salons as social gathering places (in private homes) for nobles and intellectuals	
1618–48 Thirty Years' War in Europe	
1620 Revolt of French nobles against King Louis XIII ended by Richelieu, who makes peace	
1630–43 Great Migration of Puritans from England to Massachusetts	
1636 Anne Hutchinson banished from Massachusetts for her religious beliefs	
1639 France enters the Thirty Years' War	

	Historical Events	Literary Works Set in the Period
1600	1640 New England merchants enter the slave trade	1640-55 *Cyrano de Bergerac* by Edmond Rostand
	1642–46 English civil war results in victory for Parliament	1642–49 *The Scarlet Letter* by Nathaniel Hawthorne
	1649 England declared a commonwealth; monarchy is dissolved	
	1660 English monarchy is restored	1652–94 *Robinson Crusoe* by Daniel Defoe
	1661 Louis XIV begins rule in France, suppresses noble authority	
	1666 Richelieu founds French Académie Royale des Sciences	
	1692–93 Witchcraft trials of Salem, Massachusetts	c. 1690 "Young Goodman Brown" by Nathaniel Hawthorne
		1692 *The Crucible* by Arthur Miller
		1692 *Tituba of Salem Village* by Ann Petry
		1699–1715 *Gulliver's Travels* by Jonathan Swift
1700		1706–57 *The Autobiography of Benjamin Franklin* by Benjamin Franklin
		1727 "The Devil and Tom Walker" by Washington Irving
	1729 Ireland suffers third year of famine due to lack of corn	1729 "A Modest Proposal" *by Jonathan Swift*
	1751–54 Benjamin Franklin publishes papers on his experiments on electricity	1733–58 *Poor Richard's Almanack* by Benjamin Franklin
	1754 Anglo-French War (French and Indian War or Seven Years' War) erupts in North America; both sides try to win Indian allies	
	1756 Seven Years' War breaks out in Europe	1757 *The Last of the Mohicans* by James Fenimore Cooper
	1763 Treaty of Paris ends Seven Years' War	
	1764 American Indians fight Pontiac's Rebellion in Ohio Valley	
1800		1765 *The Light in the Forest* by Conrad Richter

REVOLUTIONARY ERA

Beginning in the 1600s, a movement called the Enlightenment showed high regard for a person's power to reason and to improve the human condition. The movement taught that individuals share a few basic goals—knowledge, happiness, and freedom. These ideas helped inspire the revolutions and the post-revolutionary protests of the 1700s.

1600	1600s–1700s Movement known as the Enlightenment places high value on people's ability to reason	
1650		
	1660 English Parliament passes first Navigation Act to create a monopoly over shipping and trade in its colonies	
1700		
	1733 England passes Molasses Act to stop trade between its American colonies and the French West Indies	

Historical Events	Literary Works Set in the Period
1750	1750–99? "Rip Van Winkle" by Washington Irving
	1750–99? *Treasure Island* by Robert Louis Stevenson
1754 American colonists adopt the Albany Plan, a plan to forge a union of the colonies under one general government	1757–93 *A Tale of Two Cities* by Charles Dickens
1763–74 England exerts control over American colonies through a series of restrictive acts, culminating in Coercive Acts	Early 1770s *Common Sense* by Thomas Paine
	1771–1803 *Wuthering Heights* by Emily Brontë
1775–83 American colonists fight War of Independence from England	1775 "Give Me Liberty or Give Me Death" by Patrick Henry
1776 Thomas Paine publishes *Common Sense*	1776 The Declaration of Independence by Thomas Jefferson
1776 Thomas Jefferson drafts Declaration of Independence	1776–84 *Drums along the Mohawk* by Walter D. Edmonds
1776–85 Benjamin Franklin serves as minister to France	
1777 At first neutral, most Iroquois Indians of New York side with the British in America's War of Independence	
	Late 1780s "The Legend of Sleepy Hollow" by Washington Irving
1789 French Revolution begins	1789–93 *Mutiny on the Bounty* by Charles Nordhoff and James Norman Hall
	1790s *Frankenstein* by Mary Shelley
1791 French government entertains proposal for providing free education to its male citizens	
	1792 *The Scarlet Pimpernel* by Baroness Emmuska Orczy
	1792 *A Vindication of the Rights of Woman* by Mary Wollstonecraft
1793 French monarchs beheaded; France declares war on England	
1797 Series of mutinies break out in British navy	1797 *Billy Budd, Sailor* by Herman Melville
1798 In reaction to the Enlightenment, the Romantic movement officially begins in England with publication of *Lyrical Ballads* by William Wordsworth and Samuel Taylor Coleridge	
	1799 *Benito Cereno* by Herman Melville
1800	
1805 Admiral Horatio Nelson defeats combined force of French and Spanish	

Note: A ? by the date in which a literary work is set indicates an indefinite time period. See pages on that work for further details.

Contents by Title

Adventures of Don Quixote, The
   Cervantes Saavedra, Miguel de 1

Aeneid
   Virgil 8

Antigone
   Sophocles 14

Autobiography of Benjamin Franklin, The
   Benjamin Franklin 22

*Beauty: A Retelling of the Story of
   Beauty and the Beast*
   Robin McKinley 30

Benito Cereno
   Herman Melville 37

Beowulf
   Anonymous 44

Billy Budd, Sailor
   Herman Melville 51

Bull from the Sea, The
   Mary Renault 57

Canterbury Tales
   Geoffrey Chaucer 64

Common Sense
   Thomas Paine 71

Crucible, The
   Arthur Miller 78

Cyrano de Bergerac
   Edmond Rostand 87

Declaration of Independence, The
   Thomas Jefferson 93

"Devil and Tom Walker, The"
   Washington Irving 101

Drums Along the Mohawk
   Walter D. Edmonds 107

Frankenstein
   Mary Shelley 115

"Give Me Liberty or Give Me Death"
   Patrick Henry 122

Gulliver's Travels
   Jonathan Swift 129

Hamlet
   William Shakespeare 136

Henry IV, Part I
   William Shakespeare 144

Hobbit, The
   J. R. R. Tolkien 152

Hunchback of Notre Dame, The
   Victor Hugo 159

Iliad
   Homer 166

Inferno
   Dante Alighieri 174

Ivanhoe
   Sir Walter Scott 181

Julius Caesar
   William Shakespeare 189

King Lear
   William Shakespeare 196

Last of the Mohicans, The
   James Fenimore Cooper 204

"Legend of Sleepy Hollow, The"
   Washington Irving 211

Contents
by Title

Light in the Forest, The
Conrad Richter 219

Macbeth
William Shakespeare 225

Man for All Seasons, A
Robert Bolt 231

Medea
Euripides 238

Merchant of Venice, The
William Shakespeare 242

Merry Adventures of Robin Hood, The
Howard Pyle 250

Midsummer Night's Dream, A
William Shakespeare 258

"Modest Proposal, A"
Jonathan Swift 266

Mutiny on the Bounty
Charles Nordhoff and James Norman Hall . . . 273

Odyssey
Homer 280

Once and Future King, The
T. H. White 288

Othello
William Shakespeare 295

Paradise Lost
John Milton 301

Poor Richard's Almanack
Benjamin Franklin 309

Prince, The
Niccolò Machiavelli 316

Republic
Plato 321

"Rip Van Winkle"
Washington Irving 330

Robinson Crusoe
Daniel Defoe 337

Romeo and Juliet
William Shakespeare 344

Scarlet Letter, The
Nathaniel Hawthorne 351

Scarlet Pimpernel, The
Baroness Emmuska Orczy 358

Siddhartha
Hermann Hesse 365

Tale of Two Cities, A
Charles Dickens 371

Tempest, The
William Shakespeare 379

Three Musketeers, The
Alexandre Dumas 386

Tituba of Salem Village
Ann Petry 393

Treasure Island
Robert Louis Stevenson 400

Vindication of the Rights of Woman, A
Mary Wollstonecraft 406

Wuthering Heights
Emily Brontë 413

"Young Goodman Brown"
Nathaniel Hawthorne 420

Contents by Author

Anonymous
  Beowulf **44**

Bolt, Robert
  A Man for All Seasons **231**

Brontë, Emily
  Wuthering Heights **413**

Cervantes Saavedra, Miguel de
  The Adventures of Don Quixote **1**

Chaucer, Geoffrey
  Canterbury Tales **64**

Cooper, James Fenimore
  The Last of the Mohicans **204**

Dante Alighieri
  Inferno **174**

Defoe, Daniel
  Robinson Crusoe **337**

Dickens, Charles
  A Tale of Two Cities **371**

Dumas, Alexandre
  The Three Musketeers **386**

Edmonds, Walter D.
  Drums Along the Mohawk **107**

Euripides
  Medea **238**

Franklin, Benjamin
  The Autobiography of Benjamin Franklin **22**
  Poor Richard's Almanack **309**

Hawthorne, Nathaniel
  The Scarlet Letter **351**
  "Young Goodman Brown" **420**

Henry, Patrick
  "Give Me Liberty or Give Me Death" **122**

Hesse, Hermann
  Siddhartha **365**

Homer
  Iliad **166**
  Odyssey **280**

Hugo, Victor
  The Hunchback of Notre Dame **159**

Irving, Washington
  "The Devil and Tom Walker" **101**
  "The Legend of Sleepy Hollow" **211**
  "Rip Van Winkle" **330**

Jefferson, Thomas
  The Declaration of Independence **93**

Machiavelli, Niccolò
  The Prince **316**

McKinley, Robin
  *Beauty: A Retelling of the Story of Beauty and the
  Beast* **30**

Melville, Herman
  Benito Cereno **37**
  Billy Budd, Sailor **51**

Miller, Arthur
  The Crucible **78**

Milton, John
  Paradise Lost **301**

Nordhoff, Charles, and James Norman Hall
  Mutiny on the Bounty **273**

Orczy, Baroness Emmuska
  The Scarlet Pimpernel **358**

Contents by Author

Paine, Thomas
Common Sense 71

Petry, Ann
Tituba of Salem Village 393

Plato
Republic 321

Pyle, Howard
The Merry Adventures of Robin Hood 250

Renault, Mary
The Bull from the Sea 57

Richter, Conrad
The Light in the Forest 219

Rostand, Edmond
Cyrano de Bergerac 87

Scott, Sir Walter
Ivanhoe 181

Shakespeare, William
Hamlet 136
Henry IV, Part I 144
Julius Caesar 189
King Lear 196
Macbeth 225
The Merchant of Venice 242

A Midsummer Night's Dream 258
Othello 295
Romeo and Juliet 344
The Tempest 379

Shelley, Mary
Frankenstein 115

Sophocles
Antigone 14

Stevenson, Robert Louis
Treasure Island 400

Swift, Jonathan
Gulliver's Travels 129
"A Modest Proposal" 266

Tolkien, J. R. R.
The Hobbit 152

Virgil
Aeneid 8

White, T. H.
The Once and Future King 288

Wollstonecraft, Mary
A Vindication of the Rights of Woman 406

Photo Credits

Title page of the first edition of *Don Quixote* by Miguel de Cervantes Saavedra, 1605. Corbis-Bettmann. Reproduced by permission. —Sancho Panza discovers Don Quixote, illustration. Corbis-Bettmann. Reproduced by permission. —"Antigone Strewing Dust on the Body of Her Brother," painting. By V. J. Robertson. From *Antigones*. By George Steiner. Oxford University Press, Oxford. ©; George Steiner, 1984. All rights reserved. Reproduced by permission of The Mansell Collection Limited, London. —View from above the Herod Atticus Ancient Theatre in Athens, photograph. AP/Wide World Photos, Inc. Reproduced by permission. —Benjamin Franklin at printing press, illustration. Brown Brothers. Reproduced by permission. —Benjamin Franklin, painting. The Library of Congress. —"Beauty and the Beast," illustration. By Alfred Crowquil, 1854. —Slave ship, line drawing. Corbis-Bettmann. Reproduced by permission. —Slave auction, 1861, illustration. Corbis-Bettmann. Reproduced by permission. —Helmet from Sutton Hoo ship burial, photograph. From *From Age to Age: Life and Literature in Anglo-Saxon England*. By Bernice Grohskopf. Kingsport Press, 1968. Copyright British Museum. Reproduced by permission of the British Museum. —"Beowulf and the Dragon," illustration. By Rockwell Kent. The Rockwell Kent Legacies. Reproduced by permission. —Terence Stamp as Billy Budd in a film adaptation of *Billy Budd* by Herman Melville, photograph. Culver Pictures, Inc. Reproduced by permission. —Acropolis, etching.

From *Life in Ancient Athens*. The Macmillan Company, 1906. —Map of the Aegean, line drawing. By G. Jones. From *The Quest for Theseus*. By Anne G. Ward and others. Praeger Publishers, 1970. Reproduced by permission of Greenwood Publishing Group, Inc., Westport, CT. —Canterbury Cathedral (choir section), photograph. By Robert M. Craig. Reproduced by permission. —Tabard Inn, illustration. By Philip Norman, 1810. —Thomas Paine, portrait. By courtesy of National Portrait Gallery, London. —Title page of the first edition of *Common Sense* by Thomas Paine, 1776. The American Philosophical Society. Reproduced by permission. —Title page of *The Wonders of the Invisible World* by Cotton Mather, 1693.

Jenny Egan as Mary Warren in the original production of *The Crucible* by Arthur Miller, photograph. By Gjon Mili. Reproduced by permission. —"Trial of George Jacobs," painting. Courtesy, Peabody Essex Museum, Salem, MA. —Alfred Dreyfus, photograph. French Police, 1895. —George III, painting. By Sir W. Beechy. From an engraving by B. Smith in *Collection of Prints, from Pictures Painted for the Purpose of Illustrating the Dramatic Works of Shakspeare, by the Artists of Great Britain*. Vol. I. John and Josiah Boydell, 1803. —Draft of the Declaration of Independence. By Thomas Jefferson. Library of Congress. —The Declaration of Independence Committee, illustration. Library of Congress. —Henry Fonda and Claudette Colbert, illustration. From *Walter*

Night's Dream by William Shakespeare, photograph. By Angus McBean. Harvard Theatre Collection, Houghton Library. Reproduced by permission. —"Oberon, Queen of the Fairies, Puck, Bottom, Fairies attending, & c.," painting. By H. Fuseli. From an engraving by T. Ryder in *Collection of Prints, from Pictures Painted for the Purpose of Illustrating the Dramatic Works of Shakspeare, by the Artists of Great Britain.* Vol. I. John and Josiah Boydell, 1803. —St. Patrick's Cathedral in Dublin, Ireland, illustration. From *A Modest Proposal.* By Jonathan Swift. —George II, engraving. Corbis-Bettmann. Reproduced by permission.

"Hardened criminal being punished by the cat-o'-nine-tails," engraving. Corbis-Bettmann. Reproduced by permission. —"The Mutineers Turning Lieut Bligh and Part of the Officers and Crew Adrift," aquatint. By Robert Dodd, 1790. —Marlon Brando and Trevor Howard in a scene from a film adaptation of *Mutiny on the Bounty* by Charles Nordhoff and James Norman Hall, photograph. Springer/Corbis-Bettmann. Reproduced by permission. —City of Troy beside the sea, illustration. By Peter Connolly. From Homer's *Odyssey.* George G. Harrap & Company, 1911. —"Ulysses [Odysseus] and his companions escape the traps of the Sirens," engraving. Archive Photos, Inc. Reproduced by permission. —Map of England, line drawing. From *The New Arthurian Encyclopedia.* Edited by Norris J. Lacy. Garland Publishing Inc., 1991. Reproduced by permission. —"Desdemona, Othello, Iago, Cassio, Roderigo, Emilia, &c.," painting. From an engraving by T. Ryder in *Collection of Prints, from Pictures Painted for the Purpose of Illustrating the Dramatic Works of Shakspeare, by the Artists of Great Britain.* Vol. II. John and Josiah Boydell, 1803. —Charles I, portrait. International Portrait Gallery. —Title page of *Poor Richard's Almanack* by Benjamin Franklin. B. Franklin and D. Hall, 1756. —Four pages of *Poor Richard's Almanack* by Benjamin Franklin. B. Franklin and D. Hall, 1756. —Niccolò Machiavelli, painting. By Santi di Tito. —Socrates, bust. Corbis-Bettmann. Reproduced by permission. —Aristotle, woodcut. UPI/Corbis-Bettmann. Reproduced by permission. —Map of Dutch population in New York, line drawing . From *Stubborn for Liberty: The Dutch in New York.* By Alice P. Kennedy. Syracuse University Press, 1975. Reproduced by permission. —Title page from *The Life and Strange Surprising Adventures of Robinson Crusoe* by Daniel Defoe, 1719. The Granger Collection, New York. Reproduced by permission.

Map of Northern Italy, line drawing. From *The Works of William Shakespeare.* Vol. I. Edited by Henry Irving and Frank S. Marshall. Blackie & Son, Limited, 1898. —"Romeo and Paris dead; Juliet and Friar Lawrence," painting. By J. Northcote. From an engraving by P. Simon in *Collection of Prints, from Pictures Painted for the Purpose of Illustrating the Dramatic Works of Shakspeare, by the Artists of Great Britain.* Vol. II. John and Josiah Boydell, 1803. —Hester Prynne, painting. By George Henry Boughton. The Granger Collection, New York. Reproduced by permission. —"Robespierre Guillotining the Executioner after Having Guillotined All the French, 1793," illustration. —"Prise de la Bastille le 14 juillet 1789," illustration, 1789. —Ronald Coleman in a film adaptation of *A Tale of Two Cities* by Charles Dickens, photograph. Springer/Corbis-Bettmann. Reproduced by permission. —Cover of *A Tale of Two Cities* by Charles Dickens, illustration. By H. K. Browne. Chapman and Hall, 1859. —Scene from a production of *The Tempest* by William Shakespeare, photograph. By Angus McBean. Harvard Theatre Collection, Houghton Library. Reproduced by permission. —Mather, Cotton, painting. Library of Congress. —Salem Witch House, photograph. AP/Wide World Photos. Reproduced with permission. —Frankfort Packet schooner, painting. By F. Albinus. —Wollstonecraft, Mary Godwin, etching. By J. Chapman. UPI/Corbis-Bettmann. Reproduced by permission. —Godwin, William, painting. By James Northcote. From *Vindication of the Rights of Woman.* By Mary Wollstonecraft, 1802. —High Sunderland Hall, illustration. From *Wuthering Heights: A Novel.* By Emily Brontë. Thomas Cautley, 1847. —Moors with house in center, photograph. Yorkshire Post. Reproduced by permission. —Camp meeting, illustration. Library of Congress. —Salem witch trial, illustration. The Granger Collection, New York. Reproduced with permission.

The Adventures of Don Quixote

by
Miguel de Cervantes Saavedra

Miguel de Cervantes Saavedra lived through two distinct periods in Spanish history. The first was a "golden age" of military success, national pride, and intellectual freedom; the second, a time of economic and military weakness and religious and intellectual repression. *Don Quixote* (pronounced "kee-ho-tay") was written at the end of his life and in the midst of the second of these periods. Spain at that time was in a state of *desengaño* (a word meaning both "disillusion" and "disappointment"); the Spanish people realized by 1605 that the powerful empire of the previous century had been built on a shaky foundation—and that the foundation was crumbling.

Events in History at the Time of the Novel

Decline of the Spanish empire. In 1547, the year Cervantes was born, Spain was ruled by King Charles I, who was also the leader of the Holy Roman Empire and a member of the Hapsburg royal family. Charles ruled for many years over Spain, Austria, the Netherlands, and parts of Italy and Germany. He also controlled the territories that Spain had conquered in the New World since Columbus's first voyage in 1492, which had proved to be a valuable source of silver and gold. The wealth and power that Charles and his predecessors accumulated contributed to the discord between the Hapsburgs and the other powerful rulers of Europe. Attempting to protect and expand his empire, Charles engaged in a number of wars that heavily drained the finances of Spain and caused great losses of life.

> ### THE LITERARY WORK
> A novel in two parts set in early seventeenth-century Spain; the first part published in 1605, the second in 1615.
>
> ### SYNOPSIS
> A middle-aged gentleman imagines that he is a knight and sets out on a series of adventures with his "squire," an illiterate peasant.

Charles was a religious king, and his military policy was based partly on the desire to spread Catholicism throughout Europe and to eliminate all other religions. His son, Philip II, felt even more strongly about the importance of a Catholic world. When he took the throne in 1556, he declared that he would prefer not to rule at all than to govern over heretics. This attitude caused him to fight impractical wars and lose valuable property, leading Spain into three successive bankruptcies before his reign ended in 1598. His successor, Philip III, lacked not only his father's religious zeal but also his leadership ability and moral integrity. His crowning added moral decay to Spain's growing list of problems.

Although Spain's decline after its golden age was gradual, it was perhaps best symbolized by the destruction in 1588 of the so-called "invincible" Spanish Armada by English ships. The Spanish fleet—130 huge ships sent to the English Channel to wage war on Protestant England—was destroyed, an event that left Spain humiliated. This military disaster forced Spaniards to accept what many had been reluctant to acknowledge: the glorious days of their empire had come to an end.

SPAIN'S DECLINE THROUGH DON QUIXOTE'S EYES

~

Don Quixote bemoans the decline of Spain in the second part of Cervantes's novel, but instead of blaming it on unwise rulers, he attributes it to the death of chivalry, the principles of knighthood: "Our depraved times do not deserve to enjoy so great a blessing as did those in which knights errant undertook and carried on their shoulders the defence of kingdoms.... Now sloth triumphs over industry, idleness over labour, vice over virtue, presumption over valour, and theory over the practice of arms, which only lived and flourished in the golden age and among knights errant."

(Cervantes, *Adventures of Don Quixote*, p. 447)

Erasmus and Renaissance humanism. Under the reign of King Charles I, Spain had been an active participant in the European intellectual community. This community, led by Italy, was in the midst of the Renaissance, a period of rebirth in which artists and thinkers discovered anew the contributions that ancient Greek and Roman civilizations had made to the world. Building on what their ancient counterparts had done, Renaissance Europeans reconsidered their schools, churches, art, and politics and began experimenting with new models. Their exploration was guided by the basic idea that traditions can and should be questioned and reformed.

Among one Renaissance group, called the "humanists," this questioning led to the revolutionary conclusion that Christian faith alone should not guide humanity. These philosophers, artists, and teachers believed that practical human concerns should be studied with the same intensity applied to the study of the abstract world of God in the Middle Ages.

One such humanist, a Dutch philosopher named Desiderius Erasmus, had a great impact on intellectual and religious life in Spain. Famous for his witty satires, Erasmus thought that Catholics and the Catholic Church had strayed too far from the teachings of Jesus and that they had much to learn from Plato and other non-Christian thinkers.

He criticized the gullibility of Christians who believed in miracles, the stupidity of many theologians, and the meaningless traditions of monks. In his *Handbook for the Christian Soldier* (which also translates as "Christian knight"), he discussed the injustice of poverty and questioned the right of the wealthy to hold property.

In the early 1500s Erasmus played a central role in Catholic Spain; his ideas were the main influence behind King Charles's early policies on religion. Soon, however, the tolerant attitude of Spain's religious and political powers would end, and the humanistic ideas of the Renaissance would be stifled.

The Inquisition and loss of intellectual freedom. In the novel, the main character, Don Quixote, returns home wounded after his first adventure. Worried friends of his village, convinced that his insistence on behaving like a knight is due to his having read too many books of chivalry, hold a "great and pleasant Inquisition" during which they toss most of these books into a bonfire (*Adventures of Don Quixote*, p. 56). Although Quixote's friends have kind motives, their actions reflect an alarming trend in sixteenth-century Spain—a movement toward strict religiosity and the elimination of liberal thought and culture.

The Inquisition, a court created by the pope of the Catholic Church in 1238 to investigate and punish heresy, was made an official branch of the Spanish government in 1478; in 1481 the first heretics convicted by the court were burned to death at the stake. The court proceeded to victimize former Jews who had converted to Catholicism in order to avoid being expelled from Spain in 1492. By the late sixteenth century, no one was safe from being accused—even the famous monk St. John of the Cross was found guilty of unchristian acts.

Intellectuals were persecuted as the free thought of the Renaissance was replaced by the terror of the Inquisition. By the end of the 1500s, Catholic Spain had closed its doors to most of Renaissance Europe and any ideas that sprang from it.

Chivalry, work, and the Spanish hidalgo. *Don Quixote* is the story of a hidalgo, or nobleman. Hidalgos were people who inherited a title of nobility and supposedly had pure Christian blood. In many cases—including those of both the author Cervantes (who was almost certainly of Jewish ancestry) and his character Don Quixote—they had little more than their titles. Despite the fact that hidalgos were not required to pay taxes, they were not guaranteed wealth. Furthermore, the code of the hidalgo meant that labor of any

Title page of the first edition of the novel, 1605.

kind was frowned upon; a true hidalgo should not work for a living. As a result, many of these so-called nobles had plenty of free time but lived their proud lives in poverty.

The hidalgo's notions about work, which contributed greatly to Spain's economic problems, had their origins in Spain's Holy Wars against Muslims during the Middle Ages. The perfect hidalgo of that time was a knight who followed the code of chivalry. A courageous man of honor, he lived for war and died for Christian principles. The amount of his riches was a sign of his success as a warrior; his income came not from manual labor but from the storehouses of the lands that he had conquered. Without the profitable wars of Spain's past, hidalgos were at a loss for what to do. Many were landholders and made some money from their tenants, but a large number simply struggled from day to day, proud to have descended from the chivalric knights of Spain's past but unable to live comfortably in their high-born position.

The Novel in Focus

The plot. Alonso Quixano, a country gentleman living in the dry, desolate region of La Mancha in central Spain, is nearing fifty years of age when

his story begins. As a hidalgo, he has plenty of free time, which he has devoted almost entirely to reading tales of legendary knights and their exploits. He buries himself in these books day and night until he begins to think of himself as a knight and develops a hunger for adventure. Renaming himself Don Quixote, he gathers a rusty suit of armor, claims a neighboring peasant girl as his "lady," mounts his feeble horse, and sets off. His first round of adventures is brief. He stops at an inn that he takes for a castle and asks a startled but willing innkeeper to knight him. This new knighthood does him little good, however, for his first confrontation with evildoers earns him a harsh beating, after which he is rescued by a fellow villager and returned home.

When Don Quixote sets out again, it is with his newfound "squire," Sancho Panza, a fat peasant who expresses his insights in proverbs that convey the wisdom of the common folk in contrast to his master's book learning. With Sancho by his side, the knight Don Quixote fights giants disguised as windmills, frees a chain gang of prisoners (who then rob the knight and his squire), and engages in countless other adventures in the name of chivalry. Don Quixote's purpose in all this is plain: to restore justice and virtue to the world by battling the forces of evil, and thereby gain fame and fortune. Sancho's motives are slightly less admirable. He seeks to better his condition somehow through his association with this seemingly crazy nobleman. Don Quixote finishes this second round of exploits by once again being beaten to near death. He returns home with Sancho to recuperate and plan new adventures, at which point the first book ends.

POLICIES OF THE SPANISH INQUISITION IN THE LATE 1500S

- Punishment for importing forbidden foreign books into Spain is death.
- Study abroad is forbidden, except in Italy and Portugal (both Catholic countries).
- Unnaturally talented acrobats and circus animals are investigated for possible ties to the devil.

The second book of *Don Quixote*, though written ten years after the first, picks up the action of the story only a few weeks after the point where Book One ended. Still at home, the knight is confronted by a neighbor who has recently returned from college, where he read *The Adventures of Don Quixote.*

The neighbor explains to a pleased Don Quixote that his adventures are famous all over Europe, and discusses with him the details of some of them. Inspired by this news, Don Quixote and Sancho soon set out again to right more wrongs. This time, after a few small adventures, the knight and his squire are taken in by a country duke and duchess. The couple, who have read the first book, are happy not only to play along with Don Quixote's fantasy but to add to it for their own entertainment. Actually many of the "adventures" they devise for Don Quixote are quite cruel. The portrayal of the duke and duchess is an obvious criticsm of the idleness and injustice of much of Spain's upper class in Cervantes's time.

DON QUIXOTE RENOUNCES HIS IMPOSTOR

~

The first part of *Don Quixote* was enormously popular, and one Spanish writer, known only by the pseudonym Alonso Fernández de Avellaneda, decided to capitalize on its success. Before Cervantes published his promised continuation, Avellaneda put out a version of his own. Needless to say, this new version angered Cervantes. Since he had no legal recourse, Cervantes sought his revenge against Avellaneda by arranging a meeting between Don Quixote and one of Avellaneda's characters, Don Alvaro Tarfe, in his own Book Two. At the meeting Don Quixote asks the character to make a formal declaration that "he did not know Don Quixote de la Mancha, and that it was not he who was written of in a history entitled The Second Part of the Exploits of Don Quixote de la Mancha, composed by a certain Avellaneda" (*Adventures of Don Quixote*, p. 929). Don Alvaro complies, convinced that he has met two very different Don Quixotes, and Quixote and Sancho, greatly relieved, go on their way.

Eventually Quixote and Sancho leave the duke and duchess and embark on more adventures. These culminate in a visit to Barcelona, where the knight meets his downfall. Challenged to a joust by the Knight of the White Moon—who is actually his neighbor the college student in disguise—Don Quixote is defeated. Under the terms of the knights' agreement, Quixote must relinquish his knighthood and return home for

a year. This sacrifice proves too great for Don Quixote. He soon falls ill, and on his deathbed he renounces his knighthood, saying "I was mad, but I am sane now. I was Don Quixote de la Mancha, but to-day . . . I am Alonso Quixano" (*Adventures of Don Quixote*, p. 938). He dies shortly after speaking these words.

Fiction vs. reality. In the first part of Don Quixote's story, in the midst of his battle against another character, the action stops abruptly, and the narrator announces that the information about the conclusion of the battle is missing. This news serves as a launching point for a detailed explanation of how Don Quixote's adventures were recorded. The narrator explains that, while browsing in a market one day, he found some books written in Arabic that he soon discovered contained the history of Don Quixote, of whom he was an admirer. He bought the books and hired a translator to rewrite the knight's history in Spanish. The fact that the original version was written by an Arab led the narrator to suspect that it purposely portrayed Don Quixote unfavorably, since the Arab Muslims were bitter enemies of Spain's Catholics.

Cervantes thus introduces the idea of different versions of Don Quixote's story. Aside from catching the attention of his readers, the structure of Cervantes's novel plays with the scholarly literary standards of his day, which stressed the importance of "verisimilitude," the appearance of reality in fiction. He also may be alluding, in a much more subtle way, to the state of confusion in which Spain found itself at the time. Since the country had limited access to books and foreign knowledge and information was censored and controlled by only a few religious and political leaders, it was difficult for early seventeenth-century Spaniards to know if they were hearing "the real story" about anything. Cervantes may be drawing attention to this fact by emphasizing the manner in which his story is told.

Sources. In a conversation described in the prologue to the first part of *Don Quixote*, Cervantes's friend explains to him that "this book of yours aims at no more than destroying the authority and influence which books of chivalry have in the world and among the common people" (*Adventures of Don Quixote*, p. 30). Chivalric novels were the soap operas of sixteenth-century Spain. Widely read by commoners, hidalgos, and even some religious leaders, they told of the battles, loves, and adventures of knights, using a grandiose style that Cervantes parodies. Whether he sought to end the reading of these books or

Illustration of Don Quixote, Sancho Panza, and the windmills.

simply to poke fun at them is unclear. After all, books of chivalry, chiefly *Amadis of Gaul*, were the greatest influence on the narration and plot of *Don Quixote*. The passages below, taken from *Amadis* and *Don Quixote*, demonstrate the similarities between these two works and the comic touch that Cervantes adds to his book.

LEVELS OF REALITY IN VELÁZQUEZ

The Spanish artist Diego Velázquez, born a few years before *Don Quixote* was written, used a technique of "leveled" reality in his 1656 painting *Las Meninas*. This painting, a departure from traditional royal portraits, portrays the artist himself looking at his canvas, which the audience cannot see, while he paints the king and queen, who must be behind the audience (only their reflection, in a mirror behind the artist, can be seen). The focus of the painting is actually on several young girls positioned next to the king and queen. One of the girls is watching them pose, two are watching the audience, and the rest are watching each other. What the "real" painting is no one knows for certain.

Amadis of Gaul

And they then left that road, and taking another, journeyed all that day without encountering any adventure, and night overtook them near a fortress.
"Sir," said the dwarf, "here you may lodge, where there is a duenna who will serve you."
Amadis reached that fortress and found the duenna, who lodged him very well, giving him his supper and a very comfortable bed in which to sleep; but he did not do so, for his meditation about his lady was so great that he slept almost not at all that night; and next day, having said farewell to the duenna, he started out under guidance of the dwarf and went until noon.

(*Amadis of Gaul*, pp. 191-92)

Don Quixote

. . . at nightfall his horse and he were weary and dying of hunger. Looking in all directions to see if he could discover any castle or shepherd's hut where he could take shelter and supply his urgent needs, he saw, not far from the road he was traveling on, an inn, which seemed to him like a star to guide him to the gates, if not to the palace, of his redemption.... So he approached the inn, which to his mind was a castle, and when still a short distance

away reined Rocinante in, expecting some dwarf to mount the battlements and sound a trumpet to announce that a knight was approaching the fortress. . . . Now at that very moment, as chance would have it, a swineherd was collecting from the stubble a drove of hogs—pardon me for naming them—and blew his horn to call them together. But Don Quixote immediately interpreted this in his own way, as some dwarf giving notice of his approach.

(*Don Quixote*, pp. 37-8)

In addition to chivalric novels, there were other stylistic influences on Cervantes, including the pastoral novel and the satires of Erasmus. Pastoral novels, more popular than chivalric novels by the seventeenth century, were set in the natural world of shepherds and shepherdesses, far from the frustrations of village life or the high drama of knightly adventures. These books told stories of complicated love triangles and often included poems about the beauty of one character or the passion of another. *Don Quixote* actually includes within it two short pastoral novels (stories told to the knight and his squire in the course of their adventures). After Don Quixote's defeat at the hands of the Knight of the White Moon, he and Sancho even discuss the possibility of becoming shepherds for a year, until they can return to a life of chivalry.

The influence of Erasmus's works, though censored in Spain by the time *Don Quixote* was written, can be seen in the novel. Cervantes, who probably studied Erasmus's works as a young man in Madrid, presents many of this great humanist's ideas—and mirrors his witty style—in *Don Quixote*. Although the basic beliefs of Catholicism are never ridiculed, many of its rituals are. In the first part of the novel, for instance, Don Quixote, following the example of the legendary knight Amadis of Gaul, decides to perform penance to convince his imagined "lady," Dulcinea, that he is her devoted servant. Although acts of penance are supposed to be performed to express sorrow for a sin or wrongdoing, Don Quixote explains to Sancho that his plan is "to do it without cause" (*Adventures of Don Quixote*, p. 203). Don Quixote then informs Sancho that his penance will involve "the tearing of my garments, the scattering of my arms, the running of my head against the rocks, and other things of the kind which will astonish you" (*Adventures of Don Quixote*, p. 206). Stripped down to his underclothes, Don Quixote finally begins his penance. "He tore a great strip from the tail of his shirt, which was hanging down, and made eleven knots in it, one fatter than the rest; and this served him for a rosary all the time he was there, during which time he recited a million Ave Marias" (*Adventures of Don Quixote,* p. 215).

This passage, which raised the eyebrows of the members of the Inquisition, is one of many of Cervantes's humorous treatments of Catholic traditions. It is important to note, however, that Cervantes also includes many positive representations of the church in *Don Quixote.* The canon of Toledo, with whom Don Quixote debates the merits of books of chivalry, is depicted as a learned and distinguished man, and the priest from Quixote's village is kind and likable. Like Erasmus, Cervantes did not reject Catholicism altogether. In his view, the inward aspect of religion—an individual's relationship with God and practice of virtue—was more important than outward ceremonials. Clergymen were, after all, just human beings, subject to error and silliness like anyone else.

Although Cervantes relied on many other writers for stylistic ideas, the characters in *Don Quixote* are almost entirely his own. Cervantes is consistently praised for his realistic portrayal of people from every corner of Spanish society. The author's keen insight into the lives of his fellow Spaniards—students, priests, dukes, soldiers, innkeepers, and peasants—was gained from a life of wandering. Many of the characters in *Don Quixote,* in fact, could represent stages in Cervantes's own life. He was, at various times, a student, a cardinal's assistant, a soldier, a captive in Algiers, a purveyor in charge of buying food for the Spanish Armada, a tax collector, and, of course, a writer (a poet, a playwright, and a novelist). Many of these jobs required extensive travel throughout Spain, which allowed Cervantes to form opinions not only about the different classes of Spanish people, but about the different regions in which they lived. When Don Quixote battles a Basque, dines with a gentleman in Barcelona, or discusses literature with a priest from Toledo, Cervantes draws on his own extensive knowledge of Spanish culture to create an authentic picture of each of these characters.

Don Quixote, considered by many the first modern novel, was both a symbol of its times and a groundbreaking work. An inspiration for countless novels, including *Madame Bovary, The Adventures of Huckleberry Finn* (both covered in *Literature and Its Times*), and *Joseph Andrews,* Cervantes's story made an enormous impact on the literary world. In Cervantes's own world, *Don Quixote* was considered the funniest book of his time and was widely read by all members of society. As a comic novel, it failed to offer practical solutions for Spain's many problems, but its impractical hero, who remains positive despite his many downfalls, might have given the Spanish people a surge of optimism, and it definitely provided them with a reason to laugh.

For More Information

Anglo, Sydney, ed. *Chivalry in the Renaissance.* Rochester, New York: Boydell, 1990.

Byron, William. *Cervantes: A Biography.* Garden City, New York: Doubleday, 1978.

Cervantes Saavedra, Miguel de. *The Adventures of Don Quixote.* Translated by J. M. Cohen. New York: Penguin, 1950.

Defourneaux, Marcelin. *Daily Life in Spain in the Golden Age.* Translated by Newton Branch. New York: Praeger, 1971.

Rodríguez de Montalvo, Garci. *Amadis of Gaul.* Translated by Edwin B. Place and Herbert C. Behm. Lexington: University Press of Kentucky, 1974.

Aeneid

by
Virgil

Publius Maro Vergilius, now known simply as Virgil, was born in 70 B.C. near Mantua in northern Italy. Virgil lived during the collapse of the Roman Republic and the subsequent rise of the Roman Empire under Octavius Augustus Caesar. Virgil's poem harkens back to an idealized time in the region's history prior to the founding of Rome.

Events in History at the Time the Poem Takes Place

The city of Troy. The *Aeneid* tells the story of how Troy is destroyed by a Greek army and what happens to the Trojan inhabitants after the city's fall. Virgil's hero, Aeneas, is one of the Trojans who manages to escape. Although Virgil's story is based mainly on legends, the ruins of a city believed to be Troy were discovered in the late 1800s and are still being excavated today. These ruins are located in the northwest corner of modern Turkey (ancient Asia Minor), across the Aegean Sea from Greece. Since the traditional date of the Trojan War is 1184 B.C., it is interesting that one layer of the stacked ruins shows evidence of a war around 1200 B.C.

According to the legends, the Greeks had journeyed to Troy to take back Helen, the wife of the Greek king Menelaus. Helen had been kidnapped by the Trojan prince Paris, who was a guest at Menelaus's wedding. Assembling the largest army ever seen, the Greeks attacked Troy. The Trojan defenders, led by the great warrior Hector, kept the invaders outside the walls of Troy for ten long years. The Trojan defense was aided by bickering among the opposing Greeks. In spite of their internal problems, the Greeks

---

THE LITERARY WORK

A Roman epic poem set in ancient Italy, about 1200 B.C.; published in 19 B.C.

SYNOPSIS

Survivors of the Trojan War flee to Italy and, driven by prophecy, wage wars and overcome obstacles to found the city of Rome.

did not relent in their assault. Unable to pierce Troy's defenses, the frustrated Greek army finally decided to use guile instead of brute force to infiltrate the city's defensive walls.

They constructed a massive wooden horse and wheeled it up to the gates of Troy. At the same time, the entire Greek fleet cast off, apparently to return to their homeland. The people of Troy believed that they had finally won. The jubilant Trojans assumed the horse was an offering to the goddess Minerva to atone for the Greeks' desecration of her temple in their raids. They opened the gates and took the horse inside the city walls. But hidden in the wooden belly were fifty of the Greeks' best fighters. At night, after the Trojans had finished their victory celebration, the Greeks snuck out of the horse and cut down the few guards on duty. They opened Troy's gates from within and allowed the rest of the Greek troops, who had sailed secretly back into the harbor, to march in without resistance. Troy was then sacked mercilessly. Led by Aeneas, the remnants of the Trojan forces fled into exile.

Was Aeneas real? While there is no historical proof of the existence of a Trojan named Aeneas, there are mythical references to a Prince Aeneas in Greek literature. One such reference occurs in the epic poem the *Iliad* (also covered in *Literature and Its Times*). Probably composed in the eighth century B.C. by the poet Homer, the *Iliad* centers on the tenth year of the Trojan War. Though a Greek work, the tale spends a significant amount of time portraying the Trojan defenders. One of the Trojans depicted in the *Iliad* is a prince called Aeneas, son of Anchises and Aphrodite, the goddess of love. He is a wise counselor and a strong fighter. In one particular episode, Aeneas meets the fearsome Achilles in combat. Achilles is by far the strongest of all soldiers in the war, and Aeneas has little chance of defeating him. The gods intervene to save Aeneas, however, because he has been chosen to carry on the Trojan line. Poseidon, the god of the sea, explains:

> ... Zeus [the chief god] himself
> Will be angry if now Achilles cuts the man
>   [Aeneas] down.
> It is surely already decreed that Aeneas shall
>   outlive
> The war ...
> The mighty Aeneas shall soon rule
> The Trojans, and after him the sons of his
>   sons,
> Great princes yet to be born.
>   (Homer, *Iliad,* bk. 20, lines 297-304)

It is for this reason, then, that in the *Aeneid* Jupiter (the Roman name for Zeus) continually supports the efforts of Aeneas and appears to favor him. As the chief god, Jupiter is obligated to see that the decrees of Fate are carried out. Furthermore, Zeus/Jupiter is one of the ancient ancestors of the house of Troy, and some of his favoritism may stem from this connection.

The ancient Mediterranean. The Trojans, the Greeks, and the Romans inhabited lands in the region known as the Mediterranean Sea area. While the legendary Troy and Greece were located in the eastern Mediterranean, Italy (home of the Romans) was located further to the west. Not much is known about Italy during the period in which the Trojan War took place. The mainland inhabitants appear to have been primitive tribes with simple cultures. During the early Iron Age (c. 1000-700 B.C.), however, the various groups developed separate languages and identities. The Etruscans were by far the most powerful of these groups. Their advanced culture and superior technology were adopted by nearly all of the Italian tribes. Other tribes included the Sabines, Latins,

Volscians, Oscans, Messapians, Auruncans, and Umbrians. The various societies interacted through trade, conquest, and alliances. This complicated state of affairs was utilized by Virgil as the backdrop for the second half of the *Aeneid.*

In the eighth century B.C. Italy became an even busier region, as merchants from the Greek city-states and the Phoenician empire founded western colonies to carry out trade there. In fact, one

THE DECEPTIVE GREEKS

The ploy of the Trojan horse is the likely source of the expression "Beware of Greeks bearing gifts." In the *Aeneid,* a Trojan priest warns his comrades against taking the horse inside the walls of Troy, exclaiming:

"Have no faith in the horse!
Whatever it is, even when Greeks bring gifts
I fear them, gifts and all."
        (Virgil, *The Aeneid,* bk. 2, lines 47-9)

of Phoenicia's colonies in North Africa—Carthage—would later become a major rival of the Romans.

Rome at this time consisted of seven villages linked together for mutual defense. Its early inhabitants were part of the Latin tribe. It was not until 550 B.C. that the seven villages were united to form a recognizable city. The powerful Etruscans took control of the Latins and placed one of their own kings on the throne. Thereafter, Etruscans helped build Rome into a true city. They also reorganized the Latin military structure to make it more efficient, but the knowledge that the Latin Romans gained helped them to drive out the Etruscans four decades later. In 509 B.C. a military expedition led by the last Etruscan king, Tarquin the Proud, was routed by a combined force of Latin Romans and Greeks. The defeat plunged the Etruscans into a state of disarray. The Romans saw their opportunity and overthrew the Etruscan king. The Etruscan monarchy was replaced with a republic that would last until 44 B.C.

The Poem in Focus

The poem's contents. The poem begins with a description of the wrath of Juno, goddess of marriage and wife of Jupiter, the father of the gods.

Juno becomes angered after hearing a prophecy that Aeneas and his descendants will be the founders of a great city. The prophecy conflicts with her own goal, which is to have the inhabitants of her favorite city, Carthage, become the rulers of the world. She sends a furious storm to wreck the fleet of Trojan survivors, who are led

THE MYTHICAL FOUNDING OF ROME

In the sixth century B.C. the Romans changed from a system of rule by kings to a republic. The institution of the republic style of government marked an end to an era of Roman monarchs of both Latin and Etruscan heritage. Monarchies had been in power since the year 753 B.C., the legendary founding date of Rome by a mythic hero named Romulus. According to the legend, Romulus was directly descended from Aeneas through his mother, Rhea Silvia. His father was Mars, the god of war. Romulus and his twin brother Remus had decided to found a new city, but they could not agree on where to begin because there were seven different hills in the area. Remus chose the Aventine hill as his site, while Romulus laid down his foundations on the Palatine hill and built a wall around it as a boundary. Remus jumped over the wall in order to mock him. Romulus killed his twin on the spot and said, "So perish whoever else shall overleap my battlements" (Starr, p. 44). Mindful of the need to attract people to inhabit his new town, Romulus allowed all the criminals and bandits in the area to settle there. He became their king and lent his name to the city he founded. Thus, according to legend, was Rome founded.

by Aeneas. Ironically, the storm shipwrecks the fleet on the shores of northern Africa near the city of Carthage. Aeneas, who was separated from the rest of the Trojans in the storm, is aided by his mother, Venus (the Roman name for Aphrodite), who is the goddess of love. Aeneas and Venus enter Carthage hidden in a cloud. In this manner, no one notices the two of them or questions their presence. Once inside Carthage, Aeneas encounters Dido, the queen of the Carthaginians, who has already met and welcomed the other Trojans from whom Aeneas had become separated. The cloud that is covering Aeneas melts away. Dido welcomes him and holds a feast for the Trojans, during which she falls in love with Aeneas. Ignorant of her love for him, Aeneas relates the story of the fall of Troy and

the Trojans' adventures before reaching the shores of Carthage.

He recounts how a Greek named Sinon deceived the Trojans into taking the wooden "Trojan horse" inside the city walls. Aeneas tells of the final battle and how the gods themselves participated in the destruction of Troy. He describes his escape, explaining how he carried his father Anchises on his shoulders and took his son Ascanius by the hand. Ghosts and divinities subsequently directed Aeneas to establish a new Troy. Acting on those prophesies, he collected the survivors from the fallen city and escaped in a fleet of ships.

Aeneas notes that, after leaving Troy, the Trojans stopped many times and attempted to found new cities. But each time the gods drove him onward, instructing him to return to his forefathers' homeland. On occasion Aeneas and his people encountered monsters in their travels. Ferocious beasts such as the Harpies—creatures that are half-woman and half-bird—and the Cyclops—one-eyed giants who eat men—threatened Aeneas and his followers on their voyage.

After the feast, Dido invites Aeneas and his people to stay and help build Carthage. Aeneas agrees and settles down for a year. He even marries Dido secretly. Jupiter, however, sends down a messenger to spur Aeneas on again. He is thus forced to leave Carthage, even though Dido begs him not to go. After Aeneas's departure, Dido utters a curse in which she vows that Rome and Carthage will never know peace with each other. She then commits suicide, throwing herself on a burning pyre.

The Trojans proceed to Sicily, where other survivors from Troy have founded a city of their own. Aeneas and his people celebrate their arrival by having many contests: sailing, racing, archery, and boxing. Pressing onward despite further interference from the goddess Juno, Aeneas reaches the shrine of the Sibyl, a prophetess. She warns of the toils that the Trojans will face upon finally reaching mainland Italy. Undaunted, Aeneas declares that he is not afraid and asks if he may descend into the underworld to speak with the spirit of his father, who has died. The Sibyl states that only by finding and claiming a certain golden branch in the forest can Aeneas visit Anchises' ghost. She cautions him that the branch will only break loose for the one who has been fated to find it. Fortunately, when Aeneas finds the golden bough it yields to him. He then travels through Hades, the underworld. Hades, the Sibyl explains, is divided into two parts: Tartarus, where wrongdoers are punished, and Elysium, a paradise for heroes, philosophers, and honest men. Aeneas is allowed to visit Elysium, where the ghost of his father resides. Anchises shows Aeneas all of the future generations that will spring from Ascanius, Aeneas's son. Among them are Romulus, founder of the city of Rome; Julius Caesar, famous general and leader; and Octavius Augustus Caesar, the first emperor of Rome.

Aeneas then leaves Hades, embarks on his ship, and finally arrives in Italy. The Trojans set up a fortified camp and prepare a treaty with the Latins, the local tribe. The treaty is to be sealed by the marriage of Aeneas to Lavinia, the Latin king's daughter. But again Juno intervenes. She summons Allecto (one of the Furies, or avenging goddesses) to sow discord between the Trojans and Latins, a gambit that results in war.

The combined might of Italy's tribes, including Latins, Rutulians, Volscians, Auruncans, Sabines, and others, is thrown against the Trojans. Outnumbered and overwhelmed, the Trojans fare badly. At one point, Aeneas leaves with most of the soldiers to form another alliance with the Arcadians and Etruscans. The remaining Trojans stay inside their fortified encampment, refusing to leave its safety even though they consider such behavior dishonorable. This tactic buys them enough time for Aeneas to bring back reinforcements. When Aeneas does return, the tide turns against the enemy army. The Trojans then march on to the home city of the Latins and lay siege to it.

Determined to end the bloodshed, Aeneas challenges an enemy prince, Turnus, to a duel to decide which side shall be victorious. But Juno again intercedes, this time using her divine powers to stir up the Latins so that they will break the agreement to abide by the results of the duel. Her strategy works. The Latins attack without warning, and the duel does not take place.

During the ensuing battle, the goddess Juno keeps Turnus out of Aeneas's reach. But she protects Turnus only until she has gained an important concession from Jupiter: his decree that, although victorious in the battle with their enemies, the Trojans will lose their identity and be known forever after as Latins. Turnus is then slain in a duel with Aeneas after a mighty battle. The poem abruptly ends at that point.

The human side of Aeneas. An outstanding feature of Virgil's characterization of Aeneas is the hero's ability to feel sympathy for others, even his most dire enemy. When Queen Dido begs

Aeneas not to leave, Virgil allows his readers a glimpse into his hero's heart, showing the burden that destiny has placed on his shoulders:

> ...Duty-bound
> Aeneas, though he struggled with desire
> To calm and comfort her in all her pain,
> To speak to her and turn her mind from grief,
> And though he sighed his heart out, shaken still
> With love of her, yet took the course heaven gave him
> And went back to the fleet.
> (*The Aeneid*, bk. 4, lines 545-51)

The fact that Aeneas forges ahead makes him a hero, especially because the reader has seen the force of the love that he must overcome. Later in the poem, Virgil again gives us insight into Aeneas's psyche. In the final scene, Aeneas has at last bested his rival Turnus, who kneels at Aeneas's feet. Turnus asks for Aeneas's compassion, although he admits he has earned his fate:

> If you can feel a father's grief—and you, too,
> Had such a father in Anchises—then
> Let me bespeak your mercy for old age
> In Daunus [Turnus's father], and return me, or my body,
> Stripped if you will, of life, to my own kin.
> You have defeated me.
> (*The Aeneid*, bk. 12, lines 1268-73)

Aeneas is nearly swayed:

> Fierce under arms, Aeneas
> Looked to and fro, and towered, and stayed his hand
> Upon the sword-hilt. Moment by moment now
> What Turnus said began to bring him round
> From indecision.
> (*The Aeneid*, bk. 12, lines 1277-81)

In the end, Aeneas does kill Turnus. Nevertheless, the fact that Aeneas hesitates from striking down his worst enemy is a strong example of the hero's moral character. Indeed, it seems that Virgil believes the ability to have compassion is important, a message that he perhaps wanted to share with the society of his time. The narrative of the *Aeneid* indicates that Aeneas's beliefs in this regard were perhaps influenced by Anchises. In his visit to the underworld, Aeneas was given the following advice by his father: "Roman, remember by your strength to rule / Earth's peoples—for your arts are to be these: / to pacify, to impose the rule of law, / to spare the conquered, battle down the proud" (*The Aeneid*, bk. 6, lines 1151-54).

Sources. One of Virgil's objectives in writing the *Aeneid* was to combine the myth of Aeneas and the history of Rome. Virgil, however, was not the first Roman writer to connect Aeneas to the history of Rome. The tale of Aeneas was actually well known by the time Virgil began writing. One of the first written forms of the myth of Aeneas was authored by the poet and soldier Naevius in the third century B.C. His epic about Rome's history began with the story of Aeneas and culminated in battle between Rome and Carthage. Scholars believe that Virgil held Naevius in high regard and that he probably derived some of his ideas from Naevius's work. Another important source for Virgil was the Roman poet Ennius (239-169 B.C.), who wrote a versified chronicle of Roman history from its Trojan beginnings.

Naevius lived to see only the First Punic (Carthaginian) War; two even more devastating wars between Rome and Carthage followed. The Romans were disturbed that the resilient Carthaginians seemed only to grow stronger after their first defeat. This concern spurred the decision by the Roman Senate to completely destroy the city of Carthage. In 146 B.C. the Roman general Scipio Aemilianus razed the city and sowed the ground with salt. Virgil attempts to explain the roots of the bitter rivalry between the cities in his poem.

NO MORE WARS

In 29 B.C., Octavian ordered the Gates of Janus to be shut. When the Gates were open, it meant that Rome was at war; closing them was symbolic of the end of the hostilities that had plagued Rome during the preceding decades. Virgil must have been affected by the symbolic significance of the event because he used the Gates in the *Aeneid*. When the goddess Juno spurs on the Latins to make war against the Trojans, she descends from Mount Olympus and forces open the Gates of Janus, showing that a war has begun.

The character of Dido was based on the legendary founder of Carthage, Queen Elissa. In reality, however, the lovers Aeneas and Dido could never have met—Aeneas was a contemporary of the Trojan War, which probably took place in the twelfth century B.C., while Carthage was founded much later, in 814 B.C.

Virgil includes references to real-life people and events in a more limited way as well. In the Second Punic War, the Carthaginians were led by Hannibal, a brilliant general who, in fifteen years, was never defeated on the battlefield. The Romans managed to beat the Carthaginians anyway by avoiding a direct confrontation with Hannibal. The Roman soldiers, concerned that they could not defeat him in battle, remained in their fortified towns and awaited the return of their finest general, Scipio Africanus (grandfather of Scipio Aemilianus), from Spain. Hannibal could not storm the towns because he lacked the appropriate equipment. Virgil could very well have drawn on that episode in Roman history, for a similar situation unfolds in his poem when the Trojans face the tribes of Italy. When Virgil's Trojans refuse to give battle to the Rutulians:

> … [the] Trojans took position on the walls—
> For so on his departure their best soldier,
> Aeneas, had instructed them: if any
> Emergency arose, not to do battle,
> Not to entrust their fortunes to the field,
> But safe behind the walls to hold the camp.
> (*The Aeneid*, bk. 9, lines 56-61)

Just as the Trojans awaited Aeneas's return, the real-life Romans held out until their best general could return from Spain.

Events in History at the Time the Poem Was Written

Chaos and terror in Italy. Rome had formed a republic in 509 B.C. after driving out the Etruscan kings. Though it lasted until 44 B.C., the final fifty years of the republic were full of chaos. In 90 B.C. Roman subjects throughout Italy revolted, and the next two decades featured seven major slave rebellions. In addition, Rome experienced a civil war in 82 B.C. that caused significant bloodshed. Adding to the carnage of that conflict was the revenge that individuals such as the general Lucius Cornelius Sulla took on their opponents in the war. Sulla, the victor of the civil war, made a list of all his enemies and decreed that anyone whose name was on the list could be killed; those who murdered his foes would receive a reward. Following Sulla's dictatorship, Rome was subjected to still more internal struggles. Julius Caesar eventually emerged triumphant. Conquering his opponents, he was named dictator for life, though his reign lasted only until March 15, 44 B.C., when he was murdered by a group of senators. Virgil, a twenty-six-year-old student in Rome at the time, witnessed these events. Virgil subsequently retreated to his home in northern Italy, away from all of the turmoil in Rome.

Before his death, Julius Caesar had named his great-nephew Octavian (Octavius Caesar) as his successor. Many disputed Octavian's claim on the throne, however. More wars erupted as Octavian fought a number of foes, including the generals Mark Antony and Marcus Lepidus, for control of Rome. In 42 B.C. the three factions reached a truce and divided the rule of Rome equally among themselves.

Octavian needed to pay the troops that had supported him during the war, so he commanded that lands be taken away from others and given to his soldiers. Virgil's farm in Mantua was confiscated by one of Octavian's legionnaires as a part of this effort. Legend has it that through the influence of powerful friends, Virgil was given back his farm, but this is probably not true. Despite any conflict over the property, Octavian ultimately became Virgil's supporter as a patron of the arts and the direct sponsor of the *Aeneid*.

In the meantime, the truce had broken down. Antony, Lepidus, and Octavian resumed their battle to gain the upper hand. The contest eventually came down to just Antony and Octavian. In 31 B.C., at the battle of Actium, a naval engagement took place that secured Octavian's place as the sole ruler of Rome. Virgil was a strong supporter of the new ruler, who was granted all the powers of an emperor. Virgil glorified Octavian's triumph by describing the battle of Actium in the *Aeneid* in a scene that displays this battle of the future on a shield made for Aeneas by Vulcan, the god of fire. In the poem, the purpose of the shield is to inspire Aeneas by giving him a glimpse of the future glory of Rome. In real life, it reflected Virgil's high regard for Octavian, which probably stemmed from the fact that the new ruler finally brought peace to Italy after his defeat of Antony.

The Golden Age. After Octavian assumed the position of emperor, he set out to consolidate all of Rome's territory. Rome entered a period of unequaled prosperity and peace that Virgil describes as "an Age of Gold" (*The Aeneid*, bk. 6,

line 1065), though he only lived to see the beginning of this era. Octavian gained the title *pater patriae,* "father of the country," and also became known as the "divine Augustus." After he died, the Senate enrolled him among the gods of the Roman state.

Octavian also worked to shape the morality of the Roman people. He attempted to bring back previously extinct religious rites from the Roman past such as the worship of ancient deities and the organization of secret brotherhoods. He hoped to set an example for the Romans of his day by referring back to the proud heritage of their ancestors. In the spirit of those reforms, Octavian was in favor of Virgil's work on the *Aeneid* since the poem recounted a glorious tale of Rome's founding.

In 19 B.C. Virgil, still trying to finish revising the *Aeneid,* was returning from Greece when he suddenly became ill and died. He had given specific instructions to his two closest friends to destroy the manuscript of the poem if anything should happen to him. Octavian forbade it, however, ordering that the work be published as it was. He already knew the caliber of the work since Virgil had read several sections of the poem to him and his wife.

For More Information

Bourne, Frank C. *A History of the Romans.* Boston: D. C. Heath, 1966.

Bulfinch, Thomas. *Bulfinch's Mythology.* Edited by Richard P. Martin. New York: HarperCollins, 1991.

Frank, Tenney. *Life and Literature in the Roman Republic.* Berkeley: University of California Press, 1961.

Glover, T. R. *Virgil.* New York: Barnes & Noble, 1969.

Homer. *The Iliad.* Translated by Ennis Rees. New York: Oxford University Press, 1991.

McKay, Alexander G. *Virgil's Italy.* Greenwich, Connecticut: New York Graphic Society, 1970.

Starr, Chester G. *The Ancient Romans.* London: Oxford University Press, 1971.

Virgil. *The Aeneid.* Translated by Robert Fitzgerald. New York: Vintage Books, 1983.

Antigone

by
Sophocles

Sophocles (496-406 B.C.) came from a wealthy family in Athens and took an active role in that city-state's political life. He wrote 123 plays, but only seven of them have survived to the present. *Antigone* was a huge success for him at the dramatic festivals held in Athens. Ancient texts reveal that he was elected a general in the Athenian military because of the popularity of this work.

Events in History at the Time the Play Takes Place

Legends of the Bronze Age. The story of Antigone is drawn from Greek mythology, a great body of oral tales that inspired later Greek painting, sculpture, poetry, and theater. Scholars have used ancient Greek writings that record these oral tales, as well as inscriptions found by modern archaeologists, to determine the genealogy, or family tree, of the legendary rulers of Thebes, the Greek city in which *Antigone* takes place.

According to legend, Thebes first came to prominence and power around 1380 B.C. under the rule of a man named Cadmus, who was said to have moved there from Phoenicia (present-day Syria). The people and events that Sophocles portrays in his play were thought to have occurred in the 1200s B.C., some eight hundred years before Sophocles lived. This earlier period of time is often referred to as the "Bronze Age" because the metal was commonly used by people of the era to fashion their weapons and household tools.

Ancient myths, contemporary conflicts. The Theban "cycle" of myths (about the legendary rulers of Thebes) is one of three that were cen-

THE LITERARY WORK

A play set in thirteenth-century B.C. Thebes; first performed in 442 B.C. in Athens.

SYNOPSIS

Antigone disobeys the laws of her ruler, Creon, in favor of the unwritten laws that she feels more properly govern society. She is condemned to a chilling fate.

tral to Greek mythology; the other two are the Trojan War cycle and the stories of Jason and the Argonauts. The events in these myths are imagined to have taken place in the thirteenth and twelfth centuries B.C., although this need not imply the historical existence of these heroes at this time. Even the fifth century B.C. historian Thucydides, a contemporary of Sophocles, realized that it was unwise to regard tales from the past as being true:

> In investigating past history ... it must be admitted that one cannot rely on every detail which has come down to us by way of tradition. People are inclined to accept all stories of ancient times in an uncritical way....
>
> [P]oets ... exaggerate the importance of their themes, ... the prose chroniclers ... are less interested in telling the truth than in catching the attention of their public and [their] authorities cannot be checked and [their] subject matter, owing to the passage of time, is mostly lost in the unreliable streams of mythology.
>
> (Thucydides, 1.20-1)

In practice, Athenian playwrights often used the traditional stories to make points about their own era, and they often used mythological conflicts to portray contemporary ones to an audience. Removing the action to the mythic past, and using heroic characters, a playwright was able to touch on the profound and significant issues of his day from a safe distance. In the *Antigone*, Sophocles focuses on the possible conflicts between one's religion and one's politics. His drama pits the laws of the gods against the laws of the state as reflected in one girl's decision to, contrary to city law, perform religious burial rites for her brother, a traitor. The *Antigone* may also be commenting on the conflict in fifth-century Athens between the ancient aristocracy (which supported worship of family gods, ostentatious burial and oral tradition) and the newborn democracy (which supported respect for city gods, modest burials, and written laws).

The Play in Focus

The plot. By the time Sophocles wrote his play, the tragic dynasty of Oedipus, King of Thebes, had already been the subject of many poems and plays. The most famous of these were four plays by Aeschylus, another playwright of the same era who was regarded as the first great writer of Athenian tragedy. Athenian audiences thus knew the tale of Oedipus intimately.

The story of Oedipus was used by Sophocles to set the scene for the events depicted in *Antigone*. King Oedipus discovered that he had by accident killed his father and married his mother. Horrified to discover the manner of his father's death and the identity of his wife, Oedipus blinded himself and went into exile. One source has Oedipus commending his children into the care of his mother's brother Creon; another of Sophocles' plays has Antigone faithfully accompanying Oedipus into exile, as his attendant. Oedipus later died, as did his wife and mother Jocasta, who hanged herself. Creon, who had subsequently assumed the throne of Thebes as regent until Oedipus's two sons should grow up, is now king in his own right.

These two sons, Eteocles and Polynices, had been cursed by their father because they had twice insulted him. The curse included a prophecy that the boys would grow up to kill each other. Upon reaching adulthood, Eteocles and Polynices fought over their inheritance; they had agreed to alternate the kingship, but, once

in power, Eteocles refused to give up the throne. Polynices left Thebes in anger and married into the royal family of Argos. In Argos he assembled an army and attacked the city of his birth. The seven gates of Thebes were assailed by seven heroes, one of whom was Polynices himself. All seven heroes died during the siege. Polynices died at the hands of his brother, who was mortally wounded during the struggle as well. Oedipus's prophecy was thus fulfilled.

Sophocles's play begins with Antigone and Ismene, who were sisters of the recently deceased Polynices and Eteocles. Antigone, obviously distressed, reveals to Ismene the latest news: because Polynices has been fighting against the city of his birth, King Creon has now forbidden anyone to touch the corpse or give it a decent burial. Antigone and Ismene argue about whether or not they should bury Polynices' body. Ismene refuses to help in the illegal act, but Antigone secretly performs a ritual burial, dusting the corpse with a light sprinkle of earth. Antigone's defiance of the king's wishes causes her to be arrested by Creon's guards and brought before him. Antigone admits and staunchly defends her crime. When she is taken away, Creon's son Haemon, who is engaged to Antigone, calmly attempts to convince Creon to yield his wrath. But Creon is unbending, and Haemon leaves in a rage. Creon then sentences Antigone to be entombed in a cave with barely enough food to live on, a punishment to which she surrenders with bravery and dignity. Shortly thereafter, the prophet Teiresias arrives to warn Creon that Polynices must be buried. Creon again refuses to listen to advice. A messenger arrives with the news that Antigone has hanged herself and that Haemon, upon discovering her, killed himself also.

Religion and civic pride. Creon's anger at Antigone's disobedience may seem totally unreasonable to modern readers. But her excuse for breaking his law might have seemed equally unreasonable to an ancient Athenian audience: Antigone claims that a law higher than Creon's—the law of Zeus—has directed her to act as she has. But the ancient Greeks did not live according to a single code of ethical behavior. No single god or organized church or particular way of living was singled out as the best. Religion was viewed more as a matter of civic identity and pride. Each city-state had its own special gods that it worshipped. Citizens were free to worship other gods if they so chose as long as they did not neglect the city's gods,

Painting by V. J. Robertson depicting Antigone strewing dust on the body of Polynices.

who were expected to watch over the city's interests.

Worship practices included making public sacrifices or gifts to the city's gods and participating in ceremonies with other city-dwellers. Every community cared for its own local rituals in much the same way that it cared for its public affairs. In fact, religious activity was a significant aspect of political life in Greek society. The reverse was also true—civic duty and pride became a sort of religious obligation. This association between civic duty and religious practice was so strong in Athens in the years immediately after *Antigone* was first performed that worship of the goddess Athena had turned more or less into worship of the city itself.

This situation in fifth-century Athens is clearly reflected in the *Antigone,* despite the play's much earlier Theban setting. Here, Polynices's betrayal of his city and Antigone's rejection of the civic law that forbids her from burying her traitorous brother has serious, almost religious, implications. Although Sophocles does not mention any particular god of Thebes in the play, Antigone refers to Zeus as the source of the law by which she acts. Sophocles may have included this reference to suggest that she has perhaps abandoned her local god in favor of a more universal deity.

Unwritten laws. Antigone claims that "unwritten and unfailing rules" led her to bury Polynices. Sophocles thus alludes to an issue that was a subject of much debate in fifth-century B.C. Greek society. How much power did such "unwritten" laws have when they came into conflict with civic laws?

> *Creon:* Did you know that an edict had forbidden this action?
> *Antigone:* I knew it, inevitably. It was no secret.
> *Creon:* And still you dared to transgress these laws?
> *Antigone:* Yes, for it was not Zeus who proclaimed that edict to me, nor did that Right who dwells with the gods below lay down such laws for mankind; and I did not suppose that your decrees had such power that you, a mortal, could outrun the gods' unwritten and unfailing rules.
>
> (Sophocles, *Antigone*, 446-57)

Pericles, the great Athenian general who dominated the social and political scene at the time the play was written, addressed the issue of unwritten laws, also known as laws of conscience. As one scholar notes, he seemed to suggest "that they are concerned with various matters outside the reach of ordinary laws. At least he claims that the Athenians respect them" (Bowra, p. 161).

These "various matters" are not clearly articulated. Even the Greek historian Thucydides, who recorded the general's words, provides no additional information on specific unwritten laws. Nonetheless, Pericles held that "we [Athenians] give our obedience to those whom we put in positions of authority, and we obey the laws themselves, especially those which are for the protection of the oppressed, and those unwritten laws which it is an acknowledged shame to break" (Pericles in Thucydides, 2.37). Pericles here recognizes the power of unwritten laws but does not specify what they are or whether or not they are supposed to take precedence over civic laws.

Yet Sophocles insists in *Antigone* that such unwritten laws are more important in regulating human actions than any formal legal code worked out by men. Perhaps this commentary is a reaction to events taking place in Athens at the time Sophocles lived. Athenians were so proud of their city and its political and artistic achievements that a form of city-worship arose. "In an age when Athens was almost taking the place of her gods as an object of worship, the poet protested that the priorities were wrong and that if there is a conflict between divine and human law, there is no doubt which claims first obedience" (Bowra, p. 163). Sorting out which laws are human and which are divine could be difficult, however. The law of Zeus that Antigone claims has guided her action may actually be the law of her own conscience, as there were no universally applicable or "unfailing" laws attributable to Zeus or any other Greek deity.

Creon vs. Antigone. The conflict between Antigone and the king of Thebes exists on many different levels. Antigone is the daughter (and half-sister) of King Oedipus, to whose throne Creon has ascended. Her family history puts her in an uncertain social position in the court of the new king, who may be hostile to the relatives of his predecessor.

Furthermore, Antigone's decision to bury her brother is not only a violation of Creon's decree, but also an expression of disregard for the social constraints placed on young women of the era. Throughout ancient Greek history, women had no say in political affairs whatsoever. They could not vote or hold public office. They were rarely seen outside the home, except at such major events as festivals, marriages, and funerals. Antigone's sister Ismene reminds her of this subordinate status when she says, "We must remember, first, that we were born women, who should not strive with men" (*Antigone*, 46-47). Creon's thoughts regarding his battle of wills with Antigone are shaped in large part by her gender. When his son Haemon urges him to reconsider his terrible anger, the king responds, "While I am alive, no woman shall rule over me" (*Antigone*, 525). He seems to feel that his rule is threatened by the decision of one woman to act on her own authority. In his depiction of the tension between the willful Antigone and her uncle Creon, Sophocles suggests that the king's actions stem partly from the prevailing philosophy about the appropriate status of women.

Sources. Sophocles took the characters for *Antigone* from a well-developed body of Greek stories about the tragic family of Oedipus. He must have been especially aware of the work of his fellow playwright Aeschylus, who had already written about the Theban dynasty in his play *Seven against Thebes*. In writing *Antigone*, Sophocles created a separate tragedy that centered on one of the lesser characters in Aeschylus's play. Sophocles used the familiar characters of the royal family of Thebes but changed their actions to suit his own dramatic purposes. Antigone's defiance of Creon, for instance, is a plot element that other writers do not mention in relating the story of King Oedipus and his family.

Events in History at the Time the Play Was Written

Pericles, Creon, and Athenian democracy. According to some critics, the character of Creon was modeled at least in part on the great Athenian general Pericles, who dominated the Athenian political scene during much of Sophocles' public life. Sophocles was one of Pericles' fellow military leaders and possibly his friend. If the portrait of Creon as a power-hungry, autocratic, and harsh leader does resemble Pericles, however, the extent of that friendship is perhaps in question. In 442 B.C., when *Antigone* was first performed, Pericles' career was at its highest point. One school of thought argues that the figure of Creon, who abuses his power, may have been intended as a veiled warning to Pericles and

---

ANTIGONE HONORS THE DEAD A SECOND TIME

~

Guard: When we arrived there ... we wiped away all the dust that covered the corpse, stripped the damp body well, and sat on top of a hill to windward, taking care that the smell from the body should not reach us.... After a long time ... the girl was seen; and she uttered a piercing cry, the shrill note of a bird, as it cries when it sees, in its empty nest, the bed bereft of nestlings. So she, when she saw the corpse bare, broke out in lamentation, and called down curses on those who had carried out the deed. And at once she brought thirsty dust in her hands, and lifting up a fine bronze ewer she paid her respects to the corpse with a threefold libation.

(*Antigone*, 408-31)

---

the Athenian people about the dangers of dictatorship. In the play, Creon stubbornly insists that Antigone suffer an awful fate for her actions. His refusal to listen to any line of reasoning served to remind the Athenian audience of the terrors that tyranny could bring.

Democracy was a relatively new social development in Sophocles' Athens. It had been born

in the late sixth century B.C., after a long period of dictatorship. Concerned that dictatorship might return, the populace set up strong laws designed to protect against just such a possibility. Athenian males who were not slaves could vote on the city's political and economic business. A system was devised wherein the city was managed primarily by ten generals. Each of these ten generals came from one of the ten tribes into which democratic reformers had divided the Athenian people. To prevent power plays based on family or regional biases, each tribe included members from all over the state.

As one of the ten generals of Athens, Pericles was subject to regular electoral approval and thus could not establish a dictatorship through legislative means. Pericles did not need to establish a formal dictatorship, however; he was immensely popular and was, in essence, "the uncrowned king of Athens" (Wilcoxon, p. 207).

Other critics insist that Creon behaves as he does precisely because of the democratic ideal. He does not take into account his family ties to Antigone and Polynices when making his judgments. Instead, he treats them as though they are common citizens who have acted against the best interests of the city. In fact, when Ismene asks Creon to pardon Antigone because she is such a wonderful match for his son Haemon, the king retorts, "There are arable fields of others" (*Antigone*, 569), clearly reflecting Creon's view that Antigone is just another woman. As one scholar notes, "Creon, the political leader, categorizes and simplifies; one female equals another.... In a perverse way, Creon's refusal to distinguish, to particularize, to see differences, may make him more the democrat than the tyrant" (Saxonhouse, p. 74).

Burial rites. Funerals in Greece were largely the responsibility of women during Sophocles's time. They washed and dressed the body, adorned it with flowers, and then covered it up. Only close relatives participated in this ritual. After a death, the "prepared" corpse was laid out for two days in the home and then taken away for burial before the dawn of the third day. The funeral procession—led by men and followed by lamenting women—wound slowly outside the city gates to a cemetery, where the body would be laid to rest.

The Greeks practiced cremation as well as burial. If the former practice was chosen, the body was either burned in its grave or burned on a separate pyre, after which the ashes were buried. The dead person was typically buried with a variety of offerings, including pottery, stone vases, and

The Herod Atticus Ancient Theatre at the foot of the Acropolis Hill in Athens. The plays of Sophocles were originally performed in theaters of this type.

personal possessions. By some accounts, traitors and people who robbed temples were not entitled to be buried within Athenian territory, but the historical record is far from consistent on this. Thus, as Andrew Brown points out in his translation of *Antigone,* "whether [Creon] is justified in forbidding burial to Polynices is not clear. It was evidently normal practice, at Athens and elsewhere, to forbid burial on their native soil to men convicted of treason.... In such cases, however, the body would be cast outside the borders, rather than left in a place where it could cause pollution to the city" (Brown in Sophocles, p. 6). Left out in the sun for wild dogs to pick at, Polynices's rotting body has just this effect. Creon's refusal to let anyone touch the corpse thus seems poorly reasoned in this respect.

The sophists. Fifth-century B.C. Athens saw the rise of a revolutionary group of teachers and philosophers. Called the sophists, they turned their attention away from the gods and goddesses toward the study of mankind. The opening of *Antigone* features the famous "Ode to Man," which echoes the ideas of this philosophical movement:

> Wonders are many, and none more wonderful than man.... Subtle beyond hope is his power of skilled invention, and with it he comes now

to evil, now to good. Respecting the laws of the land and the right of oaths sworn by the gods, he is a man of a lofty city; cityless is he who recklessly devotes himself to evil.

> (*Antigone,* 332-75)

The sophists were individual teachers who differed in their views as well as their standards but agreed that the main subject of their teaching should be human actions. A particular area of study and emphasis was mankind's political views. Teachers of middle-class origin, the sophists educated the young sons of the wealthy about the practice of democracy. Pericles was closely acquainted with certain of the notable sophists in Athens and supported their influence on the city's intellectual life.

Antigone, of course, features not only the "Ode to Man" but also several dramatic events that point out a number of the faults of mankind. The Greek word deina, which is sometimes translated as "wonderful," can also mean "terrible." Some readers contend that Sophocles seems to make use of this double meaning in his work, arguing that his use of the word signifies a veiled criticism of a world view focused too intently on man.

The Athenian theater. Sophocles's plays were written to be performed in public at the great Theater of Dionysus. Located in the heart of

Athens, the theater sat with other important city buildings on the slope of the rocky hill of the Acropolis. Plays were usually staged during the festival of Dionysus, the god of growth and wine, which took place at planting time in March. Crowds of 15,000 people regularly attended the performances, and even criminals were released from prison in order to see the plays. Attendance at these dramas was perceived to be a civic duty, in part because the plays often addressed important social and political issues.

The dramatic part of the festival's program was presented as a competition between playwrights, each of whom put on four plays in the

---

THE CHORUS ADVISES CREON

*C*reon: To yield is terrible, but it is a terrible project to stand firm and so bring down the blows of ruin upon my spirit.
Chorus: Wise counsel is needed....
Creon: What should I do, then? Tell me and I will obey.
Chorus: Go and release the girl from the underground chamber, and furnish the unburied body with a tomb.
Creon: Is this really your advice? You think I should yield?
Chorus: Yes lord, and with all speed.

(*Antigone*, 1095-1104)

---

space of one day. The first three were tragedies, often related to each other. The last play was a "satyr" play that poked fun at the serious subjects and characters of the three earlier plays. The satyr play was followed by a comedy by another playwright, which was part of a separate competition for writers of comedy. "For five days the playwrights showed their productions ... and the audience made their preferences clear [by booing or cheering].... The plays were then judged by ten judges, each one selected from one of the ten tribes of Athens. These ten then cast their votes into an urn and five of the votes were drawn out at random. From these five votes the result was announced" (Taylor, p. xxiii). This complex process may have been designed to discourage cheating, an illustration of how seriously the dramatic competitions were taken.

The Chorus. The Greek word *choros* (chorus) means "dance." An important part of fifth-century B.C. drama, the chorus was a group of singers and actors who either commented on what was occurring in the main part of the drama or actually functioned as a character in the play. The chorus served as a link between the audience and the actors, often portraying a group of citizens not unlike the audience themselves. In *Antigone,* the chorus is a group of Theban elders who keep shifting their loyalty back and forth from Creon to Antigone; their indecision further confirms the complex nature of the issues under discussion.

In Greek drama, the chorus was assembled before the people involved even knew what play would be performed: "The making of plays started not with the playwright but with the Chorus. Five rich men were selected by the city authorities and each was required to select, train and produce a chorus for one of the five days [of dramatic competition]" (Taylor, p. xxi). The members of the chorus were young amateur male actors who had to be costumed, fed, and trained for their role. After the choruses were chosen, civic authorities chose the playwrights who would produce plays and matched each of them with one of the choruses and with professional actors. Choruses were thus matched with playwrights in fairly arbitrary fashion.

Reviews. When Sophocles's *Antigone* was first unveiled, the tough Athenian audience awarded it first place in the dramatic competition. But perhaps more interesting than the ancient Greek reaction to *Antigone* is the amazing "modern" history of the play. The drama has been praised over the years by a wide range of writers, including John Keats, William Butler Yeats, George Eliot, Frederich Nietszche, Martin Heidegger, and Jean Cocteau. "Between c. 1790 and c. 1905, it was widely held by European poets, philosophers, [and] scholars that Sophocles's *Antigone* was not only the finest of Greek tragedies, but a work of art nearer to perfection than any other produced by the human spirit" (Steiner, p. 1). *Antigone*'s depiction of the clash between individual conscience and governmental law has caused it to be an especially noteworthy play in times of war as well. It was immensely popular during the French Revolution and immediately after World War II, for example. The play has also been cited as an early attempt to explore the issue of equal rights between men and women.

For More Information

Bowra, C. M. *Periclean Athens.* New York: Dial Press, 1971.
Hammond, N. G. L. *The Classical Age of Greece.* London: Weidenfeld and Nicolson, 1975.

Saxonhouse, Arlene W. *Fear of Diversity: The Birth of Political Science in Ancient Greek Thought.* Chicago: University of Chicago Press, 1992.

Scodel, Ruth. *Sophocles.* Boston: G. K. Hall, 1984.

Sophocles. *Antigone.* Translated by Andrew Brown. Warminster: Aris & Philips, 1987.

Steiner, George. *Antigones.* Oxford: Oxford University Press, 1984.

Taylor, Don, trans. *Sophocles: The Theban Plays.* London: Methuen, 1986.

Thucydides. *The Peloponnesian War.* Translated by Rex Warner. New York: Penguin, 1972.

Wilcoxon, George Dent. *Athens Ascendant.* Ames: University of Iowa Press, 1979.

The Autobiography of Benjamin Franklin

by
Benjamin Franklin

Benjamin Franklin's life of eighty-four years (1706-1790) spanned most of the eighteenth century—a period in which the American colonies grew from small, isolated communities to a united nation of thirteen states. Franklin contributed greatly to the political founding of the nation and did much to help shape the American character. He thus became known by many as "the first American." In his autobiography, which stops almost twenty years before he helped to draft the Declaration of Independence and over thirty years before his death, he describes the formation of his own character as an example to others in the newly emerging nation.

THE LITERARY WORK

An autobiography detailing events in Benjamin Franklin's life from 1706 to 1757, set mostly in Philadelphia; first part published in French translation in 1791; first, second, and third parts published in English in 1818; complete version published in English in 1868.

SYNOPSIS

Benjamin Franklin relates various incidents from his life, beginning with his childhood in Boston and ending with his first period of service as a colonial agent in England.

Events in History at the Time the Autobiography Takes Place

Proprietary politics. Decades before hostilities broke out between the English government and the American colonies, a small-scale conflict was already raging in the colony of Pennsylvania, where Franklin resided. Founded as a proprietary colony by the Penn family of England in the seventeenth century, Pennsylvania had served as a haven for religious tolerance and a home to hard-working Quakers for half a century when Franklin arrived there. The Penns had advertised the colony as a land of wealth and opportunity, attracting a large number of English and German tradesmen and farmers. Settlers did, in fact, find wealth and opportunity there, but as their population mounted and the elected as-

semblies of the colony became more active, the inequalities in the distribution of this wealth and opportunity became noticeable. The origin of much of the disagreement over these inequalities lay in what the colonists viewed as unfair taxes. The Penn family, which governed mainly from England but maintained estates in Pennsylvania, had pulled strings to exempt themselves from the responsibility for paying colonial taxes. Unwilling to ignore this perceived injustice, the local assemblies fought over this tax exemption for years. In 1757 Franklin finally achieved a royal ruling in favor of the local assemblies.

Puritan virtue and Quaker individualism. The two cities in which Franklin spent the first half of his life were centers of religion. His birthplace was Boston, Massachusetts, a city founded by Puritans (also known as Congregationalists) in search of a place to practice their "pure" lifestyle of simplicity and religious strictness. His parents were devout Puritans, and Franklin's father was known to quote passages from the Bible about such subjects as the virtue of hard work. Striking out on his own, Franklin ran away from home to Philadelphia, Pennsylvania, a refuge for Quakers, who rejected professional ministers and political hierarchies.

For Puritans in New England, religion was not just something to think about on Sundays; it was an important part of everyday life. Whether they were farmers, doctors, or sea captains, they believed God had "called" them into their professions just as he had designated them his "chosen" people. Interestingly, although most Puritans attended church services faithfully, worked hard at their jobs, shunned the consumption of alcohol, and viewed untruthfulness and pride as terrible sins, their behavior was not driven by a desire to work their way into heaven. In their view, God had already made up his mind about who was fit to join him after death; God's unknowable will, not their own virtue, determined where all would spend their afterlives.

Franklin himself was not a particularly religious man. He valued the practicality of Puritan moderation, industry, and humility, but felt that "good works" should be the goal, not just a byproduct, of any religion or moral code. In a letter written in his mid-forties, he explains his sentiments:

> I wish [faith] were more productive of Good Works than I have generally seen it; I mean real good Works, Works of Kindness, Charity, Mercy and Publick Spirit; not Holiday-keeping, Sermon-Reading or Hearing, performing Church Ceremonies, or making long Prayers, fill'd with Flatteries and Compliments, despis'd even by wise Men, and much less capable of pleasing the Deity.
> (Franklin in Lopez, p. 197)

The Quakers with whom Franklin lived and worked in Philadelphia were of a different breed than the Boston Puritans, although they had descended from the same roots in England. In Boston, the sermons of Puritan ministers were the highlight of every week. The Quaker communities of Philadelphia, on the other hand, had neither sermons nor professional ministers. Quakers, who sought to establish individual relationships with God, rejected the power structure of most churches. They believed that each

"Friend" (as Quakers were called) could act as his or her own priest. As a result, Sunday gatherings of Quakers in living rooms or meeting houses did not follow a program of worship. Instead, those who had gathered sat in silence until someone was "moved" to speak—about scripture, religious concerns, or personal experiences. The Quaker emphasis on individual initiative and human equality made its way into the political structure of Philadelphia and into Franklin's own philosophy.

PACIFIST POLITICS

Although Quaker ideas about equality and individualism contributed to the democratic political philosophy of the young United States, many Quaker beliefs—especially the "pacifist" notion that no war was justified—caused continual political trouble in Pennsylvania. Finally, in 1756, Pennsylvania's non-Quaker governor declared war on two neighboring Indian tribes that had been attacking the colony's western border towns. The colony's Quaker Assembly members, unable to support the war, resigned. Their resignations relieved Franklin and other Pennsylvanians who found Quakerism incompatible with the defense of their colony.

Colonial schooling and the self-educated man. For most colonial children in the eighteenth century, school started and ended in the home. Organized schools were rare and costly to maintain, so middle- and lower-class families often had to depend on educated relatives and friends to pass along their knowledge to the young. Luckier middle-class children who lived close to schools or tutors, and whose parents could afford the expense, received more formal primary education. But few young people went on to gain a secondary education, the equivalent of high school. Fewer still attended college. Those students who did receive a college education usually entered the clergy, as Franklin's father originally intended for him to do.

One alternative to academic education was apprenticeship. Boys in their early teens would agree to work for a "master"—an expert carpenter, candlemaker, printer, or other tradesman. An apprentice learned his trade through a course of on-the-job training that typically spanned several years. Franklin's two years of school and five years of apprenticeship were typical in his day.

A lifelong devotion to learning, however, set him apart from many other colonists.

The public printer. In 1730, the year after Franklin took control of the *Pennsylvania Gazette,* seven newspapers were being published regularly in four American colonies. By 1800, ten years after his death, the United States was home to over 180 newspapers. Printing, a struggling industry in the first quarter of the 1700s, developed into a thriving business during the years that Franklin ran his print shop. A wide variety of printed material became common in this period: newspapers; public documents (in high demand, with thirteen busy colonial governments in America); advertisements; political and religious pamphlets; and almanacs, which helped farmers decide when to plant their crops and provided all readers with pithy tidbits of advice and wisdom. Because of the popularity of their publications, printing shops became town "hangouts"—especially when the building also served as a general store and post office, a common occurrence in the colonial era. Politically-minded citizens would gather at the printing press to see election results printed. Townspeople would stop to chat while collecting their mail or shopping. "Public printers" like Franklin and his counterparts emerged as men of great influence in their communities.

FRANKLIN ON THE EDUCATION OF FEMALES

In his autobiography, Franklin mentions in passing "the Propriety of educating the Female Sex," primarily in bookkeeping and accounting so that they could manage family affairs in the event of widowhood (Franklin, *Autobiography of Benjamin Franklin,* p. 60). His own daughter learned French, music, arithmetic, and bookkeeping, while his son was tutored by a famous astronomer and mathematician and an accomplished Latin scholar.

Love, marriage, and dowry. Marriage was the cornerstone of society in eighteenth-century America. As a result, men were encouraged to find wives for themselves. Bachelors were considered dangerous, prone to rowdy behavior and disgraceful behavior in regard to women. Franklin's actions during his single years confirmed this view of unmarried men; he later admitted that he was involved in "intrigues with low Women" during his youth (*Franklin, Autobiography,* p. 128). In Puritan Massachusetts, bachelors were viewed almost as criminals. If they had difficulty finding a wife, the community encouraged them to lodge with a family until they were successful in finding a mate. Financial factors also contributed to the pressure to marry. In seventeenth-century New Haven, Connecticut, for instance, taxes specifically targeted at bachelors were instituted. An additional inducement to marry was the dowry, a payment made by the family of a wife-to-be to her new husband.

Franklin thus felt plenty of social pressure to find a wife when he settled in Philadelphia. When he speaks about his frustrations in trying to find a wife with a dowry, Franklin may sound stingy and unromantic to modern readers, but his businesslike approach to marriage was typical for his time; marriage was a contractual agreement. The presence of love in a marriage was certainly valued, but its absence was not seen as a major deterrent.

In Franklin's arrangement with Deborah Read, who eventually became his wife, it seems that love—or at least affection—did play a part, because he did not receive a dowry. Their relationship began long before they were married, but then Franklin left for a trip to England. While overseas, he seemed to lose interest in Read. He eventually returned to Philadelphia and again took up his search for a wife. Meanwhile, Read had married a man during Franklin's absence, but her husband disappeared. Franklin's guilt about having abandoned her while he was in England, his frustration with efforts to find a proper wife, and his fondness for her and her family were all reason enough to endure the risk he describes in the first part of the *Autobiography:* that Read's first husband—or his debtors—would reappear and make a claim on Read or on Franklin's money. If the man had returned and Franklin and Read had been married under Pennsylvania law, they could have been imprisoned for life as bigamists. Mindful of that scenario, the couple chose instead to be joined unofficially in "common law" marriage. Read's former husband did not return.

American science in the age of the Enlightenment. While Philadelphia's colonists were busy building a new home for themselves, scientists in England and the rest of Europe were riding the wave of excitement generated by the discoveries of the Enlightenment. The Polish astronomer Nicolaus Copernicus had discovered that the earth revolved around the sun. The Eng-

Franklin (left) at his print shop.

lish physicist Sir Isaac Newton had formulated the theory of gravity. All through Europe, scientists were building on these discoveries and many others, constructing a clearer picture of how the world worked. The prevailing notion of the Enlightenment—that human reason could understand anything—fueled research and theory-building and created an elite community of European scientists. They read the works of Newton and other scientific leaders, held international meetings, and established exclusive societies. Americans, meanwhile, faced a disadvantage in conducting scientific research. With scholarly books hard to come by and European gatherings difficult to attend, some of them could only conduct experiments on their own.

Franklin was one of many amateur inventors in the colonies who were far removed from the scientific dialogue of Europe. In fact, most of them, with the limited knowledge available on their side of the ocean, understood only a small portion of the theories under discussion in European laboratories. In Franklin's case, however, ignorance had its advantages. Unaware of the complex theory of electricity that was popular in Europe at the time, Franklin embarked on his own series of experiments. He tested and developed his own theory of electricity, which proved to be simpler and more accurate than the fashionable European one. Franklin's interest in science was based largely on practical concerns: protecting homes from lightning, for example, with a lightning rod. In scientific as in other pursuits, his main tool was his own practical reasoning rather than complicated mathematical formulas or extremely involved calculations. Franklin's work marked a triumph for practical reasoning. In fact, common sense became known as the American form of reason during the Enlightenment due largely to the works of Franklin.

The Autobiography in Focus

The contents. Franklin's *Autobiography* is divided into four parts that follow the order of Franklin's life. The first, written in 1771, is the most personal; it focuses on the formation of Franklin's character. He explains that he is writing his autobiography both to provide his son and other descendants with a model life to emulate and to relive his happy experiences by recording them. Franklin proceeds to describe what he knows of his family tree, all the while pointing out similarities between himself and his ancestors. The discussion then turns to his young life. Franklin relates a series of stories about his childhood mistakes and accomplishments. Gradually a picture of a studious, hardworking, and independent-minded young man emerges.

Working as an apprentice under his older brother James, Franklin learns the tools of the printing trade while still a teenager in Boston. Frustrated by his brother's strict treatment of him, he leaves home at seventeen, arriving in Philadelphia with only a few coins in his pocket and no job. After a few false starts, including an eighteen-month stay in London, Franklin establishes himself as a printer and shopkeeper. In his early twenties, he forms the Junto, his famous discussion club. Its members, local artisans and tradesmen, debate issues such as capital punishment and slavery and discuss social news of the day. He also marries Deborah Read and embarks on his first act of community betterment: the founding of a public library in Philadelphia.

In 1784, thirteen years after writing part one, Franklin wrote part two of the autobiography. In this section, he resumes the discussion of his library project and briefly touches on his relationship with his wife. The bulk of the section, however, is devoted to a list of virtues and an explanation of the importance of each one; Franklin even includes a picture of a checklist he used to keep track of his progress on the path to "moral Perfection" (*Autobiography*, p. 148).

Part three, begun in 1788, is the longest of the four sections and marks a gradual change in focus from personal anecdotes and advice on virtue to a comparatively dry rendering of his public activities and Philadelphia's political concerns. After charting the rise of his success as a printer and local politician, he discusses in depth his involvement in the French and Indian War (which included a stint as a colonel) and his participation in the debate that raged between the city's assembly and its proprietors, the Penn family. Although his discussion of these topics lacks the intimate tone of the first and second parts, the third part does have its moments of humor. For example, at one point Franklin relates his wartime strategy for encouraging soldiers to attend prayer services: tell the minister to give out rum. This section is also interspersed with fascinating tidbits about Franklin's inventions, his experiments with electricity, and his involvement in the international scientific community in the later period of his life.

The very brief part four was probably written in the winter of 1789-90. It focuses entirely on Franklin's first diplomatic mission to England, where he served as a colonial agent charged with establishing a fair taxing policy for the Penn family's estates in Pennsylvania. His mission successful, Franklin returns to Philadelphia in 1762, and the *Autobiography* ends.

Franklin's American dream. The *Autobiography of Benjamin Franklin* is believed by many to be the first literary rendering of the American Dream. Franklin's life is a rags-to-riches story, a chronicle of one man's rise from pennilessness to power. Many readers saw his autobiography as a testament to the success that can come from hard work and high hopes. Since its discovery, America had long been linked in the European mind to the notion of new possibilities. Franklin's memoirs advertised the reality of this vision to the world. The land in which he rose to success was a land where people were not limited by class origins, where the son of a candlemaker could succeed as a diplomat, where a self-educated man could emerge as a great scientific mind—where, in short, common people could become extraordinary.

Portrait of Benjamin Franklin.

Despite his success, Franklin is realistic about the societal factors that contribute to one's success or failure. He knows the importance of a good reputation and acknowledges that appearance can be a crucial factor in attaining success. In the first part of the *Autobiography*, Franklin describes his initial strategy for business success:

> In order to secure my Credit and Character as a Tradesman, I took care not only to be in Reality Industrious and Frugal, but to avoid all Appearances of the Contrary. I drest plainly; I was seen at no places of idle Diversion; I never went out a-fishing or shooting;... and to show that I was not above my Business, I sometimes brought home the Paper I purchas'd at the Stores, thro' the Streets on a Wheelbarrow.
>
> (*Autobiography*, pp. 125-26)

Another aspect of Franklin's American Dream is that it focuses on the rise of the individual. The *Autobiography* emphasizes Franklin's younger years and the early shaping of his character. Even in the second half of the memoirs, Franklin continues to convey a feeling of progress when he describes his activities. Moving from one area to another with ease—from Philadelphia politics to the postal service to war on the frontier to diplomacy in England—Franklin is constantly challenging himself and continually learning. Even his observance of his personal improvement program, complete with a system for tallying his errors and achievements in each of thirteen categories of virtue, lasts for years. He finally becomes too busy to complete his list every night; yet he continues to carry the book of virtues with him as a reminder to aim for good behavior.

Sources. Franklin's *Autobiography* tells a new story with a fresh style in an old format. The structure of his memoirs follows patterns well established by the eighteenth century. The ancient Greek general Xenophon and the philosopher Aristotle wrote lists of virtues that were studied by many colonial schoolchildren. Plutarch, another Greek philosopher whom Franklin read as a boy, recorded the lives of great men in order to teach morality by example. A few decades before Franklin's birth, Cotton Mather, a Massachusetts Puritan, published a series called *Essays to Do Good* (1710) containing practical advice on how to "do good." Also, two major autobiographies preceded Franklin's work; one, written by an English lord (Lord Herbert of Cherbury), may have even inspired Franklin to write his own. Finally, rags-to-riches stories had already been written in England prior to Franklin's effort, although the main character's success in the English stories was generally attributed not to hard work and initiative, but rather to a stroke of luck or success in battle.

Franklin's book was different from many of its predecessors, however, because it told its story with a twist of irony and humor. Compare the excerpts below—one from the preface to a moral guide by Cotton Mather and the other from Franklin's *Autobiography*. Both deal with the topic of humility, but from very different perspectives.

> **Cotton Mather's *Bonifacius*:**
>
> I have not been left altogether uninformed, that all the rules of discretion and behavior, are embryoed in that one word, MODESTY. But it will be no breach of modesty, to be very positive in asserting, that the only wisdom of man lies in conversing with the great GOD, and His glorious Christ; and in engaging as many others as we can to join with us in this our blessedness; thereby promoting His Kingdom among the children of men; and in studying to do good unto all about us.
>
> (*Bonifacius*, p. 6)

> **Franklin's *Autobiography*:**
>
> In reality there is no one of our natural passions so hard to subdue as *Pride*. Disguise it, struggle with it, beat it down, stifle it, mortify it as much as one pleases, it is still alive, and will every now and then peep out and show itself. You will see it perhaps often in this History. For even if I could conceive

that I had compleatly overcome it, I should probably [be] proud of my Humility.

(*Autobiography*, p. 160)

Using the simple language that is his trademark, Franklin brings the ideal of virtue within reach of the common person. His honesty and directness draw in his readers, allowing them to laugh at their faults even as they strive to improve themselves. Franklin may have followed the examples of other writers like Mather, but his voice and his story are all his own.

Events in History at the Time the Autobiography Was Written

What Franklin left out and why. Benjamin Franklin lived to be eighty-four years old, a rare accomplishment in colonial times. Strangely, however, the last thirty-three years of this remarkable life—years in which he signed *The Declaration of Independence* (also covered in *Literature and Its Times*) and participated in the founding of the United States—are not discussed in his autobiography. Some scholars speculate that Franklin may have simply run out of time. Franklin's final installment of the autobiography is thought to have been composed only a few months before his death, during which time he was too weak to write and had to dictate his thoughts to his grandson. But why did he wait until the last years of his life to finish his memoirs? Why the long period of procrastination between 1771 and 1784?

Certainly Franklin was preoccupied with other concerns such as the fate of his fledgling nation and his hectic social and political life as a diplomat in England and France. A major player in world politics, his responsibilities were numerous and often time-consuming. Some historians claim that he might also have become disillusioned about his hopes of influencing the younger generation. In the time between writing the first and second parts of the *Autobiography*, the Revolutionary War had rent a painful tear in his family. While his own loyalties lay with the Americans, his only son had supported the British. If he could not even succeed in convincing his son of the need for independence, the historians contend, he may have grown discouraged about his ability to shape the hearts and minds of America's youth. Franklin may have ended the bulk of his autobiography in 1757 (though it mentions briefly later events) as a result of a combination of all these factors. Others point out, however, that perhaps Franklin felt he had finished what he set out to do.

Delay, reception, and impact of the *Autobiography*. Stories about Benjamin Franklin were told around the world long before he died, so his memoirs were eagerly awaited. Unfortunately for the reading public, the complete and original version was not printed until 1868. The delay was caused largely by Franklin's grandson William Temple Franklin, whom the elder Franklin had entrusted with the manuscript. For unknown reasons, Temple Franklin failed to print his edition (complete except for the fourth part) of the *Autobiography* until 1817-1818. By then, many copies of the first part had already been printed and read. This first printing, though, was a re-translation of a pirated French version that was probably based on a copy sent to Europe by Benjamin Franklin.

Most early reviews were overwhelmingly positive. Business people praised the *Autobiography*'s principles of hard work and practical goals, and instructors used it in their classrooms to teach virtue. Copies were printed in England, Ireland, and Canada, and translated into Danish, Dutch, French, German, Polish, and Spanish.

There were, however, some negative responses to Franklin's work. John Adams, the second president of the United States, had been one of Franklin's rivals in his lifetime. He remained a critic after Franklin's death. In an 1811 essay, Adams wrote that Franklin had enough faults of character to deserve neither applause nor condemnation. Mid-nineteenth-century preacher Theodore Parker summed up the complaints of others in a remark in the introduction to the *Autobiography*: "Franklin thinks, investigates, theorizes, invents, but never does he dream" (Parker in *Autobiography*, p. 13).

Despite such criticism, the work established Franklin as America's first symbol of the self-made man, and people heeded his advice. *The Autobiography of Benjamin Franklin* inspired many of its readers. Thomas Mellon left his Pennsylvania farm after reading the book and became a prosperous banker, while the Italian printer Gaspero Barbera, who described himself as a "lost man" before reading the book, afterwards became "healthy, cheerful, and rich" (Barbera in *Autobiography*, p. 11). A chronicle of a man on the rise in a nation on the rise, the *Autobiography* became a handbook for those around the world who wanted to better themselves.

For More Information

Boorstin, Daniel J. *The Americans: The Colonial Experience.* New York: Random House, 1958.

Franklin, Benjamin. *The Autobiography of Benjamin Franklin.* Edited by Leonard W. Labaree, et al. New Haven: Yale University Press, 1964.

Lopez, Claude-Anne, and Eugenia W. Herbert. *The Private Franklin: The Man and His Family.* New York: W. W. Norton, 1975.

Mather, Cotton. *Bonifacius: An Essay upon the Good.* Edited by David Levin. Cambridge: Cambridge University Press, 1966.

Quimby, Ian M. G. *Apprenticeship in Colonial Philadelphia.* New York: Garland, 1985.

Sweet, William Warren. *Religion in Colonial America.* New York: Charles Scribner's Sons, 1942.

Beauty: A Retelling of the Story of Beauty and the Beast

by
Robin McKinley

The daughter of a naval officer, Robin McKinley spent much of her early childhood abroad. She attended college in Maine in the early and middle 1970s, during the rise of the women's rights movement in America. Her novel *Beauty: A Retelling of the Story of Beauty and the Beast* reflects changing perceptions about fairy-tale heroines during this period, as well as her own personal interests. Set in the mythical past, the story itself is not closely linked to any specific time period. The familiar version of "Beauty and the Beast," the tale on which the novel is based, appeared in 1757 in France, where it was affected by developments in art and society that spanned more than a century. McKinley's story takes place in an era that resembles the one evoked by the familiar French version and so bears a relation to some events of that period.

Events in History at the Time the Novel Takes Place

Women, education, and salons. Upper-class French women in the early 1600s generally received a basic education. Often instructed by their nurses, they were tutored in such basic subjects as reading, writing, and geography. Some also learned to dance, sing, or play the clavichord, an early keyboard instrument. In addition, all little girls were taught social etiquette so

---

---

that they might become courtly ladies. Many girls were sent to convents to further their education, but in general their training was geared toward domestic skills. Women did not attend universities and had little access to public spheres of discourse.

In Robin McKinley's story, the character Beauty wishes to attend a university, but her longing is scorned by her governesses. Undaunted, Beauty seeks to educate herself despite social constraints. In this regard Beauty's efforts paralleled those of some upper-class women during the 1630s. These women were well connected socially; in particular, they were associated with the royal court. A number of the more intellectually curious women began meeting at salons (or drawing rooms) in Paris to talk about art, literature, love, marriage, and other subjects of importance to them.

In the salon meetings, women strove to develop their conversational skills. They emphasized particular styles of thinking, speaking, and writing that would distinguish them above others in society, placing special emphasis on wit and innovation. Skillful presentation of oneself in salon gatherings became a means of establishing individual worth.

By the middle of the 1600s, these upper-class French women began inventing parlor games to enhance their salon conversations. Among these games was the telling of stories, the object being to create the most interesting story based on a well-known narrative, such as a folktale. Although many of the tales were familiar to salon audiences, the story was supposed to seem like it was invented on the spot. Great emphasis was placed on the appearance of spontaneity, which led the women to sharpen their thinking and remarks and, at times, to question the male standards by which they lived their lives. At the same time, this type of parlor game allowed a woman to gain a reputation as an intelligent individual. She could, through storytelling, demonstrate her knowledge of courtly etiquette, fashionable manners, and proper social relations.

Fairy tales and social criticism. Many people in upper-class French society considered fairy tales vulgar and associated them with the peasant class. It was considered somewhat scandalous that French society women told such stories. Yet by the 1690s, some upper-class writers began to print the fairy tales that were told in salons. In 1690 Marie-Catherine d'Aulnoy published one of the first written fairy tales. Increasing numbers of people followed suit, submitting written versions of fairy tales for publication. For the next thirty years, the fairy tale genre became one of the most popular forms of writing. One of the reasons fairy tales became so popular is that they served as a means of social critique.

Just as the salon clientele consisted primarily of women, the majority of the writers and tellers of fairy tales were female. In their tales they sometimes gave female characters more power than women usually had in society at the time. A number of the writers who gave women the upper hand in their tales became well-known authors.

Many fairy tale writers of the seventeenth century opposed the court of Louis XIV. During the 1680s, Louis XIV waged very costly wars that were financed by heavy taxes. These exorbitant taxes left the lower classes impoverished and the higher classes in a state of severe financial distress. The harsh economic situation was further aggravated by several years of bad crops. Because people were not allowed to openly criticize Louis XIV, fairy tales became a covert means of doing so. The fairy tales often served as a protest against the king's court, illustrating the differences between the possible warmth and richness of a monarchy and the realities endured by people under the reign of Louis XIV. As one authority noted, "there was no splendid paradise in Louis XIV's court, no genuine love, no reconciliation, no tenderness of feeling. All this could be, however, found in the fairy tales" (Zipes, p. 9). Other tales pointed out faults in behavior by royal characters. The tale by the above-mentioned Madame d'Aulnoy, for example, features Prince Adolph, who puts a higher priority on the quest for glory through war than on his love for a princess. As a result, he fails to find happiness.

Marriage. During the 1700s young women from upper-class families had little control over many aspects of their lives. A young woman's marriage partner was most often dictated by her parents. Generally, the parents chose their daughter's future husband according to his social rank and fortune; often she was not consulted about their choice. Courtship, if it existed, was brief and often conducted in a businesslike manner. Extremely young when they married, many girls felt they had no choice but to accept their prescribed husbands and hope for the best. Marriage offered them a position in society, a chance to be presented at court, and possibly a life filled with luxuries and amusements such as operas, balls, and plays.

One of the main themes of the Beauty and the Beast tale is the courtship and marriage between Beauty and her monstrous husband. Regarded as serious subjects in French society of the 1700s, love, courtship, and marriage dominated many early fairy tales. The authors of these tales included women who had been forced to marry, as well as a few who had declined marriage in order to maintain their independence. *Beauty* reflects and comments on these traditions in some respects, particularly in its view of the relationship of love, class, and marriage. In McKinley's version of the tale, Beauty refuses many suitors and chooses, of her own free will, to live her life with the Beast.

Literary changes in eighteenth-century France. During the early 1700s in France, perspectives about literature began to change. As a part of this change, stories became vehicles for conveying morality, social norms, and proper manners. By this time, fairy tales had developed from a rather subversive genre to a more standardized and conventional one. The tales had become completely accepted by the upper classes and emerged as an increasingly visible element of children's literature.

The familiar plot of the Beauty and the Beast tale was fully developed by Madame Gabrielle-Suzanne de Villeneuve in 1740, well after the salon traditions had waned. Basing her story on de Villeneuve's version, another writer, Jeanne-Marie Le Prince de Beaumont, published the most familiar version of "Beauty and the Beast" in 1757. One of the first people to set down fairy tales explicitly for children, de Beaumont tended to write tales with a strong moral intent. Her version of the tale appeared in a book designed to educate little girls, and she used Beauty as a model of how to properly raise girls by emphasizing the importance of domestic skills and self-sacrifice for women.

The practice of using fairy tales as models of behavior continued into the 1800s. Due to the strict conservatism of the nineteenth century, the character of Beauty was often portrayed as meek, submissive, and docile. Betsy Hearne noted in a study of the various incarnations of the Beauty and the Beast tale that "every age modifies the traditions it receives from its predecessor," and that one version of the tale from the early 1800s contained a strong element "of dutiful contentment with one's lot" (Hearne, p. 36). Another version, in 1843, prompted the observation that English versions of the Beauty and Beast tale were filled with moralizing on such issues as education and marriage.

The Novel in Focus

The plot. The book introduces a wealthy merchant who lives in the city with his three daughters. The two older daughters, named Hope and Grace, are very beautiful. The youngest daughter, whose real name is Honour, is nicknamed Beauty despite the fact that she considers herself rather plain-looking in comparison to her sisters. More clever than her sisters, Beauty spends her time reading and dreaming of attending a university.

One day the merchant's ships are lost at sea, which reduces his family to poverty. His daughter Hope has a suitor named Gervain, who offers to take the family back to his village in the country. There, Gervain can earn a living and the family can start a new life. Everybody agrees to the plan. Before they leave, a friend of the family gives Beauty a horse named Greatheart, which she has secretly admired. The family travels for months before reaching the village.

Country life is very different for the girls. They no longer have the servants they had in the city. Instead, the girls have to wear peasant clothes, do their own cooking, and scrub the floors of their new home, which sits at the edge of the forest. Beauty grows accustomed to the new life more quickly than her sisters. But she, like everyone else in the family, is mystified by the nearby forest. Gervain warns her that the forest is haunted and that she should never wander into it or drink from the forest stream.

One day word arrives that one of the lost ships has been found. The girls' father returns to the city to take care of business and is gone for several months. Before he leaves, he asks each member of his family what he should bring back as a present. Beauty requests rose seeds. When the father finally returns, he has a strange, frightening story to tell. On his way back to the country, he became lost in the woods and stumbled upon a magical castle. Although the castle seemed empty, food appeared and he found a bed waiting. He had been unable to acquire rose seeds for Beauty in the city, so the next morning he picked a rose to bring her from the castle's beautiful gardens. Suddenly, a horrible beast appeared and demanded that either Beauty or her father return to the castle as payment for the rose.

Beauty finally convinces her father that she is the one who must return to the castle. She leaves with her horse, Greatheart, thinking that surely she will be eaten at the castle. Upon arrival, though, she finds herself the beneficiary of wondrous magic. Food serves itself to her, and she finds a giant library stocked with thousands of books. She has a beautiful room filled with gorgeous clothes. Preferring simple clothing, Beauty often quarrels with her invisible servants, who try to make her wear fine garments. She spends most of her days riding and reading. Even the weather around the castle seems magical.

In time Beauty meets the Beast, who frightens her with his horrible appearance. Surprisingly, the Beast proves to be kind, and he explains to Beauty that he wants her company. Eventually the two become good friends. Every night the Beast, who thinks Beauty is lovely, asks her to marry him. Beauty always answers "no"—she does not think that she can love the Beast.

Illustration for an 1854 publication of the Beauty and the Beast tale.

Beauty longs for her family, so she asks the Beast if she can visit them. The Beast agrees to let her go for one week, warning that if she does not return to him he will die. Once home, Beauty recognizes that she has changed during her stay in the castle. Her family does not understand magic, and she has difficulty relating to them. She also discovers that she misses the Beast. When Beauty decides to stay an extra day, she dreams that the Beast has died. Frightened, she leaves for the castle immediately and finds the Beast in a corner, barely alive. Beauty suddenly realizes that she loves the Beast and agrees to marry him. Immediately, the Beast is transformed into a handsome prince. He explains that he had been under an enchantment that could only be broken when somebody agreed to marry him in his hideous form. Beauty marries the prince, and they live happily ever after.

How Beauty thinks. Robin McKinley's version of "Beauty and the Beast" is considered a feminist story because of Beauty's character. In many American fairy tales, the heroines are beautiful and sweet, and often these are their most prominent qualities. Beauty, on the other hand, has a strong, temperamental personality. In McKinley's version, Beauty nicknamed herself when she was five years old. While she is not ugly, she considers herself very plain-looking, and as she matures her nickname makes her uncomfortable because she thinks it unsuitable. While her sisters dress up and go to parties, Beauty rejects such frivolous behavior because of her self-perception.

In one scene in the Beast's castle, she fights with her invisible servants over the garments that she should wear. She cries out that "it is a beautiful dress.... And that's why I won't wear it; if you put a peacock's tail on a sparrow, he's still a brown little, wretched little, drab little sparrow" (McKinley, *Beauty*, p. 183).

Beauty also has strong opinions and does not hesitate to voice them. When, for example, Gervain warns her to stay away from the forest because it is enchanted, she declares, "I've never heard anything about this.... Are you sure you're not making it all up to scare me into obedience? It won't work, you know; it'll only make me mad" (*Beauty*, p. 43).

Finally, Beauty is smart. While dwelling in the city, she avoids social gatherings, preferring instead to stay home and read. She actively pursues an education, describing to the reader her love for books and her secret desire to attend a university. Beauty notes that her governesses believe that scholarship is not a proper pursuit for a young woman. At the castle, however, her love for books works to her advantage, for she is able to enjoy the large library at her disposal. Her wit and education also enable her to befriend the Beast. Beauty and the Beast spend long hours discussing books and poetry.

Honor in *Beauty*. McKinley's story *Beauty* emphasizes the quality of honor. In McKinley's tale, Beauty's real name is Honour, and McKinley considers the concept of honor a central narrative element. Beauty's father promises that either he or Beauty will return to the Beast's castle in one month, presumably to be devoured by him. The father believes that since he was the one who angered the Beast, he should go. This portrayal of the father differs from his image in many versions of "Beauty and the Beast." In other versions, he is portrayed as a weak and selfish person who agrees to sacrifice his daughter because he is a coward. In McKinley's version, however, the father is willing to accept responsibility for his transgression and recognizes the importance of a vow. Beauty, however, is also honorable, and considerably more strong-willed than her father. She refuses to send him to his death, insisting instead that since the rose is hers, she should go to the castle. She declares in a typically Beauty-like manner:

> What will you do then, tie me up?... I will go, and what's more, if [need be] ... I will run off tonight while you're asleep. I need only get lost in the woods, you said, to find the castle.
>
> (*Beauty*, p. 78)

Sources. Stories of beauties and beasts are common throughout the world. In some of these tales, it is the husband who is enchanted and transformed into an animal; in others, it is the wife. In many such tales, the spell can only be broken by a kiss. Stories of this kind have been collected in India, Africa, central Asia, and the Americas. In Europe, the Beauty and the Beast tale has appeared as an oral story in places as distant as Rome and Russia.

The Roman tale of Cupid and Psyche is considered the earliest predecessor to Beauty and the Beast. In the Roman tale, the character Psyche is so beautiful that men are afraid to court her. The goddess Venus grows jealous and sends her son Cupid on a mission to make Psyche fall in love with the most vile creature on earth. Instead, Cupid himself falls in love with her. Meanwhile, an oracle directs Psyche's parents to leave her on a mountaintop as a bride for a fierce and terrible serpent. On the mountaintop, Psyche falls asleep and awakens to discover a great palace where she is magically served. Here, her husband, Cupid, visits Psyche at night. She is forbidden to look at him and believes her husband to be some sort of monster. One night she breaks her promise and shines a light from an oil lamp on Cupid. When she discovers his beauty, she kisses him and spills some of the burning oil on him, awakening Cupid. He furiously returns to Venus, who punishes Psyche by assigning her four impossible tasks. Eventually the couple is reunited. Although their tale may be at the root of the Beauty and the Beast story, key differences exist between Beauty and Psyche. Beauty, unlike Psyche, acts of her own accord in going to meet the Beast. Also, whereas Psyche is punished for her disobedience in looking at her lover, Beauty is rewarded for her cleverness and her ability to see through the ugly exterior of the Beast to find the prince within.

The first known printing of a tale about a beautiful young woman whose love for a beast frees him from an evil spell occurred around 1550; the tale appeared in a collection by Gianfracesco Straparòla called *The Nights of Straparòla*. In 1697 Charles Perrault included the story in his *Tales of Mother Goose*. In 1740 a version penned by Gabrielle-Suzanne de Villeneuve developed the plot line as it is known today. The next decade saw her version simplified by Madame Le Prince de Beaumont. De Beaumont's 1756 version became the one familiar to modern readers and a major source for versions that followed.

Events in History at the Time the Novel Was Written

Feminism. McKinley's *Beauty: A Retelling of the Story of Beauty and the Beast* was published in 1978, in a decade when the women's rights movement was at its peak. The movement had its roots in the political unrest of the 1960s, an era when minorities such as African Americans fought for and gained equal rights and social recognition. The involvement of the United States in the Vietnam War further fueled feelings of dissatisfaction with the status quo. As many women participated in minority and antiwar protests, they increasingly recognized ways in which women were oppressed. Efforts were undertaken to change the way that American society treated women. Two important laws of the 1960s helped women gain a stronger and more equitable position in the nation's work force. The Equal Pay Act of 1963 included a provision that made it illegal to pay people different rates due to gender, while a provision in the 1964 Civil Rights Act made it illegal to discriminate in hiring and firing practices on the basis of gender.

The 1970s saw the women's movement in full swing. Women challenged the traditional roles of the subservient wife and mother that had dominated American consciousness for decades. They embraced a number of nontraditional roles, and many took a more active course in seeking jobs outside the home. By 1984 approximately 50 million women were in the labor force; by contrast, only 31 million women had been counted in America's work force in 1971. The most significant increase in female employment was in the twenty-four to thirty-five-year-old demographic bracket, the age at which most women have children. Though these figures indicate the large strides females made in gaining employment in the 1970s, economic need was also a factor in the change; many families could no longer make ends meet with only one wage earner in the household. It should also be noted that the larger percentage of women in the work force did not end sexual discrimination. Female workers were paid less than men on average and they were less likely to hold powerful positions. For example, less then 3 percent of the top federal jobs were held by women in the 1970s. Nonetheless, the decade marked a period of unprecedented growth for women in the workplace.

Women also attended college in record numbers during this period. The number of women receiving doctorates rose from 14 percent in 1970 to 28 percent in 1980. McKinley herself graduated in 1975. Her love of books and education is reflected in her portrayal of Beauty. At one point in the narrative, Beauty states:

> My intellectual abilities gave me a release, and an excuse. I shunned company because I preferred books; and the dreams I confided to my father were of becoming a scholar in good earnest, and going to University. It was unheard-of that a woman should do anything of the sort—as several shocked governesses were only too quick to tell me, when I spoke a little too boldly—but my father nodded and smiled and said, "We'll see." Since I believed my father could do anything—except of course make me pretty—I worked and studied with passionate dedication, lived in hope, and avoided society and mirrors.
>
> (*Beauty*, p. 6)

Meanwhile, several major changes in the structure of the American family took place during this time. Birth rates dropped, the age at which people married rose, and the divorce rate doubled. The growing economic opportunities for women had given them new options in life besides those of being a wife and mother.

Women also began to object to the stereotypical depiction of girls and women presented in various media, including fairy tales. A number of articles published in the early 1970s objected to fairy tales presenting women as passive and helpless. Many feminists questioned whether such images hindered women's effort to achieve equal status with men. Not only did they write academic articles that challenged such stereotypes, but authors like Robin McKinley began to rewrite familiar fairy tales, populating them with strong female heroines. In the case of McKinley's *Beauty,* the author paints young Beauty as an intelligent, headstrong, and adventurous woman. She is far from helpless; rather she actively helps both her family and herself and demonstrates that women can have their own adventures.

McKinley and Beauty. There are several parallels between the main character Beauty and McKinley herself. For one thing, both love horses. McKinley recalls that as a child she always played wild-horse games, while Beauty is described as having a special talent for communicating with her horse, Greatheart. At the Beast's castle, she convinces Greatheart to walk near the Beast, something no other animal had done before.

For both McKinley and Beauty, horses and books were far more interesting than people during their adolescent years. Beauty is a shy and awkward character. As a child, McKinley also found it difficult to make friends. Beauty's disinterest in boys—at one point she rejects her male friend Ferdy's advances—reflects a similar disposition held by the author in her youth.

As a child, McKinley told herself stories about girls who do things. She noticed that boys "were the ones who got to have adventures, while we got to—well, not have adventures" (McKinley in Trachtenberg, p. 262). Beauty, however, is active and adventurous throughout the story. When she insists on going to the castle, her sister Grace remarks:

> "I see you are very determined," she said. "I don't understand why."
> I shrugged. "Well, I'm turned eighteen. I'm ready for an adventure."
>
> (*Beauty*, p. 78)

Folktales and popular culture. In the 1970s, folklorist Kay Stone documented the impact of Walt Disney's films on American women's perception of fairy tales. She found that many women were most familiar with Disney's versions, and suggested that such widely viewed movies played a role in the socialization of girls. Although this has not been proven directly, Stone noted that Disney's heroines reached new heights of passive behavior, sweetness, and beauty.

The original versions of many of the tales portrayed their heroines as being strong and intelligent, not just beautiful. These original versions, however, were often violent or sexual in nature, and Disney's target audience was the family. Thus, Disney "cleaned up" the stories for film production and distribution. Disney was not the first to do so; the Grimm brothers had similarly "cleaned up" fairy tales for audiences of their time (the early 1800s).

In *Beauty: A Retelling of the Story of Beauty and the Beast,* McKinley fights against the passive and often negative portrayal of women in fairy tales. In many versions of the story, Beauty's sisters are characterized as jealous, materialistic, and cruel. Often, they are turned to stone as punishment for their behavior. Betsy Hearne describes one version: "It is jealousy that drives these ... wicked ladies to their fate; none of them has a life of her own, but all are dependent on a miserable bunch of husbands to fulfill their existence" (Hearne, p. 18). In contrast, McKinley's version portrays Beauty's sisters as loving and supportive. They are more beautiful than Beauty, but also kind and tender.

The work of writers such as McKinley, coupled with the efforts of the women's movement, have influenced the film industry. In 1992 Disney released a new film version of the "Beauty and the Beast" tale. Although the heroine, Belle, retains many of the traits associated with American fairy tales, the movie gives her more spirited qualities as well. The film generally portrays her as inquisitive and adventurous rather than victimized.

For More Information

Gatlin, Rochelle. *American Women Since 1945.* Jackson, Miss.: University Press of Mississippi, 1987.

Goncourt, Edmond, and Jules de Goncourt. *The Woman of the Eighteenth Century.* Westport, Conn.: Hyperion Press, 1981.

Hearne, Betsy. *Beauty and the Beast: Visions and Revisions of an Old Tale.* Chicago: University of Chicago Press, 1989.

McKinley, Robin. *Beauty: A Retelling of the Story of Beauty and the Beast.* New York: Harper & Row, 1978.

Trachtenberg, Stanley, ed. *Dictionary of Literary Biography.* Vol. 52. Detroit: Gale Research, 1982.

Zipes, Jack. *Don't Bet on the Prince.* New York: Routledge, 1987.

Benito Cereno

by
Herman Melville

Born in New York City in 1819, Herman Melville took to the seas at age nineteen. His extensive travels brought him into contact with people of many races and cultures. The important legal rulings of his father-in-law, who was Chief Justice of the Supreme Court of Massachusetts, had a great impact on slavery issues and possibly also on Melville's attitudes toward slaves. Perhaps sparked by these experiences, Melville wrote the novella *Benito Cereno*. The story explores various perceptions and attitudes of the time concerning race and human equality.

Events in History at the Time the Novella Takes Place

The African slave trade. The African slave trade reached its height during the eighteenth century. Most of the slaves came from the west coast of Africa. They were cast into bondage as a result of a wide variety of circumstances. Prisoners from Africa's continual tribal feuds served as a major source of slaves, but the slave ranks were also swelled by debtors, criminals, and innocent blacks captured by slavers who made their living by kidnapping the unwary.

Slavers took their unfortunate victims to coastal cities, where they were held with other slaves in structures known as barracoons. These were huge slave pens, constructed by driving heavy logs into the ground and fastening them together with iron bands. Slaves captured during the winter sometimes languished in these primitive, uncovered prisons for months, exposed to the elements until summer winds brought slave ships from the West. After the slave ships arrived and the trading was concluded, the

---

THE LITERARY WORK

A novella set on two ships off the coast of Chile in 1799; first published in 1855.

SYNOPSIS

An American captain encounters the ship of Benito Cereno, unaware that the vessel has been rocked by a slave uprising.

---

owners forced the captured slaves to remove whatever clothing they had and climb into the ships' holds. On some ships, the hold, an interior part of the ship where cargo is stored, measured only 30 to 36 inches from floor to ceiling. For the greater part of the voyage, which could last longer than three months, male slaves remained tightly chained together. Because of the cramped quarters of the ships, slaves commonly had to lie in tight rows with their heads in the laps of the men behind them. The slaves ate meals of rice, beans, or potatoes twice each day and received seawater for washing.

On clean slave ships, the slavers washed out the holds and allowed the slaves to periodically enjoy the fresh air and sunlight on deck. These small measures were frequently insufficient to maintain sanitary conditions, and the dank recesses below deck became a breeding ground for infection and disease. Slaves who became seriously ill were often thrown overboard to keep the sickness from spreading. On one occasion, a ship loaded with 800 slaves suffered an outbreak of smallpox that reduced the slave ranks to 497 and killed 12 members of the crew.

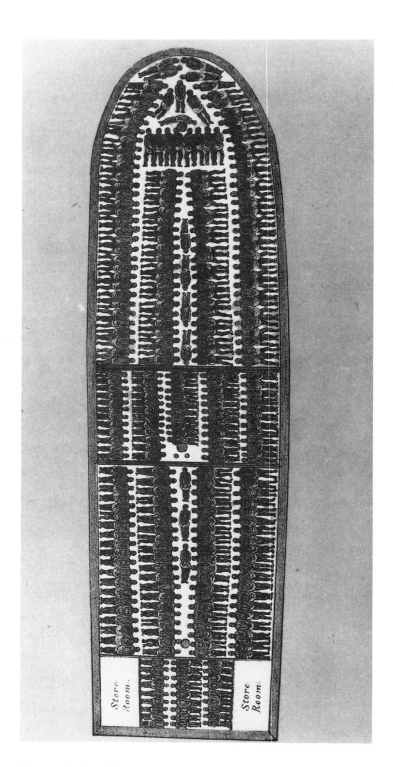

Diagram of a slave ship.

Slave ships often stopped to sell their human cargo in Cuba and Puerto Rico. From there the slaves were often sent to the sugar plantations of the Caribbean or the cotton and tobacco plantations of the United States.

Slave rebellion. At the end of the 1700s, slave uprisings became widespread in the Caribbean islands, and by 1800 this trend of insurrection had spread to the United States. Slaves revolted in Puerto Rico, Venezuela, Curacao, and Grenada, and made unsuccessful attempts in Cuba, Jamaica, and Louisiana. Greatest of all the insurrections was the complete overthrow of slavery on the island of Saint Domingue, which would become known as Haiti.

In 1789 more than nine-tenths of the island's population consisted of black slaves and a small group of free mulattos. The other 50,000 inhabitants of Saint Domingue were French landholders who formed the government of the French island colony. Inspired by the French Revolution in 1789, the slaves of Saint Domingue rebelled for their liberty. After several years of fighting and negotiating, the rebels gained full control of the colony in 1797. Fleeing the brutal violence of Saint Domingue, many French refugees took their slaves and found new homes in the United States. Virginia was one of the only southern states to admit these French immigrants and their bondsmen; other southern states, fearing that revolutionary ideas might have been planted in the minds of the newly arrived Saint Domingue slaves, denied entrance to both them and their masters.

The validity of these fears was realized as Virginia experienced a number of slave rebellions. The most notable of these uprisings was Gabriel Prosser's Rebellion in 1800. After learning to read and write, Prosser was inspired by the American doctrine that stated that all men were created equal. By the late summer of 1800, Prosser had recruited almost 100 rebels to join his revolt, and he hoped that hundreds of other slaves and poor whites would eventually join the planned uprising against wealthy white plantation owners and merchants. Unfortunately for Prosser, several of his followers informed authorities of the plot. The conspiracy was crushed before it began. Members of the plot were arrested, and a month of trials and hangings ensued. Twenty-seven slaves, including Prosser, were executed.

Racial attitudes in 1800. Englishmen and Africans experienced their first significant contact with one another in the 1500s. Negative racial stereotypes became a strong factor in their relations almost immediately. The skin color of the African people puzzled the Englishmen. Their first efforts to find scientific explanations for the Africans' skin color perpetuated negative perceptions. For example, George Best, an English geographer, claimed that the black skin of Africans "proceedeth of some naturall infection of the first inhabitants of that country, and so all the whole progenie of them descended, are still polluted with the same blot of infection" (Best in Jordan, p. 7). Such popular theories supported the perception that Africans were inferior and "polluted." Another factor that proved important in the formation of Europeans' racial attitudes toward Africans was the absence of Christianity in the cultures of Africa.

The colonization of Virginia in the early 1600s spurred a linkage of economic needs with racial attitudes, a connection that would impact African lives for hundreds of years. The cultivation of tobacco in the Virginia colony required a large supply of cheap, unskilled labor. At first, indentured servants—poor Englishmen who were promised free land after seven years' labor—filled the need. But the supply of white servants dwindled, while at the same time it grew cheaper to purchase black slaves from Africa.

Black slaves were present in Virginia by 1640. By the early 1700s black slaves had replaced the indentured servants, who were mostly whites, in the tobacco fields. As the practice of slavery grew, the earlier stereotype of Africans as "dirty" and "beastly" was used by white settlers to justify the enslavement of the black race. Moreover, enslavement led to the formation of even more stereotypes regarding the differences between whites and blacks. These beliefs remained widespread in white society, as evidenced by the 1854 statement of an Alabama farmer concerning slaves: "It wouldn't do no good to free 'em and let 'em hang round, because they is so monstrous lazy; if they hadn't nobody to take keer of 'em, they wouldn't do nothin' but, juss natrally laze round, and steal and pilfer" (Rawley, p. 69).

The perils of Cape Horn. Cape Horn, located at the southernmost point of South America, is a region that most sailors preferred to avoid. Unfortunately, this stretch of unruly winds and turbulent waters off the Cape was the only passage from the Atlantic Ocean to the Pacific Ocean at the time. Whaling and sealing vessels, and ships carrying cargo for trade with China, were thus forced to brave the life-threatening waters of Cape Horn to conduct their business.

An enslaved family on the block at a slave auction in Charleston, South Carolina in 1861.

In addition to the devastating winds and currents of the Cape, the region could be especially dangerous because of its uncharted reefs and heavy concentration of icebergs. This combination of hazards destroyed many ships seeking the warm waters of the Pacific. Even if a ship was not lost, dangers were still many for members of the crew. Captain Francis A. Thompson, who braved the Cape in 1832, gave a description of his passage "round the Horn":

> I had hard luck the whole passage and especially off Cape Horn. For five weeks I was beating and banging off that horrid place. It seems as though all the furies of the infernal region were let loose. Tremendous gales, snow and hail continually, night eighteen hours; sun nine degrees high and sometimes not see him for a week. A small vessel, all hands wet continually, and no chance to dry their clothes. Any person thinking there is pleasure in going to sea, I would advise them to double Cape Horn ... I lost my carpenter there; poor fellow, fell from the Main topsail yard and broke his head and neck; died in about ten minutes.
>
> (Thompson in Rydell, p. 50)

The Novella in Focus

The plot. Captain Amasa Delano, an American in command of a sealing expedition, observes the approach of a strange ship while he is anchored in an island bay off the coast of Chile. Concerned that the vessel might be sailing dangerously close to a bed of shallow reefs, Delano transports himself aboard the approaching vessel. Once aboard, he meets Benito Cereno, the distracted and sickly Spanish captain of the *San Dominick*, which turns out to be a slave ship.

On board the ship, slaves considerably outnumber a small Spanish crew. Cereno explains that rampant fever and rough weather off Cape Horn took the lives of many slaves and most of his crew, including Cereno's partner and best friend, Alexandro Aranda. Delano offers to help Cereno resupply his ship. As they discuss the details of this arrangement, Delano grows appalled at several incidents of violence perpetrated by the slaves against members of the crew. He sees one slave boy strike a Spanish cabin boy with a knife, then witnesses the assault of a crew member at the hands of several slaves.

Delano briefly suspects foul play of some sort, but he rejects this notion because of his belief that blacks do not possess the intelligence to organize any kind of deception. Cereno seems oblivious to the disturbances, but Delano is shocked at these "prominent breaches not only of discipline but of decency" (Melville, *Benito Cereno*, p. 14). Delano also becomes increasingly annoyed at Cereno's personal slave, Babo, who will not leave the two captains alone for even a moment. When Delano complains to Cereno about the slave's continued presence, the Spaniard replies that Babo is his "confidant" and insists that there is no reason to dismiss him.

Finally, Delano's men arrive at the *San Dominick* to retrieve their captain. Delano joins the sailors in the boat, but as his men begin rowing away from the Spanish vessel, Cereno leaps from the rail of his ship into the departing longboat. To Delano's complete bewilderment, Cereno shouts that the slaves aboard his ship had revolted, killed most of the crew, and forced him to act out his part as captain as if nothing had happened. Delano carries Cereno to the safety of his own ship and then dispatches his men to retake the *San Dominick*. The sailors kill a handful of slaves and recapture the ship. Following the victory, Delano is horrified to see that the figurehead of the *San Dominick*, which had previously been covered with a tarp, is the skeleton of a man, identified by Benito Cereno as his friend Alexandro Aranda.

Court documents continue the narrative from this point in the novella. The documents contain Benito Cereno's testimony about the events that took place on the *San Dominick* prior to Delano's appearance. Cereno explains how the slaves rebelled, killed the crew and his friend Aranda, and determined a strategy to deceive Delano so that, with his assistance, they could outfit the ship and sail back to their homes in Africa. The story concludes with a description of the execution of Babo and the subsequent death of Benito Cereno, without explanation, three months later; the implication is that the slaves' bloody acts of horror have been too much for him to live with.

Racism in *Benito Cereno*. Melville's tale of slave mutiny aboard the *San Dominick* provides both direct and indirect clues to an understanding of racism in his time. Explicit examples of racial attitudes in the book include a number of negative statements about blacks. When Delano suspects an uprising has been carried out by the slaves, he dismisses the idea, partially because he believes blacks are "too stupid" and "the whites . . . by nature were the shrewder race" (*Benito Cereno*, p. 45). Delano also dehumanizes the slaves by attributing animal qualities and descriptions to them. A black mother nursing her child is described as a "doe," while the child is referred to as a "fawn" with "two paws." Another description of Delano's attitude toward blacks perpetuates the animal comparisons: "Captain Delano took to negroes, not philanthropically, but ge-

nially, just as other men to Newfoundland dogs" (*Benito Cereno*, p. 57). Still, the novella occasionally has Delano assign positive qualities to several black slaves. When the slave Atufal appears, Delano looks upon him, "not without a mixture of admiration," and says of the "colossal" slave, "he has a royal spirit in him" (*Benito Cereno*, p. 26).

The character of Babo is described in both positive and negative terms. He is spoken of as "an uncommonly intelligent fellow," but also as someone whose servitude is "the docility arising from the unaspiring contentment of a limited mind" (*Benito Cereno*, p. 57). Ironically, Captain Delano, who finds Babo's apparent perfect servitude to be quite appealing, is disgusted when he believes that Babo has been subjected to a beating: "Ah, this slavery breeds ugly passions in man" (*Benito Cereno*, p. 63).

In presenting these contrasting comments on the qualities of the black race, Melville may have intended to highlight the diverse mix of American attitudes toward slavery during this period. In other words, he may have designed Delano "as a microcosm of American attitudes of the times towards Negroes" (Grejda, p. 140). Others speculate, however, that Melville may have created this tension between positive and negative images to encourage his readers to form their own attitudes without bias.

Sources. Melville's source for *Benito Cereno* was Amasa Delano's *Narrative of Voyages and Travels in the Northern and Southern Hemisphere*. Delano was an American sailor who commanded ships out of Boston for the purposes of trade, surveying, and sealing in the Pacific Ocean between 1790 and 1807. One of the most intriguing stories from the *Narrative* is his description of his encounter with Benito Cereno and his mutinous slaves off the coast of Chile. Melville uses this source almost without variation in the plot structure, although he changes some of the details. The novelist increased the number of slaves aboard the ship and decreased the number of crew members that survive the initial uprising. As a result, in Melville's narrative the white crew is very heavily outnumbered by the slaves, a change that may have been designed to provoke more sympathy for the hapless white crew members. Similarly Melville's addition of the skeleton of Alexandro Aranda may have been intended to inspire fear and loathing of the blacks and sympathy for the other whites aboard the ship. These changes focus the reader's attention away from the slavery forced upon the blacks and direct it toward the precarious position of the whites.

Melville also makes an important symbolic change in his novella. The name of Cereno's ship in the actual account by Delano is the *Tryal,* but Melville changes its name to the *San Dominick.* This name brings into the story the revolution of the slaves in Saint Domingue, also known as San Dominick, an event that unfolded at about the time that *Benito Cereno* takes place.

Events in History at the Time the Novella Was Written

The Kansas-Nebraska Act of 1854. As Melville was writing *Benito Cereno,* the nation was in a state of turmoil over whether Kansas would be admitted to the Union as a slave state or a free state. Such questions had haunted the United States since 1820, when the Missouri Compromise had admitted Missouri to the Union as a slave state. The Compromise was passed despite the presence of earlier legislation aimed at curbing the expansion of slavery in the South. In 1854, after weeks of heated debate, Congress passed the Kansas-Nebraska Act, which gave the citizens of Kansas and Nebraska the responsibility of deciding the slavery question themselves by a vote. The legislation enraged people in the free states of the North. They argued that the South would use the Kansas-Nebraska Act to spread slavery into the new states, an opportunity that was supposed to be denied after the Missouri Compromise. The Northern states began organizing the migration of free-soil Northerners to Kansas in an attempt to swing the vote toward free-statehood. Elections were attempted, but the effort was marked by a series of voter frauds and conflicts in the new state. A major problem with the election concerned the large number of Missouri citizens who crossed the border to vote in favor of slavery. Missouri slaveholders feared that if Kansas were admitted as a free state, it would provide too convenient a haven for fugitive slaves wishing to escape Missouri slavery.

Several elections were nullified. Tensions mounted as the federal government worked to solve the problem of voter fraud in a frontier territory with very little organization. Kansas's lack of regulations or time limits for state citizenship made it virtually impossible to enforce voting rights there. By the end of 1855, the unresolved "Kansas Question" had divided the nation. It was during this period of tension and controversy over the slave issue that Melville published *Benito Cereno.*

Racial stereotypes vs. reality. In *Benito Cereno,* Amasa Delano believes that the slaves do not possess the intelligence to successfully rebel against the whites, whom he thinks of as the shrewder race. His ideas are typical beliefs of the period, but are not at all borne out by reality. In many communities, in fact, slaves were quite adept at tricking their white masters. Thriving underground economies were prevalent among slave communities. The underground slave economy included black-owned saloons, gaming houses, and pawnshops. Although whites attempted to rid Richmond, Virginia, of these businesses, they continued in basements and other locations that remained secret from white searchers.

Blacks also were skilled at passing information among themselves without the knowledge of whites. In Richmond, such communication allowed Prosser's Rebellion to be organized. While Prosser's effort was ultimately discovered and thwarted by whites, the organizers passed along plans for the insurrection covertly for almost a year before the plans were uncovered.

Chief Justice Lemuel Shaw. In 1847 Herman Melville married Elizabeth Shaw, the daughter of Lemuel Shaw, who was Chief Justice of the Supreme Court of Massachusetts from 1830 to 1860. During his time on the bench, Chief Justice Shaw ruled on several cases that were of particular importance to black slaves in Massachusetts. Shaw tried the most famous of these cases in 1832. The case, *Commonwealth* v. *Howard,* involved a Mrs. Howard, a resident of New Orleans who brought a slave with her on a visit to Massachusetts. Because Massachusetts was a free state, abolitionists (Americans in favor of abolishing slavery) filed a case for the young slave in the hopes that it could win her freedom. Shaw had to decide whether or not a citizen of a slave state on a temporary visit to a free state could keep a slave in bondage, and whether the slave could be removed from the state against the slave's free will. Justice Shaw ruled that slaves become free as soon as they are brought into Massachusetts and that they can not be removed from the state against their will. This new precedent did not apply to fugitive cases, which were under the jurisdiction of the Fugitive Slave Law, a federal mandate that required free states to assist in the recovery of slaves who were fugitives from the South. It applied only to slaves brought into the state by their owners. Still, the decision was a significant one.

Shaw's ruling also seemed to indicate that he was a strong opponent of slavery. But while Shaw felt that slavery was "a great and acknowledged evil," he tempered such remarks by calling slavery a necessary evil because it was "too deeply interwoven into the texture of society to be wholly or speedily eradicated" (Levy, p. 60). Melville was very close to his father-in-law, and it seems possible that some elements of *Benito Cereno* could be reflections of his discussions with Shaw. For instance, the contradictory attitudes toward slaves aboard the *San Dominick* bear a striking similarity to Shaw's attitudes regarding slavery.

Changing attitudes and the *Amistad* Mutiny. In Havana in late June of 1839, a ship known as the *Amistad* was loaded with slaves. Two Spaniards, Don Jose Ruiz and Don Pedro Montes, had purchased the slaves to work the Ruiz family's sugar cane plantation in Puerto Principe. The Spaniards decided not to chain their captives because of the relatively short journey, but several days into the voyage this decision turned out to be a serious miscalculation. The fifty-three slaves revolted against the small crew of six men, killing the captain and the cook as two other crew members fled in a small boat. The slaves let Ruiz and Montes live under the condition that the Spaniards navigate the ship back to Africa. The Spaniards agreed, but secretly they sailed the ship north. After two months of deception, the ship was intercepted off the coast of New York by a United States vessel.

The capture of the *Amistad* mutineers presented the U.S. judicial system with some unique problems. The importation of slaves to the United States had been illegal since 1808, and the Spanish had agreed to stop their slave trade in 1835. Supporters of the mutineers argued that, although slavery still existed in the United States, the Africans aboard the *Amistad* had been unlawfully put into slavery. The case of the mutineers against the Spanish slave traders was argued, with the help of abolitionists, before the Supreme Court, and it was decided that the blacks had been illegally captured and so had lawfully killed to regain their liberty. The Court set the slaves free and, again with the support of abolitionists, they returned to Sierra Leone in West Africa. Melville was in New York during this widely publicized trial, and though the case occurred almost twenty years before he wrote *Benito Cereno*, the incident may have sparked an early interest in slave rebellion. A string of other incidents contributed to rising tensions over the issue of slavery during Melville's lifetime.

1822: Denmark Vesey, a free black, plans a revolt in South Carolina; the plot is discovered and thirty-five plotters are hung.

1831: Nat Turner, a slave, stages a revolt in Virginia in which some sixty whites are murdered. Panic results in the killing of innocent slaves before Turner is caught and executed.

1831-65: William Lloyd Garrison publishes *Liberator*, an antislavery newspaper, in Boston.

1839-40: Supreme Court tries *Amistad* mutineers, rules in favor of blacks.

1845: Escaped slave Frederick Douglass publishes his autobiography.

1852: White writer Harriet Beecher Stowe publishes her novella *Uncle Tom's Cabin*, which portrays slavery as an evil.

1854: Kansas-Nebraska Act states that the question of slavery in new territories should be decided by people living there. Controversy mounts in Nebraska.

1855: Melville writes *Benito Cereno*.

By 1855 attitudes concerning the justice or injustice of slavery had clashed time and again. The Kansas-Nebraska Act heightened tensions and contributed to an environment of increasing violence. The issue of slavery ultimately thrust the United States into its devastating Civil War.

For More Information

Egerton, Douglas R. *Gabriel's Rebellion*. London: University of North Carolina Press, 1993.

Grejda, Edward S. *The Common Continent of Men: Racial Equality in the Writings of Herman Melville*. London: National University Press, 1974.

Howard, Leon. *Herman Melville, A Biography*. Los Angeles: University of California Press, 1967.

Jordan, Winthrop D. *The White Man's Burden: Historical Origins of Racism in the United States*. New York: Oxford University Press, 1974.

Levy, Leonard W. *The Law of the Commonwealth and Chief Justice Shaw*. Cambridge, Mass.: Harvard University Press, 1957.

Martin, Christopher. *The Amistad Affair*. London: Abelard-Schuman, 1970.

Melville, Herman. *Benito Cereno*. New York: H. Liverwright, 1928.

Rawley, James A. *Race & Politics: "Bleeding Kansas" and the Coming of the Civil War*. Philadelphia: J. B. Lippincott, 1969.

Rydell, Raymond A. *Cape Horn to the Pacific: The Rise and Decline of an Ocean Highway*. Los Angeles: University of California Press, 1952.

Beowulf

Anonymous

The identity of *Beowulf*'s author is unknown. The writer was most likely an eighth-century West Mercian or Northumbrian monk who might better be called an editor than an author, for many sections of the poem undoubtedly had a long career in oral tradition before receiving final form in Beowulf. Whatever its source, the final version was recorded in a unique manuscript around the year 1000 A.D. It is the work of a master craftsman who was very well read, conscious of his role as a poet, and extremely skilled at making events and characters stand symbolically for universal human concerns.

Events in History at the Time the Poem Takes Place

English or Danish? There is no recorded history of the earliest of the Old English people known as Anglo-Saxons. Much of what we know about these people is derived from the artifacts they left behind, from *The Anglo-Saxon Chronicle* (a record of events in England in the first thousand years A.D.), and from the few literary works of their period that survive. Primary among these works is *Beowulf,* one of the earliest poems written in any form of English.

Beowulf is recognized as a hallmark of English literature. Yet its heroes and its setting are not English. The poem is set in two places: the first half takes place on a Danish island, and the second half takes place in Beowulf's homeland, which consists of two large islands off the southeast coast of Sweden. The hero of the poem, the warrior Beowulf, is a member of a southern Gotland tribe known as the Geats (pronounced

"yea-ots"). The warrior travels to rescue the Danish people, called Scyldings (pronounced "shild-ings"), who are being harassed by the monster Grendel.

The early Anglo-Saxons. Why should the English compose and preserve a long poem about a foreign people? One reason is that the poem champions values that were also important to the early Anglo-Saxons of Britain: bravery, loyalty, and devotion to the community. It is difficult to convey just how challenging the lives of the earliest Anglo-Saxons were. Every day was a battle to survive. The Anglo-Saxons lived in huts and dressed in animal skins to protect themselves against the miserable, bone-chilling dampness of the weather. They eked out an existence by farming the land, hunting, and venturing forth on dangerous, turbulent seas to fish. When they weren't scraping together a skimpy existence, they were fighting neighboring tribes and clans. These tough conditions created strong ties within tribes and encouraged intense loyalty to clan leaders. The environment also contributed to the high esteem in which the inhabitants held individual bravery, a quality they honored above all others.

The history of early Britain is one of foreign domination. The Angles and Saxons from the lowlands of Europe took over the rule of England (Angle-land) between 450 and 550 A.D. Viking invaders from Denmark, Sweden, and Norway made their presence felt as well, constantly raiding England during the period in which the poem was written. These seafaring warriors, descendants of Beowulf's era, were the Vikings who roamed the world and explored North America two hundred years before Columbus.

Warrior culture and society. The raw essence of life among a warrior people is celebrated in *Beowulf*. Much of its narrative is concerned with the challenges of existence, the weaponry used, and the festive celebrations of this group. The poem also portrays a strong sense of fatalism, or acceptance of death. The warriors of the era accepted their mortality and fate in a way that seems casual to the modern reader. The concept of *wyrd* (the root of the modern word *weird*), or fate, was central to the world view of the Anglo-Saxons living between the eighth and the tenth centuries. A warrior's bravery hinged upon his acceptance of the inevitable fact that at some point his courage would require the ultimate price: his life. Beowulf recognizes and draws strength from this view of the world. The warrior's grim view of destiny is ultimately fulfilled in the tale when he dies battling the fierce dragon.

In a passage that sums up the warrior philosophy celebrated in the poem, Beowulf assures Hrothgar, his Danish host in the first half of the poem, of his intention to retaliate after Grendel's mother has murdered one of his warrior companions:

> Sorrow not, wise warrior. It is better for a man to avenge his friend than much mourn. Each of us must await his end of the world's life. Let him who may get glory before death: that is best for the warrior after he is gone from life.
>
> (Donaldson, *Beowulf*, p. 25)

Another key concept of the society pictured in Beowulf is the notion of wergeld, or "man price." This signifies the amount a man's life was worth if he was killed, either accidently or in battle. The price was determined by social class distinctions—the bravest and ablest were worth the most money. Wergeld functioned as a sort of ransom that had to be paid to the dead man's relatives by the killer in order to avoid their revenge. In theory, such a payment system would allow early English society to carry on without deteriorating into a morass of never-ending feuding. But, in fact, theirs was a feuding, war-torn society despite precautions such as the wergeld system.

The Poem in Focus

The plot. The first part of *Beowulf* is set on an island off Denmark, where the Scylding (Danish) people live under the rule of Hrothgar, their king. Hrothgar has recently constructed a magnificent hall called Heorot. This hall is the site of frequent banquets and drinking celebrations that arouse the anger of Grendel, a local water-dwelling monster. Grendel lives outside the circle of human kindness and kinship: "the grim spirit ... called Grendel, known as a rover of borders, one who held the moors, fen and fastness" (*Beowulf*, p. 3). Perhaps this is one reason why the monster attacks the humans: he is envious of human society. Grendel terrorizes the local inhabitants, who live in fear, and word spreads of the monster's hold over the Scyldings.

BEOWULF'S WEAPONRY

An archaeological dig at Sutton Hoo, an estate in England, in 1939 turned up the remains of a ship containing jewelry, swords, and items believed to be part of the burial site of an Anglo-Saxon king of about 625 A.D., close to Beowulf's time. This discovery helped scholars determine how actual items described in the poem probably looked.

The hero of the poem, Beowulf, hears of their plight in his distant homeland and sails to the Scyldings' island with twelve warrior companions. Upon arriving they are greeted by a soldier guarding the coast, and the first of a series of commentaries on the weaponry and bravery of Beowulf and his men takes place. One of Hrothgar's heralds asks of them: "Where do you bring those gold-covered shields from, gray mail-shirts and visored helmets, this multitude of battle-

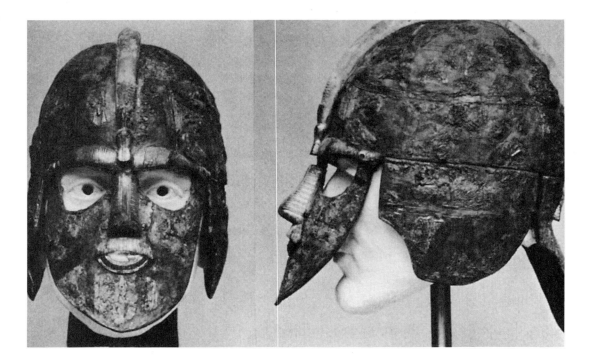

Helmet found at the Sutton Hoo burial site.

shafts ... I have not seen strangers—so many men—more bold" (*Beowulf,* p. 7).

When he is introduced to Hrothgar, Beowulf demonstrates his boldness. He pledges to "scorn to bear sword or broad shield, yellow wood, to the battle, but with my grasp I shall grapple with the enemy and fight for life, foe against foe" (*Beowulf,* p. 8). After a night of celebrating and bragging, Beowulf's bravery is put to the test. He watches as his foe devours one of his sleeping company: "He [Grendel] suddenly seized a sleeping man, tore at him ravenously, bit into his bone-locks, drank the blood from his veins, swallowed huge morsels; quickly he had eaten all of the lifeless one, feet and hands" (*Beowulf,* p. 13). Beowulf does not flee in the face of this terror but instead wrestles with the monster. Though Grendel can use magic to protect himself from many weapons, it does no good against Beowulf's bare hands. The warrior defeats the monster, and Grendel slinks off to his hideaway, mortally wounded. Another round of celebration ensues.

Beowulf is acknowledged publicly for his great bravery and rewarded with treasures by the Scyldings. The courageous men settle in for a night's rest after their fighting, feasting, and drinking. The poet again celebrates the men's warlike nature: "[As they slept] they set at their heads their battle-shields, bright wood; there on the bench it

was easy to see above each man his helmet that towered in battle, his ringed-mail shirt, his great spear-wood. It was their custom to be always ready for war whether at home or in the field...: that was a good nation" (*Beowulf,* p. 23).

The celebration is cut short, however, by the appearance of Grendel's mother. Angered by her son's death, she takes up the fight against the warriors. Beowulf, who has been housed in private quarters, is unable to do battle with Grendel's mother, who takes a prisoner and retreats to her home. Beowulf ventures forth to seek out the monster in her watery home on the moor. He descends into the monster's lair and uses a magic sword to defeat her in battle. After severing the head of the dead monster, Beowulf brings it back to his band of warriors. Yet another celebration follows.

In the final section of the story, Beowulf returns to his homeland, having fully demonstrated his bravery and generosity toward the Scyldings. He tells his own king and people about his exploits and praises the hospitality and generosity of Hrothgar's band. Time passes and Beowulf becomes king of the Geats, ruling well and wisely for fifty years. Eventually, though, a long-dormant dragon grows angry when a goblet is stolen from its hoard of treasure, and the dragon terrorizes the countryside. The fire-breathing crea-

Beowulf battling the dragon.

ture even destroys Beowulf's home and throne. This rouses the old warrior to action, and Beowulf begins his last campaign. He heads for the dragon's lair with a small group of warriors. All except the warrior Wiglaf flee before the encounter; in the end Beowulf engages the dragon single-handedly.

Beowulf is unable to do any harm to the fearsome dragon, and the old warrior is forced to take cover. Wiglaf ventures forth to help his king, and together Wiglaf and Beowulf conquer the dragon. Beowulf suffers serious wounds in the battle, however, and his end is near. As the dragon's poison works its way through his system, Beowulf instructs Wiglaf to go retrieve the dragon's treasure to comfort him in his dying. Wiglaf obeys and eases Beowulf into the next world, then takes over as leader of the Geats.

Construction of the poem. One prominent feature of the poem is its repetitiveness. Before each battle Beowulf recounts his life and hands down his legend, much as the poem itself has been handed down through time. With each victory, the hero's exploits are immediately retold to an audience of revelers as they toast his bravery and success. The action and major events of the Beowulf story are, in fact, only a tiny portion of the text; the rest of the work consists of recaps of previous events and listings of personages, weapons, and treasures. The poem actually interweaves narration about real events from history with its fictional story. Exactly how these narrated parts are related to the main story remains uncertain. It is known, however, that the repetition in *Beowulf* is due at least partly to its origins as an oral poem. Typically, an oral poem was sung by a poet who would recreate it with each telling, using complicated rhythms to relate the full tale. The repetition of long descriptive passages acted as a kind of easily remembered chorus in between the passages that described new adventures.

All Old English poetry was based upon alliteration—the repetition of consonant sounds, usually at the beginning of neighboring words. In addition, Old English poetry featured a break, or caesura, in the middle of each line, and each line typically had four beats or stressed syllables. Pauses at the caesura and at the end of each line, as well as the regular number of beats in each line, established the poem's rhythm. This rhythmic regularity helped the narrator to preserve the poem in memory and made it easier to hand down the poem in much the same form from generation to generation.

What *Beowulf* teaches. One crucial feature of *Beowulf* is its use of characters and action to create a model for the construction of a nation. The two societies in the poem, the Danes and the Geats, can be viewed as examples of all human societies. The Danes are deficient in physical prowess, and Grendel represents what happens when the intellectual strength of a nation exceeds its might: the nation becomes prey to every voracious neighbor. It is significant that Grendel conquers the Danes with his hands, showing physical prowess. Meanwhile, the Geatish kingdom, unlike the kingdom of the Danes, has great military might but lacks intellectual and moral strength. The enemy of the mighty Geats is a dragon whose breath, which can be understood to represent words or intellect, is used to conquer them. According to this model, both excesses could result in the destruction of the kingdom. The poem implies that a kingdom, and each individual, must be strong enough to discourage others from attacking. At the same time, the kingdom and the individual must be wise enough to behave justly and honorably and to refrain from attacking others unless provoked.

The major focus in the story is on bravery in the battle of good versus evil; the hero is an ideal man, brave and dedicated to doing good for its own sake. It is significant that the hero's early exploits, as he establishes his reputation, are on behalf of a foreign kingdom. He seeks out Grendel to destroy evil wherever it exists, not merely to protect his own people or his own interests. He risks his life for a group of relative strangers, demonstrating a generous bravery, although the youthful Beowulf is surely seeking fame in his adventurous quest.

His bravery is rewarded. The king and queen of the Scyldings reward Beowulf generously in goods and praise for his services. The entire issue of riches and wealth is tied into a system of bravery and merit in the poem, and rulers are presented as deserving of their wealth and status. This compensation for courage and allegiance reflects the social structure of the time. Rulers and their subjects depended upon loyal and brave warriors to support and protect them, while the warriors relied on the rulers to provide for them.

Composition and sources. *Beowulf's* history is a complicated and mysterious one. Information about who actually composed the poem or when it was written is scarce, although many believe that it was first written in Northumbria, Britain, in the late tenth century. The original text has two distinct styles of penmanship, suggesting not two authors, but two copyists, also known as scribes, usually monks whose main occupation was to produce manuscripts.

The Old English in which the original *Beowulf* was written (or spoken or sung) is quite different from the English spoken today. This Old English featured short, monosyllabic Anglo-Saxon words that were essential to the rhythm of *Beowulf* and other works of the period.

Structural similarities suggest that the *Beowulf* poet was familiar with the Roman epic poem ***Aeneid*** by Virgil (also covered in *Literature and Its Times*). Some scholars contend that the author of *Beowulf* used Virgil's poem as a model in composing his epic.

The sources of the fictional story in the *Beowulf* poem are the traditional folklore and legends of northern Europe, although Charles W. Kennedy notes in his introduction to *Beowulf* that the fact that the monster Grendel has a name is unusual in folklore. Specifically, the poem's narrative seems to derive from a common European folktale type called "The Bear's Son," in which the hero is the offspring of a bear's mating with a human. The elements of "Bear's Son" stories are remarkably similar to those of *Beowulf*: a hall built by an aged king is haunted by a spirit or monster; a young warrior fights with the spirit and wounds it, chasing it back to its lair; the hero goes underground to defeat the monster, encountering its relatives. The parallels are clear, and it is reasonably certain that this type of story constitutes the basis for the first part of *Beowulf*. The dragon story in the poem is also rooted in folk traditions, though no particular dragon story is an obvious model for the episode in *Beowulf*.

As for Beowulf himself, it is fairly certain that he is not a historical figure at all. Instead, he is a legendary being who combines many of the elements of the early Swedish and Geatish kings with superhuman strength to create a mythological figure. In this sense, he is similar to the legendary King Arthur of British lore. The *Beowulf* story in turn became a source for later tales, especially an Icelandic tale of the fourteenth century called *Grettissaga*. Tracing such tales to their *Beowulf* origins not only helps determine how ancient the *Beowulf* poem is, but also shows how literature feeds upon itself to provide the material for new and original works.

Events in History at the Time the Poem Was Written

Viking influence on England. From the eighth through the eleventh century, England was constantly raided by the Vikings. The *Beowulf* poem was composed during this age of Viking invasions. While many of these invaders limited their activities to coastal raids, others had a more lasting impact. In 866 the Viking leader Ivar the Boneless completely overran northern England. His forces moved inland and settled down in the region. These Vikings had a strong influence on the English society of the time, and a blending of northern European cultures took place. In 878 the Anglo-Saxon leader Alfred the Great defeated a force of Danes and concluded the Peace of Wedmore, a treaty that both recognized his authority over one region (Wessex) and acknowledged Danish control over a broad area to the east and north of the Thames River known as the Danelaw. Danish customs and laws became firmly embedded in the Danelaw, leaving a lasting imprint on English culture.

Poetry as entertainment. *Beowulf* is the oldest surviving northern European epic, which is a poem that tells the story of a hero or heroes and recounts a people's history or traditions. The poem's classification as an epic puts it into a select body of literature, a small family of works in world literature that capture the spirit of people at a given time in history. There was at first, though, a far less serious dimension to the poem; it provided entertainment.

The tale of Beowulf and his encounters with the monstrous Grendel and the horrible dragon was created in a world where poetry was sung for entertainment and people frequently celebrated their history. At the time of the poem's composition, the people of England practiced trades and operated small village businesses. In such communities, townspeople often gathered after work to listen to songs such as *Beowulf*. The performer at these gatherings was known as a *scop* (pronounced "shope"), a singer or maker of poems. In witnessing the scop's performance, the early residents of England celebrated the hero's qualities of bravery and loyalty and also relaxed after a hard day of work. *Beowulf* was appreciated for its entertainment value, though it was probably created with much more sophisticated purposes in mind: the development of a strong value system and a code for the construction of a balanced government.

Christianity and culture. *Beowulf* seems to straddle two worlds: it bridges the violent warrior culture that it celebrates and the Christian culture that was, at the time of its composition, displacing the earlier era.

The introduction of Christianity to the British Isles took place in 597 when St. Augustine and a group of monks arrived in England by way of Ireland. Christianity was thriving in England in the early eighth century, the time of the poem's creation. By the late tenth century, the date of the *Beowulf* manuscript, Christianity was well established in England. Careful reading of the poem reveals what seem to be insertions of Christian phrases and sections among what were originally a number of nonreligious stories.

The poem draws most heavily on Old Testament elements. The following example, which introduces the reader to the monster Grendel, illustrates the curious mix of folk legend with biblical references: "The grim spirit was called Grendel ... Unhappy creature, he lived for a time in the home of the monsters' race, after God had condemned them as kin of Cain ... From him [Cain] sprang all bad breeds, trolls and elves and monsters—likewise the giants who for a long time strove with God" (*Beowulf*, p. 3). Trolls, monsters, and elves, while unfamiliar to modern Christian orthodoxy, can be traced back to Norse mythology. *Beowulf* features many such instances where the Christian religion is melded with old stories and legends. This blending shows how one value system—that of the warrior clan, led by brave, violent leaders—was being replaced by another—that of a people obedient to a benevolent higher power who rewards virtue, forgiveness, and honesty.

For More Information

Chase, Colin, ed. *The Dating of Beowulf*. Toronto: University of Toronto Press, 1981.

Donaldson, E. Talbot, trans. *Beowulf*. New York: W. W. Norton, 1966.

Gardner, John. *Grendel*. New York: Alfred A. Knopf, 1971.

Greenfield, Stanley B. and Daniel G. Calder, eds. *A New Critical History of Old English Literature*. New York: New York University Press, 1986.

Grohskopf, Bernice. *From Age to Age: Life and Literature in Anglo-Saxon England*. New York: Atheneum, 1968.

Haber, Tom. *A Comparative Study of Beowulf and the Aeneid*. New York: Phaeton Press, 1968.

Tolkien, J. R. R. *Beowulf, the Monsters and the Critics*. 1936. Reprint, Darby, Pa.: Arden Library, 1980.

Billy Budd, Sailor

by
Herman Melville

Born in New York City in 1819, Herman Melville began a career at sea when he was nineteen years old. He served first on a merchant ship and later on an American navy vessel, his experiences furnishing him with material that inspired his later fiction. Completed at age seventy-two in his final year of life, *Billy Budd, Sailor* (also called *Billy Budd, Foretopman*), reflects the author's personal views and feelings on religion and humanity as he approached death.

THE LITERARY WORK
A short novel set aboard the HMS *Bellipotent*, a British ship, in 1797; completed in 1891 but unpublished until 1924.
SYNOPSIS
A young man is impressed into service on a British naval ship and must face the Navy's strict discipline and the jealous hatred of Claggart, the ship's master-at-arms.

Events in History at the Time the Novel Takes Place

War between England and France. France erupted in revolution in July 1789. A new government came to power, conquered Belgium and several other areas of Europe, and executed France's previous ruler, King Louis XVI, on January 21, 1793. At the outset, participants in the French Revolution set out to acquire a greater share of rights in a land that had long experienced an unequal distribution of wealth and power. Turning on French nobles with a bloody vengeance, the rebels rioted, raped, looted, and murdered in their pursuit of a government dedicated to freedom from unfair taxes and other laws they felt were prejudiced. Many English citizens, who had at first felt were some sympathy for the rebels, became alarmed at their tactics and came to fear the spread of the murderous French. Some Frenchmen, in fact, openly advocated war against the English in the hopes that the conflict would prompt a revolution similar to the one that had taken place in France.

Their wishes were granted when, on February 1, 1793, France finally declared war against England. It was a war that would last for more than twenty years, and the majority of its conflicts would be fought upon the seas. Since the English Channel separated England from France, all offensives were by necessity naval in nature. France's continued efforts to disrupt shipments of supplies to England also contributed to the mayhem on the water. Finally, the role of Ireland in the war played a part in the widespread sea battles. For centuries England had extended its authority over Ireland, a state of affairs that the Irish resented. Hoping to take advantage of Irish anger, France planned to land in Ireland and commence an invasion of English territory from this landing point. Rough weather on the Atlantic Ocean, however, prevented a large-scale landing in Ireland, and the English were able to reinforce crucial positions during the delay. As a result, France and England continued to focus on naval power throughout the war.

Life in the King's Navy. Along with England's strong reliance on naval power came the need for large numbers of sailors to man the growing fleet. Service in the navy was unpleasant at best. The ships of the era were built to accommodate armaments rather than men. Some of these weapons weighed as much as three tons and took up most of the space between decks. Sailors slept above these weapons and ate in the cramped quarters that housed the cannon to which they were assigned. Unhealed ulcers and other skin diseases became common because of the lack of soap; it was not until 1808 that the British navy finally issued soap to its sailors. The damp conditions below deck, combined with the cold work above, produced rheumatism and other ailments in the sailors. Abdominal ruptures were common among those who worked with the ship's sails, for they were often forced to lie on their stomachs across supporting poles while using both hands to complete their tasks. Worst of all, however, were the food and drink on navy ships. The sailors drank water from wooden barrels that usually became polluted with slime a couple of weeks into the voyage. Salt beef was the staple of the sailors' diet, along with salt pork, dried biscuit, oatmeal, and cheese. Pursers, the officers responsible for purchasing the ships' provisions, were notorious for selling the best foodstuffs and keeping only the poorest quality rations for their crews.

Impressment in England. Because of the horrible conditions on navy ships around the end of the 1700s, nearly half of all sailors during this period were impressed—enlisted into the navy against their will. The impressment agents scoured the coasts and waterways, taking into custody any man who did not possess apprenticeship papers, a foreign passport, or shipbuilding employment. The original intention was to enlist experienced seamen who had not volunteered. In 1797, after four years of war, most of the capable sailors had already been taken, and the impressment (press) gangs were grabbing anyone they could find, including criminals. As described in *Billy Budd,* this method of replenishing the fleet's ranks occurred with official approval: "the London police were at liberty to capture any able-bodied suspect, any questionable fellow at large and summarily ship him to the dockyard or fleet" (Melville, *Billy Budd,* p. 315). As circumstances became increasingly desperate, the impressment of criminals became even more deliberate, as Melville explained in the novel: "In the case of a warship short of hands whose speedy sailing was imperative, the deficient quota ... would be eked out by draughts culled direct from the jails" (*Billy Budd,* p. 315).

Healthy men were rarely seen in some areas where press gangs were active; they had either been previously taken or were being hidden by members of the community. Press gangs also roamed the high seas in search of potential sailors. Even privateers, privately owned ships that made up a crucial part of England's naval force, were not exempt from the gangs. As seen in the case of Billy Budd's impressment, merchant ships were regarded as acceptable hunting grounds for press gangs.

Many commanding naval officers hated impressment. Admiral Edward "Grog" Vernon, for instance, commented that "our fleets are defrauded by injustice, manned by violence, and maintained by cruelty" (Vernon in Dugan, p. 61). Still, the practice continued to be a common one.

Contrary ways of thinking. As impressment became more widespread, political criminals and radicals found themselves serving as sailors for the royal fleet. These new conscripts were attracted to ideas voiced in an English pamphlet by Thomas Paine called *The Rights of Man.* Written in 1791 and 1792 to defend the French Revolution, the pamphlet included a complaint against a military injustice of the time: "The pay of the army, the navy, and all of the revenue officers, is about the same now as it was about a hundred years ago, when the taxes were not above a tenth part of what they are at present" (Paine in Dugan, p. 63). This information almost certainly raised the sympathies of the military men who read Paine's words.

Melville uses *Rights-of-Man* as the name of the merchant ship from which Billy is seized, and the narrator of the novel comments that this ship's captain "was a staunch admirer of Thomas Paine" (*Billy Budd,* p. 297). In contrast, the captain of the *Bellipotent,* the ship to which Billy is taken, champions the rights of the state above the rights of man. The story thus echoes a controversy that was a subject of significant debate at the time. On the one side were thinkers like Paine, who believed that the rights of the individual came first; on the other were followers of another English writer, Edmund Burke, who argued that the rights of the individual must be sacrificed in the interest of the state. Burke held that in organized society the freedom of the individual needed to be given up in trust to leaders of the government so that they could preserve the liberty of all its citizens.

Punishment. A strict set of regulations governed the behavior of the sailors, and punishments were much harsher for naval offenses than they were in civilian law. The navy demanded a slavish type of obedience from the sailors it employed. In the navy's eyes, a sailor was a self-declared slave to the high notion of patriotism, a small part of a huge operation dedicated to protecting his nation's citizens. If he failed to acknowledge this and play by the rules, he risked not only his own destruction but also the destruction of his entire nation.

This general belief led to laws and punishments designed to achieve complete discipline on board a vessel. After 1790 the main forms of punishment meted out were death or flogging with a cat-o'-nine tails—a whip of nine knotted cords connected to a handle. In 1812 the Duke of York limited the number of lashes that could be administered at any single whipping to three hundred, but a man could still receive them for even a minor offense.

Impressment and the War of 1812. Following the American Revolution in the late 1700s, hostile feelings between the United States and England persisted. Because of the harsh conditions on British ships during the war against France, many Englishmen deserted to positions on American ships. British navy ships began searching for deserters among American crews in the hopes of recapturing them for service in the war against France. In the process, British ships impressed many sailors who had left England years earlier and become American citizens. British seamen seemed to ignore the outcome of the American Revolution, acting as if the Americans were not independent. Some British navy captains, desperate for men, took many American citizens who were not even former British subjects. This violation of Americans' rights was a contributing factor in the decision of the United States to declare war against the British in 1812.

The Spithead and Nore mutinies. The years 1794 and 1797 witnessed two events that shook the British navy to its core. In 1794 a mutiny of British navymen took place at Spithead in southern England. They staged an unprecedented insurrection that proved difficult to squelch. Order was eventually restored, but three years later an even greater insurrection began with the mutiny at Nore, a theater for naval operations on the east coast of England. Although the incident at Spithead had been forgotten by naval officers, the rebellious sailors had not forgotten their demands for improvements, which had been neglected after the resolution of the initial uprising at Spithead; this resentment over the unmet demands served as the major factor in the revolt at Nore in 1797.

In *Billy Budd,* the narrator repeatedly refers to these two mutinies. They are regarded as symbols of a revolutionary spirit that prompts men to rise up against real abuses. Melville uses 1797, the year of the Nore Mutiny, as the setting for his novel: combined with the ongoing conflict with France, the mutiny provides the perfect background of unrest, conspiracy, and violence for his story of human cruelty and morality.

The Novel in Focus

The plot. Billy Budd is a young sailor aboard a small merchant ship departing from England. The ship is boarded in a routine inspection by officers from the navy ship HMS *Bellipotent,* which desperately needs additional sailors. Judging Billy to be capable of the job, the officers immediately impress him into service and take him aboard the *Bellipotent.* Once aboard the gunship, Billy quickly becomes a favorite of the crew because of his innocent good looks and his easy, carefree nature.

Troubles begin for Billy when Claggart, the ship's master-at-arms (the navy officer responsible for maintaining order) begins to develop an uncontrollable hatred for the handsome young sailor. Claggart makes false accusations against Billy concerning his orderliness and uses every opportunity to reprimand Billy for minor infringements of discipline. Young Billy, unaware that Claggart is the manipulator of these events, actually believes that Claggart is one of his best allies on the ship. As Billy's troubles worsen, another member of the crew approaches him and subtly invites Billy to take part in a mutiny. Billy is outraged, and his indignation proves so great that he reveals a flaw in his seemingly perfect composure. He stutters uncontrollably, unable to form a single word in response to the mutinous sailor's proposition.

Shortly after this affair, Claggart tells Captain Vere, the commander of the ship, that he believes Billy is involved in a plot to foment a mutiny aboard the *Bellipotent.* Although he does not know Billy personally, Captain Vere is flabbergasted to think that the likable young sailor could

The hanging of Billy Budd, from the 1962 film adaptation starring Terence Stamp.

have any part in such a plan. Vere summons Billy to his cabin, where Claggart makes the accusation to Billy's face. Shocked and outraged, Billy is rendered absolutely speechless. He desperately strives to speak but can barely stutter a single syllable. Finally, he expresses himself the only way he can—by unleashing a powerful blow to Claggart's head. Claggart crumples to the cabin floor and dies from the awesome blow, which shocks Captain Vere.

The captain realizes that Billy is innocent of plotting mutiny, but the issue now at hand is Billy's guilt in killing Claggart. Vere, who witnessed the killing with his own eyes, feels obligated to charge Billy with murder, and under the provisions of the naval code, this charge means the death penalty for Billy. Despite his desire to save Billy, Vere cannot bend the rules of the sea. Billy understands this and his final words as he is about to hang from the yardarm are, "God bless Captain Vere!" (*Billy Budd*, p. 375).

Vere later receives a deathly wound in a sea battle. The Captain utters Billy Budd's name with his last breath. Ending the novel are two accounts of the young sailor's death, a navy news report that wrongly describes Budd as the ringleader of a mutiny and a poem that pictures him as a glib-speaking innocent.

From religion to politics in *Billy Budd*. Herman Melville was very familiar with the popular epic poem ***Paradise Lost*** by John Milton (also covered in *Literature and Its Times*), which details the fall of man according to the Christian faith. In his novel, Melville seems to be sharing his own personal version of this fall in a way that reveals his views on humanity and religion in the last year of his life. He compares Billy to an innocent, a character like Adam or Jesus; Claggart to Satan; and Captain Vere to a Godlike father who sits in judgment over the innocent and the guilty.

The novel establishes Billy's innocent nature early in a description of Billy aboard the *Rights-of-Man.* According to its captain, Billy's presence was enough to pacify the rough crew, which had been unmanageable before his arrival. He tells the officer from the *Bellipotent,* "But Billy came; and it was like a Catholic priest striking peace in an Irish shindy ... a virtue went out of him, sugaring the sour ones" (*Billy Budd,* p. 295). Later, however, the innocent Billy commits murder and is found guilty of the crime. In a similar reversal of guilt and innocence, the villain Claggart tells the captain that Billy is involved in a mutiny. Claggart is clearly guilty of lying, yet the court-martial regards the dead Claggart as an innocent victim of Billy's wrath. As the narrator notes, "innocence and guilt personified in Claggart and Budd in effect changed places" (*Billy Budd*, p. 354).

In Melville's view, the fault seems to lie neither in Claggart nor in Billy Budd but rather in the human makeup. Billy has a physical defect, a stutter, that leads to his committing murder. Claggart is fundamentally flawed as well. "In [Claggart]," notes the narrator, "was the mania of an evil nature … born with him and innate" (*Billy Budd*, p. 326). Both become victims of their own flaws, and Melville seems to hold God responsible for these blemishes. The Almighty, according to this view, created man as a flawed creature. Those flaws, be it a stutter or an evil nature, cause him to sin. Earlier in the 1800s, the English writer Percy Shelley had declared that "God made man such as he is, and then damned him for being so"; similarly *Billy Budd* suggests that by the end of his life Melville believed that man's fault was God's fault (Thompson, p. 361).

The question of innocence or guilt moves from the personal to the social level when Captain Vere debates the case with three other judges at the impromptu naval court. The murderer, protests one of the three, did not intend mutiny or homicide, so the death penalty seems unwarranted. In reply, Captain Vere argues that death is the only alternative if they are to maintain discipline on the ship. Any leniency would encourage mutiny and wild behavior among the rest of the crew, who, if given enough rein, might act as wildly as the king-killing populace of France. In fact, Vere argues, whether or not Billy Budd intended to commit murder or to engage in a mutiny is of little consequence. It is, says Vere, the effect of his perceived action on the crew that matters. Building on the belief that man is born with some mark of Satan in him and that society must restrain human nature, Vere places the law above individual rights. Billy Budd's life, he suggests, must be sacrificed, as Christ's was, for the greater good. Such reasoning echoes the logic of the writer Edmund Burke, who placed social order above individual rights.

The court scene in Melville's story thus opens the door to questions surrounding natural rights and their validity in the face of state laws designed to keep society whole. As Captain Vere argues for the death penalty, the three other judges move restlessly in their seats, "agitated by the … spontaneous conflict within" (*Billy Budd*, p. 362).

Melville himself may have been agitated, not only over such troubling social questions but also over a personal question of his own guilt or innocence in someone's death. A stern and difficult father, Melville had a son, Malcolm, who fourteen years earlier had shot himself to death in his own room with a pistol. Melville discovered his son's body after forcing open the door to the room. It has been suggested that in Melville's final year this memory became especially troublesome for the author. Before the climax of the novel, Captain Vere expresses fatherly regard toward Billy Budd. When Billy, on his way to his death, cries "God bless Captain Vere," he absolves the captain of guilt for the death. Billy holds him blameless, understanding that the captain is a victim of man's naval laws and God's designs. On a social level, this seems to confirm the captain's argument to the court that the laws of his society must take precedence over an individual's basic rights. On a personal level, at least one authority has drawn a parallel between this episode and Melville's own feelings of guilt in his son's suicide (Bush in Introduction to *Billy Budd*, p. xii).

Sources. In creating his sea stories, Melville typically referred to sources such as William James's *The Naval History of Great Britain* and Robert Southey's *Life of Nelson*, as well as other naval histories. But more interesting than texts from which he gleaned secondary information are Melville's personal sources for *Billy Budd*.

Melville draws heavily on his own experiences at sea, as he had in his novel *White Jacket*, which explored the abuses of seamen in the U.S. navy. He seems to have been inspired partly by a desire to capture in fiction his fond memories of Captain Jack Chase, under whom Melville had served during his stint on the *United States,* an American navy ship. Melville once wrote concerning the captain, "wherever you may be rolling over the blue waters, dear Jack, take my best love along with you" (Melville in Weaver, p. xx). Melville dedicated *Billy Budd* to Jack Chase and seems to have embodied Chase's appealing qualities in the character of Captain Vere. Captain Vere becomes a father figure to Billy Budd, a reflection perhaps of how Melville, who lost his own father at an early age, perceived Captain Chase.

Melville's plot may have also been inspired in part by the *Somers* affair, in which three young navy men—Elisha Small, Philip Spencer, and Samuel Cromwell—were hung when rumors implicated them in a mutiny. The 1842 incident raised many questions about the rights of both captains and common sailors. Forty-six years later, in June 1888, the *American Magazine* brought the episode back into the public limelight by publishing an article by Lieutenant H. D. Smith on "The Mutiny on the *Somers*." It was at this point that Melville began gathering information to write *Billy Budd*. In June 1889, *Cosmopolitan Magazine* ran another article on the

Somers affair entitled "The Murder of Philip Spencer." Melville was making revisions on *Billy Budd* at the time, a task that would keep him busy until April 1891.

Events in History at the Time the Novel Was Written

Guert Gansevoort and the *Somers* affair. On December 14, 1842, the United States brig USS *Somers* under Commander Alexander Mackenzie returned home to New York after cruising the waters off North Africa. With the arrival of the ship came the news that some men had been hung on board after being charged with mutiny. Just as in Claggart's charges against Billy Budd, there had been no overt act of mutiny, only accusations that the men had been plotting. One of the alleged mutineers was Philip Spencer, the son of the American secretary of war. Spencer had allegedly held private meetings with another member of the crew named Wales. According to Wales, Spencer was plotting to take possession of the ship by murdering the officers at night and intimidating the rest of the crew into submission. Supposedly, once in control of the brig, Spencer intended to turn pirate and rob defenseless ships in the Atlantic Ocean. Spencer had persuaded about twenty members of the crew to join him in his plan, according to Wales. Wales told the ship's first lieutenant of the plot, who then informed Captain Mackenzie, who immediately placed Spencer under arrest. The following morning, missing equipment seemed to confirm the captain's fears that unrest and mutiny were brewing in the crew. Several other men were arrested after being linked to the plot through papers found in Spencer's possession, and on December 1, 1842, Spencer and two other men were hanged from the ship's yardarm. The two other victims were Samuel Cromwell and Elisha Small, a man who was well-loved by the crew; sailors on board exclaimed "God bless the flag!" when he was hanged.

The resemblance of this case to the plot in Melville's *Billy Budd* is obvious; what makes the connection even more intriguing is that Melville's cousin served on the court that convicted the "mutineers." Lieutenant Guert Gansevoort, Melville's cousin, was seven years Melville's senior, but despite this age difference the two had spend a great deal of time together as youths, and though this closeness did not continue throughout adulthood, the relationship remained an important one. At the time of the incident, Melville was just enlisting on the *United States,* a navy ship sailing out of Honolulu. He undoubtedly would have heard of the episode. Many scholars believe that he may have heard a full account of it from Gansevoort himself. Certainly he knew of his family's belief that God approved of his cousin's role in sentencing the three men to death. Melville apparently did not share their certainty.

The critics' response to *Billy Budd.* At the time of his death in 1891, Herman Melville was a little-known author whose works remained unappreciated. The greatness of his works was not recognized until more than three decades after his death, when the publication of Raymond Weaver's biography, *Herman Melville: Mariner and Mystic,* renewed interest in his writings. In 1924, in the midst of this renewed interest, *Billy Budd* was finally published, and its publication generated a flurry of critical response. One critic of the period, Lewis Mumford, saw a greater depth in *Billy Budd* than in Melville's earlier works. According to Mumford, "*Billy Budd* is ... the story of the world, the spirit, and the devil.... Good and evil exist in the nature of things, each forever itself, each doomed to war with the other. These are the fundamental ambiguities of life" (Mumford in Harris, p. 345).

For More Information

Dugan, James. *The Great Mutiny.* New York: G. P. Putnam's Sons, 1965.

Harris, Laurie Lanzen, ed. *Nineteenth-Century Literature Criticism.* Vol. 3. Detroit: Gale Research, 1983.

Horsman, Reginald. *The Causes of the War of 1812.* Philadelphia: University of Pennsylvania Press, 1962.

Howard, Leon. *Herman Melville, A Biography.* Los Angeles: University of California Press, 1967.

McFarland, Philip. *Sea Dangers: The Affair of the Somers.* New York: Schocken, 1985.

Melville, Herman. *Billy Budd and Other Stories.* New York: Penguin, 1986.

Thompson, Lawrance. *Melville's Quarrel with God.* Princeton: Princeton University Press, 1952.

Weaver, Raymond. *Shorter Novels of Herman Melville.* New York: H. Liverwright, 1928.

The Bull from the Sea

by
Mary Renault

Born in England in 1905, Mary Renault emigrated to South Africa in 1948 and remained there the rest of her life. During her long career as an author, she wrote many historical novels set in the ancient world. *The Bull from the Sea* is a fictional interpretation of life in ancient Greece as it might have been experienced by the legendary Greek hero Theseus. While the novel focuses on a mythical figure, Renault's portrait of the society in which he is supposed to have lived is based on extensive scholarly research into the Mycenaean civilization that actually existed in Greece between about 1500 and 1100 B.C.

Events in History at the Time the Novel Takes Place

The Mycenaean Age. *The Bull from the Sea* focuses on a time early in Greek history known as the Mycenaean Age. The country known today as Greece did not exist then as a single, unified nation. Instead it was divided into many small districts, each controlled by an upper class of noble individuals. The most powerful noble in each district acted as king, serving as the supreme judge, lawgiver, and military commander. He also presided over religious ceremonies.

The king's authority rested on two factors. One was the claim of his divine right to rule because he was the direct descendant of one of the gods. The other factor was the judgment by the kingdom's nobles that the king was fit to rule, either because of his prowess in war or his wise coun-

<table>
<tr><td>

THE LITERARY WORK

A novel set in ancient Greece, about 1300 B.C.; published in 1962.

SYNOPSIS

Theseus, mythical hero of ancient Greece, has many experiences and adventures during his adult years.

</td></tr>
</table>

sel. The position of king was never absolutely secure. Rulers of Mycenaean society remained in power only as long as their military success, wealth, and political connections lasted. Power struggles between the king and nobles were frequent, for powerful rivals stood ready to grab the throne at the first sign of a ruler's weakness. Threats from ambitious relatives and neighboring monarchs lurked as well. This atmosphere explains the significance of a scene in *The Bull from the Sea* where Theseus presides for the first time as king over a gathering of the region's leaders. During the meeting he is challenged, and it becomes important for him to assert his authority. By standing up to the insolent Prokrustes and throwing him out of the meeting, he helps ensure the support of the rest of the region's leaders. He has proven to them his strength and courage—he is someone to be taken seriously.

A violent era. The Mycenaean Age was a bloody period of history. One of the most common

The Acropolis, the fortress of Theseus.

means of increasing one's wealth and power was through piracy and conquest of neighboring kingdoms. Wars were therefore frequent. Since military equipment was too elaborate and expensive for the lower classes to afford, the warriors consisted mainly of members of the upper class. In addition to weapons, these warriors used horses, chariots, immense oxhide shields, and bronze armor. The upper-class soldiers, equipped with such trappings, often fought many wars over the course of their lifetimes. Those who were defeated were often treated in brutal fashion. As illustrated by Theseus and his friend Pirithoos in *The Bull from the Sea,* warriors who conquered a city could be ruthless. They sometimes slaughtered all the men and took all the women as mistresses and slaves. After seizing as much gold, silver, and valuables as they could find, they would burn down the city and leave. In a land where such brutal warfare was common, many kings ruled from citadels. The Athenian Acropolis from which Theseus rules in *The Bull from the Sea* is an example of this kind of stronghold. These citadels were strong fortresses built on tall, steep, rocky hills, which provided a tremendous natural defense. Often the citadels were surrounded by huge protective walls that in some places were forty feet thick. Security was a very serious matter in such violent times.

Mycenaean women. In many respects, women occupied an inferior position to men in this society, where power and status were gained and held through physical prowess and military success. Much of a woman's time was spent at home engaged in such activities as raising children and attending to household chores. Before marriage, she was required to remain a chaste maiden; after marriage, she was supposed to be a faithful wife. At the same time, it was a common and acceptable practice for her husband to take mistresses.

The legendary Amazons, who play a role in *The Bull from the Sea,* led lives that differed greatly from this customary pattern. A nation of female warriors, the Amazons supposedly lived in Scythia, in Asia Minor. According to legends about the Amazons, they kept men segregated on an island and mated only to produce children. Male children would either be killed or sent back to the island reserved for men to be raised there. In contrast, young females were raised to become warriors. Skirmishes between such Greek heroes as Theseus and Hercules and the Amazons are recorded in myths and portrayed on hundreds of ancient vases and plaques. Another version of the Amazon legend, which Renault follows in *The Bull from the Sea,* is that they were a group of warrior princesses who guarded the religious

GREAT GODDESS

It was believed that the Great Goddess had power over life, death, fertility, marriage, and wisdom. Later Greek goddesses are thought to derive from the Great Goddess, and her various spheres of influence are attributed to different figures:

Goddess	Spheres of Influence
Hera	Marriage
Artemis	Birth, hunting, moon
Aphrodite	Love
Athena	Wisdom, crafts
Hestia	Hearth, home
Demeter	Agriculture

sanctuary of the goddess Artemis (goddess of birth, hunting, and the moon). They are engaged in one of their religious rituals just before Theseus appears, and a battle between his forces and theirs ensues. He successfully captures their leader, Hippolyta, but only does so after a difficult fight against these powerful women.

The Great Goddess vs. Zeus. Before the beginning of the Mycenaean Age (1500-1100 B.C.), the inhabitants of ancient Greece apparently worshipped a Great Goddess as their principal deity. Archaeologists have found many objects from this period that are connected with the worship of this goddess. These include numerous small statues of female figures (often squatting in traditional childbirth postures) with protruding breasts, large bellies, enormous thighs, and rounded contours. According to scholars, these figures indicate that the society of the time considered motherhood a sacred status. The Great Goddess seems to have been revered as the source of life and death. She was also regarded as the giver of divine wisdom, just law, and the arts, and as the protector of peace and nurturer of growth. Men held a subordinate place in this religion.

Around 1500 B.C., many generations before Theseus's legendary life, invaders from the northeast conquered and settled the Greek mainland. They brought with them the Greek language and their patriarchal religion, which featured the male god Zeus as the most powerful of all deities. The Great Goddess was apparently absorbed into this new Greek religion; each of the six main Greek goddesses worshipped in the Mycenaean Age may have been derived from the ancient Great Goddess. But the new religion made these goddesses subordinate to Zeus.

Though the reverence of Zeus became widespread in Mycenaean Greece, the ancient Goddess-centered religion of the native peoples apparently did not completely disappear. In *The Bull from the Sea,* Mary Renault refers to the continued worship by some people of a most-powerful female goddess and portrays these ceremonies as a source of tension in the area. Throughout the book, the continuing cult of the Goddess seems to be considered a serious threat by Greek society. This anxiety about the cult is due in large extent to the belief that the worship of the Goddess was intertwined with a desire to put women in a position of power over men.

The Novel in Focus

The plot. The novel opens with the arrival of Theseus in Athens. Almost as soon as he steps off the ship, he learns that his father has killed himself; it is time for him to step into position as king of Athens. Theseus soon calls his first meeting with the lords of the region. He refuses to tolerate the rudeness that Prokrustes, one of the leaders, shows him. Theseus authoritatively throws Prokrustes out of the meeting, an action that gains him the respect and support of the other lords in attendance.

Soon after becoming king, Theseus's mother Aithra insists on bringing him to a sacred grove for a religious ceremony in order to seek the forgiveness of the Great Goddess, offended by Theseus's actions as a young man. He had taken many actions against the ancient worship of the Great Goddess in the past, outlawing the Goddess worship at Eleusis and seducing and subsequently deserting Ariadne, Crete's high priestess of the Goddess religion.

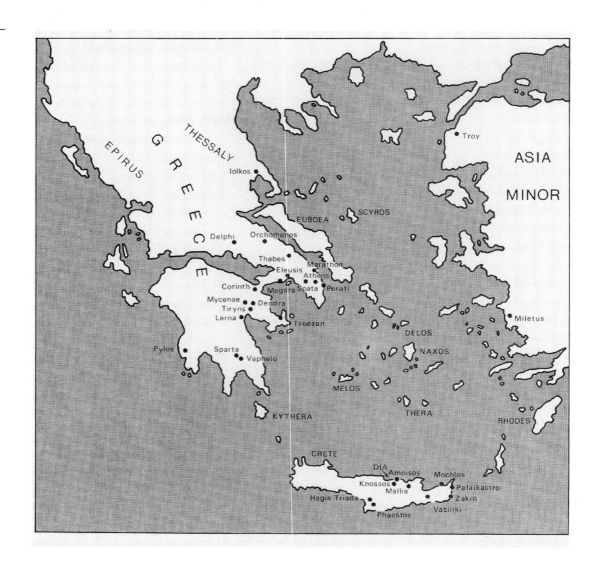

A map of the Aegean, showing the location of cities mentioned in the novel.

Once at the ceremony, however, Theseus's longing looks at a young priestess cause her to accidentally knock over the screen placed in front of a sacred statue of the Goddess that men are forbidden from laying eyes on. Sent away before the ceremony is concluded, he remains unpardoned.

Theseus spends the first five years of his reign bringing all of Attica, the eastern region of Greece, under his authority. This action marks the first time that so many individual kingdoms in Greece are united under one rule of law. He does this primarily through diplomacy rather than warfare. It is during these years that he meets Pirithoos, prince of Thessaly in northern Greece. Pirithoos becomes a good friend, and Theseus periodically accompanies him on his pirating conquests of distant cities.

As Theseus grows older, it becomes time for him to take a wife and produce a legitimate son to be his heir. He arranges a future marriage to princess Phaedra of Crete, a union that also promises to help solidify the political ties between the two kingdoms. In the meantime, Theseus ends up in battle against the Amazons while on a pirating voyage with Pirithoos. He falls in love with their leader, Hippolyta, and follows them back to their center one night with a few of his crew. The onlookers spy on the women as they perform a religious ritual that all men are forbidden to see. After Theseus is discovered, the Amazon queen, Hippolyta, challenges him to one-on-one combat. He wins, takes her back to Athens, and after an initial period of distrust, she falls in love with him.

Theseus and Hippolyta are very happy together. The Athenian people don't trust the female warrior, who behaves so differently from their own women, but Theseus ignores their discontent. Soon the couple have a son, Hippolytus. The Athenians, however, grow increasingly insistent that Theseus marry someone respectable. He finally succumbs to the pressure and marries Phaedra. Although Hippolyta remains with him in Athens, and Phaedra stays in Crete, the people are satisfied with the alliance.

After some years, the Amazons and other enemies from the north lay siege to Athens. While Hippolyta is troubled to fight against her old comrades, she ultimately demonstrates her loyalty to Theseus and takes up arms against them. She is killed when she steps in front of an arrow meant for Theseus. He sends Hippolytus to live with his grandfather and devotes more time to pirating voyages with his friend Pirithoos. Many years later, after one such adventure, he visits his son, who is now seventeen. Theseus is upset to learn that his son had made a vow to remain a virgin, never marry, and dedicate his life to becoming a healer. Before Theseus returns to Athens, however, the two come to an understanding and part as friends.

Theseus finally decides to bring his wife Phaedra to live with him in Athens. Their relationship proves an unhappy one, and she falls in love with her stepson, Hippolytus. After being rejected by him, she claims that he raped her. Theseus curses him and Hippolytus races off in his chariot. By the time Theseus finds out the truth about what happened and rides out to stop his son, it is too late; a tidal wave carrying a great bull from the sea slays Hippolytus. Theseus then returns to Athens and kills Phaedra in anger.

The aging Theseus eventually suffers a paralytic stroke. He avoids Athens during his recovery so that no one will see his weakness. He returns several years later, only to find that Athens is greatly changed and under the control of the nobleman Menestheus. Theseus leaves Athens and journeys to a friend's house in Skyros. There he kills himself, preferring to end his life before his heroic status can further diminish.

Culture clash. Before *The Bull from the Sea* opens, Medea, a high priestess of the Goddess, had tried to gain power in Athens. She is referred to by the Greeks as a dangerous and powerful sorceress "scheming to bring back the old religion and end the rule of men" (Renault, *Bull from the Sea*, p. 170). Generally, Renault portrays the Greek men of the Mycenaean Age as distrustful

of powerful women who worship the ancient Great Goddess so popular in Greece before the arrival of Theseus's forefathers. The new gods have been established, with Zeus at their head, but the men of Theseus's time fear an overthrow of their male gods and of their male-dominated social system.

When Theseus brings the Amazon leader Hippolyta back to Athens with him, the Athenians fear this strange female warrior, who comes from a society where the Great Goddess is revered. Powerful women with ties to the Goddess were commonly assumed to know magic, which added to the Athenians' fearfulness. Many people of the city believe Hippolyta bewitched Theseus into treating her well and fear that—like Medea—she has plans to overthrow the power of the men in Athens. This is far from the truth of the tale, however; she has not worked any magic on Theseus, nor does she have any plots against the people of her new homeland. Still, her presence in the royal house of Athens is never completely accepted by the public.

A TITLE DRAWN FROM LEGEND

In Greek legend, Theseus, whose father is Poseidon, the God of the Sea, calls on a bull from the sea to punish his son for raping Phaedra, a false charge leveled against him by the queen. The son's frightened horse team bolts, and he is dragged to death over the rocks. It is from this legend that Renault takes the title of her book.

The couple's son, Hippolytus, seems from a very young age to have a spiritual connection to the Goddess. On one occasion, when he is about six years old, his parents search for him at his bedtime. They scour the palace but cannot find him. Finally, they look up and see him quietly sitting on the roof of the palace, his face turned towards the sky. He appears to be meditating or praying. When his worried parents come to him, he assures them, "I was quite safe. I was with the Lady" (*The Bull from the Sea*, p. 197). Such incidents bred unfounded rumors among the people that the king's son was being taught by Hippolyta to revere the Goddess instead of Zeus. In any case, the townspeople view Hippolytus's neglect of the worship of Zeus in favor of the Goddess as highly improper. As Theseus cautions Hippolyta, "Before the people, we must see he ... shows respect to the Olympians [Zeus and his fellow gods]. You know what hangs on it" (*The Bull from the Sea*, p. 198). Theseus is concerned because gossip about his son's beliefs detracts from his own reputation and authority. It is only when Hippolyta is killed and her son sent away that the Athenian fear of a female overthrow of the male-dominated religion recedes.

Sources. *The Bull from the Sea* is a historical novel that recreates the Mycenaean Age in Greece. Renault drew from many different sources in writing the book. The first and most obvious of these was the ancient Greek myth of Theseus. She drew the basic outline of the plot from Plutarch's *Life of Theseus*. As one biographer explains, Renault's "intention was to run through the Theseus tale, episode by episode, from his return to Athens until his death" (Sweetman, p. 209).

Renault also extensively researched the Mycenaean Age. This helped her incorporate elements of the time into her narrative, giving it a realistic tone. Modern archaeological finds related to ancient Greece contributed to her knowledge of the period. She tells of a Mycenaean tomb that had been excavated shortly before she wrote her novel:

> Here with their skeleton hands still folded over their long gold-pommelled swords lay the tall princes whose descendants took Troy.... The written tablets shadowed a warlike society, well organized, aristocratic and art-loving.
>
> (Renault in Sweetman, p. 178)

Further research provided additional insights into the small details of that civilization. She investigated, for example, whether Mycenaean warriors used horses for anything but chariot teams since stirrups, which made riding easier, had not yet been invented (she discovered that warriors did occasionally ride horses). This novel, like others by the author, was thus based not only on legend but also on the results of historical research.

Events in History at the Time the Novel Was Written

The women's movement. Mary Renault published *The Bull from the Sea* in 1962. It was around this time that a movement that encouraged the political, economic, and social equality of women with men began to accelerate. The publication of Betty Friedan's *The Feminine Mystique* in 1963 is often referred to as one of the important spurs to the movement's growth. In this book, Friedan described feelings that were extremely common to many women during the preceding years:

> It was a strange stirring, a sense of dissatisfaction, a yearning that women suffered in the middle of the twentieth century in the United States. Each suburban wife struggled with it alone. As she made the beds, shopped for groceries, matched slip cover material, ate peanut butter sandwiches, chauffeured Cub Scouts and Brownies, lay beside her husband at night, she was afraid to ask even of herself the silent question, "Is this all?"
>
> (Friedan, p. 15)

During the following years, the movement took shape. In 1966 the National Organization of Women was founded. Many new books with feminist themes, such as Kate Millet's *Sexual Politics* (1970), were published. The U.S. National Women's Political Caucus was founded in 1971; the International Feminist Congress first met two years later.

Mary Renault was never an active participant in the women's movement. However, her work and opinions reflect a certain amount of sympathy with feminist attitudes. She thoroughly disliked conventional female life and once noted that:

> Sometimes I look round a lot of housewives shopping, or business men's wives stuck at some awful party when the men go off talking shop and leave them to go on about knitting or servants or something ... and I have a terribly sad feeling like looking at a lot of animals that have moulted and got silly from being kept in a cage.
>
> (Renault in Sweetman, pp. 176-77)

In *The Bull from the Sea*, her characterization of Hippolyta bears out this attitude. Hippolyta grows up among the Amazons, a society dominated by females, and occupies the stereotypical male role of a warrior king. She is skilled in combat and regularly takes up arms in battle. Instead of spinning or weaving, she enjoys spending her time in such outdoor pursuits as hunting. In fact, Hippolyta is in many respects the type of strong woman that the 1960s feminist movement held up as an ideal.

Reviews. *The Bull from the Sea* was the sequel to Renault's story of the first part of Theseus's life, *The King Must Die*, published in 1958. Many reviewers compared it unfavorably to the earlier novel. The *Times Literary Supplement*, for example, described it as a string of interesting anecdotes rather than a fully developed novel. Even so, most people gave the book at least qualified praise. The American author Granville Hicks argued that *The Bull from the Sea* was just as good as *The King Must Die*. The biographer Peter Wolfe praised Renault's creative use of myth, her psychological insights, and her ability to bring the past to life with vivid descriptions of objects and landscapes. Renault herself, however, felt that *The Bull from the Sea* was not as good as her earlier book about Theseus, "mainly because [in this novel] the legends on Theseus's life had little unity" (Renault in Sweetman, p. 217).

From Athens to South Africa. Renault lived in South Africa in 1960 during the writing of *The Bull from the Sea*. She claimed never to have felt so in touch with life as she did while living in that country. England, the nation of her birth, was a highly developed country with an impersonal government. In contrast, living in South Africa was "like being in a city state where the people in control are personally known to the community" (Renault in Sweetman, p. 199). Given this setting, she became deeply involved in politics for the first time in her life.

Apartheid, a government policy that separated the races into different living areas, had been in effect in South Africa since 1948. The country was still part of the British Commonwealth at the time, but this soon changed. During the 1950s whites who were strongly committed to the policy of racial separation gained power. Their leader, Heinrich Verwoerd, became prime minister and introduced the idea of separate homelands for blacks. Renault felt this proposal was a sneaky way to deprive blacks of territory outside the homeland areas. This and other issues set her against Verwoerd and his design to make South Africa an independent republic. Eventually, however, his plan won out. The Union of South Africa became an independent republic and left the British Commonwealth, a hateful move to Renault since the departure from the Commonwealth helped the most segregation-minded whites.

Renault touched upon racial relations in *The Bull from the Sea*. In her narrative, the populace of Athens regards Theseus's Amazon wife Hippolyta as a member of another race. Hippolyta is seen as an outsider throughout her stay in the city, despite her loyalty to Theseus. She is viewed in much the same way that the black and racially mixed people of South Africa were viewed by the conservative whites who controlled the South African government in the 1960s.

For More Information

Chadwick, John. *The Mycenaean World.* Cambridge, England: Cambridge University Press, 1976.

Friedan, Betty. *The Feminine Mystique.* New York: W. W. Norton, 1963.

Frost, Frank J. *Greek Society.* Lexington, Mass.: D. C. Heath, 1971.

Miles, Rosalind. *The Women's History of the World.* New York: Harper & Row, 1988.

Renault, Mary. *The Bull from the Sea.* New York: Pantheon Books, 1962.

Sweetman, David. *Mary Renault: A Biography.* New York: Harcourt Brace, 1993.

Canterbury Tales

by
Geoffrey Chaucer

Born in London, England, sometime between 1342 and 1345, Geoffrey Chaucer was the son of a successful wine merchant. As a result of his father's affluence, Chaucer received a good education. In 1357 he became a page in the service of Elizabeth de Burgh, the wife of Prince Lionel, one of King Edward III's sons. Chaucer later entered the king's service, working for Queen Philippe in 1367. He traveled extensively outside of England, acquiring a broad knowledge of the world, which was uncommon for his time. His travels abroad were somewhat adventurous; at one point he was taken prisoner in a battle with the French at Reims, then ransomed by the king for sixteen pounds, a sum less than the ransom paid for a nobleman's horse. Chaucer is generally considered the first great English poet, and he is among the first poets about whom we have any real biographical knowledge. At his death, Chaucer was the first artist to be buried in a place of honor at Westminster Abbey, one of England's most revered religious sites, in a section that would become known as "Poet's Corner."

Events in History at the Time of the Poem

The pilgrimage and medieval religion. The pilgrimage, such as the one Chaucer presents in the *Canterbury Tales,* was a central institution of the medieval church, perhaps second only to the institution of the parish church in its importance to religion during the period. The official purpose of the pilgrimage was to bring the participants in close contact with important religious sites, including major cathedrals like Canterbury and the holy city of Jerusalem, and also to expose them to sacred objects such as the bones and relics of saints. In practice, a pilgrimage had much of the feel of a modern-day tour to some sacred location.

Some pilgrims made the journey for personal reasons, traveling to pray for ill relatives or to seek a miraculous cure for their own ailments. Other pilgrims undertook the pilgrimage to show devotion to their religion through the sacrifice of time and energy that the journey required. In addition to those who journeyed for personal reasons or to express their devotion to God, another segment of pilgrims took the journey simply for the sake of enjoyment and recreation. This agenda is evident in several of Chaucer's pilgrims,

The choir of Canterbury Cathedral, the destination of Chaucer's pilgrims.

including the cook who becomes too drunk to mount his horse. The recreational aspect of the journey played a large part in the popularity of pilgrimages during the medieval period.

The importance of the church. The church was a central factor in medieval society. Throughout Europe, the Catholic Church owned huge tracts of land that made the institution incredibly powerful and wealthy. The church's power as a political and economic force was as significant as its role in the moral and spiritual life of its followers. Such power led to inevitable abuses, as some religious officials exploited the common people, preying upon the fears and weaknesses of the faithful for their own gain.

Chaucer depicts examples of this exploitation in "The Summoner's Tale" and "The Pardoner's Tale." While Chaucer's tales make fun of individuals who are involved in the church, they never satirize or criticize the church itself. Chaucer seems to have been a typical, faithful Christian who very much loved the church, yet felt frustrated at the individuals who used the church for their own personal benefit.

Feudalism and the late Middle Ages. The feudal system was the predominant economic and social system in England during Chaucer's lifetime. Under this system, land was farmed by a

class of peasants, or serfs, who did not own the farmland. Instead, the farms were owned by a separate class of people, known as nobles or landed gentry. The nobles reaped the profits of the peasants' labor and, in return, gave the peasants a portion of the crops and protection from outlaws and hostile armies.

The peasant classes of this period seemed in some ways to accept their lot in life; the only uprising was the Peasant's Revolt led by Wat Tyler. Wat Tyler was hanged for his role in leading the short-lived rebellion, which took place in southern England in 1381. Even in this instance, economic issues were a minor factor. The probable root of this small rebellion instead lay in the peasants' frustration at the lack of protection from the government against endless raids by the French. Offering no support to southern England's peasants, the king expected them to face the fury of the French onslaught alone.

Since the Peasant's Revolt was the only significant revolt to occur during this period, it has been suggested that there was no widespread discontent among the peasant classes at the time. If a peasant was dissatisfied with his place in society, he apparently did not blame the general social structure but rather the vices of individuals, such as greed, hatred, and lack of compassion. This sentiment is reflected in several of the *Can-*

terbury *Tales,* including "The Pardoner's Tale," which depicts characters committing the worst actions and crimes—greed, selfishness, and murder. The emphasis is on the individuals' wrongful actions rather than on any shortcomings of the medieval social system.

Society and economy in change. The economic and social system of England was undergoing a change during Chaucer's time, and a middle class largely made up of merchants gradually emerged from the previous feudal world. Chaucer himself was a prime example of one who took advantage of the new opportunities available to members of the middle class. His father was a vintner, an importer and distributor of wines, who earned a comfortable living for himself and his family. The elder Chaucer's economic security allowed him to send his son to a good school, and this educational background gave the boy the opportunity to serve in a noble household. Young Chaucer later won a position at court, where he prospered. His able service led to various annuities and administrative governmental posts, which he received in payment for his services. Chaucer's affiliation with the court was to last throughout his lifetime. Despite drastic political changes that occurred during this time, he was never out of political favor. He lived on patronage—an arrangement in which he was supported by noble sponsors—from 1357 until his death in 1400.

Literary ideals and courtly love. At the conclusion of "The Pardoner's Tale," the characters are punished for their vices. This perfect justice illustrates one of the most important aspects of storytelling in Chaucer's age: namely, the ability of stories to create a world that operates neatly by punishing vice and rewarding virtue. Tales that portrayed such a perfect world soothed the masses, whose world of reality seldom exhibited such perfect justice. Chaucer appears to have been quite comfortable with this feature of storytelling; several of his tales depict a perfectly balanced and just world in which virtuous characters overcome all opposition and are ultimately victorious.

Another important element in literature of the Middle Ages was the notion of chivalry, which included the concept of courtly love. Chivalry was the code of honor by which knights lived, pledging their allegiance to their lords and binding themselves to an elaborate system of rules and behavior. In "The Knight's Tale," two rivals, each backed by one hundred knights, fight a grand tourney for the right to woo a maiden.

Such tournaments did in fact occur, but they were usually fought as practice for war, not over a love interest.

The concept of courtly love was a literary convention that allowed the characters of romances to pursue their amorous adventures without facing social and moral consequences. Courtly love stood in direct opposition to the church's teachings and standards, yet placed as it was in the context of romantic adventure stories and poems, it did not challenge the church's influence over medieval society.

The Poem in Focus

Middle English. Chaucer's tales were written in Middle English, an earlier form of today's English language. The Middle English of the tales may at first glance seem unreadable to the untrained eye. The language features variant, unfamiliar spellings and uses vocabulary words that have become obsolete since Chaucer's day. But creative reading and a little practice allows the reader to eventually discern the word *sin,* for example, in Chaucer's *synne,* and *wild* in *wylde.*

The dramatic situation in the *Canterbury Tales.* *Canterbury Tales* was Chaucer's most popular work, although it was never finished. Even in its incomplete state, however, it reveals a level of ambition, organization, and artistic achievement unmatched in earlier English storytelling. Chaucer's tales are told by a group of travellers as they journey on a religious pilgrimage to the cathedral at Canterbury. Covering fifty-five miles, the journey from London to Canterbury could last as long as four days. Chaucer's convention of having the pilgrims entertain each other makes sense; the route to Canterbury was not especially scenic or interesting, so storytelling served as an obvious way to make the trip more interesting.

The prologue and the cast of characters. The pilgrims begin their journey at the Tabard Inn, an establishment owned by Harry Bailey, their host and the leader of the pilgrimage. They gather the night before the journey at the inn and leave on the morning of April 17, probably in the year 1387. References to the number of pilgrims on the journey—twenty-nine, plus Chaucer himself—and to the number of days the travelers take to reach their destination are confusing in places; in any case, it seems clear that Chaucer was not primarily interested in creating a "realistic" narrative with great attention to detail. Instead, he

The Tabard Inn, where Chaucer's pilgrims met and began their journey to Canterbury. This illustration shows the building as it appeared in 1810, when it was called the Talbot Inn.

wanted to provide an overall framework within which to place his characters and their stories.

Chaucer's stated intention was to have each of the thirty pilgrims tell a total of four tales, two on the journey to Canterbury and two on the road back, for a total of 120 tales. This represented a huge undertaking on Chaucer's part, an undertaking that was never finished. Only twenty-four tales were written. Chaucer also wrote the famous "General Prologue," which introduces the entire work and each of the pilgrims, as well as a retraction. In this last piece, he revokes all his writings on worldly trifles. Chaucer resorted to the retraction after realizing he would not be able to complete the original plan.

It has been said that the *Canterbury Tales* contains representations of the entire social spectrum of Chaucer's England. His characters include skilled tradesmen and craftsmen—the Miller, the Cook, and the Reeve; members of the middle and professional classes—the Shipman, the Wife of Bath, the Physician, the Manciple (a minor official), and the Merchant; figures of the upper classes and members of court—the Franklin, the Man of Law, the Knight, and the Squire; and individuals from the religious segment of society—the Parson, the Nuns, the Nun's Priest, the Prioress (head of a household of nuns), the Clerk,

the Summoner, the Pardoner, the Friar, and the Monk. Taken as a whole, these characters represent a broad and largely inclusive cross section of Chaucer's England. A summary of three of the characters and their tales follows.

The Miller's Prologue and Tale. The miller was an important character in the medieval world. His job was to turn the farmer's grain into flour by grinding it in his mill. The Miller of the *Canterbury Tales* is described in the General Prologue as a physically intimidating character: "The Millere was a stout carl for the nones / Ful byg he was of brawn, and eek of bones [The Miller was a stout fellow indeed / Full strong he was of muscle, and also of bones]" (Chaucer, *Canterbury Tales,* fragment 1, 545-46). The Miller's moral character is also revealed in the general prologue when he is described as a teller of dirty stories, "moost of synne and harlotries [most of sin and deeds of harlotry]" (*Canterbury Tales,* fragment 1, line 561).

"The Miller's Tale" is considered a bawdy tale, or fabliau, a short, comic story in verse that creates humor out of our sexual and physical nature. These tales emphasize jealousy, adultery, thievery, trickery, and the baser elements of human behavior. The liveliest of the *Canterbury Tales,* these bawdy stories delight readers largely because they make fun of human weaknesses in

PUTTING THE TALES IN ORDER

There are twenty-four tales in the work, plus the General Prologue and the Retraction. The proper order of the tales is a matter of debate. Scholars agree that Chaucer grouped the tales into ten fragments, as indicated below, but there is much discussion about how these fragments should be ordered.

Frag.   Tales

1   General Prologue, Knight's Tale, Miller's Tale, Reeve's Tale, Cook's Tale
2   Man of Law's Tale
3   Friar's Tale, Summoner's Tale, Wife of Bath's Tale
4   Clerk's Tale, Merchant's Tale
5   Squire's Tale, Franklin's Tale
6   Physician's Tale, Pardoner's Tale
7   Tale of Sir Thopas, Tale of Melibee, Monk's Tale, Nun's Priest's Tale, Shipman's Tale, Prioress's Tale
8   Second Nun's Tale, Canon's Yeoman's Tale
9   Manciple's Tale
10   Parson's Tale, Retraction

In addition to the "General Prologue," each tale except for the Knight's, Physician's, and Shipman's tales begins with its own prologue.

a way that is true to life. "The Miller's Tale," one of the best known fabliaux, is actually a story about how people shape their own lot in life.

The Miller has a motive for choosing the story he tells. He aims to tease and annoy the Reeve, another of the pilgrims, who follows this tale with one of his own, a retaliatory attack against the Miller. This interplay between tales occurs throughout the work and is used by Chaucer to convey the humanity of his characters while keeping the reader interested in the progress of the storytelling.

The subject of "The Miller's Tale" is a young student's seduction of a carpenter's wife. The student is a lodger at the home of the older carpenter, whose wife is a younger woman. Such marriages were common in the Middle Ages. The Miller describes the carpenter's jealous attitude toward his young wife:

> Jalous he was, and heeld hire narwe in cage,
> For she was wylde and yong, and he was old
> And demed hymself been lik a cokewold.
>
> [Jealous he was, and held her closely caged
> For she was wild and young, and he was old
> And deemed himself likely to be a cuckold.]
> (*Canterbury Tales*, fragment 1, 3224-26)

The student, Nicholas, is drawn to Alison, the carpenter's wife. In a bold first encounter,

he grabs her and demands her love. Alison protests, but not too much, and Nicholas convinces her that they can easily trick her husband. Following the student's plan, the two would-be lovers go to great lengths to arrange their rendezvous. Their adventures during this plotting have become one of the most famous examples of storytelling in English literature. The lovers spend a passionate night in bed while the husband sleeps in a tub; Nicholas kisses Alison's posterior instead of her lips; his own posterior receives a hot surprise; and the husband's tub comically crashes from a height to the ground.

The Wife of Bath's Prologue and Tale. In the prologue to "The Wife of Bath's Tale," specific information is given about the goodwife (female head of a household) from the city of Bath. The General Prologue reveals that she is a rich woman and a skillful weaver with a spirited personality; in the special prologue to her tale, she herself says that she has been married five times and that the deaths of her first three husbands provided her with a great deal of wealth. Scholars have argued that this explanation for her financial prosperity may be a lie fabricated by the Wife of Bath to make herself look like a successful and desirable woman. Her wealth may actually be a result of her own effort. She is described as the best weaver in England, and her skill at this profession may be the true source of her financial success.

The Wife's prologue explains her view of marriage; she believes it is an institution that allows people to enjoy their sexuality. The Wife goes on to propose that a woman receive equal or superior power to that of the man in marriage. This issue, which she calls sovereignty, is central to her tale.

"The Wife of Bath's Tale" contains a folk motif: a knight faces execution for the rape of a young maiden. The women of the court offer him his freedom if he can give the correct answer to a question the queen asks: What is the thing that women most desire? The queen gives the knight one year to go forth and seek the answer. He conducts an exhaustive search and receives many possible answers, including honor, pleasure, flattery, and freedom. None of these responses satisfies the knight, and he rides dejectedly back to the castle to face his fate. On his way, the knight encounters an old woman who gives him the correct answer—a woman wants the same level of power and mastery over her husband as she would have over a lover; neither one should be above her, and she should be equal to both. The twist in the story comes when the old woman demands that the knight marry her as payment. He complies, and this triggers a surprising and satisfying conclusion to the tale. In the end, the old woman is transformed into a young and beautiful wife.

Counterpoint and views on women. The Wife's tale so upsets the character known as the Clerk that he feels compelled to respond with a tale of his own. He tells a story that is primarily about keeping one's promises, but features a wife named Griselda who is unwilling to break her oath of obedience to her husband. Griselda, though married to a tyrant, is a long-suffering and submissive wife. In contrast, the Wife of Bath seems to have a domineering and coarse nature that reduces her chance of attracting a man's genuine affection, which, despite her focus on sex and wealth, is probably her true ambition.

There has been much speculation about Chaucer's view of the institution of marriage, and some scholars suggest that he did not hold it in high regard. But in the tale of the Wife of Bath and in other stories, such as the Franklin's, it seems as though Chaucer does have great respect for the wisdom of women and for their right to be treated fairly and gently by husbands who loved them. "The Wife of Bath's Tale" suggests that women should be recognized as equals in relationships and that men should treat them kindly.

The Franklin's Tale. The Franklin is essentially a newly rich upstart trying to act the part of the gracious, sensitive, compassionate man of wealth. He pretends that he wishes to share his good fortune and wisdom with everyone, yet his deeper intent is to draw positive attention toward himself. He is overly lavish with his hospitality, calling more attention to his own virtue than to the plight of those in need. He claims to be rough and uneducated, while also letting his audience know that he is quite familiar with Cicero, who was an authority on the subject of rhetoric.

The Franklin's Tale concerns a knight, Arveragus; his wife, Dorigen; and a neighboring squire in love with Dorigen named Aurelius. Complications arise when the husband, Arveragus, leaves his native France to go to England on knightly business for a period of two years. His wife, Dorigen, falls into a deep depression, and the squire Aurelius pursues her affections to the point even of trying to trick her into an affair with him. Aurelius approaches Dorigen, declaring his love. Dorigen, who loves her husband and feels concerned for his safety, rejects the squire, although she adds playfully,

> Aurelie, by heighe god above,
> Yet wolde I graunte yow to been youre love,
> Syn I yow se so pitously complayne."

> [Aurelius, by high god above,
> Yet would I grant to be your love,
> Since I see you so piteously complain.]
> (*Canterbury Tales*, fragment 5, lines 989-91)

Dorigen then sets Aurelius what she believes is an impossible task, thereby letting him know that she wishes to stay faithful to her husband. When Aurelius manages to complete the task, both her marriage and the moral integrity of the characters are put to the test. Her husband, Arveragus, intent on behaving honorably, orders that she keep her word and submit to her admirer, though Arveragus instructs her to keep this a secret. Aurelius, in turn, behaves in a noble way that results in a happy ending for Dorigen and her husband.

Sources. It is known that Chaucer translated a large part of the "Roman de la Rose," a French poem, as part of his training as a poet, and that some of the elements of courtly love involved in this work are found in the *Canterbury Tales*. Probably Chaucer was also aware of the work of poets such as Will Langland, author of *Piers Plowman*. It seems certain that Chaucer knew of the *Decameron*, a collection of tales by Boccaccio framed by a dramatic device similar to that used in *The Canterbury Tales*. Chaucer is said to have adopted the convention of a time-passing exchange of stories, a technique employed in the *Decameron*. Chaucer may have become acquainted with this work on his second visit to Italy in 1378. There is also evidence in the tales of the influence of Italian poets such as Petrarch, who was still living in Italy at the time of one of Chaucer's journeys there, and Dante, the author of *Divine Comedy* (**Inferno,** the first part of *Divine Comedy*, is also covered in *Literature and Its Times*).

While Chaucer's travels and readings contributed to his creation of the *Canterbury Tales*, traditional folk stories, and even tavern stories, like those so familiar to the Miller, had a greater effect. Probably Chaucer's greatest source was the living world of people around him. There is in all of the *Canterbury Tales* a celebration of our shared humanity and the humorous, difficult situations that the desire for love and companionship can create. This celebration spans the social classes of Chaucer's time, a range of people whom Chaucer was well situated to observe. He resided above one of the gates of entry into the city of London for much of his career. It seems inevitable that this location, amid the swirling masses of English society, would have encouraged and influenced Chaucer's creation of the *Canterbury Tales*.

For More Information

Chaucer, Geoffrey. *Canterbury Tales*. In *The Riverside Chaucer*. Edited by Larry D. Benson. 3rd ed. Boston: Houghton Mifflin, 1987.

Dinshaw, Carolyn. *Chaucer's Sexual Poetics*. Madison, Wis.: University of Wisconsin Press, 1989.

Herlihy, David. *Medieval Households*. Cambridge: Harvard University Press, 1985.

Howard, Donald R. *Chaucer: His Life, His Works, His World*. New York: Ballantine, 1986.

Myers, A. R. *England in the Late Middle Ages*. New York: Penguin, 1952.

Serraillier, Ian. *Chaucer and His World*. New York: Henry Z. Walck, 1968.

Common Sense

by
Thomas Paine

When Thomas Paine wrote *Common Sense,* he had been in America only slightly longer than a year. He arrived in Philadelphia in October 1774, a thirty-seven-year-old tax collector and corset-maker from England who had just started to cultivate an interest in political writing a few years earlier. By the summer of 1776, Paine's *Common Sense* had sold a remarkable 150,000 copies throughout the colonies and had persuaded probably an even greater number of colonists that they must sever their political ties to Britain. The document that Thomas Jefferson and his fellow delegates signed on July 4, 1776, may have been the colonies' official declaration of independence, but *Common Sense* was the work that convinced America's "common" people that independence was their best—or, more exactly, their only—course of action.

Events in History at the Time of the Pamphlet

Budding democracy in Philadelphia. Paine's arrival in Philadelphia, Pennsylvania, came at a time of intense political tension and excitement. As in other colonies, the Stamp Act (1765), the Townshend Acts (1767), and the Intolerable Acts (1774)—British acts imposing taxes on the colonists and limiting their rights—had stirred up questions about loyalty toward Britain. Within Philadelphia, colonial involvement in these and other political issues had broadened

> ## THE LITERARY WORK
>
> A pamphlet written in colonial America in the 1770s; published in January 1776.
>
> ## SYNOPSIS
>
> Paine explains in plain but forceful language why the American colonies should separate from Great Britain and form an independent nation.

to include a growing number of middle-class artisans. In the 1760s a great debate had raged in Philadelphia about whether to replace Pennsylvania's "proprietary" government, the colony's ownership by the Penn family, with a direct royal government. Although this issue had waned by 1770, the aristocrats in the battling Proprietary and Quaker parties had brought middle-class Philadelphians into the debate. A greater number of people than ever before had begun to vote.

Most artisans—shipbuilders, watchmakers, and other skilled craftsmen—were not legally allowed to vote. Like the members of other colonies, Pennsylvanians were required to possess a minimum amount of land or money (in their case, fifty acres or fifty pounds) to have the right to vote. The law, however, was not strictly enforced in Philadelphia. This state of affairs ensured that the voices of middle-class colonists had an increasingly significant effect on local political decisions.

Thomas Paine must have been fond of this trend, for in his post as editor of the *Pennsylvania Magazine,* a position he held during his first few years in America, he frequently criticized class divisions and aristocratic privilege. In May 1775 he reflected on the contradiction between the respectable titles and ignoble deeds of some of these aristocrats:

> When I reflect on the pompous titles bestowed on unworthy men, I feel an indignity that instructs me to despise the absurdity. The *Honourable* plunderer of his country, or the *Right Honourable* murderer of mankind, create such a contrast of ideas as exhibit a monster rather than a man. Virtue is inflamed at the violation, and sober reason calls it nonsense.
>
> (Paine in Conway, p. 46)

Most of Paine's experience with "unworthy" aristocrats came from his life in England, where he lived for many years as a common man on the verge of poverty. Before coming to Philadelphia, Paine probably shared the popular English

---

PAINE ON SLAVERY

Paine was not just concerned with the equal treatment of white colonists. He also wrote frequently about the injustice of slavery in America. In one of the first essays written after his arrival, he calls for an immediate end to the "monstrous" practice of slavery—not just the slave trade—and accuses the colonists of hypocrisy: "With what consistency, or decency [can colonists] complain so loudly of attempts to enslave them, while they hold so many hundred thousands in slavery?" (Paine in Conway, p. 7). Ironically, in the same issue of the *Philadelphia Journal* in which this essay appears, an advertisement offers a black slave for sale.

---

image of America as a land of promise where merit, not rank, determined a person's success. After a year of American life, he sought to use his writing ability to help ensure that this utopian dream could become a permanent reality. *Common Sense* was the result.

Unequal relations in American society. The politically equal society that Paine saw emerging in Philadelphia was not, however, the dream of every colonist. Many of the wealthy merchants, planters, and lawyers who controlled colonial government were disturbed by middle-class participation in politics, a growing trend throughout the colonies. These rich and powerful colonists sought better treatment from their mother country, but they feared the social and political change that might come to the colonies if independence from Britain were achieved. These colonists feared losing the power and wealth that they had accumulated.

By the spring of 1776, many of these leaders, some won over by Paine's passionate prose, had decided to support the struggle for independence. In their view, the success of *Common Sense* was a double-edged sword. It had contributed greatly to the surge of support for a movement for independence, but it had also triggered increased middle-class participation in politics. Soon after the publication of *Common Sense,* the prominent colonial politician John Adams wrote that Paine's pamphlet, in criticizing the British political hierarchy, was too "democratical"; it could spread dangerous ideas about political equality, ideas he called "Paine's yellow fever" (Adams in Foner, p. xviii). By the summer of 1776, these ideas *were* spreading, up and down the colonies. Through his writing, Paine had linked the call for independence to the movement toward more democratic political participation.

Pamphlets in the colonies. Although *Common Sense* is probably the best known of any American pamphlet, it certainly was not the only one. Short, cheap, and easy to produce, these popular reading materials initiated and reflected political debates throughout Revolutionary America. They ranged in length from ten to fifty pages, and though some contained poetry or religious sermons, most expressed political concerns. Between 1750 and 1776 alone, some 400 pamphlets dealing with British-American relations were published. Since Philadelphia was the publishing capital of the colonies, many pamphlets originated there, but by the 1770s virtually every colonial city with a printing press produced them.

Although the prevalence of pamphlets helped to bring political discussion from the colonial assemblies into churches and alehouses, no pamphlet at the time received as diverse a readership as Paine's *Common Sense.* While most American pamphlets were structured around legal and logical arguments and directed toward educated voters, Paine's essay was written with uncommon passion and simplicity, for he hoped that his words would have a powerful impact on the whole spectrum of American colonists. He must have been successful in this goal, for one Connecticut man, explaining that Paine's pamphlet was being read by "all sorts of people," exclaimed to the author that:

> You have declared the sentiments of millions. Your production may justly be compared to a landflood that sweeps all before it. We were blind, but on reading these enlightening words the scales have fallen from our eyes.
>
> (Foner, p. 79)

The twenty-five printings of *Common Sense* published in 1776 were read by farmers and tradesmen, while illiterate colonists heard its contents from neighbors who read it aloud. By means of this popular literary tool, Paine managed to widen the circle of political discussion and appeal to the "common sense" of "common people."

Religion and revolutionary thought. In England, the country that America's first colonists left behind, God and king were worshipped hand in hand. The king led the Church of England and prohibited the practice of other religions—even other branches of Christianity. Some English citizens in search of more religious freedom left their country and chose to sail to America. Consequently, from its earliest days, America was looked upon by some as a sort of "promised land." There were, to be sure, many colonists who established their own versions of England's churches and tried to remain connected to the faith of their mother country. But a number of colonists came to America to escape the religious persecution they had suffered in England.

Later, in the mid-1700s, a religious revival called the Great Awakening swept the colonies, creating a renewed sense of the importance of religious tolerance. For most Americans, religious freedom was a valued part of the colonial experience. Paine reminded his readers of its value in *Common Sense:*

> I fully and conscientiously believe, that it is the will of the Almighty that there should be a diversity of religious opinions among us. It affords a larger field for our Christian kindness ... I look on the various denominations among us, to be like children of the same family, differing only in what is called their Christian names.
>
> (Paine, *Common Sense,* pp. 108-09)

The degree of religious freedom was not the only concern of the Protestant colonists in their

Portrait of Thomas Paine.

effort to establish a just society. Since the late seventeenth century, many American Protestants had been hoping and planning for the coming of a new world, a kingdom of God on earth. Their belief was that Christ would soon return to earth, where he would rule with God for a thousand years before a final judgment day. In order to pave the way for this kingdom, many of these "millennialists" believed that they had to bring about a series of changes to create a more virtuous society. Coming to the "New World" of America had been the first step in this process of change. After reading Paine's pamphlet, many millennialists believed that American independence was the next step. In an appendix added after the first edition of *Common Sense*, Paine appears to make a direct appeal to these colonists:

> We have it in our power to begin the world over again. A situation, similar to the present, hath not happened since the days of Noah until now. The birthday of a new world is at hand.
>
> (*Common Sense,* p. 118)

Even those Christians who did not share this millennial vision, however, were easily convinced by Paine's call for separation from Britain. After all, by January 1776 the English government had already taxed their goods without their consent, outlawed the decisions of their colonial governments, and prompted its soldiers to fire on colony militias in Lexington and Concord. Colonists wondered if the king might not also seize one of their most precious remaining rights—religious freedom. To prevent this, and to create a safe haven for virtuous society, many colonists were persuaded that they must seek independence for their "promised land."

A PREJUDICE IN PAINE'S TIME

Religious tolerance was valued among the colonists, but only to a limited degree. Even they could be intolerant of non-Protestant faiths. Most Catholics were shunned by their fellow colonists, a prejudice of which Paine was keenly aware. In *Common Sense,* he played on this anti-Catholic tension by equating British monarchy to "popery" (the practices and beliefs of the Catholic Church). Paine himself rejected all organized religion, although he was careful not to share this view with the readers of *Common Sense.*

The Pamphlet in Focus

The contents. *Common Sense* is divided into four main sections that together form a convincing argument for independence from England. The essay begins with a discussion of the origins of government. Paine's aim is to distinguish clearly between society and government, and to make his readers understand that government is not a fixed institution but a creation of society. As such, it can be changed if it fails to serve its purpose—to protect the individual members of society from one another's lapses in virtue. Paine then explains how the English constitution has neglected its duty to the people of England by resting the majority of its power in the hands of the king and aristocratic legislators instead of leaders elected by society.

Paine uses the next section to expand on this claim. He describes the injustices of monarchy and of inherited government positions. He also argues that the distinction between kings and subjects is an unnatural one, insisting that "[i]t is the pride of kings which throws mankind into confusion" (*Common Sense,* p. 75). To support his position, Paine cites lengthy passages from the

Bible that proclaim the evils of monarchy and hereditary rule. He concludes with this forceful statement: "Of more worth is one honest man to society, and in the sight of God, than all the crowned ruffians that ever lived" (*Common Sense,* p. 84).

In the third section of *Common Sense,* Paine discusses the situation in America and encourages his readers to appreciate the importance of their position in history: "'Tis not the concern of a day, a year, or an age; posterity [future generations] are virtually involved in the contest, and will be more or less affected even to the end of time, by the proceedings now" (*Common Sense,* p. 85). In an attempt to dispel the notion that Americans owe loyalty to England, Paine contends that their diverse origins make the colonists children of Europe rather than England. (One-third of the white colonists in America originated from a country other than England.) Furthermore, Paine continues, England has lost her claim to the colonies by mistreating them. He then argues that the colonies have grown too large to be governed by an outside force. The third section of *Common Sense* concludes with a brief description of one possible structure by which the united colonies could rule themselves.

In the fourth section of *Common Sense,* Paine cements his argument for independence by detailing the economic resources, military potential, and unity of the colonies. The time is ripe, he claims, for these young settlements to form a government.

Paine's new political language. The ideas in *Common Sense* were revolutionary. Paine's call for democratic government was something the colonists had never heard before in any popularly accepted text, although many had practiced a form of republicanism in their local governments for years. In fact, these ideas were so new to most colonists that Paine had to change people's attitudes toward certain words to express his views. Before the publication of *Common Sense,* for example, *democracy* was a negative term. It had been used to refer only to the chaotic, undesirable system of *direct* democracy (government by the people, not their representatives). Instead Paine used it in its modern, positive sense to refer to a government by elected leaders. The very word *revolution,* so closely associated now with the war that Paine's pamphlet helped to start, was "revolutionized" by Paine. He was among the first to use it to refer to political change; before, it had been used mainly to describe the orbit of planets.

First edition copy of *Common Sense.*

Common Sense changed not only the political vocabulary of its time, but also the style of political writing that was practiced. Paine avoided the abstract, complex language of most political writing. He wrote with more simplicity and passion than his contemporaries. Moreover, he avoided making references to classical texts, aware that only educated colonists would understand such references. "As it is my design," he once explained, "to make those that can scarcely read understand, I shall therefore avoid every literary ornament and put it in language as plain as the alphabet" (Paine in Foner, p. 83). Unlike most writers of his day, Paine also drew common examples from the everyday lives of the people to illustrate the points in his text.

All of these stylistic differences set Paine apart from his fellow writers. Thomas Jefferson's original June 1776 draft of the **Declaration of Independence** (also covered in *Literature and Its Times*), for instance, included the following description of the injustices that the British government had inflicted upon the American colonies:

> These facts have given the last stab to agonizing affection, and manly spirit bids us to renounce forever these unfeeling brethren. We must endeavor to forget our former love for them, and hold them as we hold the rest of mankind, enemies in war, in peace friends. We might have a free and a great people together; but a communication of grandeur and of freedom, it seems, is below their dignity. Be it so, since they will have it. The road to happiness and to glory is open to us, too.
>
> (Jefferson in Koch, p. 27)

An example from *Common Sense* that discusses the impossibility of American reconciliation with Great Britain, on the other hand, displays a much plainer approach:

> Ye that tell us of harmony and reconciliation, can ye restore to us the time that is past? Can ye give to prostitution its former innocence? Neither can ye reconcile Britain and America. The last cord now is broken, the people of England are presenting addresses against us. There are injuries which nature cannot forgive; she would cease to be nature if she did. As well can the lover forgive the ravisher of his mistress, as the Continent forgive the murders of Britain.
>
> (*Common Sense*, p. 100)

Paine's use of graphic metaphors and his simple sentence structure reflect a language understood at the time by common Americans. While Jefferson's style is fitting for a document such as the Declaration of Independence, Paine's writing style was clearly suitable for a spokesman for the people.

Sources. Thomas Paine initiated *Common Sense* at the suggestion of a friend, Benjamin Rush, a Philadelphia doctor and closet revolutionary. Rush knew of Paine's writing ability from his essays in the *Pennsylvania Journal* and was aware that Paine had written a political pamphlet two years earlier for the tax collectors of England.

Paine did not begin to write, however, until more than a year after relocating to America. By that time he understood the major sources of colonial tensions. When he first arrived in Philadelphia, he had thought that reconciliation with Britain was still a possibility. After months of heated political discussions with other colonists—and after the battles at Lexington, Concord, and Bunker Hill—he changed his mind. By the fall of 1775 Paine felt that relations with Britain were irreparably damaged.

Although Paine was convinced that America must seek independence from England, he had a hard time putting his convictions on paper. Writing had always been a slow, painful process for Paine; it took him about two months to complete *Common Sense*. The final product, though, combined various popular ideas about government and society into one coherent and compelling argument for independence. In order to accomplish this, Paine drew on the liberal philosophy of Englishman John Locke and the notions of republicanism that were first introduced to the world by Aristotle. Paine claimed not to have read Locke, and studies on Paine suggest that he probably learned much of what he knew about political philosophy from discussion and debate rather than reading. Nevertheless, the ideas he expressed in *Common Sense* are easily traceable to these two schools of thought.

Locke's liberal ideas centered around the notion of "natural rights," freedoms that each individual is entitled to, regardless of rank or social position. Republicanism, on the other hand, focused not on individual rights but on "public good." When Paine spoke of the right of individuals to participate in government, he was referring to Locke's ideas. When he criticized the institution of monarchy, he was drawing on the notion of republicanism. Although many political philosophers see a clash between individual desires and public interest, Paine believed that both concerns were compatible. "Public good," he once said, "is not a term opposed to the good of individuals. On the contrary, it is the good of every individual collected. It is the good of all, because it is the good of everyone" (Paine in Foner, p. 89).

Success and misfortune. As Paine struggled to complete his essay, Rush advised him on his drafts and suggested the title. Paine then brought a version of it to Benjamin Franklin, whom he had met in London, the scientist David Rittenhouse, and the brewer and political radical Samuel Adams. These men edited the essay and made a few minor changes. Paine then sought out a publisher who was not afraid to print his essay. He knew that anyone associated with such a radical piece of writing could, at the very least, expect a wounded reputation. Another possibility was that the publisher of such material might be found guilty of sedition (inflammatory writing) and imprisoned (as Paine later was for a different work). Finally, a "republican printer" named Robert Bell, whose reputation was already ruined because he kept a mistress, agreed to publish *Common Sense*. In its first few printings, its author was known only as "an Englishman."

Common Sense captured the attention of the colonies, selling thirty times as many copies as other pamphlets of the day. Its language and logic succeeded in reaching and changing the minds of many who perhaps an hour before reading the pamphlet were violently opposed to the idea of declaring independence. Paine's work eventually came to be regarded by many as "the most brilliant pamphlet written during the American Revolution and one of the most brilliant pamphlets ever written in the English language" (Bailyn, p. 67).

A popular writer who spent many hours creating his essays, Paine is regarded by many historians as the first professional pamphleteer. Other pamphlet writers were mainly employed as teachers, lawyers, or ministers. They made little, if any, money from their written work.

Ironically, Paine made nothing from the sales of *Common Sense*. Bell changed the terms of their agreement and thus swindled Paine out of his share of the profits, which he had planned to use to buy mittens for American soldiers. Although multiple editions were published and over 150,000 copies sold, Paine saw not a penny of profit. Bell, on the other hand, gathered a small fortune. Fed up with the publishing business, Paine eventually gave up the rights to his pamphlet, allowing colonial publishers to print copies of the work at their own cost and profit. Paine's failure to profit from *Common Sense* was a prelude to the sad years that would follow. Although he wrote other best-selling works, his life ended in poverty and relative isolation.

For More Information

Bailyn, Bernard. *The Ideological Origins of the American Revolution.* Cambridge, Mass.: Harvard University Press, Belknap Press, 1967.

Conway, Moncure Daniel, ed. *The Writings of Thomas Paine.* Vol. 1. New York: G. P. Putnam's Sons, 1894.

Foner, Eric. *Tom Paine and Revolutionary America.* New York: Oxford University Press, 1976.

Fruchtman, Jack, Jr. *Thomas Paine: Apostle of Freedom.* New York: Four Walls Eight Windows, 1994.

Koch, Adrienne, and William Peden, eds. *The Life and Selected Writings of Thomas Jefferson.* New York: Random House, 1944.

Paine, Thomas. *Common Sense.* In *The Writings of Thomas Paine.* Vol. 1. Edited by Moncure Daniel Conway. New York: G. P. Putnam's Sons, 1894.

The Crucible

by
Arthur Miller

Dramatist Arthur Miller was born in New York City in 1915 and became one of America's most prominent playwrights following World War II. The postwar years also saw the rise of anticommunist feelings in the U.S., and Miller used *The Crucible* to draw comparisons between the American political climate of the 1950s and the Salem witch trials that had taken place in New England in the 1600s.

Events in History at the Time the Play Takes Place

Puritans in Massachusetts. A thousand Puritan settlers arrived in New England in 1630 after leaving England. In the next fifteen years the Puritan community in the New World would have almost 20,000 members. They quickly prospered, but later encountered problems. Over the years, their communities suffered from tensions attributed to illness, personal feuds, dead livestock, and other factors. In the early 1690s the Puritan community of Salem abruptly exploded in terror over claims that some of its citizens were practicing witchcraft.

The Puritans had come to Massachusetts distraught over what they saw as the corruption of the Church of England. In Massachusetts they set up a colony dedicated to God. They hoped that, by working for his ends, they would become an exemplary society, both to England and the rest of the world. To combat the harshness of life in the Massachusetts wilderness, as well as the temptations of sin, the Puritans employed a rigid

THE LITERARY WORK

A four-act play set in 1692 in Salem, a small Puritan community in Massachusetts; published in 1953.

SYNOPSIS

Hysteria sweeps a small town as accusations of witchcraft lead to an unprecedented series of trials and executions.

sense of discipline, placing the good of the group over the rights of the individual. "We must delight in each other, make others' conditions our own, rejoice together, mourn together, labor and suffer together," proclaimed John Winthrop, a governor and early leader of the Puritan colony (Morgan, p. 63). This philosophy extended to the policing of one's neighbor "as is indicated by the practice of appointing a two-man patrol whose duty was to 'walk forth in the time of God's worship to take notice of such as either lye about the meeting house, without attending to the word and ordinances, or that lye at home or in the fields without giving good account thereof, and to take the names of such persons, and to present them to the magistrates'" (Miller, *The Crucible,* pp. 4-5). Yet under this harsh discipline the Puritan communities prospered. They created a thriving economy, established the first printing press in the English colonies and founded Harvard College in 1636. The Puritan emphasis on self-denial and hard-handed justice seemed ideally suited to taming the unforgiving land of the New World.

Politics and witchcraft. Much to the Puritans' dismay, their government underwent a sharp change in the 1680s. Massachusetts was swept into the Dominion of New England, an area that also included New York, New Hampshire, Connecticut, Rhode Island, and New Jersey. The community fell under harsh rule. Sent over from England to govern the Dominion, Edmund Andros replaced the Puritans' own government and established a heavy-handed authority over the area. He confiscated all land grants and commanded that they be regranted in the king's name. Under such mandates, the villagers using the lands suddenly owed taxes to the crown for the privilege of their use. Moreover, Andros granted favors to a small group of his merchant supporters. Resentment swelled up among the colonists until it brimmed over in an angry uprising that overthrew Andros in 1689. For three years Massachusetts was subject to a vacuum in leadership; no new royal governor was sent over from England during this time. Historians speculate that this lack of leadership in Massachusetts may have been a factor in the witchcraft trials. Prior to the political upheaval, 100 New Englanders in the area had been accused of witchcraft, but the Puritan community remained relatively calm. After Andros was overthrown, however, there was no recognized authority to calm the citizens. The atmosphere eventually escalated into mass hysteria.

The "crime" of witchcraft was a felony. Of the 100 people accused before the 1690s, at least twelve were executed. Such accusations were commonplace in many regions of the world in the seventeenth century. Hundreds of people accused of witchcraft in England were killed, while thousands of suspected witches were executed in Scotland, Germany, and Scandinavia.

The cloud of suspected witchcraft passed over the region of Massachusetts as well. In 1688 Goodwife (Goody) Glover was accused of consorting with the devil and afflicting the Goodwin family. She allegedly made puppets of rags and goat hair and then wet her finger with spittle and stroked the dolls to cause her mischief. Such actions were regarded as black magic; the goat hair supposedly stood for the devil—the goat and the devil both have horns and cloven hooves—and the spittle was thought to have supernatural powers. The townspeople believed that Glover could cause one of the Goodwin

children to fall into a life-threatening fit when she rubbed the puppets.

On her way to the gallows, Goody Glover left onlookers with the foreboding news that the children's ailments would not cease with her death, for there were other witches in league with the devil besides her. Glover was then executed. A year later, in 1689, the Boston minister Cotton Mather wrote *Memorable Providences,* a book about the Goodwin case. It was published two months after the uprising against the dictatorial governor Andros and claimed that the mounting number of sins in New England proved that the devil was intent on penetrating the area with witchcraft. The book spread through the countryside in the eighteen months that passed between the Goodwin case and the beginning of the infamous Salem witch-hunt.

Witchcraft in Salem. The hysteria over witches in Salem began innocently enough with the play of young girls. Aided by Reverend Samuel Parris's slave Tituba, the girls—who ranged in age from nine to twenty—allegedly dabbled in activities that bordered on the occult. Eventually, the activities so frightened some of the girls that during the spring of 1692 they "began having fits, crawling into holes, making strange noises and contorting their bodies" (Guiley, p. 293). Believing, as they did, that witchcraft was a cause of mysterious ailments, the villagers felt that the next logical step was to discover and subsequently destroy the witch or witches responsible for the girls' misery. Reverend Parris and other villagers pursued possible practitioners of witchcraft with considerable zeal. Under interrogation by village elders and the Reverend John Hale, an expert in witchcraft from a neighboring town, the girls charged that they were being tormented by Tituba and two other women, Sarah Good and Sarah Osborne. Following the initial accusations, the number of people accused by the girls quickly multiplied, and soon other members of the town came forth with accusations of their own. These accusations led to the imprisonment of 100 members of the local community; twenty were eventually executed, many on the testimony of a single twelve-year-old girl, Ann Putnam. The scope of the trials soon moved beyond Salem Village to other nearby villages and to Salem Town. It became the most heated, terrifying witch-hunt in all of New England. People came forward on their own, confessing to orgies in the woods with sorcerers and devils, perhaps in the hope that confession would save them from a sudden accusation.

Title page of Cotton Mather's account of the Salem witch trials, *The Wonders of the Invisible World.*

Healers and fortunetellers of the time were regarded as the most likely people to be practicing witchcraft, but anyone who exhibited unusual behavior was suspect. In addition, women were much more likely than men to be targeted by accusers. The hysteria mounted as self-proclaimed witches confessed that they had ridden poles to meetings where as many as 500 of them plotted New England's ruin. Eventually, the frenzy surrounding the witch-hunts began to subside. Cotton Mather wrote another book, *Wonders of the Invisible World,* that defended the value of the tri-

als, but their days were numbered. The court proceedings continued on into 1693 before colonial leaders finally "recognized that a feverish fear of one's neighbor, rather than witchcraft itself, had possessed the little village of Salem" (Nash, p. 87). While accusations of witchcraft continued into the 1700s, no further executions of suspected witches took place in the colonies. In 1697 Samuel Sewall, one of the judges who presided over the execution of the twenty victims of the Salem witch-trials, publicly confessed that those who were executed had been falsely accused. For the rest of his life Sewall set aside one day a year to repent for his role in the affair.

The Play in Focus

The plot. The play takes place in the spring of 1692. The drama opens at the home of Reverend Parris, who is distraught over the mysterious ailment that seemingly afflicts his daughter Betty. As different members of the community come to see what is troubling the girl, the suggestion is made by the Putnam family that perhaps Betty is the victim of some sort of witchcraft. Upon the arrival of Reverend Hale, an expert on witchcraft from a neighboring town, an effort is made to ascertain whether or not the cause of Betty's affliction does lie in witchcraft. In the course of this process, Reverend Parris's slave Tituba confesses to having spoken with the devil and claims that the village of Salem is filled with witches.

Act Two opens at the home of John Proctor, a local farmer and a man who, while admired by many within the community, has come to regard himself as a fraud. His doubts stem from the fact that he has been unfaithful to his wife, having had an affair with his former housegirl, Abigail Williams. The relationship between John and his wife Elizabeth is visibly tense. As they begin to discuss the events taking place in the village, it is revealed that fourteen people have been accused of witchcraft and jailed. Elizabeth urges her husband to go to Salem to tell the court that earlier, at Reverend Parris's home, he was told that Betty's illness had nothing to do with witchcraft. This information came from Abigail, who is not only the Proctor's former housegirl, and John's former lover, but also Reverend Parris's niece. Abigail's role in the proceedings soon becomes more crucial; hoping to be rid of John's wife, she accuses Elizabeth Proctor of witchcraft, an accusation that leads to Elizabeth's arrest.

In Act Three, which takes place at the Salem meeting house, John Proctor arrives with his new housegirl, Mary Warren, in an attempt to free his wife from jail. Mary, who is one of the accusers, timidly admits to the presiding judges—Danforth and Hathorne—that she and the other girls were lying when they made their accusations. None of them had actually seen spirits or been afflicted by witchcraft. Mary also admits that she is in fact the owner of the doll that Elizabeth has been accused of using to torture Abigail. Mary also insists that Abigail knows who the true owner of the doll is.

Abigail is questioned about Mary's statements, but she and the other girls suddenly act as if they are threatened by evil spirits and accuse Mary of engaging in witchcraft practices. Proctor then confesses his past lechery to the court. Elizabeth Proctor is subsequently called before the court to confirm John's adultery. Not knowing that he has already confessed, she denies that he is guilty. Abigail then proceeds to accuse Mary Warren of witchcraft yet again. Mary, thoroughly frightened, rejoins the girls and accuses John Proctor of working for the devil. He is subsequently arrested as a suspected witch.

MARY WARREN V. JOHN PROCTOR
〜

The following is part of the actual historical document in which the real Mary Warren charged John Proctor with witchcraft. (As evident in the writing, in 1692 the colonists did not yet have a standard way of spelling and their symbol for the letter *s* looked similar to *f*.)

> The depofition of Mary Warrin aged 20 years.... I have feen the apparition of John Proctor ... among the wiches and he hath often tortured me by penching me and biting me and choaking me, and preffing me one my Stomack tell the blood came out of my mouth and alfo I faw him tortor Mis Poap and Marcey Iues and Jong Indian a pon the day of his examination and he hath alfo tempted me to right in his book. and to eat braid which he brought to me, which I refufeing to doe, Jno Proctor did moft grevioufly tortor me with variety of tortures, allmoft Redy to kill me.
>
> Mary Warrin owned the above written vpon her oath ... on ye 30 Day of June 1692
>
> *(Records of Salem Witchcraft, p. 69)*

Act Four, the final part of the play, centers on John Proctor on the morning he is scheduled to be hanged. Still plagued by guilt over his past infidelity, he has decided to forsake the truth and confess to witchcraft. By doing so, he reasons, he can save himself and return to his children. Speaking to his wife in the Salem jail, he claims that he cannot pretend to be an honest man, "I cannot mount the gibbet like a saint. It is a fraud. I am not that man.... Nothing's spoiled by giving them this lie that was not rotten before" (*The Crucible*, p. 136). After signing a confession, however, Proctor refuses to let it be presented to

Photograph from the original production of *The Crucible*, with Jenny Egan as Mary Warren and Arthur Kennedy as John Proctor.

the public because he cannot bear the idea of people seeing his name signed to a lie. Finally, he tears up his confession, an action that means that he will hang. His impending death, however, does not bother Proctor, for he declares that he can once again see a shred of honor within himself.

Private vengeance. One of the underlying themes of *The Crucible* concerns how personal vendettas served as motivation for many of the accusations leveled against members of the Salem community. Miller states in his opening remarks that one of the distinguishing characteristics of the Salem witch trials was that "long-held hatreds of neighbors could now be openly expressed, and vengeance taken, despite the Bible's charitable injunctions. Land-lust which had been expressed before by constant bickering over boundaries and deeds, could now be elevated to the arena of morality; one could cry witch against one's neighbor and feel perfectly justified in the bargain" (*The Crucible*, pp. 7-8). In the characters of Mr. and Mrs. Putnam we see this phenomenon perfectly illustrated, as the former, described as a "deeply embittered" and "vindictive" man, and the latter, the unfortunate and resentful mother of seven dead infants, are instrumental in creating the initial hysteria that sweeps Salem (*The Crucible*, pp. 14-15).

Perhaps no one element of the play better illustrates the theme of personal vengeance than the drama that unfolds between the Proctors and Abigail Williams. It is Abigail's desire for John Proctor and hatred for his wife that prompt her to fabricate a story in which Elizabeth Proctor acts as a witch. While Proctor is able to recognize the motivation behind Abigail's accusations, claiming that "little crazy children are jangling the keys of the kingdom, and common vengeance writes the law!," the presiding members of the court are so taken by the remarkable testimony that they are blinded to this simple reality (*The Crucible*, p. 77). Other observers realize the truth and denounce the proceedings. As Reverend Hale says, "I may shut my conscience to it no more—private vengeance is working through this testimony!" (*The Crucible*, p. 114). The accusations, trials, and executions continue, however. Salem sinks under the weight of the accumulating anger and fear. The reverend describes the town bleakly, noting that there are "orphans wandering from house to house; abandoned cattle bellow on the highroads, the stink of rotting crops hangs everywhere, and no man knows when the harlots' cry will end his life" (*The Crucible*, p. 130).

Sources. Arthur Miller relied on official records and court documents to recreate the dramatic essence of the events. As *The Crucible* took shape, he focused more on the individual personal struggles that, when combined, created the larger hysteria. In doing so, Miller was forced to invent dramatic scenes, though he used documents as the cornerstone of his play. The supposed extramarital affair between John Proctor and Abigail Williams, for example, required that Miller "read between the lines" of the official documents. He

---

CHARACTERS AND THEIR HISTORICAL MODELS

John and Elizabeth Proctor: Local tavern-keepers and vocal opponents of the hysteria that was sweeping Salem.

Reverend Samuel Parris: The minister of the town of Salem, his daughter Betty was among the first girls "afflicted."

Tituba: Reverend Parris's slave from the West Indies, she entertained local girls with stories of voodoo and primitive attempts at black magic.

Abigail Williams: The eleven-year-old niece of Reverend Parris, she was among the girls who dabbled in black magic with Tituba; one of the most vocal of the accusers.

Mary Warren: The Proctors' maid and one of the originally afflicted girls. She admitted that she was not suffering from witchcraft, only to rejoin the ranks of the girls after they accused her of being a witch.

Giles Corey: Local landowner, pressed to death for refusing his right to a trial. Earlier, Corey had testified against his own wife.

Judges Hathorne and Danforth: Presiding judges at the witch trials, along with Lt. Governor William Stoughton, who served as chief justice; Bartholomew Gedney; Jonathan Corwin; Nathaniel Saltonstall; Peter Sergeant; Wait Winthrop; Samuel Sewall; and John Richards.

Putnam Family: Wealthy landowning family; both Mrs. Ann Putnam and her daughter, also named Ann, were among the most vocal accusers. Their charges led to the arrest and execution of several innocent people. In 1706 the young Ann Putnam publicly begged the town for forgiveness.

---

came to believe that such a liaison did occur despite the lack of substantial proof to support such a claim. Miller did change a few of the known facts, however—such as raising Abigail's age from eleven to seventeen—in order to make the supposed affair seem more probable.

Miller changed a number of other details as well; the real John and Elizabeth Proctor, for instance, were not farmers but rather local tavern-keepers. Miller also condensed the identities of several presiding judges into the characters of just two judges—Hathorne and Danforth. Despite these changes, the basic facts surrounding the actual events remained the same, and the fate of each character was depicted accurately based on the historical evidence. As Miller himself has explained, "*The Crucible* is taken from history. No character is in the play who did not take a similar role in Salem, 1692" (Miller, *Theater Essays,* p. 27).

Events in History at the Time the Play Was Written

The rising fear of communism. Following World War II, the United States and the Soviet Union were established as the world's two dominant powers. America began to shift its attention from the threat of Nazi Germany and im-

FROM COTTON MATHER TO J. EDGAR HOOVER

As in Puritan New England, upstanding citizens of the 1950s stood in terror of a force they believed could wreak havoc on their lives. FBI Chief J. Edgar Hoover, as convinced of the dangers of communism as Minister Cotton Mather had been of the existence of witchcraft, expressed a popular conviction of his day: "This nation is face to face with the gravest danger ever to confront it. The menace of communism is no simple, forthright threat. It is a sinister and deadly conspiracy..." (Mather in Watts, p. 4).

perial Japan to the communist threat of the Soviet Union and other communist nations. With Europe essentially split between communists and noncommunists, the international spread of communism appeared to be a very real threat to many Americans.

Between 1948 and 1950 several events occurred that further heightened concern about communism and its possible insinuation into the United States. In 1948 a Soviet-led coup d'état took place in Czechoslovakia, placing the country under communist control. The Soviets blockaded Berlin, and Communist North Korea was established. A year later the Soviets exploded their first atomic bomb, and a communist government was established in China. In 1950 the Soviet Union and Communist China signed a thirty-year treaty of mutual assistance. The same year, North Korea attacked South Korea, triggering the beginning of the Korean War.

Alarmed at these ominous developments elsewhere in the world, many Americans in the early 1950s came to feel that the survival of the United States was at stake. Reports that America's atomic secrets had been leaked to the Soviets made the fight to stop communism at home seem just as vital as the struggle at the international level. This domestic battle against communism "expressed the fears and frustrations of average Americans" to whom "communism was a pervasive web of dangers that might appear in the guise of atheism, sexual freedoms, strange accents, civil rights, or whatever most threatened a particular group's sense of security" (Bailyn, p. 780). Americans of the 1950s were as terrified of the communist threat as New Englanders had been of the threat of witchcraft in the 1690s. Many previously unknown politicians, including Joseph McCarthy and Richard Nixon, took advantage of these fears to advance their own political agendas and careers. McCarthy in particular made a name for himself as one dedicated to ridding the United States of communists.

McCarthyism and the "Red Scare." In February 1950 Joseph McCarthy, a little-known first-term Republican senator from Wisconsin, claimed he had obtained a list of 205 communists who were working in the State Department. Although he possessed little or no actual knowledge of communist activity, McCarthy was nonetheless catapulted to national prominence as he exploited the press with thundering quotes and unfounded accusations. Virtually no one was safe from McCarthy's suspicion: he even went so far as to accuse the Secretary of Defense, George C. Marshall, of being a "conscious agent of Soviet Russia" (Mooney, p. 106). When his investigation was unable to turn up any communists in the State Department, he instead widened his search, attacking "books that his suspects had written, the reforms they had supported, and the people who had associated with them" (Bailyn, p. 781). When challenged, McCarthy was quick to attack the personal integrity of those who opposed him. Fearful of being accused themselves, many stood silent.

Other senators such as William Jenner joined McCarthy in his feverish search for communists in America. In 1952 Jenner said, "I charge that

Depiction of a witch trial.

this country is in the hands of a secret inner coterie which is directed by agents of the Soviet Union" (Bailyn, p. 781). Understandably, the average American was frightened to hear elected officials make such statements; soon much of the country was on the lookout for communists. Artists, writers, and university professors came under heavy scrutiny as suspicion grew to the point where virtually all forms of liberalism were suspected as communist. The environment in America became one where "a perverse kind of democracy was practiced: all accusations, no matter from whom, were taken equally seriously. Reputations, friendships, and careers popped like bubbles at the prick of the charge, 'Communist!'" (Bailyn, p. 779).

Finally, after several years of intimidation and unsubstantiated charges, Joseph McCarthy's fearsome influence began to wane. In one memorable encounter during the televised hearings, attorney Joseph Nye Welch—who had been retained by the secretary of the Army to refute charges made against him—finally commented to McCarthy that "until this moment, Senator, I think I never really gauged your cruelty or recklessness. . . . Have you no sense of decency sir, at long last? Have you left no sense of decency?" In 1954 the Senate voted by a 67-22 margin to condemn McCarthy, and his power faded away.

Arthur Miller, politics, and *The Crucible*'s inspiration. Awarded the Pulitzer Prize in 1949 for ***Death of a Salesman*** (also covered in *Literature and Its Times*), Arthur Miller wrote some of the definitive American plays of the twentieth century. Inspired by the social dramas of Norwegian playwright Henrik Ibsen as well as his own political beliefs, Miller masterfully articulated the voices of those struggling to retain pride and a sense of character in a world seen as being full of commercialism and false values. He grew increasingly alarmed at the repressive artistic climate in the United States during the late 1940s and early 1950s. Miller complained that the fear of being labeled a communist had created an atmosphere of dread and fostered a feeling that individual Americans could only operate under an officially approved set of moods and attitudes.

Inspired after reading Marion Starkey's *The Devil in Massachusetts,* Miller saw the parallels between the witch trials in Salem and the McCarthy hearings designed to expose communists.

> The main point of the hearings, precisely as in seventeenth-century Salem, was that the accused make public confession, damn his confederates as well as his Devil master, and guarantee his sterling new allegiance by breaking disgusting old vows—whereupon he

was let loose to rejoin the society of extremely decent people.

(Miller, *Timebends,* p. 331)

In writing *The Crucible,* Miller chose not to refer to any one specific individual, such as McCarthy. Rather, his intent was to show the American public that the issues (witchcraft and communism) that supposedly gave rise to the hysteria in colonial as well as present-day America were in reality covers for petty ambitions, political drives, and the fantasies of small minds bent on revenge. He aimed, moreover, to go beyond the parallel between seventeenth-century Puritans and twentieth-century Americans:

> I was drawn to write *The Crucible* not merely as a response to McCarthyism.... *The Crucible* is ... examining ... the question of ... what happens when it [a person's conscience] is handed over not merely to the state or the mores [standards] of the time but to one's friend or wife.

(Miller, *Theater Essays,* pp. 172-73)

Public reaction to *The Crucible.* Considering the mood of the United States at the time *The Crucible* first appeared on the stage, it is not surprising that public reception was less than enthusiastic. Its original run was hardly the success that Miller's previous original play, *Death of a Salesman,* had been. While *The Crucible* was at first unable to find an audience, the cast, believing in its importance, continued to perform without pay. Europeans soon applauded the play, and in time it would become Miller's most-produced work as performances were staged all over the world. *The Crucible*'s international appeal suggests that its theme is a universal one and not limited to America or the horrors of McCarthyism.

For More Information

Bailyn, Bernard, et al. *The Great Republic.* Lexington, Mass.: D. C. Heath, 1985.

Punch 231, pt. 1 (August 1956): 195.

Guiley, Rosemary Ellen. *Encyclopedia of Witches and Witchcraft.* New York: Facts on File, 1988.

Miller, Arthur. *The Crucible.* New York: Penguin Books, 1976.

Miller, Arthur. *The Theater Essays of Arthur Miller.* Edited by Robert A. Martin. New York: Viking Press, 1978.

Miller, Arthur. *Timebends.* New York: Grove Press, 1987.

Mooney, Booth. *The Politicians: 1945-1960.* Philadelphia: J. B. Lippincott, 1970.

Morgan, Edmund S. *The Puritan Dilemma: The Story of John Winthrop.* Boston: Little, Brown, 1958.

Nash, Gary, et al. *The American People.* New York: Harper & Row, 1990.

Records of Salem Witchcraft. Vol. 1. New York: Da Capo Press, 1864.

Watts, Robert. *Dynamic Freedoms.* Washington, D. C.: Supreme Council 33, 1975.

Cyrano de Bergerac

by
Edmond Rostand

The playwright Edmond Rostand (1868-1919) was born into a wealthy family whose members encouraged him to write. He studied law, then worked for a short time in a bank. Eventually Rostand devoted himself entirely to his writing. He grew fascinated by the life of the writer Savinien de Cyrano de Bergerac and avidly read all his books. Rostand based his most renowned play, *Cyrano de Bergerac,* on this writer's life. The real Cyrano lived in France from 1619 to 1655, and the events of the play take place during the last two decades of his life.

THE LITERARY WORK

A five-act play set in France during the years 1640 to 1655; first performed in 1897.

SYNOPSIS

An ugly man with a large nose writes poetry and love letters that are used by a handsome but unintelligent suitor to win the heart of a beautiful woman.

Events in History at the Time the Play Takes Place

Life in France during the 1600s. From 1618 to 1648, the Thirty Years War raged throughout most of Europe. Political dissatisfaction and religious tension from the Reformation fueled the conflict, which was fought largely in Germany. The war was mainly a struggle that pitted German protestant princes and foreign powers, including France, Sweden, Denmark, and England, against the Holy Roman Empire, which included the Catholic princes of Germany as well as the Hapsburg-controlled countries of Austria, Spain, Bohemia, and Italy. An aggravating factor in the war was the expansion of colonial trade at this time, which brought territorial skirmishes over control of various trade routes.

In 1638 France declared war on Spain, which at the time controlled the Spanish Netherlands (known later as Belgium), northeast of France. French Guardsmen marched to Arras, located in northwestern France, to protect the city from Spanish control. The war raged on, finishing for most European nations with the Peace of Westphalia, which signified the end of the power of the Holy Roman Empire and laid the groundwork for the modern European state system.

Meanwhile, France experienced a period of civil turmoil. In 1648 nobles and the parliament of Paris staged an unsuccessful revolution against Cardinal Mazarin, then governing on behalf of Louis XIV, who was only an eight-year-old child. Unreasonable taxation laws, tariffs, and road tolls triggered the uprising. The rebellion was, however, a dismal failure. Apparently the rising middle class and the aristocracy could not work together. Many members of the middle class were outraged that the nobles enlisted the aid of Spanish troops even though France was at war with Spain at the time. In the end, the disunity paved the way for King Louis XIV to become an absolute ruler.

Louis began personally to assume power in the 1650s. By the time Mazarin died in 1661, Louis had resolved that he would hold all important authority in his own hands. Most likely the peasants and the middle class alike welcomed the powerful rule of a king who would protect them from nobles interested in gaining power for themselves. Under the seventy-two-year rule of Louis XIV (1643-1715), French language, architecture, thought, and literature became the standard for all Europe.

THE REAL-LIFE CYRANO

1620: Born in Paris

1639-40: Serves in French corps of the guard in military campaigns

Early 1640s: Begins to write classical tragedies

1654: Injured by falling timber at his patron's house

1655: Dies in Paris

1656: *Histoire comique des États et empires de la lune* is published

1662: *Histoire comique des États et empires du soleil* is published

---

After the Thirty Years War ended for most of Europe, the conflict raged on between France and Spain. A Spanish army invaded France in 1653 to conquer Paris, but the Spaniards failed. In 1654 the persistent Spaniards laid siege to Arras, but were again unsuccessful. The real-life Cyrano de Bergerac fought at Arras, and the conflict found its way into Rostand's play.

Shortly after the failed attack on Arras, the French entered into an alliance with the English, who sent over six thousand soldiers to join in the fray. Together the French and English defeated the Spanish; the fighting finally ended in 1660 with the Treaty of the Pyrenees.

With a strong monarchy in place in France by the end of the Thirty Years War, many aristocrats were deprived of any significant political function. As their leisure time increased, the people of France developed a particular interest in artistic and intellectual matters. French literature focused on clarity, precision, and aristocratic tastes. The newly founded Académie Française attempted to systematize more rigorously the rules

of language and writing. Established by Cardinal de Richelieu in 1634, the Académie aimed to protect the purity of the French language against slovenly usage and grammatical inaccuracies.

Literary trends were strongly influenced during the 1600s by a small and elite audience and the writers who conformed to their tastes. Literature of the era, designed to appeal to an aristocratic and noble audience, rejected the uncouth manners of previous times in favor of a refined style that became the norm. Groundbreakers such as the playwright Molière and mathematicians and philosophers like René Descartes and Blaise Pascal elevated the arts and sciences.

Patrons. Writing paid very poorly in the 1600s. Consequently, authors of the era were either independently wealthy or extremely poor. Many sought patrons to support their artistic ventures. As long as their work attracted interest, writers could persuade nobles, wealthy landowners, and even the king to provide them with substantial money. Exaggerated praise for patrons became a common feature in books of this era as a result of their financial support. No degree of flattery to a patron was too high if the writer thought it would ensure continued backing.

At the same time, some artists rejected the creative constraints imposed upon them by patrons. The real-life Cyrano found patronage revolting and for many years refused to compromise his artistic principles by subjecting his work to the whims of a supporter. Economic circumstances, however, finally forced Cyrano to turn to the Duke of Arpajon for support. Their patronage arrangement was cut short by Cyrano's untimely death. Rostand relates Cyrano's feelings on the patronage issue, having the fictional Cyrano staunchly refuse a patron in the play:

> Dedicate my works to men of wealth?
> Become a sedulous ape, a fool who waits
> For some official's patronizing smile?
> No, thank you.... I prefer to sing, to dream, to play,
> To travel light, to be at liberty.
> (Rostand, *Cyrano de Bergerac*, pp. 80-1)

Salons. The salon was a social affair during which various pieces of literature were read and discussed. Flourishing in Paris during the 1600s, these lively gatherings brought together aristocrats, writers, and some of the finest minds of the day. Cultural opinions formed in salons strongly influenced broader literary tastes.

Commonly known as *ruelles,* the salons were often hosted by a French lady who received her guests while sitting on her bed. Members of the salons believed that contact with the ladies in this manner brought "a much needed refining influence on both the manners and language" of the noble gentlemen (Lough, p. 228). Ideas of moral virtue and polite society, commonplace in the literature of the day, were prominent subjects of discussion in the salons of France. Madeleine Robineau, whom Rostand used as a basis for his sophisticated character Roxane, was a high-minded intellectual who frequently attended salons and even hosted such events herself.

The Play in Focus

The plot. *Cyrano de Bergerac* is the story of an unpleasant-looking hero with a gargantuan nose who is in love with a beautiful woman. Cyrano, the hero, is an intellectual, a gifted poet, and a swashbuckling swordsman. Secretly in love with his beautiful cousin Roxane, he believes that she could never love him because of his long and hideous nose.

Meanwhile, Roxane loves the young soldier Christian de Neuvillette, an attractive but unintelligent man. Christian realizes that he cannot sustain Roxane's affection with his dull, tongue-tied manner. Aware that Cyrano is an eloquent speaker, Christian turns to him for help. Cyrano agrees to aid Christian by writing poems and love letters to Roxane, which Christian then uses as his own.

In the play's most famous scene, Cyrano passionately declares his love to Roxane under the cover of darkness, while Christian awaits nearby. In the scene's final moments, Cyrano steps aside, allowing Christian to kiss Roxane as if the flowing words had been Christian's all along. The ruse works and Roxane falls in love with Christian, not realizing that it is actually Cyrano who has spoken the words beneath her balcony that have won her heart.

The Count de Guiche, however, is also in love with Roxane. One evening, the Count arrives at Roxane's home just as Roxane and Christian are about to be hastily wed. Although Cyrano desperately wishes Roxane was his bride, he does not want anything to get in the way of her happiness. Cyrano comes to the aid of Christian and his beloved Roxane by intercepting the Count and preventing him from entering Roxane's house until the couple is wed. The Count is unable to stop the marriage, but since he is commander of the cadets, he secures revenge by sending Cyrano and Christian to battle in the siege of Arras.

During the siege, Cyrano continues to write love letters and prose on Christian's behalf. Cyrano writes to Roxane daily, crossing battle lines to ensure that his letters get through to her. Unexpectedly, Roxane appears at Arras. At this moment, Christian realizes that her passionate response to Cyrano's poetry can mean only one thing: Roxane must truly love Cyrano. Christian plans to tell Roxane the truth about the letters and the poems, but dies in battle before he can do so.

Following Christian's death, Roxane enters a convent. There she mourns her husband's death for fifteen years. Cyrano visits Roxane faithfully every week, yet he never reveals the secret of his love for her.

One day, Cyrano is hit in the head by a falling beam of wood. On the verge of death, he visits Roxane one last time. Faint and wounded, Cyrano asks her to let him read the final letter from Christian. The letter, which Roxane wears around her neck, is, of course, one that Cyrano himself wrote. "Roxane, farewell. It seems that I must die," recites Cyrano with his last ounce of strength. "My heart is heavy with unspoken love" (*Cyrano de Bergerac*, p. 201).

Although it is by now growing dark outside, Cyrano continues to recite from the letter. Roxane slowly realizes that Cyrano is no longer reading the letter, but knows its contents by heart. It finally dawns on her that it was Cyrano who wrote the letter and has loved her all these years. Roxane declares her love for Cyrano, who reluctantly admits that he loves Roxane. He confesses that he, not Christian, wrote her the letters from Arras and spoke to her from beneath her balcony. Sadly, no sooner does Cyrano confess his love than he staggers, falls, and dies.

Real-life parallels. The real-life Cyrano of the 1600s, on whom Rostand based his main character, was an expert swordsman and a soldier in addition to being a poet. A swaggering but heroic man, Cyrano lived dangerously. Like Rostand's character, he had a grotesque nose and an irascible temper. The fictional exploits portrayed in Rostand's play echo the real-life Cyrano's combative lifestyle. He fought hundreds of duels over insults to his unsightly appendage.

Various acquaintances of the real-life Cyrano are featured prominently in Rostand's play as well. During his school years, the actual Cyrano met Henri Le Bret, who later became Cyrano's friend and biographer. Le Bret appears in the play, as do several other personalities from the seventeenth century, including the popular poet Lignière; the military leader Carbon de Castel-Jaloux; the disliked actor Jacob Montfleury; two of Cyrano's admirers, Cuigy and Brissaille; the Count de Guiche, who married Cardinal Richelieu's niece; and two well-known actors, Bellerose and Jodelet.

After attending college in Beauvais, the real Cyrano moved to Paris, where his wild antics and extreme behavior led to trouble with his friends and father. The elder Bergerac, dismayed by Cyrano's behavior, withdrew the young man's allowance. Encouraged by his friend Le Bret, Cyrano joined the Guardsmen of Carbon de Castel-Jaloux in 1638. Cyrano fought in Flanders against Spain and, as in Rostand's drama, battled at the siege of Arras. The real-life Cyrano, however, was injured twice at Arras, whereas Rostand's fictionalized hero remained unscathed.

THE CYRANO DIVISION

News of the real-life Cyrano's heroism traveled far and wide. Long after his death, French soldiers left for the battlefront to repel invasion by the Germans in World War I. Some of these soldiers called themselves the "Cyrano Division" in honor of Cyrano's legendary bravery (Amoia, p. 123).

Cyrano's battle wounds prompted him to leave the Guardsmen. Upon returning to civilian life in Paris, Cyrano spent a large portion of his days drinking, gambling, and dueling. At the same time, he studied philosophy and literature and began to write. Cyrano's most famous works, *Histoire comique des États et empires de la lune* and *Histoire comique des États et empires du soleil* (*Comical History of the States and Empires of the Moon*

and *Comical History of the States and Empires of the Sun*), describe trips to the moon and sun. The hero of the fantasies discovers a lunar kingdom and an alien world on the sun.

Allusions to these fantasies appear in Rostand's *Cyrano de Bergerac*. In one scene Cyrano detains the pesky Count de Guiche so that Christian and Roxane can marry without interruption. Cyrano drops from a balcony and falls to the ground at the feet of the Count. Explaining that he has just landed from the moon, Cyrano begins an incredible tale of his adventures in space. His story closely parallels the other-worldly travels chronicled in the real Cyrano's *Histoire*.

> De Guiche: What's this? where did this thing—
> this man—fall from?
> Cyrano: The moon ... You must pardon me—
> I came by the last cloudburst; there is ether
> All over me. My eyes are full of star-dust.
> There's fur from some strange planet on my
> spurs.
> And—look!—here on my cuff, a comet's hair!
>
> . . .
>
> You never would believe the things I saw....
> I'm going to write a book about it all.
> (*Cyrano de Bergerac*, pp. 128-31)

One evening the real-life Cyrano, heading home for the night, was struck in the head by a large wooden beam that fell from a window. Unlike the play, in which Cyrano dies shortly after the accident, the real-life Cyrano suffered from his injury for a year before dying in 1655 at the age of thirty-six.

Sources. The characters of Roxane and Christian de Neuvillette are loosely based on the lives of Madeleine Robineau and Christophe de Neuvillette. Madeleine was a distant cousin of Cyrano, and Christophe served alongside Cyrano at the siege of Arras. Although it is true that Madeleine and Christophe married, and that Christophe died at Arras, it is unclear whether Cyrano and Christophe ever had the close friendship that was portrayed in the play. Nor is it clear whether Cyrano ever loved his cousin Madeleine.

There are also discrepancies between the play and reality. In Rostand's play, Cyrano faithfully visits Roxane at the convent every week after Christian's death. The real Cyrano saw Madeleine once in the convent, but was horrified by what he found. Grief-stricken, Madeleine's beauty had faded. Her face, hidden by long gray hair, was haggard due to tears and fasting. Repelled by the sight of her, the real Cyrano fled from the convent, vowing never to return (Amoia, p. 66).

While the characters in *Cyrano de Bergerac* are rooted in actual historical personalities, the spark for the play's central plot came from a story told to Rostand by a young man whom he met at a watering place in the Pyrenees Mountains. The sad young man told Rostand that he loved a woman who turned a deaf ear to his wooing.

> Rostand asked the unhappy man, "But what do you say to her?"
> The snubbed lover replied, "I tell her that I love her."
> "And then?"
> "I begin all over again."
> "And after that?"
> "That's all there is!"
>
> (Cohen, pp. 351-52)

Rostand decided to help the lovesick man, and, in the process, conceived of the idea for his play.

He tutored the young man in the art of poetry and literary allusion, much as Cyrano does for Christian in the play. Rostand's poetry lessons were successful. The young man earned the affection of the woman whom he loved, and Rostand walked away with the seeds of what would become his most successful drama.

Events in History at the Time the Play Was Written

France during the late 1800s. The late nineteenth century was a time of rapid and dramatic social change in France. Republican government, despite shaky beginnings, took root there in this era, with the establishment of a political framework that became the basis of modern France. The 1870s saw the beginnings of the modern party system and basic political divisions, cementing the Republican ideal and making it central to French political thought. The monarchist majority that existed in 1870 gave way to the moderate and libertarian Republicans, called Opportunists, who held power from 1879-1899.

The year 1894 gave rise to a great uproar in France over the trial of Alfred Dreyfus, a French army officer and a Jew. Dreyfus was accused of giving military information to the Germans, convicted of treason, and deported for life. The evidence used to convict Dreyfus was skimpy, however. By the end of the affair, Major Henry of the General Staff admitted that he had forged documents that were used to prove Dreyfus's guilt. Major Henry committed suicide, and Dreyfus received a presidential pardon—but not before the affair divided France and provoked a fierce dis-

Police photograph of Alfred Dreyfus, stripped of his military insignia, 1895.

play of anti-Semitism. For those convinced of his guilt, Alfred Dreyfus provided a focal point for anti-Jewish attitudes already prevalent in late 1800s France.

The Dreyfus Affair politicized many intellectual figures of the day. Various writers, thinkers, and artists united to expose the truth. Edmond Rostand, Émile Zola, Marcel Proust, and Anatole France, for example, stood in defense of the victimized Jewish captain when he was first accused. On January 13, 1898, Émile Zola published a letter in the newspaper *l'Aurore* alleging that Dreyfus had been framed. Response to the letter was swift and strong. Zola, who had denounced members of army's general staff, was tried and sentenced to a year's imprisonment and subjected to public vilification for openly supporting Dreyfus. Several other protests followed. Writers and artists signed petitions and gave speeches defending the Jewish officer. Edmond Rostand risked his literary reputation and professional standing by publicly siding with Dreyfus.

There are indications that the controversy had an impact on *Cyrano de Bergerac*. Although Rostand's play takes place in the 1600s, significant parallels emerge between Rostand's main character and Alfred Dreyfus. Both Cyrano and Dreyfus were military gentlemen, and both were honorable and dignified until the end of their respective stories. Cyrano maintained the secret of his love for Roxane until his dying moments, sacrificing his own happiness for the sake of the woman he loved. Dreyfus maintained his dignity and his principles with honor throughout his trial, until his eventual pardon. Not until 1898 did Major Henry admit that certain documents used to convict Dreyfus had been forged. A new trial followed and Dreyfus was again convicted, although a pardon was recommended. The honorable Dreyfus refused to accept such a pardon. His imprisonment dragged on until another trial in 1906 found him not guilty and granted him a complete pardon. In all, he had served an unjust sentence of twelve years, eight of them after the false evidence had been revealed.

Realism in the French theater. The arts flourished in France near the turn of the century. Theater was probably the most popular form of the arts in France during the late 1800s. Half a million Parisians attended the theater at least once a week. One observer stated that "the population of Paris lives in the theater, for the theater, by the theater" (Weber, p. 159). Technological advances of this era added to the excitement and flair of the live stage. In a time when most people still lived without electricity in their own homes, the brilliant lights of the theater enthralled the crowds. Staging techniques and dramatic dialogue became increasingly realistic during this period. Stage sets often included live horses, actual ships, and stories reflecting real-life conflicts.

There were other significant advances during this time as well. Scientific progress meant that advantages previously reserved only for the rich were more widely enjoyed. Public transportation, electricity, and improved water systems were among the modern amenities made more readily available; the Paris metro, or subway system, for example, began to operate around 1900. Problems such as political scandal and unsanitary food supplies continued to plague the nation, however, and rural peasants and urban workers still suffered from poverty.

Perhaps *Cyrano*'s overwhelming success was due in part to its imaginative, escapist plot, which transported careworn audiences back to an earlier and a more romantic tradition. For at least ten years prior to the production of *Cyrano,* the French public had been fed a steady stream of drama focusing on misery, degeneracy, and crime. The romance of the philosopher-swashbuckler's antics may have provided a welcome change from the realistic plays that permeated theater of this era. Furthermore, the play was written in verse, another throwback to the earlier, more romantic days. Despite the popularity of Rostand's fanciful play, French theater at the end of the nineteenth century remained firmly entrenched in realism. As one historian noted, *Cyrano* was a "champion without heirs" (Weber, p. 161).

How the play was received. The first production of *Cyrano de Bergerac* took place at the Porte Saint-Martin theater on December 28, 1897. Prior to opening night, there was great uncertainty about how the play would be received. The directors kept production costs to a minimum, for they expected the play to run only a few short weeks. The author was thus forced to pay for many expenses out of his own pocket. The stage sets were so inadequately designed that Rostand nearly attacked the stage designer. Only minutes before the first curtain went up, Rostand threw himself into the arms of the play's lead actor, crying, "I beg your forgiveness, my friend. Pardon me for having involved you in a disastrous adventure" (Rostand in Cohen, p. 35).

Much to everyone's surprise, the play met with sensational approval. At opening night, the audience applauded in the theater for nearly two hours after the final curtain. As described in the introduction to the play, the great French actor Constant Coquelin, who performed the lead role, described the crowd as "a house in delirium. Amid all this confusion Rostand alone seemed unconscious of his victory" (Coquelin in Rostand, p. xiii).

For More Information

Amoia, Alba. *Edmond Rostand.* Boston: Twayne, 1978.

Cohen, Helen Louise. *Milestones of the Drama.* New York: Harcourt, Brace, 1940.

Kleeblatt, Norman L., ed. *The Dreyfus Affair: Art, Truth, and Justice.* Los Angeles: University of California Press, 1987.

Lough, John. *An Introduction to Seventeenth-Century France.* London: Longmans, 1960.

Palmer, R. R., and Joel Colton. *A History of the Modern World.* New York: Alfred A. Knopf, 1969.

Rostand, Edmond. *Cyrano de Bergerac.* Translated by Louis Untermeyer. New York: Heritage, 1954.

Weber, Eugen. *France, Fin de Siecle.* Cambridge, Mass.: Harvard University Press, 1986.

Wright, Gordon. *France in Modern Times,* 4th ed. New York: W. W. Norton, 1987.

The Declaration of Independence

by
Thomas Jefferson

Thomas Jefferson's life was closely intertwined with the birth of the United States as a nation. When he wrote the Declaration of Independence, he was not just writing an eloquent document; he was laying the groundwork for a new political era in the former colonies and around the world. At age thirty-three Jefferson had been given the job of defending the most radical political act of his time—the separation of the American colonies from Great Britain.

THE LITERARY WORK

A document written in Great Britain's American colonies in June 1776; adopted by the Second Continental Congress on July 4, 1776.

SYNOPSIS

Thomas Jefferson announces and explains the decision of American colonists to separate from Great Britain.

Events in History at the Time of the Document

Rising frustration with British rule. The colonists decided to declare their independence after more than a decade of hostility against their mother country. Most of this tension dated back to the early 1760s, after King George III had come to power in England. The French and Indian War—a conflict fought on North American soil to see which European power would reign supreme there—had ended in 1763 with a British victory, but England had paid dearly for its triumph. British money, soldiers, and supplies had been sacrificed in the war, and Britain decided to recover its financial losses by imposing taxes on various goods purchased in the colonies. The first of these taxes, the Stamp Act, was instituted in 1765. This legislation was followed by the Townshend Acts (1767) and the Tea Act (1773).

These taxes were not welcome in America. The colonists were willing to tolerate Parliament regulating their trade, but prior to this new foray into the colonies' affairs, Britain had stood on the sidelines in most other areas. For decades the colonists had made decisions about taxes and other issues in their own local assemblies.

Disgruntled colonists protested Parliament's actions, claiming that as English citizens they should be protected from "taxation without representation." In other words, since the colonies did not have voting representatives in the British government, Parliament had no right to tax the colonists. While the British eventually repealed some of these acts, they never questioned their right to impose taxes on the colonists. England sent soldiers to America to help ensure that the tax laws were enforced.

STEPS TO WAR

Name of Act	What It Did	Responses/Outcome
Stamp Act (1765)	Taxed newspapers, legal documents, playing cards; first internal tax from England (previous taxes applied only to English products sold to the colonies)	Massachusetts colonists boycott British goods, harass stamp officers; colonists form inter-colonial Stamp Act Congress; act repealed by Parliament (1766)
Townshend Acts (1767)	Taxed glass, paper, paint and tea	Taxed goods are boycotted by most colonies; British troops are sent to enforce taxes; Boston Massacre occurs (1770); repealed in 1771, although Parliament retains tea tax
Tea Act (1773)	Cut price of British tea so American tea merchants would be forced out of business	Colonists send back British tea ships; Boston Tea Party occurs (1773)
Intolerable Acts (1774)	Closed port of Boston and declared local Massachusetts assembly politically powerless; intended as a punishment for Boston Tea Party	Other colonies sympathize with Boston's plight; First Continental Congress called in Philadelphia (1774)

The arrival of British soldiers aggravated tensions in the colonies. United in their anger against the British government, the colonists sent a list of grievances to the king and formed colonial militias, although they still hoped that Britain's government would reconsider its position and grant the colonists the right they felt they deserved as English citizens: freedom from taxation without representation.

Rather than attempt to appease the colonists, however, Britain sent additional troops and usurped other previously established rights. Soon after colonial assemblies and constitutions were abolished, violence erupted between the British soldiers and the colonial militias in Massachusetts. As fighting spread throughout the northern colonies, a Second Continental Congress was called to form an American army and to plan for the future of the colonies. Soon afterward, Thomas Paine's pamphlet *Common Sense* (also covered in *Literature and Its Times*) was distributed through the colonies; it convinced many of the colonists that separation from Great Britain was the only way to ensure that their rights would be protected. By June of 1776, delegates from the colonies had agreed to draft a declaration of independence from Britain. A congressional committee appointed Thomas Jefferson as its author.

The Enlightenment and the "moral sense" of Americans. In 1755 John Adams, a close friend of Jefferson in his early years, wrote that "all that part of creation which lies within our observation, is liable to change" (Aptheker, p. 87). While the words might not seem especially noteworthy today, they describe a revolutionary feeling at the time. European thinkers ranging from the Polish astronomer Nicolaus Copernicus (1473-1543) to the English scientist and philosopher Isaac Newton (1642-1727) had spent the sixteenth and seventeenth centuries contemplating the world. The conclusions of these "Enlightenment" thinkers deeply affected society.

According to Enlightenment philosophy, humans have the capacity to understand the causes of everything in the world. It contended that ideas and institutions should not be accepted

Portrait of King George III by Sir W. Beechey, engraved by B. Smith.

merely because they have always existed; they should be scrutinized and changed if a more reasonable alternative can be found. In other words, since people can depend on their own minds to understand the workings of nature and society, they should use their reasoning capacity to change the world for the better. To colonists raised on Enlightenment thought, America was the perfect place to test such beliefs. Thomas Jefferson and other colonial intellectuals used Enlightenment ideas as the backbone of their political philosophy.

COLONIAL AGENTS

Although American colonists claimed that they were not represented in Parliament, a form of colonial representation was practiced in the decades preceding the Revolution. Agents, appointed by colonial assemblies or governors, were regularly positioned in London to represent colonial interests. While these agents were not voting members of Parliament, they were able to influence government policy by acting as lobbyists; they secured acceptance of laws passed by colonial assemblies, dealt with land disputes, and often influenced trade regulations.

Even colonists who did not read Newton or Copernicus shared the idea of a moral obligation to make the world a better place. The works of Scottish philosopher Francis Hutcheson, who believed that humans have a "moral sense"—an inborn ability to tell right from wrong—convinced Protestant ministers as well as scientific-minded intellectuals in America that they must act on this moral sense. Ministers added the idea that social change was part of God's plan and told their congregations that resisting the English government was not just a right but a religious obligation. One such minister, Reverend Samuel West, made this view quite clear. Speaking to the Massachusetts House of Representatives, he explained that when British officials disobey God's law, "it is so far from being a crime to resist them, that in many cases it may be highly criminal in the sight of Heaven to refuse resisting and opposing them to the utmost of our power" (Meyer, pp. 105-06).

Strict Enlightenment thinkers might have protested that the existence of God cannot be proven. Most "enlightened" American thinkers, however, publicly accepted the religious justifi-

cations for opposition to Britain. In the Declaration, Jefferson speaks to both the nonreligious Enlightenment view of social responsibility and the Protestant one, referring to "the laws of nature and of nature's God" (Koch, p. 22). This clever mixture of two otherwise contrary philosophies demonstrates the unifying force of the American drive for independence. By July 1776, many Americans were convinced that the Revolution was not just a good idea but a moral course of behavior.

Growing unity among the colonies. Although American colonists eventually came together to fight the British, their history was a divided one. Founded by separate groups for various reasons, the colonies differed in values, economies, religious practices, and lifestyles. Most importantly, each colony had its own government that made decisions independent of the other colonies' interests.

Each colony operated under a system of government that featured an assembly and a governor, so by the time the Declaration of Independence was written, Americans were accustomed to some form of self-rule. Political power in these colonial governments was not uniformly distributed, however. Some colonies had been owned by businesses whose stockholders appointed the governors. Other colonies were ruled by wealthy families, either directly or through a hand-picked governor. Finally, a few American colonies had long histories as royal colonies, which meant that they were possessions of the British government. Under this arrangement, the British government selected their governor and exercised other forms of control. Even as royal colonies, however, they had elected assemblies of their own and maintained local control over taxes and lawmaking.

By 1776 nine of the thirteen colonies that would become the United States had changed to royal colonies. This shift in ownership during the 1760s and 1770s further encouraged the British government to assert its power over the colonies. In addition to its efforts to levy new taxes, England increasingly sought to enforce old policies that had largely been ignored in the past. The British, who for so long had allowed the colonies to govern themselves in many respects, decided that it was time to take over.

This new policy on the part of the British served to bring the colonies closer together, for it gave birth to a common yearning for independence. By 1776 most colonists could see the value of a famous statement uttered by Patrick

Henry at the First Continental Congress of 1774. Henry had proclaimed that he was not a Virginian, but an American.

The American Dream in colonial times. From its beginnings, colonial America was viewed in Europe as a land of opportunity. The colonies, known for fertile farmland, dense forests, and navigable waterways, seemed to have unlimited natural resources. These fresh areas of settlement held the promise of new possibilities and freedoms.

By the mid-eighteenth century, however, the colonies had aged in certain ways. In a number of respects the colonies came to resemble the mother country that lay across the Atlantic Ocean. Similar trends in social stratification were certainly evident, for the colonies settled into societies that were marked by the same divisions between aristocrats, middle class, and lower classes that had long been in place in England. Although generally regarded as champions of human equality, the leaders associated with Revolutionary America—George Washington, John Adams, and even Thomas Jefferson—were not common Americans but aristocrats. Yet the colonies they "represented" consisted mostly of middle-class laborers and, in the case of Washington and Jefferson, many slaves.

Class divisions—at least among white Americans—had weakened by the time of the Declaration of Independence. But most colonial charters of the time still included a provision that one must be a male property-owner in order to hold office or vote. This provision left colonial political power in the hands of the white male aristocracy and some male members of the middle class, who accounted for far less than half of the population. Most of the colonial representatives who approved the Declaration on July 4, 1776, then, represented only a certain percentage of the total number of people that populated their colonies.

Still, most of the colonists supported independence from Britain. They thought that war with Britain would open the door to greater prosperity and social mobility. Others argued that, since the clash with Britain was sparked by a cry for equal treatment with all other English citizens, the leading Americans would consider the equal treatment of their own citizens when forming a new government. Indeed, the language of the Declaration and later documents—which spoke of "equal station" and "inalienable rights"—ensured that Americans would confront the issues of social and political equality in the future.

The Document in Focus

The contents. The Declaration of Independence is divided into three sections. The first section describes the political beliefs underlying the colonies' decision to declare their independence. The second section lists the colonists' complaints about their treatment by the king. The third and final section of the document formally declares American independence.

Jefferson begins by briefly describing the purpose of the document—to explain to the world why the colonists chose to separate from Great Britain. He then lays out the political principles supporting the colonists' decision. This section explains that certain "self-evident truths" apply to the world, among them the fact that "all men are created equal" and that they are all granted certain "inalienable rights": "life, liberty, and the pursuit of happiness" (Jefferson in Koch, p. 22). In order to protect these rights, Jefferson explains, people form governments. The power of the government thus comes from the people, who can and should seize this power if a government begins to abuse it.

The second section lists twenty-seven grievances against the British government. Among this long list of abuses are complaints that the king has interfered unjustly with colonial legislatures, overburdened the colonies with his own officials, and deprived colonists of their rights in criminal cases (Koch, p. 22). To counter the notion that the colonists' fight is a rebellion, Jefferson goes on to proclaim that it is the king who has waged war on the colonists. He concludes by explaining that the Americans' decision to seek independence comes after numerous attempts to reclaim their rights through legal and peaceful means. These unsuccessful attempts left the colonists with no choice but to separate from England. Jefferson is careful here not to describe his document as a declaration of war. Instead, he closes the second section with the statement that the colonists will "hold [our British brethren] as we hold the rest of mankind, enemies in war, in peace friends" (Jefferson in Koch, p. 27).

The final section of Jefferson's document contains the actual declaration. It proclaims that "these united colonies are, and of right ought to be free and independent states" (Jefferson in Koch, p. 27). All allegiance to the king and political ties to Britain are "dissolved," thereby granting the states full political power. Recognizing that a document alone will not achieve independence, Jefferson closes with a mutual pledge by the colonies to support the Declaration.

Writing and revising. Jefferson wrote the Declaration of Independence in a lodging house in Philadelphia on a portable desk he had designed. Since he was far from his library in Virginia, he did not refer to books or pamphlets as he wrote. Instead, he relied on his memory of the political texts he had studied and other compositions he had recently written or read. Among these were a draft he wrote of a constitution for Virginia, which contained a list of charges against George III, and Virginia's Declaration of Rights, a document written by George Mason that Jefferson had earlier read. In fact, scholars note that the first section of Jefferson's Declaration resembles Mason's document. But while these works might have given Jefferson a head start on his phrasing of the Declaration, the ideas that he included were taken largely from political discussions of the time.

When Jefferson completed his draft of the Declaration, a task that probably took about two weeks, he gave copies to Benjamin Franklin and John Adams, two other members of the congressional committee in charge of drafting the document. They made some minor changes and then presented the draft to the full body of Congress, which eliminated a few passages and altered the final paragraphs. The main passages cut by Congress were negative references to the English people (as opposed to the government) and a lengthy paragraph in which Jefferson blamed King George for the colonial slave trade.

Jefferson was not happy about the editing of his manuscript but realized that it was necessary in order to win every colony's support for the Declaration. The passage about the slave trade, he explained, was removed for the benefit of South Carolina and Georgia, who planned to continue importing slaves from Africa. While other reports of the debate reinforce this claim, some historians believe that congressional delegates actually opposed the passage because they were aware of the hypocrisy—and consequent weakness—of Jefferson's position. Although he criticizes the king for allowing newly captured slaves to be brought from Africa to America, he does not acknowledge the cruelty of slavery itself, an institution that he and his fellow slaveholders were directly responsible for perpetuating.

Jefferson, slavery, and the Virginia gentry. Thomas Jefferson, a Virginia planter and slaveholder, had been born into a slave-holding society. Although he spoke out often against the cruelty of slavery, it was an unshakable part of his

A rough draft of the Declaration of Independence, written in June, 1776.

life and his livelihood. By 1776 black slaves made up 20 percent of the colonial population and 40 percent of the population in the South. Jefferson had his misgivings about slavery; he called the practice a "hideous evil" (Sheldon, p. 129). Nevertheless, he allowed it to continue on his land during his lifetime.

Jefferson's thoughts on blacks were similarly paradoxical. He respected the morality and loyalty of those slaves he knew, yet he thought the reasoning ability of black slaves was "much inferior" to that of whites, although he admitted that this belief was based on limited observation (Jefferson in Koch, pp. 256-57). Because black slaves had been so profoundly mistreated by whites in America, Jefferson doubted that the two races could ever live together in harmony. His personal wish was that slaves be freed and either returned to Africa or sent to the Caribbean, where they could start a colony of their own.

On July 2 the final decision was made to sever ties with England. Revisions to the Declaration of Independence were hotly debated for the next two days. Tensions in Congress ran high, for the delegates knew that under English law the Declaration was a betrayal of the king that was pun-

The Declaration of Independence Committee (left to right): Jefferson, Roger Sherman, Benjamin Franklin, Robert R. Livingston, and John Adams.

ishable by hanging. The official version of Jefferson's edited document finally emerged from the debate and was approved by the delegates on the night of July 4, 1776. Copies of it were printed and sent to each colony to be read in public squares to excited colonists and colonial troops.

What it means to be "created equal." When Jefferson asserted that "all men are created equal," he started a debate that still continues today. The intended meaning of those words has been the subject of essays, books, poetry, and public argument. President Abraham Lincoln later quoted this famous phrase in his Gettysburg Address, indirectly using it to support his call for the abolition of slavery. Many have followed Lincoln's lead and interpreted the statement to mean that all people have the same worth, regardless of color or other differences.

This is probably not what Jefferson meant in 1776, however, since only six years before he had claimed that blacks were inferior to whites in "beauty," in "reason," and in "imagination" (Jefferson in Koch, pp. 256-57). Others claim that Jefferson was referring simply to equality of rights, but if this is the case, then why would he list "equality" and "rights" as separate "self-evident truths"?

Most political philosophers agree that Jefferson's "equality" refers in part to basic human

needs (food, shelter, love) and abilities (speaking, reasoning). More important than these unifying characteristics, however, is the notion he shares with Frances Hutcheson that all people are "social animals" who can choose between right and wrong.

EQUALITY IN THE SOUTH

Some southern states, concerned that Jefferson's famous phrase might be used to question the morality of slavery, changed its wording in their state constitutions. Alabama, Arkansas, Florida, Kentucky, Mississippi, and Texas all eventually adopted the phrase "All freemen, when they form a social compact, are equal" (Becker, p. 240).

Jefferson stressed the importance of social interdependence in many of his letters and essays. He would probably have argued that a middle-class farmer may not be the best person to lead his state, but that he is as fit to choose a leader as an aristocratic intellectual. In Jefferson's view, people may be unequal in talents and abilities, but they share a devotion to fair government and common happiness.

Sources. Most historians are quick to link the Declaration of Independence with the English philosopher John Locke. An important Enlightenment thinker, Locke described people as naturally independent of one another. In order to protect their individual rights to "life, liberty, and estate," however, they agreed to work together to form a government (Sheldon, p. 46). These rights—which Locke considered "natural rights," or rights all people are entitled to—are the focus of the first section of the Declaration, and many of Jefferson's phrases, such as "inalienable rights" and "consent of the governed," are copied almost exactly from Locke's works.

Although Locke's influence is clear in the wording of the Declaration, Jefferson was also strongly influenced by the political ideas of Aristotle, whose works he had studied since childhood. This ancient Greek philosopher held that, far from being independent, people were naturally social and needed to participate in politics, which brought out their highest qualities. Aristotle focused not on rights but on virtue. He thought the purpose of politics was to create a good society, whereas Locke believed that the government's involvement in society should be kept to a bare minimum. When Jefferson refers to the right to "the pursuit of happiness" instead of Locke's right to hold property (or "estate"), he may be drawing from this alternate view. Historians have debated the reasons for this choice of words, but most believe that, for Jefferson, "happiness" is the product of a social practice, not a private one. Similarly, when he speaks of the "public good" in the Declaration's list of grievances, it becomes clear that Locke was not the only source that inspired Jefferson.

In Jefferson's view, the philosophies of Locke and Aristotle and others supported the colonies' quest for independence. Criticisms that the Declaration contained no new ideas, contended Jefferson, simply missed the point. As Jefferson himself explained in later correspondence, the Declaration's purpose was:

> not to find out new principles, or new arguments, never before thought of, not merely to say things which had never been said before; but to place before mankind the common sense of the subject, in terms so plain and firm as to command their assent.... It was intended to be an expression of the American mind.
> (Jefferson in Koch, p. 719)

Although the ideas stated in the Declaration echoed long-held views, the act of putting them into practice was revolutionary. Jefferson's Declaration of Independence served as the blueprint for a new nation, and thus had a significant influence on politics around the world. The Declaration was well respected in France, where in 1789 the Declaration of the Rights of Man was written into law. In the early nineteenth century, the Spanish and Portuguese colonies of South America based their wars for independence on many of the Declaration's tenets.

In these countries, and in democracies around the world, the document's most enduring concept has been that the people control government, not the other way around. Although many Americans were not granted this control in Jefferson's era, the Declaration sparked a long struggle for truly equal distribution of power among all people.

For More Information

Aptheker, Herbert. *The Colonial Era: A History of the American People.* New York: International, 1959.

Becker, Carl. *The Declaration of Independence: A Study in the History of Political Ideas.* New York: Harcourt, Brace, 1922.

Koch, Adrienne, and William Peden, eds. *The Life and Selected Writings of Thomas Jefferson.* New York: Random House, 1944.

Meyer, Donald H. *The Democratic Enlightenment.* New York: G. P. Putnam's Sons, 1976.

Randolph, Sarah N. *The Domestic Life of Thomas Jefferson.* Cambridge, England: Cambridge University Press, 1871.

Sheldon, Garrett Ward. *The Political Philosophy of Thomas Jefferson.* Baltimore: Johns Hopkins University Press, 1991.

"The Devil and Tom Walker"

by
Washington Irving

W ashington Irving was born to a wealthy family in New York on April 3, 1783. He spent almost twenty years of his life in Europe. Influenced by a movement that romanticized the preindustrial past, Irving won an international reputation as a distinctively American writer. Both Europeans and Americans considered him to be the nation's first successful professional man of letters. "The Devil and Tom Walker" first appeared in the book *Tales of a Traveler*, which he wrote in Paris in 1824.

THE LITERARY WORK

A short story set around the colonial Boston area in 1727; published in 1824.

SYNOPSIS

A man sells his soul to the Devil for pirate treasure. He becomes a moneylender in Boston and, despite his efforts to avoid his bargain with the Devil, is eventually snatched away.

Events in History at the Time the Short Story Takes Place

Puritanism. New England had been settled by Puritans in the early seventeenth century. The Puritans were a group of Protestants belonging to the Church of England who believed that the Reformation (in which the Protestant churches separated from the Roman Catholic Church) had not fully eliminated Catholic influence. Persecuted in England, Puritans emigrated to America to establish their own communal villages and worship in freedom. They were extremely religious and austere in everyday living. Puritans generally believed in the supremacy of God and the lowliness of man and that, as God's chosen people, it was their duty to govern national affairs according to his will. As a result, many aspects of everyday life in colonial New England were directly influenced by Puritan beliefs.

The fundamental doctrines of the Puritan religion were based on strict interpretations of the Bible. According to their faith, the Bible told what was right and wrong; all information necessary for a pious life could be found in the Bible. Puritans constantly strove to live a perfectly devout life. They believed that such perfection was difficult to attain, however, because of man's innately sinful nature. Puritans sought to avoid the pitfalls of sin in their lives through an emphasis on constant self-examination. They tried to eliminate such defects as pride, hardness of heart, and lust while emphasizing productivity and good works. As one author writes, the Puritans believed that "all ... acts of charity are to be undertaken not as substitutes for piety but as means by which a Christian can use the grace God has given him" (Erikson, p. 132). In some ways, Puritans were very humble because they thought of themselves as base creatures who were unworthy of God. At the same time, they saw themselves as chosen by God to convert and/or punish others who were sinful and haughty.

Because of their extreme convictions, Puritans were intolerant of other faiths and excluded from their community individuals who promoted different beliefs. The Puritans believed in one truth and thought that other religions were wrong. Tolerating other religions meant tolerating error, which was unacceptable in Puritan thinking. This philosophy is evident in a scene from Irving's short story wherein Tom Walker talks of persecuting Quakers, an action that he believes will enhance his own spiritual development.

Puritans believed strongly in the Devil (also called Satan or Old Scratch) and witches, who were his principal helpers. Puritans condemned certain people as witches and were convinced that American Indians worshipped the Devil. Irving touches on this belief as well in "The Devil and Tom Walker," although he adds a twist to the concept. Satan appears to Tom Walker in an Indian burial ground and reveals that he, along with the Puritans, presided over witch burnings. The author thus associates the Devil not with the so-called witches, but with the Puritans who condemned them.

Puritans and change. By the early 1700s, the religious zeal that characterized New England during the previous century had lost its vigor. The ideas of the Enlightenment, including scientific and rationalistic thought, had become more prevalent, weakening the religious convictions of many. The rapid economic and territorial expansion of the colonies also had an impact, for many Puritans became more interested in making money than in living a strictly religious life.

The northern colonies were gripped by a materialistic fever that was part of the developing capitalist economy in the early eighteenth century. Puritans, who despised idleness, often supported this view by stating that men had an obligation to exert themselves to avoid poverty. As people pursued wealth, however, religious convictions often became secondary concerns. While regard for the afterlife had previously dominated everyday thought, earthly comforts now took precedence.

Business and society. Merchants and manufacturers dominated the ranks of the northern rich at this time, while the emerging wealthy class in the South consisted of plantation and slave owners. Sharp social and economic divisions emerged between the poor farmers and settlers and the new business class. Those who did not fare well financially fell by the wayside. There was no safety net, such as welfare or unemployment payments, for those who could not take care of themselves.

In New England, farming conditions were less than ideal. The land available for agriculture was not very fertile, and the conventional unscientific farming methods of the time rapidly wore out the nutrients in the soil, making the farms even less productive. In addition, by the end of 1713 the population of the colonies had surged. Many people emigrated from such countries as Germany, Scotland, and Ireland, and this influx forced settlers away from the eastern coast and into the interior of the country. Others simply abandoned their poor farms and moved inward as the soil wore out. Irving's description of Tom's house, located outside of Boston, reveals the poverty of the rural countryside:

> A miserable horse, whose ribs were as articulate as the bars of a gridiron, stalked about a field, where a thin carpet of moss, scarcely covering the ragged beds of puddingstone, tantalized and balked his hunger; and sometimes he would lean his head over the fence, look piteously at the passer-by, and seem to petition deliverance from this land of famine.
> (Irving, "The Devil and Tom Walker," p. 251)

Meanwhile, business became increasingly concentrated in large commercial centers like Boston. Merchants and manufacturers resided in these growing towns, working to accumulate wealth as rapidly as possible. While many had a keen sense of business, others were often unethical in their dogged pursuit of riches. Piracy, smuggling, and privateering were all common practices. Smuggling, in particular, became a common means of circumventing restrictive British trade laws as merchants traded with the southern colonies, the West Indies, and Europe. One example of this process involved molasses. The North depended heavily on this food product from the Indies (the Caribbean islands—then colonies of various European powers). As commerce grew, demand for molasses had exceeded the supply available from the English islands in the Caribbean, and so the American colonies increased trade with the French islands in the West Indies. In response, the British Indies secured passage of the Molasses Act through the British Parliament in 1733. This legislation prohibited the American colonies from buying molasses from anywhere but the British Indies. The colonists ignored the prohibition and illegally smuggled goods from the French West Indies.

The increasing number of settlers pushing onto the frontier made land speculation a prominent means of earning a living. The speculators were often unethical and invested only to make a quick profit. Some unscrupulous speculators sold lands they did not own, while others resold "unsettled" towns that were already occupied. As Irving noted,

> ... there had been a rage for speculating; the people had run mad with schemes for new settlements; for building cities in the wilderness; land-jobbers went about with maps of grants, and townships, and Eldorados [legendary cities of gold], lying nobody knew where, but which everybody was ready to purchase. In a word, the great speculating fever which breaks out every now and then in the country, had raged to an alarming degree, and everybody was dreaming of making sudden fortunes from nothing.
>
> ("The Devil and Tom Walker," p. 258)

Slavery. After molasses was bought or smuggled from the Indies, northerners manufactured it into rum and sold the rum to ships bound for Africa. Northern slave traders used the rum to purchase slaves, who were subsequently sold to buyers in the southern colonies and the Indies. Slaves first entered North America in the early 1600s, along with indentured servants. New England used indentured servants more than slaves, but it was desperate for any kind of free labor; in 1710 Massachusetts passed an act that offered a bounty to anyone bringing male servants from ages eight to twenty-five into the colony. New England used both blacks and Indians as slaves, although Indian slaves outnumbered black slaves in 1706. As the sugar-producing islands demanded more labor, the African slave trade increased.

New Englanders, however, did not favor the slave trade. By 1712 the region had passed laws forbidding trade in Indian slaves, and heavy duties had been passed to prevent additional black slaves from entering Massachusetts. Northern slave traders often had to operate in secret and were regarded with disdain. Their lowly status is reflected in Irving's short story when Tom Walker stubbornly refuses to become involved in the trade.

Slaves were originally treated similarly to indentured servants, with the notable exception that they were bound for life. In the late 1600s, for example, slaves accused of capital offenses were entitled to a jury and police protection. As time passed, however, the severity of slave codes

increased. By 1723 the penalty for a slave found guilty of a capital offense was death. The early 1700s also sealed the fate of slave families, for children of slaves automatically became slaves themselves. Black skin color was increasingly associated with slavery, and by 1717 Maryland had instituted laws that stipulated that blacks could not testify against whites and that slaves could not own property.

Money. During the colonial period, money was difficult to obtain. The British did not allow the

---

IRVING AND THE SLAVE TRADE

By 1808 the African slave trade had closed. The states, however, engaged in active trading among themselves, and the country had grown divided over the issue. The North, which had an economy based on business and manufacturing, was not dependent on slave labor and did not support the institution. Meanwhile, the South, which was agricultural, depended heavily on slave labor. Washington Irving believed slavery was an evil practice. But he was neither an activist nor an abolitionist, and he found it difficult to believe that his country would divide over the issue. As author Johanna Johnston explains, Irving never possessed "a missionary nature, attempting to change the world and mold the future. His fancies had always played over the past, and what he brought to life was from the past and not the future" (Johnston, p. 358).

---

colonies to mint their own coins and did not import money into the colonies. Although paper money had been introduced, it was extremely unstable and caused rampant inflation that hurt large portions of the population, whose wages did not keep pace with the cost of living. Irving commented that "It was a time of paper credit. The country had been deluged with government bills" ("The Devil and Tom Walker," p. 258). By the mid-1700s an economic collapse seemed likely. Debtors demanded that more paper currency be printed and circulated in hopes of curing the situation. As a response, the infamous "Land Bank" issued paper money that had no backing or definite value. Some people turned to usurers, also known as moneylenders, to finance risky ventures or to pay mounting debts. Usurers lent money to borrowers, who had to pay a fee or pay the amount back with interest. Often, the interest was very high. For someone like Tom Walker, who had gold and silver, moneylending

Walker, who had gold and silver, moneylending was a very profitable business. Tom's customers consisted of "the needy and adventurous; the gambling speculator; the day-dreaming land-jobber; the thriftless tradesman; the merchant with cracked credit; in short, everyone driven to raise money by desperate means and desperate sacrifices, hurried to Tom Walker" ("The Devil and Tom Walker," p. 258).

The Short Story in Focus

The plot. "The Devil and Tom Walker" details the life of a prying, miserly man named Tom Walker. Tom's wife, an equally miserly and bad-tempered person, constantly fights with him about money and possessions. One day, while walking through the swamp, Tom meets the Devil. Old Scratch, red-eyed and covered with soot, is busily chopping down trees inscribed with the names of people who owe him their soul. Unafraid, Tom converses with the Devil, who reveals his knowledge of Captain Kidd's buried treasure. He offers Tom the treasure in exchange for his soul. Undecided, Tom returns home to consider the bargain. Despite their animosity toward each other, he tells his wife about the incident, and she becomes excited about the prospect of increasing their wealth. She insists that Tom accept the bargain, but Tom refuses in order to spite her.

Furious, his wife decides to seek out Satan and obtain the treasure for herself. She leaves the house with an apron full of silver and disappears. Tom, who is worried about the silver, goes to the swamp to look for her. All he finds is the apron, which contains not the silver but her liver and heart. Again the Devil appears and offers Tom the pirate treasure in exchange for his soul. This time, despite the signs of his wife's doom, Tom agrees. The Devil asks Tom to use the money to outfit a slave ship, but Tom refuses. While Tom "was bad enough in all conscience . . . the devil himself could not tempt him to turn slave-trader" ("The Devil and Tom Walker," p. 257).

However, Tom consents to become a money-lender, a business agreeable to the Devil. Tom takes the treasure and moves to Boston, where he opens a counting house and quickly becomes very rich. As he grows older, however, he regrets his sinful pact with the Devil. He attends church zealously and carries a Bible at all times, hoping to cheat the Devil out of the bargain and keep his soul. One day Tom mercilessly forecloses on a mortgage. In the process, he unwittingly sum-

mons the Devil by oath, whereupon the Devil appears on horseback and whisks Tom off forever. When officials enter the counting house to search Tom's coffers, they discover that his bonds and mortgages have turned to cinders and his gold and silver to chips and shavings.

The Walkers and greed. One of the main themes in "The Devil and Tom Walker" is greed. While Irving's characters are exaggerated for comic effect, he exposes elements of miserliness, greed, hypocrisy, and spiritual decay that existed in early eighteenth-century New England. Tom Walker and his wife, trapped in a poverty-stricken, loveless marriage, fight constantly and are despicable, greedy people. Irving writes:

> . . .they were so miserly that they even conspired to cheat each other. Whatever the woman could lay hands on, she hid away; a hen could not cackle but she was on the alert to secure the new-laid egg. Her husband was continually prying about to detect her secret hoards, and many and fierce were the conflicts that took place about what ought to have been common property.
>
> ("The Devil and Tom Walker," p. 251)

Tom and his wife are both financially desperate and spiritually barren, unable to love or care for anyone. Bound by their greed, neither one is afraid of the Devil. Tom is unconcerned when he first encounters Old Scratch and refuses the Devil's monetary offer simply to contradict his wife. She, who is as materialistic and bad-natured as Tom, journeys to the swamp in hopes of keeping the treasure for herself. She never returns. Tom searches the swamp for her only because he wants to find the silver that she has taken. When he learns of her fate, he shows no signs of sorrow for the loss of his wife. Instead, he is thankful that the Devil took her away. He even feels slightly sorry for the Devil, who he figures must have had a difficult fight.

> Tom consoled himself for the loss of his property, with the loss of his wife, for he was a man of fortitude. He even felt something like gratitude towards the black woodsman, who, he considered, had done him a kindness.
>
> ("The Devil and Tom Walker," p. 257)

With his wife gone, Tom agrees to the bargain. Throughout the story, he remains oblivious to signs of his impending doom. He disregards the fact that the Devil is chopping down trees that represent sinners, and the evidence of his wife's death does not affect his decision. Perhaps

Washington Irving saw a similar blindness in society around him and used Tom's foolhardy behavior to drive the point home to his readers.

Toward the end of Tom's life, the character regrets his pact, yet has not learned the lesson of treating others well. Tom goes to church merely to save himself. In his final moments, he refuses to "do good" to a poor customer. Greed instead drives Tom to demand his money, whereupon the Devil arrives for his promised sinner and Tom's riches disappear.

Sources. While the inspiration for "The Devil and Tom Walker" stems from lore and legends with which Irving was intimately familiar, the exact source of the story is uncertain. Some scholars believe that Irving simply retold a traditional tale exactly as he heard it. Others, however, state that Irving drew from a variety of sources, skillfully weaving diverse plot elements together to create his story.

Sir Walter Scott, a Scottish Romantic writer, had befriended Washington Irving. Both men were interested in local legends and antiquities, and Scott encouraged Irving to visit Germany to learn some of the local lore. Before writing *Tales of a Traveler,* Irving traveled in Germany for over a year and recorded German stories and legends in a notebook. He had declared his purpose before arriving in the country: "I mean to get into the confidence of every old woman I meet with in Germany and get from her her wonderful budget of stories" (Irving in Zug, p. 245). It is therefore likely that sources for "The Devil and Tom Walker" stem from his experiences during this period as well as from his own background as an American. Certainly, Irving's depiction of the Devil stems directly from Germanic tradition, which describes Satan as a large, strong black man and refers to him as the "Black Huntsman." Irving simply "Americanizes" his devil by dressing him in Indian clothing and associating him with Puritan rumors of American Indian practices.

The characters of Tom Walker and his wife are more difficult to trace. Irving may have turned to some of his own previous characters in his creation of the Walkers. Tom parallels the money-grubbing Ichabod Crane in "The Legend of Sleepy Hollow" and possibly represents Irving's idea of the money-oriented "Yankee," for Ichabod and Tom's mannerisms fit the New Yorker's stereotype of a New England character. Tom's wife, meanwhile, is similar to the wife described in "Rip Van Winkle."

Irving also incorporated the tale of Captain Kidd, considered one of the first North American legends, into his own story. In Irving's era, there was widespread belief that Kidd, a seventeenth-century pirate, had buried his treasure along the Hudson River or in southern New England.

Events in History at the Time the Short Story Was Written

Earning a living. Washington Irving came from a well-to-do family and was encouraged to practice business and law. Irving was not interested in pursuing these careers, however, and he spent much of his life avoiding traditional work. Irving worked briefly as a lawyer because he felt that he should do something, but much of his time in this job was spent daydreaming and waiting for the workday to end. He also worked halfheartedly at his family's import business, filling his ample spare time with writing.

Washington Irving's father was a deacon and a strong force in his son's early life. The author would later behave in ways that were quite opposite of his father's teachings, however. While the elder Irving told his children that all pleasures were wicked, Washington Irving made a conscious effort to enjoy himself throughout his life. He was also not religious. Washington Irving seldom attended church until he was fifty years old, and he did not take comfort in religion during any of the rough periods of his life.

Although Irving did not enjoy working, he felt guilty about not having a regular job. He considered himself a failure despite the fact that he was becoming well known as a writer. His brother had a hardware business in England. When Irving arrived in 1815, the enterprise, in which he was a silent partner, was doing fairly well. Soon after, however, the entire family business went broke. Irving quickly published *The Sketch Book,* which was enormously popular. Irving became famous and was able to support himself and his family on earnings from the book. The fact that he could support his family with his writing gave Irving hope for the future, and he resolved to permanently forgo all business in order to dedicate himself to the craft.

Economic changes. When Irving wrote "The Devil and Tom Walker" in 1824, America was experiencing rapid economic and territorial growth, much as it had in the 1720s, when the story is set. The changing economic conditions of the 1820s led to a flurry of business activity. Irving's personal distaste for all this activity is reflected in the story. In his portrayal of both Tom and the Devil as shrewd businessmen, the author makes fun of the business community.

Religious awakening. From the mid-1700s through the beginning of the 1800s, the country went through a period of religious reactions to the spiritual apathy of the early eighteenth century. Termed the "Great Awakenings" these movements increased the public's enthusiasm in Christian faith and worship and resulted in profound changes in religious viewpoints. Influenced by increased industrialism, a growing economy, and the expansion of the frontier, the Second Great Awakening dramatically changed church structure. It led to the establishment of distinct denominations in religion and the concept that no one faith was entirely correct. There was no longer an absolute way of life and therefore no longer an absolute religious truth. This unsettled atmosphere perhaps allowed Irving to examine and satirize religion in popular writing in a way that had not previously been acceptable. As individual ruggedness came to characterize the era, religion became a personal and voluntary expression of spirituality. Sin was no longer thought of as a flaw innate to man but rather, like the western frontier, as something that could be overcome and defeated.

Romanticism. During the 1800s writers, artists, and philosophers responded to the forces of nationalism that swept through Europe and the United States and questioned the notions of the Enlightenment that dominated intellectual thought. While the Enlightenment stressed rational thought, visible evidence, and universal standards of excellence, another movement, known as Romanticism, stressed the mysterious and unique nature of individual or national experience.

The Industrial Revolution fueled Romantic sentiments as well. Advances in industry and mechanization, first seen in Britain in the late 1700s, spread quickly to Europe and the United States. The Industrial Revolution triggered a period of great social and economic upheaval in the mid-1800s. People moved from the country to the city and worked in factories at tedious and sometimes dangerous jobs. Machines began to replace some workers, who were left to fend for themselves. Cities grew polluted and housing in some areas became crowded and unsanitary. Many people felt that they were losing control over their lives.

The Romantics turned to the past for comfort against feelings of isolation and despair. They believed that mankind had lost something precious in the process of modernization and that this "essence" could be found among farmers who still earned their living in traditional ways. In the eyes of the Romantics, these farmers were not yet tainted by the sins of the cities. The Grimm brothers of Germany, for example, published *Kinder und Housmarchen,* a collection of folk tales that had supposedly been gathered directly from German peasants. Many people considered these tales to contain some lost essence of true German spirit. Inspired by the Grimm brothers, hosts of other writers began to scour their own countries for legends, tales, and anecdotes, which they considered relics of a purer but dying way of life. In "The Devil and Tom Walker," Irving similarly turned from the hard science of the nineteenth century to the more magical past, incorporating legends and superstitions about the Devil as an essential ingredient of the plot.

Reviews. *Tales of a Traveler,* the collection containing "The Devil and Tom Walker," was published in 1824. Although Irving believed that the book demonstrated some of his best work, as a whole it received poor reviews. Several prominent journals stated that the stories were offensive and even obscene. The *United States Literary Gazette* criticized the story of "The Young Robber": "[a] scene most revolting to humanity is twice unnecessarily forced on the reader's imagination" (Johnston, p. 261). Others dismissed the book as dull and untrue. Irving was deeply disappointed that it received such negative press. Although he tried to put the criticisms out of his mind, he fell into a depression and eventually turned away from humorous writing.

For More Information

Emerson, Everett. *Puritanism in American 1620-1750.* Boston: G. K. Hall, 1977.

Erikson, Kai T. *Wayward Puritans.* New York: John Wiley & Sons, 1966.

Hellman, George. *Washington Irving Esquire.* New York: Alfred A. Knopf, 1925.

Irving, Washington. "The Devil and Tom Walker." In *The Complete Works of Washington Irving.* Vol. 10. New York: Thomas Y. Crowell, no date.

Johnston, Johanna. *The Heart That Would Not Hold.* New York: M. Evans, 1971.

Zug, Charles G. "Construction of 'The Devil and Tom Walker': A Study of Irving's Later Use of Folklore." *New York Folklore Quarterly* 24: 243-59.

Drums Along the Mohawk

by
Walter D. Edmonds

Born in upstate New York's Boonville in 1903, Walter D. Edmonds focused on the region's history and people in most of the novels he wrote. *Drums Along the Mohawk* centers on the experience of settlers in the Mohawk River Valley during the Revolutionary War. This book first appeared in 1936, when the United States was in the midst of the Great Depression and thousands of Americans were struggling through the same kind of poverty that the novel's main characters experience. At the same time, events were taking place throughout the world that would eventually expose this later generation of Americans to the horrors of war.

Events in History at the Time the Novel Takes Place

Life on the frontier. *Drums Along the Mohawk* focuses on the inhabitants of German Flats, the westernmost frontier settlement in the Mohawk Valley of New York in the late 1700s. As was the case throughout much of the state of New York during the time, the real-life inhabitants of German Flats and the Mohawk Valley region lived on rural farms that had only recently been carved out of the surrounding wilderness. The area attracted settlers, despite the difficulties of living on the frontier, because the land was plentiful, fertile, and relatively cheap. It offered small farmers the opportunity to develop and maintain a prosperous homestead of their own that they could proudly pass on to their descendants.

THE LITERARY WORK

A novel set in the Mohawk Valley in New York State, from 1776 to 1784; published in 1936.

SYNOPSIS

A young married couple struggles through the difficult years of the American Revolution in a New York State frontier settlement.

Most people first arrived in frontier settlements such as German Flats with a minimum of possessions. They typically began their new lives in simple log cabins; after clearing part of the land of trees and rocks, these early settlers planted wheat, corn, or other crops. The typical farmer was able to produce beyond his family's immediate needs within a few years and send surplus crops to nearby marketing centers, coastal cities, or overseas markets in Europe and the West Indies. In fact, wheat grew so successfully in the Mohawk Valley that it became the "bread basket" for much of America at the time.

The valley's rural communities were largely self-sufficient and produced nearly all of their own essentials. In German Flats and other such settlements, farmers grew food, cut lumber, and supplied wool, linen, and leather material for clothing. The women of the settlement spun, wove, and tailored the material into everyday wear. For metal work, flour grinding, and other services, the settlers turned to artisans such as millers or smiths who lived in the area. There were even a few local lawyers and doctors to meet residents' needs.

While the majority of the Mohawk Valley's population consisted of small farmers, a few wealthier men also lived there. Some of these men, such as the Johnsons, the Butlers, and Philip Schuyler, are referred to in *Drums Along the Mohawk*. Before the Revolutionary War, they dominated local politics and controlled the region's courts. These powerful men possessed large houses and greater quantities of servants, land, and luxuries than most people in the area. In colonial times they enjoyed the general respect of the rest of the region's population. When the Revolutionary War came, many of these wealthy men left to join the English forces and lost their standing in the society of the region forever.

Settlers and American Indians. Most of the Iroquois nations, which included the Mohawks, Senecas, Oneidas, Onondagas, Cayugas, and Tuscaroras, had lived in western New York long before the arrival of white settlers. In the 1700s, tension mounted between the two cultures as increasing numbers of white colonists moved into the region. The American Indians resented the encroachment of the white settlers on their lands and the threat it presented to their way of life. The settlers saw the Indians as a dangerous obstacle in their quest to secure greater prosperity on the frontier and regarded most of them as wild animals to be killed without fear of punishment from the government; it was quite rare for anyone to be punished for the murder of a Native American. Many whites felt little guilt or remorse as they steadily pushed the frontier of settlement further west, robbing the tribes of the vast expanses of land upon which they had long lived. The lack of an exact, mutually agreed-upon boundary between settlers and American Indian lands aggravated the situation, for it encouraged settlers to claim "disputed" lands and created an atmosphere of hostility between the two cultures that sometimes erupted into violent confrontations.

The Mohawk Valley during the Revolution. Another clash of beliefs became evident in the 1760s and 1770s in the Mohawk Valley and other regions. Prior to the first shots of the Revolution in 1775, disagreements accelerated between supporters of the American cause (Patriots) and supporters of the English government (Tories). Neighbors became suspicious of neighbors, and an increasing number of politically oriented meetings were held, usually at night in taverns, halls, or private homes. Sometimes these meetings became scenes of violence between Tory and Patriot factions. On the night of March 29, 1775, for example, one meeting in Caughnawaga was suddenly interrupted by the appearance of Guy Johnson and Sir John Johnson, who led a band of about thirty Tories armed with clubs. The Patriot group was ordered to end their meeting and leave. When they refused, a violent brawl broke out and more than a dozen people were hurt. After months of such confrontations, the Patriot faction managed to gain the upper hand in the region. Johnson and most other Mohawk Valley Tories left to join the British forces in Canada.

In Canada the Tories helped the British forge an alliance with the Mohawk, Seneca, and Cayuga tribes against the Patriots. These tribes, who resented the advance of the Americans onto Indian lands, sided with the British against the settlers who had been claiming Iroquois territory for years. Not all the Iroquois nations joined the Tory faction, however. Some, like the Oneidas, remained neutral at first and occasionally provided direct help to the American forces.

American Indian tribes became a major force in the Tories' campaign against the Patriots when the Revolution began. Especially important were Mohawk and Seneca raids against the Mohawk Valley settlers. The British and their allies believed that the area served as the granary for George Washington's army; by destroying its farms they would deprive the American forces of an important source of food. British forces also noted that the region was vulnerable because relatively few American troops were stationed in the Mohawk Valley, despite its strategic importance as the "bread basket" of the nation. The Revolutionary War in the Mohawk Valley region thus became a mostly defensive struggle of local militia against Tory raids on their homes and settlements.

Along the New York frontier, settlements like German Flats were attacked and destroyed by combined British and Indian forces. Homes, barns, mills, and fields, sometimes full of unharvested crops, were burned. Individuals were shot or their families savagely attacked in their homes. One man described the terrible scene he witnessed after one raid: "Such a shocking sight my eyes never beheld before of savage and brutal barbarity; to see a husband mourning over his dead wife with four children lying by her side, mangled, scalped, and some of their heads, some of their legs and arms cut off" (Evans, p. 275).

Poster for the film version of *Drums Along the Mohawk*.

The years of the Revolution (1775-1783) were a time of extreme terror and loss for people like Gil and Lana Martin of *Drums Along the Mohawk*. Not only were their farms and possessions destroyed, but they also feared for their lives. Raids often forced badly frightened farmers to desert their homes and fields and seek the shelter and protection of forts. People in *Drums Along the Mo-*

LOCAL MILITIA VS. CONTINENTAL ARMY

Before 1775 no central military organization existed in America. Instead, each state maintained its own army, called the militia. Every community organized all its able-bodied men into companies that were only called up in times of great need. For the most part, militia men lacked strict military training and discipline. This is illustrated by the description of a militia meeting in German Flats in *Drums Along the Mohawk*. "The line raggedly shouldered their guns, some to the right, some to the left.... No two of them were dressed alike. Some had coats, of homespun or black cloth; some, like Gil, wore hunting shirts" (*Drums Along the Mohawk*, p. 46). With the beginning of the Revolution, America's Continental Congress decided that a centralized military command was necessary to coordinate all the states' efforts and concentrate the Americans' strength in key areas of the nation. Congress therefore created the Continental Army, with George Washington as its commander in chief. These regular troops were all volunteers. Unlike the militias, however, they received a few months' training to gain discipline and skill. The Continental troops were therefore usually more effective than militias.

hawk, for example, retreat many times over the course of the war to either Fort Dayton or Fort Herkimer. They then live for days or weeks in cramped, unsanitary quarters. Subject to repeated attacks and miserable living conditions, the Mohawk Valley suffered enormously in the war years. The region eventually lost about two-thirds of its population and 700 buildings, while thousands of farms were left uncultivated.

The Novel in Focus

The plot. The bulk of *Drums Along the Mohawk* takes place between 1776 and 1781, although the book includes an epilogue chapter describing resettlement after the war in 1784. In 1776

Lana Borst marries Gil Martin, and together they leave her parents' New York homestead to settle thirty miles further west in Deerfield. Because of the approaching Revolution, soon after their arrival Gil must report to a gathering of the local militia called "muster day."

A month or two later, some of Gil's neighbors—the Weavers, the Realls, and Clem Coppernol—arrive at the Martin homestead to help Gil clear ten acres of his land for farming. When they are about halfway finished, Blue Back, a friendly Oneida Indian, arrives to warn them that a raiding party of Senecas and Tories is in the valley. The settlers immediately scatter for home to pack up some belongings before driving to the Little Stone Arabia Stockade for protection. Lana, who is pregnant, has a miscarriage as a result of the wild ride to the fort. The enemy destroys all the houses and fields of the Deerfield settlements, forcing Gil and Lana to rent a one-room cabin for the winter. By spring, money is scarce and Gil desperately needs work to support them. He takes a job as the hired man of Mrs. McKlennar, a widow, and he and Lana move into a house on her property. Lana later becomes pregnant again, this time safely bearing the child.

At the end of the summer, the militia is called up. It sets out westward to confront a force of Tories and Indians who have moved down from Canada to attack the Mohawk Valley. The ensuing battle at Oriskany leaves hundreds of the American militia men dead or injured. Gil returns with a bullet wound in the arm; General Herkimer, the American commander, is injured in the leg and eventually dies from his wounds.

Raiding parties continue to burn and pillage the Mohawk Valley settlements through the summer of 1778. As a result, there is hardly enough food for the Martin household the next winter. The Americans grow increasingly certain that members of the Onondaga tribe have been involved in a number of the destructive raids, although they have claimed a position of neutrality in the war. In the spring of 1779 the militia is led west by Colonel Van Schaick on a mission to strike the Onondaga settlements. The militia men arrive to find that the Indians have already fled, but the troops decide to burn down the Onondaga towns.

That summer Lana has a second child. Winter arrives, and though the Martin family has enough to eat, the cold is remarkably severe. By this time the Martins are living with Mrs. McKlennar, who has aged greatly and keeps mostly to her bed. The destructive raids continue in the

Mohawk Valley through the following spring and summer. Instead of going alone into the fields to work on their crops, farmers are forced to work in groups with armed guards.

One day Lana takes her two sons for a walk, leaving Mrs. McKlennar in the house. While Lana is gone, two somewhat drunken Indians enter and set the house on fire. Overwhelmed by her righteous indignation, they agree to carry Mrs. McKlennar's bed outside. The Indians flee as settlers rush to the scene, but it proves too late to save the house. Gil and two scouts build a cabin for the winter.

When the spring of 1781 arrives, Lieutenant Colonel Marinus Willett leads a group of American soldiers into the valley with orders to find and destroy the Tory forces in the area, which are now under General Butler's command. Butler's army is already experiencing difficulties because its food supplies are running out. When the American troops finally catch up with the Tory forces, they harass the weary army for several miles, kill Butler, and scatter his soldiers into the wilderness. The rout saves the valley from further serious harm for the rest of the war.

Three years later, in 1784, German Flats is safe. Gil and Lana return to their old Deerfield farm to raise their family. After surviving eight long years of hardship and struggle, the Martins are content to be back at home with their children and each other.

The unresponsiveness of the government. *Drums Along the Mohawk* reflects the harsh conditions that people in areas such as German Flats endured during the Revolutionary War. Tory raids were a constant threat to homes, possessions, and families. Food, money, and employment grew scarce as well, for the region's meager defenses were insufficient to withstand the onslaught of Tory and Indian enemies. General Herkimer and others wrote letters to the Continental Congress requesting regular army detachments to help protect the frontier settlements, but these requests were generally ignored. Preoccupied with other problems, Congress thought it more important to send America's troops elsewhere.

Throughout the war, the national and state governments seemed to show a tremendous indifference to the suffering of the Mohawk Valley. Edmonds highlights this government insensitivity and bureaucracy in *Drums Along the Mohawk*. When the members of the militia go to collect their pay, one of Gil's neighbors, Mrs. Reall, accompanies them. Her family is desperately in need of money, and she wants to pick up the pay earned by her husband, who had been killed at the battle of Oriskany. Because of a clerical mistake, however, Mr. Reall has not been marked on the paymaster's list as dead. The paymaster insists that Mr. Reall is officially required to pick up the money himself. Even after one of the other men in the room expresses his willingness to swear as to the time of the man's death and the fact that Mrs. Reall is his widow, the paymaster refuses to give her the money. She is required to file a claim with the government and wait for eventual results; in the meantime, her family gradually starves.

GONE WITH THE WIND VS. DRUMS ALONG THE MOHAWK

Published in the same year as *Gone With the Wind* by Margaret Mitchell, Edmonds' novel topped Mitchell's as the number one bestseller for a week before slipping below it into second place.

Edmonds provides another especially vivid example of the government's indifference to local problems near the end of *Drums Along the Mohawk*. In 1780 the settlers of German Flats, who have endured years of terror, destruction, and poverty, suddenly receive huge tax bills for land that has been abandoned, buildings that were burned in the war, and farm animals that have been killed. The shocked settlers realize that the government must have obtained the English king's old tax list. After so many years of fighting to overthrow British rule, the new American government seems not to treat them much differently. Edmonds uses such incidents to paint an unsympathetic portrait of the government in the novel.

Sources. Events and people that actually existed provide the basic framework for *Drums Along the Mohawk*. Such key military figures as General Herkimer and Captain Demooth on the American side and Tory commander General Butler on the British side are featured in the novel. Battles such as the one at Oriskany actually took place, as did the repeated raids on settlements in the Mohawk Valley.

Edmonds did a great deal of research into the history of revolutionary New York for the story. He consulted scholarly sources as well as old journals and letters that were left behind by peo-

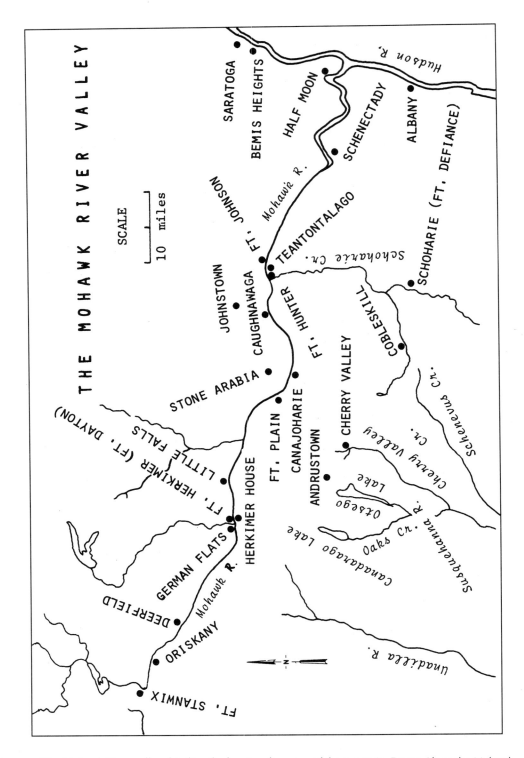

A map of the Mohawk River valley detailing the location for many of the events in *Drums Along the Mohawk*.

ple who actually lived through the events that he was describing. He also drew on personal experience, since he grew up just north of the Mohawk River Valley. His descriptions of scenery and weather are to some extent based on his own knowledge and impressions of the area.

Events in History at the Time the Novel Was Written

The Great Depression. *Drums Along the Mohawk* was published in 1936, in the midst of the Great Depression, the worst economic crisis in American history. The first visible sign of the Depression was the 1929 stock market crash, in which investors lost hundreds or thousands of dollars. Meanwhile, over 9,000 American banks either went bankrupt or closed to avoid bankruptcy in the next few years. The bank failures caused Americans to lose over $2.5 billion. By 1932, about a quarter of the work force was unemployed, while others with jobs suffered large pay cuts or reduced hours. Swelling numbers of people sought help from public relief agencies, which were overwhelmed by the tremendous demand for their services and collapsed in many cities.

In 1932 President Franklin D. Roosevelt initiated a series of economic reforms called the New Deal. One of his first acts to help impoverished Americans was to create a temporary Federal Emergency Relief Administration (FERA), which distributed a limited number of cash grants to help state relief agencies. Another temporary program, the Civil Works Administration, was established to employ millions of people in short-term projects such as the construction of roads or parks. In 1935 Congress passed the Social Security Act, which provided the elderly with federal assistance and established a pension system that would provide workers with an income after retirement. Such programs continued to be established throughout the 1930s, and while these measures provided some relief, serious financial hardship was still felt by millions of Americans through the end of the decade. Many felt dissatisfied with the government's efforts and charged that it was indifferent to their problems.

Walter Edmonds' unflattering portrayal of Congress and the government in *Drums Along the Mohawk* thus reflected the opinions of the author and many other Americans about the government during the 1930s. The author drew a direct parallel in the novel between the early frontier settlers in the Revolution and the struggling, impoverished Americans in the Depression. Families in both periods were threatened by unemployment, loss of land and property, and sometimes homelessness and starvation. Citizens of both eras appealed to the state and national governments for relief, but both times the government response was not effective enough to substantially change the terrible conditions faced by multitudes of people. As Edmonds states in his introduction to *Drums Along the Mohawk,*

> To those who may feel that here is a great to-do about a bygone life, I have one last word to say. It does not seem to me a bygone life at all. The parallel is too close to our own.... Those people of the valley ... suffered the paralysis of abject dependence on a central government totally unfitted to comprehend a local problem.
> (Edmonds, p. ix)

Threats of war. While Edmonds wrote about the Revolutionary War in *Drums Along the Mohawk,* events unfolded around the world that eventually led to World War II. The financial crisis of the 1930s had not been limited to the United States; countries around the world experienced severe shortages and financial hardships. One of the consequences of these economic conditions was the growth of fierce and intolerant nationalism in certain areas of the

A CHANGE IN THE NOVEL'S TITLE

Edmonds originally called his novel *A Starving Wilderness,* but then decided that it "was not exactly an inviting title for the Depression" (Wyld, p. 79). The title *Drums Along the Mohawk* refers to the setting of the novel in the Mohawk Valley and the way its settlers first heard about the Revolutionary War—through the sounding of drums by the American army.

world. People became desperate to eliminate their own economic problems, even at the expense of other ethnic groups, who were often blamed for a variety of social and economic ills. In a number of countries, military-minded factions gained power and began to expand their territories. The Japanese moved into China, the Italians into Ethiopia, and the Germans into the Rhineland. In 1936, the year *Drums Along the Mohawk* was published, the German dictator Adolph Hitler moved his army into the Rhineland, taking over an area that France had controlled since World War I; two years later, he also took control of Austria.

Reviews. Historical novels were very popular in the 1930s. Most followed the same pattern: they were long, involved many characters, featured plenty of action and realistic details about the period, and often ended happily. *Drums Along the Mohawk* has all these qualities, but it also featured writing that set it above many other historical novels of the period.

Drums Along the Mohawk was immediately popular. A bestseller in 1936 and 1937, the book was made into a film by Twentieth Century Fox in 1939. The novel has been called "one of the best examples of the regional chronicles ever written in America (Wyld, p. 76). A few 1930s critics disapproved of its raw descriptions of frontier and Indian brutality and its characters' use of unpolished, down-to-earth dialogue. These features, however, suited the author's intent—to capture life as it was for ordinary farmers and settlers of New York State who had been swept into the Revolutionary War. Edmonds himself sensed that his work had achieved this: "I have just finished writing a novel about the Mohawk Valley during the Revolutionary War and I feel as if I had caught a big fish" (Edmonds in Wyld, p. 75).

For More Information

Edmonds, Walter D. *Drums Along the Mohawk*. Boston: Little, Brown, 1936.

Evans, Elizabeth. *Weathering the Storm: Women of the American Revolution*. New York: Paragon House, 1989.

McElvaine, Robert S. *The Great Depression: America, 1929-1941*. New York: Times Books, 1984.

Roberts, Robert B. *New York's Forts in the Revolution*. Cranbury, New Jersey: Associated University Presses, 1980.

Sosin, Jack M. *The Revolutionary Frontier: 1763-1783*. New York: Holt, Rinehart and Winston, 1967.

Wyld, Lionel D. *Walter D. Edmonds, Storyteller*. New York: Syracuse University Press, 1982.

Frankenstein

by
Mary Shelley

Mary Wollstonecraft Shelley was the daughter of two of England's most nonconformist thinkers, William Godwin, the radical philosopher, and Mary Wollstonecraft, the author of *A Vindication of the Rights of Woman* (also covered in *Literature and Its Times*). At age seventeen, Mary fell in love with renowned English poet Percy Bysshe Shelley and fled with him to Europe. Under the influence of her husband and Lord Byron, Mary's literary talents began to flourish. After Byron issued a challenge for each of the three writers to create a ghost story, Mary began her most famous novel, *Frankenstein*. It is a product of the Romantic era and deals with several of the Romantic movement's most crucial ideas, including isolation, alienation, and the destruction that can result from man's selfish desires.

Events in History at the Time the Novel Takes Place

The Industrial Revolution in England. In the mid-1700s, Great Britain experienced a surge in population that helped initiate the Industrial Revolution. The population of England in 1700 was 6 million; by 1800 it had climbed to more than 9 million people. Advances in agriculture—which played the most significant role in the increase in population—provided a greater supply of food and better overall health for the nation's inhabitants.

Population also soared because of developments in medicine and hygiene. Beginning in 1760, inoculations for smallpox became available; the number of deaths from the terrible disease greatly decreased as a result. Another sick-

---

THE LITERARY WORK

A novel set in Europe in the 1790s; published in 1817.

SYNOPSIS

Victor Frankenstein, a young Swiss gentleman, uses his knowledge of the sciences to create a living creature, but is horrified at the result. Cursed by his maker, the monster sets out to avenge himself on mankind. It is pursued by Frankenstein, who seeks to redeem himself by destroying his creation.

---

ness that had decimated the population for centuries was typhus. Originating among rats, the disease was transmitted by fleas and lice, which thrived in the warm woolen clothing of preindustrial times. The rise of the cotton industry provided inexpensive clothing and bedding that could be washed and boiled, a process that killed the typhus louse.

Several other factors—such as growth in real incomes, a subsequent increase in demand for goods, and technological advances—also stimulated the beginning of the Industrial Revolution. This, in turn, played a significant role in the development of the Romantic movement, of which Mary Shelley and her circle were a part. The Romantics, who focused on the individual, the emotional, and the imaginative in life, considered many of the effects of industrialism as a threat to their system of beliefs. Members of the Romantic movement generally viewed many aspects of the fast-developing industrial society with alarm. They harshly criticized less desirable social developments such as the exploitation of labor, which was commonplace in the new industries in England.

The emerging textile factories, iron mills, and coal mines exacted a heavy toll on their workers. In some cities, almost 20 percent of the labor force was made up of children nine years old or younger. Furthermore, the demands for a stable labor force created a system of bonding that forced workers to remain with a company for a set period of time; in some cases cotton mills forced workers to sign five-year bonds. To the Romantics, who believed in individual liberty for the human spirit, this exploitation of the labor force was intolerable. Even the smoking chimneys of industrial plants stood in opposition to Romantic ideals. The Romantics valued natural beauty, an appreciation that is present throughout *Frankenstein* in Shelley's scenes amid the mountains and lakes of Switzerland and on the frozen seas of Siberia.

Science and technology in the Romantic period. The late 1700s were rife with new scientific theories and technological advances. Less than one hundred patents were issued in 1750, but by 1780 the number had jumped to more than four hundred. One of the greatest inventions of this period was the steam engine. There was also a growth in scientific discoveries during this period. One scientist who embodied both the technological and scientific advancements of the time was Erasmus Darwin. Considered the finest doctor of his time in England, Darwin produced numerous inventions, including a speaking machine and a horizontal windmill. His major scientific achievements included his recognition and description of biological evolution, his analysis of plant nutrition and photosynthesis, and his explanation of cloud formation processes.

Not limited to scientific subjects, Darwin was also influential in literary circles. He became immediately famous for a poem entitled "The Botanic Garden." Darwin's writings had a profound effect on the Romantics, influencing Samuel Taylor Coleridge's famous poems "The Rime of the Ancient Mariner" and "Kubla Khan." Mary Shelley's husband, Percy Bysshe Shelley, was one of Darwin's keenest disciples, and he took from the scientist his ideas of infusing science into nature poetry. He also admired Darwin for his radical political beliefs and skepticism about religion. Percy Shelley's admiration for

Darwin has led many scholars to credit him as an influence on Mary Shelley's *Frankenstein*. The specific idea for the story arose from a discussion between Byron and Shelley about Darwin's notions on the generation of life. This connection is confirmed by the first sentence of Mary Shelley's introduction to *Frankenstein,* "The event on which this fiction is founded has been supposed, by Dr. Darwin and some of the physiological writers of Germany, as not of impossible occurrence" (Shelley, p. xiii).

Echoes of the French Revolution in *Frankenstein*. The French Revolution of 1789 greatly influenced the early Romantic writers. Mary Shelley's mother, Mary Wollstonecraft, was a fervent supporter of the Revolution even after its excesses of murder and oppression began to disenchant many of its first backers. Wollstonecraft died eleven days after giving birth to Mary, but the Revolution continued to exert a strong influence on writers into her daughter's adult years. It instilled in young Romantic poets such as Lord Byron and Percy Shelley the idea that they lived in an age of new beginnings, and that everything was possible if inherited customs and procedures were discarded.

Since Shelley's mother, whom she had never known but strongly idealized, and her intimate companions were so strongly influenced by the French Revolution, it seems probable that Mary Shelley incorporated aspects and thoughts on the Revolution into her first novel. The most evident parallel between the French Revolution and the novel appears in the guise of the monster itself. The monster is an incredible, unprecedented achievement; but because it is not given careful attention and direction by its creator, Doctor Frankenstein, it becomes a monstrous murderer who torments the doctor.

This idea ties in smoothly with the prevalent thinking of English radicals during the period. Most of these revolutionary thinkers, Lord Byron and Percy Shelley among them, believed that the French Revolution offered great hope but felt that the excessive and bloody reprisals it inspired were major faults. For this reason, the conception of the French Revolution as a "monster" became a common idea at the time. Another aspect of *Frankenstein* that links the novel with the revolution is one of its crucial settings. Ingolstadt, Germany, the city in which Victor Frankenstein is educated, was also the birthplace of the Illuminati, a secret society that introduced revolutionary ideas believed by many to have helped foment the revolution in France.

Charles Ogle as the monster in the 1910 film version of *Frankenstein,* reputedly the first monster movie ever made.

The Novel in Focus

The plot. The novel begins aboard the ship of Captain Robert Walton. Walton is searching the Arctic seas for the North Pole and for a passage to the Pacific Ocean. He discovers Dr. Victor Frankenstein, a Swiss gentleman, floating on a piece of ice amid the frigid waters. Frankenstein tells Walton his story.

Frankenstein had spent his childhood in Geneva. Interested in the sciences, he travels to Ingolstadt in Germany to pursue a university education. Through his study of the natural sciences, Frankenstein becomes interested in the mysteries of life. He spends several years in study and ultimately discovers how to create a living creature. After months of exhausting labor, the experiment succeeds and the monstrous creature made from a collection of corpses comes to life. Frankenstein shrieks in horror at his creation, which prompts the monster to flee. At this point, Henry Clerval, Frankenstein's childhood friend, arrives in Ingolstadt to pursue his own studies. Frankenstein receives a letter from his father with the news that his young brother, William, has been murdered. Frankenstein rushes home to Geneva and finds that Justine, a servant and friend of his family, has been apprehended as the boy's murderer. From the details of the murder, Frankenstein realizes that his monster is responsible for the crime. The doctor watches helplessly as Justine is condemned and executed for a murder she did not commit. Disconsolate, Frankenstein wanders in the nearby mountains and is confronted by the creature.

The creature explains to Frankenstein that he has tried to live among men but that his good intentions were rewarded with hatred and abuse. Due to these experiences, he has vowed to wreak vengeance on his creator and the human species. The monster tells Frankenstein that he will cease his crime spree if Frankenstein will create a mate for him. Frankenstein finally agrees and plans a trip to England with Henry Clerval to begin the project. Before they leave, Frankenstein becomes engaged to his cousin and childhood companion, Elizabeth. He promises to return in a year.

ARCTIC EXPLORATION

The end of the 1700s saw the dawn of a new epoch in nautical exploration. Explorers pursued two major enterprises: the first was the quest to find the North Pole; the second was the pursuit of a trade route through the Arctic that would connect the Atlantic and the Pacific Oceans.

In 1811 the founding of an organization called the Hydrographic Branch created further interest in these two endeavors. The goal of the Hydrographic Branch was to chart and survey, with magnetic observations, as much of the globe as possible. The lack of knowledge about the North, as well as the incredible profit to be made from the discovery of a Northeast Passage, stimulated interest in and countless expeditions to the region.

Robert Walton, one of the chief narrators in *Frankenstein*, is the captain of an expedition that attempts to find the North Pole and also hopes to discover a Northeast Passage. Beyond this, the concept of exploration, so popular during Mary Shelley's lifetime, serves as the framework in which the narratives of Frankenstein and the monster are embedded. Walton's search for the North Pole and Frankenstein's desire to create life reflect the era of discovery in which Mary Shelley lived.

In England, Frankenstein constructs a female counterpart for the creature. He reconsiders, though, realizing that he has been wrong in attempting to control life and death, and destroys the figure before giving it life. The monster, who has followed Frankenstein to England, witnesses the destruction and threatens to visit Frankenstein on his wedding night. The next day Clerval's body is found strangled, and Frankenstein is accused of the crime. He is eventually acquitted.

Frankenstein returns to Switzerland to marry Elizabeth, even though he believes the monster plans to kill him on his wedding night. After the wedding, Frankenstein stays away from Elizabeth in the hope of protecting her, only to belatedly realize that the monster has targeted her as his victim. Frankenstein finds her strangled body and vows revenge on the monster. He pursues the monster across Europe and finally into the frozen wastes, where the explorer Walton finds him. After completing his narration, Frankenstein dies of exhaustion. Shortly afterward, Walton finds the monster standing over the corpse. The creature tells Walton that he has realized his wrongs and that he now intends to destroy himself at the North Pole; after this declaration the creature flees the ship and disappears into the surrounding snow and ice.

Responsibility and blame in Frankenstein. In her novel, Mary Shelley spends a great deal of time tracing the paths of blame and responsibility. According to the beliefs of the story's characters, one does not need to be directly responsible for an incident to receive the blame for its occurrence. An example of this indirect blame manifests itself in Frankenstein's fiancée, Elizabeth, shortly after the death of his brother William. William had asked Elizabeth to let him wear a valuable necklace for a while, and this necklace is believed to be the temptation that occasioned his murder. Because Elizabeth allowed him to wear the necklace, she feels entirely responsible for his death, wailing "Oh God! I have murdered my darling child!" (Shelley, *Frankenstein*, p. 70). Her reaction seems to be excessive. Instead of recognizing her small role in the alleged events that led to the boy's death or fastening blame on the murderer, Elizabeth views herself as the "murderer."

This concept of indirect blame also appears throughout the novel in the relationship between Frankenstein and the monster he has created. When Frankenstein visits the falsely accused Justine as she awaits execution, he realizes that she has peacefully resigned herself to her fate because she knows she is innocent. Of himself, Frankenstein says, "But I, the true murderer, felt the never-dying worm alive in my bosom, which allowed of no hope or consolation" (*Frankenstein*, p. 84). Although Frankenstein had created the monster, he did not commit the crime. Yet he, like Elizabeth, believes himself to be a "murderer" as a result of indirect blame and responsibility.

In its treatment of responsibility and blame, the novel focuses on the feelings of its characters, which was a typical concern in Romantic stories. This concern was a reaction, in part, to the preoccupation with reason and intellect that characterized the era before the Romantic movement. The novel builds on the focus of this previous era. Both of the characters who blame themselves, Elizabeth and Frankenstein, use their intellect to deduce that they bear responsibility for a crime. The emphasis, though, is on their emotional reaction, the feeling of guilt that accompanies their deductions.

Sources. Mary Shelley wrote the novel *Frankenstein* by tapping into countless literary, personal, scientific, and psychological sources. A voracious reader, Shelley found many of the central themes for her novel in works such as Goethe's *Sorrows of Werther,* which the monster reads in the novel, and Milton's *Paradise Lost.* Two literary works written by Mary's father, William Godwin, also seem probable sources. The first, *Caleb Williams,* is the story of a man bound to and haunted by another man through his knowledge of a secret crime. The second, *St. Leon,* is the story of a restless seeker of knowledge who receives the secrets of immortality, wealth, and knowledge from a mysterious stranger. This gift becomes a curse that dooms him to perpetual solitude and wandering. Both of these novels have obvious connections to Shelley's *Frankenstein.*

Percy Shelley and Lord Byron also served as inspirations for the novel. Without Byron's story-writing challenge and information gleaned from the discussions of the two men, Mary Shelley might never have created her most famous novel. Many of its characters are believed to have their origins in Percy Shelley's descriptions of actual people, and Frankenstein's professors are allegedly based on Percy Shelley's professors at Eton College. Henry Clerval is believed to be modeled after Percy's good friend Thomas Jefferson Hogg, with some hints of Byron also synthesized into the character.

Some scholars suggest that a psychological source for the monster can be found in Mary's own loneliness and in the bitterness she felt toward William Godwin, who had created her and then denied her love when she was unable to take the place of his prestigious lost love, her mother. Scholars have also speculated that Mary's stepsister, Jane Clairmont, may have been the model for the monster. "Claire" followed Mary and Percy Shelley to mainland Europe and constantly lived with them. Like the monster, she was present on the Shelleys' wedding night. Finally, the scientific discoveries of

the period probably had an impact on the novel, as seen in the influence exerted by Erasmus Darwin's writings. While their connection to the story cannot be verified, it seems likely that such discoveries played some role in the conception of the novel.

SOURCE OF DR. FRANKENSTEIN

Mary Shelley may have based the character of Doctor Frankenstein on Andrew Crosse, a British scientist whose experiments bear some resemblance to Frankenstein's fascinations. On December 28, 1814, the still-unmarried Mary Godwin and Percy Shelley attended Crosse's lecture on "Electricity and the Elements" at a lecture hall in London. Crosse discussed his attempts to harness and control electricity, which was a subject that greatly fascinated Percy Shelley. Galvanism, the belief in the possibility of reanimating life through electricity, was another subject of significant interest to Percy Shelley. He undoubtedly shared this fascination with Mary, as evidenced by her presence at Crosse's lecture.

Mary Shelley alluded to this new field of study in a passage in the novel. At one point Frankenstein witnesses the destruction of a tree by lightning. A "man of research" who is with him proceeds to describe the phenomenon in scientific terms: "He entered on the explanation of a theory which he had formed on the subject of electricity and galvanism, which was at once new and astonishing to me" (*Frankenstein,* p. 40).

Events in History at the Time the Novel Was Written

The Luddite Movement. The industrial growth experienced in England in the early nineteenth century was not without opposition. The Luddite movement came into being between 1811 and 1816, a period of unemployment, low wages, and high prices. The movement began in northern England, sparked by increases in the price of grain and potatoes without an equivalent rise in wages. In March 1811, in Nottinghamshire, the Luddites took action against an underpaying textile manufacturer by smashing weaving frames and other factory machines. Machinery was the object of Luddite violence because it was employed in areas of manufacturing that workmen wanted to ban or because it was owned by employers who did not pay fair wages or provide decent working conditions.

Ilustration of workers destroying their machines.

The machines of the industrial age, while increasing output, drastically reduced the number of workers needed, with some machines reportedly doing the work of twenty men. This lessened the need for workers and gave employers their choice of job-seekers. Operating from this position of strength, employers often paid lower wages and demanded more labor from their employees. The new machines were also frightening for reasons other than their unparalleled production rate; they threatened the way of life of thousands of craftsmen, such as handloom weavers, who were forced to shift from a comparatively independent mode of living into an anonymous position in a crowded factory.

As conditions worsened for these craftsmen and workers, the targets of their frustrations expanded beyond machines. In April 1812, William Horsfall was assassinated by Luddites, allegedly because of the great improvements he made in shearing frames. Peter Marsland, a factory owner who had made improvements on steam-weaving machines, had his life threatened and his factory burned to the ground by Luddites. As time passed, the Luddites increasingly turned to attacks against people in recognition of the impossibility of destroying the large establishments of the industrial movement. As incidents of violence spread and fears of a large-scale uprising grew, the government increasingly used the military against Luddite unrest. The Luddite movement declined after 1813, when seventeen Luddite rioters were convicted and hanged for the murder of William Horsfall, the attack on the Rawfolds woolen mill, and the theft of arms and money for the Luddite cause.

There are some possible connections from the Luddite movement to Mary Shelley and her novel, for the members of the Romantic movement shared some of the same concerns expressed by the Luddites. Lord Byron even spoke to the House of Lords in defense of the Luddites, telling of men "sacrificed to improvements in mechanism" (Byron in Thomis, p. 50). In Shelley's case, her beliefs concerning the dangers of man's technological advancements were presented through her depiction of the murderous rage of Frankenstein's monster. During the years preceding the writing of *Frankenstein,* the Luddite movement was growing. The novel's warning about the dangers of man's experimentation with technology may well have been inspired by the Luddites' fear of new industrial technology and its effects on their lives.

The resurrection men. The advancement of the sciences in England, particularly in the areas of anatomy, medicine, and biology, began a horrifying period in British social history: the age of the resurrection men. In the beginning of the nineteenth century, London surgeons and students bought and mutilated thousands of dead bodies that had been stolen by the lowliest members of society. During this period, the midnight quiet of graveyards could suddenly erupt in gunfire and confrontation between the "resurrection men" (as these grave robbers were called) and authorities.

The strange career of the resurrection men came about as a result of the severe lack of cadavers available for study and dissection. In France bodies for dissection were provided from those that went unclaimed in public hospitals. In Germany, the bodies of prostitutes and suicides were taken. In Britain, the only legal supply of cadavers came from the bodies of murderers executed within the country. After being cut down from the gallows, corpses were hauled to the College of Surgeons, where they would be dissected and given to lecturers at teaching hospitals. Because this practice provided very few bodies, resurrection men were enlisted to acquire corpses for teaching hospitals, whose students would take their tuition elsewhere unless there were enough bodies to examine. Although more stringent laws were passed as incidents of body-snatching increased, punishments were generally not enforced. This lack of enforcement was attributed to English authorities' desire to have surgeons and physicians that were as well trained as those on the European mainland.

Despite the outrage of families of the stolen dead, the resurrection men continued their morbid trade, acquiring a reputation that was known to Mary Shelley and most people in England during the period. Her acquaintance with the resurrection men and their nocturnal diggings may have been heightened by Percy Shelley's interests in anatomy and biology. In addition, she may have read about the resurrection men in the poetry of a fellow Romantic, Robert Southey, who wrote "The Surgeon's Warning," a poem that describes a dying doctor's plans to safeguard his body against the resurrection men with whom he was so well acquainted. Mary Shelley's familiarity with this practice may have been an influence on her conception of a monster made from a collection of corpses.

Critical response to *Frankenstein*. The critics greeted Mary Shelley's novel with a combination of praise and disdain. First published anonymously, the book had critics wondering at the identity of the deranged genius who had created such a tale. "Our readers will guess ... what a tissue of horrible and disgusting absurdity [*Frankenstein*] presents," wrote John Wilson Croker, a principal contributor for the *Quarterly Review*. "It cannot be denied that [it] is nonsense—but it is nonsense decked out with circumstances and clothed in language highly terrific" (Croker in Abbey, p. 249). Another attack on the story, this time without praise for the language, was published in the *Monthly Review*: "An uncouth story ... setting probability at defiance and leading to no conclusion either moral or philosophical. A serious examination is scarcely necessary for so eccentric a vagary of the imagination as this tale presents" (Summers, p. 94).

Despite the critical attacks, *Frankenstein* caused a literary sensation in London. The novel fit smoothly into the popular gothic genre, the style of fiction known for its aspects of horror and macabre details. The work was also considered innovative because of its introduction of a synthetic human character. Less obviously, the novel became one of the triumphs of the Romantic movement due to its themes of alienation and isolation and its warning about the destructive power that can result when human creativity is unfettered by moral and social concerns.

For More Information

Abbey, Cherie D., ed. *Nineteenth-Century Literature Criticism*. Vol. 14. Detroit: Gale Research, 1987.

Cole, Hubert. *Things for the Surgeon: A History of the Resurrection Men*. London: William Heinemann, 1964.

Coleman, D. C. *Myth, History, and the Industrial Revolution*. London: Hambledon, 1992.

Haining, Peter. *The Man Who Was Frankenstein*. London: Frederick Muller, 1979.

King-Hele, Desmond. *Doctor of Revolution: The Life and Genius of Erasmus Darwin*. London: Faber and Faber, 1977.

Shelley, Mary. *Frankenstein*. New York: Penguin, 1983.

Spark, Muriel. *Mary Shelley*. New York: E. P. Dutton, 1987.

Summers, Montague. *The Gothic Quest*. New York: Russell and Russell, 1964.

Thomis, Malcolm I. *The Luddites: Machine Breaking in Regency England*. Newton Abbot, England: David & Charles, 1970.

"Give Me Liberty or Give Me Death"

by
Patrick Henry

Born in 1736 in Hanover County, Virginia, to a family of modest means, Patrick Henry became a self-educated lawyer with a gift for speechmaking. In 1775 he delivered his most famous speech, "Give Me Liberty or Give Me Death," in which he encouraged the colonists of Virginia to use military force to defend individual freedom from British laws. His passionate speech ignited in many listeners a militant spirit that helped propel the colonists into the Revolutionary War.

THE LITERARY WORK

A speech delivered at St. John's Church in Richmond, Virginia, at a revolutionary convention held on March 23, 1775.

SYNOPSIS

Patrick Henry urges his fellow Virginians to arm themselves and form a united military force to face the increasing tyranny of the British government.

Events in History at the Time of the Speech

Communication in colonial America. Speech served as the main means of communication in colonial America. Printed newspapers and pamphlets existed, but most of the population was unable to read and write. Speeches thus became a popular avenue for people to disseminate and receive information. A standard style of speechmaking prevailed in legislatures and church services of the era. The style featured formal language and a roundabout rather than direct method of discussion. A flat tone of voice was often employed as well. Typically, speeches were not made up on the spot; instead, they were delivered from a prepared manuscript.

Another style of speechmaking appeared with the growth of a religious movement known as the Great Awakening, which lasted from about 1720 to 1760. The aim of this movement was to reform the Anglican Church from within and in-fuse new life into it. Speakers promoting the reform delivered emotionally charged sermons rather than the old flat-tone speeches of previous years.

The Great Awakening, inspired in large part by Reverend George Whitefield, reached out to all people at a time when organized churches involved only a minority of the American population. Whitefield, an Englishman, captivated audiences, calling on them to put their beliefs into action and live by their faith. In 1745 he visited Hanover County, Virginia, and roused colonists there with his fiery preaching.

Two years later, a Reverend Samuel Davies, who preached in the same style as Whitefield, arrived in Hanover County to stay. Sarah Henry, Patrick's mother, attended his services regularly. She brought her son along on those occasions. Patrick delighted in Davies's powerful speeches, and regarded the preacher as the finest orator he had ever heard. Davies's style of preaching was direct and emotional, yet dignified. He and other experimental preachers delivered heart-touching sermons in plain style, peppering their speeches with references to the Bible and nature. As time passed, Henry seemed to adopt some of Davies's characteristics in his own speeches about political issues.

Henry's speechmaking. Henry, like other colonial leaders of his time, had been schooled in the writings of the Greeks and Romans. Tutored by his father after reaching the age of ten, Henry learned Latin, Greek, math, and ancient and modern history. In this manner, he became familiar with the works of the Greeks and Romans who had perfected the art of persuasive speechmaking. Cato, to whom Patrick Henry was often compared, was one of the first to successfully use speech as a tool of persuasion in the Roman senate. Cato's fellow Roman, Cicero, had an eloquent style that became the model upon which succeeding lawyers based their legal arguments.

Though he drew on his knowledge of the classics in creating his speeches, Henry was also willing to violate many rules of classical speechmaking and to employ the techniques he had learned from the religious speakers of his time. Henry expressed himself in everyday language and made references to things that were familiar to his audience—the Bible, nature, and current events—thereby avoiding the most formal aspects of traditional speaking. He offended many Virginia aristocrats, who were taken aback by the unrestrained passion with which he spoke, his unrefined clothing, and his failure to mention Greek and Roman teachings. Another possible reason for his unpopularity with the Virginia aristocrats was his habit of delivering speeches not only to wealthier gentlemen in courts, legislatures, and conventions, but also informally to the general public as a spontaneous stump speaker, or traveling political speechmaker.

Henry was also influenced by the cultural movement known as the Enlightenment, which promoted reason and science as the way to truth. Practitioners felt they had an obligation to make the world a more perfect place. Henry applied the concept that people should behave in accordance with their beliefs to the political arena, contending that such a philosophy, when applied to government, could improve it. Henry spoke about political reform with as much passion as the new preachers of his day. He also utilized religious themes—such as the assurance that there is "a just God who presides over the destinies of nations" (Henry in McCants, p. 125)—to support his views.

The speaker in action. One of Henry's first law cases established the young lawyer as an orator to be reckoned with. In 1763 Anglican church officials had challenged Virginia's right to impose laws and determine the officials' salaries. The parsons contended that the British government alone had authority in such matters and that British law superseded Virginia law. The church officials won their case, and a final hearing was scheduled to determine the amount of back pay due the parsons. At this point, Henry took the place of the defeated lawyer who had earlier argued the case against the parsons. Henry argued at the hearing that Virginia did have the sole right to impose laws on her citizens. He further charged that the church officials' requests for salary increases at a time when the colony could not afford it was an affront to the common good.

As a result of Henry's powerful argument, the parsons—though they had won the initial judgment—were awarded just one penny in compensation. The case set a precedent for colonial independence from the Crown and made Henry the most prominent lawyer in Virginia. Though Henry's speech in the case proved effective, no record of it exists. In fact, many of his early speeches were not preserved. Only the reports of others convey the contents of these works.

Stamp Act rebellion. While American colonists were obliged to pay taxes to the distant British government, they had no say in the policies their taxes helped to finance. It was a situation that bred discontent, yet the colonists mostly complied with British policies through 1763. Only when the British Parliament started imposing limits on personal freedom, tighter trade restrictions, and heavier taxes did the colonists begin to revolt.

Open rebellion erupted in 1765 when the Stamp Act was passed. The Stamp Act affected nearly every segment of the colonial population, for it required the purchase of stamps for newspapers, games, marriage licenses, and other common goods. It raised the price of commodities and services and further offended the colonists because the income from selling the stamps was used to pay for the continued presence of British troops in America. The presence of British soldiers was already a source of frustration to colonists since their purpose after the French and Indian war was to enforce the laws of the Crown and suppress rebellion in the colonies.

Recently elected to serve in Virginia's assem-

A portrait of Patrick Henry painted by Thomas Sully.

bly, which was known as the House of Burgesses, Henry entered into the thick of the Stamp Act debate. He drafted a series of resolutions condemning the British Parliament for enacting the legislation. Laying the foundation for his future call to arms against the Crown, Henry blasted the measure as "illegal, unconstitutional, and unjust" (Henry in Wirt, p. 92). In a fiery speech—the first of several he would deliver on the subject—he insisted that only the colonists themselves had the right to determine and enforce laws in America. Henry argued that "the inhabitants of this

colony, are not bound to yield obedience to any law or ordinance whatever, designed to impose any taxation whatsoever upon them, other than the laws or ordinances of [its own] General Assembly" (Henry in Wirt, p. 93).

Henry's words were treasonous. He had attacked the supremacy of the British Parliament and the king. Marked as a traitor in the eyes of the British Crown, Henry would come to view the delivery of the speech as one of his proudest moments. Later, in preparation for his death, he included a sealed copy of his Stamp-Act resolutions with his will, along with the following comment:

> The within resolutions ... formed the first opposition to the stamp-act.... Violent debates ensued.... The great point of resistance to British taxation was universally established in the colonies. This brought on the war, which finally separated the two countries, and gave independence to ours.
>
> (Henry in McCants, p. 46)

Galvanized by Henry's words, the Virginia Assembly passed his resolutions declaring the Stamp Act illegal, and the American colonists launched a campaign to repeal it. In October 1765 they formed the Stamp Act Congress, which led to a boycott of British goods. British manufacturers, crippled by the boycott, also called for repeal of the legislation. Yielding to all this protest, the British Parliament abolished the Stamp Act in March 1766.

Parliament, however, passed other restrictive measures, including a Tea Act that actually reduced the price of British tea sold to the Americans. Great Britain's intent, however, was to edge out the competition—Dutch tea—and gain even tighter control of the American colonies. The legislation gave certain tea merchants monopolies while unfairly excluding other merchants. In the end the Tea Act backfired. Colonists dumped British tea into Boston Harbor, an action that became known as the Boston Tea Party. In response the British sent more troops to Boston, halted imports of food and other goods, outlawed public gatherings, and replaced locally named officials with their own British appointments. The colonists, in turn, formed the Continental Congress to decide how to stop British tyranny once and for all.

Continental Congress. Delegates from every colony except Georgia met at Carpenter's Hall in Philadelphia on September 5, 1774. One of the most prestigious gatherings of leaders ever assembled, the first Continental Congress included Patrick Henry, George Washington, Richard Henry Lee, John and Samuel Adams, and Joseph Galloway. Along with Richard Henry Lee, Patrick Henry was singled out as the most effective speaker in the group. It was here, at a gathering in which the colonies struggled to protect their separate interests yet act cooperatively, that Henry informed his fellow countrymen that "distinctions between Virginians, Pennsylvanians, New Yorkers, and New Englanders are no more. I am not a Virginian, but an American" (Henry in Willison, p. 245). A delegate from Connecticut, Silas Deane, predicted that if Henry's future

speeches were equal to the small samples he delivered at the Continental Congress, they would indeed be remarkable. "I can give you no idea of the music of his voice, or the high-wrought yet natural elegance of his style and manner" (Deane in Willison, p. 246).

The first Continental Congress endorsed another boycott of British goods and agreed not to export any American products to Great Britain or her territories. The representatives also drafted a list of grievances against the British Crown and set a timetable of six months for the Congress to meet again and prepare for war if colonial demands were not met by the British government.

Birth of Virginia's army. In November 1774, two months after the first Continental Congress, Patrick Henry called a meeting in Hanover County, Virginia, to discuss the formation of an army. With British troops flowing into Boston and New England, he saw the need to prepare for the forthcoming military conflict with Great Britain. In another of his animated speeches, Henry urged the formation of a volunteer army organized into independent companies. Hearing of his efforts in Hanover, other counties followed his lead; by the end of 1774, there were at least seven independent companies in Virginia and dozens more throughout the other colonies.

VARIETY OF LEADERSHIP

The success of the American Revolution can be attributed in large part to a variety of extraordinary leaders. Thomas Jefferson provided the philosophical basis; George Washington the military expertise; and Patrick Henry the powerful oratory that roused the colonists to action. He swayed people with forceful speech: "We have done everything that could be done, to avert the storm which is now coming on. We have petitioned—we have remonstrated—we have supplicated—we have prostrated ourselves before the throne ... we must fight! ... An appeal to arms and to the God of hosts, is all that is left us!" Even colonists previously opposed to fighting the British were moved to Henry's side by such fiery speech (Henry in McCants, pp.124-25).

Henry's rallying cry. Four months later, in March 1775, the colony of Virginia assembled delegates to meet in a Convention of the People. It was the second such convention to be held in the colony. The delegates met at St. John's Church in Richmond, Virginia. After three days they had made no definite progress in regard to the rebellion against England. Then, on March 23, 1775, Henry made his move. Convinced that the newly formed independent companies needed to consolidate into a united colonial army, he drafted resolutions to that effect. Departing from traditional rules of protocol, Henry delivered his most famous speech in support of his motion to organize a colonial army and prepare for war. The church was filled to capacity, and spectators flowed into the streets. Others peered through windows to catch a glimpse of the proceedings and hear the inspiring oratory.

A PATRIOT'S VIEW OF SLAVERY

In his "Give Me Liberty or Give Me Death" speech, Patrick Henry compared the plight of the colonists to that of black slaves, proclaiming that peace should never be "purchased at the price of chains and slavery" (Henry in Willison, p. 267). He personally found slavery a miserable practice, "inconsistent with the Bible and destructive to liberty," yet Henry, like so many of his fellow Virginians, owned slaves. He remarked that he could not justify this, and noted that the practice could bring trouble in the future: "I could say many things on the subject, a serious view of which gives a gloomy perspective to future times" (Henry in Willison, p. 267).

The Speech in Focus

The contents. Henry brought before the assembly of convention delegates three resolutions:

1. That Virginia form a militia of gentlemen and yeoman (farmers).
2. That such a militia is necessary to protect Virginians from further violations of their freedoms.
3. That the militia be formed immediately and that a committee be established to organize, arm, and discipline the militia.

Other colonies had already passed similar proposals, yet Henry's met with heated objection by men who considered such a move premature. There was a great deal of debate among the delegates. While Thomas Jefferson sided with Henry immediately, Richard Henry Lee opposed the measure. George Washington remained silent in pensive deliberation, presumably waiting for further argument to sway him one way or another. Realizing he needed to prove his case, Henry stood up and delivered his most famous and rousing speech. He relied on sudden inspiration, for his remarks were delivered off the cuff, without preparation. As a result, no official transcript of the speech exists. The speech was instead pieced together later through eyewitness accounts.

Henry addressed the entire convention at St. John's Church, but he specifically appealed to its president, Peyton Randolph. Arguing that the occasion was no time for ceremony, Henry asked that he might openly address the assembly out of turn. After a brief apology for daring to disagree with some of his distinguished fellows, Henry launched into his speech.

According to one listener, the judge St. George Tucker, Henry began with the warning that the times called for him to speak his mind without concern for whom he might offend. He proceeded to address the gentlemen who hesitated to take up arms and begin the fight. He used riveting words to rebuke these gentlemen, whom Henry felt had fooled themselves into thinking that the conflict could be resolved through means other than war:

> Were we disposed to be of the number of those, who having eyes, see not, and having ears, hear not, the things which so nearly concern their temporal salvation?
>
> (Henry in McCants, p. 124)

Henry asked them to open their eyes to the warlike preparations that Great Britain was already making, noting that the colonists had been trying to settle their differences with England through peaceful means for the previous ten years. He pointed to the presence of British troops in New England and contended that they would soon launch a full-scale attack on the colonists: "Has Great Britain any enemy in this quarter of the world to call for all this accumulation of navies and armies? No, sir, she has none. They are meant for us; they can be meant for no other" (Henry in McCants, p. 124). Henry informed the assembly of colonists that they had already petitioned, boycotted, and pleaded, and all in vain. He compared the British to slavers trying to cast the Americans in chains and declared that the colonists could no longer rely on wishful hopes for peaceful solutions: "If we wish to be free . . . we must fight!—I repeat it, sir, we must fight!!!" (Henry in McCants, p. 125).

Anticipating objections that the colonies were too weak to defeat Britain, Henry pointed to their advantages—their numbers, resources, and the likelihood that other nations would come to their aid: "Three millions of people armed in the holy cause of liberty, and in such a country as that which we possess, are invincible.... Besides, sir, we shall not fight our battles alone. There is a just God who presides over the destinies of nations, and who will raise up friends to fight our battles for us" (Henry in McCants, p. 125). Henry insisted that the Americans would also not be fighting alone because they would have the aid of a just God. "The battle, sir," he continued, "is not to the strong alone; it is to the vigilant, the active, the brave" (Henry in McCants, p. 125). Henry's speech rose to a feverish climax when he stated his own preference for death over political enslavement to the British. His appeal was an implicit exhortation to listeners to follow his example and prepare to put their lives on the line in a desperate struggle for liberty:

> Is life so dear, or peace so sweet, as to be purchased at the price of chains and slavery? Forbid it, Almighty God!
> I know not what other course others may take. But as for me—give me liberty, or give me death!
>
> (Henry in Willison, p. 266-67)

According to reports by another listener, John Roane, Henry's speech showed a mastery not only of words, but also of gestures, delivery, and facial expressions.

> When he said, "Is life so dear, or peace so sweet, as to be purchased at the price of chains and slavery?" he stood in the attitude of a condemned galley slave.... His form was bowed, his wrists were crossed.... He turned toward the timid Loyalists in the house, who were quaking with terror at ... participating in proceedings which would be visited with the penalties of treason by the British crown, and he slowly bent his form nearer to the earth and said, "I know not what course others may take".... After remaining in this posture of humiliation long enough ... he arose proudly and exclaimed, "But as for me" ... then the loud, clear, triumphant note, "Give me liberty" ... and as each syllable of the word "liberty" echoed through the building, his fetters were shivered, his arms were hurled apart ... his hands were open, and his arms elevated and extended.... He let his left hand fall powerless to his side, and clenched his right hand firmly, as if holding a dagger with the point aimed at his breast.... He closed the grand appeal with

the solemn words, "or give me death".... And he suited the action to the word by a blow upon the left breast with his right hand, which seemed to drive the dagger to the patriot's heart.

> (Roane in Willison, p. 267-68)

At the conclusion of Henry's speech, the convention exploded with enthusiastic support. Henry's resolutions to create a Virginia militia passed by five votes, and war preparations began. As time passed, it became clear that Henry's words continued to linger in the minds of those who heard them. One man, Colonel Edward Carrington, was so moved by the oratory that he asked to be buried at the spot where he heard the speech, just outside St. John's Church (he was in fact buried there in 1810). Another listener called the speech "one of the most vehement and animated pieces of eloquence that ever had been delivered," while another listener commented that Henry created a "tempest" with his oration, and compared Henry to Cato addressing the Roman senate. When the Virginia assembly officially convened three months later, in June 1775, every member dressed in homespun rather than imported clothing and had "Liberty or Death" sewed or painted on the breast of his coat. Henry's words became a rallying cry and helped ensure that the unplanned speech would be remembered as one of the finest in history.

A REBEL TRIUMPHS

Initially opposed to Henry's resolution to arm the colonists, Edmond Randolph changed his mind after hearing Henry's powerful speech. "Henry trampled on rules," observed Randolph, "yet triumphed ... perhaps beyond his own expectation" (Randolph in Wirt, p. 260).

Years later, the American leader Thomas Jefferson would look back and say of Henry, "He left all of us far behind.... He gave the first impulse to the ball of Revolution.... He was the idol of the country beyond anyone that ever lived" (Jefferson in Willison, p. 9).

For More Information

Handlin, Oscar, and Lilian Handlin. *Liberty in Expansion.* New York: Harper and Row, 1989.

MacLeod, D. J. *Slavery, Race, and the American Revolution.* Cambridge, England: Cambridge University Press, 1975.

McCants, David A. *Patrick Henry, the Orator.* New York: Greenwood, 1990.

Willison, George F. *Patrick Henry and His World.* Garden City, New York: Doubleday, 1969.

Wirt, William. *Patrick Henry: Life, Correspondence, and Speeches.* 3 Vols. New York: Burt Franklin, 1969.

Gulliver's Travels

by
Jonathan Swift

orn in Ireland in 1667, Jonathan Swift spent many years in England working closely with the British government. During this time, he witnessed corruption, waste, and fierce power struggles between rival political parties and religious factions. When he returned to Ireland in 1714, Swift saw firsthand the ill effects of Britain's social and economic policies on the Irish people and became a leading advocate for Irish independence. He also belonged to the Anglican Church (Church of England; known in Ireland as the Protestant Church of Ireland). *Gulliver's Travels,* a story set and written in the same historical era, was published after Swift returned to Ireland and became dean of the Protestant St. Patrick's Cathedral. Drawing on his experience of the times, he created a series of outrageous adventures that exposed aspects of government, war, and human nature.

Events in History at the Time of the Novel

Restoration England: Tories vs. Whigs. In 1660 the Restoration began when Charles Stuart (Charles II) became king of England and thus "restored" the Stuart family to the British throne. The return of the Stuarts to the monarchy meant the return of the Anglican Church as the dominant national religion and ultimately the establishment of the Tory party as the leading political power. The Tories, mainly landowning nobles and high church officials, were strong supporters of the Crown as well as the Anglican Church.

> **THE LITERARY WORK**
>
> A novel that takes place from 1699 to 1715; published in 1726.
>
> **SYNOPSIS**
>
> A seafaring doctor has a series of wild and enlightening adventures on four separate voyages overseas.

Protestants themselves, they vehemently opposed Protestant "Dissenters"—the minority of Protestants who rejected the Anglican Church. These Dissenters joined with the Roman Catholics to form the Whigs, the opposition party to the Tories.

The Test Act. The major factor that prompted hatred between the two parties was the passage of the Test Act in 1673. This act required all government employees—civil and military—to receive the sacrament according to the Anglican Church and profess their belief in Anglican doctrine. It was a law that prevented most Whigs from holding office or serving in the military, thereby strengthening Tory power. The Whigs naturally opposed the act, while the Tories supported it. It became a major point of debate during the 1700s and was championed by Swift after he joined the Tory party in 1710.

As the years passed, the rivalry between the Tories and Whigs mounted. The two parties disagreed not only on religion but also on nearly every political issue. Most Tory and Whig government officials voted strictly according to party lines. They rarely compromised even for the good of the nation. As a result, little was accomplished except by force and domination. Each party carried out its own policy when it had the majority in Parliament and the favor of the Crown, but

---

FROM WHIG TO TORY

In 1710 Swift shifted loyalties from the Whigs to the Tories. Swift explained that he simply realized he was more in line with the views of the Tories than the Whigs. In truth, however, Swift's political philosophy lay somewhere in the middle of both extremes. His primary loyalties were to only two causes: Ireland and the Anglican Church.

---

when the tide turned and the opposing party took power, members of the ousted party sometimes faced exile and imprisonment. In *Gulliver's Travels,* Swift mocks the behavior of the Tories and Whigs in his portrayal of the Tramecksans and Slamecksans of Lilliput (also known as the High Heels and the Low Heels because of their respective footwear). Gulliver explains:

> The animosities between these two parties run so high, that they will neither eat nor drink, nor talk with each other.
>
> (Swift, *Gulliver's Travels,* p. 35)

Gulliver goes on to describe the careful balance that the incoming ruler of Lilliput must strike between the two parties—a feat he accomplishes by wearing one high heel and one low heel. Here Swift is directly comparing the future Lilliputian emperor to the future British monarch, George II, who surrounded himself with Tories and Whigs so that he would gain the throne no matter which party controlled Parliament.

Whigs and Catholics rebound. In 1681 the Whigs found an unlikely ally: the Crown. The Whigs included Catholics, and King Charles II had underlying Catholic sympathies. His brother James was a Catholic and next in line for the throne. When Parliament tried to force Charles to sign a bill that would deny James his right to the throne, Charles refused and defeated the measure. This event was known as the "Popish Plot," and its outcome led to the crowning of

James II and the return of Catholic power to Great Britain in 1685.

From James II to the Glorious Revolution. King James immediately repealed the Test Act and began to fill military and government posts with Whigs. Outraged by his actions, the Anglican-dominated Parliament entered into secret negotiations with William of Orange, the Protestant Dutch husband of James's Protestant daughter, Mary, to assume the throne. William arrived in England in December 1688, and James fled to France without a fight. William became king after this "Glorious Revolution"—so called because no blood was shed.

William and war. Shortly after William became king, he entered into a war with France. Known as William's War, the conflict concerned trade and religion. With King Charles II of Spain childless and nearing death, England and its Protestant allies wanted to ensure that Spain and its numerous European holdings would remain in friendly hands and not fall under control of the French Catholics, who were rivals in trade and religion. Louis XIV, France's Catholic king, declared war on Spain in 1689 and wound up fighting against the English, Dutch, Spanish, and German allies.

Though supportive of the allied war effort on the continent, England was simultaneously at war with Ireland. An uprising had erupted, led by Irish Catholics who were sympathetic to the French and wanted freedom from British domination. William feared that the Irish, if left unchecked, would enable a French invasion of England through Ireland's open ports. Fighting on two fronts, England mounted massive war debts during nearly a decade of battle. A peace treaty known as the Partition Treaties was finally signed in 1697. Land was partitioned among the allies, but England received little acreage. Spain's possessions were instead divided among Europe's two leading noble families, the Bourbons and the Hapsburgs. William was widely criticized for allowing this to happen. To save face—and perhaps his life—he declared war on the Spanish and French and thus began the War of Spanish Succession.

Queen Anne, last Stuart monarch. In 1702 William died and Queen Anne assumed the British throne. England under Queen Anne continued to fight the War of Spanish Succession, trying to make sure that neither the Bourbons nor the Hapsburgs gained too much power in Europe. During Anne's reign, the war became in-

Portrait of Jonathan Swift.

creasingly brutal. In 1709 the English author Daniel Defoe lamented the hate-filled atmosphere in England:

> We fight not like men but like devils, like furies; we fight not as if we would kill one another only, but as we would tear one another's soul out of our bodies.
>
> (Defoe in Collins, p. 103)

Defoe was referring not only to the physical war in France and Spain but to the ongoing power struggle in Parliament between the Tories and Whigs. The Whigs, whose merchants and manufacturers were profiting from the war, wanted the fighting to continue, while the landowning Tories wished the war would end because of its negative impact on property values.

Swift, Harley, and the end of the war. While the Whigs pursued the total destruction of France through 1710, the Tories began a campaign to end the war. Their efforts were greatly aided by Swift, who had just defected from the Whig party. Swift became editor of the *Examiner*, a Tory newspaper. His daily attacks on the Whigs and the war swayed public opinion in favor of peace. While the Tory leader Robert Harley ne-

gotiated a settlement with the French, Swift wrote pamphlets supporting Harley's efforts, and these pamphlets helped ensure Harley's success. The result in 1713 was the Treaty of Utrecht, an agreement that officially ended the war.

Swift moves back to Ireland. Though Swift loyally served the Tory ministry under Queen Anne and helped end the war that was bankrupting the nation, he was not rewarded for his service. Instead, he was passed over for preferment to a good post in the Church of England and was forced to press all the contacts he had in order to get a position as dean of St. Patrick's Cathedral in Dublin, Ireland. In *Gulliver's Travels,* he satirizes his mistreatment by the queen. Gulliver, a giant among the Lilliputians, saves the queen and her castle from great calamity by urinating on a fire that had engulfed the royal palace. While Gulliver feels he has done the queen and nation a great service, she is appalled by the "vulgar" manner in which he saved her and puts him on trial for treason. Similarly, Queen Anne viewed Swift as too vulgar to be a leader in the Church of England because of his sharp tongue—even though his biting words had helped end the war. In 1714 Queen Anne died and George I became king of England. A strong Whig supporter, the king detested Swift.

Ireland's tumultuous history with England. Beginning in the fifteenth century, the British monarchy tried to exert control over Ireland. The monarchy feared that Irish Catholics would back invasions by France or Spain and so sought to oust them from power and install a friendly, Protestant government. Beginning with England's King Henry VIII, Irish officials and nobles were forced to swear an oath of allegiance to the crown. If they refused, their lands were confiscated. These and other policies led to open rebellion, and a series of wars between Ireland and the Crown.

In 1603, after nine years of war, the English finally conquered Ireland, but success came just as Queen Elizabeth died. She was succeeded by James I, who offered hope to Irish Catholics. To the disapproval of his English subjects, James pardoned all who had participated in the war, officially proclaimed Ireland a separate kingdom, and granted it civil rule. Yet English influence spread across Ireland, and the nation became increasingly dominated by England's king and Protestant Parliament. Irish land was again confiscated and redistributed. Much of the land was handed over to Protestant English settlers who were sent in droves to "colonize" Ireland. By 1660 Protestants made up the majority of the Irish population.

Trade restrictions. With the help of this Protestant majority, England began to tighten its reign over Ireland. In 1666 it instituted trade restrictions on Ireland's imports and exports. The restrictions included a ban on exporting live cattle—the mainstay of Ireland's economy. In 1670 the Navigation Act required that all imports bound for Ireland pass first through British ports, where they would be taxed. Other trade laws were imposed as well. In 1699 Ireland was prohibited from exporting wool goods to any nation but England. The Irish were devastated by these restrictions; poverty increased rapidly, as did civil unrest.

WRITERS SHOULD BE HEARD, NOT SEEN

Like most men of his age, Swift believed that writers should remain anonymous. He never attached his name to anything he published, though most knew he was the author. He felt that when an author was known, it limited his freedom of expression because of fear of government persecution.

Anti-Catholic policies. Catholics were systematically stripped of power and rights by the English Crown. In 1691 the British Parliament passed an act requiring all Catholics to denounce their faith. Four years later the government prohibited Catholics from sending their children to religious schools abroad and from owning weapons. In 1704 Catholics were stripped of all political power, land, and individual rights unless they joined the Protestant Church of Ireland. The Crown also tried to devalue Irish money by issuing "Wood's coins"—these coins would have made Ireland wholly dependent on England for trade because no other nation would accept them.

Perhaps most disheartening to the Irish people, however, was the British government's effort to replace the Irish Gaelic language with English. From 1711 to 1800, nothing was printed in the Irish language. The language and culture of Ireland ceased to be taught in public schools, inciting a growing hostility in the Irish people over the decline of their heritage and national identity.

Irish politics. When Swift returned to Ireland in 1714, he saw firsthand the crushing effects of the British government's social and economic policies on the Irish. Poverty and famine were rampant, and the countryside was ravaged from centuries of warfare. Swift began to use his literary talent as a pamphleteer for the Irish cause. First he wrote *A Proposal for the Universal Use of Irish Manufacturers,* a pamphlet that urged the Irish to buy only Irish-made products and to boycott English goods until the restrictive import/export laws were repealed. The tract was published anonymously, as were all of Swift's writings, and was banned by the British government. The pamphlet's printer was arrested, but he was acquitted of charges after nine attempts to convict him. The Irish had achieved their first small victory.

After that mild success, Swift began his famous M. B. Drapier letters, which urged the public not to accept Wood's coins and to seek independence from England. He aimed to inspire the Irish to take action: "By the laws of God, of nature, of nations, and of your country, you are and ought to be as free a people as your brethren in England . . . All government without consent of the governed is the very definition of slavery" (Swift in Collins, p. 185). Incensed by the pamphlets, the Crown offered substantial monetary rewards for anyone who would name the author. Though it was commonly known to be Swift, no one turned him in, and his efforts led to the withdrawal of Wood's coin patent in 1725. Swift was hailed as a national hero and remains so to this day.

The Novel in Focus

Plot—Book I. *Gulliver's Travels*—which contains four books chronicling four separate journeys—is the story of the adventures of Lemuel Gulliver, a humble English ship's surgeon. The first book, *A Voyage to Lilliput,* begins in 1699 when Gulliver accepts a job as a ship's doctor aboard a cargo vessel bound for the East Indies. During the journey, a violent storm wrecks the ship and Gulliver lands on the shore of an unknown island. Exhausted from combating the storm and swimming to shore, he falls asleep on the beach and wakes to find himself tied to the ground by dozens of tiny ropes. He soon learns he has landed on the island of Lilliput, which is inhabited by six-inch-tall people. The Lilliputians hold him captive but feed and clothe him and generally treat him well.

Gulliver learns that there are two rival parties in Lilliput, the Tramecksans and the Slamecksans, also known as the High Heels and Low

Heels on account of the height of their shoes. He also learns that there is a bitter feud between Lilliput and a neighboring country, Blefuscu, due to an edict issued by an ancient emperor that required all subjects to break their eggs on the small end only. A civil war broke out between those who wanted to break their eggs on the big end and those who adhered to the law and broke their eggs on the small end. The Big Endians and Little Endians, as the two groups are known, became bitter rivals—much like the Protestants and Catholics—and the Big Endians went into exile in Blefuscu.

The Lilliputians gradually accept Gulliver and give him limited freedom in exchange for his help. He is asked to aid Lilliput in the war against Blefuscu. Gulliver does so by wading into the water and capturing the Blefuscu fleet. After refusing to destroy Blefuscu, however, he begins to lose favor with Lilliput's emperor. Gulliver's troubles increase when the royal castle catches fire and he urinates on the inferno to put it out. Although his action saves the castle and queen, he is accused of high treason because of the "vulgar" means he employed to douse the blaze. He escapes back to England before punishment can be exacted.

Book II. Within two months of his return, Gulliver sets sail for the West Indies. Again a storm overtakes the ship and he winds up on an island called Brobdingnag. He quickly realizes that he is in a land of giants and scrambles to keep from being crushed. Discovered by a farmer who is sixty feet tall, as are all the inhabitants of this empire, Gulliver is given to the farmer's nine-year-old daughter, Glumdalclitch. He is then made to perform for the people of Brobdingnag. The queen is so amused that she buys him for herself. He and Glumdalclitch move to the royal residence and become intimates of the king and queen.

Curious about Gulliver and his homeland, the royal couple question their small guest about his origins and culture. He fascinates them with talk of British politics and his own life. But the king and queen grow appalled when he tries to share his knowledge of weapon construction, for the Brobdingnags have no concept of modern warfare or offensive weapons.

A box is constructed to transport Gulliver so that he can accompany the king and queen on excursions and tour the countryside with Glumdalclitch. On a trip to the sea, his box is picked up by an eagle, carried for miles over the ocean, and dropped into the water. The box is eventu-

ally discovered by some British sailors, who tow it back to England.

Book III. Restless again after a few months with his family in England, Gulliver gains passage aboard a ship bound for Indochina. He arrives at his destination, and then, in order to make some money, sails to some neighboring islands to trade. Before reaching the islands, Gulliver is overtaken by pirates and set adrift on a dinghy to die. Instead he lands on a deserted island, from which he is rescued by a flying island called Laputa. Laputa, a large land mass that floats in the sky, rules its various territories by pelting rocks—like bombs—at inhabitants who rebel or step out of line.

Gulliver visits territories such as Glubbdubdrib, which is filled with sorcerers and magicians. These magicians are able to conjure any ancient person for a period of twenty-four hours. Gulliver is at first delighted at this ability. At Gulliver's request, Aristotle, Descartes, and other distinguished men are called up by the sorcerers. The reality of these legendary figures proves gravely disappointing, however, and Gulliver departs for another island. He then sails for Japan and home to England.

A MAN OF COMPROMISE
~

Swift was a man of moderation and always worked for compromise. Having served as both a Tory and a Whig, he saw the danger of the extreme positions on each side. "In order to preserve the Constitution in Church and State, whoever has a true value for either would be sure to avoid the extremes of Whig for the sake of the former, and the extremes of the Tory for the sake of the latter" (Swift in Collins, p. 58). In *Gulliver's Travels*, Swift expresses his philosophy in his depiction of an adviser's solution to a conflict over which end of an egg to break, the big end or the little one; the adviser states simply: "all true believers shall break their eggs at the convenient end" (*Gulliver's Travels*, p. 36).

Book IV. After five months at home, Gulliver makes his final voyage as captain of a ship bound for Barbados. He is captured by pirates and again set adrift in a dinghy to die. But, as before, he lands safely on an island. When he first arrives, he sees the most hateful-looking creatures he has ever encountered. The creatures, which he learns later are called Yahoos, walk on their hind legs and have hair very similar to human hair. Gulliver then encounters a horse called a Houyhnhnm, who makes Gulliver feel welcome. Gulliver soon realizes the Houyhnhnms are the most intelligent, rational, and good-hearted creatures he has ever met.

SCRIBLERUS CLUB

In about 1712, Swift and fellow writers in London formed the Scriblerus Club to encourage literary pursuits. The others in this famous society included English playwright William Congreve, Scottish historian David Hume, and Irish nationalist leader Charles Stuart Parnell.

Gulliver stays with the Houyhnhnms, who treat him graciously even though they regard him as a Yahoo. He learns that among the Houyhnhnms there is no disease, unhappiness, or violence. The longer he lives with them and the more he learns about their nature, the more he loves them. He decides to spend the rest of his life with these perfect creatures. But in Houyhnhnm society Yahoos are subservient because of their unreasonable and violent natures. They do not live with the Houyhnhnms, and Gulliver is unable to convince the Houyhnhnms to make an exception in his case. To his deep disap-

---

SWIFT IN A LETTER TO CHARLES FORD

I have finished my Travells, and I am now transcribing them; they are admirable Things, and will wonderfully mend the World. (Swift in Smith, p. 122)

---

pointment, he is forced to return to England and the "European Yahoos." Thoroughly disgusted with these European Yahoos, Gulliver buys two horses and teaches them the Houyhnhnm language. Thereafter Gulliver communes with his horses and shuns the rest of the world.

How Gulliver's hosts treat him. In Lilliput Gulliver is a giant among men. He is treated first with fear, then with curiosity, and finally is seen as an ally to be used in the Lilliputians' war with Blefuscu. All of Gulliver's personal possessions—

penknife, gold coins, comb—become menacing and overwhelming objects because of their grotesque proportions. For example, the gold in his possession is enough to make Lilliput rich beyond measure, while his knife is so massive that it is capable of wiping out dozens of Lilliputians at a single stroke. In drawing Gulliver larger than life, the novel illustrates the human tendency in Swift's time to blow things out of proportion. The story shows how easily real-life religious and political differences can be inflated and lead to tragic consequences, such as the War of Spanish Succession.

In Brobdingnag, Gulliver is tiny compared to his hosts and inspires great curiosity and intrigue. Because he is so small, he is not seen as a threat. He is instead exhibited as a sort of circus side-show performer. Here Gulliver serves as the counterpart of the real midgets, monkeys, puppets, and freaks used to entertain the English in the eighteenth century. Gulliver fears that his giant hosts will find him a mate to bear his children. In fact, such a family was put on display in 1712 in London. The exhibit, which became known as the "Little Family," featured a man who was only three feet tall, his pregnant wife, and their little horse.

In Houyhnhnm-land, Gulliver is seen as a Yahoo—the lowest of all creatures. He is eventually forced to leave the island against his will because his hosts fear that he will corrupt the pure Houyhnhnms. The incident reflects Swift's view of human beings based on his own experiences and observations. Swift felt that, although people are capable of acting reasonably, the quest for power and other such "treasures" overwhelms rational thought and decent behavior, causing them instead to act like Yahoos.

Sources. The naive or "gullible" traveler was a well-known literary device, used earlier by writers such as Plato, Lucian (a personal favorite of Swift's), and Sir Thomas More. Swift himself had created such a character as early as 1711 in his story *A New Journey to Paris.* The traveler in this story, whose name is Sieur du Baudrier, is a translator or reporter, much like Gulliver, who describes how the Tories negotiated peace in the War of Spanish Succession.

Other possible sources for *Gulliver's Travels* include conversations that Swift had with fellow writers in the Scriblerus Club over a plan to create a group novel. The group agreed that the novel would satirize "all the false tastes in learning"—a theme that is conveyed in parts of *Gulliver's Travels.* Swift also drew on personal experiences in creating the novel. Models for characters and political intrigue depicted in *Gulliver's Travels* came directly from his own knowledge of the British government.

Reviews. Swift wrote the first two books of *Gulliver's Travels* from 1721-1723. The fourth was written by January 1724, but the third book wasn't completed until 1725. With the help of Swift's close friend and printer, Alexander Pope, the novel made money. The first printing sold out in one week, in large part because the novel appealed to people of all stations in life. Contemporaries of Swift viewed Gulliver as "a happy man" and the book as nothing more than a humorous adventure (Hunting, p. 96). By the end of the eighteenth century, however, the underlying messages of the book were detected, and they prompted public outrage. Only the third book was deemed acceptable, while the rest—especially the last book—was considered highly offensive. This sentiment was echoed through the nineteenth century. In fact, Swift's stated purpose of the book was "to vex the world rather than divert it" (Hunting, p. 96). The epitaph on Swift's grave declares that all his life he fought for liberty and that he hoped to serve as a model for all who struggle for justice. With *Gulliver's Travels*, Swift was most successful, for the novel continues to stimulate thoughts on the quest for both liberty and justice.

For More Information

Beckett, J. C. *The Making of Modern Ireland: 1603-1923.* New York: Alfred A. Knopf, 1966.

Collins, John Churton. *Jonathan Swift: A Biographical and Critical Study.* London: Chatto & Windus, Picadilly, 1893.

Kamen, Henry. *The War of Succession in Spain 1700-15.* London: Weidenfeld & Nicolson, 1969.

Hunting, Robert. *Jonathan Swift.* Revised Edition. Boston: Twayne, 1989.

Plumb, J. H. *The First Four Georges.* New York: Macmillan, 1957.

Smith, David Nichol, ed. *The Letters of Jonathan Swift to Charles Ford.* Oxford: Clarendon Press, 1935.

Swift, Jonathan. *Gulliver's Travels.* New York: Pocket Library, 1957.

Hamlet

by
William Shakespeare

William Shakespeare was fascinated not only by human nature but also by the tumultuous history of rulers. From the combination of these two interests came a number of plays concerning the corrupting influence of power and ambition. Shakespeare wrote *Hamlet* in approximately 1600, after completing a series of history plays (*Richard II*, **Henry IV Part I** [also covered in *Literature and Its Times*], *Henry IV Part II*, and *Henry V*) in which he detailed the complex and often deadly subject of succession to the throne. By the time Shakespeare created *Hamlet*, his characters had gained a high degree of realism and he had become adept at portraying both the positive and negative effects of power. Though a Danish prince of the legendary past, Hamlet was developed into a character whom English audiences of the early 1600s could well understand.

Events in History at the Time the Play Takes Place

Historian of Denmark. A mixture of legend and fact, the story of Hamlet harks back to Iceland in the 800s. A poem by Snaebjorn (preserved by Snorri Sturluson in the *Prose Edda*) mentioned a semi-historical character named Amleth (Hamlet). Two hundred years later, an assistant priest in Denmark, Saxo Grammaticus, included the legend in his history of Denmark (*Gesta Danorum*, or *The Exploits of the Danes*). Saxo had set out to record Danish history, a task that he completed up to the year 1185 in sixteen books, the first nine of which dealt with the legendary past and introduced Prince Amleth. Catching the fancy of the public, Saxo's Amleth tale found its

THE LITERARY WORK

A play set in Denmark before the Viking Age (before 780 A.D.); first performed about 1601.

SYNOPSIS

The king of Denmark is murdered by his brother, who subsequently marries the king's widow and takes the throne. The king's son, Prince Hamlet, suspects treachery and then sets out to discover the truth about his father's death. In the end, he exacts a revenge that leads to tragic consequences.

way into popular song at the end of the 1400s. In 1514 a translation of Saxo's work appeared in English, including the tale of Amleth. Such a prince probably did exist, but there is no positive evidence to prove this; how much of Saxo's history is fact and how much is fiction remains uncertain. Historians question the accuracy of Saxo's tale, but there are few other sources from which to glean information.

Medieval Denmark. Scholars date the beginning of the Middle Ages from the 400s A.D., after the fall of the Roman Empire. According to tradition, Prince Amleth came from an area of Denmark known as Jutland around this time. One scholar maintains that Amleth was "in truth a historical character regnant [ruling] in Jutland, toward the close of the sixth century" (Johnston, p. 192). Although less specific about the time in which he lived, similar information about Amleth appears in Denmark outside the castle that served as the model for the one in

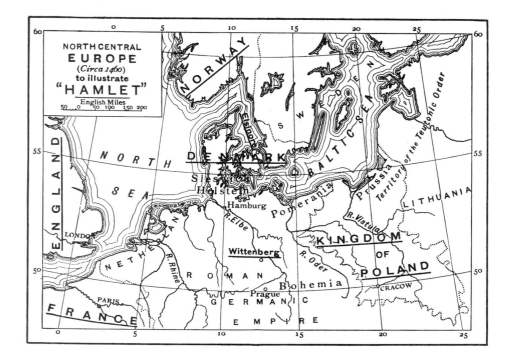

A map of north central Europe showing Denmark, the setting of Shakespeare's *Hamlet*.

Hamlet. On a sandstone plaque are the following words:

> The legend tells of a king's son Amleth who lived in Jutland before the Viking Age. In the Middle Ages Saxo wrote down the tale about him. In the Renaissance, Shakespeare retold Hamlet's life and set it at this castle.
>
> (Dollerup, p. 236)

Due to the lack of early sources, little is known about the Danish Middle Ages. The earliest documentation on Denmark concerns the period around 720, when the area included places known as south Jutland, Scania, and the Danish Isles. By 810 it had grown into a kingdom of three main provinces: Jutland, Zealand, and Scania, and some smaller provinces. Especially Scania and Jutland showed a willingness to act independently, suggesting these provinces or portions of them had operated as separate chiefdoms or kingdoms in the past.

The three provinces elected a common king, whose authority and royal family were all that bound them together. While the king became the most important and powerful landowner among the nobles, he did not claim to have a God-given right to rule, for Christianity had not yet been adopted in Denmark. Not until 960 would the Catholic Church become firmly established in the land. Yet Shakespeare clearly includes Christian touches in his play, such as the concept of a hell in which unrepentant sinners suffer everlasting torment. Such touches are but a few of many details from Shakespeare's own era that the playwright grafted onto the older setting. As noted above, the Elsinore castle in *Hamlet* was modeled after the palace built under Denmark's King Frederick II (1559-88). Intended as a fortress, the castle had red brick walls enclosed in sandstone and fine brass guns that sat visibly on the ramparts for protection. The splendidly furnished fortress, called Kronberg Castle, became known far and wide as one of the most marvelous palaces in all of Europe at the time.

Foreign relations. In *Hamlet,* the conflict between Norway and Denmark is a backdrop to the main action of the play. The Danish king—Hamlet's father—has killed King Fortinbras of Norway in a duel of honor and has confiscated Norwegian land. In response, Prince Fortinbras, the son of the previous king and nephew to the new king of Norway, vows revenge and plans an attack to wrest back the conquered land. He is acting without the knowledge of his uncle. An embassy from Denmark to the king of Norway prevents the prince from carrying out the invasion.

In fact, relations between Denmark and Norway wavered between war and peace over the centuries. Raiders journeyed from one land to the other, and a long-standing rift between the two lands began around 800 A.D. About the same time, conflict broke out between Denmark and England when Danish Vikings began to raid the English coast about 835 A.D. The Danish Vikings finally conquered part of England in 1014 and for a time they would also rule Norway, but within forty years, after the rule of Canute the Great (1018-1035), their empire collapsed. His son Hardicanute laid claim to the thrones of both Norway and Denmark after his father died. But Norway's young king, Magnus the Good, threatened to protect his crown by going to war. Noblemen in both lands made the two young kings compromise; it was agreed that each would rule his own country for the time being, but the one who lived longest would be entitled to take over the other's kingdom. This compromise shows that Hamlet's pronouncement at the end of Shakespeare's play was a plausible way to handle the succession to the Danish throne; after the deaths of its king and queen, the dying Prince Hamlet designates Norway's Prince Fortinbras to take over the rule of Denmark.

Christian/pagan ideals and supernatural belief. Though most of the Vikings had adopted Christianity by 960, and all of the subsequent Danish monarchs declared themselves Christians, the people retained beliefs in mythology and supernatural forces. Because the Danes were generally farmers and fishermen, they were heavily dependent on nature for their livelihood. Hence, even after they adopted Christianity, they retained a strong connection to forces they believed controlled nature—human and otherwise. Like the Romans, the Danes and others in the far North had developed an elaborate mythology based on gods of thunder, the sun, and other natural forces. The people often paid homage to these gods in ceremonies that were held before a fishing fleet set sail or during the crop-planting season. The hope was that such ceremonies would guarantee good returns. In *Hamlet* Shakespeare refers to pre-Christian myth as well as Christianity, drawing on Roman mythology, which was more familiar to his audiences in England than Danish myths and legends. While there are clear references to Christian ethics throughout *Hamlet*, such as Queen Gertrude's imminent judgment by heaven, there are also ample references to figures such as Neptune, the Roman god of the sea. Thus Shakespeare's character Horatio refers not to the watery empire (the sea) of one of the

Norse gods but rather to "Neptune's empire" (Shakespeare, *Hamlet*, 1.1.119).

The Play in Focus

The plot. *Hamlet* opens with Prince Hamlet returning from his studies at the University of Wittenberg in Germany. His father, King Hamlet, has recently died. As the play reveals, he was murdered by his brother, Claudius, who has become king and married the older Hamlet's widow, Gertrude. Young Hamlet is naturally distraught over the events, though at the outset he does not know that his father has been murdered. He only senses, as does his friend Marcellus, that "something is rotten in the state of Denmark" (*Hamlet*, 1.4.89).

Soon a ghost appears to Hamlet and several of his friends. It is the spirit of Prince Hamlet's dead father, who has come to inform the prince of his murder. His brother Claudius has killed him by pouring poison in his ear. The spirit declares that Claudius is "the serpent that did sting thy father's life," imploring Hamlet to exact revenge (*Hamlet*, 1.5.40). This news sends Hamlet into a frenzied rage and melancholy depression. He promises to avenge his father's murder and begins behaving strangely. To others, who do not know the truth, the young Hamlet appears to have gone mad. By pretending to be insane, Hamlet hopes to conceal his knowledge of his father's murder at his uncle's hands.

But rather than deflect suspicion, Hamlet's behavior arouses the curiosity of the king and queen, who try to ferret out the cause of his mad behavior. Polonius, the lord of the treasury, believes the cause is his own daughter, Ophelia, who has on his advice rejected the prince's advances. Though it is clear that Hamlet once loved Ophelia deeply, he now denies it to her face and rejects her completely, displaying what Ophelia interprets as a distraught noble mind "here o'erthrown" (*Hamlet*, 3.1.158).

As part of his plot of revenge, Hamlet produces a play about murder to "catch the conscience of the king" (*Hamlet*, 2.2.606). Hamlet intends to see if the ghost has been truthful about Claudius by watching how the king reacts to the play. But the play yields more than its desired effect. The king becomes so shaken and enraged by it that he begins to plan Hamlet's murder. Though unaware of the king's real intent, Polonius offers to aid the king and eavesdrops on Hamlet while he speaks to his mother. Hamlet senses someone's presence and stabs the figure behind the curtain in the mistaken belief that it is Claudius. Instead, Polonius is instantly killed by the assault.

Claudius now fears Hamlet and devises a plan to send him to England and have him killed there. Meanwhile, Ophelia, who is already distraught over Hamlet's rejection of her, learns of her father's murder and goes insane. Her brother Laertes returns from France, demanding revenge for his father's death. Claudius, of course, encourages Laertes and helps him develop a plot to kill Hamlet, who manages to return from England unharmed. Laertes will challenge Hamlet to a duel, which honor demands that he accept; to guarantee that Hamlet loses, the conspirators will poison not only his wine but also the tip of Laertes' sword. The queen then arrives and informs them that Ophelia has drowned; after hearing of his sister's death, Laertes breaks down weeping.

The duel between Hamlet and Laertes takes place as scheduled with the king, queen, and court watching. The poisoned wine is set out for Hamlet, but the queen accidently drinks some of it. As the fierce duel continues, Laertes and Hamlet wound each other with the poisoned sword, which changes hands during the fight. Hamlet witnesses his mother's death and learns from Laertes that the king poisoned the wine. Enraged, Hamlet runs the fatal sword through Claudius and forces him to drink the deadly wine. Laertes and Hamlet forgive each other and then die; Hamlet's dying request is that Horatio explain Hamlet's motives to the world. Finally aware of Prince Hamlet's agonized last days, the court mourns him as a hero who has avenged his father's death.

Sources. Shakespeare's *Hamlet* is based on the legend of fabled Danish Prince Amleth (also known as Amlodhi), who feigned insanity to veil a plot of revenge against his uncle for his father's murder. Set down by Saxo Grammaticus at the end of the twelfth century in the *Historiae Danicae*, the legend included two parts: Amleth's rise to power and his reign. About 1570 François de Belleforest published a translation of Saxo's Amleth story in French in his collection *Histoires Tragiques*. There is, however, no evidence that Shakespeare came into contact with either of these versions. The most direct source for his drama seems to have been another play of around 1588 now known as *Ur-Hamlet*, which was based on Belleforest's version but is now lost. Thomas Kyd is credited with having written *Ur-Hamlet* as well as *The Spanish Tragedy*, a revenge play published in 1592 that also influenced Shakespeare's work.

In Saxo's version of the tale, Amleth not only killed the eavesdropper (the Polonius character in *Hamlet*) but also cut "his body into morsels, he seethed it in boiling water, and flung it through the mouth of an open sewer for the swine to eat" (Watts, p. 5). In contrast, Shake-

Hamlet

MENTAL ILLNESS IN *HAMLET* AND IN SHAKESPEARE'S TIME

In *Hamlet* the main character feigns insanity while Ophelia, the woman he loves, actually does go mad. These developments reflect a preoccupation in Shakespeare's time with melancholy and insanity. There was a hospital for the insane in London called Bethlehem, a name that popular usage changed to Bedlam, which came to stand for "utter madness." So fascinated were Londoners by the insane that they would go to Bedlam to ogle the fewer than thirty inmates who occupied the hospital in the late 1500s and early 1600s. Meanwhile, doctors, preachers, and dramatists spoke about grief and insanity in their works. These shapers of public opinion warned especially against excessive grief, which, they believed, could drive people to distraction the way the death of Ophelia's father and Hamlet's rejection drive her mad in *Hamlet*. Hamlet acts the part of a genuine madman, which the English classified into two main types—the violent madmen and the raving ones who talked nonsensically, the way Prince Hamlet does. The English also recognized a less serious mental disorder called stupor or mopishness, which referred to a disturbance in a person's five senses. Hamlet assigns this ailment to his mother to explain her hasty marriage to Claudius: "Eyes without feeling ... Ears without hands or eyes, smelling sans all, / Or but a sickly part of one true sense / Could not so mope" (*Hamlet*, 3.4.78-81).

---

speare's Hamlet feels remorse after the murder of Polonius:

> I do repent; but heaven hath pleas'd it so,
> To punish me with this, and this with me,
> That I must be their scourge and minister.
> (*Hamlet*, 3.4.180-82)

Hamlet's speech reflects the more Christian viewpoint of Shakespeare's time. Though his quest for revenge was probably understandable

Michael Redgrave as Hamlet and Dorothy Tutin as Ophelia in Glen Byam Shaw's 1958 Stratford-upon-Avon production.

to audiences of the early 1600s, Amleth's barbaric treatment of the eavesdropper would have been condemned. Also Shakespeare's Hamlet plans to punish only the murderer, Claudius, whereas in Saxo's version the whole court is marked for destruction.

An actual event inspired the idea of murdering Hamlet's father by pouring poison in his ear. In 1538 in Italy a barber-surgeon killed the Duke of Urbino by pouring a lotion in his ear. He had been hired to do so by Luigi Gonzaga, whose name Shakespeare uses in the play that Hamlet stages to prick the conscience of the murderer Claudius. It is uncertain whether Shakespeare took the event directly from real life or whether the earlier play Ur-Hamlet used it first.

Hamlet's ghost and Shakespeare's time. The presence of a ghost character in Hamlet reflects a general acceptance of the supernatural during the Elizabethan Age. The ghost gives Hamlet an insight into life that cannot be seen or transmitted by others living on this "distracted" globe. Shakespeare's drama suggests that there are a great many things human beings do not understand and that such things can affect human destiny.

The concept that unseen forces or Fortune have influence or control over human destiny was common in Elizabethan tragedy. Much earlier, the Roman philosopher Seneca had written of the Roman goddess Fortuna's ability to control destiny with her wheel of fortune. Elizabethan playwrights adapted Seneca's concepts, combining medieval and classical elements in their tragedies.

Events in History at the Time the Play Was Written

Succession to the throne. Great Britain has a long and violent history regarding succession to the throne. From 1399 to 1485 the Wars of the Roses raged and produced continual political instability throughout England. Then came Protestant, Catholic, and Puritan conflicts as well as Tudor and Stuart rivalries that continued through the reign of Elizabeth (1558-1603). One of the rivalries between the Tudor and Stuart dynasties involved Queen Elizabeth of England (a Tudor) and Queen Mary of Scotland (a Stuart). There were remarkable similarities between the events in Mary's life and Hamlet. On February 10, 1567, Queen Mary's husband, Lord Darnley, was murdered by Lord Bothwell. Three months later the queen married her husband's murderer,

Bothwell. He died in 1576 after confessing his crime, and Mary herself came to trial for other alleged crimes ten years later. In 1587 the English convicted and executed her for conspiring to destroy Queen Elizabeth, England, and its commitment to the Protestant faith. The public was

Hamlet

PLOT SOURCES

Saxo's and Belleforest's Versions:

Brother murders brother, takes throne, and marries queen.
Son returns home for funeral of his father, learns of murder, and plots revenge.
Son feigns insanity to conceal his knowledge of murder, draws attention of king and queen.
Son kills eavesdropper character.
King tries to kill avenging son by sending him abroad, but son foils plan and king's agents die instead.
Son finally kills king.

Ur-Hamlet

A ghost urges revenge.
Son seeks to verify truth about the murder and stages a play for that purpose.
Son contemplates suicide.
Female character goes insane and commits suicide.
Son laments delay in getting revenge.
Son dies after killing the king.

---

overjoyed. However, her son James, a prince in some ways like Hamlet, expressed indignation. James, however, took no action, and went on to rule England after Queen Elizabeth. Assuming the throne in 1603, he must have reacted emotionally when he saw a performance of Hamlet, whose plot recalled similar events in his own life.

Denmark and England. The sport of fencing was popular in both England and Denmark in the early 1600s. In 1606, during James's reign, King Christian IV of Denmark visited England. Over the years he and James had corresponded with each other on friendly terms. King Christian watched fencing matches daily while in England. The fencing match in the last act of Hamlet may reflect the popularity of the sport. Other elements of the play that reflect life in Denmark during the early 1600s are names such as Polonius,

Rosencrantz, and Guildenstern; the braying of trumpets at certain points in the action; and the idea that nobles would leave Denmark to study abroad at Germany's University of Wittenberg.

Corruption and ambition in the play. Through the character of Claudius in the play, Shakespeare illustrates the potentially corrupting influence of ambition and power. Claudius's desire to assume the throne was so great that he was willing to kill his own brother, an action that he regards as terrible.

> O, my offense is rank, it smells to heaven;
> It has primal eldest curse upon 't,
> A brother's murder.
>
> *(Hamlet, 3.3.36-8)*

He further confesses that he committed the murder to satisfy his own ambition. But Shakespeare does not place all the blame squarely on Claudius's shoulders. He hints that an uninvolved and ignorant society is also to blame for corruption. The characters Rosencrantz and Guildenstern are representatives of a society willing to turn a blind eye to evil in order to prosper or to avoid punishment. In the play's own

---

BELIEF IN GHOSTS

The Elizabethan Age has been called the Age of Uncertainty. Science was on the rise, as "experts" created maps, experimented with plants, and concocted new medicines. Concurrently, the debate about the reality of ghosts and apparitions grew. Perhaps this is why Hamlet delays his revenge even though the ghost has clearly instructed him to kill Claudius. Hamlet, like Shakespeare and his contemporaries, may have been unsure if the ghost was real or a figment of his imagination.

---

words, they are "the indifferent children of the earth" (*Hamlet,* 2.2.227). Hamlet, on the other hand, struggles to embody the heroic ideal, which stresses fairness in battle and the duty to revenge a lawless killing. He vows vengeance, though he feels tormented by this duty: "O cursed spite, / That ever I was born to set it right" (*Hamlet,* 1.5.189-90).

From the heroic ideal to humanism. Prince Hamlet reflects, in part, the evolving humanistic attitude of the Renaissance era. In contrast to the earlier medieval belief that death was the proper

and necessary punishment to revenge a murder, Hamlet conveys a growing pacifist sentiment that denounces killing in general. In an era that saw rampant human destruction from war and the bubonic plague, the English were beginning to regard killing—even to avenge a lawless murder—as a less heroic action than had the people of the Middle Ages. This changing viewpoint contributes to Hamlet's delay in avenging his father's death, which causes the prince much inner turmoil.

> Why, what an ass am I! This is most brave,
> That I, the son of a dear father murder'd,
> Prompted to my revenge by heaven and hell,
> Must, like a whore, unpack my heart with words,
> And fall a-cursing, like a very drab,
> A scullion! Fie upon 't, foh! About, my brain!
>
> *(Hamlet, 2.2.583-88)*

Hamlet is torn between the conflicting concepts of vengeance as honorable and murder as sin, a struggle that Renaissance society was grappling with as well. A law called the Bond of Association of 1584, for example, legalized revenge against anyone who attempted to overthrow or malign the queen. Yet when the Earl of Essex was killed under that law for attempting to overthrow the government, society in general condemned his execution, as did Shakespeare. Hamlet's ongoing indecision reflects the society's debates about the legitimacy of vengeance and humane treatment of wrongdoers and seems to suggest that there are elements of merit and dishonor in both.

Revenge tragedy. Revenge tragedies became very popular in England during the late 1500s and early 1600s. Stemming back to classical Greek and Roman drama, they were widely introduced to English audiences through the works of the ancient Roman playwright Seneca. His plays became required reading at most universities, and English theater companies performed derivatives of them on stage.

Shakespeare figured among the British playwrights who created new revenge tragedies, a genre that appealed to English audiences, who could easily apply them to history in their own times. England's Queen Elizabeth publicly condemned the execution of her rival Queen Mary of Scotland, but it was regarded as a prudent measure by many in England and proper revenge due to the rumored plans by the Scots to murder Elizabeth. Similarly, the execution of the Earl of Essex was punishment for his attempt to overthrow Elizabeth, although she, like Hamlet, was uncertain that killing Essex was the proper penalty.

Hamlet also reflects beliefs about sin and damnation that were common to Shakespeare's time. In the play, Hamlet sets out to kill Claudius in a particular manner. He wishes to ensure his victim's damnation according to his, and the audience's, understanding of God's judgement. It was believed that a sinful person could be sentenced to eternal doom if he or she were killed before they had time to pray or if they were killed in one of the conditions that Hamlet envisions—in the act of drinking, gambling, swearing, or some other disgraceful act. When Hamlet finds Claudius praying, this type of damnation is not possible, and he decides not to kill him at that time. Shakespeare's audience would have likely viewed this decision as proper.

Reviews and early stage history. In 1604 Antony Skoloker wrote that the play was able to "please all" (Skoloker in Watts, p. xix). Richard Burbage played the role of Hamlet during Shakespeare's lifetime, and it is thought that in some productions Shakespeare himself performed the part of the ghost. The most popular of all Shakespeare's plays, *Hamlet* was performed 358 times through the year 1750. In fact, the play was so popular that it was "pirated" or copied by hack writers and published in what is now known as the bad quarto in 1603. Shakespeare's own version was first published in response to the illegitimate copy in 1604 or 1605.

For More Information

Dollerup, Cay. *Denmark, Hamlet, and Shakespeare.* Vol. 2. Salzburg: Institut für Englische Sprache und Literatur, 1975.

Johnston, William Preston. *The Prototype of Hamlet and Other Shakespearian Problems.* New York: Belford, 1890.

Lauring, Palle. *A History of Denmark.* Copenhagen: Høst & Søn, 1986.

MacDonald, Michael. *Mystical Bedlam: Madness, Anxiety, and Healing in Seventeenth-Century England.* Cambridge, England: Cambridge University Press, 1981.

Ogburn, Charlton. *The Mysterious William Shakespeare.* New York: Dodd, Mead, 1984.

Shakespeare, William. *Hamlet.* Edited by David Bevington. Toronto: Bantam, 1988.

Watts, Cedric. *Twayne's New Critical Introductions to Shakespeare: Hamlet.* Boston: Twayne, 1988.

Wright, Louis B., ed. *Shakespeare's England.* New York: Harper & Row, 1964.

Henry IV, Part I

by
William Shakespeare

Although he may have learned some aspects of successful play writing from other dramatists of his time, William Shakespeare remains a major innovator of the English history play. Such early Shakespeare plays as *Henry VI* and *Richard III* were among the first to achieve any sort of commercial success. In *Henry IV, Part I,* Shakespeare continues his tradition of re-enacting the history of his native land.

Events in History at the Time the Play Takes Place

The reign of Henry IV. Because he had actively opposed Richard II, the reigning king of England from 1376 to 1399, Henry Bolingbroke was living in exile when he succeeded his father as Duke of Lancaster. Immediately following this inheritance, King Richard seized Henry's lands and his title and ordered him into exile for life. Henry soon returned to England with a band of supporters and sought to usurp the kingship. Charging Richard with whimsical and oppressive rule, the rebels rather easily overthrew his regime in 1399. Although Richard had named Edmund Mortimer as his successor, Henry's leadership during the revolt earned him the crown. The distribution of England's political power following the revolution, however, made it difficult for Henry to maintain his authority.

There was a division of loyalties best explained, perhaps, by the complicated lineage from which both Henry and Richard descended. The following family tree helps to clarify this point.

THE LITERARY WORK

A play set in England during the year 1402; probably first performed in 1597.

SYNOPSIS

King Henry IV, a recent successor to the English throne, battles rebels and attempts to teach his son the lessons of leadership.

As the family tree indicates, Henry had, in fact, overthrown his cousin when he dethroned the king. According to rights of inheritance, the throne should then have passed to the second-eldest son in the family line, Edmund Mortimer. Because Edmund had died in 1381 and Roger, his eldest son, had died in 1385, Richard's rightful successor should have been Roger Mortimer's son Edmund. The boy was too young to rule or resist, however, so Henry claimed the title. By ignoring the established royal lineage, Henry knew that it could prove difficult for him to maintain his seat on the English throne for long. He would, in fact, reign from 1399-1419, when he died at age forty-six.

During the revolution and the early years of Henry's reign, the Percy family acted as his chief supporters. In the north, Harry Percy, known as "Hotspur," led the English military against Scottish revolters. Elsewhere, Henry Percy, the Earl of Northumberland, assisted King Henry IV in matters of the court. Henry Percy's brother

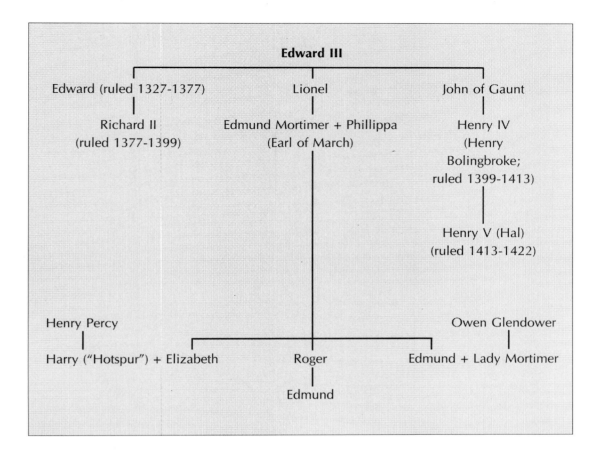

Thomas, the Earl of Worcester, counseled Henry IV as well, even though Thomas had previously assisted Richard II. The loyalty that the Percys originally exhibited, however, did not last for any great length of time. Hotspur's marriage to Elizabeth Mortimer (called Kate in *Henry IV, Part I*), a woman from a family unfriendly to Henry IV, created a serious breach. King Henry could only be suspicious of an ally who would so readily marry into his rival's family. King Henry's subsequent refusal to ransom Elizabeth's brother Edmund after his capture by the Welsh, combined with his demand for Scottish prisoners that Hotspur had claimed, served to burn the shaky bridges of loyalty that Henry had established. His government, new and weakened from the previous civil strife, faced rebellion in 1402.

Edmund Mortimer's father-in-law, Owen Glendower, led the revolt. Given their new ties to the Mortimer family via Hotspur's marriage, the Percy clan quickly joined the rebels. The events of their rebellion are portrayed in Shakespeare's *Henry IV, Part I*. Henry's first defeat of the rebel group took place at the Battle of Shrewsbury in 1403, in which Hotspur was killed. Although the curtain of Shakespeare's play closes without the promise of victory for

Henry IV, by 1408 all of his enemies had met with defeat.

England and Scotland. One of the principle reasons why Henry could not unite his nation was the constant wars that England faced along its borders. Since the reign of Edward I of England (1272-1307), Scotland had lived under English rule. Although the Scots had managed to defeat the English in 1314, England took advantage of weak Scottish leaders to restore its claim. The rule of Henry IV occurred during what became a seesaw period of constant struggle between the two forces. Having known autonomy for a brief time, Scotland attempted to assert its independence. England, however, unwilling to relinquish one of its holdings, refused to lose Scotland again. In the opening of Shakespeare's work, the king receives a briefing on the condition of the Scottish uprising. Although Hotspur does quell the attempt, the debate over the fate of his prisoners eventually causes the internal rebellion against Henry.

Pilgrims. In Shakespeare's play, Falstaff, one of the drama's comedic figures, attempts to rob a group of pilgrims making their way to Canterbury. The Catholic Church often ordered such pilgrimages as penance for sins. In 1170 Thomas Becket, the Archbishop of Canterbury, had been cruelly murdered inside his cathedral walls. For the members of the congregation who had looked to Becket as a spiritual leader, the murder elevated him to the status of a martyr. Two years following his death, Thomas Becket was canonized as a saint, and the English faithful began making journeys to his burial place.

Such pilgrimages involved long and often dangerous travel. Along the way, the travelers stayed at inns and private hostels. Since they had to pay for all their food and lodging, pilgrim parties often carried relatively large sums of money. By the fifteenth century, pilgrimages had evolved into festive events. These elaborate parties proved tempting to thieves such as Shakespeare's Falstaff.

Education of Henry V. Although Shakespeare paints young Prince Hal (Henry V) as a novice soldier, the actual Henry V (1387-1422) received an extensive education in the skills of a knight. Records show that on Henry's tenth birthday he participated in a tournament at Pleshey Castle in Essex that tested skills such as horse riding and archery. In 1403, at the age of sixteen, Henry was called on to assist his father in battling the rebels. While the playwright credits Hal with the slaying of Hotspur, in actuality this slaying was accomplished by an unnamed figure. The real Henry V, though he fought with vigor in other wars, was not present at the Battle of Shrewsbury. Nonetheless, from his first moment on the battlefield, Henry V established himself as both a prominent soldier and leader. He would reign in England from 1413-1422 and become the subject of Shakespeare's later history play *Henry V*.

The Play in Focus

The plot. The action of *Henry IV, Part I* begins where Shakespeare's *Richard II* leaves off. A chronological series, Shakespeare's histories are connected to one another. The opening of *Henry IV, Part I*, therefore, finds a newly seated Henry who has not fully established his authority. With the civil distress of the revolt against Richard in the recent past, Henry desires to unite his countrymen in a crusade to the Holy Land. He cannot accomplish this ambition, however, due to the several wars England is waging on its own fronts. In the north, a Scottish uprising threatens the English borders, while in the west, the Welsh present a similar problem. Although his noble compatriots, Harry Percy ("Hotspur"), Henry Percy (the Earl of Northumberland), Thomas

Percy (the Earl of Worcester), and Edmund Mortimer (the Earl of March) ably lead the king's armies into battle, civil unrest clearly exists. Since Richard II left no direct heir to the English throne, Henry IV realizes that the Mortimer family is his chief rival. At the opening of *Henry IV, Part I*, the rift between Henry IV and the Mortimers is already a significant one. Phillippa Mortimer's son Edmund has been captured by the Welsh. King Henry IV, much to the distress of Edmund's relatives, refuses to ransom him.

Henry IV's problems, however, do not stem solely from political affairs. His son Hal provides the king with several domestic concerns. An untried soldier, Hal possesses neither the ambition nor the acclaim enjoyed by Hotspur. He prefers to spend his days with his tavern friends, chief among them the portly thief John Falstaff. During one episode, Falstaff and his men rob a group of pilgrims traveling to Canterbury. For amusement, Hal and another man, in turn, rob Falstaff. While these events provide great fun for the young Prince of Wales, they do not amuse his father. During a soliloquy in Act I, however, Hal recognizes his seemingly immature behavior. He promises that his wildness will make his future behavior "show more goodly and attract more eyes / Than that which hath no foil to set it off" (Shakespeare, *Henry IV*, 1.2.202-03).

Incensed over both the king's refusal to ransom Edmund and the king's rather despotic rule, Hotspur, Glendower (Edmund's father-in-law), and a few others plot their revolt. They divide the map of England according to who shall rule which territory after their victory. Once Henry IV receives word of the conspiracy, he speaks with his son. For almost the entire conversation, the king expresses disapproval of the prince. He marvels at how barren pleasures and rude company could please a man of Hal's position. In response Hal vows to "salve / The long-grown wounds of my intemperature" (*Henry IV*, 3.2. 155-56). Joining with those still loyal to the crown, the king and his son plan their military strategy. Hal even enlists Falstaff's aid in defending his father.

The two armies meet at Shrewsbury in western England. Through one of his messengers, Henry IV tells the rebels that he will pardon their conduct if they abandon their plans. Hotspur, the rash leader of the band, refuses the offer. He sends the rebel Earl of Worcester as a messenger to inform the king of his decision. In a bid to avoid mass bloodshed, Prince Hal offers to fight Hotspur in one-on-one combat to settle the

A depiction of Falstaff by H. Fuseli, engraved by W. Leney.

grievances. But Hal's father, King Henry, dismisses this idea, instead offering the rebels one last chance to surrender with a promise not to punish them. Because Worcester fears for his life, he does not inform Hotspur of these developments. He worries that Hotspur may be tempted to surrender and that the king would then punish an old rebel such as himself despite the promise of amnesty.

A battle ensues, costing many men their lives. In one of the final scenes, Hal kills Hotspur. The prince receives no credit for this victory, however, due to the ever-scheming Falstaff. After losing their leader, the rebels Worcester and Vernon surrender to the enemy and the gallows. Although the close of the play does not entirely

---

FALSTAFF

The character of Falstaff proved the most problematic for Shakespeare when the play first went into production. Originally the rogue bore the name of Sir John Oldcastle. The real Sir Oldcastle had been executed for heresy against the Catholic Church. Although revered by the Protestants, he endured many posthumous attacks by the Catholics, who described him as a "ruffian-knight" (Parsons in Kay, p. 213). In presenting this figure as a comedic one, Shakespeare offended Oldcastle's living descendants and ran the risk of angering Protestants. William Brooke, one of Oldcastle's relatives, served as one of Queen Elizabeth's advisers and therefore also as a patron of Shakespeare's company. In order to avoid conflict, the name of the character was changed to Falstaff in both public performance and print.

---

resolve the conflict, the king expresses confidence that his side will crush the remaining forces that oppose him. More importantly perhaps, the king acknowledges Hal's progress: "Thou hast redeemed thy lost opinion, / And showed thou mak'st some tender of my life" (*Henry IV*, 5.4.47-8).

Shakespeare's morality play. Although drama had become a more sophisticated art form by Shakespeare's time than it once was, some vestiges of fifteenth-century theater still remained. Shakespeare added to these, developing a livelier, more complicated play. In Middle English times, the main focus of the theater was the

morality play. These productions featured universal characters, with names like "Lechery," who attempted to lead the protagonists astray from moral behavior. Shakespeare both drew and deviated from this structure within his work.

The corpulent figure of Falstaff, for instance, resembles physically the character "Gluttony" who appears in several older works such as *The Castle of Perseverance* and Edmund Spenser's *The Faerie Queene*. Likewise, Falstaff's drunkenness finds its roots in similar stock characters. Although not as clearly allegorical as these figures, Falstaff's lifestyle represents the immoral world into which Hal may fall.

Within morality plays, the alternatives of vanity and vice are presented to the protagonist in the form of a choice. The scenes alternate between serious probabilities and ridiculous representations of the immoral world. *Henry IV, Part I* similarly alternates between the serious scenes of the court and the ridiculous ones of the tavern. Until Act 3, Scene 2, when Hal promises a reformation to his father, this pattern does not falter. In this manner Falstaff becomes a foil against which the figure of the king is played. Both men offer role models to young Hal; in the end the prince must choose whom to follow.

Sources. Because Shakespeare based his play on English history, all characters and events come from historical works. The playwright relied heavily on the third volume of Raphael Holinshed's *The Chronicles of England*, published in 1587. Most critics agree, however, that Shakespeare's play far outreaches its historical roots. Other than a brief account of conflict between King Henry IV and his son found in *The Chronicles of England*, this entire subplot comes from the playwright's own imagination. Shakespeare, not history, described the familial strife between the king and the prince.

In addition, the conflict that Henry IV faces with his nobles seems to have been embellished, or even misrepresented, in Shakespeare's play. Like Holinshed, Shakespeare confused which of the Edmund Mortimers could lay rightful claim to the English throne. In reality, the first Edmund Mortimer's *grandson* (the son of his second son), not his third son, would have been next in line for the position of king. Throughout the play, however, Shakespeare indicates that Owen Glendower's son-in-law, the second Edmund Mortimer, would inherit the throne. The playwright cannot be faulted entirely for this error; his source, Holinshed, misrepresented this situation as well.

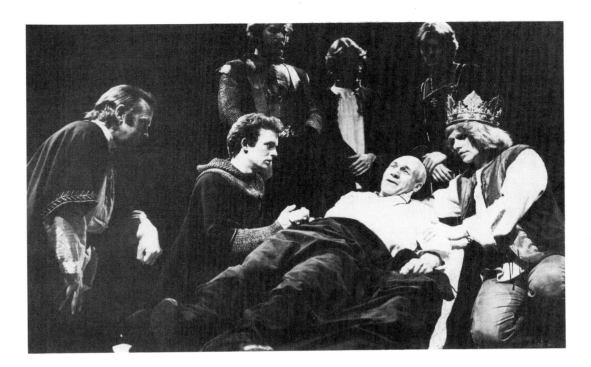

A Royal Shakespeare Company production of *Henry IV* staged in London in 1982.

Shakespeare seems to take poetic license in his interpretation of Hotspur as well. Indeed, the man's hot-tempered disposition, as well as his prominent contribution to the rebellion, appear to have been entirely the work of the playwright. Moreover, the rivalry between Hal and Hotspur could not have been so intense. The real-life Hotspur, aged thirty-nine when he died in 1403, was quite a few years older than Hal, then aged sixteen, so the two men probably had only limited interactions with each other. Certainly Hal never challenged Hotspur to one-on-one combat. Another of Shakespeare's sources, Samuel Daniel's *The First Four Books of the Civil Wars,* does credit the prince with the slaying of Hotspur, but both the historian and the playwright are incorrect in this regard, as they interpreted preceding historical texts.

Events in History at the Time the Play Was Written

England and Scotland in Shakespeare's lifetime. By the time of Queen Elizabeth I's reign (1558-1603), England had become a rather small country and did not have large holdings in other areas. The English empire in the Americas had only just begun to take shape with the settlement of Virginia in the 1580s. Although England still ruled Wales and Ireland, the English crown no longer held the lands it had once controlled on the continent of Europe. Scotland had also managed to gain its independence from England in 1314 and did not become a part of Great Britain until 1707. In fact, 1603 would see the ascension of a Scot (King James I) to the English throne.

The rule of King James I resulted from the tangled lineage of English and Scottish royalty. Because Elizabeth I was the daughter of Henry VIII by his second wife, Anne Boleyn, many Roman Catholics would not recognize her as the proper inheritor of the throne. They considered Henry's second marriage invalid because it contradicted Catholic law. Instead of Elizabeth, the Catholic faction recognized Mary Stuart, Queen of Scots, as the proper queen of England. Her claim to the throne lay also with Henry VIII. Mary's grandmother, Margaret Tudor, was Henry VIII's sister. She and Elizabeth I, therefore, were cousins of sorts.

Following Henry VIII's death in 1547, his only son, the boy king Edward VI, ruled until 1553. After his death, Mary Tudor, Edward VI's older sister, ascended to the throne. Because Mary died childless in 1558, the throne then passed to Elizabeth I. In 1587 Mary Stuart, Queen of Scots, found herself implicated in a plot to assassinate Elizabeth I. She was beheaded at Elizabeth's command for her alleged participation. When Elizabeth I died without an heir in 1603, James I, the son of the executed Mary, protested his mother's wrongful death and gained the throne. He began the Stuart dynasty that retained control of the English throne for about eighty years. The Stuart monarchy ruled the territories possessed by both England and Scotland. After Scotland lost this family connection with the English throne, it resumed its battle for independence from England.

Elizabethan history plays. Queen Elizabeth, despite the power struggle that preceded her rule, managed to unite England as no monarch had before her. When a 1570 papal decree excommunicated Elizabeth I from the Catholic Church, her subjects rallied around her in opposing the placement of Mary Stuart on the throne. Elizabeth's advancement of England's commercial profits overseas further strengthened this feeling of national unity. The climate proved perfect for the birth of the history play.

Because such productions took their characters and scenes from the pages of English history, their popularity was virtually assured. The nature of the historical productions enhanced the importance of the royal dynasty and the transfer of royal power. This question of inheriting the throne proved to be of vital interest to the people of England. Most critics agree that Shakespeare addresses this interest best in his two cycles of history plays. His *Henry IV, Part I* is perhaps his supreme achievement in this regard. The popularity of such productions in Shakespeare's time was due partly to a unique aspect of Elizabeth's rule. Known as the "Virgin Queen," Elizabeth would remain unmarried and childless, insisting that England was her only spouse. Questions and speculation about the eventual successor to the throne after Elizabeth's death were thus fairly common.

Corruption from abroad. For the Elizabethans, increased trade meant increased contact with foreign influences. While these new markets provided the English with exciting goods such as new clothing and spices, they also exposed England to what moralists would call foreign corruption. Contemporaries of Shakespeare such as John Marston and Thomas Middleton wrote plays that centered on Italian debauchery and styles of murder. Other angry Englishmen condemned the French for introducing vanity in dress. Foreign influence in general was credited for bringing cosmetics, tobacco, gambling, wine, and a variety of other vices to the English shores.

Shakespeare himself seems to touch on these issues in *Henry IV, Part I*. His character Hotspur shows no tolerance for a fawning member of Henry's court who comes to the battlefield to deliver a message from the king. His contempt for the man, who is "perfumed like a milliner," exemplifies the general dislike of those who took too many pains in primping themselves (*Henry IV*, 1.3.36).

Fathers and sons. To Elizabethan parents, a child's first duty was loving obedience. At the same time, new thoughts of individual freedom were gaining ground. Elizabeth's father, King Henry VIII, had defied the Catholic Church by marrying her mother Anne Boleyn, an act that boldly gave precedence to individual preference over established rules. Outside court, people strayed more willingly from their social class. In England a noblewoman might marry a commoner, whereas in other countries, such as Germany, social conventions remained fixed in this regard. People in these other countries insisted that proper marriages required husband and wife to be of equal social rank.

Perhaps the wildness of Prince Hal in Shakespeare's play reflects, to some degree, the greater tendency to experiment and satisfy personal whims in Elizabethan England. Certainly Hal was not the only wayward son in Elizabethan drama. The playwright Ben Jonson, in *Every Man in His Humour,* includes a father's considerations of how to deal with his son's wildness. He resolves "not to stop his journey; / Nor practice any violent means to stay / The unbridled course of youth in him" (Johnson, *Every Man in His Humour,* 1.2. 122-24). Shakespeare's King Henry IV seems to adopt a similar stance with Prince Hal, although his son's misbehavior pains him.

Reception of the play. First staged, scholars believe, in 1597, *Henry IV, Part I* enjoyed continued popularity among playgoers until 1642, when the government closed theaters during the political upheaval of the civil wars. After the monarchy was restored and the theaters were reopened in 1660, *Henry IV* became one of the first plays to resurface. Performances occurred in 1660 and periodically thereafter, with the play again enjoying popularity. Public approval, however, faded in the second half of the 1800s during Queen Victoria's reign. The proper English audiences of this period took offense at the rogue Falstaff's coarse and bawdy brand of humor. Interest in the play revived with a superior production in 1896 and has persisted ever since.

For More Information

Earle, Peter. *The Life and Times of Henry V.* 1972. Reprint, London: Weidenfeld and Nicolson, 1993.

Johnson, Ben. *Every Man in His Humour.* 1601. Reprint, London: Methuen, 1986.

Kay, Dennis. *Shakespeare: His Life, Work, and Era.* New York: William Morrow, 1992.

Loxton, Howard. *Pilgrimage to Canterbury.* Totowa, N.J.: Rowman and Littlefield, 1978.

Shakespeare, William. *Henry IV, Part I.* In *The Oxford Shakespeare.* Edited by David Bevington. New York: Oxford University Press, 1987.

The Hobbit

by
J. R. R. Tolkien

J. R. R. Tolkien was a student of classical and Norse mythology who used his knowledge in these areas to inform his creation of the imaginary land of Middle-earth, the setting for *The Hobbit* and other works. Tolkien, who hoped to create a mythological past for England, used his imagination to present an account of the European world before the recorded history of humankind. Although *The Hobbit* was directed primarily at young people, the novel led into the series *The Lord of the Rings,* a more complex, adult narrative. Because of its mythological trappings, *The Hobbit* does not adhere to any strict chronological placement in time. The author intended only that the setting evoke images of a time of paganism and chivalry prior to the recorded history of man.

Events in History at the Time the Novel Takes Place

Internal chronology. Although Tolkien's series of books are not based on any specific historical time period, the author created and maintained a strict history for Middle-earth within his novels. He divided this history into four ages, entitled the First through the Fourth Age. According to the chronology, the events of *The Hobbit* take place sometime during the last century of the Third Age. Each novel in *The Lord of the Rings* series is set within that same world and century.

Because of his scholarly interests, Tolkien knew that calendars themselves carried mythological associations. The English calendar, for in-

THE LITERARY WORK

A novel set in the fantasy world of Middle-earth during a mythological time; published in 1937.

SYNOPSIS

Mr. Bilbo Baggins, a Hobbit, accompanies a band of dwarves on an adventure to slay the dragon Smaug.

stance, names several of its days of the week after Anglo-Saxon gods who derive from Norse counterparts. These days correspond to individual gods as follows:

> Tuesday: The day of Tiw, the god of war
> Wednesday: The day of Woden, the chief god
> Thursday: The day of Thor, the god of thunder
> Friday: The day of Frigg, the goddess of the heavens.

With this in mind, Tolkien created and adhered to an elaborate calendar to chart the passage of time on Middle-earth. In the shire, or county, where the hero Bilbo Baggins lives, Tuesday is known as "Trewsday," the day of trees, followed by "Hensday," the day of Heavens. These close associations with the English days of the week are not the only parallel between our world and Middle-earth. According to *The Lord of the Rings,* the Middle-earth year has "365 days, 5 hours, 48 minutes, 46 seconds" (Kocher, p. 7). In other words, time passes in Middle-earth just as it does in our world. To further depict his calendar year for readers, the author provides details such as the names of seasonal holidays. The dwarves in The Hobbit are told that they can only gain entrance to the dragon's lair on Durin's Day, the last day of autumn. This attention to the calendar underscored Tolkien's interest in creating a mythological history for England.

England in the Middle Ages. By "Middle-earth" the author refers to the area known as *Midgard* in the Old Norse language, *Middangeard* in Old English, and *Middlered* or *Meddelearth* in Middle English. According to Norse mythology, this region is the area between heaven and hell that is composed of land and sea. While Tolkien never directly linked this area to a definite place or time, the world's name and the social customs that are described in the narrative suggest that the author drew inspiration from England's Middle Ages, around the fifth century A.D.

The Anglo-Saxon invasion of England began in the first half of the fifth century. In actuality, these invaders belonged to three different tribes—the Angles, the Saxons, and the Jutes. Primarily Germanic in origin, they shared a relatively common language and set of customs. The loosely structured government that these tribes established in England was determined by family units and lines of kinship. In this manner, several kingdoms coexisted at once throughout Britain. A similar social construction can be seen in Tolkien's work. While the elves, dwarves, eagles, and goblins depicted in *The Hobbit* do not necessarily aid one another, they live in virtual harmony unless otherwise provoked.

A king of the Middle Ages had to conform to a strict heroic standard. The king, whose title comes from an old Germanic word for "chief," had to excel in such areas as sailing in storms, horse taming, hall construction, and fighting. If successful, the king could command absolute loyalty from his followers. They would defend him in battle, sacrificing their own lives for his. In return, his subjects were entitled to a share of the profits of war. In *The Hobbit*, the dwarves offer Thorin, the rightful heir to the dwarf throne, this same degree of loyalty. At one point, Thorin decides to wage a battle against armies made up of men and elves, hoping to gain the whole treasure that he is trying to reclaim. Although some of the dwarves disagree with Thorin's greed, they are nevertheless prepared to die for his cause. In

the ensuing clash, a number of these loyal soldiers do, in fact, perish.

Oral narrative tradition. Stories were handed down only by oral poems and songs during the early Middle Ages; written work did not appear until the eighth century A.D. These oral narratives were composed by bards, then memorized and handed down through countless recitations. Cultural beliefs in some societies made it very important to a warrior to strive to become a subject of one of these narrative works. Early Germanic religion, for instance, carried with it no promise of an afterlife. The sole means by which one could attain immortality was through the enduring fame of poetry.

Beowulf. The only surviving poem from Old English literature is the epic ***Beowulf*** (also covered in *Literature and Its Times*). Tolkien, a scholar of Beowulf, incorporated the importance of poetry and song into his work. When the dwarves return to slay the dragon Smaug, the people of Laketown rejoice that predictions contained in old songs will finally come to pass:

> Some began to sing snatches of old songs concerning the return of the King under the Mountain....[They] spoke confidently of the sudden death of the dragon and of cargoes of rich presents coming down the river.
> (Tolkien, *The Hobbit*, pp. 196-97)

Beowulf was composed in the eighth century A.D. A manuscript of the tale that dates back to the tenth century A.D. is the oldest surviving work of literature written in a European vernacular, or common spoken language. The poem focuses on two Scandinavian tribes, the Danes and the Geats, who were among England's Germanic forefathers. The epic tells of Beowulf, a hero whose task it is to kill monsters and dragons. As the work unfolds, his feats convey the basic notion of the heroic ideal.

Dragons, along with dwarves, elves, and trolls, were considered actual threats in the epic world of *Beowulf*. Tolkien used this premise in composing *The Hobbit*. Like the author of *Beowulf*, Tolkien likewise utilizes the lore that surrounds the dragon, having once asserted that "whatever may be his origins, in fact or invention, the dragon in legend is a potent creation of men's imagination" (Tolkien in Helms, p. 4). Finally, Tolkien includes a scene in which Bilbo steals the dragon Smaug's golden cup. The incident echoes similar events found in the story of *Beowulf*.

The Novel in Focus

The plot. Although the novel opens at a hobbit hole in the Shire, between the River Brandywine and the Far Downs, its setting covers a vast territory. The story centers around Bilbo Baggins, one of the little creatures known as hobbits. Bilbo belongs to a respectable family, and as the story opens, he leads an average hobbit life. Prior to his encounter with the wizard Gandalf, Mr. Baggins' main worry is the preparation of his next meal.

Gandalf and a band of twelve dwarves, however, alter this quiet lifestyle forever. Paying a visit on the hobbit, the wizard enlists Bilbo as a reluctant burglar to aid the dwarves on a mission of revenge. Bilbo learns that the town of Dale, a village north of the Shire where the dwarves used to dwell, is now ruled by a wicked dragon named Smaug, who maintains a reign of terror over the people in the region. Long ago Smaug killed Thror, the dwarf king who lived under the mountain, and stole the dwarves' stores of gold. Thorin, the old king's grandson, now seeks to overthrow the dragon and reclaim his kingdom and its riches. Although he certainly does not intend to join in this quest, Bilbo finds himself coerced into accompanying the wizard and the dwarves on the adventure of a lifetime.

The party winds through the Wilderland of Middle-earth as it journeys toward the town of Dale. Along the way, Bilbo, a most inexperienced thief, learns the tricks of his new profession and proves his worth to the entire expedition. During one escapade, he becomes separated from the rest of the party inside the goblin tunnels of the Misty Mountains. In order to make his way out of the confusing maze, the hobbit trades riddles with a slimy creature named Gollum. During his encounter with the treacherous Gollum, Bilbo manages to secure a magic ring that renders its wearer invisible. Bilbo escapes from the goblin lair to rejoin his friends, and his ring proves its value time and again throughout the journey.

Eventually, after many harrowing experiences and narrow escapes, the dwarves and Bilbo reach the land of Smaug. Although the dragon is rather easily killed, Thorin finds that the creature is not his only enemy. Numerous tales concerning the riches beneath the mountain encourage several armies to lay claim to the dwarves' gold. Some of these claims are, in fact, legitimate. In his greed, however, Thorin refuses to part with any of the treasure, and a great battle ensues. The dwarves reinstate their kingdom eventually, although not without the loss of several lives. Thorin is among those who are killed.

Bilbo returns to his hobbit hole, a hero in most respects. Although the other hobbits now regard him as a peculiar and rather disreputable character, Gandalf and the dwarves vow to never forget the central role Mr. Baggins played in their adventure.

Bilbo as an autobiographical figure. In one account Tolkien wrote, he declared that "I am in fact a hobbit in all but size. I like gardens, trees, and unmechanized farmlands; I smoke a pipe, and like good plain food.... I like, and even dare to wear in these dull days, ornamental waistcoats ... I do not travel much" (Tolkien in Carpenter, p. 176). Bilbo is similarly attached to his hobbit hole and fond of food and tobacco. When Gandalf comes to visit, Bilbo remarks that it is "a very fine morning for a pipe of tobacco out of doors" (*The Hobbit,* p. 4).

Other parallels between the author's life and that of his central character can be easily found. The very hole in which Bilbo lives, called "Bag End," is named after Tolkien's aunt's Worcestershire farm. Furthermore, Tolkien was the son of Mabel Suffield, an independent and enterprising young woman, and the author considered himself a product of his mother's side of the family in "tastes, talents, and upbringing" (Carpenter, p. 19). His mother and her two sisters were born to a man who lived to be over one hundred years old. Likewise, Bilbo's mother, Belladonna Took, was one of "three remarkable daughters" (*The Hobbit,* p. 2) who descended from a family patriarch. Just as Tolkien was influenced by his mother's family, Bilbo "got something a bit queer in his makeup from the Took side" of his family (*The Hobbit,* p. 3). It is this "queer" aspect of his makeup that prompts Bilbo's adventure.

While the author may have originally conceived of Bilbo as an autobiographical figure, hobbits serve as an embodiment of the English people throughout Tolkien's *Lord of the Rings* series. According to the author himself, "Hobbits are just rustic English people, made small in size because it reflects the generally small reach of their imagination—not the small reach of their courage or latent power." He adds that he is continually surprised "that we [the English] are here, surviving, because of the indomitable courage of quite small people against impossible odds" (Tolkien in Carpenter, p. 176). In other words, the hobbits carry within them the determined bravery that Tolkien believed characterized the nation of England during World War I. These comparisons between the hobbit population and the people of England, however, were not made

Portrait of J. R. R. Tolkien.

until the publication of the *Lord of the Rings* tales. *The Hobbit* was written primarily for amusement.

Sources. The primary source for the characters in *The Hobbit* is Tolkien's own imagination. The setting of Middle-earth, however, rings familiar to anyone who has visited England. As Tolkien stated in a 1932 lecture at the University of St. Andrews, "secondary" or fantasy worlds must have both "freedom from ... and domination of observed fact" (Tolkien in Kocher, p. 1). Tolkien's world thus contains fantasy figures such as dwarves and dragons within more realistic surroundings. The climate, geography, flora, and fauna described in his tales do not differ greatly from those found in England. Finally, Bilbo's village of Hobbiton is based on the English village of Warwickshire. Tolkien wanted his setting to possess the climate and soil of Britain as well as its subtle beauty.

After *The Hobbit,* Tolkien expanded his geographic setting for the *Lord of the Rings* novels. The extensive maps of Middle-earth that illustrate the settings of Tolkien's later sagas resemble what Europe may have looked like prior to ages of geological erosion. Likewise, the constel-

---

LANGUAGE AND NAMES IN THE TEXT

Tolkien drew upon vocabulary from approximately fifteen separate languages, including Modern and Middle English, in his series of books. He often used this vocabulary in selecting character and place names. For instance, the name for Smaug, Tolkien's dragon, was created from the Germanic verb *smugan,* which means "to squeeze through a hole." Tolkien had originally called him Pryftan, but he changed the name to Smaug, perhaps as a pun on the dragon's size. Gandalf, the name originally intended for the head dwarf, was later given to the wizard in accordance with its Icelandic meaning, "sorcerer-elf." The name Balin, given to one of the dwarfs of Middle-earth, recalls Sir Balin, one of King Arthur's legendary knights.

---

lations mentioned throughout the series resemble those we see in today's sky. References to Orion, Great Bear, and Venus all appear within Tolkien's works.

The exact time in history to which Tolkien's Middle-earth novels are set, however, remains ambiguous. As one reviewer noted, Tolkien seems to say, "Choose some interglacial period if you

must ... but do not expect me to bind myself by an admission that you are right" (Kocher, p. 6).

While England proved to be fertile ground for Tolkien's imaginary efforts, he also found inspiration for some of his characters outside that country's borders. On a trip to Switzerland he came across a postcard reproduction of *Der Berggeist,* a painting by J. Madelener, a German artist. The work, whose title means "The Mountain Spirit" in English, was a painting of an old man with a white beard and long cloak seated under a pine tree. Tolkien kept the postcard and later labeled it "Origin of Gandalf" (Tolkien in Carpenter, p. 51).

Events in History at the Time the Novel Was Written

Oxford. Tolkien entered Oxford University as a student of classics in 1911. He became involved in activities with several clubs, including the Essay Club and Stapeldon, the college debating society. He did not perform as expected in his first term, however, and Tolkien began to question his course of study. After taking a class with Professor Joseph Wright, Tolkien decided to alter his major to philology (the study of literary texts and written records) and English. His previous interest in Old Norse (the language of Norwegians who sailed to Iceland during the ninth century) resurfaced during his studies. He studied the *Younger Edda* and *Elder Edda,* collections of prose and poetry that provide heroic and mythological accounts. Tolkien would later adopt the name "Gandalf," as well as all dwarf names used for his tales, from the *Elder Edda.* This background also served as the foundation for Tolkien's own invented language, which was based on Finnish. The young student felt that if he wrote any stories in the future, his invented language could serve as a strange fairy language. Following is an example of Tolkien's language:

> Ai lintulinda Lasselanta
> Pilingeve suyer nalla ganta
> Kuluvi ya karnevalinar
> V'ematte singi Eldamar
> (Tolkien in Carpenter, p. 76)

The words *Lasselanta,* or "Autumn," and *Eldamar,* or "elvenhome in the west," are used by Tolkien throughout his *Lord of the Rings* series. Another language invented for that series featured an alphabet with letter shapes that corresponded with the intended sound of the letter. Based on the runes (letters) of the *Elder Edda,* Tolkien invented his own "runes." These appear

A World War I battle.

in *The Hobbit* as a form of secret writing used on a map that directs the party to Smaug's cave. Tolkien believed that any complex tongue must have a history in which it developed. He thus began to conceive of a mythology based on his language and set in his native England.

T.C.B.S. Prior to college, Tolkien had attended the highly competitive King Edward's School in Birmingham. As a senior he was a member of the elite "Tea Club," a group that maintained the school library. It was here that Tolkien became intimately acquainted with classmates Christopher Wiseman, Rob Gilson, and G. B. Smith. This group became informally known as T.C.B.S. (T.C. for Tea Club, and B.S. for the Barrovain Society, where it conducted after-school meetings). Tolkien maintained these friendships throughout his Oxford years, continually exchanging letters and writing samples.

With Smith as a contributor and critic, Tolkien composed a series of poems known as his "Earendel Verses." These centered around a heroic figure, Earendel, and his travels through a strange and wonderful fantasy world. The poems marked Tolkien's first attempts to create his own mythology. Smith was later killed in World War I. The final line of his last letter to Tolkien read, "may you say the things I have tried to say long after I am not there to say them,

if such be my lot" (Carpenter, p. 86). This, perhaps more than anything else, inspired Tolkien to continue his efforts to flesh out his own mythological world.

World War I. On June 28, 1914, a group of Serbian conspirators assassinated the Austro-Hungarian Archduke Francis Ferdinand. Since the Serbian government had known of the plot and done nothing to prevent its execution, the Austrian government decided to immediately retaliate. The tense political climate in Europe provided the perfect breeding ground for a conflict that quickly escalated into a world war. By late summer, the British government had joined the Allied forces of Russia, France, and Serbia against the Central Powers of Austria and Germany. The United States later entered the war with the Allies in April 1916. While battles raged in France, Russia, and Belgium, Great Britain defended the Allies at sea. The British cut off Germany from virtually all food and supplies with their naval blockade. World War I finally came to a close with the signing of an armistice agreement on November 11, 1918. The years of conflict exacted a heavy toll on its participants, however. In addition to material losses, the war killed 8.5 million people and wounded another 21 million. While all nations involved in the war were significantly weakened, Britain emerged from the war as a country that had lost a great deal during the conflict. In fact, it had spent the most money among the Allies.

Although Tolkien wanted to enlist in the armed forces at the onset of World War I, his primary objective was the completion of his Oxford degree. He therefore underwent military training while at the university and took a draft deferment until after graduation. In 1916 he enlisted with the 11th Battalion, stationed at Étaples, France. Both Rob Gilson and G. B. Smith of T.C.B.S. were killed in the war effort during that same year.

C. S. LEWIS

C. S. Lewis, a fellow Oxford scholar and author of *The Chronicles of Narnia*, another notable children's series, was one of the first people to read Tolkien's manuscript of *The Hobbit*. A reviewer for *The Times Literary Supplement*, he helped convince *The London Times* to print a notice of the publication of his friend's new novel.

Tolkien's wartime experiences had a significant impact on the young writer. One chapter in *The Hobbit*, entitled "The Gathering of the Clouds," deals with the rising tensions prior to the Battle of Five Armies in the novel. On one side are the Elves, Men, and Dwarves; the other side consists of the Goblins and the wild Wolves. The parallel to the division of Allied and Central powers cannot be missed. Like World War I, the novel's battle rages without an end in sight until a sixth army, the Eagles, enters to aid the Dwarves.

Tolkien's war also featured tragic casualties. In an incident that perhaps recalls the incredible loss of young men in World War I, the two youngest dwarves, Fili and Kili, are killed in Tolkien's epic battle. Finally, the character Thorin almost certainly echoes the author's own thoughts when he states on his deathbed that "if more of us valued food and cheer and song above hoarded gold, it would be a merrier world" (*The Hobbit,* p. 288).

Reception of the work. Although some critics found *The Hobbit* to be lacking "the courageous freedom of real adventure" (Carpenter, p. 182), most greeted Tolkien's novel with rave reviews. The novel was published on September 21, 1937, and by Christmas of the same year the first edition had sold out. The American reprint that was issued a few months later included four color illustrations by the author that had not been included in the original version. In 1938 *The Hobbit* received the *New York Herald Tribune* prize for best juvenile novel of the season.

For More Information

Carpenter, Humphrey. *J.R. R. Tolkien, A Biography.* London: George Allen and Unwin, 1977.

Helms, Randel. *Tolkien's World.* Boston: Houghton Mifflin and Co., 1974.

Kocher, Paul H. *Master of Middle-earth.* Boston: Houghton Mifflin and Co., 1972.

Tolkien, J. R. R. *The Hobbit.* 1937. Reprint, New York: Ballantine, 1973.

The Hunchback of Notre Dame

by
Victor Hugo

The poet, novelist, and dramatist Victor Hugo was born in 1802, a decade after the end of the French monarchy. He was a child during the dictatorship of Napoleon Bonaparte and grew to manhood during a sweeping period of political unrest in France. Even as a young man—he was twenty-eight when he began *The Hunchback of Notre Dame*—he looked to France's past to orient himself in the present and sort out what it meant to be French.

Events in History at the Time the Novel Takes Place

France in 1482. During the exhausting Hundred Years' War, Joan of Arc and her cohorts had helped to expel the English from French soil. By 1482, the year the novel takes place, the French monarchy had recovered much of the authority it had lost during the war and had consolidated its power. The menacing Black Plague, which had devastated Paris in the previous century, had subsided, and the population began to grow and prosper again. Yet the world was still seen as a confusing and volatile place where the forces of good and evil battled constantly. For someone living in Paris during that period, the memory of the Black Death and its suffering and pain remained vivid and contributed to the belief that dark forces were ever present. People's outlook on the future was very much conditioned by the dismal recent past.

Positive changes were taking place at the end of the fifteenth century that began to dislodge the

THE LITERARY WORK

A novel set in Paris, France, in 1482 during the reign of Louis XI (1461-83); published in 1831.

SYNOPSIS

The grotesque hunchback, Quasimodo, bell-ringer of Notre Dame cathedral, suffers the torture of an impossible love that he harbors for the sublimely beautiful Esmeralda, a mysterious street dancer.

firmly implanted belief that people had no control over their destiny. These changes took some time to take effect, however. At the time, French society was still organized along feudal lines, with power in the hands of nobles and the church. Their lands were worked by peasants, mostly serfs who could not leave their estates and were forced to lead slave-like existences. Europe, however, was poised on the brink of the Renaissance, a period in which people would gain a greater sense of human achievements of the past and of the potential of humanity to shape its own destiny.

Feudal France. Feudalism was a political and economic system that was common in Europe from the eleventh to the sixteenth century. Under this system, land was controlled by a small number of powerful individuals. The large peasant class was forced to provide services, dues, and an oath of allegiance to the landowners in exchange for the right to farm parcels of the nobility's land. In feudal France, the countryside was full of powerful nobles—the Duke of Burgundy, the Count of Britanny, and others—who exercised kingly powers over their separate territories.

LANDMARK DATES IN FRENCH HISTORY THROUGH THE 1830S

800-814: Emperor Charlemagne gives the church a share in the government of his empire.

887: Empire that includes France, Germany, and Italy dissolves; rise of feudal system places control with nobles inside and outside the church.

1163: Construction of Notre Dame cathedral begins.

1453: End of the Hundred Years' War.

1461-1483: Louis XI overpowers the nobles and concentrates authority in the hands of the king; period in which *The Hunchback of Notre Dame* is set.

1470: The printing press, invented twenty years earlier by Johannes Gutenberg of Germany, finds its way into France.

1789: French revolution begins, leads to fall of Bastille prison, which represents the power of the monarchy.

1792: Monarchy is abolished; mob attacks Notre Dame cathedral, destroys many of the sculptures on the face of the building.

1804: Napoleon names himself emperor.

1814-1815: Napoleon gives up power; monarchy is restored.

1830: Rebellion leads to constitutional monarchy with more power for the people; Hugo begins writing *The Hunchback of Notre Dame.*

Feudalism grew, with more and more castles dotting the countryside, serving as fortresses against invaders from the north. Most of the nobles played both a superior and an inferior role. They had serfs who worked for and received protection from them, while at the same time the nobles provided military support to lords with even greater power. Called duke, count, or lord like the nobles, the clergy (officials of the church) held perhaps even more power than did members of the nobility. The clergy managed large, rich parcels of land in the name of the church and controlled education in the country. Combined, the clergy and the nobles governed most of France.

Louis XI. Louis XI gained power in 1461. He attacked the nobles and recovered their lands and authority for the Crown. In some instances, he won the noble families over to his side. On other occasions, he mercilessly crushed those who opposed him. One historian paints a gruesome picture:

> Many perished, being hanged to the trees along the roads or thrown into the river sewn in sacks on which was written, "Let the justice of the king proceed."
>
> (Duruy, p. 436)

The ruthlessness of Louis XI's reign from 1461 to 1483 was greatly felt. No French king had ever imposed himself so totally and tyrannically. He was the first ruler to have the powers of the realm of France so firmly in hand. He therefore wielded much authority over the lives of his subjects. Cursed as a tyrant and hailed as a peacemaker, Louis XI also ushered in a period of growth. He was, for example, the first to welcome the printing press into France, twenty years after its invention. With his death in 1483, the year after the novel takes place, France entered the modern era.

Fate. Fate must have seemed a fickle force to someone living during the Middle Ages. Sometimes cruel, sometimes kind, it weighed heavily on the life of medieval man. The concept of fate as a wheel of fortune turning this way and that, with abrupt reversals, is reflected by the twists and turns of plot in *The Hunchback of Notre Dame.* In one scene of the novel, for instance, the king inspects at length the construction of a wooden cage. Inside the cage, a prisoner wails for mercy. The king does not notice the prisoner because he is preoccupied with the cost of the wood for the cage. Yet when another prisoner appeals for mercy, the king frees him on a whim. Like fate, the king's actions seem to have no rhyme or reason.

"Time of Trials." The development of Paris had been hindered by the Hundred Years' War (1337-1453) and the Black Plague. This span of turbulence, which straddled two centuries, is known in French history as the "Time of Trials." After this period, marked not only by war and the Black Plague but also by famine, peasants began to move back to urban centers such as Paris, searching for security in numbers and for increased opportunity. The safety that Paris afforded was relative, however, for bands of roving thieves harassed the city dwellers. These pillaging groups had sprung from the droves of mercenary soldiers left idle by the conclusion of the Hundred Years' War. They terrorized the

One of the gargoyles on Notre Dame cathedral.

elements in a grotesque union of opposites: depictions included winged lions with hooves, goat men, raven cats, and dragon frogs.

The Novel in Focus

The plot. The story opens on the day of the Festival of Fools, the highlight of which is the selection of a Prince of Fools, celebrated for his ugliness. After rejecting many contestants, the Parisians choose as the winner Quasimodo, the hunchback who rings the bells of Notre Dame cathedral to sound the hours and call people to prayer. His grotesque features (including a misshapen eye, protruding teeth, a huge hooked nose, and apelike arms) make him appear monstrous to others. Parading him through the streets of Paris, the crowd encounters the enchanting gypsy girl Esmeralda and stops to watch her dance.

populace with impunity, and all but the most privileged feared for their lives.

This state of affairs is reflected in *The Hunchback of Notre Dame*. At one point in the novel, the poet Pierre Gringoire inadvertently wanders into the *Cour des Miracles* (*Court of Miracles*), a haunt of beggars and lair of bandits controlled by the powerful Clopin Trouillefou, who is known as the King of the Thieves. Trouillefou mercilessly condemns Gringoire to be hanged for the poet's supposed trespass into his domain.

Notre Dame, spiritual and historical epicenter. Paris was a settlement in the immediate area surrounding Notre Dame as early as the third century. The cathedral, begun in 1163, took about a century and a half to complete. It is built on a spot that Parisians have always dedicated to the practice of religious rites. Before Christianity it was the site of a temple to the Roman god Jupiter. Both a historical and spiritual monument of France, Notre Dame has witnessed many important events in French history. Kings and queens have been married and crowned inside its walls.

In building Notre Dame, the architects ringed the spires of the cathedral with statues of fearsome-looking gargoyles. As messengers of the divine wrath of God, the gargoyle supposedly warded off evil spirits. A fantasy creature, the gargoyle was a combination of natural and imagined

PLACE OF GATHERING—NOTRE DAME

During the Middle Ages, the Notre Dame cathedral was one of the few havens in Paris for commoners and the less fortunate. It provided shelter and served as a place of religious pilgrimage and prayer. Within its walls one could perhaps find spiritual solace in religion, or take comfort in being around other people in the large public square—the *Place du Parvis*—in front of the cathedral.

People frequently gathered for commerce or to meet each other in this square, which, like other public squares, was also the site of punishments for heresy or other crimes. Justice was, by today's standards, arbitrary; one could be accused of evil deeds on the slightest suspicion. Heretics might be burned at the stake, and public torture was prevalent. These public displays of punishment calmed popular fears and satisfied a widespread obsession with sin and damnation. Many people felt that evil had to be stamped out at all costs, even if it meant killing or punishing someone in error. In *The Hunchback of Notre Dame*, Hugo depicts the punishment of Quasimodo and the execution of Esmeralda before thronging crowds full of morbid curiosity. Such scenes reflect the sometimes tragic quest for purity and the destruction of perceived evil.

Secretly, the evil archdeacon Claude Frollo lusts after Esmeralda. Deeply loyal to Frollo, who rescued him as an abandoned baby, Quasimodo assists the archdeacon in an attempt to kidnap

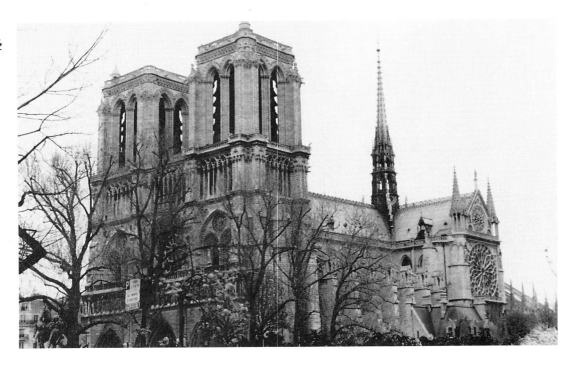

Notre Dame as it looks today.

Esmeralda. The attempt is witnessed by the poverty-stricken poet Gringoire, whom Quasimodo attacks with a blow. The kidnapping,

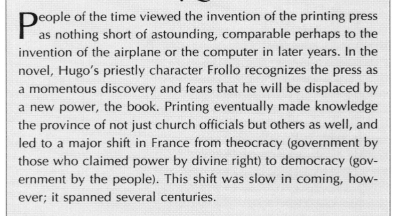

THE PRINTING PRESS, A PIVOTAL INVENTION

People of the time viewed the invention of the printing press as nothing short of astounding, comparable perhaps to the invention of the airplane or the computer in later years. In the novel, Hugo's priestly character Frollo recognizes the press as a momentous discovery and fears that he will be displaced by a new power, the book. Printing eventually made knowledge the province of not just church officials but others as well, and led to a major shift in France from theocracy (government by those who claimed power by divine right) to democracy (government by the people). This shift was slow in coming, however; it spanned several centuries.

however, is foiled by a rescuer, Phoebus de Châteaupers, a handsome scoundrel who is captain of the Paris city archers.

Gringoire is then captured by thugs in a dangerous section of the city. His captors threaten to execute him if none of the women present will marry him. Faced with hanging, he is rescued by Esmeralda, who suddenly appears and, out of pity, offers to marry him, although the marriage is not consummated. Meanwhile, Frollo is suspected of sorcery and Quasimodo is accused in court of associating with him and is publicly flogged. Esmeralda, although she is in love with her rescuer Châteaupers, offers the thirsty Quasimodo a drink, and this kindness gains her Quasimodo's undying love.

Frollo, still determined to possess Esmeralda, tricks Châteaupers into leading him to a rendezvous with Esmeralda, at which Frollo stabs Châteaupers. Frollo makes his escape, and the crowd accuses Esmeralda, who had fainted during all the mayhem, of having slain Châteaupers. Esmeralda, also accused of witchcraft, is taken to prison. On her way to do penance in the square of Notre Dame before being hanged, she glimpses Châteaupers, who has survived Frollo's attack; but he does nothing to help her. Frollo offers to save her if she will be his, but she refuses. Finally Quasimodo appears and whisks Esmeralda off, giving her refuge in the cathedral tower.

A crowd of Parisian commoners attacks the cathedral in an attempt to free Esmeralda from Quasimodo, whose noble motives are unknown to the throng. Frollo intercedes, delivering Esmeralda to her executioners. Having witnessed her body swaying from the gallows pole, an enraged Quasimodo then pushes Frollo from the heights of Notre Dame to die below. The novel's last chapter, "The Marriage of Quasimodo," provides a haunting gothic description of the discovery of the skeletons of Quasimodo and Esmeralda locked in eternal embrace.

The central role of Notre Dame cathedral. The novel's usual title in English, *The Hunchback of Notre Dame,* has perhaps fostered too much fascination with the grotesque as exemplified in the physically repulsive body of Quasimodo. Faithfully translated, the title of Hugo's novel is simply *Notre Dame of Paris,* an indication of the central place the cathedral occupies in the story. Indeed, the cathedral emerges as an essential "character" in the novel. It serves as the point around which the action and the main characters gravitate. Book (or chapter) III of Hugo's work is devoted in large part to bringing the cathedral alive through descriptions of its underlying historic and spiritual importance to the culture of France. "Every face, every stone of the venerable monument is a page ... of the history of the country" (Hugo, *The Hunchback of Notre Dame,* p. 102).

Hugo points out that as Notre Dame was built over a period of 150 years its architects combined two different styles—Romanesque and Gothic. He further details all the trials and damage it had suffered at the hands of pillagers and various architects as if he were describing the ravages of time a living person had suffered.

The medieval multitudes and the way they spoke. In *The Hunchback of Notre Dame,* Hugo attempted to recreate the archaic diction and grammar of the 'common' people of the Middle Ages. He led his fellow French Romantic writers of the first half of the 1800s in breaking the old barrier between the common speech of the people and the 'noble' or high and rigid vocabulary of the aristocrats that had dominated poetry and drama since long before the French Revolution. In rendering the language of the general populace, Hugo gave them the possibility of being represented in fiction; he gave them a voice. Never before had the common man played such an important role in fiction. Hugo intended that such details, coupled with his careful description of Gothic art and architecture, enhance the authenticity of the historical setting of the novel.

Sources. Hugo began to research *The Hunchback of Notre Dame* in the early 1820s. Contrary to the legend that Hugo wrote the entire novel from scratch in five months, it was the fruit of many years of preparation. Hugo studied chronicles of medieval life, borrowing historical details and names for his characters from annals of the fifteenth century. In this way, he hoped to accurately and naturally recreate the atmosphere of medieval Paris.

DIVINE INSPIRATION

In the preface to the first edition of *The Hunchback of Notre Dame,* Hugo discusses the inspiration for his novel. During a careful exploration of the Notre Dame cathedral, he had come across a Greek inscription in the wall of one of the corner towers that translates as "fate" or "destiny." He was struck by the "dark and profound significance of the word" and noted that its Gothic calligraphy identified it as the work of a medieval scribe. It set Hugo to wondering about the life of the person who left such a trace. It was on this word that he founded the project for his book.

His characters share traits with others in literature and history. To create the gypsy street dancer Esmeralda, for example, Hugo turned to popular tales and myths from Italian, Spanish, and French stories. To create the character of Phoebus de Châteaupers, the cad who is unworthy of Esmeralda's longing, Hugo combined the traits of a nobleman of the same name who actually lived during the 1400s with traits of Phoebus, the Greek sun god who was reputed for his physical beauty. Similarly, Hugo's Pierre Gringoire was based on a real-life Gringoire, a court poet for King Louis XII, who ruled after the time span of the novel. The real Gringoire was only seven years old when *The Hunchback of Notre Dame* takes place.

Events in History at the Time the Novel Was Written

Revolution of 1830. Hugo began writing *The Hunchback of Notre Dame* right after the Revolution of July 1830. The initial French Revolution in 1789 had toppled the king from his throne, but over the next two decades, power again became concentrated in one man as Napoleon seized control of France and crowned himself emperor in Notre Dame cathedral. After his defeat by opposing European forces in 1814,

France returned to a system of monarchy and the powers of the people were greatly reduced. Freedom of the press was abolished and the vote was restricted primarily to landowners. In 1830 the people rebelled once again, raising havoc for three days until a new citizen-king, Louis Philippe, came to power. Hailed as a monarch devoted to the revolutionary spirit of 1789, he increased the freedom enjoyed by the population. His actions included lowering the voting age from thirty to twenty-five and dropping the tax on voters from 300 to 200 francs. But there was more unrest. Mob action in December 1830 led to the sacking of the archbishop's palace and the tossing of his books into the river.

Though the December unrest was a potential threat to Louis Philippe, he managed to maintain his position as ruler of France. He was successful in large part because he used newspapers to appeal to the people and staged public rallies that proved he had support among French citizens.

SAVE NOTRE DAME

In 1829 Hugo wrote a pamphlet that he hoped would inspire people to a greater love and appreciation for the monuments and cathedrals left from the Middle Ages, which had fallen into neglect. Hugo was especially concerned about the state of Notre Dame cathedral. A symbol of the monarchy and the church's power, it had been sacked during the anti-monarchical and anti-clerical frenzy of the French Revolution. His pamphlet, "On the Destruction of Monuments in France," called for the compatriots of his day to save the France of old to which the traditions of the people are tied. In 1845, not many years after the publication of *The Hunchback of Notre Dame*, a complete restoration of the neglected and ransacked cathedral was undertaken.

But the events surrounding the Revolution of 1830 made it clear that the masses would have to be reckoned with in determining the political future of France. Increasingly conscious of their roles as actors in history, the commoners began to see themselves differently. They had gone from being the subjects of a king to the citizens of the French Republic. The degree of power they would ultimately wield, however, remained unclear. Members of the French population grappled with questions about their country's place in history

and their own place in the new social order. Consequently, nineteenth-century France developed a thirst for all things historical in an effort to explain uncertain issues of their own time.

Revolution and *The Hunchback of Notre Dame*. The Revolution of 1830 affected many of the views presented in Hugo's novel. The book predicts revolution and includes a scene where a crowd of characters from the Paris underworld assault the cathedral. This plot development was based on the mob action that actually took place during the 1789 French Revolution.

A primary feature of Hugo's novel is its focus on the rise of the common people. He views them as a significant political force capable of weighing decisively on the course of history. This is reflected in the prominent place they occupy in the story. By including a vast cast of characters in his novel, Hugo attempted to portray people from all walks of life and to represent society as a whole.

Hugo's personal political views were unfixed. At one time he had been a royalist, a supporter of the king. He broke away from this set of beliefs, however, and gradually moved closer to a democratic view. Though he supported Louis Philippe when he came to power in 1830, in the rebellion of 1848 he opposed the citizen-king. Hugo took to the streets with others that year, forcing Louis Philippe from power.

Personal unrest. In addition to experiencing the great historical changes that faced his country in the 1830s, Hugo encountered unstable relations in his personal life while writing the novel. His wife Adéle became involved in an affair with Sainte-Beuve, a prominent literary critic and Hugo's best friend. In 1827 Hugo and Sainte-Beuve had co-founded a *cénacle,* or literary salon, comprised of prominent Romantic writers such as Prosper Mérimée, Théopile Gautier, and Gérard de Nerval. When Sainte-Beuve became Adéle's lover, Hugo's marriage underwent a profound change. Though Adéle and Victor remained married, they became ever more estranged. Hugo soon engaged in relationships with other women, including a life-long affair with actress Juliette Drouet.

In addition, Hugo's brother Eugéne had been confined in an insane asylum since 1823, a situation for which Hugo felt somewhat responsible. Eugéne had been Victor's rival in two ways; he was an aspiring writer, and he was interested in Adéle before she married Victor. On the night Victor and Adéle were wed, Eugéne had a mental breakdown and was later committed to the asylum. Hugo's feeling of guilt over this turn of events is echoed in *The Hunchback of Notre Dame*. In the novel, the character Frollo feels responsible for the death of a younger brother.

The birth of the historical novel. The creation of the historical novel in France was spurred by the works of the Scottish writer Walter Scott (1771-1832) and the book *The Genius of Christianity* by the Frenchman François René de Chateaubriand. In Scott's novels, which Hugo had studied, the common people were represented for the first time as conscious agents of history. Chateaubriand held that Gothic architecture, as embodied in Notre Dame, was a symbol for the old French Catholic spirit which could, in his eyes, be traced all the way back to France's primordial beginning and, ultimately, nature. Guided by these two major influences, Victor Hugo looked to the past for inspiration for *The Hunchback of Notre Dame*.

In the early 1800s Hugo was among the leading young writers in search of new literary forms.

His historical novel satisfied the taste of the day for books dealing with the history of France, especially its Middle Ages. Hailed by some as the first great historical romance in French literature, the novel also received criticism. Writers of the 1800s called it everything from a magnificent book that brought Old Paris alive to melodrama and bad art.

For More Information

Bayer-Berenbaum, Linda. *The Gothic Imagination*. Rutherford: Associated University Presses, 1982.

Brombert, Victor. *Victor Hugo and the Visionary Novel*. Cambridge: Harvard University Press, 1984.

Duruy, Victor. *A Short History of France*. New York: E. P. Dutton, 1917.

Hugo, Victor. *The Hunchback of Notre-Dame*. New York: Dodd, Mead, 1947.

Maurois, André. *Victor Hugo and His World*. London: Thames & Hudson, 1966.

Stevenson, Robert Louis. "Victor Hugo's Romances." *The Cornhill Magazine* 30, no. 176 (August 1874): 179-194.

Iliad

by
Homer

The Greek poet Homer is credited with composing the *Iliad*, although the authorship of the epic remains uncertain. It is believed that Homer probably lived in the eighth century B.C. While scholars have made educated guesses about aspects of his life, nothing is known for certain. His birthplace may have been an island on the eastern edge of the Aegean Sea, or perhaps a city on the nearby coast. The population of both areas probably spoke of legends of the Trojan War—the subject of the *Iliad*. It is believed that the author of the *Iliad* composed the work before writing the **Odyssey** (also covered in *Literature and Its Times*), another narrative attributed to Homer, that describes events following the war.

Events in History at the Time the Poem Takes Place

The legend of the Trojan War. The *Iliad* is set during the Trojan War, in the ninth year of the legendary ten-year conflict, which ended in either 1184 or 1250 B.C., depending on the source consulted. The epic itself offers no explanations for why the war began or how it ends; Homer assumes that this information is familiar to his audience.

The legend of the Trojan War appears in many different Greek stories. All of these tales agree that the war started over a woman named Helen, who was reputed to be the most beautiful woman in the world. Helen was the wife of Menelaus of Sparta. Her married status, however, did not stop a Trojan prince named Paris from seducing her.

Paris traveled to Menelaus's palace to collect

THE LITERARY WORK

An epic poem set in ancient Greece, around 1200 B.C.; written around 750 B.C.

SYNOPSIS

A Greek army has been at war for nine years when an internal quarrel breaks out between Achilles, the greatest warrior, and Agamemnon, the most powerful king. The wrath of Achilles—its genesis, its effects, and its resolution—underlies an exploration of what it means to be a war hero.

Helen, who was given to him as a prize from Aphrodite, the goddess of love. Paris had gained Aphrodite's favor because of his judgment that Aphrodite was more beautiful than either Athena, the goddess of wisdom, or Hera, the goddess of marriage. Aphrodite rewarded his judgment of the contest by granting him possession of the most beautiful mortal woman in the world. Paris carried Helen off to Troy and married her; whether or not this turn of events was to her liking is a matter of conjecture, but many versions of the story insist that she aided and abetted Paris in his abduction of her. In any event, Helen's husband Menelaus was enraged. He took prompt action, beseeching his brother, King Agamemnon, for help in winning Helen back. Agamemnon assembled a huge fleet from all over Greece and sailed to attack Troy.

Although the Greek army was vast, the Trojans managed to hold out for ten years behind the city's strong walls. Finally, realizing that Troy

SOME CHARACTERS IN THE LEGEND OF THE TROJAN WAR

Greek Spelling	Latin Spelling
Achilleus	Achilles
Hektor	Hector
Menelaos	Menelaus
Patroklos	Patroclus
Athene	Athena

could not be taken by force, the Greeks devised an ingenious plan to infiltrate the city. They built a massive wooden horse and left it just outside the city walls. The Greek ships then sailed away, bearing their army. The Trojans believed that this signaled the end of the war, so they opened their gates and dragged the horse inside their city, taking it as a gift from their vanquished foes. Hidden in the horse's wooden belly, however, were the Greeks' finest warriors, who spilled out of their hiding place late at night and opened the city gates for the rest of their returned army. They sacked and burned Troy, slaughtering its inhabitants. Helen was then returned to her husband.

The existence of Troy. Ancient people claimed to have visited Troy and seen the graves of the heroes that died during the war. Although they recorded their findings in some detail, it was not until the late 1800s that archaeological digs in Turkey finally discovered the fabled city. A German businessman by the name of Heinrich Schliemann, who had been fascinated by ancient Greece since boyhood, was determined to find the legendary city of Troy. He reportedly used Homer's own description of the city's location to pinpoint a hill at the Turkish site of Hissarlik. Between 1871 and 1890, he and his Greek wife Sophie oversaw excavations there that unearthed a whole series of ancient towns built one on top of the other over the course of thousands of years. The earliest town, which was named Troy I, dates back to the fourth millennium B.C., and so was much too old to be Homer's Troy. But evidence found in the ruins of Troy VII (the remnants of the seventh civilization to live on that site) indicate that it was destroyed violently around 1220 B.C., a discovery that makes it the most likely model for the legendary Troy. No other archaeological evidence supporting the tale of the Trojan War has been found, however. Scholars speculate that the legend was based loosely on facts that were embellished as they were told and retold.

History vs. legend. Although the *Iliad* concerns ancient Greek heroes, the poem's major characters are referred to not as Greeks but as groups of "Achaeans," "Argives," and "Danaans." Originally from western Asia, these Greek-speaking peoples invaded the Mediterranean area around 1900 B.C. Within 400 years of their arrival in Greece, these peoples had founded the highly developed civilization that provides the background for Homer's tale.

This culture is known as "Mycenaean," named after the city of Mycenae that has been excavated by modern archaeologists. Mycenae is thought to be the model for the cities in which Homer's Greek heroes lived. The Mycenaeans were city-dwellers who were ruled by kings and governed by well-organized bureaucracies; the ruling classes were clearly militaristic.

Discrepancies can be found between discoveries about Mycenaean culture and details in Homer's epic. For example, characters in the *Iliad* cremate their dead, but the Mycenaean civilization practiced burial of their dead. It was not until later in history, closer to Homer's time, that cremation became widespread. These discrepancies may simply be errors. While a great deal of information about the Mycenaeans was passed on to Homer's society through tales and legends, Mycenaean culture had disappeared long before the creation of the *Iliad*. Homer could not have known about every aspect of their civilization.

Around the year 1200 B.C., many of the great Mycenaean palaces were violently destroyed, and the entire Mycenaean culture dwindled. It is not clear who the attackers were, or why the palaces were assailed, but historians speculate that a series of local disputes may have been responsible. For the next 400 years, the Greeks sank into an obscure era that is sometimes referred to as the "Dark Ages" (1150-800 B.C.).

Who were the Trojans? While archaeologists were unable to find the kind of evidence that

Painting by R. V. Deutsch depicting the abduction of Helen by Paris.

would help them understand the lives of the Trojans in Troy VII (the seventh civilization to live on that historical site), Troy VI (the sixth civilization) contained ancient remains that helped them draw conclusions about the inhabitants of Troy VII. The discovery of a wide variety of Mycenaean artifacts, including arrowheads, daggers, and sword pommels, within the ruins of Troy VI indicate that the two civilizations were trading partners. The ruins of Troy VI also contained a large number of horse bones, which suggests that the Trojans were horse breeders. Supporting this theory are passages in Homer's poem that describe the Trojans as "breakers of horses" and praise the quality of Trojan horses (Homer, The Iliad, 3.127).

The gods. Pinning down the religious beliefs of Homer's Greeks is difficult because archaeology and the literary record offer conflicting evidence, and views varied from region to region and from one time period to another. The Iliad deals extensively with the interactions between the gods and men. As the oldest Greek poem known, it has been studied by scholars searching for clues to the spiritual beliefs of the people represented by its characters. Some evidence indicates that the ancient Greeks conceived their gods' appearances to be much different than those of the deities who populate the Iliad, indicating that the ancient Greek deities could be human-shaped, half-human and half-animal, or even take the form of a rock. In the Iliad, however, all of the gods appear as human beings. While they have the power to change shape—appearing, for example, as animals if it suits their purposes—their normal appearance is human.

In the Iliad, many events are influenced by the involvement of gods, an idea that seems to have been popular in ancient Greece. This belief was based on the idea that all events, ranging from earthquakes to plagues to unsuccessful efforts to throw a spear, were the result of divine intervention in human lives rather than luck or other factors. If any misfortune befell a person, it was probably because that person had not performed the proper rituals to the appropriate gods.

But it was also possible that the misfortune was predestined. There was a belief among the ancient Greeks that, on the day of every person's birth, his or her fate was decided. Some sources speak of a Greek belief that even the gods themselves could not control fate. According to Greek tradition, one's destiny was determined by three daughters of Zeus known as the three Fates. These Fates were thought of as old women; one

spun the thread of life that carried the person's lifelong destiny, a second measured its length, and the third cut the thread and ended the life. In the Iliad, however, Zeus himself is portrayed as the supreme deity who ensures that the course of each person's fate is completed.

The Poem in Focus

The plot. The Iliad is the story of the Greek hero Achilles. Although he is a mortal man, his mother is the sea-goddess Thetis. Achilles's impressive skill as a warrior makes him one of the most important Achaeans in the army, and his skills on the battlefield are a source of pride to him. But despite his prowess as a warrior, he must remain subordinate to King Agamemnon, who is leading the expedition against Troy.

A NOBLE HERITAGE

~

The Iliad was so influential in ancient Greece that the noble families of Athens used to pay specialists to create family trees in which their ancestors were listed as the heroes of the Iliad. Alexander the Great, who conquered the known world in the fourth century B.C., declared that he was the direct descendant of Achilles. It is recorded that Alexander visited the tomb of Achilles at Troy before beginning one of his military campaigns. The Iliad's influence also extended to the Romans. Julius Caesar and his son, the emperor Augustus Caesar, claimed that they were descended from the Trojan hero Aeneas.

As the poem begins, the Achaeans have just sacked a small city in the area around Troy. They have taken all of the women captive, including the daughter of a priest of Apollo, the god associated with healing. This priest comes to Agamemnon and begs him to release his daughter in return for a ransom, but Agamemnon refuses. The priest then calls on Apollo to punish the Achaeans until they return his daughter. The god fulfills his wishes, spreading a deadly disease throughout the army. The Greek soldiers continue to die in large numbers until Achilles convinces Agamemnon to release the priest's daughter. But Agamemnon will return the girl to her father only if Achilles, in turn, gives Agamemnon a captive woman named Briseis. Achilles agrees to give his beloved Briseis to the king, but he is infuriated. The warrior views Briseis as his

DIVINE AID

Numerous gods and goddesses participate in the Trojan War. They support their respective sides for many different reasons. Since Aphrodite's son, Aeneas, is a Trojan warrior, Aphrodite assists the Trojans. Hera and Athena, on the other hand, help the Achaeans; they are angry because the Trojan prince, Paris, had judged that Aphrodite's beauty was greater than theirs. Following is a list of the principal gods and goddesses that support each side in the epic battle taking place on earth:

Achaeans	Trojans
Hera—goddess of marriage	Apollo—god of healing
Athena—goddess of wisdom	Aphrodite—goddess of love
Poseidon—god of the sea	Ares—god of war
Hermes—messenger god	Artemis—goddess of the hunt
Hephaestus—god of fire	

rightful war prize and evidence of his prowess. He feels dishonored, a very serious offense to a man whose entire life revolves around competing successfully against other men.

Achilles and his troops withdraw from the Achaean army and return to his ships. Humiliated by Agamemnon's treatment of him, Achilles calls on his divine mother, Thetis, for help in securing revenge. She appeals to Zeus, the father of the gods, to punish the Achaeans until they have recognized the superior qualities of Achilles in proper fashion. Zeus agrees, in part because he wants to make certain that Achilles fulfills his destiny.

A prophecy surrounds the life of Achilles: he can either live a long, happy life and die without recognition, or he can fight at Troy and gain everlasting fame. The prophecy promises that he will be doomed to a short, painful life if he chooses fame over happiness. Because Achilles chooses to go to war, Zeus must ensure that the hero gains the most acclaim of all the warriors at Troy. The god's plan is to bring the Achaeans to the brink of defeat so that Achilles can save them and win honor in the eyes of others.

To carry out his plans, Zeus inspires the Achaeans to go into battle against the Trojans. He also allows the gods and goddesses of Olympus to choose sides between the Achaeans and Greeks and to support them in battle if they desire.

The battle seesaws as the gods take turns helping their favorite mortals. The Achaeans first take the upper hand, killing every Trojan who faces them. But the Trojans recover and turn the Achaeans back with the help of the gods who are sympathetic to their cause. The Trojans are led by a number of heroes, particularly the magnificent warrior Hector.

The Achaean heroes almost kill Hector several times, but he always recovers. Eventually, Hector manages to overrun the Achaean camp and threatens to set fire to the Achaean fleet. The only person who can save the Achaeans is Achilles, who has refused to join the battle because of his anger at Agamemnon. The king, desperate to convince his best warrior to return to the field of battle, offers to return Briseis and pay him a vast amount of treasure. Agamemnon's efforts fail, however.

The best friend of Achilles, Patroclus, who had been wearing Achilles's armor in order to fool the Trojans into thinking that Achilles had rejoined the fighting, is then killed by Hector. Only at this point does Achilles reenter the war. He meets Hector in combat and slays him. Achilles afterward ties Hector's body to his chariot and drags it around the walls of Troy to dishonor his enemy. The *Iliad* ends when Hector's father, the king of Troy, goes to the camp of Achilles in secret and asks for the return of his son's body for burial. Advised by the gods to be merciful, Achilles agrees and calls for a truce so that the Trojans can properly bury Hector.

Women as spoils of war. Although the *Iliad* is primarily about the heroic exploits of male warriors, women are actually central to the action of the poem. In most instances, they serve as prizes that the men battle one another to win. The entire Trojan War is triggered by Helen's great beauty, which causes the goddess Aphro-

Engraving of an 18th-century drawing of Homer.

dite to give her away to a man who is not her husband; if, as in some versions of the tale, she grows to like her fate, it does not change the fact that her fate is largely controlled by men. The treatment of the captive woman Briseis is further evidence of the subservient status of women in the poem. Taken from her home when the Achaeans sack her city, Briseis is given to Achilles, traded to Agamemnon in compensation for his loss of another woman, and then traded back to Achilles in the hope of winning his agreement to fight. Helen and Briseis are both loved by the men who have taken them, but the women's value as a social asset or political prize is more important than the personal bonds that tie them to their men.

Whether the poem reflects the actual status of women in archaic Greece is a matter of debate. The more plentiful documents of later Greek culture indicate that women had very little control over their lives. Such evidence suggests that Homer's depiction of the standing of women during that period may be fairly accurate.

War in the *Iliad*. Although the *Iliad* emphasizes Achilles's prowess as a warrior, there are several points in the poem at which the heroes are critical of war and acknowledge it to be evil. At one point, a truce is called so that Menelaus and Paris can fight a duel. Rather than continue with the war, the winner gets to keep Helen. Menelaus agrees to the duel, saying to the Trojans:

You have suffered much evil
for the sake of this my quarrel since
　　Alexandros [Paris] began it.
As for that one of us two to whom death and
　　doom are given,
Let him die: the rest of you be made friends
　　with each other....
So he spoke, and the Trojans and Achaians
　　[Achaeans] were joyful.
　　　　　　　　　　　　　　(*The Iliad*, 3.99-111)

The prospect of a duel to settle the dispute fills both the Trojans and Achaeans with joy, an indication that both sides would much prefer to avoid a battle. Achilles himself discovers that winning glory is of little value next to the loss of his best friend. Throughout the epic there is an insoluable tension between the human ties that bind and the martial prowess that kills.

FORGOTTEN ALPHABETS

The Mycenaeans had developed a form of writing, now known as Linear B, but it disappeared completely during the Greek Dark Ages. Without a written language to record events, the people who lived during that period left archaeologists with very little reliable information about events that took place during the Dark Ages. The situation did not change until the ninth century B.C., when Phoenician traders from what is today Syria brought with them the prototype of what developed into the Greek alphabet.

Sources. Since the *Iliad* is the earliest piece of Greek literature that has survived to the present, it has no single identifiable source. The poem emerged out of a predominately oral culture in which stories and information were passed from generation to generation by word of mouth. In fact, it may be that the *Iliad* was originally composed to be sung and was written down because of its great length (at festivals in ancient Greece, the *Iliad* took three full days to recite).

In creating his poem, Homer probably drew on a whole tradition of stories about the Trojan War. The *Iliad* tells only a tiny fraction of the entire legend, but contains references in the narrative to episodes that would have occurred both before and after the time frame of the *Iliad*. For instance, at one point Helen stands on the walls of Troy and sees her former husband, Menelaus, far below. She recalls that it was her decision to

leave that caused the war: "I wish bitter death had been what I wanted, when I came hither / Following your son [Paris], forsaking my chamber, my kinsmen, / My grown child..." (*The Iliad*, 3.173-75). In another scene, Achilles admits that he has been told that he will die. Neither of these episodes takes place in the *Iliad*, but Homer's references indicate his expectation that his audience knows the entire story of Troy. He is thus free to focus on just one section of it.

The entire legend of the Trojan War was told by many different authors in a series of eight poems known as the Epic Cycle. *Cypria, Iliad, Aithiopis, Little Iliad, Sack of Troy, Returns, Odyssey,* and *Telegony* make up the cycle. Of the eight, only the *Iliad* and the *Odyssey* remain in existence. The rest are known only through summaries written by ancient Greeks. Nevertheless, it is clear that the Epic Cycle begins with an account of the causes of the war and ends by explaining the fates of the Achaean heroes after they return home from Troy.

Events in History at the Time the Poem Was Composed

The Dark Ages. At the height of the Mycenaean civilization, most of the region around the Aegean Sea was unified, and peace was maintained. The period that followed the fall of the great Mycenaean cities offered a stark contrast to those stable and sophisticated times. Greece fragmented into many individual kingdoms that were constantly at war with one another. This period has been called the Greek Dark Ages because its people left behind little in the way of art and architecture by which later peoples could know them.

Somehow, in the midst of the chaos, progress took place. The Greeks learned how to shape iron and use it for weapons. Previously, the soft metal bronze had been the only metal that could be effectively molded into useful shapes. The invention of stronger and more durable iron weapons and other tools was one of the first and most important steps in the renaissance of Greek civilization that pulled Greece out of the Dark Ages. It was then, at the birth of this renaissance, that epic literature began to flourish, and the works of Homer made their appearance.

Who was Homer? While most scholars believe Homer was an individual poet, some theories suggest that "Homer" was really a pseudonym for a group of poets who collaborated in creating the *Iliad* and the *Odyssey*. Others contend that Homer composed only the *Iliad*, and that the *Odyssey* was composed by someone else. The ancient Greeks, however, never doubted that Homer was the creator of both epics. They fleshed out his sketchy character by claiming that he was the blind son of Orpheus, a mythical poet.

The Greeks were uncertain about Homer's birthplace. Several different islands in the Aegean Sea claimed him as one of their own. Some scholars suggest that he may have been born on the island of Chios. They point out that a group of epic singers named the "Homeridae" (the sons of Homer) lived on Chios during the sixth century B.C., but it is not known whether they were members of Homer's family or just a group that adopted his name. Strong evidence has also been offered that suggests that the poet lived on the mainland of Asia Minor, possibly in the town of Smyrna, to the south of Troy.

How the *Iliad* was communicated. The *Iliad* probably originated as a poem that was sung aloud. Reciting the long and complex *Iliad* required enormous work, and certain skills were necessary to sing it correctly. A specialized group of artists known as rhapsodes developed over time. These artists concentrated on the singing of poetry. Working within a strict poetic meter, the rhapsodes actually created the poem anew with each retelling. The rhapsodes earned a living by traveling around and reciting their poems at such public events as religious festivals. Scholars speculate that Homer may have been a rhapsode himself.

Influence of the *Iliad*. The *Iliad* is the oldest surviving example of Greek literature. Others in Homer's time (such as the authors of the other Epic Cycle poems) probably wrote down their poetry as well. Their works, however, have been lost through the ages, perhaps because they were not so highly regarded as Homer. Homer was considered the supreme poet by the Greeks of subsequent centuries, and his *Iliad* was considered the first piece of Greek national literature. In the fourth century B.C., the philosopher Plato wrote that some members of Greek society thought that they should direct their lives by following the writings of Homer.

At the time the *Iliad* was written, Greece was divided into many different regions, with peoples who spoke different versions of the Greek language, worshipped different gods, and maintained different cultures. The *Iliad*, however, told the story of how many different groups within Greece united to fight a foreign enemy. The Greeks who read or heard the *Iliad* began to see the common traits and practices of the groups rather than the differences.

Another aspect of the *Iliad* that helped shape a Greek identity was Homer's depiction of gods common to all the people of Greece. It is believed that before Homer's time, each of the gods in the *Iliad* was originally the god of a very specific area. Different deities were worshipped in each geographic region. In the *Iliad*, though, all of the gods live together on top of Mount Olympus. By placing the gods in a place removed from any one specific region, Homer treated them as common to all of Greece.

GREEKS AND BARBARIANS

The development of a Greek national identity contributed to feelings of discrimination. The Greeks began to make strong distinctions between those who spoke Greek and those who did not. All peoples who did not speak Greek were called "barbarians." The first pan-Greek Olympic Games, established in 776 B.C., reflected this prejudice; no man who was not Greek was allowed to participate.

For More Information

Edwards, Mark W. *Homer: Poet of the Iliad.* Baltimore: Johns Hopkins University Press, 1987.

Forsdyke, John. *Greece before Homer: Ancient Chronology and Mythology.* New York: W. W. Norton, 1957.

Homer. *The Iliad.* Translated by Richmond Lattimore. Chicago: University of Chicago Press, 1951.

Luce, J. V. *Homer and the Heroic Age.* London: Thames and Hudson, 1975.

Morford, Mark P. O., and Robert J. Lenardon. *Classical Mythology.* 2nd ed. New York: Longman, 1977.

Stubbings, Frank H. *Prehistoric Greece.* New York: John Day, 1973.

Inferno

by
Dante Alighieri

> **THE LITERARY WORK**
>
> A poem in thirty-four cantos, set in Hell in 1300; written in Italy between 1307 and 1314.
>
> **SYNOPSIS**
>
> Written during Dante's exile from Florence, *Inferno* maps Hell, which, according to the narrative, contains many of Dante's political rivals, as well as wrongdoers from many periods of history.

Exiled from his native town of Florence, Dante Alighieri wrote the *Divine Comedy*, the first part of which is *Inferno*, as he wandered from city to city in northern Italy between 1301 and 1314. The poem reflects the political and social turmoil that plagued the region at the time.

Events in History at the Time of the Poem

Florentine politics. In the early fourteenth century, Italian cities were engaged in making important decisions about their methods of government. The cities had a confusing array of choices, each championed by elements of society that were competing for control. Competitors included the popes in Rome, who wanted to incorporate the cities of Tuscany (an area of northern Italy) into the "Papal States"; the Holy Roman Emperors, German aristocrats who claimed an ancient right to rule Christendom; the local noblemen, who favored rule by a small, select group; and the rapidly rising merchant classes, who sought to establish a system of rule that would protect their newly acquired wealth. The personal vendettas and personality conflicts at the root of most of the trouble emerge clearly in the *Inferno*, as Dante, a staunch supporter of the Holy Roman Emperors, accuses—and punishes—individuals for the actions they have taken in public life.

The civic politics of Florence during Dante's life were dominated by the strife between two rival factions, the Guelphs and the Ghibellines. In general, the Guelphs represented ordinary citizens and were aligned with the papacy; the Ghibellines sided with the emperors. Dante came from a family of Guelphs, but he himself came to favor the Ghibelline cause, especially their promise to bring Florence within a stable empire.

The Guelphs and the Ghibellines were divided on the political issue of empire. Among Italy's city-states, Florence provided the leading Guelph opposition to the idea of a pan-European state. The city fought to maintain and increase its own independence. Meanwhile, Dante was convinced that only under the wider authority of an empire could human beings enjoy the fullest freedoms and most moral lives. The sort of Christian empire favored by the popes in Rome did not appeal to Dante, however, primarily because he thought that the church was greedy, corrupt, and ambitious. In Dante's *Inferno*, the fourth circle of Hell, reserved for the greedy, is filled with nothing but churchmen; the part of the eighth circle reserved for barratry (graft, including the buying and selling of church positions) is dominated by popes. Distrustful of the church and its leaders, Dante instead placed his hopes for political stability in the leaders of the Holy Roman Empire.

Florence during Dante's lifetime was the fourth largest city in Europe, with a population of some 90,000. As the city became increasingly powerful, however, it also fell victim to increased corruption. Florence's wealth was derived in large part from the trade and banking connections that it enjoyed all over the continent, from the city of London in the west to Constantinople in the east. Dante's Hell is filled with people associated with the misuse of money and goods: usurers who lend money at interest, thieves, counterfeiters, and frauds.

Dante's life. Born into a nonaristocratic but respectable Florentine family, Dante had to assume responsibility for other family members after the death of his father. This new responsibility hurtled him into Florentine politics, where he reached his height of influence in 1300, when he was made one of the city's seven prefects, or civic governors. The struggle for power in that city was such that prefects governed for only two months at a time—the city changed hands six times a year. During his brief term in office, the decision was made to banish the feuding leaders on both sides of the political conflict between the Guelphs and the Ghibellines. This ban included two sets of Guelph families—the populist "Whites" and the pro-papal, pro-aristocratic "Blacks"—who had been in dispute with one another.

As part of a small city group, Dante went to Rome to negotiate with Pope Boniface VIII, who had been interfering in the dispute between the White and Black Guelph families. While Dante was in Rome, the new prefects of Florence, who assumed power during his absence, canceled the banishment of the Blacks. In addition, the new prefects exiled Dante for two years for his involvement in the original decision to exile the Blacks. When Dante refused to return to Florence to answer the charges against him, he was sentenced to death and permanently exiled from the city.

Of Dante's life in exile not much is known with certainty; it is said that for a while he plotted the overthrow of the Florentine factions responsible for his downfall, but that effort did not last very long. He was for a time in the court of Verona. Dante died in Ravenna with his daughter by his side. She had become a nun and had taken the name Sister Beatrice. This name was significant, for Beatrice was also the name of Dante's lifelong love.

Beatrice. According to another work by Dante, *Vita nuova* (1293-94), he was nine years old when he first set eyes on Beatrice and fell in love at first sight. Although she married someone else and died young, Dante's love for her lasted the rest of his life. She figures prominently in many of his works, including those penned long after her death, and appears in works created throughout Dante's marriage to another woman.

Beatrice's identity and the relationship that she had with Dante have been a subject of considerable debate over the years. Although some critics wonder if the woman ever really existed, the consensus now is that she was the daughter of a powerful Florentine family, the Portinaris, with whom Dante had a passing acquaintance. As to their relationship, it should be remembered that marriage at that time did not necessarily exclude romance with a person other than one's spouse. A highly ritualized form of romantic love

---

DIVINE "COMEDY"

Inferno, Dante's poem about Hell, forms one-third of the monumental epic known as the *Divine Comedy.* The other two parts are *Purgatorio* and *Paradiso,* which have Dante visiting the souls in Purgatory and Heaven, respectively. The term *comedy* may seem problematic since Dante's trip through Hell is not a humorous one, but in fact the word is used in its classical meaning: "a story with a sad beginning and a happy ending." Beginning in Hell and culminating in a heavenly vision of divinity, the *Divine Comedy* is in this sense a true comedy.

---

could exist between unmarried people. Often this sort of love was the subject of lyrical poetry in which the lady became an ideal, an unattainable object. In the *Inferno,* Beatrice is an angelic representative of the Virgin Mary, which puts a Christianized spin on a common romantic situation of the times.

Beatrice appears in the *Divine Comedy* as an image of spiritual love. Her largest role is in *Paradiso,* in which she helps guide Dante through Heaven. In Dante's poem about Hell, the *Inferno,* she is one of three heavenly ladies—the Virgin Mary (Mother of Christ) and St. Lucy (to whom two churches in Florence were dedicated) are the other two—who watch over Dante. That Beatrice serves as a symbol of divine love marks a significant departure from the way in which Dante wrote of her earlier in his life. In the *Vita nuova*, Dante spoke of her in sacred terms, but in a manner that was rather shocking for the times; he appropriated wholeheartedly the language of religious devotion and applied it to a mortal woman. One critic points out that this action "approaches the limits of sacrilege" (Harrison in Jacoff, p. 36). The *Divine Comedy* treats Beatrice in a less controversial manner. While Beatrice has a heavenly role in the work, she is placed in an entirely Christian framework.

Pope vs. emperor. As one historian explains, "Italy in Dante's time was a mass of self-seeking smaller states: the cities of northern Italy, the kingdoms of southern Italy and France ... and the papal states. All had constantly shifting alliances" (Ferrante, p. 51). One subject of particular controversy concerned the amount of influence the popes in Rome ought to have in worldly affairs. The Holy Roman Emperor, who was in effect the king of all Christian lands (although this was a hard claim to back militarily), was supposed to be the ruler of rulers, and hence the king of the rulers of England, France, and Norway. But the pope, who had the sole authority to crown the Holy Roman Emperor, also claimed, on the basis of his absolute spiritual authority over all Christians, to be the supreme power in Europe. This tension is played out throughout the *Inferno*, primarily in the recurrence of evil churchmen in Hell's many circles.

Matters came to a head in the late 1200s as Pope Boniface VIII and Philip IV of France ("Philip the Fair") fought for control of Europe. Boniface's immediate predecessor, Celestine V, was the only pope ever to abdicate; he lasted in the papal office for only five months. The College of Cardinals, the group of elite authorities and highest-ranking churchmen, had elected Celestine, a simple hermit, because they did not want to elect the most obvious candidate, the acidic and power-hungry Benedict Gaetani. When they eventually gave in and elected him, Gaetani took the name Boniface VIII. The new pope's enemies, of whom there were many, accused him of forcing or tricking Celestine into resigning his duties.

One of Dante's passages in the *Inferno* may refer to Celestine. There is some speculation that Dante places Celestine in Hell for relinquishing his sacred duties; he may be the person referred to in the lines "I saw and knew the shade of him who from cowardice made the great refusal" (Dante, *Inferno*, 3.59-60). While the identity of this person is not established decisively, the poem does accuse Boniface of tricking the old man into resigning. Canto 19, which takes place in Hell's eighth circle, recites much of the political tension between kings and popes that dominated European society during Dante's life. One of the sinners there, who cannot see because his head is buried, mistakes Dante for Boniface, and asks: "Are you already standing there, are you already standing there, Bonifazio? ... Are you so quickly sated with those gains for which you did not fear to take by guile the beautiful Lady, and then do her outrage?" (*Inferno*, 19.52-7). The "beautiful Lady" referred to in this instance is the church.

Boniface and Philip first came into conflict when the French king insisted that he had the right to levy a tax upon the clergy who lived in his kingdom. Boniface was furious at what he saw as an attack upon his own authority and tried to excommunicate Philip, an act which amounts to denying a person all church sacraments, rituals believed to be necessary for the saving of one's soul. Philip won this round of sparring, however, by cutting off the export of all money from France. Since Pope Boniface needed the rich revenues that came from the French clergy, he caved in and "allowed" Philip to tax the clergy in his country.

Round two began when Philip accused a French bishop (the priest responsible for church affairs within a certain jurisdiction, usually a city) of treason. Philip and the pope each claimed to be the final authority on such matters. Their battle escalated to the point where Philip's men actually captured the pope and held him prisoner for several days before releasing him.

The power-hungry and unpleasant Boniface and the equally powerful French monarchy both earned Dante's hatred; their perpetual wrangling and political maneuvering prevented the crowning of a rightful Holy Roman Emperor. Although the German Hapsburg dynasty continued to insist that it was entitled to the role of Holy Roman Emperor, the family had many rivals for the position. Nothing ever came of the Hapsburg efforts. Not until 1308 was another emperor (Henry VIII of Luxemburg) crowned in Rome; Boniface died in 1303.

The Poem in Focus

The plot. On Easter weekend, in the year 1300, Dante discovers himself at the brink of Hell. Afraid and threatened by a trio of wild animals, he feels relieved to see a figure approaching him from afar. He is wildly delighted to discover that this figure is Virgil, the great Roman poet and one

Painting by Eugène Delacroix, *Dante and Virgil.*

of Dante's literary heroes. The Roman poet has been sent by the heavenly Beatrice, Dante's true love on earth when she was alive. Beatrice watches over Dante's best interests from Heaven as he takes a tour of the Inferno, another name for Hell.

Dante's Hell consists of nine concentric circles, with the widest at the top and the narrowest at the bottom, in the manner of a cone or funnel. In each of the nine circles live specific sorts of sinners, with the less serious offenders in the higher regions, and Satan, accompanied by Judas Iscariot, Brutus, and Cassius, in the lowest.

Virgil has been denied the possibility of going to Heaven because he was a pagan worshipper of many gods instead of one god. Along with a company of classical writers, philosophers, and legendary characters, Virgil inhabits Limbo, the least awful section of Hell. The first people that Dante meets are Virgil's fellow poets: Lucan, Ovid, Homer, and Horace. They inhabit a self-contained city in which the citizens are unhappy but not tortured like the other residents of Hell. Also in the walled city that occupies the first circle of Hell are heroes and philosophers, including Aristotle, Julius Caesar, Socrates, and Plato.

From the relatively pleasant enclosure of the good pagans, Virgil leads Dante downward to the other circles of Hell. As the circles get smaller toward the bottom, the torments inflicted upon the sinners grow increasingly horrible. People are boiled in mud, transformed into hybrid snake-men, ripped to shreds by demons with pitchforks, embedded in ice, or subjected to having their brains eaten by lifelong rivals. Time and again among the sad company of the damned, the character of Dante recognizes people that he knew or had heard of from Italian politics and draws moral conclusions about the state of affairs in Italy.

Passing by horrific monsters and awful tortures, Virgil leads Dante to where Satan stands at the very center of the earth, embedded in ice from the waist down. Satan is a gigantic figure who is uglier than anything else in Hell. The two poets inch between Satan's fur and the ice that surrounds him and end up on the other side of the world. *Inferno* concludes here. *Purgatorio,* the second part of the *Divine Comedy,* features Dante's climb up the mountain that was pushed up at the point on earth directly opposite to where Satan fell.

Easter in the year 1300. Pope Boniface VIII proclaimed 1300 to be a Jubilee Year, the first such event in church history. It featured a festival that celebrated the church and the papacy. Since Boniface was an unpopular man, he may have ordered the festivities as a show of strength and unity.

Dante set the *Divine Comedy* on Easter weekend of 1300, the year in which he himself reached the estimated halfway point of a human life. According to Psalm 89:10 of the Bible, "Seventy is the sum of our years," and Dante, born in 1265, was thirty-five when he wrote the poem. He set its beginning on Good Friday, the most solemn day of the Christian church calendar; on this day, says the New Testament, Christ died on the cross after being crucified.

HELL

D ante's Hell is comprised of concentric circles, nine in all, each inhabited by a different kind of sinner, ranging from those who commit the relatively common sins, such as greed and lust, to the deepest circle of all, where Satan is punished for his treachery to God. The scheme is as follows:

UPPER HELL

    The River Acheron

        Circle 1: Limbo (for the unbaptized: Virgil, good pagans)

        Circle 2: Carnality (sins relating to bodily desires)

        Circle 3: Gluttony (sins relating to overeating and drinking)

        Circle 4: Greed

        Circle 5: Anger, sloth (laziness)

    The River Styx

LOWER HELL: THE CITY OF DIS

        Circle 6: Heresy (denial of or opposition to Christian teachings)

        Circle 7: Violence (against others, against oneself, against God and nature)

        Circle 8: Fraud (panderers and seducers, flatterers, those who lend money at a high rate of interest, diviners, barrators who buy or sell church or government positions, hypocrites, thieves, bad counselors, schismatics who separate or divide from the church, forgers)

    Cocytus: The Frozen Lake

        Circle 9: Treachery (traitors to family, to country, to guests, to lord or patron)

In Canto 34, line 117, Dante uses the word *Giudecca* to describe the lowest point of Hell. This word refers to Judas Iscariot, the betrayer of Jesus Christ, who inhabits the place with Satan, but it was also used in Dante's time to describe the ghettos of European cities in which Jews were confined.

The poet's next journey, into Purgatory, is related in *Purgatorio*. This journey takes place on Holy Saturday, the day on which Christ freed from Hell all the good people who could not go to Heaven until he opened the way. In Christian theology, Purgatory is a transitional place where souls that are not evil but are not yet holy enough to enter Heaven are purified. The final section of the epic, *Paradiso,* is set on Easter Sunday, the holiest day in Christian life, when Christ rose from the dead. In this section, Dante visits Heaven.

Virgil. Virgil, the Latin poet (70-19 B.C.) who wrote ***The Aeneid*** (also covered in *Literature and Its Times*), the national epic for the Roman Empire, leads Dante through Hell and Purgatory. By associating himself with Virgil, Dante is perhaps making a claim for the comparable importance of his own work as a celebration of a Christian empire. This certainly fits with Dante's lifelong political aspiration of seeing Florence and the other Italian city-states welcome the Holy Roman Emperor as the leader of a unified land.

Book VI of Virgil's *Aeneid* features a visit to the underworld, and Dante makes use of the details and imagery in that work to describe Hell in the *Inferno.* Virgil explains to Dante that, no matter how virtuous he and others like him might have been while alive, they are sentenced to Hell because they were pagans who worshipped many gods and did not receive the Christian initiation sacrament of baptism:

> "[T]hey did not have baptism, which is the portal of the faith you hold; and if they were before Christianity, they did not worship God aright, and I myself am one of these. Because of these shortcomings, and for no other fault, we are lost, and only so far afflicted that without hope we live in longing."
>
> (*Inferno*, 4.33-42)

In the upper circles of Hell, Virgil's power is quite strong; he is able to command other spirits to do his bidding and is confident that Heaven approves of his role as Dante's tour guide through Hell. As the two poets descend, however, Virgil grows less sure of himself; in Lower Hell, where they encounter the heretics (people who disagree with official church teaching), he must have angelic help before he is allowed to enter the gates of the City of Dis. This may be because, as a pagan, he is unfamiliar with church controversy and is therefore out of his league. With such scenes, *Inferno* shows how pagan figures stand in a Chris-

Satan embedded in ice.

tian concept of the afterlife, and it also upholds the supremacy of the Christian religion. There is also an implied suggestion that, as a baptized poet of the church, Dante himself will surpass the works of Virgil and the other pagan poets.

Sources. The *Divine Comedy* is a thoroughly Christian poem, and so it is no surprise that allusions to and quotations from the Bible permeate the entire work. But quotations from Virgil are also plentiful. In Canto I, Dante states that whatever fame he has already earned has followed from his imitation of Virgil: "O glory and light of other poets, may the long study and the great love that have made me search your volume avail me! You are my master and my author. You alone are he from whom I took the fair style that has done me honor" (*Inferno,* 1, 82-7).

Legacy. Dante was the most famous European poet ever at the time he died in Ravenna in 1321. Immediately upon his death, a whole industry of commentators swung into production; Dante's poetry became the subject of translation, speculation, and inspiration. In 1371 the Florentines established a public lectureship on Dante; they appointed Boccaccio, the famous poet, to take up the position. Boccaccio made it only part way through a discussion of the *Inferno* before his worsening health forced him to resign his post.

Maps of Hell. One of the more interesting offshoots of the *Divine Comedy* is the spate of mapmaking that arose in the Renaissance. Some scholars took very seriously the dimensions of Hell that Dante mentions from time to time in the *Inferno.* Debating the various aspects of Dante's description, they created detailed maps of the circles, ditches, walls, and rivers of the underworld. Two Florentine architects, Antonio Manetti and Filippo Brunelleschi, started the project. Christophoro Landino, who published a literary commentary on the *Inferno* in 1481, included Manetti's figures in his own work, and the following twelve editions of the Landino commentary generally featured Manetti's work. In 1506 Girolamo Benivieni discussed Manetti's work and provided "the first drawings of Hell to qualify unambiguously as maps" (Kleiner, p. 25). Even Galileo Galilei delivered lectures on the subject of infernal cartography, or Hell-centered mapmaking. To this day, very few editions of the *Divine Comedy* appear without an accompanying map of Hell.

For More Information

Chubb, Thomas Caldecot. *Dante and His World.* Boston: Little, Brown, 1966.

Dante Alighieri. *The Divine Comedy: Inferno.* Translated by Charles S. Singleton. Bollingen Series 80. Princeton: Princeton University Press, 1970.

Ferrante, Joan M. *The Political Vision of the Divine Comedy.* Princeton: Princeton University Press, 1984.

Hibbert, Christopher. *Florence: The Biography of a City.* New York: Viking, 1993.

Jacoff, Rachel, ed. *The Cambridge Companion to Dante.* Cambridge: Cambridge University Press, 1993.

Kleiner, John. *Mismapping the Underworld: Daring and Error in Dante's 'Comedy.'* Stanford, Calif.: Stanford University Press, 1994.

Ivanhoe

by
Sir Walter Scott

Sir Walter Scott was born in Edinburgh, Scotland, in 1771. Scotland had only recently (in 1707) united with England to form the United Kingdom. At the time of union, Scotland was still a relatively undeveloped country, with half of its population made up of Highland clansmen. It was not until 1745 that Scotland began to close the technological and social gap with England. The forced merging of an advanced culture and an unsophisticated culture into one society became a common theme of Sir Walter's novels. During the era in which *Ivanhoe* takes place, tension existed between the advanced Normans and the less sophisticated Anglo-Saxons.

Events in History at the Time the Novel Takes Place

The Norman Conquest. In 1066 A.D., Duke William of Normandy (a section of modern-day France) landed in England with an army, defeated the English at the battle of Hastings, and became king of England. The English of the eleventh century were Anglo-Saxons, descendants of Germanic tribes that had conquered the British Isle sometime in the sixth century A.D. The Norman invaders spoke a different language, had their own customs, and were technologically more advanced than the Anglo-Saxons.

Although the Normans were foreigners, their leader William was distantly related to the Anglo-Saxon king. His claim to the crown was thus regarded as semi-legitimate and was not strongly contested by the English after the Battle of Hastings. Nevertheless, many Anglo-Saxon nobles had their property taken away by William and

given to the Norman knights who had fought for him. Scott points this fact out in the opening pages of *Ivanhoe:* "The whole race of Saxon princes and nobles had been extirpated or disinherited, with few or no exceptions; nor were the numbers great who possessed land in the country of their fathers ..." (*Ivanhoe,* pp. 8-9). As a result, much of the power in England was transferred to the Norman conquerors. They helped to support the descendants of Duke William, who became the subsequent kings of England.

Richard the Lion-Hearted. The third king to descend from the line of William of Normandy was Richard the Lion-Hearted. He earned a reputation as a strong warrior and brilliant general, yet those same qualities hindered him from becoming a good ruler. During Richard's ten-year reign (1189-1199 A.D.), he visited England only twice for just a few months. In fact, although he was born in England, he never learned the English language. There were two reasons for his neglect of England. The first was that Richard was much more interested in his kingdom in France (the Norman kings ruled both countries at once). In addition, Richard spent his entire life fighting wars, an occupation that left him little time to concentrate on other responsibilities. At the age of fifteen, he commanded an army in a revolt against his father, and before the age of twenty, Richard had besieged and destroyed his first fortress. His greatest military feat was to organize

---

HIGH TECHNOLOGY

When the Normans invaded England, they had an important advantage—the knight. The armored knight was the tank of the Middle Ages. When protected by armor, the knight was a fearsome sight on the battlefield. Such a transformation, however, required significant technological advances. Different devices, like the stirrup, had to be developed so that a knight could stay seated on his horse during the shock of combat, where impact speeds could approach fifty miles per hour. At the Battle of Hastings, the main strength of the Normans lay in their force of mounted knights. The Anglo-Saxons, on the other hand, all fought on foot. This difference proved crucial as the Norman cavalry gradually wore down and then utterly defeated the Anglo-Saxon army, thereby making Duke William the undisputed victor. In *Ivanhoe,* knighthood becomes a symbol for Norman culture. The Anglo-Saxon patriot Cedric, for instance, dislikes all discussion of knights and jousting—combat between knights on horseback—because of what he calls "the fantastic fashions of Norman chivalry" (Scott, *Ivanhoe,* p. 56).

---

and lead the Third Crusade.

Richard's crusade. In 1099 a crusade by the Christian kings of Europe had resulted in the capture of Jerusalem from the Saracens and its transformation into a Christian kingdom. The attack on the city had been made, according to the crusaders, to ensure safe passage for all Christians who were making their pilgrimage to Jerusalem. The kingdom of Jerusalem remained in European hands until 1187, when it was retaken by the Saracens. As soon as Richard heard the news, he vowed to undertake a crusade to recapture Jerusalem. The king spent three years trying to reach Jerusalem, but he was ultimately unsuccessful due to rivalries within his army. As Richard began the journey home to France, he

was captured by his enemies in Austria. This is the historical backdrop on which *Ivanhoe* is played out. King Richard is still imprisoned when the novel opens, and the hero Ivanhoe has not yet returned home from the Crusades.

The Templars. During the First Crusade, certain knights took it upon themselves to defend both the kingdoms of Christianity in the Holy Land and the pilgrims who traveled there. The knights took religious vows that made them roughly equivalent to monks in the eyes of the Catholic Church. One particularly successful group of knights was named the Poor Knights of Christ and of the Temple of Solomon. They were more commonly known as the Knights Templars, or simply, the Templars.

Although the Templars' original duties lay in the Holy Land, they later acquired and maintained estates throughout Europe, including England. Since the order was made up of well-manned and skillful armies, they became a force in European politics and warfare. They also expanded into trade and banking and amassed great fortunes. In the early 1300s, the Templars were accused of heresy, and these charges were vigorously promoted by King Philip IV of France. Though the truth of these allegations is still a matter of dispute, Pope Clement V banned the Templars in 1312. In some areas, members were imprisoned and executed and their assets were taken by other orders. Certain countries, such as Spain and Portugal, gave the Templars better treatment, with some groups of knights continuing their activities under different names. In *Ivanhoe,* the main antagonist or enemy is Sir Brian de Bois-Guilbert, a high-ranking Templar who has returned from the Third Crusade.

The Jews. Life in England was very difficult for the Jewish people during the twelfth and thirteenth centuries. Even though many Jews had immigrated to England after the Norman Conquest, they were not allowed to become citizens and were shunned by the English population. They had to live separately from the rest of the community, and English laws did not protect them. One of the only businesses open to a member of the Jewish people was that of moneylending, a practice that the Catholic Church had forbidden Christians from pursuing. Still, moneylending proved to be a profitable profession because the English kings and nobles often required money to finance their military ventures. The English king, aware of this need for their money, saw that it was in his best interest to protect the Jews from his own subjects so that he could obtain favorable rates on his loans. Despite royal protection, the Jews were often persecuted or murdered. In 1190, on the eve of Richard's coronation as King of England, many people in the country took note of the king's idea of a crusade against those who did not believe in Christianity. In response, they massacred all Jews living in the town of York. Perhaps Sir Walter Scott was unaware of this historical event when he wrote *Ivanhoe;* one of his characters, Isaac, is a Jew who lives in the town of York during the reign of Richard.

The Novel in Focus

The plot. The story opens four generations after the Norman conquest of England. Although most of the former Anglo-Saxon rulers lost their wealth and power as a result of the conquest, there were some exceptions. One Anglo-Saxon who retained both his wealth and position is Cedric of Rotherwood. The setting of the first chapter is Cedric's woodlands. Two of his slaves—Wamba, a jester, and Gurth, a pig-herder—are asked for directions to Cedric's castle by two Norman aristocrats. One is a priest and the other is Brian de Bois-Guilbert, a knight who has just returned from the Crusades. The travelers are on their way to participate in a large jousting tournament held by Prince John. Both are men of the church, yet they are making a detour in order to see Cedric's beautiful ward, Rowena.

Misled by the jester, the two Normans become lost. They encounter Ivanhoe, Cedric's son, who has recently returned from the Holy Land, where he had gone with King Richard to fight in the Crusades. Ivanhoe is disguised as a pilgrim, however, and he is not recognized. Remaining disguised, he leads the Normans to his father's castle. Ivanhoe does not want his identity discovered because his father has disowned him for leaving his family lands to fight under a Norman king in a foreign country. Cedric gives the travelers lodging and a place at his dinner table. During the course of the feast, two important events occur. Another traveler arrives and asks for lodging at Cedric's castle. The man, a wealthy Jew named Isaac, is temporarily without money or food. Although he is allowed to enter the castle, he is shunned because he is a Jew. Ivanhoe gives up his own seat so that Isaac can eat. In the meantime, Brian de Bois-Guilbert boasts of the unsurpassed skills of his knightly order, the Templars. The pilgrim contradicts Sir Brian and reminds him that both King Richard and Ivanhoe have defeated the Templars in the past. The angered Tem-

plar then issues a challenge against Ivanhoe, who he believes is still in the Holy Land, to do battle at anytime. Rowena, who was engaged to Ivanhoe before he left for the Crusades, accepts the challenge on Ivanhoe's behalf. Later, in the middle of the night, Ivanhoe departs with Isaac, who gives the warrior a good suit of armor and a strong horse for use in Prince John's tournament.

A NEW LANGUAGE

The language that we know as English developed as a result of the Norman Conquest. Before 1066, the primary language spoken in England was Old English, a close relative of the German language. When the Normans took over, French became the official language of England. It was the tongue used by all those who ruled, or aspired to rule. Gradually, though, Old English and French began to merge into one language, a melding that formed the basis of modern-day English. A scene in *Ivanhoe* illustrates this early language barrier between the Normans and the Anglo-Saxons. Cedric the Saxon greets Sir Brian de Bois-Guilbert and says, "You will excuse my speaking to you in my native language, and that you will reply in the same if your knowledge of it permits; if not, I sufficiently understand Norman to follow your meaning." In response Bois-Guilbert explains, "I speak ever French, the language of King Richard and his nobles; but I understand English sufficiently to communicate with the natives of the country" (*Ivanhoe*, pp. 41-42).

On the first day of the tournament Ivanhoe defeats five knights in the joust. He refuses to take off his helmet, thus keeping his identity secret. The second day of contests features a mass fight between two forces of fifty knights each. At the end of the day-long battle Ivanhoe is declared the most worthy of all the knights in the battle, although at one point he was almost defeated, only to be saved by a mysterious Black Knight. Grievously wounded in the contest, Ivanhoe falls unconscious after receiving his prize. His helmet is removed and his identity discovered. Isaac and his beautiful daughter Rebecca, a talented healer, proceed to save the wounded Ivanhoe.

After the tournament one of the royal henchmen devises a plan to kidnap Rowena and force her to marry Sir Brian. Cedric and Rowena's party is ambushed as they travel through the woods on their way home. The kidnapped group includes Isaac, Rebecca, and the still wounded

Illustration of Richard the Lion-Hearted dressed as a Norman knight, wearing armor and mounted on a horse.

Ivanhoe, though his identity is once again disguised. They are all brought to the castle of a Norman warrior and held captive. Two of Cedric's followers, Wamba and Gurth, manage to escape. They meet up with a group of bandits led by the legendary Robin Hood, who vows to raise an army to free the captives. He is aided by the Black Knight, who turns out to be none other than King Richard himself. Led by Robin Hood and Richard, a large force of bandits and local woodsmen attacks the castle, sets fire to the fortress, and manages to rescue all of the prisoners except for Rebecca

Sir Brian, who has fallen in love with Rebecca, hides her in one of the churches overseen by the Templars. Sir Brian takes a number of precautions, but she is still discovered by the visiting Grand Master of the Templar order. He believes that Rebecca is a witch because of her Jewish faith and her wonderful healing powers. The Grand Master blames Rebecca for Sir Brian's behavior as well, contending that she enchanted the knight, causing him to break his holy vows of celibacy.

A trial is held and Rebecca is condemned to be burned at the stake. Her only remaining chance is to demand that her guilt or innocence be determined by combat between two champions. Sir Brian is chosen to fight against Rebecca's cause. In the final hours before Rebecca is to be burned alive, Ivanhoe appears to defend her. Exhausted from riding all day to arrive there and still recovering from the wounds suffered in the earlier tournament, he can barely sit in his saddle. Yet Ivanhoe makes a single pass against Brian de Bois-Guilbert and kills him. Ivanhoe's lance barely grazes Sir Brian, but he dies from his own guilt. Rebecca is subsequently set free.

King Richard restores order to England, having captured his rebellious brother John, and all is set right again. The story ends with Ivanhoe's marriage to his lifelong love Rowena and Rebecca's departure from prejudiced England for a safer home in the south of Spain.

Staying true to one's self. An important facet of the characters of Ivanhoe is that they do not stray from the path that they have chosen for themselves. For example, although Ivanhoe cares for Rebecca and saves her life, he does not marry her. He instead weds Rowena, to whom he had previously pledged himself before leaving for the Crusades. In much the same way, Rebecca remains true to herself throughout the course of the novel. Sir Brian offers to save Rebecca from being burned at the stake if she will leave Eu-

rope with him and become his wife. She is resolute in rejecting him, though it means her certain death: "Put not a price on my deliverance, Sir Knight—sell not a deed of generosity—protect the oppressed for the sake of charity, and not for a selfish advantage" (Ivanhoe, p. 443). In the last scene of the novel, Rebecca visits Rowena and asks her to thank Ivanhoe for saving her life. She then tells Rowena that she will be leaving for Spain and that she will not marry but will devote her life to healing the sick.

THE WELL-DRESSED TEMPLAR

The Templar uniform was a white mantle with a red cross. Famous for their military skill, the uniformed Templars attracted many recruits and were frequently employed by kings, popes, and lords. Included in the order were noblemen-knights, priests, craftsmen, and temporary members. Only the knights were allowed to wear the uniforms.

When Ivanhoe was first published in 1820, many of Scott's readers were disappointed with the conclusion. They argued that since Rebecca was the heroine of the book, she should be the one to marry the valiant Ivanhoe. Scott heard the criticisms, but he did not agree with them. Expressing his thoughts on the subject in the introduction to the 1830 edition of Ivanhoe, he writes:

> Not to mention that the prejudices of the age rendered such an union almost impossible, the author may, in passing, observe, that he thinks a character of a highly virtuous and lofty stamp is degraded rather than exalted by an attempt to reward virtue with temporal prosperity [marriage].
>
> (author's introduction to Ivanhoe, p. 544)

Anxious to set a good example for his readers, particularly the young ones, Scott felt that it was his responsibility to portray life as close to reality as possible. He knew that it was highly unlikely that a Christian who had fought in the Crusades would marry a Jew.

Sources. Scott believed that there were kernels of truth in the fiction of the past. To give Ivanhoe the feel of the Middle Ages, he relied upon earlier books, poems, and plays. For example, Scott drew upon his memory of an old ballad when he chose the name "Ivanhoe," thinking that it had an old English sound. Also connected to

Joan Fontaine and Robert Taylor in the 1952 film version of *Ivanhoe*.

earlier literature is the character Friar Tuck, inspired by an obscure tale entitled the "Kyng and the Hermite." Among the numerous sources Scott used was the ancient Greek epic **The Odyssey** (also covered in *Literature and Its Times*), which tells the story of a Greek warrior who returns after the Trojan War to find his home in disarray, then restores order and exacts revenge with the help of his son and a faithful swineherd. Scott's novel paralleled the Greek epic in several respects. Both works feature similar plot lines and include a character who is a loyal keeper of the hero's swine. Scott refers also to Shakespeare's **The Merchant of Venice** (also covered in *Literature and Its Times*), beginning several chapters with quotes from this play. In Shakespeare's drama, the main characters are a Jewish moneylender and his beautiful daughter; *Ivanhoe* has two similar characters—Isaac the Jew and Rebecca. In addition to earlier literature, Scott's novels plainly draw on actual historical personalities—for example, the real king Richard the Lion-Hearted and his brother Prince John.

Events in History at the Time the Novel Was Written

The difficult union. In 1707 Scotland and England signed the Act of Union, which formally united the two countries to create a single nation, the United Kingdom. The Scottish, however, did not welcome the union, and many problems arose in the decades that followed. The conflict stemmed from the differences between Scotland and England. Scotland was an undeveloped country with large regions dominated by clans of Highlanders. These Highlanders were the descendants of the Celts, the people whom the Anglo-Saxons had conquered in the sixth century. They spoke a different language, Gaelic, and had different customs from the English. Their political system was based on old laws of feudalism, which gave the clan chiefs all the power. The English, on the other hand, had already passed through their stage of feudalism to more advanced forms of government. By the time of the union, the English practiced limited democracy, a form of government that spread power more evenly throughout the population.

The differences between the two countries eventually exploded into war. On two occasions—1715 and 1745—the Highlanders rose in arms against the English. On both occasions they were defeated. After 1745 the English implemented harsh laws to destroy the power of the clan chiefs, whom they saw as the main threat to the union. The Highlander feudal system disintegrated, a development that greatly affected Sir Walter Scott. He apparently saw the defeat of the Highlanders as a type of victory for Scotland. Scott felt that, while many of the Highlander customs such as loyalty to clan and adherence to pledges were noble, those customs ultimately held Scotland back. Scott seemed to believe that the strongest society would develop from a combination of Scottish and English customs, politics, and technology.

This desire to blend the two cultures is evident in many of the novels that Scott wrote about eighteenth-century Scotland. Forced to choose between the two ways of life, Scottish or English, Scott's heroes choose the middle ground. *Ivanhoe,* although it deals with a much earlier time, addresses similar problems. On one side is Cedric the Saxon, and on the other is the Norman Prince John. Both are unswervingly devoted to their respective cultures, Cedric to the Anglo-Saxon monarchy and John to the Norman feudalism. In the middle is Ivanhoe, a faithful Anglo-Saxon defender of England who has learned the Norman customs, and, to the displeasure of his father, the codes of Norman chivalry. *Ivanhoe* was the only one of Scott's novels to feature the beginnings of the feudal era in England; his other novels dealt with the end of feudalism.

Scott's historical fiction. By the time Scott began *Ivanhoe,* he had already written many successful novels about eighteenth-century Scotland. Those books were the first examples of historical fiction, the type of story based to a greater or lesser degree on facts and actual occurrences. Most of Scott's novels were rich repositories of information on Scottish culture and politics. For example, before writing a story about the famous Scottish outlaw Rob Roy, Sir Walter Scott first spoke with men who had personally known Rob Roy. *Ivanhoe* surprised his readers because, despite the sources about the Middle Ages that he had used, it lacked much of the historical accuracy of his previous works. Even so, it became Scott's most successful novel.

Popular acclaim for *Ivanhoe*. Immediately popular when it was first published, *Ivanhoe* inspired operas and plays throughout Europe. Scott was amazed at the response. Six years after the publication of *Ivanhoe,* after viewing an opera in Paris based on his novel, Scott commented that it "was strange to hear anything like the words which I ... dictated ... now recited in a foreign tongue and for the amusement of a strange people" (*Ivan-*

hoe, p. xvi). Scott's novel influenced architecture and painting as well, and there were eccentrics who tried to recreate details from the book in real life. In 1839 one English lord, inspired by Ivanhoe's knightly skills, held a jousting tournament on his estate; in America a group of gentlemen formed a society called the Knights Templar, naming themselves after the Templars of Scott's novel.

Critical reviews. While *Ivanhoe* was a commercial success, critics have subsequently found fault with a number of aspects of the novel, including its historical inaccuracies. Many historians feel that Scott's portrayal of the conflict between the Anglo-Saxons and Normans is overblown, arguing that the cultural differences cited in the book were no longer an issue by the time of Richard I. They also believe that Scott's grasp on the particulars of the time period was weak. In text that accompanies his novel, Scott himself admits that he may have made mistakes:

> [I]t is extremely probable that I may have confused the manners of two or three centuries, and introduced, during the reign of Richard the First [Richard the Lion-Hearted], circumstances appropriated to a period either considerably earlier or a good deal later than that era.
>
> (*Ivanhoe,* p. 530)

Unchanging human nature. Scott's objective in writing *Ivanhoe* was to illustrate that the passions that drove the people of the 1100s were the same ones that drove inhabitants of the 1800s. In the text accompanying his novel, he clarifies this point by quoting several lines from *The Merchant of Venice:*

> Our ancestors were not more distinct from us ... they had "eyes, hands, organs, dimension, sense affections, passions"; were "fed with the same food, hurt with the same weapons, subject to the same diseases, warmed and cooled by the same winter and summer," as ourselves.
>
> (Scott, *Ivanhoe,* p. 528-29)

Scott gleaned information from old manuscripts in his attempt to understand the personalities of historical figures such as King Richard. To fill in details, he used his intuition about people, whom he assumed had not changed much in the more than 600 years that had elapsed from their time to his own. His estimation of earlier personalities proved surprisingly accurate. In Ivanhoe, King Richard, disguised as the Black Knight, helps Robin Hood storm a Norman castle. Scott created this scene based on his understanding of the adventurous personality of King Richard, not on any knowledge of historical events. Yet in 1882 an old manuscript of 1219 was discovered that speaks of a disguised King Richard taking part in a siege of the castle of Nottingham. It is only when the attackers demand the surrender of the castle's defender that the king reveals his true identity.

For More Information

Anderson, James, and Ross G. Roy. *Sir Walter Scott and History.* Edinburgh: Edina, 1981.

Gillingham, John. *Richard the Lion-Hearted.* London: Weidenfeld and Nicholson, 1978.

Hilton, R. H. *Peasants, Knights and Heretics: Studies in Medieval English Social History.* Cambridge: Cambridge University Press, 1976.

Johnson, Edgar. *Sir Walter Scott: The Great Unknown.* New York: Macmillan, 1970.

Lunt, W. E. *History of England.* New York: Harper & Row, 1965.

Parker, Thomas M. *The Knights Templars in England.* Tucson: University of Arizona Press, 1963.

Scott, Sir Walter. *Ivanhoe.* Edited by A. N. Wilson. New York: Penguin, 1984.

Julius Caesar

by
William Shakespeare

Born in England in 1564, William Shakespeare wrote *Julius Caesar* in 1599. The play follows events that actually took place in ancient Rome in the first century B.C., but also reflects to some degree the realities of English life in the late sixteenth century, during what is known as the Elizabethan era.

THE LITERARY WORK

A play set in ancient Rome, about 45 B.C.; first performed in 1599.

SYNOPSIS

Julius Caesar is assassinated by a conspiracy of senators, a murder that has important consequences.

Events in History at the Time the Play Takes Place

The Roman Senate. All the central characters of *Julius Caesar*—Caesar, Mark Antony, the conspirators—are members of the senate, Rome's main governing body. The senate controlled both domestic and foreign policy, publishing decrees, arresting and convicting citizens, levying fines, and convening public assemblies. Senate members generally worked hard; their meetings started very early in the day and often continued until dark. Though its size varied over the years, the Roman Senate had about 600 members during the time covered in *Julius Caesar*. Any adult male citizen automatically became a senator after serving as a junior government official. In practice, the body was dominated by Rome's aristocrats, who were called patricians. This dominance of the senate by rich citizens was due in part to the low salaries pulled in at even high-level government posts; one had to be wealthy to be able to afford to take such a position.

The principal officials of the senate, and of Rome, were two consuls. Selected from among the senators by the general population, they each served during alternate months for about one year. A consulship was the supreme honor available to a Roman citizen. Consuls summoned and presided over the senate, conducted the main elections, and commanded armies during wartime. Though they wielded great influence, their power was checked by the presence of the second consul with whom they served and the short duration of their term in office.

The rise of Julius Caesar. In 60 B.C., about fifteen years before the events depicted in *Julius Caesar* took place, Caesar, Gneius Pompeius (Pompey), and Marcus Licinius Crassus were three of the most powerful senators in Rome. They decided to form a pact to support each other politically. This pact, which became known as the First Triumvirate, allowed each to support the others in accomplishing their respective political goals. Armed with such power, the three allied senators were able to get laws passed more easily than they had been able to do individually. The alliance served each of the senators well for a number of years. In 53 B.C., however, Crassus was killed in a war and the alliance between Caesar and Pompey gradually began to disintegrate. Caesar tried to salvage the relationship. He offered to divorce his wife, Calpurnia, and marry Pompey's daughter, Pompeia. At the same time, Pompey would marry Caesar's great-niece Octavia. Such intermarriage between families was a common way of solidifying political bonds. Pompey refused the proposal, however, and married the daughter of one of Caesar's enemies, a certain sign of hostility. Before long, violence and civil war broke out between supporters of Caesar and supporters of Pompey. In 49 B.C., Caesar's army forced Pompey and his followers out of Italy. Battles continued between the two for a number of years in such places as Greece, Egypt, and Africa. Caesar finally emerged victorious in 45 B.C. at the battle of Munda, Spain.

ROMAN NAMES

Men in patrician or aristocratic families had three names—*praenomen, nomen,* and *cognomen.* For example, Caesar's full name was Gaius Julius Caesar. The *nomen*—Julius—indicated the person's clan. The *cognomen*—Caesar—specified the family branch of the clan. This was the name that a person was normally called by colleagues. The *praenomen*—Gaius—was only used by relatives or close friends. Women of the period legally had no name. They were called by the feminine form of the *nomen,* their clan name. Thus, Caesar's daughter was called Julia. If a family had more than one daughter, affectionate personal names could be used within the family to avoid confusion.

Caesar's popularity grew tremendously during the civil war. In 46 B.C. the senate appointed him to be "dictator" for ten years. This new status as Rome's supreme leader made him much more powerful than a consul. Upon his triumphant return to Rome in 45 B.C., the senate voted him a great number of honors. He was awarded the title *pater patriae* (father of the country). His statue was placed in all the temples of Rome and the towns of Italy. He was also allowed to use several significant emblems of power on all occasions. These symbols included a wardrobe of a purple triumphal toga and a laurel wreath and use of a gilded chair. Other honors

followed as well. A religious temple—where festivals in his honor would be celebrated annually—was to be built in memory of the peace Caesar had restored. An ivory statue of his likeness was to be carried with those of the gods in processions. His birthday was made a public holiday and the month Quinctilis renamed as July in his honor. On February 15, 44 B.C., he assumed the title *dictator perpetuus:* "dictator for life." Previously, dictators had only been appointed to serve temporarily to deal with state emergencies. As *dictator perpetuus,* however, Julius Caesar was assured that he would be the most powerful man in Rome for the rest of his life.

What Caesar was really like. Though not described as a particularly likable man, Caesar had such skill in politics, generalship, public speaking, and writing that he has been called a genius. So generous was he to the enemies he had defeated (if they were Roman) that he forgave some without doling out punishment. Sometimes he even gave them posts in his own government. Two such former foes were Cassius and Brutus. Both would later turn against Caesar. Caesar's pained cry, "Et tu, Brute?" (And you, Brutus?) became famous; it is often used today by those who wish to convey feelings of betrayal.

How well did Caesar rule? As dictator, Julius Caesar proved generous in granting Roman citizenship to foreigners. He also had the cities of Corinth and Carthage rebuilt for his discharged soldiers and for the workers of Rome. He further increased the size of the senate and made it better represent all of Rome. But Caesar also had an air of haughtiness that apparently contributed to his downfall. He, for example, disregarded public opinion when, in 46 B.C., he welcomed the Egyptian ruler Cleopatra to Rome. Along with other ill-considered acts, such disdain for public sentiment was one factor that prompted old friends to turn against him.

While Caesar had the support of the senate, some members were not happy about his rise to dictatorship. They chafed under a political arrangement that greatly diminished their influence. In addition, Rome's republican tradition seemed to be in tremendous jeopardy. Prior to Caesar's ascendancy, even the most influential Romans had checks on their powers in the form of popular elections and term limits for consuls. No single person had ever before wielded so much power. So, as reenacted in Shakespeare's play, a conspiracy that included about sixty senators formed. Led by Gaius Cassius Longinus

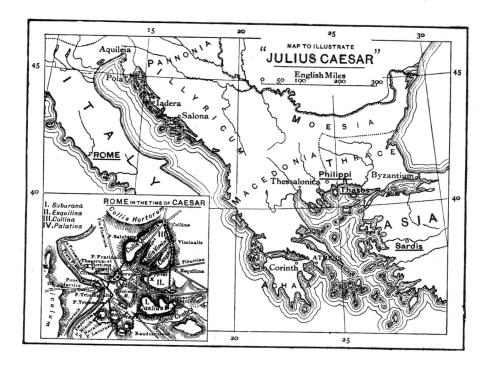

A map showing locations that figure in the plot of the play, with an inset map of the city of Rome at the time of Julius Caesar's rule.

(Cassius) and Marcus Junius Brutus (Brutus), the conspirators assassinated Caesar on March 15, 44 B.C.

Roman religious holidays. The Romans believed in a pantheon of gods, each linked to a particular human activity. For example, there were gods of war (Mars), home life (Vesta), and agriculture (Ceres). Every activity was performed under the authority of a particular god. Before beginning any significant action, people customarily performed a ritual or made a sacrifice in honor of the appropriate god. The Roman calendar also consisted of a large mixture of regular daily, monthly, and yearly religious rituals celebrating the cult of a particular god or gods. Some of these holidays, such as the Ides of March and the Feast of Lupercal, are mentioned in *Julius Caesar*.

The Feast of Lupercal was a major public event that took place yearly on February 15. The Luperci were a group of priests associated with Mars, the god of war. Every February 15 they met at Lupercal, a sacred cave at the southwest foot of the Palatine hill in Rome. According to legend, this was the place where a wolf had suckled Romulus and Remus, the twin sons of Mars and the mythic founders of Rome. The ritual began with a sacrifice of goats and a dog, and an offering of sacred cakes. The priests smeared blood on the foreheads of two young men from noble families. Afterwards the blood was wiped off with wool dipped in milk and the young men laughed in accordance with the rules of the ritual. A feast followed. Next the priests cut up the sacrificial goat skins into strips. Naked except for the skins, the priests ran from Lupercal, traveling several times around the Palatine hill. Along the way they struck bystanders—especially women who wanted to be cured of barrenness—with thongs. Mark Antony is portrayed in *Julius Caesar* as one of the Lupercal runners. Caesar alludes to this when he tells him:

> Forget not in your speed…
> To touch Calpurnia, for our elders say
> The barren, touched in this holy chase,
> Shake off their sterile curse.
> (Shakespeare, *Julius Caesar*, 1.2.6-8)

Jupiter, the god of the sky, was also the supreme god of the Roman pantheon. In fact, the city of Rome was a domain dedicated to him, and his temple on the capitol was the center of national religious life. The Ides, or midpoint, of every month was devoted to him; honorary rituals called for a number of sheep to be led along a road called the Via Sacra and then sacrificed to Jupiter. In addition to this ritual of recognition of the Ides of March, another festival dedicated to Anna Perenna was celebrated. In ancient Rome March was the first month of the year, and Anna Perenna was honored as the goddess of the new year. Her festival took place in a grove near Rome's Tiber River. After a formal sacrifice and public prayers to secure a healthy year, people spent the day socializing, drinking, singing popular songs, and dancing. It was in 44 B.C., on the same day these festivities would have been taking place, that Caesar was killed in the senate.

BRUTUS AND THE ORIGINS OF THE REPUBLIC

According to Roman legend, the city of Rome was founded in the eighth century B.C. Before then, it was one of many small, independent cities in Italy ruled by a line of kings. Its oppressive seventh king, Lucius Tarquinius Superbus, was overthrown toward the end of the sixth century B.C. Lucius Junius Brutus, who led the revolt, was known as the traditional founder of the Roman Republic and served as one of its first consuls. Marcus Brutus was the descendant of this esteemed leader, a fact that is referred to in *Julius Caesar.* As Cassius says to him:

O, you and I have heard our fathers say
There was a Brutus once that would have brooked
Th'eternal devil to keep his state in Rome
As easily as a king.
                    (*Julius Caesar,* 1.2.158-61)

Brutus later remarks that "my ancestors did from the streets of Rome / The Tarquin drive when he was called a king" (*Julius Caesar,* 2.1.53-4). Brutus ultimately follows the precedent set for him by his famous ancestor and joins the conspiracy to destroy Caesar, seen by the plotters as the contemporary threat to the republic.

The Play in Focus

The plot. The play opens on the Roman religious feast of Lupercal. In addition to the feast, Julius Caesar's triumph over Pompey and his followers and his recent return to Rome are also being celebrated. Caesar is cautioned by a soothsayer to beware the Ides of March, but he decides to ignore the warning. A number of senators express concern about Caesar's rapidly increasing power and popularity, especially after he is publicly offered a crown by Mark Antony. Though he refuses it, Rome's long tradition as a republic—and

the senators' positions in it—seem to be in great jeopardy. Cassius forms a conspiracy to kill Caesar that includes a large number of senators.

Brutus, a well-respected senator, is approached by Cassius and informed of the plot. He deliberates over whether to become involved in the conspiracy. During a night full of ominous thunder, lightning, storms, and strange happenings, he finally decides that his duty is to help save the Roman republic; Caesar must be killed. The conspirators meet Brutus at his house, and they agree to carry out their plan that day.

The foreboding storms of the night, along with her own nightmares, have disturbed Caesar's wife Calpurnia. Interpreting them as warnings that something terrible is about to happen to Caesar, she begs him to stay home that day. The conspirators convince him otherwise, however, and escort him to the senate. Soon after his arrival, he is stabbed to death by the conspirators.

Despite Caesar's popularity, the conspirators believe that they will be able to convince the Roman people of the rightness of their action. At Caesar's funeral, Brutus's speech does win them over, but only temporarily. After Brutus leaves, Mark Antony convinces them instead that Caesar's death was unjust, and he manages to work the crowd into a fury against the murderers.

Brutus and Cassius flee Rome and gather an army. At Philippi, in Macedonia, they fight a battle against the armies of Mark Antony and Octavius, who is Caesar's great-nephew. Cassius, believing the war to be lost, commits suicide. Soon after, Brutus decides to run upon his own sword, held by his faithful servant Strato, rather than die at the hands of enemies. Rome is thus left in the control of Mark Antony and Octavius.

The character of Brutus. Brutus seems to be guided in the play at least partly by the philosophy of stoicism, a school of thought that was popular among the ancient Romans. Stoics believed that there was a rational force pervading reality and guiding all things to their perfection. Every person had a share of this force. It was one's duty to try to identify oneself with the force while training oneself to feel indifference to everything else. According to the Stoics, the rational soul should dominate one's actions. Personal emotions, which are motivated by service to oneself rather than by rational consideration of what is universally beneficial, are seen as powerful and disabling distractions. The Stoics believed that only by putting aside passion, unjust thoughts, and self-indulgence, and by performing

Calpurnia pleads with Caesar not to go to the Senate. Act II, scene ii of *Julius Caesar.*

one's duty with the right attitude, could a person live consistently with nature.

Brutus can be seen striving against his emotions throughout the play. In the first act he is at "war with himself" and tells Cassius,

Vexed I am
Of late with passions of some difference ...
Which give some soil, perhaps, to my
     behaviors.
                          (*Julius Caesar,* 1.2.39-46)

The stoic philosophy strove to be detached and aspired to a feeling of passionless indifference, an approach that appears to be favored by Brutus during his deliberation over what to do about Caesar. He separates his personal feelings for Caesar from his rational assessment of what must be done. For example, in his speech to the Roman people after Caesar's assassination, he states, "I slew my best lover [friend] for the good of Rome" (*Julius Caesar,* 3.2.38). In other words, he killed Caesar because he rationally came to the decision that his existence threatened the general good; therefore it was his duty to do so. "Not that I loved Caesar less," Brutus says, "but that I loved Rome more" (*Julius Caesar,* 3.2.19-20).

In the last scene of the play Brutus decides that he himself must die. He appears to come to

this decision, and face the act itself, with the passionless indifference of a stoic. He and his army are fighting a losing battle against the enemy forces of Antony and Octavius. He states that it makes the most sense for him to kill himself before his enemies can do it; it is the most honorable course of action to take. Furthermore, he has seen the ghost of Caesar twice since the assassination, and he calmly takes this to mean that his "hour is come" (*Julius Caesar,* 5.5.19). After meditating, he requests that one of his trusted servants hold his sword while he runs upon it. He kills himself, saying "Caesar, now be still; / I killed not thee with half so good a will" (*Julius Caesar,* 5.5.50-1). His manner of death indicates a mastery over his feelings even in the last moments of his life.

Sources. *Julius Caesar* is based on characters that actually existed and events that actually took place in ancient Rome. For his interpretation of the facts, Shakespeare seems to have drawn on Sir Thomas North's 1579 *Lives of the Noble Grecians and Romanes.* North's book was a translation of Plutarch's *Parallel Lives,* a work originally written in Greek toward the end of the first century A.D. In particular, Shakespeare drew on Plutarch's articles about the lives of Caesar and Brutus. In fact, some of the passages in *Julius Cae-*

sar incorporate phrases that are very similar to those employed by Plutarch.

Plutarch

"I dare assure thee, that no enemy hath taken nor shall take Marcus Brutus alive ... for wheresoever he be found, alive or dead, he will be found like himself."

(Dorsch in Shakespeare, p. xiv)

Shakespeare

"I dare assure thee that no enemy shall ever take alive the noble Brutus / ... When you do find him, or alive or dead, / He will be found like Brutus, like himself."

(*Julius Caesar*, 5.4.21-5)

Other similar examples can be found throughout the play. Still, while Plutarch evidently provided a basis for some of the elements of Shakespeare's Julius Caesar, there were marked differences between the versions. For example, Shakespeare condenses the actions described by Plutarch a great deal. The play moves very quickly from scene to scene. What really took place over the course of two years seems in Shakespeare's play to unfold in less than a month. Moreover, the scene in which Cassius and Brutus first speak about Caesar is presented in much more detail by Shakespeare. Finally, the playwright added the speeches Brutus and Antony give to the Roman people after Caesar's death. Though Plutarch's narrative seems to have been an important influence, the play that Shakespeare wrote is ultimately his own interpretation of the story.

Numerous other plays were written about Julius Caesar in the Elizabethan era. These included *Caesar Interfectus,* presented at Oxford in 1582, the anonymous *Caesar's Revenge,* and Sir William Alexander's *Tragedy of Julius Caesar.* Shakespeare's work was first staged in September 1599 and proved immediately popular. The play was later included in the first published collection of Shakespeare's plays, the *First Folio,* in 1623.

Events in History at the Time the Play Was Written

Shakespeare and Elizabethan politics. Although the political events that take place in *Julius Caesar* do not correspond directly to events of the Elizabethan era, there were similarities between the two. Like the rule of Julius Caesar, Queen Elizabeth's monarchy was not immune to plots and conspiracies against it. The career of Robert Devereux, Lord of Essex, which reached its high point around the time Shakespeare wrote this play, illustrates this fact.

In the 1590s the charismatic Essex became a favorite of the queen and one of the most popular men in England. His career began to decline toward the end of the decade, however. He was appointed to crush a rebellion in Ireland and left on March 27, 1599. After six months there, he concluded a truce that was extremely favorable to the Irish and returned to England against orders. Bursting into Queen Elizabeth's chamber early on September 28, 1599, he threw himself on her mercy. The next day he was taken prisoner. He underwent trial and was eventually freed from custody on June 5, 1600. Disgraced by the experience, Essex was also financially ruined when the queen deprived him of a monopoly on sweet wines from which he drew his income.

Essex's anger against the queen grew; he raved to one colleague about "the old woman, as crooked in her mind as in her carcase" (Essex in Halliday, p. 226). In those times, it was a very serious matter to criticize the monarch in this way. Essex went further, however. He began to form a conspiracy against the government. On February 3, 1601, he and five other conspirators laid plans for seizing the court and gathering the support of the people. The next day some of Essex's followers staged Shakespeare's *Richard II* (a play that chronicles the successful overthrow of a monarch), most likely as a means of gathering support for their cause. On the morning of February 8 about 300 followers met at Essex's house. Essex and his followers marched into London, brandishing swords and appealing to their fellow citizens to rise up and join them. None did. When a royal herald publicly proclaimed Essex to be a traitor, his own followers deserted him. The plot quickly deteriorated. Essex turned back toward home and was soon arrested. Within two weeks he was convicted of treason. He was executed on February 25, 1601.

Shakespeare finished *Julius Caesar* during 1599, the same year of Essex's disgraced return from Ireland. By the time of the failed conspiracy of 1601, the play was widely known. The English people took note of the similarities between the play and the actual events that unfolded and marveled anew at Shakespeare's work.

The Elizabethan conception of the world. Though *Julius Caesar* takes place in ancient Rome, Shakespeare's Elizabethan conception of the world influenced the content of the play. One element reflected in his work is the common belief in a direct connection between the phenomena of the natural world and the course of human events. A belief in the influence of the stars upon weather, plant and animal life, people, and events was probably held by a majority of Shakespeare's audience. While many were skeptical of claims of specific knowledge about individuals based on astrological information, general predictions about future events were quite respected. A number of distinguished astronomers, including Tycho Brahe (1546-1601) and Johannes Kepler (1571-1630), were also practicing astrologers. Furthermore, it was common for people of the Elizabethan period to interpret comets, eclipses of the sun or moon, earthquakes, and unusual sights as portents or warnings. When something of major importance was about to happen, or people were in any particular danger of suffering from divine anger for misdeeds, they believed that God provided warning in the form of portents.

Such ominous signs are plentiful in *Julius Caesar*—thunder, lightning, storms, and many strange happenings occur the night before Caesar's murder. The characters experiencing these phenomena interpret them as omens for the future. As Casca says,

> . . . never till tonight, never till now,
> Did I go through a tempest dropping fire.
> Either there is a civil strife in heaven,
> Or else the world, too saucy with the gods,
> Incenses them to send destruction.
> (*Julius Caesar,* 1.3.9-13)

He goes on to describe other strange images he has seen that night—a man's hand on fire yet not burned, a lion near the capitol, and a hundred ghastly women who swore they saw men on fire walking the streets. Caesar's wife Calpurnia is concerned as well, disturbed by accounts of strange sights seen by the night watchmen—graves opening up, blood drizzling upon the capitol, and ghosts. She also has nightmares of Caesar being murdered. She takes these portents very seriously and begs her husband not to leave the house the next day. He does so anyway and is subsequently killed.

Another Elizabethan belief reflected in *Julius Caesar* is that human beings were composed of four elements, or humours: choler, phlegm, sanguine (blood), and melancholy. These humours were constantly flowing and never completely stable. When these elements were in balance, a person was at the height of mental and physical health. Any humour could become dominant for a period of time, however, thus affecting personalities in particular ways.

Humour	Associated Personality Traits
Choler	Impetuous, cunning, quick to anger, lean, greedy
Phlegm	Sluggish, forgetful, dull, slow
Sanguine (Blood)	Cheerful, talkative
Melancholy	Stable, grave, deliberate

Cassius is characterized in *Julius Caesar* as choleric. While arguing with him, Brutus says, "Must I give way and room to your rash choler?... Go show your slaves how choleric you are, / And make your bondmen tremble" (*Julius Caesar,* 4.3.39-44). In accordance with Elizabethan belief, Cassius's choler made him quick to anger but also quick to calm down. Though extremely angry at the beginning of the discussion, Cassius becomes immediately apologetic when he learns that Brutus's wife, Portia, is dead. Other characteristics associated with choler were leanness and greediness, two qualities linked to Cassius during the play. Caesar notes at one point that he distrusts such a lean, cunning-looking man, while Brutus later accuses him of accepting bribes and having "an itchy palm" (*Julius Caesar,* 4.3.10).

On the other hand, Brutus is remembered as a man whose humours were well-balanced. Antony says of Brutus,

> His life was gentle, and the elements
> So mixed in him that Nature might stand up
> And say to the world, 'This was a man!'
> (*Julius Caesar,* 5.5.73-5)

For More Information

Crawford, Michael. *The Roman Republic.* Cambridge, Mass.: Harvard University Press, 1992.

Dodd, A. H. *Life in Elizabethan England.* New York: G. P. Putnam's Sons, 1961.

Dupont, Florence. *Daily Life in Ancient Rome.* Translated by Christopher Woodall. Cambridge, Mass.: Blackwell, 1989.

Guy, John. *Tudor England.* Oxford: Oxford University Press, 1988.

Halliday, F. E. *Shakespeare in His Age.* London: Gerald Duckworth, 1956.

Kay, Dennis. *Shakespeare: His Life, Work, and Era.* New York: William Morrow, 1992.

Scullard, H. H. *Festivals and Ceremonies of the Roman Republic.* Ithaca, N.Y.: Cornell University Press, 1981.

Shakespeare, William. *Julius Caesar.* Edited by T. S. Dorsch. London: Methuen, 1977.

King Lear

by
William Shakespeare

Forty-one years old when he wrote *King Lear*, Shakespeare created the play to be performed for King James, who had assumed the English throne in 1603. Shakespeare's play features a ruler quite different from the one that James I was proving to be. Despite some disharmony with parliament and other problems during his reign, James gained a reputation as a ruler with a peaceful nature, a concern for justice, and an interest in unifying Britain. In contrast, the ancient King Lear divided his kingdom, which led to bloodshed and war.

Events in History at the Time the Play Takes Place

English history—fact and legend. Scholars describe Shakespeare as being less interested in historical accuracy than in the passions and psychology of his own time. Nevertheless, although the setting of *King Lear* is not firmly fixed, the play appears to take place in the southern portion of the British island in the first thousand years B.C. Cornwall, Kent, and Gloucester, the names of characters in Shakespeare's play, are likewise names of regions in the southern portion of the island. According to the early English scholar Geoffrey of Monmouth, in his *Historia Regum Britanniae* (*History of the Kings of Britain*, 1136), the events on which *King Lear* is based took place in the era before recorded history, around 750 B.C. Later scholars have questioned the accuracy of Geoffrey's information. New facts about the Celts uncovered since his work sug-

gest that such a kingdom would have existed sometime later in the first thousand years B.C.

Historians look to both facts and legends to piece together information about England in the time before recorded history. Tales about such ancient English rulers as King Arthur, with his court at Camelot, are studied intently. A character in Shakespeare's play, the Fool, places the events of *King Lear* before the time of Camelot by mentioning King Arthur's magician Merlin: "This prophecy Merlin shall make for I live before his time ..." (Shakespeare, *King Lear*, 3.2.95-96).

Shakespeare set his play among the Britons, one of the peoples who inhabited the island in the first thousand years B.C. The Britons are known to have been part of a larger group, the Celts, who in ancient times had migrated to the island from western continental Europe. By examining Celtic legends, scholars have traced the name of Shakespeare's title character to *Llyr*, a Celtic sea god. Turning to early histories of England, they have further traced the character to a King Leir, who, according to these records, once ruled over all the Britons. He is thought to be a separate character from the Celtic sea god, despite the similar name. Other plays from Shakespeare's time, such as *The True Chronicle History of King Leir*, also discuss this monarch. There is, however, no real evidence to prove that a historical King Leir actually existed.

Celtic society. "The whole nation ... is warmad, both high-spirited and quick for battle" (the Greek writer Strabo in Powell, p. 76). The Greeks and Romans had encountered the Celts (or Gauls, as the Romans called them) on continental Europe, where the groups traded and fought with one another. The Celts possessed a highly aristocratic society, with kings, priests, a warrior class, freeman farmers, and slaves. Their social structure survived in large part in the early Celtic communities of both Ireland and southern Britain.

In Celtic Britain, society consisted of kings, nobles, free commoners (farmers), and an unfree population. As a rule, the people lived in kin or extended family groups. Land in early Celtic communities was owned not by individuals but by the kin group. Evidence suggests that several hundred years after Shakespeare's play is set, it was common among Britain's Celts for a father to divide his estate among his children. There is uncertainty about when this custom began or how widespread it was, but it parallels Lear's division of his kingdom at the outset of *King Lear*.

Among the ancient Celts, nobles and commoners related to each other in a system known as clientship. The commoners provided military and other services to a noble, who in return protected them and helped them meet basic needs. Unlike peasants in a feudal society, they were free and could own property.

In Shakespeare's play, King Lear's forces include an army of knights. Knights appeared in later, feudal societies, in which they fought for a king in exchange for land grants. But, while rulers in early Celtic culture did have bands of skilled warriors, there is no evidence that their armies included knights. A king could amass a powerful fighting force, but in another way. A local king would sometimes enter into a pact of friendship with less powerful kings, becoming their overlord. The less powerful kings would pledge armed services to the overlord in return for his military protection.

The power of women. *King Lear* concerns a father's efforts to divide his kingdom among his daughters indirectly, by distributing portions to his sons-in-law. He plans to give Cordelia's share to the man she will marry. The play seems to suggest that only male Britons could own property, which may not have been the case. In fact, daughters may have been able to inherit property directly and wives to own it independently of their husbands.

The Play in Focus

The plot. *King Lear* is remarkable for its skillful integration of parallel plot lines. The play tracks King Lear's tragic fall as well as the Earl of Gloucester's undoing. As the play opens, the Earl of Gloucester jests crudely about the conditions leading to the birth of his bastard son Edmund.

It is this son's evil plan that will lead to the earl's undoing. Gloucester suffers a fate similar to Lear's in the play—both believe their deceitful offspring and fail to trust their honest children, and both meet with disaster.

The aged and weary King Lear then turns his kingdom over to his daughters' husbands. His daughters must pledge their love to him in order to earn their share of his estate. While the words of his elder daughters, Goneril and Regan, win his approval, his youngest daughter, Cordelia, is unwilling to play this game of hollow flattery. Lear banishes her in a fit of rage and divides her share between Goneril's and Regan's husbands. The Earl of Kent objects, but his continued protests result in his banishment as well.

PUNISHMENT IN ELIZABETHAN ENGLAND

The blinding of the character Gloucester may seem a horrifying punishment, but even in Shakespeare's day many punishments were grisly. If a man was convicted of high treason, the law demanded that he be hanged and cut down while still alive. Next his bowels were to be taken out of his belly and burned before his eyes while still alive. Finally, his head was cut off and his body divided into four quarters. The head might afterward be displayed on a pike along London Bridge or some other public venue. Punishment for a female traitor was somewhat milder; she was to be burned by fire until dead. Although the law was supposed to be carried out as written, in fact mercy was often shown by hanging the male until he was dead before mutilating his body.

King Lear's decision to banish his youngest daughter affects her two suitors. Both the Duke of Burgundy and the King of France had expressed a desire to marry her. Stripped of her dowry, she is no longer attractive to the duke, but the king feels drawn to her and takes her to France.

Meanwhile, Gloucester's bastard son, Edmund, schemes to advance himself. A central motivation unfolds—Edmund aims to get even with his legitimate brother, Edgar, and his father, Gloucester, by gaining control of their estate. He gives Gloucester a letter, written by himself but signed with Edgar's name, that talks about the younger generation's right to inherit their elders' wealth without waiting for their parents to die.

Gloucester feels betrayed by Edgar but wants further proof of his treachery; therefore, Edmund sets up a meeting in which he frames the unwitting Edgar. Feeling trapped, Edgar flees, and Gloucester calls for his arrest.

The banished Earl of Kent, meanwhile, returns in disguise to serve King Lear. Gloucester's son Edgar, too, has resorted to disguising himself, masquerading as Poor Tom, or Tom o' Bedlam, a homeless madman tormented by "foul fiends." Another servant to the king, the Fool, sees the folly of Lear's actions and attempts to warn Lear of his error in judgment in a series of riddles and songs. Lear highly values the Fool and tolerates much criticism from him; he does not, however, understand the Fool's message.

Meanwhile, Goneril and Regan have launched a plot to deflate their father's power. Lear, who has decided to divide his time between his daughters' castles, has set a condition that 100 knights accompany him on his journeys back and forth. His daughters, each in her turn, coldly refuse to support such a large contingent of knights. The outrageousness of these actions drives Lear from first Goneril's and then Regan's castle.

Homeless and exposed to a lashing storm, Lear rails at nature. Kent and the Fool attempt to coax him into a nearby hovel or hut. Soon the exertions of his ranting and his growing madness weary the old king, and he collapses in exhaustion. Although Goneril and Regan have forbidden him to do so, Gloucester finds Lear and his companions and offers them shelter. He informs Kent of a plot against Lear's life, and the king leaves for Dover to meet the forces of the King of France and Cordelia, which are coming to his aid.

Upon returning to his castle, Gloucester is arrested and brought before Goneril, Regan, and Regan's husband, Cornwall. They condemn Gloucester for treachery and punish him by plucking out his eyes. Edmund is then named Earl of Gloucester, a development that makes it appear that he has managed to usurp his father's place, just as Lear's daughters have usurped their father's. Soon, however, Cornwall is fatally wounded by a servant still loyal to the old Gloucester. Cornwall's death proves to be the first step in the disintegration of the wicked new rulers' power. Goneril and Regan become entangled in a competition for Edmund's affection and physical love that eventually leads to both their deaths. Out of jealousy, Goneril poisons Regan and subsequently Goneril commits suicide.

At Dover a tender reunion takes place between Lear and Cordelia, but her French forces

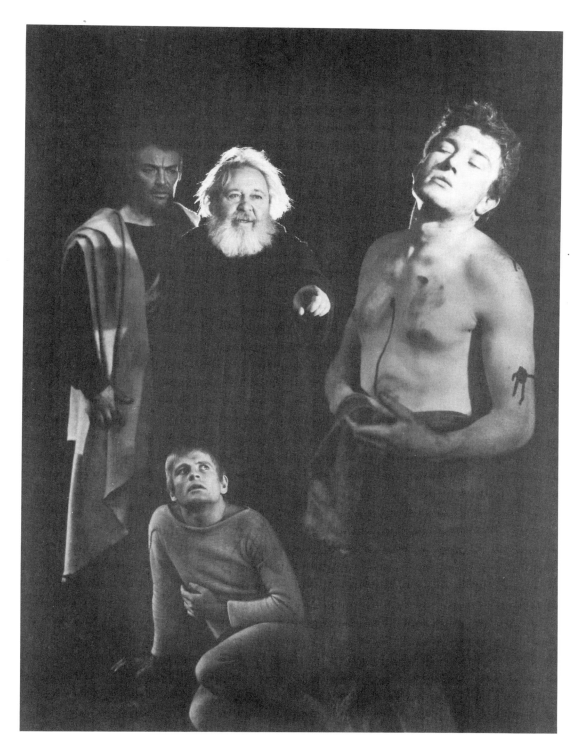

A scene from a stage production of *King Lear*.

lose to Goneril and Regan's army, and the father and daughter are arrested. Goneril's husband, the Duke of Albany, who has come to hate his evil wife, has Edmund arrested for treason. Edmund, in turn, offers to fight anyone who calls him a traitor. Still in disguise, Edgar meets Edmund in one-to-one combat and mortally wounds him. Edmund makes a last-minute attempt to do some good before his death, confessing that he has ordered the deaths of Lear and Cordelia. This information, however, is given too late to countermand his order. King Lear, having recognized Cordelia's loyalty and love, dies grieving over her breathless body. With the death of most of the principals—Lear, Cordelia, Goneril, and Regan, among others—Edgar declares that those remaining must, "Speak what we feel, not what we ought to say" (*King Lear*, 5.3.325). This allusion to the false flattery that triggered the play's tragic events thus links the end of the drama to its beginning.

Science vs. nature in *King Lear*. The words *nature, natural,* and *unnatural* appear some forty times in *King Lear*. There were two views of nature in Shakespeare's England, and they competed with each other. Inherited from the Middle Ages was the image of nature as closely tied to God; man, according to this image, must cooperate with the natural order and behave with human decency to succeed. In Shakespeare's play, Lear considers his cruel treatment by two of his daughters as an offense against nature, which demands that children honor their parents. He holds the medieval view of a naturally moral universe and shows an increasing human decency as the play progresses.

At first, King Lear seems unaware of the disparities and inequalities in his world. But as he loses his land, his power, and ultimately his identity, he comes to understand the vulnerability of the poor. When Lear is exposed to a lashing, wind-driven rain, he laments his earlier insensitivity to them:

> Poor naked wretches, wheresoe'er you are,
> That bide the pelting of this pitiless storm,
> How shall your houseless heads and unfed
>   sides ... defend you
> From seasons such as these? O, I have ta'en
> Too little care of this!
> (*King Lear*, 3.4.28-33)

The character Edmund represents another, competing view. He is the "new man" of the post-medieval Renaissance period, a creature who is, above all, a political animal driven by self-inter-

est and a desire for power. The century leading up to Shakespeare's play had seen the appearance of such politically driven and scientific men. Perhaps most notably, Europeans had seized on and perverted ideas from Nicolò Machiavelli's 1529 book **The Prince** (also covered in *Literature and Its Times*). These ideas, which concerned strategies for acquiring and retaining power, helped foster the image of the new man and became part of a larger, scientific view of nature. Instead of being connected to God, nature was regarded as an independent machine that God had created but then left to run of its own accord. Man, according to this view, need not worry about having to cooperate with nature to excel. Rather he could discover nature's laws and manipulate them for his own purposes. Even human nature could be manipulated, as shown by Edmund in *King Lear*; when Goneril and Regan compete for his love, he ruthlessly exploits their feelings for his own personal gain.

The two views—that of nature as including man and tied to God and that of nature as independent of God and controllable by man—co-existed uneasily in Shakespeare's society. Shakespeare himself takes a position in *King Lear*. Favoring the first view, he casts Edmund, the new-age man in the play, as the villain. But Edmund shows some human decency at the end, when he tries to save Lear and Cordelia from death, an act that suggests his character is a complex mixture in which old values have not altogether been displaced by the new.

Sources. Shakespeare almost certainly drew upon the play *The True Chronicle History of King Leir* (c. 1590) in developing his own drama. He definitely drew upon Raphael Holinshed's *Chronicles of England, Scotland, and Ireland* (1587) and probably upon Geoffrey of Monmouth's *Historia Regum Britanniae* (c. 1135) as well. The similarities between Shakespeare's *King Lear* and the stories of King Leir in the *Chronicles* and the *Historia* are remarkable. Those documents describe Leir as a king of ancient England with three daughters. The two elder ones, Goneril and Regan, earn a share of his kingdom; Cordelia, the youngest, refuses to flatter her father. She is banished, only to return at a later time. The key difference between Shakespeare's work and the earlier accounts is found at the end. In the sources, Cordelia rescues Leir from his wicked daughters and establishes a peaceful kingdom (although she is later driven to suicide by her sisters' sons). Other publications of the era in which the same basic storyline appears are Edmund Spenser's *The Faerie Queene* (1590 and 1596) and John Higgins' *The First Parte of the Mirror for Magistrates* (1574).

Shakespeare apparently developed the Gloucester subplot from Sir Philip Sidney's *Arcadia* (1581 and 1583). Sidney's work also had a tragic ending, with the equivalent of the Gloucester character dying of a broken heart, which may have influenced the tone of the conclusion to *King Lear*.

Shakespeare drew inspiration from several other quarters in his creation of a number of characters in *King Lear*. For the figure of Tom o' Bedlam, Shakespeare used Samuel Harsnett's *Declaration of Egregious Popishe Impostures* (1603), a work dealing with demons. The devils and fiends who torment Tom are derived directly from this piece.

The character of the Fool dates back to ancient times. By Shakespeare's era, fools had become servants in the homes of nobles. Mentally impaired or physically deformed, fools were thought to be touched by God and so enjoyed a privileged position. They were expected not only to amuse but also to criticize their masters. Queen Elizabeth, who ruled before and during Shakespeare's lifetime, is known to have scolded one of her fools for not being critical enough with her.

Events in History at the Time the Play Was Written

From Queen Elizabeth to King James. England under the rule of Elizabeth I (1558-1603) became a vigorous land of growth, opportunity, and fierce competitiveness. The queen proved to be a unifying force whose leadership helped propel her island nation to new levels of achievement. An intellectual and a writer of poetry herself, she was a patroness of the arts as well as a forceful ruler.

Queen Elizabeth never married or had any children. Because of this, there was no direct heir to the throne; as she grew older, the question of who would succeed her as monarch became one of increasing concern to her subjects. Internal politics and religion complicated the problem. There was great concern that ambitious rivals for the throne would plunge England into a civil war. The transfer of power, however, proved to be a smooth one. Before her death, Elizabeth arranged for James VI of Scotland to give up his Catholic religion, convert to the Anglican Church, and rule England as James I. James proved to be a capable king.

King Lear was first performed in 1606, only three years after Elizabeth's passing. Some readers feel that Shakespeare may have used the play to pay tribute to the queen, his late patroness. By focusing the play's plot on the difficulties that can arise in determining succession to the throne, he may have been indirectly praising her—as well as King James—by showing how dangerous the transfer of power can be. Certainly, Shakespeare presents a startling contrast to James I's relatively untroubled ascension to the throne.

As king, James concluded a peace with Spain, ending a war that had lasted nearly twenty years at great expense to England. On the first day of Parliament after his coronation, he promoted plans for a formal union between Scotland and England (which, despite his efforts, would not occur during his reign). James tried to resolve disputes in the church, too. He clearly kept the well-being of his kingdom in mind when mak-

---

THE MODEL FOR LEAR?

Brian Annesley was a nobleman who lived during Shakespeare's lifetime. He went insane, and two of his daughters took him to court to have him committed to an asylum and to win control of his estate. A third daughter, Cordell, protested. As a result of a letter she wrote to King James, her father was allowed to live out his life in the care of a friend. In his will Annesley left Cordell his estates, a move that her sisters contested unsuccessfully in court. A friend of Shakespeare's knew the family, and it is likely that Shakespeare was aware of the case.

---

ing decisions and taking action. Moreover, his efforts on behalf of unity contrast sharply with the divisions and subsequent decay in the kingdom of *King Lear*.

Great Chain of Being. Although the world of *King Lear* sometimes seems to lack any sense of order, Shakespeare's audiences were familiar with a certain hierarchy, or system of organization by rank or authority. This hierarchy was based on a model of the world known as the "Great Chain of Being," a name given to the model only after Shakespeare's time. The name alludes to a chain of existence that begins with God and descends downward through the angels, to humans, then to beasts, and finally to rocks and other inanimate objects.

Portrait of James I by David Mythens. He succeeded Elizabeth as the English monarch, ruling during the time *King Lear* was written.

In *King Lear,* Shakespeare focuses on the position of humans between angels and beasts. Angels, it was assumed, already knew themselves and therefore had little interest in self-understanding. Humans did not have automatic self-knowledge but could learn to understand themselves, which helped explain why they occupied a higher position on the Great Chain than beasts, who were incapable of self-knowledge. At the outset of the play, Lear suffers from poor self-understanding and so would drop down to the position of beast on the chain. As the drama progresses, however, he realizes the truth about his own foolish misjudgment of his daughters. To educated playgoers, Lear's growing awareness allows him to assume his proper place on the Great Chain of Being.

Treatment of the insane. In Shakespeare's time, the insane were thought to be possessed by evil spirits. Edgar, disguised as Poor Tom, speaks of these spirits—Flibbertigibbet, Modo and Mahu, Frateretto, and Hoppedance—as fiends who prey upon him. The name Tom o' Bedlam is taken from the name of a hospital in London (Bedlam, a corruption of *Bethlehem*) dedicated to the "treatment" of the mentally ill. In treating the insane, the hospital typically prescribed whipping as a "cure" for madness. Patients released from Bedlam were almost always poverty-stricken, and they usually resorted to begging for their existence.

Family life in Shakespeare's England. Life in England during the 1600s was still very precarious. People died suddenly of diseases and injuries for which no cure existed. Despite the all-too-likely risk of sudden loss, though, people formed close attachments and institutions of the time concentrated on preserving and promoting the immediate family. Church courts penalized people for straying from their loyalty to a husband or wife, and a divorce was virtually impossible to obtain. Severe punishments were handed down for those who murdered or attacked their parents or husbands. Living in such a society, audiences must have regarded the actions of Lear's two elder daughters as especially wicked and contrary to nature more than just evil. In Act 1, Lear rages against Goneril, expressing his desire that she might feel, "How sharper than a serpent's tooth it is / To have a thankless child" (*King Lear*, 1.4.279-80). This sums up the revulsion that most playgoers probably felt toward Goneril and

her sister Regan, especially in view of Lear's generous gift of his kingdom to them. In fact in Shakespeare's England, children who challenged the authority of their elders were generally considered "brainsick" (MacDonald, p. 165).

A CRITIC APPROVES OF SHAKESPEARE'S ENDING

After surviving so many sufferings, Lear can only die ... if he is also to be saved and to pass the remainder of his days in happiness, the whole loses its signification.

(Schlegel, p. 413)

Reviews. Although *King Lear* is a play of great power, in its action and its depiction of characters, as well as in its themes and tragic mood, some early audiences were dismayed by the play's bleak conclusion. In 1681 the English playwright Nahum Tate altered the tragedy by giving it a happy ending that included victory for Cordelia's army and Lear's return to the throne. Tate's popular version was staged with greater frequency than the original for the next 150 years. Not until the 1800s would critics prefer Shakespeare's own tragic ending as the most realistic, effective one for his play.

For More Information

Burgess, Anthony. *Shakespeare.* Chicago: Elephant Paperbacks, 1994.

MacDonald, Michael. *Mystical Bedlam: Madness, Anxiety, and Healing in Seventeenth-Century England.* Cambridge: Cambridge University Press, 1981.

McIlwain, Charles Howard. *The Political Works of James I.* Cambridge, Mass.: Harvard University Press, 1918.

Powell, T. G. E. *The Celts.* 1958. Revised edition. London: Thames and Hudson, 1980.

Schlegel, August Wilhelm. "Criticisms on Shakespeare's Tragedies" in *A Course of Lectures on Dramatic Art and Literature.* 1846. Reprint. New York: AMS Press, 1965.

Shakespeare, William. *King Lear.* New York: Penguin, 1970.

Tatlock, J. S. P. *The Legendary History of Britain.* Berkeley: University of California Press, 1950.

The Last of the Mohicans

by
James Fenimore Cooper

Born in 1789, James Fenimore Cooper grew up in a small town on the edge of the frontier in upstate New York. Over thirty years before, the area had been embroiled in the French and Indian War. This dispute, also known as the Seven Years' War, thrust England, France, the colonists, and the American Indian population into a bitter conflict that permanently reshaped the future of North America.

Events in History at the Time the Novel Takes Place

North America in the middle 1700s. During the eighteenth century, North America was home to many different groups of peoples who sought to secure a claim on the vast territory. English, Irish, and Scottish settlers filled the English colonies, while the French and Spanish settled the territory of Canada and Florida as well as the wilderness interior, which was also home to large numbers of American Indians. The desire to control the various parts of this vast territory led to a number of conflicts between these groups. France and England, for instance, fought four wars against one another between 1689 and 1763. In North America the conflicts between France and England were primarily the result of the rapid growth of the English colonies. The population in those settlements exploded from less than a quarter of a million people in 1700 to over 1.5 million by 1760. This surge in population sent many English settlers further into the interior of the continent, where they challenged

THE LITERARY WORK

A novel set in 1757 during the French and Indian War in the forests of what was later to become the upper portion of New York State; first published in 1826.

SYNOPSIS

The frontiersman Hawkeye and his two Indian friends become involved in a struggle to guide two English girls to see their father. They later rescue the girls after their capture by a renegade Indian.

not only France's New World territories, but also those of the powerful Indian tribes that inhabited the region.

In order to stop the English expansion and protect its own economic interests in the region, the French drove the English out of the Ohio Valley and built a series of forts to prevent further English encroachment. The French also made several attempts to seduce American Indian leaders to sympathize with the French cause. In 1754, angered by this challenge and anxious to clear the Ohio Valley of the French, the British parliament decided to send several thousand troops to destroy French control in North America once and for all. In response, France sent more than 3,000 of its own soldiers in preparation for a final showdown with the English in the New World.

The French and Indian War. This first major conflict of the war resulted in a crushing defeat for the English. General Braddock of the English forces was inexperienced in the subtleties of forest warfare. He led the British troops into battle in a remote part of rural Virginia, where they were routed by a small force of French soldiers and Indians. This decisive victory brought more Indians to the side of the French, and for the next two years they carried on a series of attacks and raids that created tremendous fear among the British colonists, who "believed that the yells of the savages mingled with every fitful gust of wind that issued from the interminable forests of the west" (Cooper, *Last of the Mohicans,* p. 3).

Fort William Henry—the massacre. The French maintained a clear advantage in the struggle. In 1756 they advanced against the English at Fort William Henry, which was in the command of Lieutenant Colonel George Monro. Monro had only 2,372 men at his disposal against an oncoming force of 7,626 French and Indians. Despite the odds, Monro and the English held out for four days. They then received word from a superior at a nearby fort that no aid would be forthcoming. Forced to surrender, Monro arranged with the French leader, the Marquis de Montcalm, to evacuate men, women, and children from the fort. In the process, however, forty to fifty of Monro's followers were murdered by Indians fighting on the side of the French. Cooper describes the bloodbath, known in historical records as the "massacre of William Henry," in his novel.

The Iroquois choose sides. In 1757 the British decided to focus the whole of their military might on the struggle in North America. The following year, the tide of battle turned in favor of the British, and they began to amass significant victories on the battlefield. Yet they still suffered some crushing defeats. On one occasion, a British-led army of over 15,000 men—the largest ever yet assembled in North America at that point—was badly beaten when it attempted to storm a French fort on Lake Champlain. The French, however, found it increasingly difficult to hold off the concerted effort by the British, who closed out 1758 with a string of decisive victories. Using their navy to bottle up French shipping, the British were also able to convince the powerful Iroquois Indian Confederacy that an English victory in North America was inevitable. The Iroquois nation, which had previously remained neutral, cast their lot with the probable winner. The British thus captured Quebec and Montreal, the major French strongholds in Canada, with the help of the Iroquois.

As their numbers dwindled and their power bases were destroyed, it became clear that the French had been thoroughly defeated in North America. While they continued to fight the British in the Caribbean as well as in Europe, England's dominance in the New World was firmly established. When the Treaty of Paris was signed in 1763, French control of North American land was virtually erased. Canada and all of France's holdings east of the Mississippi were officially handed over to England.

The American Indian role in the French and Indian War. American Indians were pivotal figures in the French and Indian War. Grouped into many tribes, their diverse interests and concerns dictated different allegiances during the conflict. At first the French attracted an overwhelming amount of Indian support, due in part to the fact that their colonial population was not as large as that of the British and was thus not as great a territorial threat. Tribes that joined forces with the French included the Wyandot, Shawnee, Chippewa, Potawatomi, Ottawa, Miami, Abenaki, Micmac, and Delaware. Interestingly, some tribes switched alliances during the war. The Cherokee originally sided with the British. Displeased over their treatment, however, they moved over to the French side.

FROM JAMES FENIMORE COOPER TO JOHN MILLER, A LONDON BOOKSELLER

~

Dear Sir,
Carey Published the "Mohicans" on the 6th of February [1826].... The book is quite successful, in this Country, more so, I think, than any of its predecessors.

(Cooper, *Letters and Journals,* p. 127)

Evidence of the importance of American Indian support came in 1759 when the powerful Iroquois Confederacy joined the British attack on the French Fort Niagara. Supported by the Iroquois, the British wore down their French opponents. The Iroquois received much of the credit for the victory, which drove the French off. Of course, their long-term goal was to drive not only the French but all Europeans from their territory.

Tribal conflict. In the novel, the villain Magua belongs to the Mohawks, a division of the Iro-

A map of North America at the time of the French and Indian War, 1689-1763, showing forts, native villages, and white settlements.

quois, while the Mohican character Uncas explains that he descends from Delaware Indians. (Magua is called a Huron, but the novel explains that only by birth does he belong to this nation. The Iroquois have adopted him as one of their own.) In reality, the Delaware and Iroquois actually did compete with one another. Their competition began around 1681, when the founding of Pennsylvania put the Delaware tribe in a separate colony from the Iroquois of New York. The two groups increasingly competed for status and prestige in the area. When the Iroquois tried to dominate some of the Delaware in 1756, the Delaware rebelled, insisting they would speak for themselves at treaty councils.

The Novel in Focus

The plot. Set during the third year of the French and Indian War, the novel opens as Cora and Alice Munro are preparing to journey to Fort William Henry to meet their father, Colonel

Munro, who is commander of the fort. Accompanied by Major Duncan Heyward, and later joined by the traveling psalm singer David Gamut, the group is led to the fort by Magua, a mysterious and fierce-looking Huron. Soon the group meets up with Hawkeye, a skilled frontiersman, and his two Mohican friends, Chingachgook and his son Uncas. Major Heyward tells Hawkeye and his friends that he believes Magua is leading the group astray. Hawkeye and his companions then attempt to seize Magua, but the guide escapes into the forest. Hawkeye attempts to shoot him down but fails.

Fearing an attack by unfriendly Indians, Hawkeye leads the group by canoe to Glenn's Falls, where they hide in a series of caves behind the waterfall. After leaving the caves the next morning, the group is ambushed by a band of Iroquois. The small group retreats to the caves where they leave the women, accompanied by Gamut, to hide. Out in the forest Hawkeye, Heyward, and the two Mohicans engage the Iroquois in a bloody struggle. Running out of ammunition, the two Mohicans and Hawkeye slip downstream in order to get help for the others. Soon, however, a group of Hurons led by Magua enters the caves and captures the people within, as well as Heyward.

Magua, who has taken control of the prisoners, reveals a bitter hatred for Cora and Alice's father, Colonel Munro. Despite this animosity, he claims he will release Alice if Cora will become his wife. When she refuses, Magua stirs up the other Indians into a fit of rage directed at the captives. Just as Heyward is about to be killed, Hawkeye and the two Mohicans charge the group. Although Magua again escapes, the rescue proves successful and the captives—Alice, Cora, Gamut, and Heyward—are freed.

The group continues its journey towards Fort William Henry, only to find that their arrival at the fort has coincided with the beginning of an assault on it by 10,000 French troops. The band makes a mad dash for the fort that proves successful. The girls are joyously reunited with their father, Colonel Munro.

The British forces, however, are forced to surrender to the French siege and leave the fort. General Montcalm, the French leader, neglects to arrange for a troop escort for the defeated British. Suddenly a group of 2,000 Indians descend on the British, massacring them in a bloody attack. Magua recaptures Alice and Cora and leads them into the forest, with Gamut following behind.

Munro, Heyward, Hawkeye, Chingachgook, and Uncas go out to rescue the girls, following their trail north through the forest. The group encounters Gamut and learns from him that the girls have been separated. While Heyward attempts to rescue Alice from the Huron camp, Uncas is brought in as a captive. Heyward succeeds in carrying Alice out of the camp, and Hawkeye rescues Uncas by using an elaborate disguise. They then rush to the camp of the Delawares to rescue Cora. Arriving at virtually the same time as Magua, Heyward and Hawkeye are tied up by the Delawares, only to be released when Uncas reveals himself a chief and a descendent of the Delawares. Hawkeye and Heyward are cut free. Cora, however, is judged to be the rightful prisoner of Magua, and he is allowed to leave with her.

Magua and Cora leave the Delaware village for the Huron village, but they are followed by Hawkeye, the Mohicans, and a band of warriors, all of whom are intent on freeing Cora. After another bloody conflict, Uncas, Hawkeye, Heyward, and Gamut pursue Magua and two warriors into a cave. Cora, a stubborn prisoner, refuses to move in accordance with the instructions of her captors. Magua threatens to kill her, and another Huron steps in and stabs her to death. At the same moment, Uncas leaps from an overhanging ledge in a desperate attempt to save Cora. A deadly battle between the two sides follows and Uncas is one of those who are slain.

The final chapter is one of mourning as the Indians and whites grieve their respective losses. As the rest of the whites leave, Hawkeye remains with Chingachgook, who laments the fact that he is the last of his tribe.

THE FIRST MOHICAN

The real Uncas might more properly be called the First Mohican (Mohegan) rather than one of the last. A rebel in the nation of his birth (the Pequots), he founded his own tribe and turned it into a strong force in eastern Connecticut. Though friendly toward the English, the real Chief Uncas often quarreled with neighboring Indian groups.

Lineage. A major focus of *Last of the Mohicans* is the idea of the survival of one's lineage, reflected not only in the title but also in the words and deeds of the characters. Lineage comes to represent both the continuance of a family and the way of life of a people. Even Hawkeye can be seen in this light.

By his own admission, Hawkeye is a man with no "kin" and no "people," so he too represents the last of his line. In a grander sense, he also represents the life of the frontiersman, an increasingly rare occupation with each passing generation.

The focus on lineage is most clearly seen in Cooper's depiction of Chingachgook and Uncas, whose bond as father and son is strengthened by the knowledge that they represent the last of the Mohican tribe. The demise of his once-great tribe is articulated by Chingachgook when he laments, "Where are the blossoms of those summers!—fallen, one by one: so all of my family departed, each in turn, to the land of spirits. I am on the hill-top, and must go down into the valley; and when Uncas follows in my footsteps, there will no longer be any of the blood of the sagamores (chiefs), for my boy is the last of the Mohicans" (*Last of the Mohicans*, p. 26).

TWO STORIES OR ONE?

A s was a common practice of the day, *The Last of the Mohicans* was originally published in two separate volumes. This publishing tactic forced Cooper to treat each volume as a separate story and helps to explain why the novel really reads like two separate stories, with the two long chase and rescue sequences divided by a short and peaceful interlude at Fort William Henry.

While *The Last of the Mohicans* is an adventure story, it also pays tribute to a way of life that was rapidly being overrun by the constantly expanding white population. Chingachgook pays this tribute after burying his son: "As for me, the son and the father of Uncas, I am a blazed pine, in a clearing of the pale faces. My race has gone from the shores of the salt lake, and the hills of the Delawares. But who can say that the Serpent of his tribe has forgotten his wisdom? I am alone" (*Last of the Mohicans*, p. 373). The novel, in fact, ends with an Indian lament for a dying way of life. A chief of the Delaware Indians, Tamenund, mourns the fate of the Indian peoples: "The pale faces are masters of the earth, and the time of the redmen has not come again. My day has been too long. In the morning I saw the sons of Unamis happy and strong; and yet, before the night has come, have lived to see the last warrior of the wise race of the Mohicans" (*Last of the Mohicans*, p. 374).

Sources. While *The Last of the Mohicans* was obviously centered around the French and Indian War, it was never intended to be an exact account of actual events. Authors of the day, such as Sir Walter Scott, were often concerned more with the telling of a story than the recreation of history. Cooper, in fact, modeled his novels of romantic action after those penned by Scott. Inventing almost the entire story, Cooper includes only a few references to real people and events, although he does mention the Fort William Henry massacre and a few real military figures such as the British colonel George Monro and the French general Marquis de Montcalm. He uses some actual tribal names as well, including Delaware, Huron, and Mohawk. Cooper apparently had little actual contact with Indians, however, relying instead on written accounts that discussed the various tribes. He did have a few personal interviews with chiefs, including Ongpatonga, a noble Omaha Indian who became the model for Chingachgook in *The Last of the Mohicans*.

Cooper took some creative liberties, however, with Indian names and other details. For instance, the Mohican tribe, which nears extinction in the novel, was a name that Cooper seems to have taken from an actual tribe, the Mohegans. In reality, the Mohegans did not suffer the same fate as the Mohicans in Cooper's novel. Members of the tribe still exist today. Historians, though, generally agree that Cooper took his inspiration from the Mohegans. They note that the tribe was once led by a chief named Uncas, who befriended the British. Yet even in this respect, the similarities between fact and *The Last of the Mohicans* are minimal. The real Uncas lived a hundred years earlier (circa 1606-1682) than the one in the novel.

Events in History at the Time the Novel Was Written

National Indian policy. Much of *The Last of the Mohicans* can be seen as a tribute to American Indian tribes and a dying way of life. At the time Cooper was writing the novel, the United States government was implementing plans that were to lead to the destruction of the American Indian lifestyle. While the government attempted to treat each tribe as a separate nation, it did so with the private understanding that "the expansion of White civilization should not be obstructed or prevented by hunter or agricultural societies, thinly spread over the land and not fully using the resources according to White standards" (Washburn, p. 40).

Portrait of Ongpatonga, an Omakas chief and Cooper's real-life model for Chingachgook, painted by Charles Bird King, c. 1821.

By the 1820s it was obvious to white observers that the "Indian problem" was growing very serious. Most of the Indians had resisted absorption into the white lifestyle, a stand that threatened to have greater consequences as more and more whites pressed westward. Many white settlers and travelers began calling for the United States government to remove the Indians from their path. Indiana, Illinois, Michigan, Wisconsin, Iowa, and Minnesota all had large portions of land opened up to settlement through the removal of Indian tribes. In the Southeast, however, the Cherokee, Creek, Choctaw, Chickasaw, and Seminole refused to give up any more land and stated their expectation that the United States would honor the treaties it had previously signed with them.

This conflict was debated on and off for the first twenty years of the nineteenth century. The debate culminated in 1824 when U.S. President James Monroe declared in his State of the Union address that the only solution to the problem was the removal of the Indians to lands further west. Soon after, Cooper began writing *The Last of the Mohicans,* which was published in 1826.

With the discovery of gold in Georgia in the latter portion of the 1820s, the situation for the Indians grew more precarious. Many Cherokee held firmly to their territory, and their presence created many conflicts with settlers who came in search of gold. During this era, President Monroe and his successors, John Quincy Adams and Andrew Jackson, were consumed with the problem of Indian territorial claims. Eventually, all three recommended the removal of the Indians to land further west, and during Jackson's presidency such measures were passed into law. Cooper himself seems to have approved of the removal policy as the most humane solution for the Indians if executed with a fair and generous spirit. He clearly did not foresee its deadly consequences. The last chapters of *The Last of the Mohicans* though, are seen by some modern readers as emblematic accounts of the doomed existence led by all American Indians of the nineteenth century.

AN 1826 REVIEW

Mr. Cooper's Indians are somewhat of the visionary order ... but then he has interwoven with his vision more of what really belongs to the aboriginal character than any other writer of poetry or romance. (*North American Review*, p. 166)

The birth of American literature. First published in 1826, *The Last of the Mohicans* was written at a time of tremendous transition for the United States. It had held its own against the mighty British in the War of 1812, had defeated tribes on the Great Plains, and had gone on to wage battle against Florida's Indians and win control of Florida from Spain in 1821. A year earlier, the South had become the world's largest cotton producer, a status that spurred the construction of numerous new textile mills in the North. But while the United States had advanced quickly in terms of its economy, territorial gains, and military strength, its cultural growth paled in comparison to that of the much older European nations. A combination of many different peoples, the United States was already developing a truly distinct folk culture, but one that was not regarded as "high culture." It was not until *The Last of the Mohicans* that the United States produced a novel that was considered significant in Europe.

Reviews. While some critics found fault with aspects of *The Last of the Mohicans,* such as the numerous dangers and narrow escapes that mark the novel, the public embraced it. The book was the second in Cooper's series of novels featuring the frontiersman in the American wilderness (*The Pioneers*—1823, *Last of the Mohicans*—1826, *The Prairie*—1827, *The Pathfinder*—1840, and *The Deerslayer*—1841). *The Last of the Mohicans* out-

shone all the others in popular appeal and became a wild success in Cooper's lifetime.

Cooper's trademarks. By drawing from the folklore of the day, Cooper's work did much to influence the growth of American literature, including his use of two settings that were to become trademarks of American literature: the frontier and the sea. Cooper's novel, while accepted by intellectuals, remained rooted in the essence of folk culture, especially in terms of plot and theme. He created almost mythic characters who confronted and conquered terrible odds while simultaneously living up to a strict code of morals and values. Cooper's frontiersman Hawkeye, for instance, chooses to live like a hermit in the wilderness, valuing the wild game around him and resenting the advancing settlers. Holding values that in some respects differed greatly from traditional European values, the character of the frontiersman helped establish a view that was distinctly American and a voice through which the United States could speak to the rest of the world.

Cooper also depicted Indian characters that were either noble or wickedly savage. Later writers would model their Indians on his, and although historians called his characters unrealistic, they became commonplace stereotypes held by whites of his time. In any case, Cooper's descriptions of North American Indians were apparently more realistic than those that had appeared in earlier romances and works of poetry.

For More Information

Champagne, David. *Chronology of Native American History.* Detroit: Gale Research, 1994.

Cooper, James Fenimore. *The Last of the Mohicans.* New York: Bantam Books, 1988.

Cooper, James Fenimore. *The Letters and Journals of James Fenimore Cooper.* Vol. 1. Edited by James Franklin Beard. Cambridge, Mass.: Harvard University Press, 1960.

"Cooper's Novels." *North American Review,* vol. 23 (July 1826).

House, Kay Seymour. *Cooper's Americans.* Columbus, Ohio: Ohio State University Press, 1965.

Jennings, Francis. *Empire of Fortune: Crowns, Colonies and Tribes in the Seven Years War in America.* New York: W. W. Norton, 1988.

Josephy, Alvin J. *500 Nations.* New York: Alfred A. Knopf, 1994.

Ringe, Donald A. *James Fenimore Cooper.* New York: Twayne, 1961.

Steele, Ian K. *Betrayals: Fort William Henry and the "Massacre."* New York: Oxford University Press, 1990.

Washburn, Wilcomb. *History of Indian-White Relations.* Washington D.C.: Smithsonian Press, 1988.

"The Legend of Sleepy Hollow"

by
Washington Irving

Washington Irving was born in New York in 1783. He was strongly influenced by the Dutch culture of that area, which maintained a distinctive identity into the early 1800s. Successfully integrating both European and American elements into his stories, he gained an international reputation as the first distinctively American writer. Irving lived abroad from 1815 to 1832; "The Legend of Sleepy Hollow" was first published while the author lived in England. Although the story is set shortly after the Revolutionary War, Irving's characters draw on traditions of the pre-Revolutionary days of the colonial English and Dutch in his home state of New York.

THE LITERARY WORK

A short story set in a New York Dutch community after the Revolutionary War; published in 1819-20.

SYNOPSIS

Icahbod Crane, a greedy Yankee schoolteacher, vies with a local youth for the affections of a rich farmer's daughter. On his way home one day, the schoolteacher is accosted by a figure who appears to be the legendary headless horseman of Sleepy Hollow. Crane is never seen again.

Events in History at the Time the Short Story Takes Place

Regional conflict. In colonial America, the region that is now the state of New York was first settled by the Dutch and called New Netherland. In 1664 the British conquered New Netherland and changed the name to New York, yet the influence of the Dutch immigrants continued to be felt long after this conquest. Tensions had existed between the Dutch in New Netherland and the English immigrants in New England from the early days of colonization. They quarreled over the fur trade, property issues, and relations with American Indian tribes. As early as 1640, the Dutch complained of being mistreated by the English and charged that the English accused them of crimes that they had not committed. In

1661 Governor Winthrop of Connecticut wrote a memo referring to the Dutch as "noxious neighbours," and after their colony was conquered by the English in 1664, the Dutch were considered an alien culture by the English colonists. This view of them persisted until approximately 1800.

A series of border wars between New England and New York and continuing economic competition fueled tensions over the years. But the most important source of early conflict appeared just after the Revolutionary War. At this time, immigration from New England into New York increased rapidly. The tide from New England grew even greater after 1783, when New Englanders swept "up the Mohawk gateway, and . . . out across the fertile lands of central and western New York" (Ellis et al., p. 189). These settlers, who sought to secure rich farmland and escape the high taxes in place in Massachusetts, immigrated in such great numbers into the Hudson-Mohawk valleys that they overwhelmed most Dutch and German communities. By 1820 a clear majority of New Yorkers were of New England origin. The consequence was ill feeling among the Dutch and Germans toward the New Englanders. This tension is reflected in Irving's tale, which pits the Dutchman Brom Bones against the New England schoolteacher Ichabod Crane, who has recently come to New York.

The Dutch character. Bones is a rough and tumble character who exhibits many qualities shown by rural Dutch settlers before the American Revolution. A simple country fellow, he is quick to show both his anger and his sense of humor, and he is prone to storytelling, exaggerating, joking, and fighting.

FUN AND GAMES

The raucous personality of Brom Bones draws on the boisterous nature attributed to early Dutch colonial youths, some of whose games would be considered cruel by today's standards. "Clubbing the Cat," for example, consisted of placing a cat inside a barrel and suspending the barrel in midair. The participants competed to see who could set the cat free by hurling clubs at the cask. Another favorite was "Pulling the Goose." In this game, a goose with a greased head was hung upside down from a rope strung across the road. The object was to see which horseback rider could pull the goose free as he rode under the rope.

Both practical jokes and fighting were common elements of colonial Dutch society. In the story, Brom Bones and Ichabod Crane compete for the affections of Katrina Van Tassel. According to the tale, Bones "had a degree of rough chivalry in his nature, (and) would fain have carried matters to open warfare, and have settled their pretensions to the lady according to the mode of those most concise and simple reasoners, the knights-errant of yore—by single combat" (Irving, "Legend of Sleepy Hollow, p. 343). Ichabod, who is much smaller than Brom Bones, refuses to fight, much to Bones's frustration. "There was something extremely provoking in this obstinately pacific sys-

tem; it left Brom no alternative but to draw upon the funds of rustic waggery in his disposition, and play off boorish practical jokes upon his rival" ("Legend of Sleepy Hollow," p. 37). To get even with Ichabod, Bones and his friends smoke out the schoolhouse, turn the furniture upside down, and teach Bones's dog to mimic Ichabod's singing. Brom's tricks demonstrate his frustration, and indeed his final jest becomes the climax of "The Legend of Sleepy Hollow."

Although Irving lets his readers draw their own conclusions about Ichabod's fate, the story suggests that Ichabod was the brunt of an elaborately orchestrated prank designed to run him out of town. While this trick may have been rather elaborate, it was not unusual for jests of the time to go to great lengths. A common prank, for example, involved surprising a newlywed couple at their home on their wedding night and placing large, decorated poles by the door. It was also common for Dutch youths to disturb the nighttime peace by firing their guns and shouting loudly; some would run their horses through the town at high speeds.

Often such pranks led to trouble of a more serious nature, resulting in fights or other types of punishment. One story tells of two Dutch youths who brought a soldier-friend into a tavern and introduced him to the owner as a hero of the Revolutionary War. The owner bought them drinks for the rest of the night. When it became known that the friend was no such hero, the youths were forced to pay the large bar bill and placed in stocks. (An instrument of punishment, stocks were a wood frame with slots for locking in a prisoner's ankles and wrists.) In another alleged incident, a trumpeter blew his instrument directly into the ears of his comrades as a joke. Startled and angry, they pounded the trumpeter fiercely. Such anecdotes indicate that Brom Bones's desire to fight Ichabod Crane reflected the habits of pre-Revolutionary Dutch youth.

Education. Though "The Legend of Sleepy Hollow" takes place after New York became part of the United States, some critics believe that Irving included some of the attributes of the colonial Dutch education system that date back to the existence of New Netherland. New Netherland was the only colonial province that used public monies to pay for elementary instruction for both boys and girls. Elementary education in New Netherland included all children without regard to sex, class, or social condition, a remarkable state of affairs for that historical era.

Despite these good intentions, however, the early Dutch had problems with some of the schoolmasters, and Irving's characterization of Ichabod Crane as a somewhat shady person may reflect a vestige of this aspect of the Dutch colonial experience. One of the earliest teachers, Adam Roelantsen, was quarrelsome; he found himself in court several times for slander and drunkenness. He sued his neighbors often, married a widow in order to possess her property, and once landed in court for refusing to pay for his passage on a boat. Later teachers proved unsavory in similar ways.

In "The Legend of Sleepy Hollow," Ichabod is depicted as a rather dubious scholar. The narrator mentions that he had read only a couple of books completely. His favorite is a book not on history or science or literature, but on witchcraft. Furthermore, Ichabod exploits his position as a schoolteacher in the community. He freeloads off the hospitality of others, yet maintains the respect of the community because of his education.

Ichabod often beats his students, which was a common practice in both Dutch and New England schools. In Ichabod's case, he beats the larger boys but not the smaller ones. In many Dutch schools, corporal punishment was normal, and such items as a willow rod or a plank were used for beating children. The plank, which could be either rough or smooth, consisted of a piece of wood on a stick. Rough planks could draw blood. Irving himself was a rather lazy student who was uninterested in school as a youth; perhaps his own disdain for academics is embodied in the story.

Witches, ghosts and goblins. Tales of the supernatural provided source material upon which Washington Irving continually drew. Ghost stories and tall tales permeated the Dutch community, and the Dutch were reputed to be fairly superstitious. In fact, the Dutch settlers contributed a great deal of folklore to the Hudson River Valley area. This influence can be felt in such enduring place names as Hell-gate, Storm King, Pirate's Spook, and Spuyten Duyvil (which means "in spite of the Devil"). Legends of ghosts and headless horsemen were common in Dutch society, and their folk tales also made use of the devil, curious phantoms, and other horrid creatures of the night. Rumors of haunted ships and pirate treasure also abounded. Irving's story of the headless horseman thus fit neatly into the Dutch community's stream of supernatural tales.

New Englanders were also superstitious, as demonstrated by the character of Ichabod Crane.

Furthermore, Ichabod hails from an area noted for its heritage of religious intolerance. This heritage is recalled by the story's mention of Ichabod's favorite book, *A History of New England Witchcraft* by Cotton Mather. Cotton Mather was an influential Congregationalist minister in Massachusetts during the late 1600s. He believed that God's will entailed ridding the community of witches, and his views became closely associated with the Salem witch trials of the early 1690s. While he helped his community in a number of ways, his name is often connected with Puritan excesses.

> ### THE HAUNTED TREE
>
>
> Throughout "The Legend of Sleepy Hollow," recurring references are made to a haunted tree near Sleepy Hollow. A popular soldier on the British side, Major John André, was captured by American soldiers near this tree during the Revolutionary War. Major André had met with the traitor Benedict Arnold, who smuggled American army plans to the British. André snuck off a British warship and across enemy lines to meet with Arnold. Afterward, Major André put on a disguise for protection and started to cross back over American lines on land, but he was captured near the haunted tree in September 1780. Sentenced to hang, André was executed in October of that year. His fate moved even some of the Americans, who considered Benedict Arnold the true villain of the whole affair. While André suffered the consequences, Arnold escaped. In Tarrytown, says Irving, the common people regarded the tree "with a mixture of respect and superstition," partly in sympathy for Major André "and partly from the tales, strange sights, and doleful lamentations, told concerning it" ("Legend of Sleepy Hollow," p. 47). Near the end of Irving's short story, Ichabod Crane grows frightened when he reaches this tree, and soon after the headless horseman appears.

Despite the superstitious nature of the Dutch communities, they never convicted anybody of witchcraft. The Dutch proved fairly tolerant of religious differences in their own communities. By contrasting Ichabod's intolerance with Dutch folk beliefs, the story emphasizes differences that its author perceived in regional character.

Tarrytown and the Revolutionary War. About two miles from Sleepy Hollow is the larger village of Tarrytown. References to Tarrytown's par-

Portrait of Washington Irving, who is often described as the first uniquely American author.

ticipation in the Revolutionary War permeate "The Legend of Sleepy Hollow." The exploits of soldiers engaged in battles there provided much fodder for the Dutch storytellers. As Irving himself observed, by his era just enough time had passed since the Revolution for storytellers to dress up facts with fiction and make themselves heroes. The passage of time also served to fuel Dutch superstition in regard to the war. Supernatural attributes came to be associated with a number of soldiers who died in the conflict. Indeed, the headless horseman of Irving's tale was alleged to be a trooper for the British who was decapitated by a cannonball during the war.

The Short Story in Focus

The plot. "The Legend of Sleepy Hollow" details the mysterious fate of Ichabod Crane, a Connecticut schoolteacher in the Dutch community of Sleepy Hollow, a few miles from Tarrytown, New York, sometime after the Revolutionary War. A thin, spindly man, Ichabod is also a glutton and a freeloader. The village people accept him as a gossip; he often stops to visit women in order to be fed and to talk.

Because of his status as the schoolteacher, Ichabod is respected in the community as a man of learning. In reality, however, he is not well-read, and his extremely superstitious nature includes a belief in witches and demons. Despite the fact that he lives at his pupils' houses, Ichabod often beats his bigger students, supposedly to help them learn better. He meanwhile tells them they will thank him for the beatings later and otherwise attempts to stay on good terms with his students so that they will invite him over for dinner.

Ichabod falls in love with a well-to-do farmer's daughter named Katrina Van Tassel. He also admires her wealth and wants to marry her so that he can possess her family's productive farm. Every time he sees her, he imagines himself feasting on all the potentially good things to eat:

> The pedagogue's mouth watered, as he looked upon this sumptuous promise of luxurious winter fare. In his devouring mind's eye, he pictured to himself every roasting pig running about with a pudding in its belly, and an apple in his mouth.
>
> ("Legend of Sleepy Hollow," p. 32)

Ichabod seeks to win Katrina's heart. Katrina, however, has many suitors, including Brom Bones. In contrast to Ichabod, Brom is a man who likes to jest. An athletic, rough, good-humored, and somewhat overbearing man, Brom resents Ichabod's advances to Katrina. The flirtatious Katrina, though, basks in the attentions of each man.

One night the Van Tassels have a quilting party. After spending a great deal of time primping, Ichabod rides to the party on a broken-down horse that he borrowed from a farmer. Attending the party are guests from all over the county, including many beautiful women. Ichabod, however, is enchanted not with the women but with the sumptuous food that fills the house. He eats heartily and dances with Katrina, "while Brom Bones, sorely smitten with love and jealousy, sat brooding by himself in one corner" ("Legend of Sleepy Hollow," p. 43).

After the dancing and feasting, the guests begin to tell ghost stories. Sleepy Hollow is especially known for its tales of ghosts, and the most famous story of the region concerns the legend of the headless horseman. A Hessian soldier (a German mercenary in the British army), the headless horseman had been decapitated by a cannonball during the Revolutionary War. He was rumored to sometimes haunt a particular covered bridge near a church in Sleepy Hollow. The legends told that the ghostly horseman would pursue any traveler that passed while he was around. The partygoers tell tales of the horseman and how he vanishes as suddenly as he appears.

The party breaks up. Ichabod, who has convinced himself that Katrina is in love with him, asks for her hand in marriage, but she refuses. Heavy-hearted, he starts on his way back home long after the other guests have left. During his ride home, he recalls the supernatural tales he had heard earlier in the evening, and a feeling of fear begins to settle over him. When he approaches the covered bridge, another rider suddenly appears nearby. The horseman, a huge and silent figure, does not answer Ichabod's greeting. Ichabod and the apparition each ride forward slowly. Ichabod then rides quickly, but the other rider keeps pace. As Ichabod mounts a hill in the road he sees his mysterious companion silhouetted against the darkness: the man has no head atop his shoulders, but he seems to be carrying one on the front of his saddle. Terrified, Ichabod spurs his horse through the bushes. He loses his saddle but clings to his horse, thinking that he will be safe if he can only make it across the bridge. He risks one final glance backward to see if his pursuer has vanished at the bridge as the legends described. The goblin hurls his decapitated head after Ichabod, hitting him squarely on the skull.

Engraving from "The Legend of Sleepy Hollow" showing Ichabod Crane pursued by the headless horseman.

Ichabod is never heard from again. The farmers find his horse and the lost saddle, as well as some pieces of smashed pumpkin along the bridge near the church. Some people guess that he left town after Katrina's rejection, while others conclude that the headless horseman carried him off. Whenever they speak of him, though, Brom Bones "burst into a hearty laugh at the mention of the pumpkin; which led some to suspect that he knew more about the matter than he chose to tell" ("Legend of Sleepy Hollow," p. 52).

Sources. Since the publication of "The Legend of Sleepy Hollow," scholars have argued about the origin of Irving's ideas. Some people believe that he derived his material from the German folklore in which he immersed himself, while others believe that his creations stem from his native New York. What is most likely, however, is that Irving derived his ideas from both of these sources.

While Irving's main themes may have German origins, he introduces elements—such as the quilting party and the Van Tassels' black servant—that are native to the United States. Local detail is also incorporated into the story; the graveyard of the real Sleepy Hollow holds a soldier whose head was knocked off by a cannonball. Finally, a biographer of Irving argues that the setting for "The Legend of Sleepy Hollow" and the character of Brom Bones stemmed from the narratives of Washington Irving's brother-in-law, who had spent time in Tarrytown and was familiar with a person similar to Brom Bones.

Events in History at the Time the Short Story Was Written

The Yankee stereotype. Washington Irving viewed the New Englanders with mistrust, a fact which manifested itself in his writing. Many New Yorkers believed that the New Englanders, also called Yankees, were only interested in money. They also believed that the Yankees were cold and calculating, interested only in progress, change, and movement. Irving distrusted Yankees and felt that their dominant traits included restlessness and continual pursuit of development. He once complained that the Yankees were always on the move. New York society, on the other hand, was more rooted and conservative. Those who viewed Yankee society as a threat to their own solid existence were convinced that their own standards of order, tradition, and family values were at risk.

The theme of the poor native against the rich invader became common in American literature. By Irving's time, New Englanders were often depicted in stereotypical fashion by New Yorkers. New York writers commonly satirized the Yankees, portraying them as lean, mean gossips who questioned everybody about his or her business. The portrayal of Ichabod Crane in "The Legend of Sleepy Hollow" was thus fairly representative of New York views. Ichabod's enormous appetite might even be viewed as a metaphor; he means to devour the best of Tarrytown's innocence by marrying Katrina Van Tassel. Even the manner in which Ichabod courts Katrina is self-serving. He loves her inheritance as much as he does the girl. He hopes to turn the prosperous, bountiful, and stable farm into cold hard cash and move away after securing Katrina's hand in marriage.

Art and progress in the early 1800s. During the beginning of the nineteenth century, Americans struggled to break free from European influences. Society emphasized practical goals to achieve national growth. With this in mind, the government initiated a systematic program of de-

velopment and doubled the size of the nation's territory. Society took a conservative turn, valuing usefulness.

Industry took precedence over the arts, and many Americans rejected artistic endeavors as unpatriotic. They argued over whose standards should determine national culture. Many were afraid that English taste would become the norm, and because the United States had just attained independence, they did not wish the English to dominate in any manner. Americans spurned the arts as the products of old wealth, social privilege, and moral decay—an attitude that resulted from the tendency of monarchs and aristocrats in Europe to sponsor the arts. From the viewpoint of some Americans, painting, sculpture, and fiction seemed out of keeping with the nation's republican values of simplicity, social equality, and moral behavior. Most Americans considered poetry and fiction useless endeavors and regarded creative writing with disdain. Irving's writings, which drew on the American heritage and so helped establish a patriotic element to the nation's literature, were largely responsible for changing these attitudes.

Romanticism. Science and reason had been held in high regard in both the United States and Europe for much of the 1700s. This continued in the early 1800s as the growth of industry began to bring about great changes in society. Moving out of their quiet villages, people began crowding into cities. The Romantic movement developed in response to these trends. Romanticism placed high regard on the emotional, the mysterious, and the imaginative as well as on the uniqueness of personal or national experience. Romantic artists turned to the past for comfort against feelings of isolation and despair that they felt had been caused by society's emphasis on rational thought and progress. As artists in Europe and the United States looked to the past, they paid increasing attention to national customs and origins. This reexamination was especially strong from about 1805 to 1830.

The tensions Irving felt between progress and an idealized past can be found in "The Legend of Sleepy Hollow." Irving portrays the Dutch community as a magical, dreamy, and idyllic place. As one scholar notes, "Tarry Town emerges as a symbol of the colonial past, in which we tarry for a moment before moving on. The atmosphere is simple, uncomplicated, pastoral. It is established by such adjectives as quiet, listless, drowsy, dreamy and such nouns as murmur, lull, repose, tranquillity" (Bone, p. 170).

Reviews. "The Legend of Sleepy Hollow" was included in a book called *The Sketch Book,* which Washington Irving published in 1819 and 1820. He had been working with his brother in the family's business, but when the business suddenly went bankrupt, Irving's family was in danger of impoverishment. Irving, who never had great aspirations as a businessman, had already made something of a name for himself as a writer, so he quickly wrote *The Sketch Book,* which was published simultaneously in England and the United States.

The Sketch Book was an immediate success on both sides of the Atlantic Ocean. Irving was able to support his family because of its success, and *The Sketch Book* cemented his reputation as a writer. The book was an important publication because America had not yet produced literature that Europeans considered quality work. As one reviewer noted in *Blackwood's Edinburgh Magazine* in 1820, "Mr. Washington is one of our first favourites among the English writers of this age—and he is not a bit the less for having been born in America..." (Mullane and Wilson, p. 367). In addition, Irving's book was considered one of the first distinctly American works of fiction, notable for its use of local humor and folklore. Another reviewer raved:

> [W]e are now tempted to notice it as a very remarkable publication,— and to predict that it will form an era in the literature of the nation to which it belongs. It is the work of an American, entirely bred and trained in that country.
>
> (Mullane and Wilson, p. 367)

For More Information

Bone, Robert A. "Irving's Headless Hessian: Prosperity and the Inner Life." In *American Quarterly* 15, no. 2, part 1 (summer 1963): 167-75.

Ellis, David M., James A. Frost, Harold C. Syrett, and Harry J. Carman. *A History of New York State.* Ithaca: Cornell University Press, 1967.

Hults, Dorothy. *New Amsterdam Days and Ways.* New York: Harcourt, Brace and World, 1963.

Irving, Pierre. *The Life and Letters of Washington Irving.* New York: Putnam's, 1862-1864.

Irving, Washington. "The Legend of Sleepy Hollow." In *Two Tales.* New York: Harcourt Brace Jovanovich, 1984.

Mullane, Janet, and Robert Wilson. *Nineteenth-Century Literature Criticism.* Vol 19. Detroit: Gale Research, 1988.

The Light in the Forest

by
Conrad Richter

A native of Pine Grove, Pennsylvania, Conrad Richter (1890-1968) had a natural love for the woodsy countryside in which he grew up and a deep appreciation of the region's history. As both a journalist and a novelist, he focused on the lives of pioneers and American Indian tribes affected by colonial expansion. Richter had deep feelings for both the Indians and the immigrant-pioneers and saw a distinct connection between American events in the eighteenth and twentieth centuries. *The Light in the Forest* reveals the adverse impact that immigrant development had on native peoples and landscapes. Through the novel, Richter attempted to show that U.S. domination of third world countries in the 1950s was producing many of the same negative results as the colonization of the American wilderness in the 1750s.

Events in History at the Time the Novel Takes Place

The Lenapes. The Lenape, or Delaware, Indians thrived in the mid-Atlantic region of North America, which they called "Lenapehoking," for more than three thousand years. By approximately 700 A.D. they had developed a culture and lifestyle that would persist until European settlers arrived on the East Coast in the 1500s.

The Lenapes lived in small independent communities located on waterways of the region. These communities are thought to have been made up of clans, or family groups, based on the mother's family lineage. In Lenape society, chil-

THE LITERARY WORK

A novel set in Pennsylvania and wilderness to the west (in present-day Ohio) in 1765; published in 1953.

SYNOPSIS

A boy who has been raised by Delaware Indians is forced to return to his white parents and finds himself caught between two worlds.

dren took the last name of their mother rather than their father, and all property belonged to the females. While males served as chiefs, leadership was usually transferred in such a way that the leadership of the community remained in the mother's family line.

The Lenapes farmed, hunted, fished, and trapped for food and trade. Women performed most of the farming and domestic chores, while men took care of hunting, fishing, and trading duties. A religious people, they held deep spiritual beliefs based on the worship of nature. They developed the land only to a limited degree and killed no more than was needed to survive.

The Lenape people built permanent dwellings—wigwams and longhouses—and planted various crops (corn, beans, pumpkins, squash, and tobacco). But the men also migrated with the seasons, to follow herds and to fish. Women and children often went along on these trips, leaving the elderly behind in the village.

The Lenapes, who centered their lives around the family, highly valued children and showed deep respect for elders. Because the Lenapes prized the family so greatly, the premature death of a child often prompted the parents to adopt an outside child—usually a white boy or girl taken during a raid on a colonial township. They proceeded to raise the child as a full-blooded clan member. In *The Light in the Forest*, True Son is an example of an adopted child taken to replace a deceased son. Raised as a full member of the clan, he comes to cherish his family and culture. His unwillingness to adapt to a colonial lifestyle when forced to return to white society illustrates the strong bonds formed in such relationships and the vast differences between the colonial and Lenape cultures.

THE WALKING PURCHASE

Often the Lenapes were cheated outright. In a well-recorded incident known as "The Walking Purchase," Lenapes were forced to sell William Penn's sons as much land as could be walked on in one-and-a-half days. Hiring professional runners and clearing a road beforehand, the Penns acquired more than twice the land the Lenapes intended to sell.

Colonization. The Lenapes experienced peace and prosperity until Europeans arrived in North America in 1524. Dutch, English, French, and Swedish colonists, lured to the New World by promises of instant wealth, religious freedom, and unlimited opportunity, competed for land throughout the mid-Atlantic region. They drove the Lenapes further and further west, out of Lenapehoking and into the wilderness of present-day Ohio. By 1650 there were more than five thousand Europeans in the region, and over the next hundred years their members would grow to 750,000. Meanwhile, Lenape numbers drastically declined due to diseases such as smallpox and measles, warfare, and alcoholism—all elements that were introduced or intensified by contact with the Europeans. By 1700 the Lenape population had dwindled from 24,000 to less than 3,000.

European immigrants took Lenape land by barter and by force. Superior in number and military strength, the immigrants physically drove the Indians from their land and purchased property—most often paying nominal fees because the Lenapes did not comprehend land ownership in the same way as Europeans. The Lenapes believed they retained hunting, fishing, and migrating rights on the land they sold because, according to their faith, all land belonged to the Creator, Kishelemukong. People could develop the land but no one could "own" the earth—that was as ludicrous a concept to the Lenapes as owning a star. When the Lenapes were killed for hunting on or traveling through sold land, however, they realized they had made a fatal mistake in selling the land. By the 1760s most of the Lenape homeland had been lost to the European settlers.

French and Indian War, 1754-1763. Pushed back into the wilderness that became present-day Ohio, the Lenapes established a trading partnership with French fur traders who trapped there. When armed conflict erupted in 1754 between Great Britain and France—a clash that became known as the French and Indian War—the Lenapes of the Ohio River Valley naturally sided with the French. Lenape warriors were among those who killed British General Edward Braddock at Fort Duquesne in an early French victory. Soon they began raiding English townships in their former homeland in Pennsylvania. Terrorizing English settlers, the Lenape raiders drove them from western Pennsylvania and back east across the Allegheny Mountains.

British troops greatly outnumbered the Lenape and French forces, however, and it seemed likely that they would eventually gain the upper hand in the conflict. Aware of this, the Lenapes signed a peace treaty in 1758. They agreed to stop the fighting and return all prisoners taken during colonial raids (a term of the treaty that was not followed through on until several years later). The truce with the Lenapes helped the British troops to defeat the French. They captured Fort Duquesne (which they renamed Fort Pitt) and pushed the French north, out of the Ohio River Valley, effectively ending the war in 1763.

The 1763 Paxton Boys massacre. After the war ended, British troops remained in the Ohio River Valley and Lenape territory. As a result, area tribes led by Chief Pontiac of the Ottawas rallied and attacked in an attempt to oust the British from Indian land once and for all. They captured three key forts, including Fort Pitt, and killed and captured many English settlers. Unable or unwilling to fight the tribes on their territory, the British responded by killing innocent Indians who lived among them in Pennsylvania. A notorious group known as the Paxton Boys murdered

Engraving of the Lenapes concluding a treaty with William Penn, founder of Pennsylvania.

a band of unarmed Conestogo Indians—including their children—who had not been involved in any of the fighting. The incident inspired others to attack peaceful Indians throughout the colonies, outraging the tribes of the area. In *The Light in the Forest,* True Son is forced to live with his birth family in Paxton, but detests the town and its citizens because of this incident. The Paxton massacre is legendary among his clan and is recalled to reinforce their hatred for colonists.

Bouquet expeditions. Fighting against part of Pontiac's forces, Colonel Henry Bouquet, a Swiss officer in the British army, attacked and defeated a group made up largely of Lenapes at Bushy Run in August 1764. From there, he led a series of successful forays against the Lenapes. In November 1764 he forced the Lenapes to surrender and return all prisoners taken since the start of the war in 1754. The prisoner return that had been promised in the treaty of 1758 finally occurred in 1765. This was more than ten years after many of the prisoners had been captured. Most of the young prisoners, like the character of True Son, had lived the bulk of their lives as Lenapes and did not want to return to their European families. Bouquet enforced the terms of surrender, however, and "weeping Indian families led crying children or gently pushed sullen,

reluctant teenagers toward waiting soldiers, church officials, and families of settlers hoping to recognize and reclaim loved ones lost to Indian raiders" (Grumet, pp. 59-60).

The Novel in Focus

The plot. As the novel opens, fifteen-year-old True Son is being sent back to his white parents after living for eleven years with his Lenape Indian family. True Son's Lenape father and mother, Cuyloga and Quaquenga, are the only family he has known, and he is terribly distraught over being forced to leave them and his Indian way of life. Though his skin is white, he is thoroughly Lenape; he treasures his Indian lifestyle of hunting and fishing and living in harmony with nature in the lush woods and rugged terrain of western Pennsylvania. True Son has learned to hate the white man and his so-called civilization and abhors even the sight or smell of him. Although he is being returned because he is considered a "white prisoner," he decides that he will never give up his Indian life (Richter, *Light in the Forest*, p. 4).

After trying to hide in the woods, True Son is tracked by his Lenape father, who tells him he must "go like an Indian" and give his father no more shame (*Light in the Forest*, p. 6). Clearly the father does not want to lose his son, but he intends to keep his promise to return the boy. He accompanies True Son to a British military camp and places him in the care of a soldier assigned to bring the boy to eastern Pennsylvania. Outwardly, True Son complies with the plan, but inwardly he vows: "Once my hands are loose, I'll get his knife. Then quickly I'll kill him" (*Light in the Forest*, p. 8).

The soldier assigned to True Son, Del Hardy, is on an expedition with Colonel Bouquet, a well-known officer from the French and Indian War. Presently, Bouquet is leading a mission to reclaim white prisoners taken prior to and during the war. Hardy was himself captured by Indians as a boy and has seen the tremendous emotional torment both Indian families and the so-called "prisoners" go through upon being separated. But while he empathizes with the Indian families affected by his mission, he is a loyal soldier and has in fact volunteered for duty. Like most other soldiers, he has a deep dislike of the "Injuns," whom he considers his enemy. He brands them as "devils" who have "scalped plenty of our people in their time" (*Light in the Forest*, p. 11).

Of all the prisoners Hardy has seen, True Son is the wildest. Speaking to him in the Delaware language, Hardy tells him he had better not try to escape; he is a white boy and should be happy to be returning to his parents. True Son retorts that his parents are Cuyloga and Quaquenga and that he is Indian, adding, "I spit on white people!" (*Light in the Forest*, p. 14). He boldly announces that he will never go back to Pennsylvania, and Hardy realizes it will not be an easy task returning this boy to his white parents.

Half Arrow, True Son's Indian cousin, accompanies him on the journey, along with an Indian friend named Little Crane. The journey back to Fort Pitt is an arduous trek through untamed wilderness. While True Son must sleep next to the British soldiers in tents at night, the Indians who are accompanying him sleep in the woods next to their mother, earth. During the day, they walk alongside True Son to the next encampment. To pass the time and relieve anxiety brought on by their impending separation, True Son, Half Arrow, and Little Crane discuss their lives and the beliefs of their people.

As they near Fort Pitt, Little Crane and Half Arrow must return to their home. It is not safe for Indians to be inside the colony of Pennsylvania, especially near a military camp, just as it is not safe for whites to be in "Indian country"

outside the colony's western boundary. A sad parting follows; the boys will perhaps never see each other again.

At Fort Pitt, True Son is introduced to his birth father and told that his own name is really John Butler. He is defiant and hostile toward his "father," who sends him on to the Butler home in Paxton township in western Pennsylvania. The only thing True Son knows about Paxton is that a group of men from the town murdered some young Conestogo Indian boys.

When True Son arrives at the Butler home, he is introduced to his birth mother, brother and sisters, and an aunt. He does not remember any of them and is cold to all except Gordie, his younger brother, whom he has never met before. His "mother," Myra, tells him that he has a lot of lost time to make up for. Concerned that he has been raised as an uneducated savage, his parents intend for him to embark on a rigorous educational program. He is given white peoples' clothes and shoes and told to change his ways.

True Son tries to explain to his white family his Lenape philosophy of life, his elaborate spiritual beliefs, and the well-rounded education he has received. But the Butlers cannot understand what he is saying. Only his young brother Gordie admires his Indian ways.

For the next year, the Butlers try to "civilize" True Son, but to no avail. Although he is forced to wear pants and button-down shirts, his soul remains pure Lenape. He has few people to talk to—only a black slave who knows some of his native language. His white uncles, who are Indian fighters, kill Little Crane when he comes with Half Arrow to rescue True Son. Half Arrow finds True Son, and the two avenge Little Crane's murder. They nearly scalp True Son's white uncle but are forced to flee before he dies. They escape through the woods and travel the long distance back to the wilderness of Ohio to their Lenape homeland.

But when True Son returns to his village, he is not wholly welcomed. Greeted with suspicion, he must prove his loyalty to his Lenape tribe. He goes on a scalping expedition with the male leaders of the tribe; his role is to act as a decoy to lure whites into ambush. When he is asked to stop a boat filled with a group of women and children, however, he cannot do it. He thinks about his little brother and decides that he cannot willingly allow a youngster he spots in this group to be murdered. He warns the whites of the ambush and they escape downriver. His Indian brothers and father cannot believe what he has done. They immediately hold a meeting to decide what should be done to punish him. True Son's father saves him from being killed, but he is told to leave the tribe and never return. He has truly disgraced himself and is now considered an enemy to all Lenapes, including his father. The novel ends with True Son left in the forest alone, caught between the white and Indian worlds. Homeless and without a family or culture to call his own, he is left to wander in solitude or assimilate into the white world he detests.

Culture clash. Richter gives insight into the Lenape culture and its sharp contrast to European society through the dialogue of Little Crane, Half Arrow, and True Son. En route to Fort Pitt, they discuss how the "Indians are an original people"—pure of stock and therefore superior to the whites, who are mixed and sickly-looking (*Light in the Forest*, p. 27). They discuss how the whites must be hard of hearing because they never listen and blind because they see building sites rather than beauty when they look at nature. "They are young and heedless like children," Little Crane says. "You can see it in the way they heap up treasures like a child, although they know they must die and can't take such things with them" (*Light in the Forest*, p. 28). True Son, Little Crane, and Half Arrow consider the puzzling behavior of the white man, but the Lenapes are unable to comprehend the ways of the colonists. They puzzle over concepts such as locks, which are part of white society. Little Crane concludes, "They're a peculiar race and no sensible man can understand them" (*Light in the Forest*, p. 29). By revealing the views of True Son and his family, Richter illustrates the near if not total impossibility of a Lenape adapting to the white way of life. He further indicates, through his description of the long and rich history of the tribe and their acquired wisdom, that contemporary American society could learn a great deal from this ancient culture.

Sources. Richter was a careful student of history and pored over early documents to compile his novels. He read newspaper articles, uncovered scrapbooks, maps, and manuscripts, and spoke to older residents of the region—Indian and white—to form an accurate picture of frontier life in the 1700s. Drawing from actual events as well as from a personal boyhood desire to live among the Indians, Richter blended fact and fiction to make *The Light in the Forest* realistic. His stated aim, as described in his acknowledgments, was "to give an authentic sensation of life in early America" and, through the trials of True Son, encompass the true stories of "the numbers of returned white captives who tried desperately to run away from their flesh-and-blood families and return to their Indian foster homes and the Indian mode of life" (Richter, p. viii).

Events in History at the Time the Novel Was Written

American empire and global expansion. America emerged as the leading world power after World War II. The United States exerted its influence commercially, economically, and militarily throughout the world. Under the postwar Marshall Plan, the United States helped war-torn countries in Europe by lending them money and shipping supplies to the region. Furthermore, the U.S. took an active role in many underdeveloped or "third world" nations, shaping and maintaining political systems that seemed to be favorable for American interests. With the increasing cold war tensions between the U.S. and the major communist powers, American intervention often sought to counter the danger of growing Soviet or Chinese influence in specific areas. In the Korean War (1950-53), the United States brought its power to bear in Asia, with American forces promoting democracy and seeking to destroy communism on the Korean peninsula.

There was also a commercial aspect to the U.S. role in world affairs. The American economy benefited from increased exports to other countries. Corporations based in the U.S. often became powerful forces in foreign lands, sometimes influencing the political situation so that their trade interests would be protected. Along with this commercial dominance came American cultural influences that changed foreign countries. From India to South America, Coca-Cola became a household word, its popularity signaling the extent of U.S. influence on developing and developed nations. American music and fashions gained favor around the world, especially among the wealthier citizens of foreign countries. Just as in *Light in the Forest*, however, American influence was not always welcomed. Some groups in foreign countries wanted U.S. products, from soft drinks to blue jeans, removed from their markets; in their view, the goods were hateful symbols of American cultural penetration. Resistance to these items was also a means of voicing opposition to the political and economic power of the U.S. The immigrant-pioneers of the 1700s and 1800s had displaced tribes and eradicated American Indian cultures from mainstream life in America; foreign nationals of the 1950s feared that a similar scenario would unfold on a global scale.

Baby boom. Along with a thriving economy, the postwar baby boom—the great increase in the number of children born in the United States in the years following the conclusion of World War II—caused massive growth nationwide. Suburban housing developments sprang up from Maine to California, and communities initiated extensive building programs. Schools, high-rises, highways, and shopping malls were built en masse to meet the needs of a rapidly growing population. Similar to the colonial era, the 1950s in America were years of rapid expansion and change. Most of the population viewed the development as progress, but some, like Richter, did not. Richter saw the potential dangers of overdevelopment and argued for preservation of wildlife and land.

American Indian rights. The 1950s marked a major turning point in U.S. government policy regarding American Indian tribes. Since 1934, the government had promoted the survival of reservations. In 1953 it reversed this position in an attempt to extract the national government from some of its involvement in Indian affairs. It ended federal jurisdiction over tribes and relegated regulation to the states.

In 1953, the year that Richter's novel was published, the U.S. government adopted the "termination policy." In essence, this policy set out to eliminate all reservations by offering money to Indians who agreed to relocate to cities. The plan was to do away with the Indian nations and merge their members into the mainstream society. *The Light in the Forest*, however, shows how difficult it is to meld such vastly different cultures.

From the ideas and characters in Richter's novel, a view of Indian life emerges that argues against homogenization of tribal members and for the preservation of native lifestyles. Not until 1970, however, would the policy be reversed and the U.S. government again support the separate existence of the American Indian tribes.

Reviews. Though it is not regarded as Richter's strongest work, *The Light in the Forest* received mostly positive reviews when it was published in 1953. The book was described as a thought-provoking study of conflicting loyalties. Lewis Gannett of *The Nation* hailed the work as a study of so-called "civilization," which "presents a sorry contrast to the Indians' oneness with nature" (Gannett, p. 176). Although some reviewers felt that the novel's portraits of white colonists were one-sided and shallow, Richter's detailed description of frontier life was highly praised. It was reprinted eleven times from 1953 to 1972, an indication of its enduring popularity.

For More Information

Gannett, Lewis. "Indian Idyl." *The Nation,* June 6, 1953.

Grumet, Robert S. *The Lenapes.* New York: Chelsea House, 1989.

Levernier, James. *The Indians and Their Captives.* Westport, Conn.: Greenwood, 1977.

McCutchen, David. *The Red Record.* Garden City Park, N.Y.: Avery, 1989.

Richter, Conrad. *The Light in the Forest.* New York: Alfred A. Knopf, 1972.

Rockland, Michael Aaron. *America in the Fifties and Sixties.* University Park, Pa.: Pennsylvania State University Press, 1972.

Stevens, S. K. *The Pennsylvania Colony.* London: Crowell-Collier, 1970.

Macbeth

by
William Shakespeare

Some details of William Shakespeare's life are still shrouded in uncertainty. What is known is that he rose to prominence as a playwright in London toward the end of the sixteenth century and that he died on April 23, 1616. He wrote *Macbeth* sometime between 1605 and 1606, shortly after the ascension of King James of Scotland to the English throne. Scotland, previously a land of mystery to the people of England, came into the public limelight during a period of political plotting, violence, and religious conflict.

THE LITERARY WORK

A play set in Scotland during the eleventh century; first performed probably in 1606 at Hampton Court before King James I.

SYNOPSIS

An ambitious nobleman usurps the Scottish throne and uses murder and tyranny to solidify his power.

Events in History at the Time the Play Takes Place

Macbeth's Scotland. Scotland during the eleventh century was still a very primitive land. Until the beginning of the tenth century, it had been under the authority of England, but during the time in which *Macbeth* is set, Scotland was able to establish its independence because England was forced to channel its resources toward defending itself against continuing Viking invasions. During this transition period, living conditions in the rugged hills of Scotland were crude at best. Houses were simple structures built of wood or turf around a central hearth. Even the "castles" of the higher classes were primitive in style. Macbeth's castle, of which Duncan says, "This castle hath a pleasant seat" (Shakespeare, *Macbeth,* 1.6.1), was most likely a rough fort. It probably consisted of a central hall built of wood upon a mound of raised dirt that was circled by a log wall.

Succession and feuding in Scotland. When King Malcolm II of Scotland died in 1034, his last command was that the throne should pass to his oldest grandson, Duncan. This last request went against the Celtic tradition of succession, which stipulated that the inheritance of the throne alternate between different branches of the family. The historical Macbeth, who was also a grandson of King Malcolm, felt that he should succeed the old king, as prescribed by tradition. He further supported his claim through the ancestry of his wife, the Lady Gruoch, who was a direct descendent of two earlier Scottish kings, Malcolm I and Kenneth III. Despite the fact that Macbeth's claim on the throne was valid, it was rejected in favor of Duncan's claim. The old king's will continued to exert power even from the grave.

Macbeth was not immediately hostile to the new king, but several years into Duncan's reign, he raised an army and openly opposed him. Duncan led his own forces against Macbeth and was killed in the ensuing battle. With Duncan finally out of the way, and his two young sons out of the country, Macbeth became king of Scotland. He held the throne without incident for seventeen years until Duncan's oldest son, Malcolm III, returned to Scotland with an army. Macbeth was defeated in a clash that in many ways resembled his usurpation of Duncan's throne nearly two decades earlier. Malcolm killed Macbeth when their armies met at the Battle of Lumphanan. With the death of Macbeth, the final obstacle to Malcolm's ascension to the throne was Lulach, the son of Macbeth's Lady Gruoch from an earlier marriage. Lulach claimed the Scottish throne through the ancestry of his mother and was actually crowned king immediately following Macbeth's death. Malcolm did not let this development deter him; he had Lulach murdered and took the crown in 1058.

THE HEBRIDES: ISLES OF THE VIKINGS

The Hebrides is a chain of islands off the western coast of Scotland. Often referred to as the "Western Isles," these islands served the Vikings as bases from which they could launch their attacks and became a region absolutely controlled by these Scandinavian marauders. It is from here that the rebel Macdonwald gathers his soldiers in *Macbeth*.

The Norse invasion—raiders and settlers. During the ninth century Scotland found itself invaded by raiders who came across the North Sea from Norway and Denmark. These "Norsemen," also known as Vikings, came to Scotland for several reasons. The most basic explanation for their presence was simply that the prevalent pattern of winds on the North Sea was favorable to this enterprise. These winds blow west in the spring and east in the autumn, which made Scotland a natural destination. Another attraction for these northerners was the remarkable similarity between the landscapes of Scotland and Norway. Both countries possessed offshore island chains, deep inlets or fjords, and rugged mountains. Perhaps the most important reason for the arrival of the raiders, however, was the opportunity for conquest and plunder. The remote monasteries and villages of Scotland were easy targets for the Norse rovers, who dominated the bloody northern seas for several hundred years. The monasteries were especially ripe for plunder, as they generally housed valuable religious artifacts and other treasures. The Scandinavian pirates launched raids on Scotland from the surrounding islands, and few monasteries or villages could

hope to defend themselves from these attacks. In his play, Shakespeare depicts such an invasion when he portrays King Sweno of Norway attacking Scotland from the Hebrides island chain. The character Macbeth's defeat of Sweno's forces is the incident in the play that serves as the foundation of his rise to power.

As time passed, many of these hostile invaders found that, amid the rocky hills and bogs, Scotland offered some fertile land for farming. A growing number of northerners gave up their warring and turned to the soil to make their living. The similarity of the terrain to their homeland meant that very little adjustment was necessary for the Norse settlers to establish communities. Through intermarriage and conversion to Christianity in the tenth century, these settlers assimilated completely into the Scottish culture.

The status of women in Scotland. With the beginning of the Viking Age in Scotland, the position of women changed drastically. While women in other societies of the time were bound to home and farm activities, the Viking influence spurred greater freedom and independence for women in Scotland. The most famous matriarch of the period was Aud the Deep-Minded, a Norse woman who rose to a position of power in Scotland. After the death of her husband, Olaf the White, who was the King of Dublin, Ireland, Aud lived as an independent monarch. She held power for several years following his death and finally moved north to Iceland, where she founded the first of the Icelandic dynasties. This tradition of strong-willed women is represented in Shakespeare's play in the character of Lady Macbeth, who tells her husband,

> We fail?
> But screw your courage to the sticking-place,
> And we'll not fail.
> (*Macbeth*, 1.7.59-61)

Lady Macbeth is depicted by Shakespeare as an equal of Macbeth in the realm of ambition and ruthlessness; without her, in fact, Macbeth's courage may never have reached the "sticking-place."

The Play in Focus

The plot. Macbeth is a minor Scottish noble who leads the Scottish army to victory over the forces of Norway. Following the battle, Macbeth and Banquo, a fellow nobleman, encounter three witches. These mysterious old women greet Macbeth with prophecies. They tell him that he will rise in rank and eventually become king. The hags also inform

Macbeth with the three witches, who foretell his rise to kingship.

Banquo that although he will not be king, his descendants will hold the Scottish throne.

Following this encounter, Macbeth is rewarded by King Duncan, who proposes to stay with him at his castle. Lady Macbeth persuades her husband that he should murder the king during his visit and take the crown for himself, fulfilling the witches' prophecy. Giving in to her persuasion, Macbeth murders the "gracious" Duncan. Duncan's two sons, Malcolm and Donalbain, flee from Scotland and are blamed by Macbeth for having orchestrated the assassination. Macbeth then assumes the kingship, just as the witches foretold. Worried about the witches' prophecy concerning Banquo's family gaining the throne, Macbeth hires assassins to murder the nobleman and his son, Fleance. Banquo is slain, but Fleance escapes.

The witches then warn Macbeth that another nobleman, Macduff, is also a threat to his power. Macbeth attempts murder again, only to find that Macduff has fled to England. Angry at the nobleman's escape, Macbeth has the wife and children of Macduff brutally murdered. In England, Macduff meets with Malcolm and decides that Malcolm is worthy of ruling Scotland. Together they gather an army and march against Macbeth. A guilt-ridden Lady Macbeth loses her sanity and dies as the opposing army surrounds the castle.

Macduff kills Macbeth in combat, and Malcolm is crowned king of Scotland.

Witchcraft and the supernatural. Among the traditions of Scotland was a belief in witches, including their ability to make prophecies and to affect the outcome of certain events. During the reign of King Kenneth, one of Lady Gruoch's ancestors, witchcraft was considered an unsavory practice and a serious problem. King Kenneth proclaimed that witches who called up spirits and asked their help should be burned to death.

Macbeth's encounters with the witches build on this tradition and were inspired in part by the *Chronicles of England, Scotland, and Ireland* (1577), a volume written by Raphael Holinshed. An incident that reflects the strong beliefs of these Scottish people in the supernatural comes from Holinshed's account of strange occurrences that began to happen after the death of Duncan. Holinshed writes, "horses in Louthian, being of singular beauty and swiftness, did eat their own flesh and would in no wise taste any other meat" (Holinshed, p. 140). These lines helped shape Shakespeare's scene between the nobleman-messenger Ross and an old man outside Macbeth's castle. As they discuss the bizarre happenings that are being reported in the countryside, Ross says,

Vivien Leigh as Lady Macbeth and Laurence Olivier as Macbeth in a 1955 stage production of *Macbeth*.

> And Duncan's horses ...
> Beauteous and swift ...
> Turned wild in nature....
>
> (*Macbeth*, 2.4.14-16)

The old man responds by saying, "'Tis said they eat each other" (*Macbeth*, 2.4.18). Clearly, the fact that strange events and witch appearances are incorporated into Holinshed's text on history indicates how strong an influence the supernatural world exercised upon the society of eleventh-century Scotland.

The play's focus on witchcraft also reflected an interest in the subject in Shakespeare's England more than five centuries later. The succession of King James VI of Scotland to the English throne as King James I in 1603 had an important influence on Shakespeare's writing of *Macbeth*. King James had multiple interests encompassing many of the period's important issues. One of James's greatest passions was the subject of witchcraft. The king's interest in this topic was so great that in 1597 he wrote *Daemonologie*, a text in which he contended that witchcraft was a reality and that its practitioners must be punished. In addition to writing on the subject, King James also attended the examinations of Dr. Fian, a Scottish schoolmaster who was an alleged witch. Fian was accused of practicing wicked acts with other witches. Charges of which he was ac-

cused included making curses against the king and the possession of an attendant spirit much like the "Paddock," "Graymalkin," and "Harpier," which are the attendant spirits of Shakespeare's witches. Dr. Fian's spirit was reputed to have caused several marine disasters, including an attempt against the ship of King James himself. This episode is reminiscent of the witch's curse against a ship captain in the play: "Though his bark cannot be lost, / Yet it shall be tempest tossed" (*Macbeth*, 1.3.24-5).

Sources. Following the process used in the creation of several of his plays, Shakespeare drew the plot for *Macbeth* from a historical source. In this case, the source was Holinshed's *Chronicles of England, Scotland, and Ireland,* and Shakespeare used this book as a source of historical information on other occasions as well. This text, though fantastic by modern standards, was the authoritative historical text of the period.

The story of Macbeth's treacherous murder of Duncan was actually drawn from Holinshed's description of King Malcolme Duffe's murder at the hands of Donwald. In this episode, King Malcolme, just like Duncan, puts his trust in his noblemen and is murdered. The characters of Macbeth, Duncan, and Banquo were all drawn from Holinshed's text as well. Macbeth and Banquo were noblemen of King Duncan, who was described by Holinshed as too kind and gentle to be an effective monarch. Realizing this, he enlisted the aid of Macbeth and Banquo to fight off the invasion of Macdonwald from the western islands. Macbeth and Banquo defeated this invasion, as well as a subsequent invasion by Sweno of Norway. Other elements of *Macbeth* that can be traced to Holinshed's *Chronicles* include Macbeth's attempt to murder Banquo and Fleance, and Macbeth's death at the hands of Macduff.

Events in History at the Time the Play Was Written

The Gowrie Conspiracy. On August 5, 1600, an assassination attempt on King James of Scotland was undertaken. The resulting scandal came to be known as the Gowrie Conspiracy. King James was in residence at Falkland Palace when the plot began. Just before embarking on a hunting expedition, the king was approached by Alexander Ruthven, the oldest brother of the Earl of Gowrie. Ruthven told the king that he had captured a suspicious character whom he thought the king would be interested in questioning. He explained that the captured man had been carrying a substantial quantity of gold and could provide no explanation for his possession of this great wealth. After much persuading, the king agreed to examine this mysterious character and set off with Ruthven. Ruthven led the king and his party to Gowrie House. Once there, the king was taken to a locked chamber in which he was greeted by "not a bondman, but a freeman, with a dagger at his girdle" (Clark, p. 77). Ruthven left the king in the man's custody and went to fetch his brother, the Earl of Gowrie. When Ruthven returned and attempted to bind the king, the king yelled out the window. His noblemen, who were preparing to leave, heard his cries. They rushed to the scene, and with their assistance, the king killed Ruthven. Meanwhile, the Earl of Gowrie gathered his forces together and attacked the king and his men. The king's noblemen fought valiantly and killed the traitorous earl and his henchmen. This attempt on the king's life became a major event of the period—pamphlets were written about the affair, including one penned by the king himself. Numerous sermons were also presented throughout England and Scotland focusing on the blasphemy of the attempted murder. Shakespeare was certainly acquainted with the incident, which may have influenced his decision to use the murder of a king as the central plot element of his play.

The Gunpowder Plot. On November 5, 1605, London reeled under a whirlwind of wonder and horror. A blanket of terror had settled over the city as a result of the Gunpowder Plot, in which a group of Catholics violently opposed to the Protestant monarchy had formulated a plan that was intended to kill the king, the royal family, and dozens of government officials. The plotters planned to blow up the Parliament House during a ceremony at which the majority of the English government would be present. The plan was to dig a tunnel into the basement of the Parliament building, place large quantities of gunpowder in the vaults, and explode them during the ceremony. On the night before the ceremony, during an inspection of the cellar, one of the conspirators, Guy Fawkes, was found waiting in the darkened basement ready to ignite the explosives. Several of the plotters were immediately arrested. The rest were captured a few days later, after a failed attempt to rouse Catholic citizens to action against the Protestant government. The capture of these renegades was bloody and resulted in the deaths of the plot's key figures, Thomas Percy, John Wright, and Robert Catesby.

ROBERT CATESBY: PORTRAIT OF A PLOTTER
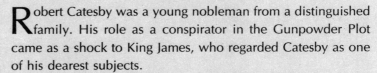

Robert Catesby was a young nobleman from a distinguished family. His role as a conspirator in the Gunpowder Plot came as a shock to King James, who regarded Catesby as one of his dearest subjects.

Catesby grew up near Shakespeare. In fact, many scholars have speculated that the two were acquainted and that Catesby was the model, not for Macbeth, but for the treacherous Thane of Cawdor, the rebellious lord whose property was given to Macbeth by King Duncan, about whom Duncan says:

> There's no art
> To find the mind's construction in the face:
> He was a gentleman on whom I built
> An absolute trust.
>
> (*Macbeth*, 1.4.12-13)

The King's Book, a text written about the plot and the subsequent capture of the rebels, stated that people wanted to view the traitors, "as the rarest sort of monsters; fools to laugh at them; women and children to wonder; all the common people to gaze." This line expresses sentiments almost identical to those in Macduff's address to

Macbeth during their final encounter in Shakespeare's play:

> Then yield thee, coward,
> And live to be the show and gaze o' the time:
> We'll have thee, as our rarer monsters are,
> Painted upon a pole.
>
> (*Macbeth,* 5.8.23-6)

In the actual Gunpowder Plot, the surviving traitors were tried in court, convicted of treason, and executed on January 30, 1606. The event proved that the conflict between the Catholics and Protestants in England had not been resolved and that the threat of further violence was a real one.

The trial of Father Henry Garnet, the great equivocator. An examination of the issue of "equivocation" gives further evidence of the religious conflicts in England during the period. Equivocation was a doctrine of the Jesuits that justified the giving of untruthful responses to interrogation. This practice involved the use of words with equivocal or unclear meanings. A person being interrogated about their religious actions would speak such words so that they wouldn't have to admit to wrongdoing. This practice became crucial for staunch Catholics in Protestant England, where one's Catholic faith could have dire consequences. Indeed, under the Protestant King James, being Catholic was considered a crime.

Equivocation came to be regarded as a punishable form of treason in England. The trial of Father Henry Garnet stands out as the climax of the Protestant attack on equivocators. The trial took place in March 1606; Garnet was found guilty in fifteen minutes and was executed at Saint Paul's Church in London. Shakespeare undoubtedly followed the event, as did the rest of London, and although *Macbeth* may have been almost completed at the time of the trial, he was still able to incorporate the subject of equivocation into his text. Following the death of Duncan, a porter appears whose speech seems to be a direct reference to Father Henry Garnet. The porter says, "Faith, here's an equivocator, that could swear in both the scales against either scale; who committed treason enough for God's sake, yet could not equivocate to heaven" (*Macbeth,* 2.3.8-11). This episode would have been understood by every member of the audience during this period as a mockery of Catholics and the practice of equivocation.

The political interests of King James. The attempts against the king's life in the Gowrie Conspiracy and the Gunpowder Plot could have been influential in Shakespeare's choice of the treacherous murder of a Scottish king as the plot for his play. In *Macbeth,* Shakespeare depicts this type of murder as the most loathsome treachery possible. When Macduff discovers the body of the slain Duncan, he cries,

> O horror, horror, horror!
> Tongue nor heart
> Cannot conceive nor name thee.
>
> (*Macbeth,* 2.3.66-8)

Throughout the play Shakespeare portrays Macbeth as the foulest of murderers, and its depiction of the extreme guilt and resulting insanity that plague Macbeth and Lady Macbeth sends a warning about plots against monarchs. This moral lesson, implicit in the play, certainly enjoyed the support of King James, who had felt the threat of murder himself. Shakespeare also touches on other subjects of interest to his king. James's interest in ancestry and his desire to maintain friendly relations between England and Scotland are represented in the play. Shakespeare addresses his monarch's interest in ancestry by including a scene wherein the witches in the play conjure an image of King James's ascent to the throne. This ascent is traced unbroken back to the line of Banquo. Finally, the king's desire for friendly interactions between his kingdoms of England and Scotland is supported in the play. Safe harbor is offered to the exiled Malcolm by the king of England following Duncan's murder.

For More Information

Adam, Frank. *The Clans, Septs, and Regiments of the Scottish Highlands.* Edinburgh, Scotland: W. & A. K. Johnston & G. W. Bacon, 1960.

Clark, Arthur Melville. *Murder under Trust or The Topical Macbeth.* Edinburgh, Scotland: Scottish Academic Press, 1981.

Cromartie, Roderick Grant Francis Mackenzie, Earl of. *A Highland History.* Berkhamsted, England: Gavin Press, 1979.

Holinshed, Raphael. *Chronicles of England, Scotland, and Ireland.* Edited by Sylvan Barnet. New York: Signet Classic, 1987.

McMurtry, Jo. *Understanding Shakespeare's England.* Hamden, Conn.: Archon Books, 1989.

Nicholls, Mark. *Investigating the Gunpowder Plot.* Manchester, England: Manchester University Press, 1991.

Shakespeare, William. *The Tragedy of Macbeth.* Edited by Sylvan Barnet. New York: Signet Classic, 1987.

Sharpe, Charles Kirkpatrick. *Witchcraft in Scotland.* London: Hamilton, Adams, 1984.

A Man for All Seasons

by
Robert Bolt

Born near Manchester, England, in 1924, Robert Bolt writes about what he calls the human conflict—the struggle between living by one's principles and selling one's soul for earthly rewards. *A Man for All Seasons* studies the human tendency to conform rather than to stand for one's principles—and risk being ostracized or even condemned to death. Bolt concentrates on a controversy of the 1500s that dramatically incorporated these choices, which he portrays in the characters of the Common Man and Sir Thomas More.

THE LITERARY WORK

A play set in England in the early 1500s; written in the early 1950s, first performed for the London stage in 1960.

SYNOPSIS

Sir Thomas More refuses to endorse King Henry VIII's divorce from Queen Katherine and marriage to Anne Boleyn. Though More does not condemn the king's actions, he is nevertheless beheaded.

Events in History at the Time the Play Takes Place

Henry VIII. In 1509 Henry VIII was crowned King of England after the unexpected death of his brother, Henry VII. By special decree from Pope Leo X, Henry was allowed to marry his brother's widow, Katherine of Aragon. He eventually sought to have this marriage annulled, however, for several reasons, including her inability to bear him a son and his desire to marry the much younger Anne Boleyn—daughter of Sir Thomas Boleyn, a wealthy aristocrat. Henry argued that his marriage to Katherine should not have been allowed in the first place because it was contrary to canon law—the official law of the Catholic Church. But the pope, agitated at Henry's convenient reversal of sentiment after twenty years of marriage, refused to grant the king's request. Not easily dissuaded, Henry embarked on a campaign to convince church leaders to allow the divorce and recognize his marriage to Anne Boleyn, which took place in 1533. He needed church approval so that any children he might have with Anne would be considered legitimate heirs to the throne.

The Reformation. In November 1517, Martin Luther, a Catholic priest who was attempting to rid the church of corruption, inadvertently started a movement. This movement, the Reformation, resulted in the creation of a Protestant Church separate from the Catholic Church. Luther—who was concerned with religious principle above all else—felt that the pope and other Catholic Church leaders were usurping God's authority, placing themselves on near-equal footing with God. Luther was also opposed to church leaders who had become feudal lords, protesting that they were acting contrary to their roles as Christian leaders by exacting forced labor from peasants.

Proposing to cleanse the church of such corruption, Luther nailed ninety-five theses, or statements of his ideas, to a church door in Wittenberg, Germany. He expected his views to spark calm debate, but instead they resulted in indignant reactions on the part of the Catholic clergy and in mass revolution among disillusioned Catholics. Luther was proclaimed a heretic and ousted from the Catholic Church; he went on to found his own religion—Lutheranism.

Anglican Church formed. Although he was a Catholic and an earlier critic of Luther, Henry VIII became one of his staunchest supporters. Luther's concept that only God—not popes—can determine religious law provided a rationale for Henry's divorce of Katherine and marriage to Anne. After exhaustive and futile attempts to get his second marriage sanctioned by the Catholic Church, Henry broke off relations with the pope and declared himself head of his own branch of Christianity, the Church of England, also known as the Anglican Church.

In 1534 Henry VIII drafted the Acts of Succession and Supremacy, declaring himself "Supreme Head on Earth" of the Anglican Church. The acts officially recognized his union with Anne and the legitimacy of their children and required all state officials to swear an oath of allegiance to the new Anglican Church. At the same time, Henry eliminated all tax revenue designated for the Roman church and closed all Catholic monasteries, churches, and nunneries in England. Rome viewed such actions as all-out war. Henry was excommunicated from the church, and Rome launched a political attack on his heirs and the Anglican Church that would last for centuries.

Sir Thomas More. While most English officials quickly and quietly renounced Catholicism and adhered to the Act of Supremacy, Sir Thomas More, Henry's lord chancellor (the presiding member of the House of Lords and chief advisor to the king), could not do so. A man of principle, More was a devout Catholic as well as a staunch supporter of the king. When Henry VIII founded the Anglican Church and required the approval of his marriage to Anne in the Act of Succession, More was torn between his loyalties to the Catholic Church and the king of England. For two years he struggled with this dilemma. He found a middle ground by remaining silent, a stance that proved ultimately unsatisfactory to the king. Henry wanted to either get an oath of allegiance from More or destroy him.

Sir Thomas More resigned his position as lord chancellor, a step that did not prevent him from

Martin Luther, whose disagreement with the Catholic Church gave Henry VIII the excuse he needed to break away and to form his own church, with himself as the head.

being persecuted. Henry believed that More's silence and resignation signaled his disapproval of the Anglican Church and Henry's remarriage, although More never indicated one way or the other what his silence meant. Convinced that More was acting like a traitor, the king had him jailed in the Tower of London until he would comply with the Act of Supremacy. After years of imprisonment, it was clear that More was not going to break his silence. Henry's frustration became so great that, through his secretary of state Thomas Cromwell, he had More charged with high treason under penalty of death. A skilled lawyer who ably defended himself, More was nonetheless found guilty. He was beheaded in 1535. Four hundred years later he was named a saint by the Catholic Church, which regarded him as the martyr of the popes.

Tudor women. Henry VIII belonged to a family dynasty of English rulers known as the Tudors. The role of women in English society changed in important ways during the Tudor era (1485-1603). For example, the era saw a budding movement, led by Sir Thomas More, for the public education of women. More belonged to a group of men who were reforming the educational system in England, seeking to establish a more liberal and practical school curriculum. He was the first to propose that the new course of study be applied also to the education of girls. More received strong support from Katherine of Aragon for his proposal (which may explain in part his reluctance to publicly sanction Henry's divorce from her). In fact, More's own daughters received fine educations—his household was described as a kind of "utopia" for women, a place where in many respects they were treated as equals (Plowden, p. 34). More's daughter Margaret, who is featured in the play, became a highly respected scholar.

British women would go on to exercise great political influence in the 1500s. Following Henry VIII, Queen Elizabeth I, daughter of Anne Boleyn, assumed the throne and became the most powerful queen England had seen. She forever changed the notion that a woman could not effectively lead a great nation.

In the play, Bolt shows the emergence of strong women leaders through the actions of More's wife and daughter (Alice and Margaret). When More implies that his conflict with the king is not his wife's concern—she should mind her own house—his wife retorts that she is minding her house. During Henry's reign, women such as Alice More began stating their opinions and raising daughters who would do likewise.

Schools of thought. During the early 1500s a literary and philosophical movement called "humanism" emerged in England. The movement involved the study of ancient Greek and Latin literature, the examination of human ideals and social conventions, and the promotion of social reform. Sir Thomas More was the leading supporter of humanism in England. His book *Utopia* (1516) commented on what he saw as the sad state of human affairs in the 1500s by contrasting English society with an ideal society, a utopia, where peoples' actions are all based on reason rather than personal interest. Like *A Man for All Seasons, Utopia* promotes the idea of maintaining personal integrity in a greedy and corrupt world. More's book mentions Henry VIII's conflict with the Catholic Church and gives an example of a perfect society that could not conceive of and would not tolerate such a controversy.

Humanism in many ways challenged traditional thinking. In essence, the philosophy placed social responsibility on man and deemphasized the role of God. While Thomas More held fast to his religious beliefs in God, heaven, and life after death, he also became convinced that man should try to create a heaven on earth.

People, he thought, had a responsibility to one another and to the world.

During his life, More combined two views about who controls fate—man or God—hinting that God works through man but that man determines his own actions. Bolt captures this combination in his play. While the Common Man—Bolt's archetypical character who embodies all the baser qualities of human beings—chooses to live like a rat and avoid all controversy in order to survive, Sir Thomas More—the heroic figure—behaves like a lion by standing firm for what he believes, even if it costs him his life.

CATHOLIC AND ANGLICAN: DEGREES OF DIFFERENCES

~

Henry VIII thought he could break away from Rome and establish his own branch of Catholicism without altering the doctrine of the church. He envisioned the Church of England remaining identical to the Roman Catholic Church in every way except that Henry, and not the pope, would be recognized as its ultimate human authority. But others, who supported the reform ideas of Luther and sought power in the new Church of England, significantly influenced its doctrines. In the Ten Articles of 1536, the Anglican Church did away with all sacraments of the Catholic Church except baptism, holy communion, and penance. Further, the Anglicans denounced the practice of praying to saints and the dead and pushed for modern translations of the Bible. Other reforms followed, making the Church of England markedly different from the Catholic Church.

In addition to humanism, other philosophies and ideas wielded great influence in the early 1500s. The writings of two individuals, Niccolò Machiavelli and the ancient Greek thinker Aristotle, presented arguments concerning the ideal ruler. Both schools of thought were important during the era, though they were quite different. In Machiavelli's view, any quest for attaining or keeping power is permissible. This philosophy came to be summarized in the phrase, "the end justifies the means." In his 1513 book *The Prince* (also covered in *Literature and Its Times*), Machiavelli qualified his argument by cautioning that cruelty should only be used if it is serving a greater good, but readers tended to ignore this condition and focus solely on the notion of resorting to any action, however cruel, to secure power. Aristotle, on the other hand, argued that without virtue, power and life are meaningless.

A Man for
All Seasons

Henry VIII, who had Thomas More imprisoned and executed because More would not endorse Henry's annullment of his marriage to Katherine of Aragon.

The Play in Focus

The plot. A two-act play, *A Man for All Seasons* opens with an introduction by the Common Man, whom Bolt uses as a kind of Everyman, or representative of the ordinary person. He will assume various roles in the tragedy that follows, serving as the butler, jailer, boatman, and executioner as the story dictates.

The curtain rises on the house of Thomas More in Chelsea, England, in the early 1500s. He has not yet been made lord chancellor but is in the service of King Henry VIII as speaker of the House of Commons. Thomas, his wife Alice, and daughter Margaret (Meg) are preparing to host a small dinner party at which Richard Rich and the Duke of Norfolk are guests. As the party begins, all begin discussing current events, which include the Reformation and the publication of *The Prince,* a controversial book by Niccolo Machiavelli. More is clearly opposed to the book and the Reformation, but Rich is in favor of both. Rich, however, does not openly defy More because he wants a recommendation for a government appointment. He is courting More and any person of influence who might help him secure such a post. More, illustrating his view that power corrupts, advises Rich to become a teacher. "A man should go where he won't be tempted," he says, giving Rich a silver cup that a woman tried to bribe More with when he was a judge (Bolt, *A Man for All Seasons,* p. 7). Disregarding this advice, Rich later becomes the collector of revenues. Jealous of More's power, he schemes to use the silver cup to implicate More in the crime of accepting a bribe. Rich's scheme ultimately fails, however.

The Duke of Norfolk enters next and all in attendance briefly debate the philosophies of Aristotle and Machiavelli. More sides with Aristotle's views, while Rich touts Machiavelli's ideas. The party breaks up when More is summoned to court. Arriving at one o'clock in the morning, he takes a boat upriver to meet with Cardinal Wolsey, the lord chancellor. Wolsey wants More to review a request about to be sent to Rome asking that King Henry's marriage be annulled.

Wolsey is trying to convince Pope Leo X to annul Henry's marriage to Katherine of Aragon and to win permission from the pope for Henry to marry Anne Boleyn. As the meeting progresses, More is clearly taken aback by Wolsey's willingness to break church law. Wolsey argues that the marriage must be annulled so that the king will not die without an heir (Katherine has been unable to bear a male heir, and it is assumed that the much younger Anne Boleyn will furnish a

son). In the style of Machiavelli, who holds that the end justifies the means, Wolsey insists that disobeying church law is justifiable if it keeps Henry's family in power. More responds:

> I believe, when statesmen forsake their own private conscience for the sake of their public duties ... they lead their country by a short route to chaos.
>
> (*A Man for All Seasons,* p. 22)

After More leaves Wolsey to return home, he encounters Secretary of State Cromwell, who prizes power above all else. He then meets Chapuys, the Spanish ambassador. Chapuys is a deeply principled man who is vehemently opposed to King Henry's divorce. Chapuys works for King Charles of Spain, brother to Henry's wife, Katherine. Any offense against Katherine, he warns More, is an offense against Charles, Spain, and the Catholic Church. By this point, the audience realizes how complex the issue of Henry's divorce is, and that the personal actions of the king may be disastrous for millions of people.

More returns home to find Will Roper asking for the hand of his daughter Margaret More in marriage. Roper is adamantly in favor of the Reformation because he believes the Catholic Church to be morally bankrupt. Despite Roper's anti-Catholic stance, More respects Roper for being so concerned about morals and for speaking his mind on a controversial subject.

As the drama continues, Wolsey dies and More becomes lord chancellor. Despite his best efforts, Wolsey had not been able to win approval from the pope for the king's divorce and was therefore executed. King Henry himself visits the More home in an effort to make sure that his new lord chancellor will not fail him as Wolsey had. More assures the king of his loyalty but never agrees to champion his divorce. To the audience, More reveals his inner torment: as a Catholic he wants to remain loyal to his church and God, but as lord chancellor he wants to remain loyal to his king.

Act 2 opens two years later, in May 1532. Unable to get a dispensation from Pope Leo X, King Henry has founded his own church, the Church of England, and proclaimed himself its "Supreme Head" (*A Man for All Seasons,* p. 83). More remains silent on this development despite pressure to endorse the king's action. Specifically, the king wants him to take the Oath of Supremacy, which acknowledges Henry as leader of the Anglican Church. More refuses to state his true views or to endorse or denounce the king's actions. He opts instead to remain silent, attempting to carry on his duties as lord chancellor as best he can. The king, however, will not tolerate his silence, for he feels that it conveys disapproval. In light of the king's feelings, More resigns his post and hopes to live a life of obscurity.

Aided by Cromwell and Rich, Henry persecutes More in an effort to get him to publicly voice his approval of his church and children. More is thrown into the Tower of London for two years, but despite repeated efforts to get him to speak out one way or another, he remains silent. Finally, using contrived evidence, Cromwell charges More with high treason, an offense punishable by death. More's family pleads with him to give his approval to the king and seek refuge in Spain. Margaret begs her father to "say the words of the oath and in your heart think otherwise" (*A Man for All Seasons*, p. 140). But More responds that he cannot do so because "a man's soul is his self!" (*A Man for All Seasons*, p. 153). At his trial, More presents a legal precedent that says silence gives consent. He argues that his silence should be taken as consent for, not disapproval of, the king's actions. Nevertheless he is found guilty and beheaded.

Male-female tensions. Scattered through Bolt's play are references to male-female tensions in English society at the time of Henry VIII. Sir Thomas More's wife Alice is a strong-willed character in her own right and continually reminds the others that the actions of a husband deeply affect the life of his wife. Her daughter, Margaret, is also strong-willed and steadfast like her father. Moreover, she is so well schooled that when King Henry visits the More home, he feels threatened by her knowledge of Latin and Greek and compelled to show his superiority on some level. Clearly inferior in his knowledge of foreign languages, he finally discovers that he is a better dancer. Margaret cleverly praises his talent and laments her lack of it, which leaves the king with a self-satisfied feeling.

At the small dinner party that begins the play, Margaret displays her cleverness when the men debate ideas of their time. The Duke of Norfolk observes wryly that she will be unable to find a husband because of her intellectual prowess. His reaction reflects a common view at the time; that women would become too "forward" and "discontent" if they were educated. Citing such beliefs, many people felt that it would be "not profitable and probably harmful" to provide them with schooling (Plowden, p. 36). Later in the play, Will Roper asks for Margaret's hand in marriage, disproving Norfolk's words. The majority of Englishmen, though, were skeptical about educating women, an attitude that would endure for several more centuries.

Prejudice against women leaders also contributed to King Henry's desire for a divorce from Katherine. She had borne a daughter but no male heir with Henry. For statesmen of that era, having a queen on the throne was out of the question. This mindset would give way in a few decades, when Queen Elizabeth assumed the throne in 1558. Her ascension to the throne served as another indication that society was slowly changing.

Sources. Bolt looked carefully into the historical circumstances surrounding this episode in English history before writing the play. In his research he unearthed not only facts but also feelings. King Henry, he discovered, viewed the pope as just another bishop with no divine authority to appoint other bishops; a king, on the other hand, ruled by the grace of God and, in Henry's mind, did have such divine authority. The popes of Rome, he felt, had set up a rival monarchy without any right to do so. This state of affairs would send King Henry into fits of anger. Looking for a bishop independent enough to grant him his divorce, Henry in fact appointed Thomas Cranmer to be the archbishop of Canterbury.

The character of Cranmer in Bolt's play is based on the actual person in history, as are the other characters. An exception is the Common Man; intended by Bolt to represent qualities with which anyone could identify, he came instead to represent unsavory qualities in human nature.

Attempting to understand Sir Thomas More's feelings as well as his actions, Bolt determined that he was a very orthodox Catholic with a strong opinion about oath-making. More enjoyed a fine life—he was adored by his family and visited by some of the greatest minds of the time, such as the renowned humanist Erasmus. But Sir Thomas More saw the society that surrounded him as subservient to the larger society of Christ, which held that an oath was an invitation to God to serve as witness and judge to a man's act. The punishment, in More's mind, for lying about one's feelings when making an oath was eternal damnation, a penalty that he was simply not willing to pay.

Reviews. Based on the true story of the martyrdom of Sir Thomas More, *A Man for All Seasons* was the third play by Robert Bolt to reach the stage. It proved to be his most successful drama. It appeared in 1960 on the London stage and ran for nine months before playing on Broadway through 1961. Bolt won awards from the New York Drama Critics Circle and from the American Theater Wing for the production.

Critic Walter Kerr of the *New York Herald Tribune* called *A Man for All Seasons* "an extraordinarily lucid play about an extraordinarily difficult subject: the authority of the individual conscience." Robert Coleman of the *New York Mirror* praised it as "wonderful theater—something we too seldom get now-a-nights—for the thoughtful" (Kerr and Coleman in Bolt, p. i). The play was enormously popular with the public, as evidenced by its long runs in London and New York. Bolt wrote the screenplay for a film adaptation of the drama as well.

Events in History at the Time the Play Was Written

Churchill and More: reluctant heroes. Robert Bolt lived in England during Winston Churchill's long tenure as prime minister. Much like Thomas More, Churchill was a controversial figure. Churchill became one of England's greatest national heroes after overseeing Great Britain's successful resistance of Nazi invasion in World War II. Also like More, Churchill was a very literate and inspirational man, known for his eloquence, candor, and strong leadership. In 1953 Churchill won the Nobel Prize for literature.

Although he remained politically active in the postwar era, Churchill's reputation suffered a decline in this period. He lost his post as prime minister in 1945 when the Conservative Party was defeated in elections, though he was returned to the office with the party's victory in 1951. Throughout this period, Churchill retained his conservative beliefs; he refused to support Labor Party demands for nationalized industry and socialized government. An imperialist, he also resisted efforts to grant independence to nations, such as India, that sought to separate from the British Commonwealth. These efforts succeeded without his approval when the Labour Party took control of Parliament in the 1950s. Ironically, Churchill was sometimes blamed for the decay of the British Empire, though he opposed its breakup.

Like Sir Thomas More, Churchill was a curious combination of rebelliousness and conservatism, a man of principle who never wavered publicly from his core beliefs. In describing Churchill as one of the few heroes of the twentieth century, the American statesman Henry Kissinger commented that heroes pursue success as the outgrowth of their inner values. This comment also recalls Thomas More's steadfast commitment to his personal code of conduct.

England 1950-1960. *A Man for All Seasons* was written in the 1950s, a period of postwar recov-

ery for Great Britain. World War II had ended in victory for the British, a result that instilled immense national pride. But the British empire, economically devastated by the conflict, was crumbling. While America and even the defeated nation of Germany enjoyed significant economic growth during this period, Britain experienced a deep recession because of its crippling debt to the United States, which had helped England finance the British war effort. Rationing of basic foods became more common in the early 1950s than it had been during the war.

In 1951, after a decade of belt-tightening with no economic recovery in sight, the British people voted out the Labour Party and voted in the conservatives. After regaining power with such slogans as "Thirteen Wasted Years" and "Set the People Free," the conservatives propped up the economy by increasing the national debt and lowering taxes on the rich. The late 1950s and early 1960s saw the appearance of affluence in Great Britain. British millionaire J. Paul Getty, owner of the Getty Oil Company and a man who projected the quintessential image of British prosperity, was listed as the richest man in the world in 1957. Consumerism and the acquisition of material goods became markers of success. New refrigerators, television sets, vacuum cleaners, pop-up toasters, and luxury cars became the goal for most consumers. Debt increased rapidly during this period of consumerism, as did crime. The values of personal integrity and social responsibility were, to some degree, superseded by greed and self-preservation. Bolt's play, then, featured a man whose values contrasted sharply with those of the time in which it was performed.

For More Information

Bolt, Robert. *A Man for All Seasons*. New York: Random House, 1960.

Chapman, Hester W. *The Challenge of Anne Boleyn*. New York: Coward, McCann & Geoghegan, 1974.

Churchill, Winston S. *Great Destiny*. New York: G. P. Putnam's Sons, 1965.

Cross, Colin. *The Fall of the British Empire*. New York: Coward-McCann, 1968.

Lamont, Peter. *The Philosophy of Humanism*. New York: Frederick Ungar, 1977.

Machiavelli, Niccoló. *The Prince*. London: Penguin, 1981.

Plowden, Alison. *Tudor Women*. New York: Atheneum, 1979.

Simon, Edith. *The Reformation*. New York: Time-Life, 1966.

Medea

by
Euripides

Euripides (485-406 B.C.) is regarded as one of the greatest of classical tragedians. Creator of more than ninety plays (although less than twenty are available in complete form), Euripides is cited by scholars as a dramatist who cultivated a more realistic tone than most of his contemporaries. His works often featured flawed, unheroic characters.

Events in History at the Time the Play Takes Place

Medea as an Athenian play. An Athenian citizen, Euripides revolutionized Greek tragedy by treating his mythic characters as if they were people of his own time, subject to the political and social pressures faced by everyday citizens in fifth-century B.C. Athens; although the play is set in Corinth, Euripides has his characters live according to Athenian customs. Medea's characters are drawn from Greek myth, a body of stories and legends that were passed on orally and regarded as historical accounts by the Greeks who eventually wrote them down. Roughly a thousand years separate Euripides from the mythic past in which Medea and Jason were imagined to have lived; however, the dramatist compresses this time so that the earlier characters seem to inhabit the same historical moment as the audience.

The Play in Focus

The plot. Medea and Jason were best known to Athenians of the fifth century B.C. as the main characters in the legend of the Golden Fleece. This tale concerned Jason's search for the magic fleece of a ram that was sacrificed by Phrixus and

---

THE LITERARY WORK

A play set in ancient Corinth, performed in Athens in 431 B.C.

SYNOPSIS

Medea, a foreign princess and sorceress, is abandoned by her Greek husband Jason, who has married the princess Creusa. Medea takes terrible vengeance upon her former husband. She murders Creusa and Creusa's father, then kills her own two sons—Jason's only children—in retribution.

---

transformed into the constellation of Aries. The character of the nurse in *Medea* recounts part of this legend in the opening scene of the play, and other characters mention the legend liberally throughout.

In the legend, Jason and his troop of young Greek heroes arrive in Medea's home of Colchis, located on the farthest shores of the Black Sea. Jason is continuing his search for the magnificent golden fleece that is in her father's possession. Medea falls in love with Jason and betrays her father by helping the adventurer win the treasure. Jason, Medea, and her brother flee Colchis with the fleece. In some versions of the story she kills her brother and throws pieces of his body overboard to delay her father, who is in pursuit. When the fugitives arrive in Jason's homeland, Medea commits another murder by dispatching Jason's uncle, who has usurped the throne. Forced to flee once again, the pair settle in Corinth, where Euripides's play takes up the story.

Jason becomes involved with Creusa, the daughter of King Creon of Corinth, entering into a relationship he believes is politically advantageous. Creusa and Jason decide to marry despite the presence of Medea. When Medea learns of this, she curses the wedding and the king. Because King Creon fears Medea, he exiles her from his city. She obtains a reprieve for one day to put her affairs in order and to make provisions for her two sons, who are to accompany her. But she has fooled the old king. Instead Medea intends to exact revenge. Although she at first considers killing Jason, his new bride, and Creon, upon second thought she realizes that it would be a greater punishment to let Jason live once she has killed his new family—and the children she had with him.

To further her scheme, she begs King Creon to let her sons remain in Corinth with their father Jason. Medea involves the unwitting boys in her evil scheme, sending them to Jason's new bride with poisoned gifts—a golden robe and diadem (crown). The horrible poison melts the princess's skin from her bones. Creon embraces his afflicted daughter and is killed as well. Medea later turns on her own two sons with a sword, confident that the impact of those murders will crush the spirit of her faithless husband. The play concludes as Medea flies off in a dragon-drawn chariot laden with the bodies of her two dead sons, leaving behind a devastated and childless Jason.

Sources. Medea appears in many different guises in the mythological stories on which Euripides based his play. She is sometimes portrayed as the rightful queen of Corinth, or as the granddaughter of the sun, Helios (in whose chariot she departs at the end of Euripides's play). In some traditions, she is the niece of Circe, a wicked enchantress. The extent to which she is an evil figure varies from story to story; Euripides's own contribution to the tradition is the grim variation in which Medea purposely kills her own children. Previous versions of the story explained that the Corinthians killed the boys in retaliation for the death of their king and his daughter, or that Medea killed them accidentally while trying to make them immortal.

Women and marriage in fifth-century Athens. Women in fifth-century B.C. Athens were kept cloistered within the home and could not act on their own behalf. In political, economic, social, and legal terms they were largely powerless. The powerful Medea flouts this state of affairs, however. At one point she announces, "Women of Corinth, I have come outside to you" (Euripides,

Medea, line 214). Some speculate that this announcement may have signaled to the audience in Athens her rejection of the traditional social role of wife and mother. She protests against the unfairness of such a system, which extends to all Greek women: "Great Themis, lady Artemis, (goddess of oaths), behold the things I suffer, though I made him promise, my hateful husband" (*Medea,* lines 160-62).

> ## A NASTY RUMOR
>
> Slander ... accrued to Euripides at some point after production of the *Medea*: that Euripides had accepted a bribe from the Corinthians to saddle Medea instead of them with the murder of her children.
>
> (McDermott, p. 98)

When Medea rages at being put aside by Jason in favor of Creusa, she assumes sympathetic overtones. Tradition, however, is clearly on Jason's side. One of her sharpest accusations against Jason is that he has broken his marriage oath to her. But as a Greek man, Jason was not obligated to honor such an oath—a woman could not legally promise herself in marriage, and Medea's father did not sanction the union. Medea herself had no authority to marry Jason. In fact, the ceremonies surrounding the betrothal were traditionally negotiated by a woman's prospective husband and the man responsible for her, usually her father. The transaction was finalized by the father's pronouncement, "I give my daughter to you to plow for legitimate children" (Rabinowitz, p. 4). Marriage was seen as the means of producing offspring who would be citizens and not as a romantic attachment. Jason says as much when he complains: "It would have been far better for men to have got their children in some other way, and women not to have existed" (*Medea,* lines 573-75).

Like marriage, divorce was initiated exclusively by men and was easily accomplished. All a man had to do was publicly renounce his marriage, which is what Jason does, and send his ex-wife home with the dowry with which she had entered the union. The woman had no say in the matter. Athenian men were also allowed to keep a foreign concubine (mistress) with whom they could have children in addition to their "real" Athenian wives. Such was the domestic arrangement that Jason hoped to achieve when the play began. The only reason that Jason's action might have been considered improper to Euripides's audience was that Medea had nowhere to go, no father or male protector to turn to. The dramatization of these commonplace aspects of Athenian domestic life served as an important element in Euripides's tragedy.

ARISTOPHANES ON EURIPIDES AND WOMEN

Another Athenian writer, the playwright Aristophanes (448?-388? B.C.), poked fun at Euripides in his work. The following is a comic exchange between Euripides and another character that is featured in one of the plays of Aristophanes:

> Euripides: "I fear that this day will be my last. The women have been plotting against me. And today, at the Thesmophoria, they're going to discuss my liquidation (death)."
> "But why on earth . . .?"
> "They say I slander them in my tragedies."
> "Well, so you do. Serve you right if they did get you!"
>
> (Powell, p. 32)

Events in History at the Time the Play Was Written

The Age of Pericles. Pericles dominated Athenian politics from 447 B.C. until around 431 B.C., the year that *Medea* was performed. An empire builder, he was always searching for ways by which he might increase the number of Athenian colonies and bolster the city's power throughout all of Greece. His ambitions led Athens to war, but the city also grew in beauty and wealth under his leadership. Huge amounts of money were directed toward buildings, festivals (including dramatic productions), and religious monuments.

THE COLOR OF THE CHARACTER'S SKIN

Herodotus [a Greek historian] mentions that Colchis [Medea's homeland] was first an Egyptian settlement. According to this evidence, then, Medea was not only a foreigner but also a woman of color and, more important, a member of a well-established civilization, not at all barbaric.

(Rabinowitz, p. 137)

The most famous building in Athens, the Parthenon, was finished in 431 B.C.; this temple was dedicated to Athena, not as the goddess of wisdom but as the patroness of Athens. A cult of city-worship rose during this era; the famous ode to Athens sung by the chorus in *Medea* might have been a reflection of this trend. Also during this time, the new philosophical school known as Sophism became popular, with Socrates emerging as its most famous teacher. Socrates challenged commonly held beliefs about religion and ethics. The psychology of the average man was studied for the first time, and important questions about truth and virtue were considered through the use of philosophical dialogue. In fact, Socrates is thought to have been an influence on Euripides's dramatic technique, which mimicked cultural trends of the time, such as the study of psychological motivations behind individual actions.

Drama and Athenian politics. The theater was squarely at the heart of fifth-century B.C. social and political life in Athens; Pericles actually dipped into the civic treasury so that people could go to the great festivals at which drama was presented (Ehrenberg, p. 248). Ten to fifteen thousand people would sit on the grassy slopes in the middle of the city to watch the highly ritualized performances. These began with a parade of representatives from the Athenian colonies who presented tributary money to the city, along with a dance performed by youths dressed in military gear. The festival was very competitive: each play was judged by a panel drawn from the audience, and the results were set down permanently in the public record. How well a playwright did in these competitions would naturally influence whether, and how often, he would be allowed to have his work performed publicly. Although it later became one of Euripides's most famous plays, *Medea* was not his most successful effort in the dramatic competitions, possibly because it challenged rather than affirmed traditional values regarding the role of women in Greek society.

Reviews. *Medea* placed third out of three tragedies that were performed in the spring of 431 B.C. Yet Aristotle, who thought that Euripides produced particularly tragic poetry, held up *Medea* as an example of a drama that successfully inspires pity or terror in the audience: "The action may be done consciously and with knowledge of the persons, in the manner of the older poets. It is thus too that Euripides makes Medea slay her children" (Aristotle, *Poetics*, 14.6). Euripides, though, was occasionally the target of later comedies, particularly those written by Aristophanes.

The citizenship law of 450–451. In the play, Jason protests to Medea that his new Corinthian wife is necessary in order to protect the position of his first family: "I wished to preserve you and breed a royal progeny (set of children) to be brothers to the children I have now, a sure defense to us" (*Medea*, lines 595-97). Medea scoffs at this justification, but it is possible that Euripides is referring in these lines to a law that had been recently enacted in Athens. Under this new law, which was passed by Pericles, only those people whose parents were both Athenian could be citizens of the city. Therefore, the children Jason had with Medea were barred from obtaining citizenship. Even the son of Pericles, who was born to the general's Milesian lover, could not be a citizen. Some historians feel that the law was drawn up in order to limit the power of certain aristocrats who opposed Pericles's policies. Others suggest that it was the increasingly large number of resident aliens that necessitated the concentration of power among a relative few. Whatever the case, the citizenship law was probably not far from the minds of Euripides's Athenian audience as they considered the plight of the foreign princess Medea and her children.

Preparing for war. At the time Euripides was completing *Medea*, the treatment and status of foreigners became important for other reasons. The play was staged in Athens in 431 B.C., on the eve of the first major war in which Greeks fought among themselves. The Peloponnesian War was named after the Peloponnesus peninsula, which forms the southern part of Greece. The war was the result of tensions between Athens and the cities of the Peloponnesian League—Sparta and Corinth, primarily. A preliminary skirmish broke out between Corinth and one of the allies of Athens, Corcyra. Previous battles had pitted the Greeks against foreign forces such as the Persians, a people with different customs and appearances. Because the warring Greek cities of Corinth and Corcyra shared the same culture and traditions, a different definition of foreign or alien had to be formed. The struggle to arrive at this definition would continue for almost thirty years, until the end of the Peloponnesian War.

For More Information

Aristotle. "Poetics." In *Criticism: The Major Texts.* Edited by W. J. Bates. New York: Harcourt Brace Jovanovich, 1970.

Bulfinch, Thomas. *Bulfinch's Mythology.* New York: Crown, 1978.

DuBois, Page. *Centaurs and Amazons: Women and the Pre-History of the Great Chain of Being.* Ann Arbor: University of Michigan, 1991.

Ehrenberg, Victor. *From Solon to Socrates: Greek History and Civilization during the 6th and 5th Centuries.* 2nd ed. London: Methuen, 1973.

Euripides. "Medea." In *Euripides 1, The Complete Greek Tragedies.* Translated by David Greene and Richmond Lattimore. Chicago: University of Chicago, 1974.

Hammond, N. G. L., ed. *A History of Greece to 322 B.C.* Oxford: Clarendon Press, 1959.

McDermott, Emily A. *Euripides' Medea: The Incarnation of Disorder.* Philadelphia: Pennsylvania University Press, 1989.

Powell, Anton, ed. *Euripides, Women, and Sexuality.* London: Routledge, 1990.

Rabinowitz, Nancy Sorkin. *Anxiety Veiled: Euripides and the Traffic in Women.* Ithaca, N.Y.: Cornell University Press, 1993.

Thucydides. *History of the Peloponnesian War.* Translated by Rex Warner. New York: Penguin, 1972.

The Merchant of Venice

by
William Shakespeare

A lifelong resident of England, William Shakespeare may have visited Venice, Italy, on tour with his acting company. Certainly many of his well-to-do countrymen made the trip, for shipping was a major business in both lands, and Venice served as a main port of trade between Asia and Europe. Whether or not Shakespeare knew any Jews is also unclear, since Jews had been expelled from England three hundred years earlier. But he was undoubtedly familiar with a 1590s scandal that involved a Jew, as well as the contents of at least one other popular play of the decade that featured a Jewish character.

Events in History at the Time the Play Takes Place

The city of Venice. In the 1300s to 1500s the region that is present-day Italy consisted of separate territories ruled by various governmental bodies, including single-ruler states, the Papal States (a region controlled by the pope and the Roman Catholic Church), and a few regions that had a republican form of government. One of these republics was Venice, located in the northeastern portion of the peninsula, on the Adriatic Sea. The city, which also exerted its rule over nearby towns, was an oligarchy—a state ruled by a few noblemen who did all the voting and governing, sometimes even serving as judges in court cases.

The members of this oligarchy organized themselves into a Great Council of 1,000 to 2,500 members, a Senate of Sixty, a Council of Forty, and an all-powerful Council of Ten. Members of

THE LITERARY WORK

A play set in Venice, Italy, most likely in the late 1300s or in the 1500s; first performed between 1596 and 1598.

SYNOPSIS

A rich heiress must marry the man who solves a riddle contained in her father's will. To woo her, one of her suitors borrows money from a friend who, in turn, takes a loan from a Jewish moneylender. The friend promises a pound of his flesh should he default on the loan, an unlikely event that becomes much more probable when his ships are reported lost at sea.

the smaller bodies could arrest, try, and execute people at will. Among the ruling noblemen was an elected chief, the doge of Venice. This magistrate was treated like a prince in accordance with his status as the city's leading oligarch, although his powers were limited. This is the position filled by the Duke of Venice in Shakespeare's play.

The nobles of Venice were involved not only in government but also in shipping, the major activity of the city. Spices, silks, wine, and gold came and went through its docks. Indeed, ships and seafaring were so central to Venice's existence that every year on Ascension Day (a holiday that commemorates Christ's ascent into heaven), the republic commenced a series of carnival festivities with a ceremony in which the doge of Venice, seated in an elaborately decorated boat, married the Adriatic Sea. A ring was dropped into the water to seal the ceremony.

The time of the play. Shakespeare does not identify an exact time in which *The Merchant of Venice* is set, and pinpointing the precise era in which it takes place is difficult. The background of shipping and trade does, however, suggest a time frame. For centuries, the merchants of Venice shipped cargo at their own risk without the benefit of insurance that would reimburse them if they encountered misfortune on the voyage. The wealthy shipper in Shakespeare's play, Antonio, does not insure his cargo though it seems likely that he would have done so if the option existed; the cargo, after all, represents his entire fortune. Marine insurance first became available in Venice in the 1400s. Since Antonio does not have this protection, the play may have been set earlier, perhaps in the 1300s.

The case for a setting in the late 1300s is supported by the character of Shylock, the Jew who lives in Venice. Not until 1366 were Jews invited to live in the city, and from 1396 to 1509 Venice expelled Jewish people. These data suggest that Shakespeare's plot might be set between 1366 and 1396, or in the 1500s, when Jews were again permitted to live in Venice. Since marine insurance existed by the 1500s, however, the late 1300s appears to be a more likely time period.

Foreigners and the law. All of the trade that flowed in and out of Venice made it advantageous for the city not only to tolerate foreigners, but also to give them equal treatment under the law; if powerful foreigners had received mistreatment in Venice they might have avoided the city when conducting trade. Over the years Venice earned a high reputation for legal fairness. Commoners as well as foreigners supposedly had equal standing with nobles in court. In Shakespeare's play, Antonio fears that strict observance of the law will cost him his life; nevertheless he recognizes the necessity of upholding it:

> The Duke cannot deny the course of law,
> For the commodity that strangers have
> With us in Venice, if it be denied,
> Will much impeach the justice of the state,
> Since that the trade and profit of the city
> Consisteth of all nations.
> (Shakespeare, *Merchant of Venice*, 3.3.26-31)

Jews in Venice. Despite all the foreign traffic and Venice's reputation as a place of legal equity, prejudice existed in the city. Such prejudice was reflected by Shakespeare in the character of Portia. Among her suitors is Morocco (an African), who, much to her relief, fails the test her father has devised for her suitors. "Let all of his [Morocco's] complexion," wishes Portia aloud, "choose me so" (*Merchant of Venice,* 2.7.87). This indicates Portia's feelings about all men with dark skin; she hopes they would make the wrong choice so that she would not have to marry them.

The Jews were an openly persecuted minority. This persecution was first evident in southern Italy, where many Jews lived. During the 1290s, synagogues were changed into churches in this region, and Jews here were forced to convert. Many instead retained their Jewish faith and fled north. They were welcomed by northern authorities—though not necessarily by the citizens—because Jews filled a desperate need. Christian church leaders had forbidden all Christians to practice usury (to charge a fee for letting someone "use" their money). Jewish law, however, allowed a Jew to charge fees on loans made to Christians, though Jews were not allowed to charge other Jews with such fees. Given this situation, northern city-states invited Jews to open loan-banks so that money could be lent to needy Christians of their towns. The businesses were pawnbroking establishments, not banks as they are known today. Money was loaned in exchange for an object taken as security, normally for twelve or eighteen months. The fee charged for the loan ranged from 15 to 25 percent a year.

THE OLD TESTAMENT ON USURY

Thou shalt not lend upon usury to thy brother; usury of money; usury of victuals; usury of anything.... Unto a stranger thou mayest lend upon usury; but unto thy brother thou shalt not lend upon usury.

(Deuteronomy 23:19-20)

Very careful conditions were laid down between a city-state and its pawnbroking establishments. These conditions were recorded in a document called a *condotta* (which means "conduct"); once such an agreement was made, a Jewish settlement generally sprang up in the city. The city-state typically limited the length of the agreement to no more than ten years, then renewed it. This arrangement prevented the Jews from becoming permanent residents of a city;

they could be expelled at the end of the agreement if the rulers so chose.

Some two hundred to three hundred Jews lived in the average Jewish community of the north in the 1300s. In Venice the non-Jews would have outnumbered the Jews by about five hundred to one. Still, the Jews were conspicuous. As one historian noted, "a civic Jewish loan-banker became nearly as universal a figure in many regions [of Italy] as the civic physician or schoolteacher, and [in the beginning] enjoyed very much the same status" (Roth, p. 107).

Though the Jews served a vital function, Jewish settlement was tightly controlled in Venice. For more than half a century, Jews were allowed to live in the republic of Venice but not in the city itself; instead they had to settle across the lagoon in Mestre. This stipulation was due in part to anti-Semitism, but the ban may have also resulted from the city leaders' desire to maintain control of trade. The distant location of the Jewish institutions proved inconvenient for its citizens, however, and Venice finally relented.

A FRIAR STIRS UP ANTI-JEWISH FERVOR

~

Accordingly all the saints and all the angels of paradise cry then against [the usurer], saying "To hell, to hell, to hell." Also the heavens with their stars cry out, saying, "to the fire, to the fire, to the fire." The planets also clamor, "To the depths, to the depths, to the depths."

(Fra Bernardino in Homer and Sylla, p. 69)

In 1366 Venice invited the Jews to set up three loan-banks in the city, which led to the birth of the first Jewish community in Venice. The city renewed its agreement with the Jews until 1394, when anti-Jewish feeling swelled to such a pitch that Venice finally expelled the Jews, who returned to Mestre. Legal measures were adopted that permitted Jews to "visit" Venice in the 1400s, but even these stays were limited to two weeks at a time.

Racism. In 1394 the Jews of Venice were ordered to wear a yellow *O* on their clothing to signify that they were Jewish. Venice was not the first community to prescribe such a sign; this distinguishing badge had been ordered by church authorities a century earlier and periodically enforced in Italy over the years. In *The Merchant of*

Venice, Shylock mentions another identifying garment—a gabardine cloak—that serves the same purpose as the yellow circle.

Requirements such as the wearing of the yellow *O* reflected a growth in Judeophobia in Italy that continued in the 1400s. These feelings were due largely to the anti-Jewish speeches of Franciscan friars such as Fra Bernardino da Feltre. A believer in his own fiery words, the friar led his listeners to adopt the erroneous idea that Jews murdered children and consumed their blood during the Passover season. The pope in Rome defended the Jews, helping to clear them of any guilt in an incident in which a baby was found murdered. Undaunted, the friar continued his rabble rousing, appearing in Venice itself in 1492.

Conditions worsened in the 1500s. Venice was embroiled in war, and an invasion in 1509 left Mestre in ruins. Its residents, including the Jews, fled to Venice, where they were allowed to stay. In 1516 the Christian leaders of Venice confined them to an area known as the New Foundry, or *Ghetto Nuovo*. This idea of designating a section of the city to which Jews were restricted would spread throughout Italy over the next few decades; the term *ghetto* stemmed from this first neighborhood in Venice. A gate was erected at the entrance to this section, and from sundown to sunrise Christian watchmen made sure that the Jews did not venture out.

Although earlier popes had protected the Jews, in 1555 Pope Paul IV issued an edict, or bull. It required Jews in the Papal States (central Italy) to live in special areas and to wear a yellow hat or veil. The edict also prohibited them from owning real estate and from hiring Christian servants. The pope's declaration even limited Jews to only a few occupations: loan-banker, seller of secondhand clothing, and doctor (confined to treating Jewish patients only). Rules were strictly enforced. Authorities examined the account books of loan-bankers and, in the event of a dispute, seized all his property to ensure payment in case he owed a penalty.

This state of affairs is reflected in *The Merchant of Venice.* In Shakespeare's play, the judgment against the Jewish moneylender calls for all his goods to be seized and confiscated. This sort of punishment was not uncommon in the Papal States. The new laws reduced some well-to-do Jews to poverty, and were enforced so harshly that some members of the Jewish community converted to Christianity.

Conversion to Christianity. King Edward I had ejected some sixteen thousand Jews from Eng-

Act 2, scene 5 of *The Merchant of Venice*: Jessica, Shylock, and Launcelot at Shylock's house.

land in 1290, and many other European countries followed suit (France in 1306, Spain in 1492, and Portugal in 1497). Eventually about nine thousand of these Jews found their way into Italy, one of the few places where it remained possible to practice the Jewish faith. Even in Italy, though, serious restrictions were in place. Jews were subject to regulations about where they could live, how they could work, and what they could wear.

But while Venice enforced a number of unfair laws, it did not experience any bloody anti-Semitic riots and though for a time Venice expelled Jews, they were not forced to convert. The powers of Venice did have a serious interest in converting Jews if they truly embraced Christianity, however. In 1557 a House of Catechumens was founded in the city to provide Christian training to candidates for conversion. Despite such measures, few Jews converted.

There is no evidence that Shakespeare knew anything about the emotional struggle that a Jew went through when faced with the question of converting. He may have also been unaware of the stubborn strength with which people held on to the Jewish faith, even if they went through the motions of conversion, and unaware of the degree to which the religion bound a child to a parent. The fifth commandment from the Old Testament, to "honor thy father and mother," was considered the highest obligation of a Jewish child, indicating that in most cases it would not be so easy for a Jewish daughter to abandon her father and her faith, as Shylock's daughter Jessica does in *The Merchant of Venice*.

The Play in Focus

The plot. Antonio, a wealthy and generous merchant of Venice, is melancholy despite his wealth. His friends Bassanio, Gratiano, and Lorenzo try to cheer him; they eventually succeed when Antonio hears that the spendthrift Bassanio has decided to woo Portia, a beautiful and virtuous woman whose father's death has left her extremely wealthy. But Bassanio has no money to compete with Portia's other suitors, who come from wealthy foreign royal families. Antonio, whose funds are temporarily tied up in his shipping ventures, volunteers to borrow the money needed by Bassanio to support his efforts to win Portia's heart.

Bassanio orchestrates the loan with the Jewish moneylender Shylock, despite the fact that Bassanio and Antonio detest Shylock for his practice of charging fees for loans. Since Antonio has made no secret of his disgust for Shylock, the moneylender is not eager to make the loan, but in the end he offers not to charge any fee at all. Instead, as a bizarre joke, Shylock asks that a penalty of one pound of Antonio's flesh be paid if the money is late. Antonio, certain his repayment will not be late, agrees to the stipulation.

Meanwhile, in nearby Belmont, the wealthy heiress Portia is also weary of the world, despite her riches. Her friendly servant Nerissa cheers her by joking about Portia's suitors, none of whom please either of the women. Portia's father's last will and testament has prescribed a test for her suitors; his daughter is to marry only the man who chooses the correct casket among three—one gold, one silver, and one lead. Each is inscribed with a phrase, but only one of the chests contains Portia's portrait, the indication that the man has chosen correctly.

Lancelet, Shylock's Christian servant, leaves the Jew's employ to work for Bassanio, who sets out for Belmont with Gratiano to woo Portia. In the meantime, Bassanio's friend Lorenzo takes advantage of the festivities and costumes of carnival to elope with Shylock's daughter Jessica, who departs with much of her father's wealth and converts to the faith of her new Christian husband. The blows of losing his daughter and his fortune, both to a Christian, leave Shylock thirsting for revenge.

Back in Belmont, the prince of Morocco has failed Portia's father's test by selecting the golden casket with the inscription, "Who chooseth me shall gain what many men desire" (*Merchant of Venice*, 2.7.5-6). Having incorrectly equated Portia with golden coins and treasure, he has been rewarded with a carrion death (skull). The prince of Arragon also fails. When Arragon selects the silver casket, which reads "Who chooseth me shall get as much as he deserves," he is rewarded with a portrait of a blinking idiot (*Merchant of Venice*, 2.9.53-4). Bassanio, who has already gained Portia's love, selects the lead casket, which reads, "Who chooseth me must give and hazard all he hath" (*Merchant of Venice*, 2.7.11-12). He is rewarded with a portrait of Portia, thus winning the right to marry her. Gratiano and Nerissa fall in love during this period as well.

All this happiness is threatened, however, when bad news suddenly arrives. They learn that Antonio's ships are lost at sea and probably wrecked, and that Shylock, bereft of his daughter and his money, demands his pound of flesh as payment for the loan.

The two couples are quickly married and the wives bestow rings on their husbands. After the service, however, Bassanio and Gratiano immediately depart for Venice to be with Antonio. Portia and Nerissa depart secretly as well, planning to dress as a doctor of law (lawyer) and his clerk as part of an effort to rescue their husbands' friend. In court, Portia (the doctor of law) begs Shylock to show mercy, but Shylock refuses, so the doctor of law rules that Shylock may collect his pound of flesh. A significant stipulation is added, however; Shylock may not take any blood with the flesh.

Furthermore, Shylock's attempt to collect his bond is regarded as the attempt of a foreigner to murder a Venetian. For this crime, Shylock must pay with his life and all his earthly goods. Showing mercy, the Duke of Venice spares Shylock's life, and Antonio contents himself with the use of only half of Shylock's earthly goods. Shylock may keep the other half if he becomes a Christian and bequeaths all that he owns upon his natural death to his newly Christianized daughter, Jessica.

Bassanio and Gratiano offer a reward to the wise doctor of law and his clerk. The disguised women, though, demand the rings that they themselves have given their husbands as a reward. Eventually the men give up their rings, hoping for merciful forgiveness from their wives. Arriving back in Belmont just a step ahead of the others, Portia and Nerissa change into their usual garments and welcome their returning husbands. They needle the men about giving up the rings for a time. Finally, though, the women let everyone in on the joke they played on their new husbands.

Friendship and love vs. money. *The Merchant of Venice* has been classified as a comedy. In Shakespearean comedy, the central goal of the play's participants is marriage. In this play, money makes the perfect antagonist. Ducats (a coin used as currency) and the commercial world of Venice are set against romance and Portia's inherited wealth in nearby Belmont, and usury is condemned in the process. The cold metal of the coin is sterile and inert; it cannot naturally reproduce itself, which makes it the ideal foe in a genre devoted to creating couples who will be fruitful and multiply. By the end, the play has reshuffled its characters into a trio of such couples—Bassanio and Portia, Gratiano and Nerissa, and Lorenzo and Jessica—with Antonio and Shylock left out of the nuptials, perhaps because they are too closely linked to the cold world of money, be it invested in a ship's cargo or in usury.

Usury, of course, was regarded as the more offensive of these investments. In Shakespeare's time, some people still viewed the making of a loan not as a business venture, but as an aid to a neighbor in distress. To profit from that distress seemed at worst purely evil and at best plainly unjust. Italy's priests called usury a sin and declared that anyone who committed it would not receive a Christian burial. This fate weighed heavily on the conscience of Christian merchants.

Christians had tried to meet the need for loans themselves in the 1400s by opening public pawnshops, known as *mons pietati*. They made money available for a fairly nominal fee, called interest, to cover the cost of running the shops. The idea that the lender was taking a risk in making the loan was not viewed as an acceptable reason to charge interest, perhaps because most loans at the time were secured by property worth many times the amount of the loan. In any case, a distinction arose between usury and interest, and usury ultimately came to mean "overcharging" for the use of money.

By Shakespeare's time, then, people were charging interest (Queen Elizabeth set the maximum interest rate at 10 percent) and distinguishing it from usury. But some still found the very idea of a fee on a personal loan repulsive. This attitude is exemplified in the views of Shakespeare's merchant Antonio. In Act 1, Shylock recalls being mistreated by Antonio in the past, but offers to loan him money anyway as a gesture of friendship. Antonio objects. No friend, he rails, would charge for a loan:

> I am as like to call thee so [a dog] againe;
> To spet on thee againe, to spurne thee too.
> If thou wilt lend this money, lend it not
> As to thy friends, for when did friendship take
> A breed for barren metal of his friend?
> (*Merchant of Venice*, 1.3.140-44)

The play's Christians, including Antonio, seem to urge self-sacrifice over profit. Yet they too are motivated by money. Antonio risks all his money in shipping to make money, then risks his life to secure money for his friend Bassanio. Bassanio's first words about the lovely Portia describe her wealth; and Lorenzo steals not only Jessica, but her father's money. These examples show that the profit motive is as strong in the Christians as in Shylock, and that they too connect money to love. Written in an age of Christianity and commercial growth, the play appears to examine the coexistence of love and money, and to contend that the hazards and risks taken in the name of love are superior to those taken in purely monetary ventures.

Sources. Shakespeare utilized a number of sources in creating the play. The "pound of flesh" storyline stems from a tale written as early as 1378; it first appeared in print in 1558 in a collection of stories called *Il Pecorone* (*The Big Fool*) by Giovanni Fiorentino. The tale, which was not translated into English during Shakespeare's life, tells of two friends, a loan involving a pound of flesh, a contest for a woman, the default on the loan, the woman's disguise at the trial, and a ring. While the contest for her love takes place in Belmont, it does not involve caskets. The most likely source for the casket storyline is another collection of tales, *Gesta Romanorum*, compiled around 1300, printed in 1472, and translated into English first in 1577 and then in an improved version in 1595, close to the time of Shakespeare's play.

There is uncertainty about the influence that other plays of Shakespeare's time had on his creation of *The Merchant of Venice*. Among them was *The Jew* (1579), which no longer exists but may have been an important source, and *The Jew of Malta* (1590), a tragedy by Christopher Marlowe that was a smashing success in Shakespeare's day. It features a villainous Jew named Barabas who is referred to in Shakespeare's play. At one point Shylock laments his daughter's elopement, noting that "Would any of the stock of Barabas / Had been her husband, rather than a Christian!" (*Merchant of Venice*, 4.1.309-10). As in Shakespeare's play, Marlowe's drama featured a daughter of the principal Jewish character. In *The Jew of Malta*, however, the daughter, named Abigail, converts to Christianity and enters a convent.

Events in History at the Time the Play Was Written

Jews in England. After they were expelled in 1290, fewer Jews lived in England than in almost any other European country. A half dozen or so Jews arrived in 1310, perhaps to see if they would be allowed to return. One or two Jewish doctors were invited to settle in the country over the years, and an occasional wandering adventurer passed through. After the Jews were expelled from Spain and Portugal, some who had been forced to convert to Christianity came to England. They were known as *Marranos* (a negative term meaning "pigs"), and at one point their community in England grew to include one hundred members. Among them were Sara Ames and her husband, Dr. Roderigo López, a refugee from Portugal who was invited to serve as a medical consultant to

England's Queen Elizabeth and her favorite member of the court, the Earl of Essex. In 1594 López was swept up in a scandal that probably affected the creation of Shakespeare's play.

Aside from acting as the queen's personal physician, López was assigned to serve as an interpreter for Antonio Pérez. Pérez was a pretender to the throne of Portugal—that is, he made the false claim that he was a rightful heir to the kingship. It was alleged that agents from Spain, an enemy of Portugal at the time, lured López into a plot to assassinate Pérez. The Spanish feared that Pérez would oppose their interests should he gain power. It is true that López's sympathies were with Spain, but little else is certain.

The Earl of Essex, meanwhile, had anti-Spanish sympathies. He accused López of being drawn into a plot not only to kill Pérez but also to poison England's Queen Elizabeth. López denied the accusation. Essex provided evidence to support his claim, which some thought to be false. The queen herself doubted López's guilt. Still, he was convicted.

López ended up confessing to the charges so that the authorities would not torture his body on the rack before hanging him. He died professing his love for Jesus Christ, but evidence suggests that this declaration was not in earnest. López had strong ties to the Jewish faith; he had been sending funds to help maintain a Jewish synagogue in Antwerp, Belgium, and Jewish religious services were held in the home of one of his English friends. He was, it seems, a convert due to political necessity rather than belief. López was hanged, drawn, and quartered on June 7, 1594, in front of a scornful crowd that hurled ridicule at the Jewish doctor. Marlowe's *The Jew of Malta* was brought back to the stage and performed during the time between López's trial and his hanging; altogether *The Jew of Malta* would be performed fifteen times that same year.

Jews in Italy. Insincere converts were also on the minds of Venetians in the late 1500s. A group of Jews who had converted to Christianity and immigrated to Venice were expelled from the city in 1550, perhaps more because of the competition they posed to other Venetian businessmen than for any other reason. Some of these converts belonged to a new wave of ex-Jews that had begun to appear in Venice in the early 1500s. Called the Levantines, they came from the rival Ottoman Empire to the east. Many such Levantine Jews were actually former residents of Spain or Portugal who had settled further east before coming to Italy. Some of the refugees excelled in trade.

One Jew who remained further east, Joseph Nasi, operated from Constantinople, the center of the Ottoman Empire and a rival city of Venice. Nasi developed an organization that competed with Venice's trade, purposely bypassing the port of Venice for other ports in Italy whenever possible. When Nasi died in 1579 trade through Venice increased, and conditions soon improved for Jews in the city. By the 1590s, Christians were attending concerts in the ghetto, while Jews were able to attend theater events outside its gate. The Marranos who redeclared themselves Jews were allowed back into Venice. The population of the city's Jewish ghetto neared twenty-five hundred as the century drew to a close.

Popular and critical reception. Appearing in print in 1600 as *The Comical History of the Merchant of Venice,* the play was performed repeatedly that year, an indication of its initial popularity. Its alternate title, *The Jew of Venice,* suggests that the character Shylock had a strong impact on its first audiences. As time has passed, reviewers have divided into several camps regarding the tone of the play. Some have argued that Shakespeare shared the view of the Christians in the play, who regard themselves as superior to the Jew. Others have argued that the play's Christians are, in fact, no better than Shylock, to whom they show little mercy in court, and that Shakespeare wanted to rouse some sympathy for the Jew. Still others say that the play is preoccupied less with religion and more with a major conflict of Shakespeare's time—that of love versus material riches.

For More Information

Andrews, Mark Edwin. *Law versus Equity in The Merchant of Venice.* Boulder: University of Colorado Press, 1965.

Curiel, Roberta, and Bernard Dov Cooperman. *The Venetian Ghetto.* New York: Rizzoli, 1990.

Homer, Sidney, and Richard Sylla. *A History of Interest Rates.* New Brunswick, N.J.: Rutgers University Press, 1991.

Roth, Cecil. *The History of the Jews of Italy.* Philadelphia: Jewish Publication Society of America, 1946.

Shakespeare, William. *The Merchant of Venice.* New York: Washington Square Press, 1992.

Shapiro, James. *Shakespeare and the Jews.* New York: Columbia University Press, 1996.

The Merry Adventures of Robin Hood

by
Howard Pyle

H oward Pyle was a well-known children's author and illustrator during the late 1800s. He was the first graphic artist in the United States to be associated with high artistic standards. One of the first American artists to train solely in the United States instead of Europe, Pyle eventually founded the Brandywine school of art in Delaware. He was fascinated by the Middle Ages and immersed himself in English history and legend.

Events in History at the Time the Novel Takes Place

Angles, Saxons, Normans. The Angles, the Saxons, and the Jutes were originally Germanic tribes who made inroads into England around the fifth century, when the lands were controlled by a weakening Roman Empire. An early form of English was spoken by these West Germanic invaders, who combined to form the Anglo-Saxon peoples. This group developed a rich Anglo-Saxon culture from the seventh to the eleventh centuries.

In the mid-eleventh century, however, William the Conqueror led an invading force from France. The Norman people conquered the Anglo-Saxons in 1066 at the Battle of Hastings. The Normans, who were of Viking stock, were the last successful invaders of England, and their conquest had immediate political, social and cultural consequences.

Although only 10,000 Normans lived among a hostile population of one or two million peo-

THE LITERARY WORK

A novel based on British legend; set in England from about 1154-1247, spanning the reigns of kings Henry II, Richard the Lion-Hearted, and John I; published in 1883.

SYNOPSIS

Robin Hood and his band of outlaws live in Sherwood Forest, where they often steal from passing nobles and give part of their plunder to the poor. Robin Hood and his group of warriors experience a series of adventures, many of which pit them against their chief foe, the Sheriff of Nottingham.

ple, the Normans successfully took over the majority of Anglo-Saxon institutions. The influence of the invaders was soon noticeable in nearly all aspects of English society and culture. Norman French became England's official language, despite the fact that most common people still spoke English. English politics became part of French politics, and English culture came to be dominated by the French, especially under the rule of King Henry II (1154-1189) and Eleanor of Aquitaine. In the church, Norman bishops replaced old Saxon bishops. Land was redistributed as well, and many Anglo-Saxon thanes—freemen who held the king's land—lost their possessions. Meanwhile, the Normans built numerous castles. By 1207, 80 percent of the property owners in Winchester were Normans, a sharp rise from the earlier figure of 30 percent. As one historian notes, "It is hardly surprising, then, that generations of patriotic Englishmen should have looked upon the Battle of Hastings as a national catastrophe" (Gillingham, p. 108).

Comments made by the characters in *Robin Hood* reflect disputes between the Saxons and the Normans. A palmer (pilgrim), for example, laments to David of Doncaster, one of Robin's men, that: "It grieves my heart to see one as gallant as this Stutely die, for I have been a good Saxon yeoman in my day, ere I turned palmer, and well I know a stout hand and one that smiteth shrewdly at a cruel Norman or a proud abbot with fat money-bags" (Pyle, *Merry Adventures of Robin Hood,* p. 34). Despite the grievances of the Saxons, however, the Norman Conquest also led to the beginning of a strong royal government, the emergence of English common law, population growth, and the expansion of agriculture.

Services rendered and taxes paid. English society was broken into many levels during the eleventh and twelfth centuries. In rural areas, most people lived under the manorial system. Under this system, lords and abbots received land from the king that they paid for not with money but instead with promises of loyalty to the Crown. This allegiance meant that they would fight and die for the king if necessary. The lords and abbots then exacted goods, services, and loyalty from the villeins, or peasants, who worked the manorial land. Villeins worked very hard to earn a living. Records show that some villeins, for example,

1. Ploughed four acres of land for the lord in the spring;
2. Supplied two oxen for the lord's plough team for three days in winter, three days in the spring, and one day in the summer;
3. Worked three days a week on the lord's land or paid a yearly toll;
4. Had to follow the lord to war and uphold justice as determined by the lord's courts;
5. Paid inheritance taxes to lords and were subject to their commands about using the mill, oven, and winepress.

During his reign, King Henry II developed extensive laws to govern the possession of land and curb the excesses of the great lords. Several lords had become tyrants who often violated and abused the customs that governed their relationship with their tenants. Henry II also experimented with new taxes to increase his income.

He encouraged his own vassals (lesser lords who held land from him) to substitute a payment of money, called scutage, for their military service. Another source of income, the tallage, was a percentage tax of the total value of an individual's movable property—this tax enabled the king to tap the riches of the growing towns. In order to pay for his wars in the Holy Land, Henry's successor, King Richard the Lion-Hearted, imposed yet another tax on England, a land tax called a carucage. King Richard visited England only twice during his reign (1189-1199), and each time it was to raise money.

The ruler most notorious for raising taxes during the time of Robin Hood, however, was King John I (ruled 1199-1216). John has been portrayed throughout history as a greedy, cruel, and poor leader—he is considered one of England's worst kings. In 1203 John lost his holdings and raised taxes to recover the lost inheritance. At about the same time a string of price hikes in England plunged many families and religious houses into financial difficulties. The population blamed the king for the situation, paying little attention to other economic causes. Price hikes further reduced the value of John's royal tax income. He reacted by levying new taxes and tightening up the laws governing the forest, actions that made him even more unpopular.

The forests. The Normans had created the royal forests, an institution that grew especially strong under King Henry II. Laws governing the forests were considered different than regular laws. Some historians contend that as early as the twelfth century, separate courts may have been established to consider violations of forest law apart from violations of general law.

Forest laws protected the king's hunting rights. It was forbidden for anyone to hunt animals such as deer and wild boar. Poaching of the king's deer was regarded as a serious matter, and penalties for violations of forest law became known for their severity. Those who broke forest laws were sometimes blinded, emasculated, or even killed. In later years, the king's exclusive rights to the forests at the expense of other people came to be regarded as an abuse of royal power.

The outlaw Robin Hood and his men lived in Sherwood Forest. They had no other means of getting food, and so they illegally poached the king's deer. The hunting skill of Robin Hood and his band, however, enabled them to poach deer without being apprehended. The royal forest was an extensive game preserve which, at its

An illustration by Pyle that shows Robin and another character, the Tinker, as they relax at an inn.

greatest size, covered as much as one quarter of England.

Law and outlawry. Outlawry, one of the most ancient of legal charges, places a person outside of the law. The concept of outlawry, which dates back to at least the tenth century, is commonly found in governments with a weak central authority. Originally, charges of outlawry were leveled against accused felons who ran away from the law instead of facing trial. Such flights took place after the wronged party launched an appeal against an accused person. If the accused person could not be found, the sheriff demanded that he appear at one of the next four court sessions. If the accused failed to show up, the sheriff pronounced him an "outlaw." Out-

lawry was commonly called "bearing the wolf's head," and the sentence of outlawry was punishable by death, for the outlaw's flight was viewed as an act of defiance against the king and community. Members of the community were duty-bound to kill an outlaw, and it was a crime to harbor a person who had been labeled as such. The accused thus fled the community, which was licensed to pursue the fugitive. Robin Hood was one of the outlaws who fled to Sherwood Forest to escape punishment. His practice of giving money to the poor might have been partially motivated by a desire to make friends with people who otherwise might have captured or killed him for a reward.

The number of outlaws rose dramatically during the time of Robin Hood, because of changes in English law. These changes allowed the king (as well as a wronged party) to institute an appeal against an alleged criminal, and they obligated juries to furnish the names of suspects in a legal case.

Games. Games were an important part of life in England in the twelfth and thirteenth centuries because they were a means of proving skill as well as establishing status and dominance. In Pyle's version of *Robin Hood,* Robin and his men continually compete with each other and outsiders in both formal competitions and among themselves. Archery and quarterstaff fencing are the most common modes of competition for the band of outlaws.

Archery dates back to ancient times. The Anglo-Saxons used bows and arrows well before the Norman Conquest, although archery seems to have been reserved as a hunting skill or as a recreational pastime. The Normans, however, developed archery into a military skill. During the age of chivalry the skillful use of a bow and arrow was seen as part of the required education of young men. Talented archers, noted and admired for their expertise, became featured characters in many English ballads. As proficiency with bow and arrow assumed greater importance, the value and significance of archery equipment increased as well. One historian observed that "an old ballad of Robin Hood says, that he and his followers had an hundred bows furnished with strings, and an hundred sheafs of goose arrows, with bright burnished heads; every arrow was an ell long, adorned with peacocks' feathers and bound at the notching with white silk" (Strutt, p. 60).

Another, less familiar, activity practiced by Robin and his men was quarterstaff fencing. A quarterstaff (also called a cudgel) is a long, heavy, wooden stick that was used both as a weapon of attack and a weapon of defense by fighters in England during the 1100s and 1200s.

Formal competitions for sports such as quarterstaff fighting and archery were arranged so that men could determine who was the best. Competition hosts often offered a prize for the winner in an effort to attract contestants. Nottingham's matches, for instance, provided a cask of ale to the winner of one match and a golden arrow to the winner of the other. While distinctions between the upper and lower classes were significant during the Middle Ages, everyone attended such competitions, albeit in separate and

unequal manners. Matches were thus a festive and communal affair.

The Novel in Focus

The plot. *The Merry Adventures of Robin Hood* details the exploits of Robin Hood and his band of merry men. According to Pyle's version, Robin Hood never intends to become an outlaw, but his temper and pride lead him into trouble. When Robin Hood is eighteen years old, he meets a group of drunken men who poke fun at him and challenge him to an archery contest. Robin wins by illegally shooting one of the king's deer. As Robin departs, one man fires an arrow after him. The arrow misses, but an angry Robin shoots back and kills the man. The now doubly guilty Robin flees into the forest. Shortly thereafter a £200 bounty is set upon his head.

A FESTIVE DAY FOR ALL

~

A fair sight was Nottingham Town on the day of the shooting-match. All along upon the green meadow beneath the town was stretched a row of benches, one above the other, which were for knight and lady, squire and dame, and rich burghers and their wives; for none but those of rank and quality were to sit there.... Across the range from where the seats for the better folk were raised was a railing to keep the poorer people from crowding in front of the target. Already, while it was early, the benches were beginning to fill with people of quality, who kept constantly arriving in little carts, or upon palfreys that curveted gayly to the merry tinkle of silver bells at bridle reins; with these came also the poorer folk, who sat or lay upon the green grass near the railing that kept them from the range. (*Merry Adventures of Robin Hood*, p. 25)

In Sherwood Forest Robin gathers together a group of Anglo-Saxon men—including famous characters such as Little John and Friar Tuck—who swear their loyalty to him. Robin's band vows to despoil their Norman foes and other oppressors and take back the money that had been squeezed from the poor through unjust taxes, land rent, or wrongful fines:

> To the poor folk they would give a helping hand
> in need and trouble, and would return to them
> that which had been unjustly taken from them.
> Besides this, they swore never to harm a child

nor to wrong a woman, be she maid, wife or widow; so that, after a while, when the people began to find that no harm was meant to them, but that money or food came in time of want to many a poor family, they came to praise Robin and his merry men, and to tell many tales of him and of his doings in Sherwood Forest, for they felt him to be one of themselves.

(*Merry Adventures of Robin Hood*, p. 5)

The band becomes famous for its archery and fighting skills as well as its ability to strip the wealthy of their money. One strategy employed by Robin and his men consists of "invitations" to wealthy people to visit Sherwood Forest. Once inside, these guests are treated to a huge feast and entertainment. Payment for the festivities is then demanded. On such occasions Robin Hood typically appropriates one-third of the guest's money for his men and one-third for the poor, leaving the hapless traveler with one-third of his original sum. In this way, Robin becomes known as a most courteous and gentlemanly thief.

Robin's main adversary is the Sheriff of Nottingham. The sheriff is a greedy villain who cheats people, abuses his power, and is determined to capture Robin and collect the reward. In one famous incident, the sheriff sponsors a shooting match in Nottingham in order to trap the outlaw. He reasons that since Robin Hood is regarded as the best archer, he will enter the contest to show his skill. Robin Hood does indeed enter the contest, but in a cunning disguise. He wins the first prize, a golden arrow, without being recognized by the sheriff.

While Robin Hood had long before incurred the wrath of King Henry and others, he becomes a favorite of the next king, Richard the Lion-Hearted. One day King Richard, who had heard of Robin's talents, passes by Sherwood Forest disguised as a friar. Unaware of the stranger's identity, Robin Hood takes King Richard into Sherwood Forest to entertain him with a feast and demand money of him. Richard instead tests Robin's loyalty to the king and eventually reveals his identity, after which he employs Robin and his merry men as fighters in the Crusades.

Robin Hood eventually becomes an earl and retires from his life in the forest. After the death of Richard the Lion-Hearted, however, Robin begs King John to let him visit Sherwood Forest. The king gives permission for a short visit, but upon returning to Sherwood Forest in 1247 Robin decides to forgo the easy life of an earl and stay. Furious with this decision, King John swears that he will capture Robin dead or alive and sends the Sheriff of Nottingham after him. A great battle ensues and Robin falls sick. He seeks out his cousin, a prioress (nun), to have her bleed him, utilizing a common ancient medical practice in which people purposefully shed a little blood because they believed it would make them well. Robin's cousin, however, is furious with Robin for throwing away his wealth. Fearful that the king will turn on her because she is Robin's cousin, she cuts his artery and Robin Hood bleeds to death.

The king and the law. In one of Robin's many adventures, Queen Eleanor summons him to participate in a royal shooting match despite his status as an outlaw. Robin Hood presents himself before the queen immediately:

Here am I, Robin Hood. Thou didst bid me to come, and lo, I do thy bidding. I give myself to thee as thy true servant, and will do thy commanding, even if it be to the shedding of the last drop of my life's blood.

(*Merry Adventures of Robin Hood*, p. 185)

Queen Eleanor has wagered with King Henry that her archers will beat his. Concerned that no harm should befall Robin Hood, the queen makes King Henry promise that if her archers are victorious, they will be free to roam for forty days even if they are outlaws. The king agrees, unaware that Robin Hood and two of his band are scheduled to shoot on behalf of the queen. Robin wins the tournament and reveals his identity. King Henry is outraged, for his earlier promise means that he is unable to capture a famed outlaw who is now within his grasp. Afraid of looking like a fool, King Henry breaks his promise to the queen and sends many men to hunt down Robin Hood. Unable to return to Sherwood Forest, Robin grows desperate and throws himself upon the mercy of the queen.

King Henry's utter disregard for his promise aptly characterizes the power of the crown in the twelfth and thirteenth centuries. While the king proclaimed laws for others to follow, he himself was not bound to anyone. There was no check on his power, and nobody could force him to keep his promises or obey his own laws. This absolute power angered many people, especially the barons and nobles who wanted more power for themselves. When King John came to the throne, they seized an opportunity to correct what seemed to them a grossly unjust situation.

John was a weak king with many enemies. His hold over his barons, who chafed under his rule, became a tenuous one. In 1215 they revolted, refusing to pay yet another tax and insisting on political reform. The financially desperate king withered under the pressure of a hostile kingdom. On June 19 he was forced to sign a document called the Magna Carta. The Magna Carta stated that the law itself was the highest power in the land and stipulated that even the king himself must obey the laws of the kingdom. King John believed that he would eventually regain his previous degree of power. He never intended to uphold the Magna Carta. The king remained weak for the rest of his reign, however, and by the time of his death the Magna Carta was firmly established. It became one of the most important political documents of all time.

Sources. The modern image of Robin Hood was largely constructed by writers and actors of the sixteenth and seventeenth centuries. The figure of Robin Hood, however, appears in texts prior to those eras; early allusions to the notorious outlaw can be found in medieval ballads and a handful of historical references. One of the earliest texts that mentioned Robin Hood was the second edition of William Langland's *Piers Plowman*, which appeared around 1377. The work cites a priest who declares that he can recite the rhymes of Robin Hood and Randolph, the earl of Chester. Other references to Robin Hood can be found in literature, ballads, and records throughout the fifteenth and sixteenth centuries. While in some instances Robin Hood is not prominently featured, in other cases he is a central character.

Robin Hood and his colorful career remain the subject of much debate. Some scholars consider him an outlaw, others regard him as a murderer, and still others view him as just a kindly robber. In any case, while it is generally believed that the legend of Robin Hood is probably founded on a historical person or persons, the character's origins remain mysterious. Some historians contend that the legendary Robin Hood is based on the exaggerated deeds of a now-anonymous leader of a band of outlaws, which were plentiful in the twelfth and thirteenth centuries. Some speculate that he was really the Earl of Huntingdon, while others identify him as Robert Hood or Robert Fitzooth. It is also possible that the stories about Robin Hood originate from the exploits of two or more figures.

Other aspects of the Robin Hood legend are a subject of debate as well. Some versions of the tale state that Robin Hood was a noble who aligned himself with the common people, while other versions state that he was of moderate origins but had noble qualities. Robin Hood's exact dwelling is more easily traced. Apparently he (or

they) originally inhabited Barnsdale, which is located fifty miles north of Nottingham.

As an "outlaw hero," Robin Hood represented a different type of protagonist than the aristocratic and romantic heroes to which audiences of the later Middle Ages were accustomed. Robin Hood was not a noble yet clearly possessed aristocratic manners. He was a poor man's hero and represented the beginnings of a tradition of "noble bandits." The earliest known depictions of Robin Hood, however, did not portray him as

---

A ROBIN HOOD BALLAD

Lithe and lysten, gentylmen,
That be of frebore blode;
I shall you tell of a good yeman,
His name was Robyn Hode.
Robyn was a proude outlawe,
Whyles he walked on grounde,
So curteyse an outlawe as he was one
Was never none yfounde.
Robyn stode in Bernysdale,
And lened hym to a tree,
And by hym stode Lytell Johan,
A good yeman was he;
And also dyde good Scathelock,
And Much the millers sone;
There was no ynche of his body,
But it was worth a grome.
Than bespake hym Lytell Johan
All unto Robyn Hode,
Mayster, yf ye wolde dyne betyme,
It wolde do you moch good.
Then bespake good Robyn,
To dyne I have no lust,
Tylee I have some bolde baron,
Or some unketh gest,
[Or els some byshop or abbot]
That may paye for the best;
Or some knyght or some squyere
That dwelleth here by west.
(Ritson, pp. 2-3)

---

overly concerned with the well-being of the poor. In these stories, the principal figure whom Robin helps is a poor Lancashire knight, and his concerns are with the people who enforce the laws of the forest.

Events in History at the Time the Novel Was Written

Lore, life and art. Howard Pyle was born to a Quaker family in Wilmington, Delaware, on March 5, 1853. As a young child, his parents often read to him aloud, and he immersed himself in the various books of fables and literature found in his parents' home. The young reader matured into a person with a penchant for drawing, a love of heroes and fantasy, a keen eye for observation, and an unmistakable sense of spirituality, all of which were later reflected in his works.

Pyle was one of the first purely American-trained artists. During the middle of the nineteenth century, aspiring writers and artists considered Europe the center of culture. Most American artists studied in places such as Paris, France. Howard Pyle's parents could not afford to send him to Europe, however, so he trained in Philadelphia. At the time, Europeans generally ignored American art and artists, a stance that irritated Pyle. Unable to decide whether to become a writer or an illustrator, Pyle became both. Despite his American training—or perhaps because of it—his art eventually earned respect on both sides of the Atlantic.

Pyle was also a mystic and a realist. His mysticism stemmed from his Quaker background and was further fueled by the writings of Emanuel Swedenborg, the Swedish mystic. Quaker practices were not concerned enough with art in Pyle's view, yet such Quaker characteristics as "usefulness" manifested themselves in his life. Instead of working as a canvas painter, he chose to become a print illustrator, creating art that reached the entire population instead of a select few.

The Merry Adventures of Robin Hood was Pyle's first lengthy project of any kind. While his illustrations for magazines usually contained obviously American material, Pyle's books demonstrated that his imagination ran far beyond continental borders despite the fact that he traveled very little.

> The fascination of Europe was deeply imbedded in him. Although he sometimes rebelled against it, perhaps considering it a disloyalty to his Americanism, he could not erase those childhood hours spent poring over the old fables, folktales, and legends of Europe, nor his delight with reproductions of old pictures of sea monsters, ancient towns, great castles, men in armor, ancient ships and strange animals.
>
> (Pitz, p. 68)

As Pyle grew older, he became so concerned with standards of American illustration that he founded the Brandywine school in Delaware. The school produced many renowned artists and gained a large following. When Pyle died in 1911, he was considered the greatest illustrator of the day.

Reviews. Pyle envisioned projects of grand scale well before he actually began work on *Robin Hood*. The concept of uniting art and literature had been important to him for a long time. When *Robin Hood* was published in 1883, it quickly received recognition in both England and the United States as a work of great quality. The public and critics immediately perceived that his text was not merely a frame for the pictures, nor were his pictures subordinate to the narrative. There was a type of discourse between the two; the illustrations rounded out the characters and vice versa. Pyle, in fact, gained the recognition of English illustrators whom he himself had long admired. Biographer Henry Pitz commented that "with the publication of Robin Hood, Howard Pyle established himself in the first rank of both writers and illustrators of children's books. There was no uphill struggle for recognition, it came in abundance with this first book and remained with him to the end of his days and beyond" (Pitz, p. 70).

American frontier. The frontier has always played an integral role in the development of American character and in fueling the American imagination. The middle and late nineteenth century, however, brought the realization that the frontier was not limitless. By 1883 the railroad was an established entity that provided a direct link from one coast of America to the other. The image of the "wild west," however, was still strong. Primitive western conditions made law enforcement difficult, if not impossible, and numerous bandits sought out the seemingly endless resources of California and the Rocky Mountains. The promise of gold and silver tempted both honest and dishonest men into parts of these lands well beyond the reach of eastern standards and practices. Such notorious figures as Billy the Kid, Black Bart, and Jessie James all gained notoriety during this time as road agents and train robbers. Some robbed miners of their hard-earned riches, while others engaged in cattle rustling or fought for control of the range. Law enforcement was often so weak that local groups called vigilantes took the law into their own hands. Suspected criminals were occasionally shot or hanged without a trial at the hands of vigilantes.

Despite their criminal status, however, many bandits were made into folk heroes and compared to such legendary outlaws as Robin Hood. Robin Hood lived beyond the law in Sherwood Forest; many of these men lived beyond the law on the frontier. The average frontier outlaw, however, did not steal from the rich to give to the poor. Instead, he generally stole from anybody and kept it all. Some of the legends that sprouted up around these western personalities, however, depicted characteristics such as bravery, battle prowess, and rebelliousness that were reminiscent of Robin Hood. Pyle, however, did not fantasize about or identify with the western frontier. His love lay with history and not with contemporary phenomena.

Battle for land. Some general conditions that characterized the American West during the time of *Robin Hood*'s publication might be compared to the conditions of early medieval Britain. Both eras were times of extreme upheaval and transition in which land was a central issue. The land of the Saxons had been wrested away by the Normans more than 100 years before Robin Hood's

arrival, yet the pangs of the conquest were still sharply felt. Similarly, American Indian tribes were losing the battle for their land against the onslaught of encroaching civilization in the 1800s. Unlike the Saxons and the Normans, however, America's Indian and white populations did not manage to coexist. In fact, many American Indian tribes were decimated by the struggle.

For More Information

Briggs, Asa. *A Social History of England.* New York: Viking, 1983.

Gillingham, John. "The Early Middle Ages." In *The Oxford Illustrated History of Britain.* Edited by Kenneth O. Morgan. Oxford: Oxford University Press, 1984.

Pitz, Henry. *Howard Pyle.* New York: Clarkson N. Potter, 1975.

Pyle, Howard. *The Merry Adventures of Robin Hood.* New York: Charles Scribner's Sons, 1951.

Ritson, Joseph. *Robin Hood.* London: Jon C. Nimmo, 1885.

Rowling, Marjorie. *Everyday Life in Medieval Times.* New York: G. P. Putnam's Sons, 1968.

Strutt, Joseph. *The Sports and Pastimes of the People of England.* London: Methuen, 1903.

A Midsummer Night's Dream

by
William Shakespeare

Shakespeare borrows from the history of ancient Greece for the framework of his play *A Midsummer Night's Dream*. Using the Greek legend of Athens' king Theseus and the Amazonian woman Hippolyta, the play features Theseus as the Duke of Athens, which places the text historically during the twelfth century B.C., at the time of the Mycenaean rule of Greece.

THE LITERARY WORK

A play set in Athens, Greece, during the twelfth century B.C.; first performed between 1595 and 1596.

SYNOPSIS

Four Athenian youths, the victims of fairy magic, experience a night of confusion and love in the woods outside the city.

Events in History at the Time the Play Takes Place

Greece during the Bronze Age (1700-1000 B.C.) The progression toward the well-known democratic model of government in fifth-century classical Athens involved a long and gradual process. Prior to this early democracy, the Mycenaeans, who were early Greek settlers, had established a society based on a royal hierarchy. The Mycenaeans ruled primarily in the Peloponnesus, a peninsula of southern Greece that included the towns of Mycenae, Pylos, and Tiryns. In central Greece, Athens and Thebes were the main Mycenaean outposts.

Shakespeare's play depicts a time when this system of aristocratic rule was in place. According to this system of government, Theseus is able to dictate his wishes to his subjects. At one point in the play, for instance, he decides the fate of one of the young female characters—Hermia—with one command. Unlike the democracies that later evolved, in early Greek societies the king's command was law.

The palace lifestyle. The scarcity of records detailing the names and accomplishments of Mycenaean kings makes it difficult to determine their actual role in the society. However, it is certain that the towns of Greece were governed in a highly aristocratic fashion during the Bronze Age, with higher nobles overseeing the major territories in each king's district. This arrangement helps explain the familiarity that Hermia's father, a prominent citizen of Athens, had with Theseus in *A Midsummer Night's Dream*. The epics of the Greek poet Homer indicate that the relationship between the king and his men was somewhat feudal in nature: The citizens retained control of their land in exchange for a portion of the goods they produced. Although most archaeological findings provide clues as to the nature of the aristocratic lifestyle, the majority of the Mycenaean citizens were probably of a much lower class. These free peasants held common plots of land allotted to them by the king. At the lowest end of the social scale resided the slave population. Handled like possessions, Mycenaean slaves were in fact sometimes skilled craftsmen, and such characters are found among the mechanicals (a term for persons in the lower, artisan class) of *A Midsummer Night's Dream*.

The role of women. Women in ancient Greece were expected to bear male children for the community, which relied on such offspring to replenish their warrior ranks. Homer's *Odyssey* suggests that a woman had some degree of choice in whom she would marry. Her rights were limited, however. Fathers might arrange a marriage to bond two powerful families together or, according to tales by Homer about the time, a man might capture a bride for himself or win her in a contest.

It is evident that most women in ancient Greek society were inferior in status to their husbands. Both royal and slave women depended on the men, and in daily life the two types of women performed similar household tasks. Men viewed even royal women as property—"the prizes of contests and the spoils of conquest" (Pomeroy, p. 25)—and domination of a woman increased a man's prestige. Shakespeare's play incorporates this view of the female gender; the maiden Hermia is treated like the property of her father.

The legend of Theseus. Shakespeare found his Theseus character in the pages of classical folklore. While many legends surround this hero, perhaps none is quite so remarkable as Theseus's battle with the Minotaur. After his son has been killed by the Athenians, King Minos of Crete demands that the city send seven youths and seven maidens every year (or every nine years, depending on the source) as food for the Minotaur, a half-bull and half-human monster. Theseus sails to Crete to battle the monster. Upon arrival, though, Minos's daughter promptly falls in love with him. Her love for Theseus proves valuable to the warrior in his encounter with the Minotaur. Because the Minotaur inhabits a maze (known as a "labyrinth"), the monster's human victims usually become lost, quickly exposing themselves as prey. Minos's daughter gives Theseus a ball of thread so that he can retrace his steps out of the labyrinth. Armed with this tool, Theseus is able to slay the monster and find his way out of the labyrinth. He begins his voyage back to Athens, which has been liberated from the threat of the Minotaur by his bravery. Unfortunately, the young warrior forgets a promise he made to his father Aegeus (or Egeus) when he departed—that he would signal a victorious expedition by raising white flags on his returning ship. After seeing the black flags on the incoming vessel, Aegeus draws the mistaken conclusion that Theseus was defeated and throws himself into the sea in grief. The body of water in which he drowned himself thus became known as the Aegean Sea. Theseus, the legend concludes, succeeds his father to the Athenian throne and rules for many years.

THE PYRAMUS AND THISBE MYTH

According to mythology, Pyramus was a young Babylonian youth in love with his neighbor, Thisbe. Because their parents forbade their marriage, they had to communicate with each other through a wall that separated their properties. One night they agreed to hold a clandestine meeting at the mulberry tree near the tomb of Ninus. Thisbe, the first to arrive, was frightened away by a lion whose bloody jaws bore the remains of a fresh kill. As she fled, however, she dropped her veil, and it was subsequently shredded by the lion. When Pyramus arrived to find Thisbe's torn veil stained with blood, he was convinced that she had been killed. The heartbroken young man then took his own life with his sword. Thisbe returned to find her dead lover and killed herself with the same sword. Because their blood stained the nearby mulberry tree, its fruit was changed from white to crimson.

Hippolyta and the Amazons. At the outset of Shakespeare's play, mention is made of the Amazon queen Hippolyta. The Amazons were a group of warrior women who, according to legend, lived east of Athens in Asia Minor, across the Aegean Sea. Their society was limited to warrior women and female children and was ruled by Queen Hippolyta. Legends of the Bronze Age describe a number of battles between male heroes and the Amazons. The male warriors ultimately win all these encounters, and the various accounts of the story of Theseus and Hippolyta are no different. One version tells of an attack led by Theseus against the Amazons. Defeating the warrior women, Theseus rapes Hippolyta and kidnaps her. The Amazons retaliate by attacking Athens but are driven back. Other accounts maintain that the queen accompanies Theseus willingly. All stories agree that Theseus later takes a second wife, Phaedra, who is Greek. Tales of the manner of Hippolyta's death, however, vary.

The mechanicals rehearse "Pyramus and Thisbe." Charles Laughton as Bottom in a 1959 Royal Shakespeare Company production of *A Midsummer Night's Dream*.

Some accounts say that after being discarded for another woman, Hippolyta attacks her husband at his wedding feast only to be killed by a guest. But others contend that she gave her life in defense of Theseus or was slain by Hercules.

The Play in Focus

The plot. The opening act of *A Midsummer Night's Dream* presents the primary plot of the work. As the curtain rises, the audience finds Theseus, the Duke of Athens, anxiously awaiting his marriage to Hippolyta, queen of the Amazons. A conflict is quickly revealed when Egeus, an Athenian citizen, beseeches Theseus to reprimand his daughter Hermia. The distraught father explains that, although the girl has been betrothed to a young man named Demetrius, she wishes to marry Lysander. While both men seek her hand in marriage, the choice of a husband does not rest with Hermia, but with her father.

After listening to Hermia's father, Theseus commands that Hermia choose to marry Demetrius, join a cloister of nuns, or be put to death. The young girl, though, decides to elope with Lysander and reveals the plan to Helena, her best friend. Helena, however, is in love with Demetrius. She plots to tell him of his fiancée's planned elopement with Lysander in hopes of winning his favor.

The following scene finds a group of Athenians, "the mechanicals," practicing a play they wish to perform for the court at the event of Theseus's marriage. The skit is based on the tragedy of Pyramus and Thisbe, but in the bumbling hands of these actors the drama becomes a comedy. This glimpse of the mechanicals establishes them as comic characters whose antics will affect the course of the play.

Hermia and Lysander, meanwhile, escape into an area of woods that houses a community of fairies. Oberon and Titania, the king and queen of the fairies, reign here. Because of a domestic dispute, Oberon plots with his attendant Puck to play a trick on Titania by placing in her eyes the juice of a "western flower." This juice makes those who have been exposed to it fall in love with the first person he or she sees. But Oberon and Puck also overhear an argument between Helena and Demetrius. She has told him of Hermia's betrayal, but instead of shunning Hermia as Helena had hoped, Demetrius is determined to find the couple and stop the elopement. Oberon feels pity for Helena and asks Puck to place the flower juice in Demetrius's eyes so that he might fall in love with Helena.

Oberon drugs Titania with the flower's juice. Afterward, Puck comes across the mechanicals as they practice their performance. The mischievous

Titania and Bottom with the head of an ass.

Puck alters one of the actors, Bottom, so that he possesses the head of an ass. Titania awakens and promptly falls in love with the "ass," who is then treated like royalty.

The attempt to drug Demetrius fails, however. Puck makes the mistake of dropping the potion into Lysander's eyes. Oberon realizes that an error was made and drops the juice into the eyes of Demetrius, creating a situation where both Demetrius and Lysander now love Helena instead of Hermia. When the four youths again fall asleep, Puck remedies the mix-up by squeezing an antidote into Lysander's eyes. The lovesick fairy queen Titania receives a remedy as well.

After awakening, Titania tells Oberon of a dream she had in which she was "enamored of an ass." The young Athenians stir, and it becomes clear that they too appear to believe that the romantic events of the recent past were only dreams. Because Demetrius was never remedied of his love for Helena, the two couples appeal to Theseus to take back his previous ultimatum that Hermia should marry Demetrius. The king consents, and the couples plan for their weddings. Not only will Theseus be wed to Hippolyta, but also Lysander to Hermia, and Demetrius to Helena.

At the same time, Bottom awakens from his ass-like state, believing that he too has had a fan-

tastic dream. He quickly finds the other mechanicals to practice the play they are to perform at the approaching wedding feast. The final act of the play presents this performance to both the Athenian court and to Shakespeare's audience.

The romantic comedy of the Athenian youths. *A Midsummer Night's Dream* opens with the promise of a happy ending. Theseus complains that the slow moon "lingers [his] desires" (Shakespeare, *Midsummer Night's Dream,* 1.1.4) to wed Hippolyta. From the onset, the expectation of a union between the individuals is apparent. It is this trust in a satisfactory conclusion that Shakespeare's audience bears in mind when confronted with the troubles facing Hermia and Helena. Perhaps due to the unmarried status of their queen, Elizabeth I, playgoers in Shakespeare's time did not wish to see female characters in a play remain unloved. As one author explains, audiences were "loathe to see the charm of an attractive heroine 'withering on a virgin throne'" (Holzknecht, p. 181).

In addition, Elizabethan audiences would not accept a romantic comedy in which all couples were not happily matched by the close of the curtain. Shakespeare hints to his audience early in the drama that they need not worry. Helena remarks in the opening scene of the play that "through Athens I am thought as fair as she [Hermia]" (*Midsummer Night's Dream*, 1.1.227). Her suggestion of equality instills in the viewer a desire for both girls to marry their respective loves.

Sad Helena and distressed Hermia are eventually transformed into "lovers full of joy and mirth" (*Midsummer Night's Dream*, 5.1.27), but the passage toward this happy destination is not direct or entirely natural. The play concludes with Demetrius still under the influence of the magical flower nectar. In order for the union between this character and Helena to work, he must remain under the spell of this power. Demetrius remarks, upon returning to the palace, "Are you sure / that we are awake? It seems to me / That yet we sleep we dream" (*Midsummer Night's Dream*, 4.1.189-91). He is, indeed, the only character who does still sleep. The audience's quest for a union of all the young lovers, though, as well as its ability to immerse itself in the fanciful plot, allow Shakespeare to employ the nectar as an effective matchmaking tool. After all, his Elizabethan audience's primary desire was to see a happy ending.

Because of the centrality of the wedding theme, it is possible that Shakespeare composed the play with a specific marriage in mind—perhaps the marriage of Elizabeth Carey and Thomas Berkeley on February 19, 1596. The bride's father was Lord Chamberlain, the patron who owned Shakespeare's production company.

Sources. Shakespeare borrowed from Roman poet Ovid's work *Metamorphoses* when he created *A Midsummer Night's Dream*. The setting, theme, and several characters in Shakespeare's drama were influenced by the Roman poem. Study of classic literature was a central element in the education of a young English male of Shakespeare's era, and Ovid's work was widely studied at the time.

Metamorphoses is a collection of more than two hundred Greek myths and legends. Included are elements such as the character of Theseus, the Pyramus and Thisbe myth, and concepts of physical transformation. Shakespeare's character Bottom, for example, is given the ears of an ass, a fate also suffered by the fabled King Midas in Ovid's work. In drawing on *Metamorphoses*, Shakespeare used a significant work. The collection has been called "the most important source of mythical lore for all writers since Ovid's time" (Goold in Ovid, p. xii).

Shakespeare was also influenced by English poet Geoffrey Chaucer. Some 150 years earlier, Chaucer had told a story quite similar to *A Midsummer Night's Dream* in "The Knight's Tale," one of the verse narratives in his book ***Canterbury***

Tales (also covered in *Literature and Its Times*). Shakespeare used Chaucer's general plot as well as several character names.

"The Knight's Tale"	*A Midsummer Night's Dream*
Theseus—Duke of Athens	Theseus—Duke of Athens
Hippolyta—Amazon Queen	Hippolyta—Amazon Queen
Palamon and Arcite—young knights	Demetrius and Lysander—male youths
Emily—female love interest	Hermia—female love interest
Egeus—Theseus's father	Egeus—Hermia's father
Philostrate—Arcite's alias	Philostrate—palace official

The cast of fairies can also be traced to several sources. When Henry VIII converted his nation from Catholicism earlier in the sixteenth century, he eased a fear among England's citizens that a person might be labeled a heretic (a rebel against Catholic teachings) on the basis of statements that person made or the stories he or she told. This in turn allowed for a surge in fairy stories. Many English households blamed minor mishaps or lost possessions on the work of fairy magic.

In old English society the name Robin Goodfellow, or Puck, represented the figure of a mischievous spirit. He belonged to the second of four fairy classes: (1) trooping fairies, (2) hobgoblins, (3) mermaids, and (4) giants, monsters, or hags. Although hobgoblins could sometimes be endowed with evil traits, Shakespeare's Puck retains the merry jesting qualities found in most ballads, legends, and dramas of the time. A similar character is found, for example, in Ben Jonson's *Love Restored*, produced in 1616. Prior to the sixteenth century, fairies were considered to be of average or above-average human stature. The small size of later English fairies can be directly attributed to the inventions of Shakespeare. Quickly adopted by other writers, this notion of miniature size eventually developed into national folklore.

Events in History at the Time the Play Was Written

Elizabeth I. From her ascent to the throne in 1558 to her death in 1603, Queen Elizabeth I ruled England with a political genius that few monarchs before her had possessed. Although she has been described as difficult, pompous, and strong-willed, Elizabeth identified herself wholly with her nation. Unmarried, she used her single status to play her suitors off one another and do her bidding. Eventually Elizabeth would confess that England was her only spouse. She became totally identified with the nation and left it independent and united, though she had no heirs. Many scholars interpret Oberon's mention of a "fair vestal throned by the west" (*Midsummer Night's Dream*, 2.1.158) as a direct reference to the virgin queen. Bottom's waking speech discusses the enticing yet impossible notion of possessing such a figure. For the population of England, Elizabeth was the ultimate, unattainable love.

Elizabeth's court was not without its social intrigue, however. During her reign, royal patronage (support for select individuals favored by the queen) reached new heights. Elizabeth transformed local noblemen and gentry into advisors known as courtiers who depended on her favor to prosper. Still, she won an allegiance that few monarchs have equaled. This quality, combined with her lengthy rule, made her one of the century's leading figures. In acknowledgement of her rule, the second half of the 1500s came to be known as the Elizabethan Age.

Shakespeare's own company was not supported by the Elizabethan court but was privately employed. It still seems to have labored under certain obligations to the court, however, including the production of two new plays each year—a comedy and a tragedy (or historical play).

Elizabethan drama. Both comedy and tragedy were composed of a mixture of classical and medieval traditions. Developed from earlier Latin models, comedies of the Elizabethan era involved the lives of noblemen, and their often romantic plots centered around confusion over love. Typically, actors representing the higher classes spoke in verse, while characters of a lower class had prose speeches, a method used in *A Midsummer Night's Dream*. While the fairy nobles and the Athenian court members all speak in blank verse in the drama, the mechanicals speak only in prose.

Reception of the play. It is likely that *A Midsummer Night's Dream* was first performed as a private production for nobility and occasionally performed publicly by Shakespeare's company, Lord Chamberlain's Men. Aside from this, little is known, as is true of most dramatic productions prior to the Commonwealth period that began in 1648. The existence of a separately published work or spin-off entitled "The Merry Conceited Humours of Bottom the Weaver," however, indicates that the play was originally well received. *A Midsummer Night's Dream* has since then taken its place as one of Shakespeare's unfailingly successful plays. The popular comedy has been regularly staged over the years.

Marriage. Elizabethans, confined by gender (in the case of women) as well as class expectations, did not exercise much control in marriage. That Queen Elizabeth defied Parliament and public opinion by refusing to marry and bear children set her apart from most Englishwomen. She shocked the world with her statement that "in the end, this shall be for me sufficient, that a marble stone shall declare that a Queen, having reigned such a time, lived and died a virgin" (Elizabeth I in Jones, p. 88). It would be some time, in fact, before the general public came to

MUSTARD

According to Elizabethan lore, mustard supposedly contained a devil in its seed. Shakespeare was probably recalling this lore when he named one of Titania's fairy attendants "Mustardseed."

terms with her defiance of so-called female responsibilities.

The concept of marital duty ran deep throughout Elizabethan society. It taught that a man, according to the edict of God, should care for his wife as if she were a part of his own flesh; she, in turn, should consent to the rule of her husband. Furthermore, love for a spouse could only be earned through the proper enacting of one's role. Passion, thought to render the mind senseless, was regarded as an emotion to be avoided and suppressed. Hermia's father rebukes Lysander for an unearned and therefore false profession of love for his daughter, stating, "Thou hast by moonlight at her window sung / With feigning voice verses of feigning love" (*Midsummer Night's Dream*, 1.1.30-1).

As in ancient Athens when the play is set, marriage in Shakespeare's day was a social relationship involving the community as well as the couple. It was rarely desirable to marry out of love for one's partner. Instead, families arranged marriages for their children, paying particular attention to matters of age, social rank, and, of course, wealth. Both the family name and the accumulation of property depended on a proper union. The couple, as adults, willingly recognized their role in this social institution. When Hermia denies her union with Demetrius in *A Midsummer Night's Dream*, she jeopardizes the future of her entire family. Therefore, her father's anger is not entirely unwarranted. Until her marriage, a female child in Shakespeare's day lived according to a code of obedience to the male head of the household. When, in the play's setting of ancient Athens,

---

SHAKESPEARE'S MARRIAGE

Shakespeare's own wedding was not without elements of awkwardness and gossip. The Registry of the Bishop of Worcester shows that on November 28, 1582, William Shakespeare was wed to Anne Hathaway. Records also prove that in May of the following year, some six months after the ceremony, the couple christened their first child. The hasty wedding, however, did not mar the marriage or the reputation of the playwright. Anne survived her husband by seven years and is buried next to him. Although rumors persist about affairs Shakespeare may have had, both with a "Dark Lady" and a young boy, they remain unconfirmed.

Hermia's father remarks that her acceptance of his wishes is "due to [him]," he is also stating a fact of Elizabethan society (*Midsummer Night's Dream*, 1.1.36).

In the end, though, Hermia does win the right to marry the husband of her choice. Because Queen Elizabeth broke social protocol by refusing to marry, certain deviations from the standard became more accepted during her time. The queen's independence perhaps inspired Shakespeare to have Hermia break with the past and attain a partner of her own choosing. These social issues—the unfairness of forced marriages and the idea of permitting young people to select their own mates—were tackled in other plays of the era, too, such as

The Miseries of Inforst Mariage, by George Wilkins.

Dream study in sixteenth-century Europe. In sixteenth-century England, there was a wealth of books on the topic of dreams. The most notable of these was *Oneirocritica* by a scholar named Artemidorus. He suggested that a dream might have a number of different meanings depending on the circumstances of the dream and the dreamer's life. Artemidorus thus introduced the idea that a dream had to be interpreted, a belief that contrasted with earlier theories that a dream was by nature either good or evil. Another important work, the *Dream Book of Daniel,* was written by an unknown author. Printed in English in 1542, this book, like others of the era, focused on the difference between divine and devilish dreams. Going further, the scholar Macrobius attempted to classify dreams, paying most attention to those that led to higher knowledge or special insights. Church leaders also focused on "higher" dreams.

In Shakespeare's play, the dream world is a transforming place, from which the dreamers return greatly changed and more in harmony with their world. Their dreams lead them toward an enlightenment of sorts, perhaps to a greater self-knowledge. This use of dreams in the play reflects the great degree to which dream study captured the popular English mind in the 1500s. In fact, the folk calendar included a few holidays related to prophecy and dreams. Among them was Midsummer Eve and Day (June 23-24), a holiday also associated with fairies, love, and madness. Midsummer Eve was sacred to lovers, who celebrated the holiday by dancing around bonfires, calling on spirits to aid them in matters of love, and trying in various ways to divine who their future mates might be. At noon on June 23, for example, a maiden might take a mirror to a water well and reflect the sun's rays into the water. Such a maiden would be careful not to speak because that would break the spell. In a few minutes, the image of her future mate was supposed to appear.

For More Information

Amos, H. D., and A. G. P. Lang. *These Were the Greeks.* Chester Springs, Pennsylvania: Dufour Editions, 1979.

Camden, Carroll. *The Elizabethan Woman.* Houston: Elsevier, 1952.

Garber, Marjorie B. *Dream in Shakespeare*. New Haven, Connecticut: Yale University Press, 1974.

Holzknecht, Karl J. *The Backgrounds of Shakespeare's Plays*. New York: American Book, 1950.

Jones, Norman. *The Birth of the Elizabethan Age*. Cambridge, England: Blackwell, 1993.

Kay, Dennis. *Shakespeare, His Life, Work and Era*. London: Sidgwick and Jackson, 1991.

Ovid. *Metamorphoses*. Edited by G. P. Goold. In *Ovid in Six Volumes*. Vol. 3. Cambridge, Mass.: Harvard University Press, 1984.

Pomeroy, Sarah B. *Goddesses, Whores, Wives, and Slaves: Women in Classical Antiquity*. New York: Schocken, 1975.

Shakespeare, William. *A Midsummer Night's Dream*. Edited by R. A. Foakes. New York: Cambridge University Press, 1984.

"A Modest Proposal"

by
Jonathan Swift

As dean of St. Patrick's Cathedral in Ireland, Jonathan Swift saw firsthand the devastating consequences of famine on the poorer segments of the Irish population. Conditions in Ireland reached a crisis point in 1729. Thousands of men, women, and children suffered homelessness and poverty as the result of crop failures, high unemployment, rising prices, and trade restrictions imposed by the British government. Responding to the public outcry for a remedy, Swift wrote "A Modest Proposal" as a satire—a literary work that ridicules a subject through the use of irony and wit and is intended to create amusement, contempt, or anger in the reader. The essay blasted those whom he believed to be responsible for Ireland's state of affairs—the British government, corrupt landlords and merchants, and Absentees (those who fled the country in 1714 when George I took control of the government). He also criticized the "projectors," people who offered often absurd and simplistic solutions to very complex problems; "A Modest Proposal" provides just such a solution as obvious satire.

Events in History at the Time of the Essay

Irish politics in the early 1700s. The Tory political party came to power in England from 1710 to 1714, employing Swift to write as a political journalist. It was a happy period in his life that ended abruptly with the death of Queen Anne and the downfall of the Tory government. The

THE LITERARY WORK

An essay written and published in 1729 in Ireland.

SYNOPSIS

Responding to the desperate state of Ireland's poor, "A Modest Proposal" offers an absurd solution: Breed the children of the poor for profit and eat them.

opposing political party, the Whigs, came to power with King George I, whose reign would last from 1714 to 1727. Prime Minister Robert Walpole became the dominant party and government leader under King George. A strong leader, Walpole believed firmly in the right of the British government to oversee and regulate Irish affairs.

As early as the 1500s, England had exerted power over Ireland and fought to make the country a subordinate kingdom, a colony loyal to the British monarchy. By 1700, however, the Irish, who had their own Parliament and cultural identity, felt they were an independent nation that simply shared a king in common with the English. The British government recognized the Irish Parliament as a legitimate body, but felt that the Irish House of Lords was subordinate to the British House of Lords and passed a law to that effect in 1720. Known as the Act of 1720, the measure increased a trend set by

St. Patrick's Cathedral in Dublin. As the Dean of St. Patrick's from 1713 to 1745, Swift directly witnessed the suffering of Ireland's poor. His observations inspired the writing of "A Modest Proposal."

the long-standing Poynings Law of the 1500s, which had removed the right of the Irish government to meet or pass laws without England's approval. Together the two acts eliminated the rights of the Irish to make their own laws, mint their own currency, or exercise supreme judicial and legislative authority in their country. This enraged many Irish nationalists. These "Patriots," as they came to be known, initiated an aggressive fight for Irish independence from Great Britain.

The rise of the Irish Protestants and patriotism. Among those Patriots calling for Irish independence was Jonathan Swift. Although he had lived much of his life in England, Swift was born and died an Irishman. Appointed dean of St. Patrick's Cathedral in 1713, Swift was a devoted Protestant who supported the so-called Protestant Ascendancy. This was the coming to power of the Protestant landed class in the largely Catholic country of Ireland. These Irish Protestants included Patriots such as Swift who were fiercely anti-English and strongly supported the Church of Ireland—the equivalent of the Church of England in Ireland. Swift spent a considerable amount of effort defending the Church of Ireland from Protestants who dissented or refused to join it, such as the Presbyterians.

Irish Patriot tradition. The Irish Patriot philosophy was espoused most prominently by Swift, William Molyneux, and Charles Lucas. Swift and Molyneux in particular called for parliamentary independence and opposed the presence of the English in Irish government. They called for implementation of a number of measures to reverse English influence, including Irish settlement on lands seized by the British; Catholic containment; cheap government and lower taxes; investment in the Irish economy; and the right of the Irish Parliament to print its own currency. Moving beyond these general wishes of the Patriots, who were largely the landed Protestants, Swift's "A Modest Proposal" also called for help to be extended to Ireland's poor and working-class majority.

Trade restrictions. The English economy prospered in the early 1700s, partly due to the country's colonies and trade. Ireland, meanwhile, was in a period of decline. In the 1690s the English restricted Irish exports of wool and wool products. They then further restricted Ireland's agricultural trade with the European continent, at the same time increasing English imports into Ireland. These decrees had a devastating effect on the Irish economy. Because it could not export many of its products, Ireland lost domestic industries, especially in agriculture. As Ireland's economic health deteriorated, it became less self-sufficient and fell victim to high unemployment and inflation. The Irish became overly dependent on potatoes and pigs for subsistence, and when disease and drought harmed both during the 1720s, nationwide famine occurred.

The series of bad harvests continued into the late 1720s, and a devastating crop failure occurred in 1727. During this period, the English Crown tried to further devalue Irish currency by issuing "Wood's Coins." The coins would have made Ireland wholly dependent on England for trade because no other nation but England would accept them.

Public reaction. Irish nationalist cries for independence from the English Crown and pleas that citizens consume only domestic products echoed across the country in the 1720s. Patriots urged the masses to take matters into their own hands and rebel against the tyranny of the British monarchy. Pamphlets calling for independence circulated throughout the country, and Swift began using his literary talent as a pamphleteer for the Irish cause.

His first piece of protest literature was *A Proposal for the Universal Use of Irish Manufacturers,* a pamphlet that urged the Irish to buy only Irish-made products and to boycott English goods until the restrictive import/export laws were repealed. The tract, published anonymously (as were all of Swift's writings), was banned at once by the British government. The government arrested the printer, but after nine attempts to convict him, he was finally acquitted. The Irish people had achieved their first small victory in an incident sparked by Swift's writing.

Swift emerges as national hero. After that mild initial success, Swift began his famous M. B. Drapier letters, which implored the Irish to reject Wood's Coins and to seek independence from England. He tried to incite his countrymen into action: "By the laws of God, of nature, of nations, and of your country, you are and ought to be as free a people as your brethren in England.... All government without consent of the governed is the very definition of slavery" (Swift in Collins, p. 185).

Incensed by the pamphlets, the English Crown offered substantial monetary rewards to anyone who would name the author. But while the identity of the pamphleteer was well known in the Irish community, no one turned Swift in. His efforts led to the withdrawal of the patent for Wood's Coins in 1725, a victory that catapulted

Swift to national hero status. He would soon attempt to deal an even more lethal blow to the English in his biting essay, "A Modest Proposal."

Pamphleteering and "projectors." Political writing grew in the first two decades of the 1700s, ushering in a number of new developments in literature. Several newspapers were born, including *The Tatler, The London Examiner,* and *The Spectator,* and Swift wrote for all of them. The newspaper was first used as a political tool in this era, joining the pamphlet, which had continued to serve as a primary means by which a writer could influence public opinion. Daniel Defoe and Swift were the leading pamphleteers of their day.

Swift's *Drapier's Letters* are a fine example of pamphleteering at the time. Like most pamphlets of the era, they were published anonymously. With *Drapier's Letters,* Swift chose to use the pseudonym M. B. Drapier. But the pen name did not interfere with the heavy influence the letters exerted on public attitudes. Swift wrote a variety of other pamphlets as well. Some ridiculed a quack astrologer who called himself John Partridge. Another work, *A Tale of a Tub,* made fun of literary and scientific showoffs as well as others in society. But while his writings were influential, Swift lamented that the pamphleteers' advice was seldom put into practice. He complained about his own ineffectiveness:

> This kingdom is grown so excessively poor ... which I have been telling them [the public] in print all these years, to as little purpose as if it came from the pulpit.
> (Swift in McMinn, p. 127)

Such comments indicate Swift's growing disillusionment with the Irish people by the late 1720s and his inability to move them to action either from the pulpit or with his pen.

Age of Reason. The 1700s were part of an era called the Age of Reason, largely due to huge advances in science and technology. This "scientific revolution" fueled the belief in reason over emotion and promoted the idea that humans could achieve perfection through rational thought and scientific achievement. This concept applied not only to scientific endeavors but also to government and social institutions.

By 1729, however, Swift and others saw that the Age of Reason had not produced a more capable government or responsible society. In fact, society was stained by corruption and extreme social inequality. This was especially true in Ireland, where landlords (who were mostly English) focused primarily on making money. They did little or nothing to improve or maintain their property and became notorious for their ill treatment of poor Irish tenants. Such landlords reasoned coldly that profit was more important than people's welfare, an attitude that allowed them—as well as merchants and government leaders—to ignore the famine and unemployment that had cast the poor into such a wretched state by 1729.

Swift's biting pamphlets and satires emerged in response to what he considered the failure of the Age of Reason to improve society. He believed that "although reason were intended by Providence to govern our passions, yet it seems that ... God hath intended our passions to prevail over reason" (Swift in Bullitt, p. 10).

Religious battles. The Church of Ireland represented less than a quarter of the population but served as the official state religion. An off-shoot of the Church of England, the Irish Church was Protestant and opposed to both Catholics and Dissenting Protestants who refused to join it. Fear of a Catholic uprising (Catholics comprised 75 percent of the population) prompted the all-Protestant Irish parliament to impose severe restrictions on Catholic freeholders. All citizens, including Catholics and Dissenters, were made to swear an oath of loyalty to the Church of Ireland and pay "tithes," or taxes, to support it. In 1729 the legislature passed a measure that forbade Catholics from voting. This law, coupled with previous restrictions, prompted many to leave Ireland (as others had been doing since 1688). The Absentees, as they were known, were Catholics and Dissenters who fled to other lands. While some went to France, another popular destination was the islands of the West Indies; by 1729, a total of 4,200 people had left Ireland for these Caribbean islands, where religious freedom and employment were possible.

A supporter of the Church of Ireland, Swift opposed Catholics and, in particular, Absentees. Reflecting the view of the majority of Protestants, he blamed Absentees and their failure to pay taxes for many of Ireland's economic and social problems. The Church of Ireland saw emigration as an evil, as did Swift, who sought to have Absentees pay taxes to the government of Ireland while living abroad. This idea is one of many articulated in "A Modest Proposal."

Wretched state of Ireland. In 1727 King George II assumed the throne of England, and Prime Minister Walpole gained even more power.

Hopes for political and social reforms and for Irish independence were all but dashed. Just two years after George II's accession, Ireland experienced its worst year on record. Severe restrictions on the woolen trade by the English, coupled with the impact of famine, draught, devalued currency, and the continual threat of war, had disastrous effects on Ireland. The nation's poor were particularly brutalized during this period. As the economy declined, job competition became fierce. Violent outbreaks in the nation's slums—often between Catholics and Protestants—were common. Population growth among the poor drastically increased, and homeless men, women, and children became a familiar sight in city streets.

TARGETING THE ABSENTEES

In addition to decreasing the tax base, the loss of citizens boded ill for those who subscribed to the idea that people are a nation's most valuable resource. A popular economic theory at the time held that economic prosperity is proportionate to population size. Since this theory was widely believed, it generated hostility toward the Absentees. In "A Modest Proposal," Swift parodies this concept, insisting that if people are so valuable, we should eat them!

Walpole and the Irish Parliament did virtually nothing to aid the nation's poor. Instead, they aggravated the situation by raising taxes on goods sold in the country. Even the Church of Ireland failed to provide for the poorer classes, as it catered primarily to the landed elite. It was this sad state of affairs that prompted Swift to write "A Modest Proposal," a bold effort to change society's perception of Ireland's poor and provide for their welfare.

The Essay in Focus

The contents. Under the heading "A Modest Proposal for Preventing the Children of Poor People from Being a Burden to Their Parents or Country, and for Making Them Beneficial to the Public," Swift's essay opens by noting that anyone who can find a remedy for Ireland's devastating economic problems will be a national hero. He briefly describes the deplorable state of the king-

George II, under whose rule Ireland experienced its worst economic decline, leading to outbreaks of violence and soaring rates of homelessness.

dom of Ireland in 1729 and then goes on to define a solution to the nation's ills.

Utilizing a deadpan tone, Swift says he has thought long and hard about this issue and has "weighed the several schemes of our projectors," finally coming up with this proposal (Swift, "A Modest Proposal," p. 258). Before stating what his scheme is, he lists the many benefits his proposal will yield. One benefit, he says, would be that poor children will no longer be a burden to society; on the contrary they will "contribute to the feeding and partly to the clothing of many thousands" ("A Modest Proposal," p. 258). To add weight to his argument, he lists the exact costs of raising children, calculates approximately how many poor children would be affected by his remedy (120,000), and computes the profit to be derived from his own solution. Parodying serious journalists, pamphleteers, projectors, and politicians, Swift matter-of-factly points out the sound reasons for murdering the nation's poor children and using them for food, providing facts and figures to substantiate his claim.

Swift's proposition—that Ireland raise the children of the poor for sustenance, thereby reducing the nation's poor and creating a profitable, domestic industry untaxed by the English—is put forward in a reasonable tone. He insists that small children make very tasty and wholesome food. He has been assured of this by an American (who is presumably from a country where savages prevail). He then lists the many benefits of his plan in detail: poor people will finally have something of value to sell; Ireland's gross national product will increase £50,000 per year from the profit earned by the sale of 100,000 children annually; restaurateurs and vintners will profit because they will invent new gourmet dishes, wines, and ales that will sell for a high price to the upper classes; the country will no longer have to rely on pork and potatoes—food sources that are prone to disease and draught; and finally, the plan will promote marriage, reduce wife and child abuse, and induce landlords to treat their tenants better, as they will now view the poor as an asset rather than a liability.

Once he lists his manifold reasons for killing poor children, Swift states that he is making his proposal strictly for the good of Ireland. He realizes his plan may be a bit controversial but says the alternatives—increasing taxes, urging people to boycott English goods, and generally making do with less in order to help their neigh-

bor—are far more outrageous. Swift thus cleverly lists his true proposals for elevating the suffering of the Irish people, disguising them as a list of solutions that he would never propose. He warns readers:

> Let no man talk to me of other expedients:
>
> Of taxing our absentees at five shillings a pound:
>
> Of using neither clothes, nor household furniture, except what is of our own growth and manufacture:
>
> Of utterly rejecting the materials and instruments that promote foreign luxury:
>
> Of curing the expensiveness of pride, vanity, idleness, and gaming in our women:
>
> Of introducing a vein of parsimony, prudence, and temperance:
>
> Of learning to love our Country... :
>
> Of quitting our animosities and factions... :
>
> Of being a little cautious not to sell our country and conscience for nothing:
>
> Of teaching landlords to have at least one degree of mercy toward their tenants.
>
> Lastly, of putting a spirit of honesty, industry, and skill into our shopkeepers....
> ("A Modest Proposal," pp. 264-65)

SWIFT'S LETHAL PEN

Before he wrote "A Modest Proposal," Swift told his good friend Dr. John Arbuthnot of his intentions to display his frustration with the government in his writing. "I have a mind," he said, "to be very angry, and to let my anger break out in some manner that will not please them at the end of a pen" (Swift in Bullitt, p. 4).

Swift concludes his essay by stating that he welcomes response from any politicians bold enough to reply or offer their own solutions. But as an admonition to himself as well as other projectors, he insists that no remedies should be offered unless "there will ever be some hearty and sincere attempt to put them into practice" ("A

Modest Proposal," p. 265). He further comments that those who think it cruel to kill the poor at birth should ask them whether they would not have rather been killed at age one "and thereby have avoided such a perpetual scene of misfortunes as they have since gone through" ("A Modest Proposal," p. 266). Swift concludes "A Modest Proposal" as he begins it, insisting he is writing the tract unselfishly for the benefit of the Irish people. His proposal is not intended to bring him any personal gain.

Reviews and response. Published by Sarah Harding, whose husband, John, had printed *The Drapier's Letters,* "A Modest Proposal" was well received. It was reprinted several times in both London and Dublin within months of its first edition. Swift was already a national hero because of his *Drapier's Letters,* and "A Modest Proposal" added to his acclaim; though neither of the works were published under Swift's name, the identity of the author was well known.

Despite the commercial success of the essay, Swift was deeply disturbed at the nation's response—or lack of it. He had hoped the Irish people would take action against the British government and aid the poor. Instead, the situation worsened on all fronts. Swift became exasperated with the Irish people (and probably at society in general) and withdrew completely from politics.

Role of satire in the 1700s. In the late 1600s and early 1700s, satire became a popular literary genre. Developed about seventeen hundred years earlier by Roman writers such as Horace, Juvenal, and Persius, the style was perfected by Englishmen of Swift's time. British satire emerged partially in response to the failure of the Age of Reason, the inability of cold science to improve life in a way that would ease mass suffering.

Swift, John Dryden, and Alexander Pope became known as the era's most talented practitioners of satirical writing, and "A Modest Proposal" is considered the best short satire in the English language. The essay's central idea, to solve Ireland's hunger problem by eating poor children, turns on irony and wit, the key ingredients of satire. In Swift's view, satire exposed the injustices of life:

> Many great abuses may be visibly committed, which cannot be legally punished.... I am apt to think, it was to supply such defects as these, that satire was first introduced to the world.
>
> (Swift in Bullitt, p. 17, 22)

Known as the golden age of satire, the 1700s produced a host of acclaimed writers who, like Swift, attempted to "laugh men out of their follies" (Swift in Bullitt, p. 7). Satire was an acceptable form of ridicule during the Age of Reason, whereas outright attacks could be deemed treasonous and punished by death. Whether out of fear of government persecution or because he felt satire was a more powerful form of persuasion, Swift used the medium to urge change and vent his anger. He himself best explained how satire served him:

> Like the ever laughing Sage,
> In a Jest I spend my Rage:
> (Tho' it must be understood,
> I would hang them if I cou'd.)
> (Swift in Bullitt, p. 8)

In other satires, such as his 1726 novel *Gulliver's Travels* (also covered in *Literature and Its Times*), Swift views man as a sort of ridiculous creature, but one who is capable of doing good. "A Modest Proposal," however, has been called "the darkest pamphlet he ever wrote," and it reflected Swift's growing cynicism toward society (McMinn, p. 129).

For More Information

Bullitt, John M. *Jonathan Swift and the Anatomy of Satire.* Cambridge, Mass.: Harvard University Press, 1953.

Collins, John Churton. *Jonathan Swift.* London: Chatto & Windus, 1893.

Foster, R. F. *Modern Ireland, 1600-1972.* London: Penguin, 1988.

McMinn, Joseph. *Jonathan's Travels.* New York: St. Martin's, 1994.

Swift, Jonathan. "A Modest Proposal." In *A Modest Proposal and Other Satires.* Amherst, N.Y.: Prometheus, 1995.

Mutiny on the Bounty

by Charles Nordhoff and James Norman Hall

Charles Nordhoff and James Hall were two pilots who shared a common love of writing and adventure. Disenchanted with the post-World War I civilization, they decided to visit a place where money was not the only important medium of exchange. They subsequently journeyed to the South Seas. Shortly thereafter the two men wrote a historical novel based on an actual eighteenth-century mutiny that erupted on board a ship sailing near the island of Tahiti.

THE LITERARY WORK

A novel set mainly aboard naval vessels traveling between England and the South Seas from 1789 to 1793; published in 1932.

SYNOPSIS

A young midshipman relates the travels of the *Bounty* and the mutiny that takes place aboard the vessel.

Events in History at the Time the Novel Takes Place

The mutiny. On April 28, 1789, His Majesty's Ship (HMS) *Bounty* was seized from its captain and taken by mutineers. The decision to wrest control of the ship from its captain was a serious one. According to the strict naval code that ruled British ships at this time, those participating in the mutiny would be subject to the hangman's noose.

While the events that provoked this incident vary depending on whose side of the tale one hears, the act of mutiny itself has been recorded with the utmost care. Two of the *Bounty's* sailors, Fletcher Christian and Charles Churchill, entered Captain William Bligh's cabin on the morning of April 28. Armed with bayonets, these men seized the captain and forced him on deck in only his nightshirt. There they tied him to one of the ship's front masts and told him of their intent to take the vessel. During the passage from his cabin to the deck, Bligh could see that ap-

proximately twenty-one sailors were participating in the mutiny. Originally the mutineers had planned to set the captain and any of his followers adrift in the *Bounty's* small cutter, a single-masted sailing vessel. Upon noting some damage to the cutter, however, they decided to give the captain the launch, a larger utility boat. They loaded this boat with the captain and eighteen faithful crewmen, along with some meager provisions. Although the mutineers knew of the hostility of some of the natives in the area, they gave the sailors in the launch only four cutlasses (short, curved swords) with which to defend themselves. Historian George Mackaness noted that the mutineers hurled insults such as "damn his eyes" and "blow his brains out" at their former leader as the launch was lowered into the water (Mackaness, p. 133).

Captain Bligh's account. Although several accounts of the mutiny have been recorded, no history seems able to determine who deserves the blame for the events on board the *Bounty*. Certainly Captain Bligh's tyrannical behavior could have driven his men to mutiny, but the navy contended that Bligh's actions did not excuse the behavior of Fletcher Christian and the other mutineers. Bligh stated in the records he sent to the navy upon his return home that the desire to return to Tahiti provided the mutineers with their main motivation.

During their sojourn on the island, the sailors, normally accustomed to a life of hard labor, had enjoyed the pleasures of a paradise in the South Seas. This paradise had included native women. Bligh remarked that "the allurements of dissipation [on Tahiti] are more than equal to anything that can be conceived" (Bligh in Mackaness, p. 161). Indeed, one account of the mutineers' struggles after taking the *Bounty* has them arguing among themselves about the seizure of women.

Bligh also asserted that the mutiny must have been long in its planning. While docked at Tahiti, two of the *Bounty's* three anchor cables had been cut. Although at the time the captain assumed this to be the work of mischievous natives, he later maintained that the mutineers had played a part in the destruction.

Prior to his stint at the helm of the *Bounty,* Bligh had been regarded as a fair and capable sailor whose main concern lay with the health of his crew. Records show that he was involved in such acts of kindness as hiring fiddlers to entertain the men on the journey and giving up his bunk for sailors whose berths were wet. He blamed the problems experienced during the *Bounty's* voyage on the ineptness of his officers.

Christian's account. As the leader of the mutineers, Fletcher Christian has become a figure of much debate in naval history. Was he or was he not correct in his actions? Private journals of other sailors aboard the *Bounty* state that Captain Bligh frequently used insulting language toward his men. It often amounted to what today would be called "verbal abuse." He also regularly flogged (whipped) the sailors for minor offenses, such as insolence toward a superior. Although this type of conduct was not uncommon on naval ships in the eighteenth century, the severity with which Bligh carried out his punishments appears to have been unique. Each of the men whipped in such a manner eventually joined forces with the mutineers. It seems that the captain's abuse of power formed a lasting impression on his men. Bligh did not reserve his short temper only for those under his command, either. During the stopover at Tahiti, Bligh had one of the natives

whipped for supposedly stealing some of the *Bounty's* goods. His crewmen, however, were the primary recipients of Bligh's discipline. In fact, three men—Charles Churchill, John Millward, and William Muspratt—attempted to desert the ship when it was at Tahiti. Bligh caught the offenders soon enough, and these men later joined the other mutineers.

The crux of the problem between Bligh and his men appears to have stemmed from his dual role of captain and purser, or supply officer. Bligh frequently rationed food and drink as a form of punishment. The sailors viewed this action as an excuse for Bligh to line his own pockets with some of the ship's wealth. On Tahiti several of the sailors made friends with the natives, who provided the crew with gifts of pork or fruits. Bligh seized these private stores and did with them as he pleased. When the men complained of these actions, he threatened to whip any sailor who appeared dissatisfied with his operation of the ship.

The patience of the crew finally gave way the day before the mutiny, when Bligh accused some of his officers of stealing from the ship's store of coconuts. Out of thousands, four had been taken, yet the captain flew into a rage, cutting off all alcoholic beverages until the offender stepped forward. Reasoning that they had endured enough, over half of the crew joined together to overthrow their captain.

From slaves to breadfruit. The latter half of the 1700s saw a reduction in England's involvement in the African slave trade. By 1807 Parliament had outlawed any British participation in the international exchange of slaves. Until this point, however, slave trading had provided a lucrative business for many English merchants. Ships leaving England would journey to the coast of Africa, where they would exchange their goods for slaves. They would then travel to the West Indies or to the American colonies to trade the slaves for the sugar and molasses produced in these regions. On the last leg of the triangle, the vessels would journey back to England for a repeat of the trip. These routes composed the "Triangle Trade."

The purpose of the *Bounty's* voyage was the acquisition of breadfruit trees in the South Pacific. In the novel Captain Bligh states, "Considering that the breadfruit might provide a cheap and wholesome food for their Negro slaves, several of the West India merchants and planters petitioned the Crown, asking that a vessel be fitted . . . to convey the breadfruit from Tahiti to the

A criminal being flogged with a cat-o'-nine tails, a punishment similar to the whippings allegedly ordered by Captain Bligh.

West Indian islands" (Nordhoff and Hall, *Mutiny on the Bounty*, p. 10). Although Bligh's original journey to obtain these plants did not prove successful, he returned some years later to gather this crop.

The Novel in Focus

The plot. Told from a first-person point of view, the book records the travels of Roger Byam aboard the HMS *Bounty*. In the early spring of 1787, Byam and his mother entertain Captain William Bligh at their home in Withycomb, England. Enchanted by the Captain's tales of adventure on the high seas, Byam postpones his Oxford University studies for an opportunity to sail with Bligh on his next voyage aboard the *Bounty*.

Destined for Tahiti, the vessel's crew intends to gather the breadfruit trees that grow in abundance on the island. The breadfruit is viewed as a perfect food staple for black slaves being shuttled to the New World. Along with attending to other duties, Byam intends to compose a dictionary of the Tahitian language. Those in charge of the project hope that such a book will prove useful for future sailors' interactions with the natives in the South Seas. On December 23, 1787, the *Bounty* heads out for Tahiti.

On board, Captain Bligh proves a more formidable character than his manner at Withycomb had suggested. He rules his sailors with an iron fist, frequently issuing floggings at the slightest provocation. Byam, meanwhile, works diligently at his duties and makes the acquaintance of almost every sailor on the ship. He takes a particular liking to one of the master's mates, Fletcher Christian.

Once the *Bounty* reaches Tahiti, Byam spends most of his time on the island at the household of his *taio,* or native friend, Hitihiti. Because Hitihiti speaks English with relative fluency, Byam's dictionary develops with rapid progress. When the *Bounty* sets sail a few months later, all of the sailors express regret at having to leave this tropical paradise. The days proceed without incident until the afternoon of April 7, 1789. Upon hearing that four coconuts among several thousand that had been collected are missing, Bligh flies into a rage. He accuses every sailor on board of thievery, attacking even his officer Christian. The next morning the captain awakens to the bayonets of the mutineers. Led by Christian, the men force Bligh and eighteen other sailors into a small boat and lower them overboard. Although Byam wishes to leave with the captain, the lack of room in the small boat prevents him from doing so.

An illustration by Robert Dodd showing Captain Bligh and his supporters being set adrift from the *Bounty*. This aquatint etching was published in 1790, the same year that Bligh returned to England.

The other sailors then turn the *Bounty* back toward Tahiti, confident that they have seen the last of their oppressive leader.

The mutineers realize that the British naval forces will soon come after the missing vessel. As a result, they decide not to drop anchor at so obvious a port as Tahiti. They do, however, allow those wishing to do so to abandon the *Bounty* and make their home on the tropical island. Byam and several others agree to this arrangement. For the following eighteen months, Byam lives with his Tahitian hosts and even marries one of the women, with whom he has a daughter. Soon enough, however, the British ship *Pandora* arrives at the island. Captain Bligh had apparently made his way to England and reported the mutiny.

The captain of the *Pandora* orders Byam and the others taken as prisoners. They find themselves caged like animals on the ship, which sets out for England. Before leaving the South Seas, however, the *Pandora* falls victim to a squall and sinks along with thirty-three of its sailors and four of the prisoners. Byam, along with some of the other prisoners and sailors, manages to escape this initial disaster, only to encounter harrowing times ahead. For the next ten months, the survivors drift slowly along, making their way to a Dutch settle-ment on the island of Timor. By the time they arrive at the settlement, they are barely alive.

Byam and the other prisoners are then shuttled in another vessel to England, where they will stand trial for their part in the mutiny. On June 19, 1793, more than four years after the departure of the *Bounty,* the sailors return to the English port from which they had sailed.

Although all men are initially found guilty, a last-minute witness clears Byam of any wrongdoing. The lives of two other sailors are spared by the king, but the remaining ones hang for their actions. Although Byam remains much disturbed by the events that took place on the *Bounty,* he rebounds and eventually embarks on a successful naval career.

Captain Bligh. Captain Bligh is a complex figure. While the events of the *Bounty* have labeled him a tyrant, few histories deny the captain's capabilities at sea. A liberal user of floggings to maintain discipline, Bligh also accomplished feats equaled only by a select number of navy men. He survived the mutiny of over half of his crew and led the remainder of his men to safety. Moreover, the captain returned to Tahiti in 1793 to fulfill his original mission of gathering the breadfruit trees.

Nordhoff and Hall present a rather unbiased account of the mutiny against the captain. The authors side neither with the mutineers nor Bligh in restating the fairly complicated case. Although *Mutiny on the Bounty* only touches upon Bligh's achievements in sailing the launch to safety and eventually returning to England, a subsequent novel dealt with this episode of his life in great detail.

Leading eighteen men, Captain Bligh sailed an open boat 3,618 miles across uncharted waters. He rationed the few provisions they had to a sip of water, an ounce of salt pork, and an ounce and a half of bread per man each day. In addition, said Bligh,

> I issued for dinner about an ounce of salt pork to each person. I was often solicited for this pork, but I considered it better to give it in small quantities than to use all at once or twice, which would have been done if I had allowed it.
>
> (Bligh adapted from McFarland, p. 35)

Although he attempted to land the launch at several islands to replenish supplies, the hostility of the natives quickly led the sailors back out to sea. Navigating through rain and coral reefs, Bligh landed his men at the safety of a Dutch settlement on June 14, 1789, more than two months after the mutiny.

Once he returned to England, Bligh continued with his navy career. It seems that the experience of the mutiny did not change his temperament. Later, serving as the governor of an Australian settlement, he again faced rebels who resisted his tyrannical rule.

Sources. Because the mutiny referred to in Nordhoff and Hall's novel actually took place, the authors had several historical accounts to use as reference guides. Through Dr. Leslie Hotson at the British Museum and Elery Sedgwick, a trusted friend, the two authors began their research. They copied every report, chart, picture, and transcript that the museum held, and Commander E. C. Tufnell of the British navy sent them the deck and rigging plans of the *Bounty*. They searched booksellers and engravers for historical accounts pertaining to the period and for pictures of Captain Bligh. Finally the two men gathered their evidence and shipped off to Tahiti, where they co-authored the novel.

Some of the manuscripts Nordhoff and Hall may have used include the following:

1. A factual account of the mutiny by Sir John Burrows

2. Captain Bligh's "A Narrative of the Mutiny on Board His Majesty's Ship *Bounty*; and the Subsequent Voyage of Part of the Crew in the Ship's Boat, from Tofoa, on to the Friendly Islands, to Timor, a Dutch Settlement in the East Indies"
3. Letters from Bligh sent to Secretary Stephens of the British Admiralty, to Bligh's wife, and to Sir Joseph Banks
4. The log book of the HMS *Bounty*
5. The journal of midshipman James Morrison
6. The minutes of the court-martial of the mutineers upon their return to England

These documents would have provided the authors with the primary sources for interpreting the events that took place aboard the HMS Bounty.

Events in History at the Time the Novel Was Written

The Royal Navy in World War I. Published in 1932, *Mutiny on the Bounty* was written by two men who had participated in World War I, flying for a French naval squadron. Always a naval power, Great Britain entered World War I with the largest and probably the most modern fleet of ships. The nation amassed eight hundred fighting ships, over twice the size of the fleet that its enemy Germany boasted. Furthermore, the British were engaged in their annual naval maneuvers when Archduke Francis Ferdinand was assassinated in July of 1914 and the European powers moved toward war. As a result, they were already mobilized and prepared for action when hostilities began. Until the United States joined the other Allied forces (including England, France and Russia) in 1917, these nations relied on Great Britain for protection at sea.

Germany, however, was able to inflict some damage with its own navy, especially through the actions of Admiral von Spee in 1914. Von Spee commanded a fleet of German ships that was active in the South Pacific and Indian oceans, sinking British merchant ships and bombarding ports controlled by the Allies. Von Spee's fleet won a decisive victory over a British fleet in November 1914 but was defeated a month later near the Falkland Islands, off the coast of South America. Von Spee himself was killed in the battle when his ship was sunk.

Later in the war, the Germans used submarines extensively. They adopted a policy of sinking any ships that provided supplies to England and other Allied countries. As a result, ships from the United States were torpedoed and Americans killed. These attacks were one of the main reasons that the U.S. entered World War I in 1917, siding with the Allies and fighting against Germany and the Central Powers. The U.S. Navy joined with the British in battling the German submarines and soon proved decisive. When the war ended in 1918, a total of 1,000 warships had been destroyed on all sides, and more than 300 of these belonged to Great Britain. The Royal Navy also lost 34,000 naval and merchant marine personnel—the largest human loss experienced by any participating navy.

Tahiti during and after World War I. After the war, anxious to escape to a remote area of the world untouched by the ills of modern society, Nordhoff and Hall went to Tahiti. Although it seemed to present a paradise, in actuality the island, a French colony since 1880, did not escape the First World War unscathed. In Papeete, the town off the bay where the *Bounty* originally docked, the Tahiti Yacht Club serves as a visual reminder of the island's participation in the war. A great hole in one wall remains unmended, having been damaged by shellfire in a 1914 battle. In September of that year, two German ships, the *Scharnhorst* and the *Gneisenau,* docked in Tahiti to restock supplies. While in port, they were attacked by a French gunboat, the *Zéelée.* After sinking the French boat, the Germans dropped a few shells into the center of Papeete, then headed out to the South Seas. During the shelling, the Yacht Club incurred the damage it still shows today. The two German vessels were later sunk by ships of the Allied forces. Each year, the island celebrates the anniversary of the attack as a holiday. In honor of its participation in the war, the Tahiti Yacht Club has preserved the giant hole.

Other evidence of modern society had found its way to the island by the time Nordhoff and Hall took up residence there. In addition to a smattering of hotels and commercial retailers, Tahiti boasted one of the first movie theaters in the South Seas. Not all of this exposure to the outside world resulted in welcome changes, however. By the early twentieth century, as one historian notes, "white man's diseases [had] carried off whole generations of the best [natives]" (Eggleston, p. 21). In addition, many young men who left the island to participate in World War I and World War II lost their lives in the trenches of France.

In the novel, the character Roger Byam ob-

serves the beginnings of Tahitian loss. During his navy career, the former midshipman of the *Bounty* returned to the island he had so loved. He found that "war and the diseases introduced by the visits of European ships, had destroyed four fifths of the people ... and the future of the island appeared dark indeed" (*Mutiny on the Bounty,* pp. 374-75).

Nordhoff and Hall in Tahiti. Although Nordhoff and Hall had met while flying together for the navy in the war, neither one was anxious to pursue an aviation career. In addition to their love of flying, the two men also shared an affection for writing. They agreed to live together following the war and to jointly pursue the writing of travel articles. After a short period of time, Nordhoff and Hall convinced *Harper's Magazine* to finance a series of articles about the South Seas. In 1920 the two men sailed to Tahiti to write the articles.

Like the character Byam, Hall's first experience on the island involved the study of the Tahitian language. In his autobiography, he writes, "Their speech has great charm for a stranger from the northern latitudes. Only children of nature, isolated for centuries on such islands as these, could have fashioned words so warm and fragrant with the breath of the land" (*My Island Home,* p. 255). In *Mutiny on the Bounty,* Byam echoes these words stating, "It [Tahitian] is a simple language and a beautiful one.... It is rich in words descriptive of the moods of Nature" (*Mutiny on the Bounty,* pp. 85-6).

By 1929 the two authors had not experienced their anticipated literary success. They decided to collaborate on a novel and set off in search of a story that interested them. Hall proposed that they base their work on the history of the *Bounty,* using Sir John Barrow's factual account as a guide. After reading Barrow's book in one sitting, Nordhoff could not believe that no other novelist had written about so incredible a tale. He and Hall then set out to collect research and begin the book.

Reception of the novel. Originally Hall envisioned the tale of the *Bounty* as a trilogy. One novel would deal with the account of the mutiny; one would discuss Bligh's open-boat voyage back to England; and the third would treat the subject of the mutineers who sailed with Fletcher Christian. Neither author, however, anticipated that public interest would be so great as to warrant the writing of all three novels. To their great shock and excitement, the first novel was widely popular. Eventually they completed the trilogy

A scene from the 1962 film version of *Mutiny on the Bounty*. Marlon Brando (center) as Fletcher Christian stops the flogging of Captain Bligh (Trevor Howard) after seizing control of the ship.

with their novels *Men against the Sea* and *Pitcairn's Island.*

Critics praised *Mutiny* for its suspense, faithfulness to reality, and inclusion of picturesque details. A review in the magazine *Punch,* however, criticized its portrait of Captain Bligh.

> Bligh in sober truth was no monster.... If anything, Bligh seems to have been ahead of his time in his care for his crew, and, had he been the bloodthirsty ogre this book paints him, it would have been incredible that so many of his ship's company should have elected to follow him to what must have seemed at the time the virtual certainty of a lingering death from starvation and thirst.
>
> (*Punch,* p. 504)

This criticism, however, was a minority opinion. Other reviews described Mutiny on the Bounty as a skillfully wrought novel and a thrilling read.

For More Information

Eggleston, George T. *Tahiti.* New York: Devin-Adair, 1953.

Hall, James Norman. *My Island Home.* Boston: Atlantic Monthly, 1952.

Halpern, Paul G. *A Naval History of World War I.* Annapolis: Naval Institute, 1994.

Mackaness, George. *The Life of Vice-Admiral Bligh.* New York: Farrar and Rinehart, 1931.

McFarland, Alfred. *Mutiny in the "Bounty" and Story of the Pitcairn Islanders.* Sydney: J. J. Moore, 1884.

Nordhoff, Charles, and James Norman Hall. *Mutiny on the Bounty.* New York: Back Bay, 1932.

Punch 184 (May 3, 1933): 504.

Odyssey

by
Homer

Homer is one of the most romantic figures in the history of Western literature. According to popular belief, he was a blind poet who orally composed and recited both the *Odyssey* and the closely related Greek epic, the *Iliad* (also covered in *Literature and Its Times*). Today there is considerable doubt that the same poet wrote both of these poems. Some scholars also think it likely that Homer was not blind and that he had traveled extensively. Scholars also debate whether he wrote down the poem himself or just created the oral version that was later written down by others. It is widely believed, however, that the written poems are polished examples of the type of epic tales that existed in ancient Greece. Herodotus, the Greek historian of the fifth century B.C., claims that Homer was writing around 850 B.C., but modern critics contend that he flourished between 700 and 750 B.C. In view of the poem's ancient setting some 500 years earlier, only a few details of the tale can be confirmed as historical. Others are either the product of Homer's imagination or the remnants of epic tradition.

Events in History at the Time the Poem Takes Place

The Bronze Age. The events in the *Odyssey* occur in the Bronze Age, a period of ancient history from 1900-1150 B.C. The age takes its name from the metal that people of the era used for their weapons and household tools. In Greece and surrounding areas, Bronze Age civilization was highly sophisticated; kings lived in opulent palaces and commissioned artists to produce beautiful ceramics, mosaics, and metalwork.

THE LITERARY WORK

An epic Greek poem set around 1200 B.C. in Greece and surrounding lands; probably written in the eighth century B.C.

SYNOPSIS

The *Odyssey* recounts the wanderings of the hero Odysseus through the Mediterranean region, where he encounters a fantastic array of Bronze Age monsters and heroes on his journey homeward from the Trojan War.

Well-made roads and a highly developed trading system linked Greece with the Near East, northern Africa, and Italy.

Large, partially walled cities dotted the landscape. The kings, whose palaces and citadels towered over these communities, made certain that the region's food supply was secure and provided a basic framework of law and order. A simple system of writing emerged, but subsequently disappeared when the large cities were destroyed shortly after 1200 B.C. Archaeologists speculate that a series of local disputes as well as climatic changes and possibly earthquakes probably led to the fall of the cities.

Troy's demolition heralded the end of the brilliant culture of Bronze Age Greece. Legends of a great war in Troy (located in modern-day Turkey) portray it as the most remarkable battle of the Bronze Age, drawing fighting men from all over the eastern Mediterranean region. It is this war to which Homer's hero Odysseus is called from his native island of Ithaca.

An illustration of Troy as it is thought to have looked on the eve of the Trojan War.

The legendary Trojan War. According to the story, the war in Troy began when Paris, son of Troy's king, abducted the beautiful Helen, the Queen of Sparta, and took her home to Troy with him. In retaliation, Helen's husband, Menelaus, assembled a huge fleet that included Odysseus and his followers. The Greeks initiated a ten-year siege against the Trojan stronghold of Troy. They finally won the city through a clever ploy devised by Odysseus himself. The attackers built a huge wooden horse, filled its hollow belly with armed warriors, and then made a show of sailing away, as if defeated. The Trojans did not know what to make of this lone horse outside their walls, but they were eventually persuaded that it was left by the Greeks as a gift. Despite the warnings of a prophet and other signs of doom, the Trojans were reassured by their enemy's departure and dragged the horse inside the city. Under cover of night, the hidden warriors streamed out of the horse, opened the gates for their fellow Greeks (who had sailed back into the harbor), and sacked Troy.

The *Odyssey* includes a scene in which a singer relates the story of Troy's destruction and the slaughter that took place there. Hearing this song on his long journey home, Odysseus breaks down and weeps, but not because the hero feels guilty about the havoc he caused in Troy. Instead, Odysseus laments his long absence from home and his separation from friends. He even mentions that, upon leaving Troy, he sacked yet another city, known as the city of the Ciconians: "I sacked their city and killed their people, / and out of their city taking their wives and possessions / we shared them out" (Homer, *Odyssey*, 8.40-2). Such events illustrate the day-to-day life of a warrior in the world of Homeric epic.

Mycenaean navigation. The people of Mycenae and other towns on the southern Greek mainland spread their influence throughout much of the area. Their impact on the region was so great that an era in Greek history—the Mycenaean Age (1400-1150 B.C.)—was named after them. Memories of seafaring in the western Mediterranean at this time may provide the background for Odysseus's wanderings after he leaves Troy. A standard trade route went past Odysseus's island home of Ithaca, located off the northwest coast of Greece. The route continued toward the "heel" of Italy and then extended to Sicily and Malta.

Greek sailors regularly voyaged more than five hundred miles from home, and Mycenaean artifacts and influences have been traced as far away as Sweden, Italy, and Slovakia. Such findings suggest that the stories of Odysseus's journeys may not have been merely fables; perhaps they were based in part on reports of actual journeys. When, near the end of the *Odyssey*, the sorceress Circe tells Odysseus how to return from her enchanted island to his home, her directions are so specific that some historians believe that Homer relied upon an actual sailing manual of sorts. Historians have long battled over the exact geographic location of Odysseus's wanderings, but no one is really certain about the route that he allegedly took. Homer's own eighth-century society did not explore or trade nearly to the same extent as the previous society, so much of the geographic material contained in the *Odyssey* may have been preserved and passed down in legends.

ORAL POETRY AND THE HEROIC AGE

Many of the subjects of Greek oral poetry come from events of the so-called Heroic Age, the legendary age in which Homer's heroes lived (imagined to be 1250-1150 B.C.). The main function of the oral poet was to preserve the memory of the great deeds of a society's heroes by composing and transmitting in song a narrative of their exploits. Such songs were usually embellished with the passage of time.

The Poem in Focus

The plot. The epic opens with a dialogue between the gods Zeus and Athena, who discuss the fate of Odysseus, who has been struggling to return home from the Trojan War for ten years. He has been kept from his goal by the wrath of the god Poseidon, whose son (the one-eyed Cyclops) Odysseus had injured. Because of Poseidon's grudge, Odysseus has been forced to wander the known world, experiencing countless adventures along the way. These include encounters with the sorceress Circe and the beautiful and seductive nymph Calypso. He also visits the Land of the Dead, where he speaks to the spirits of his mother and slain comrades.

While Odysseus sails through these foreign lands in his struggle to return to his beloved family, his wife—the beautiful, clever, and wealthy Penelope—is courted by 108 suitors who are hopeful that Odysseus has died. Each of these men would like nothing more than to seize Odysseus's power and property for himself. Vague threats are leveled at Telemachus, Odysseus's son, who is

coming of age and will soon be able to assume his father's place. The suitors all move into Penelope's palace at the same time and refuse to budge, pressing her for a decision, but she remains faithful (as she has for twenty years) to the hope that Odysseus will one day return.

All along Penelope has manipulated the suitors in an effort to keep her options open and acquire valuable gifts. The suitors, however, caught her at one of her tricks. Penelope had claimed that before she remarries she must finish weaving a funeral shroud for Laertes, Odysseus's aging father. But although she wove all day, at night she undid her own progress, secretly unraveling the work accomplished in public the previous day. When the *Odyssey* opens, the suitors have now learned from this episode and are forcing Penelope to make daily progress in her weaving.

Odysseus, whose name in Greek means "man of pain," finally returns to Ithaca, although he has been stripped of every possession. Odysseus dons a disguise and, with the help of his now-adult son, disposes of the suitors. In a touching recognition scene, Penelope comes to realize that the disguised stranger is her long-lost husband. Odysseus then is finally reunited with the wife he has sought for so long to rejoin.

The gods. In the beginning of the *Odyssey*, Odysseus is trapped in the "hollowed caverns" of the nymph Calypso, who wants the warrior to be her husband. She promises to make him immortal should he stay with her. But Odysseus remains adamant in his desire to rejoin his family—and indeed this is the fate that has been decided for him by the immortal gods: "But when in the circling of the years that very year came / in which the gods had spun for him his time of homecoming / to Ithaca, not even then was [Odysseus] free of his trials / nor among his own people" (*Odyssey*, 1.16-18).

The gods speak to Calypso, who reluctantly allows Odysseus to leave her island. In the *Odyssey*, gods and goddesses are often involved in events that affect the hero. But Zeus, the father of the gods, insists that the gods themselves are not responsible for what happens to human beings. Instead, humans bring misery on themselves: "Oh for shame, how the mortals put the blame upon us / gods, for they say evils come from us, but it is they, rather, / who by their own recklessness win sorrow beyond what is given" (*Odyssey*, 1.32-4).

In the *Odyssey*, the Greek gods are portrayed as "anthropomorphic"—that is, they take the form and attributes of human beings. Athena, the goddess of wisdom, for example, dons different human disguises and takes frequent walks among the mortals. Like human beings, the gods and goddesses have unique personalities and motivations, fighting battles among themselves as well as with human beings. Athena and Zeus, her father, support Odysseus and try to help him reach home. Poseidon, the god of the sea, strives against him, seeking vengeance because Odysseus put out the eye of one of Poseidon's sons.

The religious aspect of the relationship between the gods and the mortals of the *Odyssey* remains rather shadowy. Sacrifices to the gods are the strongest element of worship shown in the poem. It is, in fact, because Odysseus has sacrificed more to the gods than any other man has that he wins the support of the father of the gods, Zeus, in his struggles to return to Ithaca.

Sacrifice involved the ritual slaying of an animal, generally a cow or a sheep, in the name of a god or goddess. One of the most detailed descriptions of a sacrifice in the *Odyssey* occurs when Nestor, to whom Odysseus's son Telemachus goes for advice, sacrifices a heifer to Athena. The ritual combines painstaking preparations, such as dipping the cow's horns in gold, with determined blood-letting:

> Stratios and the noble Echephron led the cow
> by the horns, and Aretos came from the inner
>   chamber carrying
> lustral water in a flowered bowl, and in the
>   other hand
> scattering barley in a basket. Steadfast
>   Thrasymedes
> stood by with the sharp ax in his hand, to
>   strike down the heifer.
> Perseus held the dish for the blood, and the
>   aged horseman
> Nestor began with the water and the barley,
>   making long prayers,
> to Athene [Athena], in dedication, and threw
>   the head hairs in the fire.
>
> (*Odyssey*, 3.439-46)

Hades. In a section of the poem, Odysseus visits the Greek underworld, which is ruled by the Greek god of death, Hades, and his bride Persephone. The hero speaks there to the spirits of his mother and his companion Elpenor, who recently died. He also converses with a variety of Greek heroes of both sexes.

The dead spirits are summoned to Odysseus by a blood sacrifice that seeps into the ground; the spirits flock around the blood in order to drink it, and only then may Odysseus speak to the souls of the dead:

> [Now gathered] brides, and young unmarried
>   men, and long-suffering elders,
> virgins, tender and with the sorrows of young
>   hearts upon them,
> and many fighting men killed in battle,
>   stabbed with brazen
> spears, still carrying their bloody armor upon
>   them.
> These came swarming around my pit from
>   every direction
> with inhuman clamor, and green fear took
>   hold of me.
>
> (*Odyssey*, 11.34-43)

The land of the dead appears to be a place of despair and unhappiness. Even the names of places in Hades are sorrowful, as shown by the names of the mythic rivers in the underworld: Grief Flood, Fireblast River, Wailing Stream, and Loathing Water (*Odyssey*, 10.513-14). Homer's grim picture of the afterworld is reinforced by the words of Odysseus's mother, who has died of grief at the prolonged absence of her son. Her spirit appears and tells Odysseus what happens to human beings after death:

> The sinews no longer hold the flesh and the
>   bones together,
> and the spirit has left the white bones, all the
>   rest
> of the body is made subject to the fire's
>   strong fury,
> but the soul flitters out like a dream, and flies
>   away.
>
> (*Odyssey*, 11.219-22)

RELEVANT DATES AND AGES

Bronze Age: 1900-1150 B.C.

Mycenaean culture: 1400-1150 B.C.

Troy is destroyed: c. 1200 B.C. (traditional dates—1184 B.C. or 1250 B.C.)

Greek Dark Ages: 1150-800 B.C.

Homer writes the *Odyssey*: 750-700 B.C.

According to Homer, the spirits of all people, whether good or evil in life, wind up in the same place. The Greek word *psuche* (psyche), which means "soul," is used in the *Odyssey* to refer to the image of a person visible in Hades or in dreams. According to the poem, this visual image, which always goes to Hades, is all that remains after the death of the body.

Odysseus and his companions escape from the Sirens: Book 12 of the *Odyssey*.

The land of Hades is a dark world of sorrowful shadows where the spirits of the dead lament forever. Odysseus's visit reinforces the seriousness of his choice to leave Calypso to rejoin his beloved family. His decision indicates that he prefers the temporary joys and pains of a human life with family and a home on earth, even if it means eventual residence in Hades, to an eternal life of bliss with an immortal nymph.

Family ties. In many respects, the center of the *Odyssey* is the hero's wife back in Ithaca, Penelope. Odysseus struggles to be reunited with her, but uncertainty about their relationship runs through the poem. Questions about whether Odysseus will return home in time and whether Penelope will have waited for him are raised throughout the *Odyssey*. Odysseus's long absence has put their marriage in jeopardy because he had previously given her permission to do as she pleases regarding future matches should he fail to return:

> I do not know if the god will spare me . . .
> there in Troy; here let everything be in your
>   charge.
> You must take thought for my father and
>   mother here in our palace,
> As you do now, or even more, since I shall be
>   absent.
> But when you see our son grown up and
>   bearded, then you may
> marry whatever man you please, forsaking
>   your household.
>
> (Odyssey, 18.265-70)

If Penelope had gone ahead and married another man—for example, one of the suitors—without knowing whether Odysseus were dead or alive, that second marriage would have been valid in the eyes of society at that time, even if Odysseus returned at a later date. Marriage was approached from a practical, rather than legal, perspective. If a relationship between a man and a woman had the appearance of marriage, then the partnership was viewed as a marriage by others in the community. A long-absent husband, or one who failed to provide for his wife, called the validity of marriage into question. Penelope's future, however, was not entirely in her control because of the limits placed on women in her society.

"Homeric" society, the society of the poet's characters, was organized according to the *oikos*, or family unit. An *oikos* consisted of a male, a female, children, and other people or animals that fell under the protection of the male. There was an emphasis on continuing the family unit in the future, and thus it was important for the sons of the family to produce male heirs. The leader of the *oikos* was always the most prominent male, generally the father/husband, but in the event of his death that responsibility fell on the eldest son. If the sons were too young to assume the family leadership, the wife was permitted to control the possessions and home of the *oikos*.

Penelope was in just such a situation. If, having concluded that her husband was actually dead, Penelope had decided to leave Odysseus's house, she was free to return to the house of her father and rejoin his *oikos*. She was in fact free to do this at any time in their marriage; to do so constituted getting a divorce. When Telemachus, son of Penelope and Odysseus, was old enough to assume the role of leader of the *oikos,* he could also send his mother back to her father, although he would be obligated to pay for that option. If the death of Odysseus was confirmed, Telemachus would be able to marry his mother off as he liked.

Sources. Homer was part of a mainly oral culture by which people received most of their information not from written sources but from word of mouth. As a member of a migrant people who had been driven out of their sophisticated cities by war and other misfortunes, it is almost inevitable that Homer would have heard tales about heroes of the glorious past such as Odysseus: "In Homer . . . the oral tradition which went back to Mycenaean times reached its culmination and its end. . . . Centuries of history have gone into the making of . . . [the] *Odyssey*" (Ehrenberg, p. 10).

Reviews. The *Odyssey* became the first Greek text to be translated for use by Roman schoolboys, and its fame continues unabated. For the Greeks, Homer's *Iliad* and *Odyssey* became a primary source for the mythology and legend that dominated much of their artistic culture. At least one Greek, however, remained torn about the value of Homer's work: some three hundred years after the *Odyssey* was written, Plato blames Homer for telling unpleasant tales about the gods, heroes, and Greek underworld.

Plato had positive comments about Homer as well. For instance, he praised the poet for presenting images of self-control in Odysseus, particularly when the hero, in a moment of rage, wants to slay all the suitors himself rather than wait for assistance. He wisely waits, saying "Endure, my heart, you have suffered more shameful things than this" (*Odyssey*, 20.18). This declaration is significant, as throughout Odysseus's long journey he has been a victim of his own lack of self-control, giving in to emotional reactions without considering the consequences. In contrast, near the end of the *Odyssey*, Odysseus has finally gained a great degree of self-mastery.

In the fifth century B.C., the Greek historian Herodotus credited Homer with having "made" the great gods and heroes about which he wrote; in fact, the word *poet* comes from the Greek verb "to make." Herodotus singled out Homer as the finest transmitter of the Heroic Age that ancient Greece had produced.

PLATO ON HOMER'S HADES

Three centuries after Homer wrote the *Odyssey*, Plato reacted strongly to the lines in which the hero Achilles claims: "I would rather labor on earth in service to another, / to a man who is landless, with little to live on, / than be king over all the dead" (*Odyssey*, 11.489-91). Plato responds to this declaration in the ***Republic*** (also covered in *Literature and Its Times*), which features Socrates as the primary speaker:

> What if [men] are to be brave? Should not one tell them things that will make them least afraid of death? Or do you think anyone ever becomes brave if this fear possesses him?... Further, can he be without fear of death, and prefer it to defeat in battle and to slavery, if he believes in an underworld full of terrors?... We must then ... supervise such tales and those who undertake to tell them, and beg them not to rail at things in the underworld in the unrestrained manner they do, but rather to praise them, as their stories are neither true nor beneficial to future warriors.

> (Plato, *Republic*, 386B-C)

Events in History at the Time the Poem Was Written

Homer's culture. Homer's culture emerged out of the Dark Ages, a historical period of obscurity and decline that ended around 800 B.C. It was formed by exiles who migrated away from the Greek mainland toward Asia Minor after the fall of the Mycenaean cities. During this period of destruction, the Greek mainland underwent a devastating decline in population, as well as the almost complete disintegration of urban life. Those who remained tended to huddle together in small hamlets that were probably organized around a tribal system called the *ethnos*.

People resettled in the general vicinities of the great Mycenaean cities over time, but in an entirely different way from their predecessors. They encircled the entire city, or *polis*, with a wall; earlier designs featured walls that only enclosed the area where the aristocracy lived. Inside the walls, people were able to remain organized within a tribal system. This *polis* was the forerunner of the later Greek city-state; "it was in fact, both more and less than a state, rather a human community, often very small indeed, always held together by narrow space, by religion, by pride, by life" (Ehrenberg, p. 7).

In the eighth century B.C., the period when Homer probably composed the *Odyssey*, the *polis* underwent a political change. Those people in control of the land surrounding and within the city walls began to concentrate their power. Since kings and royal families were no longer a feature of these societies, powerful landowners emerged as a new aristocracy. The towns in which the landowners lived began to grow in importance. A new type of human community wherein citizens were ruled by a class of noble landowners gradually formed. The emergence of this new noble class may have inspired the reappearance of tales such as the *Odyssey*, which depicts the exploits and problems of wealthy leaders. In all probability the noble class liked to trace its ancestry to the same legendary heroes that Homer's tales depict.

The people of Homer's culture, whose ancestors were almost certainly Mycenaean-era refugees, were largely responsible for reviving the legends of the Heroic Age. This cultural revival took various forms, including the production of lengthy poems that recounted the heroic exploits of earlier days. From Homer's descriptions of cities in the *Odyssey*, historians have speculated that he must have lived in one of the walled cities that were sprouting up in this era. Smyrna is often mentioned as a possible home of the poet.

The alphabet. In the eighth century B.C., the Greeks were in regular contact with the Phoenician culture that was based in present-day Syria. Important trading partners with the Greeks, the Phoenicians brought with them what was probably their most significant contribution to Greek culture and ultimately to the history of the world: the alphabet. The Phoenician alphabet, which had characters for consonants only, first appeared in Greece around 850 B.C. Building on this base, the Greeks modified it by adding symbols for vowel sounds and for other sounds that were uniquely Greek. In fact, the word *alphabet* comes from the first two letters—the vowel *alpha* (*a*) and the consonant *beta* (*b*)—of the Greek alphabet. In time the system of writing became fairly uniform throughout the land. The writing of Homer's poem, which occurred sometime in the eighth century B.C., thus dates from shortly after the introduction of the alphabet.

For More Information

Ehrenberg, Victor. *From Solon to Socrates: Greek History and Civilization during the 6th and 5th Centuries B.C.* London: Methuen, 1973.

Hammond, N. G. L. *A History of Greece to 322 B.C.* Oxford: Clarendon Press, 1959.

Higgins, Reynold. *Minoan and Mycenaean Art.* New York: Oxford University Press, 1981.

Homer. *Odyssey.* Translated by Richmond Lattimore. New York: HarperPerennial, 1991.

Lacey, W. K. *The Family in Classical Greece.* London: Thames and Hudson, 1968.

Plato. *Republic.* Translated by G. M. A. Grube. Indianapolis: Hackett, 1974.

The Once and Future King

by
T. H. White

Born to English parents in Bombay, India, in 1906, Terence Hanbury White came to England in 1915 at the height of World War I. Throughout the early years of his life, Europe was in a constant state of flux. A communist government came to power in Russia, while fascist sentiments grew in Italy, Spain, and Germany. Underlying the plot in *The Once and Future King* is a discussion of politics and values that can be traced to these events.

Events in History at the Time the Novel Takes Place

The historical King Arthur. Populated with magicians, knights, crusades, and damsels in distress, legends of King Arthur have fascinated the Western world for many centuries. There is, despite this continuing popularity, no proof of a historical King Arthur, but tantalizing clues to his possible existence reach back into the dim past.

Arthur is generally imagined to have lived in the fifth or early sixth century, an era of turmoil for Britain. The Roman Empire, which had invaded the British Isles and governed its native Celtic peoples since the first century B.C., suddenly pulled its troops out of Britain. This left the region's inhabitants defenseless against attacks by the Saxons, invaders from ancient Scandinavia. Many details of the Arthurian legend clearly place it in this historical period of change for Britain. Arthur's very name, a Welsh form of the Roman name *Artorius,* suggests that he lived

THE LITERARY WORK

A collection of novels set in the fifth or sixth century A.D.; written between 1938 and 1958, first published in a single volume in 1958.

SYNOPSIS

A young boy grows up under the guidance of Merlyn the magician to become King Arthur of England. As king, he attempts to bring order to the realm, then experiences a series of personal trials as his kingdom deteriorates around him.

during the fifth century, when inhabitants of the British Isles often used Roman names.

Most stories of King Arthur are inextricably bound up with fictional accounts of his exploits. It is widely believed, however, that there was a historical King Arthur upon whom these accounts were based. Less certain, however, are the details of this person's life. Whether Arthur was a local leader or a national one; whether he lived in the fifth or early sixth century; or whether his territory was in the north or south of Britain—these are issues that may never be satisfactorily resolved, unless new literary or archaeological resources are discovered.

King Arthur in literary history. Early Welsh and Scottish literature provides sources for the earliest Arthurian traditions. A series of Scottish poems, known as *The Gododdin,* were written

A map of England during Arthur's time, roughly the 5th or 6th century A.D.

around 600 A.D., less than a century after Arthur's presumed death. These poems greatly exaggerate Arthur's feats in the style of Greek and Roman epics. Welsh texts from the ninth and tenth centuries seem to substantiate Arthur as a historical figure, calling him the war-leader of the kings of the Britons (native people of the isles) and listing battles that he won against the invading Saxons. The legend grew, and by the latter part of the eleventh century, Welsh sagas portrayed Arthur as a powerful warrior prince connected with both historical and imaginary characters.

In the twelfth century, Arthur appears as a quasi-historical figure in *History of the Kings of Britain,* a Latin work by the historian Geoffrey of Monmouth. The work is clearly fictional, and for this reason modern historians find Geoffrey of Monmouth an untrustworthy source. When, for example, he was unable to find a historical record of the birth of Arthur, Geoffrey of Monmouth made one up based on the legendary accounts of the birth of the Roman god Hercules. Geoffrey claimed to have access to Arthur's lost archives. Although the supposed manuscripts from these archives were unverifiable, Geoffrey's work became the primary source for subsequent medieval and modern tales of King Arthur.

The fantastic legends of Arthur became popular with later medieval authors, who embroidered them with contemporary issues and medieval culture. This is especially evident in the prose work *Le Morte d'Arthur* (1470). Its author, Thomas Malory, created a version of the King Arthur story that paralleled his own experiences in the turbulent years of civil strife that tore through England during the War of Roses. In the works of Malory and twenty-six other medieval writers, the fifth-century warriors of the fictional world of Arthur are transformed into knights of a much later era; similarly, the simple hill forts of the Dark Ages become medieval castles, and the ancient Celtic culture of Britain becomes a medieval one.

Feudalism. Feudalism was a popular social and political system in Western Europe during the Middle Ages, the period that Malory (and White, who based his work on Malory's text) uses to give color and shape to the Arthurian tales. After the fall of the Roman Empire, small counties of Britain were governed by the local lords, who maintained a certain amount of authority and control over other individuals in their jurisdiction. Although the lords were technically subservient to the king, often the king had little or no authority over these counties. Instead, the lord of the county enjoyed full military and administrative power.

The small size of these areas, however, invited attacks from neighboring communities. This state of affairs made military defense an important consideration for the lords. Much of the military force that was created in the various communities came from the vassals, underlings who received land within a district and in return owed service to the lord who granted the land. The land grants were called fiefs, and they were worked by numerous peasants who paid rent to the vassals in the form of crops and dues for the use of markets, mills, and ovens.

In 1066 the Duke of Normandy invaded England and divided it into fiefs under his jurisdiction. Most of the land fell under the control of the duke (who became known as King William I) either directly through his own vassals or through the vassals of his vassals. Everyone who held land owed military service to the throne. Not only did a lord or vassal have to protect his own homestead with knights, he also had to have enough knights to travel with him to battle. To escape military service, a man could pay money, called *scutage,* to hire substitute professional soldiers; in other words, he could buy his way out of the armed forces.

Knighthood. Knights first appeared in England after 1066. Until the early 1100s the term referred only to someone skilled in the art of fighting on horseback. This simple definition grew much more complex as the duties of a knight expanded during the twelfth century. Military service remained the primary role for the knights, who formed the core of the medieval army. Often the knight became an officer in command of about five hundred foot soldiers. Over the years his responsibilities came to include legal duties; he might, for example, serve on a jury or act as an investigator in criminal cases. Various types of knights became common as well, ranging from the comparatively unskilled country variety to the skilled knight of high noble heritage. In addition, some knights actually waged war, while others rarely, if ever, fought.

Training for knighthood began at a boy's birth. At the age of seven, a boy would be placed under the care of a knight other than his own father to learn the skills and values of the profession. He served as a page in this knight's household, mastering hawking and hunting skills, exercising the lord's battle horse, learning religion, and practicing courtesy and obedience. Hawking—the practice of training hawks to catch other birds and small animals—was held in particularly high esteem; nobles rarely appeared without their hawks, and strict hawking laws were in place to protect the interests of the owners.

As the trainee progressed he became responsible for carving meat and serving wines. He also attended the knight of the household when he prepared for a joust or battle. The trainee armed the knight before a fight and practiced wearing armor himself, gradually learning to move with agility under the overwhelming weight of the steel armor. He also learned to ride a battle horse and to wield weapons while so encumbered.

A youth could be knighted as early as age fifteen, but most were officially inducted at twenty-one. Recognition of this achievement often involved an elaborate ceremony in which the candidate received expensive clothes and the trappings of knighthood from his master. The ceremony often coincided with a religious day, wedding, coronation, or other occasion. Held in highest regard was a battlefield ceremony. The rituals of the ceremony varied to some degree, but in each case the high point was the dubbing of the new knight. This typically involved giving the new knight a slight blow on each shoulder with the flat blade of a sword. In some cases, however, a kiss or embrace replaced the touch of a sword to the shoulders.

The Crusades. The Holy Wars of the Middle Ages, called the Crusades, were fought in the name of Christianity under the direction of popes and kings alike. The Crusades gave the knights a sense of purpose and a chance to use their warrior skills. *The Once and Future King* makes note of this as a reason for sending knights to fight in the Crusades. As King Arthur observes,

> We have run out of things to fight for, so all the fighters of the Table are going to rot. While there were still giants and dragons and wicked knights of the old brigade, we could keep them occupied: we could keep them in order. But now that the ends have been achieved, there is nothing for them to use their might on.
> (White, *The Once and Future King*, p. 456)

The Crusades were imagined to give knights a chance to put concepts of chivalry into practice. The war would allow them to fight on behalf of loyalty, love of God, and personal honor. In fact, however, the motivation for the Crusades stemmed in large part from the greed of powerful nobles, who assumed that great hoards of treasure were available for plunder in the Middle East. Unfortunately, some of the original ideals of chivalry were also changed as a result of the experiences of the Crusades. Mercy, a characteristic often

shown by Lancelot to his enemies in legends and a quality revered among the Knights of the Round Table, was abandoned by knights in their dealings with non-Christians. Muslims, Jews, and other "infidels" were cruelly slaughtered and maimed in the name of Christianity. In *The Once and Future King,* Arthur perceives the contradiction between the knights' ideals and their behavior and recognizes this gap as a violation of the code of chivalry.

Tournaments. Tournaments were military contests on horseback between knights who divided themselves into opposing groups to fight each other as if they were enemy armies. The tournaments provided practice for war and an opportunity to display personal skill. There were two kinds of contests: the tourney, which involved combat with swords between troops; and the joust, a battle with lances between two individuals. The object of the joust was to knock the other warrior off his horse and, if possible, break his lance. The lances were blunted to reduce the danger of breaking through armor, while the grounds of the tournament fields were covered with sand and wood shavings in an attempt to prevent serious injuries or death when riders were thrown off their mounts.

In spite of these precautions, men were killed or disabled in the contests. Tournament armor weighed nearly 120 pounds, and contestants needed a stepladder just to mount their horses. The physical toll sometimes proved significant to those who were thrown to the ground while encased in these outfits of steel. The church vehemently opposed the games. Its representatives complained that the tournaments wasted valuable horses, men, and money. The various kings of England alternated between allowing and forbidding the holding of tournaments in the 1100s and 1200s. It was not until the reign of Edward I (1272-1307) that they became an official social event attended by the royal family.

The Novel in Focus

The plot. *The Once and Future King* follows King Arthur's life from childhood to the end of his reign. It is a combination of four smaller novels: *The Sword in the Stone, The Queen of Air and Darkness, The Ill-Made Knight,* and *The Candle in the Wind.*

The central plot features the son and rightful heir of King Uther Pendragon and Queen Igraine. The boy is sent away from home at birth to live with Sir Ector and his son Kay. At Sir Ector's home, "the Wart," as Arthur is nicknamed as a child, receives a proper education in jousting, horsemanship, hawking, fencing, archery, and chivalry. From his tutor Merlyn, who is a magician, the boy gains further knowledge about the nature of man and animals. Peculiarly, Merlyn is moving backward through time, traveling from the future into the past. Merlyn claims this past to be his own future and therefore unknowable to him. Due to the circumstances of living backward, Merlyn often mentions events, characters, and objects from the future that are not familiar to Wart and his contemporaries.

Merlyn turns Wart into several different creatures over the course of his childhood; each adventure in the animal kingdom presents the boy with an understanding of the unique political and social structure in which different species of animals exist. A pike, for example, trying to show Wart that "Might is Right," demonstrates the supremacy of big fish. The falcon teaches him about military life. Even the ants teach Wart a particularly memorable lesson about thoughtless dictatorships and cannibalism. Wart abhors the behavior of the ants, which causes a goose to ask in astonishment, "what creature could be so low as to go about in bands, to murder others of its own blood?" (*The Once and Future King*, p. 172). The parallel to human beings is clear, and Arthur remembers the lesson that "Might" should not be used for its own ends.

When the adolescent Wart, searching desperately for a sword for Sir Kay to use in a tournament, accidentally pulls one out of a stone, he finds that he has fulfilled a task at which many men have failed and has thus proven himself the true and rightful King of England. He is then able to use Merlyn's teachings to implement a new political philosophy. Wart, now known as King Arthur, decides to use "Might for Right," that is, to have his knights do battle against evil for the good of the human race.

Arthur then has the famous Round Table built, his idea being to minimize the traditional hierarchy within the court by placing everyone on an equal level. Despite this attempt at equality, the ugly "ill-made" knight, Sir Lancelot, clearly stands above the rest of the knights in his ability to fight and play games. Unfortunately, this romantic knight falls in love with King Arthur's wife, Queen Guenever. He stifles his desire for her by leaving on lengthy quests, thus removing himself from her presence. Lancelot, though, is ultimately tricked into losing his prized virginity by Elaine, a woman whom he has gallantly saved. No longer pure, Lancelot allows himself to eventually enter into a risky, adulterous relationship with Queen Guenever.

Meanwhile, Arthur finds that he and his knights have killed all the threatening beasts and dragons in the kingdom and saved all the virgins and damsels who were at risk. While justice may have prevailed, the knights are growing bored at the lack of challenges. Arthur decides to send them on a crusade to find the Holy Grail, the cup from which Jesus and his disciples drank at the Last Supper.

The Holy Grail is discovered in a church in Israel and brought home to England by the knights Galahad, Pelles, and Bors. Several of the other knights were not so successful; in fact, many met untimely and tragic deaths. The tone at the Round Table is forever changed, for "it seemed that the best knights had gone to perfection [in finding the Holy Grail], leaving the worst to hold their sieges" (*The Once and Future King*, p. 504). Moreover, Sir Lancelot, the greatest of all knights, has been punished by God for his immoral love affair with Arthur's wife. He was excluded from the pursuit of the Holy Grail, a punishment that makes him try to end the affair. When a knight named Sir Meliagrance kidnaps Guenever, however, Lancelot saves her and their love is consummated once again.

Knowledge of this love affair becomes the means by which Arthur's enemies, the Orkneys, are able to destroy him. Gawaine, Gaheris, Agravaine, and Gareth Orkney are Arthur's nephews through his half-sister Morgause. These knights have since childhood been poisoned with tales of evil attributed to Arthur's father, King Uther Pendragon. These tales accuse the king of stealing their grandmother Igraine from the Orkneys' grandfather.

Arthur's half-sister Morgause, one of three witches born to Igraine, ultimately punishes Arthur for the sins of the past by seducing the unsuspecting king and conceiving a son by him, called Mordred. Arthur tries to kill Mordred but does not succeed and instead must bear Mordred's hatred for the murder attempt. Meanwhile, the nephews' hatred of Arthur leads them to plot to trap Guenever and Lancelot in bed. They know that if Arthur learns of their romantic involvement, he will be forced to excommunicate Lancelot, who is his best friend, and to have his wife burned at the stake. Lancelot accidentally kills two of the four nephews, which spawns further hatred.

A chain of events draws away Arthur to do battle in France, leaving Mordred free to usurp the throne and plan to marry Guenever. Arthur returns to England to protect his queen and fight Mordred. The book ends before this fight begins, leaving the outcome unresolved. At the novel's end, Arthur relates his tale to a young page named Tom (presumably Thomas Malory), asking him to circulate to the world the story of King Arthur and his ideas for a nonwarring civilization.

Sources. White credits Malory's *Morte d'Arthur* as his main source, although he made major changes to Malory's version. A most notable difference in the two tales is the ages of Guenever, Arthur, and Lancelot at the end of the tale. Malory presents them as figures in their thirties, while White argues that they were considerably older, probably closer to their mid-forties and fifties. The second important change made by White is to the character Elaine, seducer of Lancelot. In Malory's version two Elaines appear, the young maiden who gives birth to Galahad and a rather pathetic fat woman. White condenses these two characters into one by transforming the young maiden at the beginning of the tale into a disturbed suicidal woman at the end, greatly simplifying a story that he felt was probably misinterpreted by Malory in the first place. A final change made by White concerns the character of Lancelot, whom he decides to paint as horribly ugly.

A reflection of T. H. White? Many of the changes to the tale that were made by White may be instances in which he imposed his own emotions and experiences onto the characters. By transforming the handsome Lancelot into an ugly man, White may be drawing on his own feelings. His friend Sylvia Townsend Warner claimed that White "was a self-tormented person and I imagine he saw himself very much as Lancelot in *The Ill-Made Knight*" (Warner, p. 93). White shared with his character Lancelot a sense of guilt that probably began sometime in childhood. Throughout his life, White struggled with homosexual desires that may have found form in Lancelot's own self-hatred and shame.

But while the characters of Lancelot and the young boy Wart bear some resemblance to White, it is the character of Merlyn who is most closely modeled after the author. Like Merlyn, White was an instructor of young boys (he taught public school) and a lover of animals. Most significant is the use of Merlyn as spokesman for White's own political theories, which White felt compelled to contribute to civilization as his "war effort" since he did not serve directly in World War II. In the novel Merlyn teaches White's theories to young Arthur so Arthur can improve the world.

White's physical surroundings are also utilized as a resource in the creation of the novel. In the first part of *The Once and Future King*, White imposes features of his own twentieth-century England onto the twelfth century. The gamekeeper's house in which Wart discovers Merlyn is really a description of a cottage in which White was living when he began writing the novel. Like Merlyn, White housed several animals within his home. Two creatures in the work, the owl Archimedes and the hawk Cully, are both animals owned by White that he paints into the novel. In addition, the hunting, hawking, and shooting that take place in the novel are an extension of his own lifestyle. White lived close to nature and was skilled at many of the games described within the text.

Events in History at the Time the Novel Was Written

Naturalism. One of the great influences on literary works and social conditions in the early part of the twentieth century was naturalism. This philosophy, influenced by Darwinism, proposed that individuals had little control over life; circumstance and environment determined one's future.

These new scientific studies closely linked human nature to animal nature. It had been previously believed that reason, unique to human beings, enabled them to build political and social systems impossible to duplicate in the animal kingdom. The new ideology, however, forced intellectuals to examine animal habits and systems when studying human ones. In keeping with this trend, White suggested approaching politics from a naturalistic point of view. "Animals have politics," he said, "and most interesting ones.... Think of ants, bees, wasps, wild geese, elephants—in fact, think of any animal you like, nearly all have politics, and some have politics very close to the great nostrums of our century" (White in Gallix, p. 125-26).

Fascism. Was it the evil leader who led innocent populations to slaughter, or did evil populations choose leaders after their own hearts? This was a question pondered by White in *The Once and Future King*, giving voice to a dilemma of his age. Nationalist movements of the late 1800s and early 1900s gained strength in the years after World War I and became official policy in some countries. The most extreme of these movements were fascist regimes in which dictators ruled their countries with an iron fist, exercising strict social and economic control and suppressing opposition through terror and censorship.

Although fascism had touched many nations, only Italy, Spain, and Germany seriously embraced it. Italy and Germany were propelled by beliefs in their own national superiority and a desire to expand their borders. Adolf Hitler, leader of the National Socialist Party (the Nazis) in Germany, recognized that "state boundaries are made by man and changed by man," and it was his will "to secure for the German people the land and soil to which they are entitled on this earth" (Eubank, p. 46). His dangerous reasoning became a rallying call for German nationalists, whose army dared to invade other European countries. White was well aware of the dangers inherent in this brash seizure of territory. In his novel, when King Arthur ends his lifelong quest for peace, it is political geography—the imaginary lines of frontiers—that he singles out as the sole cause of conflict.

Reviews. White published his first book on the Arthurian legends in 1938. *The Sword and the Stone* received rave reviews in both England and America and became a Book-of-the-Month Club selection. Also well received were the next two installments, *The Witch in the Wood* (1939—later titled *The Queen of Air and Darkness*) and *The Ill-Made Knight* (1940). Despite this acclaim, it was not until 1958 that his entire Arthurian tragedy—including the fourth installment, *The Candle in the Wind*—was published.

Several changes were made to the original three novels for the 1958 release. The earlier novels were written in the earlier stages of World War II and reflected hope for the possibility of worldwide cooperation. The 1958 revision, one reviewer claims, is a "tale [that] has been refashioned by a writer who remembers the gas chambers" (Locher, p. 18). White felt disturbed by man's warring nature and wished to make some

sense out of it. He observed the animals, how they treated one another, and how they acted in comparison to man. As one reviewer noted:

> [White] one day discovered that only men and ants make war upon one another, and he was shocked at the way men of the 1930s, 1940s, and 1950s followed blindly into battle because leaders, haranguing on national patriotism, baited them to it.
>
> (Locher, p. 18)

The accounts of young Wart's adventures in the animal kingdom are not found in the 1938 version of *The Sword and the Stone* but are an important part of the plot of the 1958 version. Critics who once dismissed White as a writer who was directing his work only at a young audience were forced to re-examine his work after the publication of the 1958 version. They generally came to appreciate his attempt to both moralize an ancient story and link the past with the present.

For More Information

Eubank, Keith. *World War II: Roots and Causes.* 2nd ed. Lexington, Ky.: D.C. Heath, 1992.

Gallix, Francois. *Letters to a Friend: The Correspondence between T. H. White and L. J. Potts.* New York: G. P. Putnam's Sons, 1982.

Goodrich, Norma Lorre. *King Arthur.* New York: Harper & Row, 1986.

Lacy, Norris J., ed. *The New Arthurian Encyclopedia.* New York: Garland, 1991.

Locher, Frances Carol, ed. *Contemporary Authors.* Vols. 73-76. Detroit: Gale Research, 1978.

Warner, Sylvia Townsend. *T. H. White.* London: Butler & Tanner, 1967.

White, T. H. *The Once and Future King.* Glasgow, Scotland: William Collins Sons, 1958.

Othello

by
William Shakespeare

Wtilliam Shakespeare adapted the tragic Italian tale of *Othello* to appeal to a British audience and, in particular, to the new king, James I. Shakespeare was a child at the time of the Cyprus Wars and was familiar with the famous Battle of Lepanto—a grand victory for Christian forces that serves as the backdrop to the main action of the play. The religious and social conflicts depicted in the drama reflect events and changes occurring in both Italy and England during the sixteenth and seventeenth centuries. Shakespeare's tragedy *Othello* was a tale that, despite the Venice setting, addressed concerns of his own time.

THE LITERARY WORK

A tragedy set in Venice and Cyprus around 1571; first performed for King James I in 1604.

SYNOPSIS

Desdemona, the young daughter of a powerful citizen of Venice, marries Othello, an older Moorish commander. Doomed from the start, Othello and Desdemona become embroiled in a terrible plot of jealousy and revenge that results in tragedy on a grand scale.

Events in History at the Time the Play Takes Place

Venetian history. Up until the 1500s, Venice was a powerful, independent state that controlled territories throughout Italy and the Mediterranean. Situated on the Adriatic Sea at the gateway of the overland route to the Spice Islands of eastern Indonesia, it was a thriving port that served as the link between the Far East spice trade and the European market. Venetians (citizens of Venice) became wealthy as brokers of exotic spices and manufacturers of silk imported from the East.

When Portuguese explorer Vasco da Gama sailed around the Cape of Good Hope in 1499 and established a sea route from Europe to the Far East, Venice began to decline. The city reeled under the consequences of a public panic that forced most major banks to close and a devastating outbreak of bubonic plague. The state became increasingly weak and vulnerable to outside attack.

By the late 1400s the once-powerful Venetian military was also in decline, struggling to man its

formidable naval fleet. The increasingly wealthy and luxury-loving citizens of the city showed little appetite for risking their lives at war. Where once it had been considered a duty or honor to serve the state in battle, military involvement during these years became less appealing, and as a result the state was defended mainly by reluctant recruits, convicts, and debtors.

As Venetian defense capabilities waned, the Ottomans (Turkish rivals whose empire included the Middle East, Asia Minor, and North Africa) initiated attacks on Venetian territories in the Mediterranean in 1463. Venice suffered a series of humiliating defeats. In several instances, a majority of Venetian forces retreated or surrendered to the advancing enemy without engaging in combat. The Turks captured key Venetian outposts and by 1500 controlled virtually all of mainland Greece, territory that had previously belonged to Venice.

Turkish religious wars. The war between the Turks and the Venetians raged for more than 100 years. The conflict grew from a territorial battle into a religious war. The Ottoman Turks were Muslim, while the Venetians were Christian. To Christian Europeans, the threat of Muslim Turk control of the Mediterranean was a serious one, for such control increased the potential for a Turkish invasion of western Europe. As the Turks captured key Venetian territories, including the island of Cyprus, Europeans became increasingly alarmed. Several states rallied to Venice's defense and joined in the war effort in the name of Christianity. Spain, Genoa, and the Holy Roman Empire—together known as the "Holy League"—allied with Venice against the Turks, who formed their own Muslim alliance with Berbers, Levantines, and corsairs (pirates) of the Barbary Coast.

CERVANTES AND SHAKESPEARE

Miguel de Cervantes, a contemporary of Shakespeare's who later wrote *Don Quixote,* fought at the Battle of Lepanto as a twenty-four-year-old Spanish soldier. In the battle he injured his left hand, a wound that maimed him for life. Shakespeare and Cervantes never met, but they died on the same day—April 23, 1616—and became two of the best known and most acclaimed authors of their time.

War of Cyprus. The island of Cyprus, a Venetian territory, was vital to the economy of Venice. It produced honey, saffron, cotton, wax, salt, sugar, indigo, and wine, as well as abundant tax revenue. Its geographic location, however—close to the Ottoman Empire and distant from Venice—made it a likely target for Turkish invasion. By September 1570 almost all of Cyprus was in the hands of the Turks, and the Holy League had been formed to recapture it. In September 1571 Pope Pius V predicted a Christian victory over the Turks and backed his vision with strong military participation. A fleet of 209 ships was amassed, and the allied forces set sail from Italy toward Cyprus, intent on defeating the Turks and retaking the island for Venice.

Cyprus was well fortified, though, and the Turkish fleet of 309 ships outnumbered the attackers. In addition, Venetian troops had suffered a crushing defeat at the Port of Famagusta in Cyprus after holding out against the much more formidable Turkish military for over a year. The victorious Turkish forces subsequently killed the

leaders of the Venetian troops in brutal fashion. News of the fall of Famagusta reached Venice's troops at sea. They realized Cyprus was totally lost and probably could not be recaptured. Rather than abandon hope, though, the Christian forces became enraged over the deaths of their comrades and vowed revenge against the Turks. With that in mind, they sailed forth to meet their enemy at sea.

Lepanto, 1571. Confident in their ability to defeat the Venetians and their allies in the Holy League after their earlier successes, the Turks deployed their fleet to attack the approaching Europeans. The enemies met at the Port of Lepanto and a famous sea battle ensued. The ships of the League, which sailed under an azure flag that depicted Christ on the cross, encircled the Turks, whose ships flew white and gold flags inscribed with phrases from the Muslim holy book, the Koran. For two hours the bloody conflict raged. Kettle drums pounded as cannons fired, swords clashed, and arrows soared. Though greatly outnumbered by the Turks, the League managed to trap the Turkish fleet in the Lepanto harbor and set fire to hundreds of their ships. The commander Sebastiano Venier, described as a ferocious old Venetian, fought valiantly against the Ottomans and helped ensure the League's victory. The Turks were forced to retreat, their fleet in tatters. The Holy League lost 7,600 men and 12 ships in the battle, but the Turks lost 240 ships and 30,000 men. It was a stunning victory for the Holy League and was seen by some Christians as a validation of the pope's prophecy. Although Cyprus was not recaptured, the victory restored European confidence and virtually ended the Turkish wars. Venice emerged once again as a formidable power with a strong military.

Wild Venice. Late sixteenth-century Venice was known by many as a city of sin. Venetians were famous for their wild dress and behavior. Upper- and middle-class existence was often marked by flamboyant costumes, elaborate carnivals, a passion for gambling, and sexual practices that resulted in epidemic rates of syphilis. Even the popes of the era were allowed to have intimate relations with women; they fathered a number of children during this period. In *Othello* Shakespeare portrays this liberal atmosphere in the celebration that follows the defeat of the Turks. Each Venetian in attendance is given full freedom to engage in "what sport and revels his addiction leads him" (Shakespeare, *Othello*, 2.2.5-6). The general climate of debauchery helps explain how easily Othello could be convinced of his wife's adultery.

The Moor question. The Moors were originally a nomadic people of northern Africa. They became Muslims in the eighth century and invaded Spain in 711, where they established a kingdom (the Umayyad emirate) in the south at Córdoba. The transplanted Moorish culture thrived in Spain, establishing splendid centers in other Spanish cities as well. But the Moors never established a strong central government, and by the fifteenth century the various Moorish strongholds had surrendered to stronger rulers, including Christians like Ferdinand and Isabella of Spain. Most of the Moors were driven from Spain to other European countries.

In sixteenth-century Italy, the terms "Moor" and "pagan" were almost interchangeable. By and large, Moors were considered barbarians, were treated as slaves, and often were made scapegoats for crimes or seen as causes of society's problems. Though attitudes slowly began to shift by the seventeenth century, when the slave trade died out, the Moor was still considered a second-class citizen.

Some Moors, however, were able to escape the negative stereotypes and integrate successfully into Venetian society. Citizens of Venice, in fact, insisted that theirs had always been a multiracial and multicultural society. They pointed out that in the fifteenth century the city had imprisoned a prominent nobleman for raping a black slave girl. Such instances of social justice may lend legitimacy to Shakespeare's depiction of Othello, a Moor, as a general in the Venetian army. As the play shows, he was still subject to racism. At the same time, however, he was respected for his ability as a warrior. The treatment of the Othello character illustrates both a shift toward tolerance and the lingering seeds of prejudice in the real Venice of the late 1500s.

A second explanation for how Shakespeare's Othello could have become such a powerful member of the Venetian military is that the historical model for this character may not have been a Moor at all. Some Venetians insist that an earlier writer named Cinthio (or Cinzio)—who has been cited as a source used by Shakespeare—and Shakespeare himself misinterpreted the story of a Venetian general named Moro who hailed from Morea. A statue of Moro dressed in battle armor even stands outside the palace at the Campo dei Carmini.

The Play in Focus

The plot. Set in Venice in approximately 1571, *Othello* opens with the Venetians at war against the Turks over possession of Cyprus. Iago, Othello's "ancient" or ensign, expresses his anger at being passed over for promotion and plots revenge. Othello, a Moor and distinguished war hero, has appointed Michael Cassio as lieutenant and has just secretly married Desdemona, a much younger Venetian. The jealous and evil Iago desperately wants to destroy Othello and Cassio. To that end, he first tries to get Othello's marriage annulled. Appealing to Desdemona's father's racist attitude, Iago announces brashly to him: "Sir, y'are robb'd... an old black ram is tupping your white ewe" (*Othello,* 1.1.87, 89-90). Brabantio, Desdemona's father, is outraged by the news and becomes convinced that Othello has used witchcraft or black magic to lure his daughter into marriage.

REVERSING NEGATIVE STEREOTYPES

~

The Moors were ousted from Spain in 1492 by the Catholics, who, like the Venetians, considered them pagans and treated them as intruders who were disruptions to Christian society. Yet Shakespeare paints Othello as the Christian leader of allied forces that include Spain. Othello appears as the exact opposite of the negative stereotype so commonly associated with Moors of the day.

Brabantio levels his accusation at Othello at a meeting of the duke's war council, which has been convened to discuss an impending Turkish attack on Venetian-controlled Cyprus. Othello and Desdemona eloquently explain how they fell in love. Othello had told Desdemona his life story—including his days as a slave and his exploits as a victorious general defending Venice—and she naturally fell in love with him. Hearing this, the duke declares: "I think this would win my daughter too" (*Othello,* 1.3.173). Brabantio, however, is not convinced and plants a seed of doubt about his daughter's honesty in Othello's mind. He tells him: "Look to her, Moor, if thou hast eyes to see. / She has deceiv'd her father, and may thee" (*Othello,* 1.3.295-96).

Brabantio's words play right into Iago's next plot. Iago makes plans to destroy Othello and Desdemona's union by arousing Othello's jealousy. The devious Iago schemes to make it appear as if Cassio is Desdemona's lover, thereby ruining the marriage and Cassio at the same time.

The reunion of Othello and Desdemona at Cyprus: Act 2, scene 1 of *Othello.*

Once the issue of Othello's marriage is settled, the duke's council makes plans for the defense of Cyprus against the Turks. Othello is sent to Cyprus as its new governor, and Desdemona is to follow in a later ship, escorted by Iago. Meanwhile, a great storm nearly destroys the Turkish fleet, and the ship carrying Othello has disappeared. Iago arrives in Cyprus with Desdemona, and shortly afterward Othello too arrives safely.

Iago travels to the city to set his evil plot in motion. First, he gets Cassio drunk and incites him to fight a fellow officer. When Othello learns of the fight, he reduces Cassio's rank. Desdemona innocently promises to help Cassio get his position back. Iago baits Othello, openly questioning why Desdemona should take such a keen interest in Cassio. He further hints that a white woman marrying a black man is somehow "unnatural" and suggests that it is only a matter of time until she will return to her "natural" course and pick a Venetian man. Iago implies that the relationship between Desdemona and Cassio could be a romantic one. In reality, such suggestions are utterly false. Desdemona is completely in love with Othello, and Cassio has no designs on her.

Iago quickly manages to paint a picture of adultery. Playing on Othello's insecurity—he's an outsider among the Venetians and has been subjected to racist treatment much of his life—Iago spins a web of lies that turns Othello into a man consumed by jealousy. Othello believes he finds proof of Desdemona's unfaithfulness when he finds Cassio has been in possession of her handkerchief. Convinced of her guilt, Othello confronts Desdemona and smothers her while she lies in her bed. Emilia, Desdemona's maid, enters as Desdemona, near death, comes to momentarily and protests her innocence—and Cassio's. Emilia explains to Othello Desdemona's innocence and Iago's lies. Iago's evil plot is finally uncovered, but Emilia pays for her honesty with her life when Iago, who has arrived on the scene, stabs her in an effort to keep her quiet. Overcome with anger and remorse, Othello first wounds Iago and then kills himself. Iago is apprehended and it is clear that he will be punished for his crimes, but it is too late for Othello and Desdemona, who have been destroyed by the dark power of jealousy and hatred.

Sources. Like **Romeo and Juliet,** (also covered in *Literature and Its Times*). *Othello* was apparently based on a collection of Italian tales, in this case a story included in *Gli Hecatommithi* by Giovanni Baptista Giraldi Cinthio. The specific naming of Desdemona and her marriage to a Moorish general is owed to him. Other details may have come from Geoffrey Fenton's *Certain Tragicall Discourses,* a book published in 1567 that Shakespeare apparently consulted to locate plots for his tragedies. The story also incorporates details from the true history of the Cyprus Wars and the Battle of Lepanto. The play may or may not have been expressly written for King James I, but its subject matter was certainly of great interest to him. Before becoming king, James wrote a poem about the Holy League's famous victory at Lepanto and was known as an expert in witchcraft. Shakespeare may have added several witchcraft references and shaped his portrayal of the evil Iago with the king's interest in mind.

Events in History at the Time the Play Was Written

Africans in Elizabethan England. The English of the sixteenth century had access to a variety of source materials regarding Africa, some factual and some fictional. Legends and tall tales rooted in the popular imagination—due in some part to classical historians' stories of monsters and strange creatures—gradually became replaced by the more accurate accounts of sea and land travelers, who also provided more accurate maps than before. It has been suggested that Shakespeare probably knew one of these books, *A Geographical History of Africa* by Johannes Leo Africanus, a North African Moor, and that its background material on, for example, the adventures of its author may have influenced the creation of *Othello*. In addition, with the advent of the slave trade in the 1560s, more and more Africans began to be brought into England. From the mid-sixteenth century onward, therefore, the English in London and other ports had ample exposure to both dark-skinned and light-skinned Africans. They also encountered blacks as free men in official capacities; they traded with them, and in 1600 a Moorish nobleman was sent as an ambassador to Queen Elizabeth.

The reign of King James. At the time the drama was written, King James I had just ascended to the English throne, ending years of bitter feuding over who would succeed Queen Elizabeth I. Though James took the throne peacefully, the religious and social conflicts that marked the end of Elizabeth's tenure remained. Protest against the powers of the Church of England increased, as did calls for lower taxes and fairer representation in Parliament. The country began to divide into religious and political fronts. Puritans broke from the mainstream and threatened to close theaters and taverns, while moderates urged religious and racial tolerance. The debate over reforming the established church grew as heated as the challenge to the power of the

monarch, and in 1642 civil war finally erupted. James's son and successor, Charles I, was beheaded by Oliver Cromwell's government in 1649.

Arts. Though the nation was rocked by turbulent debates about various issues, the arts flourished under King James. Dramatists such as Shakespeare received as much or even more support from the king than they had under Queen Elizabeth, who was considered a great patron of the arts. James, who considered himself an artist and intellectual as well as a theologian, enjoyed reading and writing poetry. He sponsored his own theater company, the King's Men, for which Shakespeare was the primary playwright. The King's Men performed regularly at court. In addition to writing new works for the king's company, Shakespeare also revived several of his older plays, such as *Romeo and Juliet,* which James had not seen at its opening.

Religious conflict and prejudice. As a largely Protestant nation, England was often in conflict with neighboring Catholic countries such as Spain. In 1588, the Spanish Armada was pummeled by a sudden, violent storm while on its way to attack England. This event made many people in England believe that God had intervened on their behalf as a sign of approval of their Anglican Protestant religion. Similarly, in *Othello* the Turkish fleet is destroyed at sea by a wild wind storm, a development that brings victory to the Christian Venetians. Shakespeare does not, however, paint a perfectly rosy or one-sided picture of religion and holy wars. He shows the hypocrisy of so-called Christians such as Iago and the ill-treatment suffered by truly Christian characters such as Othello. Clearly the most Christian of all the men at the outset of the play, Othello is accused of being a pagan and practicing witchcraft simply because he has dark skin.

The term "Moor" historically refers to the lighter-skinned African race of partial Arab descent, rather than the darker-skinned blacks of Africa. Yet Shakespeare, like other men of his day, does not draw any distinction between the two types and portrays Othello as a distinctively black African, in full appreciation of the racial tensions that would be evoked by his union with the fair Desdemona.

Shakespeare's depiction of Othello reflects an emerging shift in attitude in seventeenth-century British society. Prejudices and long-held notions about the roles of men and women and racial and religious differences were beginning to break down. By the end of the civil wars—which Shakespeare did not live to see—some British began to realize that "individuals ... could hold differing views about foreign policy, the nature of Christ's presence in the sacrament ... without necessarily precipitating social chaos" (Abrams, p. 1053). The growing concept of tolerance, an underlying but powerful idea in *Othello,* may be seen as affecting the subsequent course of British history.

Shakespeare's emerging genius. By 1604, the year that *Othello* was first performed, Shakespeare had established himself as London's premiere playwright. The tragedies that had beset his personal life—the deaths of his son and father, imprisonment of his patron Southampton, and execution of his friend the Earl of Essex—were in the past, and he was able to devote his time to developing his skills as a writer.

Othello is considered an inspired play that cemented Shakespeare's popularity with the new government and the general population. To his audience, tragedies were considered the highest form of drama and something all legitimate playwrights should strive to perfect. *Othello* was another of Shakespeare's attempts to master the form; he had had a similar goal when he wrote **Hamlet** (also covered in *Literature and Its Times*) some three years earlier.

Mature understanding. The major issues raised in the play—jealousy, racism, aging, evil, social and religious conflict—illustrate Shakespeare's growth as a playwright and his interest in a wide range of contemporary issues. Whereas many of his previous plays had dealt primarily with political intrigue, *Othello* examined social issues and human behavior; politics are here relegated to secondary status. In looking at the subject of age—and situations wherein romance was complicated by differences in age—Shakespeare may have drawn on personal experience. Shakespeare himself, it has been speculated, was previously involved in some sort of love triangle with his patron, Southampton, and an unnamed mistress. Whether true or not, Shakespeare did express much jealousy and frustration in his own poetry—sentiments that are also exhibited by Othello. Shakespeare remarks in Sonnet 57, for example, that love has made him a slave:

> Being your slave, what should I do but tend
> Upon the hours and times of your desire?
> ...Nor dare I question with my jealous thought
> Where you may be, or your affairs suppose,
> But like a sad slave, stay and think of nought
> Save where you are....
> (Shakespeare, "Sonnet 57," lines 1-2, 9-12)

Othello's lines, like Shakespeare's poems, show a man confused and frustrated by love. Othello's lament "I think my wife be honest and think she is not" (*Othello,* 3.3.389-90) is strikingly similar to one found in Shakespeare's Sonnet 138: "When my love swears that she is made of truth, I do believe her, though I know she lies" (Shakespeare, "Sonnet 138," lines 1-2).

A common experience. When it became apparent that Shakespeare was one of the great writers of his age, rival playwrights harshly criticized his works. Writers from Cambridge and Oxford universities denounced the output of this playwright who was self-educated and had not gone to college. Even the great dramatist and Shakespeare's friend Ben Jonson said that Shakespeare wrote too much and should have "blotted" or deleted a thousand lines (Rowse, p. 49). By the time he wrote *Othello,* then, Shakespeare, like his main character, had distinguished himself and experienced the resentment of others firsthand.

For More Information

Abrams, M. H. *The Norton Anthology of English Literature.* Vol. 1. New York: W. W. Norton, 1986.

Bevington, David. *The Complete Works of Shakespeare.* London: Scott, Foresman, 1980.

Crow, John. *Italy: A Journey through Time.* New York: Harper & Row, 1965.

Kay, Dennis. *Shakespeare: His Life, Work and Era.* London: Sidgwick & Jackson, 1991.

Rowse, A. L. *What Shakespeare Read and Thought.* New York: Coward, McCann & Geoghegan, 1981.

Shakespeare, William. *Othello.* Edited by David Bevington. Toronto: Bantam Books, 1988.

Thubron, Thomas. *The Venetians.* Alexandria, Va.: Time-Life Books, 1980.

Wright, Louis B. *Shakespeare's England.* New York: Harper & Row, 1964.

Paradise Lost

by
John Milton

Events in History at the Time the Poem Takes Place

War in Heaven. The immediate prehistory of *Paradise Lost* is the War in Heaven, during which the rebel angels, under Lucifer (Satan), try to overthrow God the Creator and are flung into Hell as punishment. Lucifer refuses to be subordinate to God or his divine Son (Christ) and decides to achieve a perverse revenge by seducing God's newest creation, Adam and Eve, to his party, or forcing God to destroy them. This subject of heavenly clashes for dominion has a rich history, not just in the Judeo-Christian tradition but in other belief systems as well. Prominent among these are the classical Greek myths upon which Milton draws so frequently in his poem.

Biblical passages that discuss the War in Heaven are actually rather scant; in the New Testament Gospel of Luke, Christ says "I beheld Satan as lightning fall from heaven" (Luke 10:18); the Book of Revelation speaks of the dragon (Satan) whose tail swept down "the third part of the stars of heaven, and did cast them to the earth" (Rev. 12:4) and who was "cast out into the earth, and his angels were cast out with him" (Rev. 12:9). In Milton's poem, the rebels who fall with Lucifer amount to one-third of the angels in Heaven.

Greek myths about fallen deities are much fuller. Several versions of such tales exist, and Milton seems to have been familiar with them all. In his poem, for example, when Christ routs the devils from Heaven, forcing them into the abyss, they fall "Nine times the Space that measures Day and Night / to mortal men" before they find

---

THE LITERARY WORK

An English epic poem, set in Heaven, Hell, and the Garden of Eden at the time of the creation of humanity; first published in ten books in 1667, published in its final form of twelve books in 1674.

SYNOPSIS

Milton relates the biblical story of Adam and Eve's (humanity's) fall from grace in a poem that deals with the issues of evil, disobedience, damnation, and salvation.

---

themselves in Hell (Milton, *Paradise Lost,* 1.50-51). In Greek myth, a nine-day fall is the fate of the Titans, who attempted to oust Zeus and his younger group of gods, the Olympians, who had seized control of the heavens. Hundred-armed giants come to Zeus's aid, hurling hundreds of boulders at the enemy Titans and driving them beneath the earth; the fall down to the depths takes nine days and nine nights. Milton almost certainly had this scene in mind when he described enemy angels throwing mountains at each other in *Paradise Lost.*

Adam, Eve, and the Garden of Eden. Milton's poem is based on the Judeo-Christian Book of Genesis, in which God creates the entire universe in six days. Beginning with light and darkness on the first day, God proceeds to create waters, plants, stars, fish, birds, and other animals, in-

REBEL ANGELS IN *PARADISE LOST*

Lucifer (also called Satan): leader of the fallen angels

Beelzebub: Lucifer's first lieutenant, favors seducing man to the fallen angels' side

Belial: fallen angel who favors doing nothing; counsels ignoble ease, and peaceful sloth

Moloch: toughest rebel angel, who argues for violent war against God

Mammon: rebel angel who favors building a kingdom in Hell to rival God's kingdom in Heaven

Sin: Lucifer's daughter

Death: son of Sin and Lucifer

Mulciber: architect of a palace in Hell called Pandemonium

cluding the first man and woman. Genesis 2:18-25 describes God's creation of Eve out of Adam's rib, an act that Milton refers to in his poem.

Eve is created as Adam's helper. Although the Bible and Milton agree that their home, the Garden of Eden, is beautiful, it is also a place in which humankind can live and work, not just bask in the splendid surroundings.

The Bible describes this lush garden as located in the "east," which to the ancient Hebrews would have meant Mesopotamia, in today's Iraq. Four rivers flow from the center of the garden, including two that are known today—the Tigris and the Euphrates. The other two are either purely mythical, or located in another geographical area, which makes it impossible for modern scholars to settle on a precise location for the garden.

Two trees grow at the center of the garden—the Tree of Life and the Tree of Knowledge of Good and Evil; Adam and Eve are forbidden to eat from the latter, but despite God's prohibition, they eat the forbidden fruit. The immediate consequence of Adam and Eve's disobedience is expulsion from the Garden of Eden; the long-term consequence is the loss of immortality.

The Poem in Focus

The plot. *Paradise Lost* begins in Hell, where Lucifer and the rest of the fallen angels have newly alighted.

As *Paradise Lost* begins, the rebel angels convene at Satan's palace in Hell to determine their next move. Beelzebub informs the congress that God has created Earth and peopled it with humans, who are good beings. He proposes that they seduce humanity to the side of the fallen angels.

Lucifer, the leader of the revolt against God, sneaks out of Hell to confirm the rumor of the creation. God notices Lucifer winging his way toward Earth but does nothing to stop him, knowing that Adam and Eve are destined to fall prey to Lucifer and disobey God. (This betrayal of God's trust is referred to as the "Fall of Man.")

Christ, the Son of God, offers at this point to take upon himself the responsibility of making amends to God for what man is about to do; his offer is accepted. Meanwhile, Lucifer arrives in Eden, which is guarded by one of God's angels, Gabriel. At Gabriel's command, the angels Ithuriel and Zephon find Lucifer whispering into the ear of the sleeping woman, tempting her to taste the fruit from the Tree of Knowledge of Good and Evil, the only act that God has forbidden.

Lucifer returns temporarily to Hell, and another of God's angels, Raphael, is sent to instruct Adam about the War in Heaven and inform him about the enemy. Despite this forewarning, when Lucifer disguises himself as a serpent and tempts Eve to eat the forbidden fruit, she does. Adam's love of his mate is so great that he eats the fruit too, so that Eve will not suffer punishment alone.

God sends his son, Christ, to the garden to pass judgment. Eve's sorrow will be to bear children in pain, and she must serve Adam forever. Meanwhile, Adam must earn his bread by hard labor. Asking Christ for mercy, Adam and Eve beseech him to speak to God on their behalf.

God administers both hardship and hope. He replaces perpetual springtime with a stormy round of seasons and condemns the creatures of Earth to prey upon one another. Soon to be turned out of Paradise, Adam and Eve contemplate suicide. They dismiss the notion, though, after God's angel Michael brings Adam a vision of the future. According to this vision, evil is to grow on earth until a great flood destroys everything but Noah and his ark full of creatures. A return to evil will follow until the crucifixion and resurrection of the Christ on Earth takes place. Moreover, the corruption will persist in the church up to Milton's day and beyond until the Second Coming of Christ.

Satan—hero or villain? During the late 1700s and early 1800s, the notion that the real hero of *Paradise Lost* is not the hapless human couple, nor God the Creator, but rather Lucifer (Satan), became a popular one. The poem opens with a scene wherein Lucifer bravely shakes off his terrible fall into Hell and resolves to do something about it: "To wage by force or guile eternal War / Irreconcileable to our grand Foe" (*Paradise Lost*, 1.121-22). Lucifer is a compelling figure. Beautiful and brilliant, he is engaged in a battle against insurmountable odds, angry about his subordinate position to God:

> Who can in reason then or right assume
> Monarchy over such as live by right
> His equals, if in power and splendor less,
> In freedom equal?
>
> (*Paradise Lost*, 5.794-97)

In fact, such reasoning led Milton and many of his fellow Englishmen to condone the 1649 execution of England's King Charles I. One reason for the execution was the king's decision to act alone in important matters, such as raising funds and starting battles, without consulting or heeding Parliament. The English king was supposed to be subject to certain limitations imposed by the members of Parliament, the elected representatives of the people. Charles, however, felt that the king ought to be set far above the people whom he ruled. Unrepentant until the very end, he is reported to have said just before he was beheaded that "a subject and a sovereign are clean different things" (Tomlinson, p. 160). Milton had written a heated defense of the decision to kill the king, arguing that Charles overstepped his bounds in ignoring Parliament: "Parliament is the supreme council of the nation, established and endowed with full powers by an absolutely free people ... the king was created to carry out all the decrees of ... [Parliament]" (Milton in Tomlinson, p. 168).

Despite his own involvement in unseating the king, Milton defends the right of God to unopposed monarchy throughout *Paradise Lost*. For Milton and others of his deeply religious time, there was a profound difference between a divine king and an earthly one. People of the era viewed Lucifer's heavenly revolt as unjustifiable and

purely evil. Certainly they did not regard Lucifer as the hero of *Paradise Lost*, no matter how intelligent and brave his character might seem. Milton himself did not view Lucifer as a heroic figure, although his rebellion bore some resemblance to one stage of Milton's own political views.

Milton probably did have politics in mind when he wrote his poem. After the beheading of Charles I, England had experimented with a kingless form of government, ruled by a council in which Milton held a position, but this government collapsed. Milton, who had wholeheartedly embraced the commonwealth, must have taken its downfall particularly hard. Like others of his time, he firmly believed that God took part in human history and that changes came about as a result of God's almighty will.

MILTON'S PREFACE TO *PARADISE LOST*

*P*aradise Lost is written in "blank verse," iambic pentameter verse that does not rhyme. Before Milton, blank verse was used in composing dramas, such as Shakespeare's plays. For poetry, the most popular verse forms in Milton's culture were probably the sonnet and heroic couplets, which used rhyme. In the preface to his poem, Milton felt compelled to defend his choice of blank verse: "The measure is English Heroic Verse without Rime, as that of Homer in Greek, and of Virgil in Latin; Rime being no necessary Adjunct or true Ornament of Poem or good Verse, in longer Works" (Milton, *Paradise Lost*, p. 210).

Milton regarded the beheading of the king as God-inspired. He may have attributed the failure of the experimental government to God as well. In seizing and attempting to reshape England's government, perhaps the rebels whom he so admired had interfered with God's timing. The inability of the rebels and Parliament to work together may have been proof of this interference. Their noble effort to overcome the tyranny of King Charles I had collapsed due to their own vicious squabbling. In his poem, Milton appears to be looking closely at human weakness in an effort to comprehend why good turns to evil. He might then understand why the political experiment in his own time went amiss.

Sources. Before his blindness, Milton was able to read works in six foreign languages—French, Italian, Hebrew, Latin, Greek, and Spanish—and

King Charles I, who was executed by Parliament in 1649.

Paradise Lost is teeming with references to classical literature, the Bible, other national epics, and Jewish historical and literary works.

The scientific discoveries of his time also influenced Milton. The dominant model of the universe—and one that Milton used because his audience was familiar with it—was that of the ancient Greek astronomer Ptolemy. According to this model, the earth was the center of the universe, and the other heavenly bodies, including the sun, revolved around it. Copernicus's *On Celestial Motions* (1543) demonstrated that the reverse was in fact true, that the earth revolved around the sun. The idea had obvious theological consequences that were not popular at the time; if the earth was not the center of God's universe, then it was possible that mankind was not the center of God's plan.

Well aware of the scientific discoveries, Milton seems fairly unconcerned about such religious fears. He visited the groundbreaking astronomer Galileo and referred to both him and his telescope in the poem. The poem also mentions the concept of possible life in other worlds and includes the opinion, voiced by Adam, that the earth may be only a "punctual spot" in a vast universe (*Paradise Lost*, 8.23).

Events in History at the Time the Poem Was Written

Civil war and the Restoration. The England in which Milton studied and wrote was a nation troubled by civil war, the execution of King Charles I, and a confused period of government. The poet had his own personal trials during this period as well.

1642: Civil war breaks out in earnest in Great Britain

1649: Rebels execute King Charles I; Milton publishes *The Tenure of Kings and Magistrates,* a pamphlet defending rights of citizens to kill a tyrant-king; Milton is appointed the Secretary for Foreign Tongues in new government

1652: Milton goes totally blind; his first wife, Mary Powell, dies

1653: Puritan leader Oliver Cromwell is named Lord Protector of the new English government; Milton works under him

1656: Milton marries Katherine Woodcock, who dies in February 1658

1658: Cromwell dies; Milton begins *Paradise Lost*

1660: Puritan government collapses; monarchy restored with Charles II on the throne; Milton is jailed

1663: Milton likely completes *Paradise Lost,* marries Elizabeth Minshull

1667: *Paradise Lost, A Poem in Ten Books* published

1674: *Paradise Lost, A Poem in Twelve Books* published; Milton dies on November 8

England's civil strife arose in part from the financial difficulties of the monarchy, which had been selling off property ever since the time of Henry VIII (1509-1547). Charles I was heavily invested in waging wars against France and Spain. He financed his political ambitions by levying huge taxes on his subjects, particularly London merchants. He also refused to summon Parliament between 1629 and 1640. Unable to meet without his bidding it to do so, the government was therefore unable to stop the king.

THE MILTONS AT HOME

By the time he produced *Paradise Lost,* Milton was completely blind. He composed the poetry in his head and then dictated it to a scribe, sometimes one of his two youngest daughters. His daughters also had to read to him in any one of the six foreign languages that he—but not they—knew: "[Milton's two youngest daughters] were condemned to the performance of reading ... all the languages of whatever book he should at one time or other think fit to peruse.... All ... without understanding one word" (Phillips in Milton, pp. 1036-37).

At the heart of the battle between the king and the people was the question of authority—the king thought he was justified in acting alone, while his opponents, the Parliamentarians, thought that the people had the right to regulate the king's actions. By 1640 Charles needed more money than he could raise on his own to fund his Scottish war, so he was forced to summon Parliament. It remained in session until 1653, becoming known as the "Long Parliament." The Long Parliament resisted Charles's plans, threw out his favorite ministers, and abolished the king's "Star Chamber," a secret court. The conflict climaxed when Parliament pronounced itself the sole authority in the land. Hearing that he had been ousted from power, the king attempted to seize the rebellious leaders, but failed. Civil war became inevitable. It erupted in August 1642.

Religious fears added to the tension between the king and the people of England. Back in the

1530s, the English had separated from the Catholic Church and formed their own Protestant-based Church of England. Those worshippers who belonged to this new church were called Anglicans. Catholic-Anglican tensions became a factor in England almost immediately.

King Charles I was Anglican, but he married a Catholic woman, Queen Henrietta Maria, and many of his closest advisors were Catholic. Charles embarked on a program of religious control in which he tried to force everyone, including the Scots, to use the same prayer book. Society balked at the idea, for it smacked of the old authoritarian ways of Catholicism. To make matters worse, the powerful Archbishop of Canterbury was slowly reintroducing certain Catholic practices. The Scots rebelled against the king in 1637. Two years later, in the first act of the civil war in 1639, the king tried to carry out his religious program with armed force. Unable to raise an army of sufficient strength, he failed. Meanwhile, in 1641 the Irish, mostly Catholics, rebelled against English settlers. Charles's Catholic tendencies were blamed for the loss of English life in Ireland, an almost certain injustice.

Paradise Lost is rife with insurrection—Lucifer's, Adam's, and Eve's. By the poem's conclusion, it is clear that obedience to God ought to provide a system of ordering man's behavior in the world. But it is equally clear, according to the poem, that political struggle is a sad fact of fallen humanity, one that perhaps may never be satisfactorily resolved, and that this struggle is rooted in the original battle in the Garden of Eden, in which desire was allowed to overpower reason. God's angel Michael says as much to Adam just before the human beings are thrust from Eden.

> Since thy original lapse, true Liberty
> Is lost, which always with right Reason dwells
> Twinn'd, and from her hath no dividual being:
> Reason in man obscur'd, or not obey'd
> Immediately inordinate desires
> And upstart passions catch the Government
> From Reason, and to servitude reduce
> Man till then free. Therefore, since hee permits
> Within himself unworthy Powers to reign
> Over free Reason, God in Judgment just
> Subjects him from without to violent Lords.
> (*Paradise Lost,* 12.83-93)

In this dark philosophy, upon which the poem ends, one perhaps sees Milton's own hard-learned political lessons.

Heavily involved in political events of the period, Milton had fired off writings on behalf of the reformers. In 1649 he assumed the post of Secretary for Foreign Tongues to the new interregnum ("between rulers") government run by those who had beheaded Charles I.

New relations had to be established with foreign governments; Milton's job demanded that he translate letters for the governing council and serve as interpreter and advisor, although he had no vote on the council. Troubled by repeated conflict between rebel leader Oliver Cromwell and Parliament, the new government foundered. Finally, Parliament voted for a return to kingship, a move known as the Restoration. They invited Charles II to take the throne with reduced powers, a condition that would apply to all monarchs after him.

After the king's coronation in 1660, Milton was jailed for his role in the now disgraced regicidal ("king killing") government. He probably expected to lose his life, but he had certain powerful friends in the new regime. He may also have been pitied because of the blindness that had by this time become complete. Some of his enemies suggested that God had stricken Milton blind because of his wicked political writings.

"The Divorcer." In *Paradise Lost,* Adam loves Eve so much that he takes a bite of the forbidden fruit on purpose. Adam's actions illustrated his willingness to join in her fate, whatever it might be, rather than live without her or force her to live without him. In addition, while the fallen couple bicker and place blame for their plight on each other, Adam intends to remain with his mate no matter what the consequences may be. His position reflects the perfect state of marriage before the fall of man and woman.

Milton was regarded as something of an expert on marriage because he wrote extensively on the subject of divorce. Perhaps it was his personal circumstances that drove him to tackle the topic: his first wife, the eighteen-year-old Mary Powell, left him after a month or so of their marriage. She returned to her parents' home, where she remained for three years. The reason for her departure remains a mystery. During his wife's prolonged absence, Milton wrote a tract on divorce, in which he maintained that the perfect marriage was sacred and worth pursuing to such an extent as to make divorce from an unsuitable spouse a socially desirable thing. His *Doctrine and Discipline of Divorce* (published in 1643, revised 1644) was such a huge bestseller that for twenty years he was popularly known as "Milton the Divorcer." He was rumored to have had many wives, all still living.

Milton's work on divorce also got him in trouble with the authorities; in 1644 he was forced to appear for questioning before the House of Lords. He stopped writing for publication for the next five years, during which time his wife returned and the first of his children was born. In 1652 his wife died. Altogether Milton would marry three times—in 1642, 1656, and 1663—perhaps gaining greater expertise on the subject through personal experience.

The Puritans. Milton's religious beliefs were similar to his political beliefs in that they were difficult to pin down to a convenient category. He wrote tracts in defense of Puritan ideas, showing his disenchantment with mainstream Anglican religious politics, but he also acted in ways that went against the spirit of Puritanism.

Broadly speaking, the Puritans were a Protestant sect, composed generally of people from the citizen and craftsman classes (as opposed to the nobility). They were practical in their religion, studying those passages in the Bible that could teach them how the individual soul might best struggle for salvation. Much of their study thus focused on the subjects of sin and the devil. In *Paradise Lost,* Milton's Puritan leanings are probably most evident in his treatment of the character of Satan and his clever seduction of Eve. The Puritans were also revolutionaries, convinced that the world, though teetering on the brink of chaos and iniquity, could be set right if sufficiently dramatic changes were made. To set it right, they were willing to stage a civil war. Milton apparently agreed with this drastic action, in which he took part.

But Milton's views also differed from the Puritan ideal in important ways. His ideas about divorce—that a man should be able to obtain one without any bother if he really wanted or needed it—shocked the Puritan mainstream, and his attention to beautiful poetic wording ran counter to the Puritan ideal of the straightforward use of language. Clearly Milton did not consider Catholicism to be a reasonable choice under any circumstances. His views were atypical, though, in that he seems also to have believed that man owes allegiance not to any one sect or religion—but to God alone.

America and Milton. Milton tried to reform English society throughout his lifetime; perhaps this explains why he was so popular in early America, a country filled with people who had recently fled the very same England that Milton wanted to change. His writings on many social issues, from marriage to church government to the relative merits of monarchy and republics, assumed a huge importance in early American culture. It was reported that his example inspired the liberal laws of Rhode Island and that Thomas Jefferson scoured Milton's characterization of Satan for evidence of heroic rebellion. *Paradise Lost* was quoted from pulpits and bandied about in national political debates.

Popular for the ideas that it contained, the poem also became the model for a flood of imitation American epic poems. Not until the 1800s, when the nation had calmed significantly in its discussion of competing views on how a nation should be run, did the American public fall out of love with *Paradise Lost.*

Reviews. English critics of the 1700s produced some of the most important reviews of *Paradise Lost.* In the influential English literary journal *The Spectator,* Joseph Addison wrote a series of eighteen short essays on *Paradise Lost.* His introductory essay, published on January 5, 1712, puts Milton in the same class as Homer and Virgil, and speaks of Milton's careful enlargement of the Bible's scanty descriptions of the fall of the angels and man:

> [Milton] was ... obliged to proceed with the greatest caution in everything that he added out of his own invention. And, indeed, notwithstanding all the restraints he was under, he has filled his story with so many surprising incidents, which bear so close an analogy with what is delivered in Holy Writ, that it is capable of pleasing the most delicate reader, without giving offense to the most scrupulous.
> (Addison in Abrams, p. 2205)

On the other hand, Samuel Johnson's *Lives of the Poets* (1779) contains a section on Milton in which Johnson criticizes *Paradise Lost* as a dull work:

> The want of human interest is always felt. *Paradise Lost* is one of the books which the reader admires and lays down, and forgets to take up again.... Its perusal is a duty rather than a pleasure.
> (Johnson in Abrams, pp. 2427-28)

Throughout its history, *Paradise Lost* has inspired variations on these two opinions. There is, meanwhile, general agreement that the impact of the poem has been enormous. For centuries, observed one writer, *Paradise Lost* "determined the way in which the majority of the English-speaking world read and interpreted the Bible" (González, p. 163).

For More Information

Abrams, M. H., et al. *The Norton Anthology of English Literature.* 5th ed. New York: Norton, 1986.

Ashley, Maurice. *The English Civil War.* London: Thames and Hudson, 1990.

Goldberg, Jonathan, and Stephen Orgel, eds. *John Milton.* Oxford: Oxford University Press, 1994.

González, Justo L. *The Story of Christianity.* Vol. 2. San Francisco: Harper San Francisco, 1985.

Milton, John. *Paradise Lost.* In *John Milton: Complete Poems and Major Prose.* Edited by Merritt Y. Hughes. Indianapolis: Odyssey, 1957.

Newlyn, Lucy. *Paradise Lost and the Romantic Reader.* Oxford: Clarendon Press, 1993.

Sensabaugh, George F. *Milton in Early America.* Princeton: Princeton University Press, 1964.

Tomlinson, Howard, and David Gregg. *Politics, Religion and Society in Revolutionary England, 1640-1660.* London: MacMillan, 1989.

Poor Richard's Almanack

by

Benjamin Franklin

From a childhood of poverty, Benjamin Franklin rose to become a successful businessman and a founding father of the United States. Born in 1706 as the son of a candlemaker, Franklin earned a position of wealth and respect in the Philadelphia community through hard work and thrift. He filled *Poor Richard's Almanack,* a bestseller for more than twenty years, with advice on how to acquire wealth through industry.

Events in History at the Time of the Almanacs

Franklin as an early example of the American dream. America has always been considered a land of freedom and economic opportunity. Immigrants who possessed nothing in Europe dreamed of coming to the American colonies to make their fortunes. This concept of working one's way out of poverty into wealth has been a driving force since the early colonists stepped off their vessels onto the raw American continent. A living example that this dream could come true, Franklin spread the belief that anyone willing to work hard could succeed.

Franklin was the fifteenth child in his family. He attended school for two years, after which he stayed home to help his father make candles and soap. His father observed that young Benjamin liked to read, and so he apprenticed the boy to his brother as a printer in Boston, Massachusetts. Franklin developed writing skills during his apprenticeship, and he showed great promise. The

two brothers did not get along, though, and Franklin ran away after five years.

Nearly broke, Franklin arrived in Philadelphia, Pennsylvania. He hungrily entered a bakery and paid the baker three pennies to give him anything he could for such a paltry sum. The baker gave him three bread rolls that were so large they would not fit inside Franklin's pockets. Instead, he carried one under each arm and ate the third. Franklin often referred back to this point in his life to show the poor beginnings that he had overcome through hard work.

Staying in Philadelphia, Franklin began a period of determined labor. He borrowed money and used his printing skills to rise out of obscurity, developing habits that enabled him to do well. Franklin did not want his creditors to think him frivolous, so he dressed plainly and continually sought to appear industrious and frugal. Entering into a number of successful business ventures, Franklin owned a printing press at the age of twenty-four. Franklin's efforts included publication of the *Pennsylvania Gazette,* the second newspaper to open in Pennsylvania. He continued to expand his printing business and served as a public official in the colony. Some of the positions Franklin held included the job of clerk to the Pennsylvania Assembly and the job of Postmaster of Philadelphia. Both of these positions enhanced his printing business.

Franklin retired after only twenty years in the printing business, yet he was busy and successful for the rest of his life. He became a soldier, commissioner, diplomat, scientist, and inventor. He also helped found Philadelphia's first library, fire company, college, and militia. Franklin went on to help draft both the **Declaration of Independence** (also covered in *Literature and Its Times*) and the Constitution of the United States of America. His rise to prominence and the range and impact of his activities remain impressive. As one biographer noted, it is important to remember that Franklin "began as a businessman, and his success in business paved the way for grander successes" (Baida, p. 30).

Dreams of prosperity in the early 1700s. During the first half of the 1700s, colonial America underwent a time of rapid economic expansion and change. Manufacturing and commerce grew at enormous rates in the northern colonies, and business was concentrated in large commercial centers like Philadelphia. Pennsylvania emerged as once of the richest and fastest-growing provinces during this period. In the South, a wealthy class of plantation owners began to emerge.

The period found many colonists actively engaged in the pursuit of wealth. People invested in "get rich quick" schemes or bought and sold land to make rapid profits. Other economic issues emerged as well. A problem that troubled Franklin during the early and middle 1700s was the great scarcity of "real" money. The colonies were not allowed to mint coins, so people often conducted business by bartering, trading one kind of good for another, or using credit. People who paid with cash were rare, and credit accounts often ran on indefinitely. Franklin advocated the introduction of paper money as a means to solve this problem.

The emergence of industry and commerce brought economic flux, and the nation experienced booms and busts. Occasionally, the financial slumps left people homeless or reduced them to beggars. Many historians question how much of the population benefited from the economic prosperity of the times. As places like Philadelphia grew, so did urban poverty, especially after 1720. Many of the poor were recent immigrants or rural farmers who had moved to the expanding city in order to improve their financial situation. Poverty was so widespread that poorhouses were established in order to feed the growing number of needy.

Heavy immigration during this time also affected the economy. Previous waves of immigrants had been mostly Anglo-Saxon and included many people from the upper classes. During the 1700s, however, many black slaves were brought to the colonies, and a significant number of poor people of German, Scottish, and Irish descent streamed into Pennsylvania, sparking fears of foreigners among the English inhabitants. By 1720 Pennsylvania had surpassed New York in terms of population. While reliable statistics are difficult to find, some estimate that the city of Philadelphia grew from less than 2,500 people in 1700 to 5,000 inhabitants in 1720 to over 20,000 by 1770.

Franklin believed that these newcomers tended toward financial speculation and did not know how to save. He felt that the immigrants coming to Pennsylvania sought easy shortcuts to riches. Franklin wanted Philadelphia to become a notable city, but believed that it would never reach that point if its inhabitants did not learn how to be industrious and frugal. Persuading them to share this belief became one of the goals of his almanacs.

Printed material in the colonies. Most colonists did not have easy access to books other than the Bible and religious tracts. There were not many printers and publishers in the early 1700s, and the few books that were published sold for high prices. A single book might cost twice the amount a common laborer earned in a day. Even newspapers were not widespread. Almanacs, however, were circulated by the thousands. Easy to write and publish, they were purchased by some 60 to 65 percent of colonial households.

Originally, almanacs consisted of single sheets with eight pages to a side. This sixteen-page format gradually evolved to twenty-four pages by the end of the 1600s. Almanacs generally had no cover and varied in their dimensions. A standard almanac measured approximately six by four inches, while pocket almanacs measured approximately four and one-half by two and three-fifths inches. Most almanacs included a title page, a preface, and instructions for use. Many began the calendar year with March and allotted one to two pages per month.

Almanacs played an important role in the lives of the colonists. Providing information that was otherwise difficult to obtain, almanacs were calendars supplemented with weather forecasts, tidal predictions, and astronomical tables. Some almanacs provided other information as well, including timetables for court sessions, listings of the royal European families, road conditions, conversion tables for currency, and weight and measurement tables. Almanacs also incorporated elements of popular science, literature, current events, humor, and other forms of entertainment, providing food for thought, conversation, or gossip. Some people used almanacs as diaries because they had wide margins, while others used the publications to teach their children to read.

Ben Franklin and the Enlightenment. The growing materialistic attitude in the United States during this time can be traced back to the philosophy of the Enlightenment. The Enlightenment, which is also known as the Age of Reason, was based on the ideas of French philosophers such as François Voltaire and Jean Jacques Rousseau. It was a movement that embraced science, rational thinking, progress, individualism, and the acquisition of knowledge based on fact. Proponents of the Enlightenment valued mankind's ability to reason above all other things.

The influence of the Enlightenment was manifested in the changing values in the United States during the eighteenth century. People began to concentrate on the pursuit of material rewards in this world rather than spiritual ones in the next. Franklin, who was not a religious man, is often considered a strong figure of the Enlightenment in America. He firmly believed that it was an individual's duty to better himself, and that the community would eventually benefit from individual success. A person who betters himself through hard work and diligent saving habits, for instance, eventually provides material wealth for both the person and the town or settlement.

Franklin believed in the quest for moral improvement as well as the pursuit of money. He listed thirteen virtues that he considered necessary for moral perfection—temperance, silence, order, resolution, frugality, industry, sincerity, justice, moderation, cleanliness, tranquillity, chastity, and humility. A man who acted on his beliefs, Franklin resolved to develop these virtues in himself one by one. He even kept a moral ledger with which he measured his progress.

Puritans, poverty, and politics. Franklin felt an affinity for common people and he specifically geared his almanacs toward them. He purposefully prefaced his pseudonym with "Poor" as a means of identifying himself with the masses. Although Franklin was not religious, he grew up in a strongly Puritan household, and *Poor Richard's Almanack* reflected his Puritan heritage in relation to poverty. Puritans generally believed that hard work indicated a virtuous character and that the pursuit of wealth was a praiseworthy goal—views promoted by Franklin's almanacs.

Franklin also suggested that those who remain poor deserved to be poor, another notion firmly rooted in Puritanism. Wealth came to those who applied themselves and took advantage of opportunities that came along. Furthermore, Franklin reasoned, citizens ought to help such hard-working poor people because everybody suffers temporary misfortunes.

Almanacs provided a forum outside the government and churches for discussion of politics, bringing the subject to the average Americans of the day. Franklin encouraged his readers to become involved politically and urged poor people to shape their own destinies by following the maxims in *Poor Richard's* and assuming a role in public affairs. While he did not believe that political involvement was appropriate for all members of society (he excluded immigrants and women from such duty), he did believe in opening up the political process to middle-class white males. During the 1700s, this was a revolutionary notion.

Benjamin Franklin began publishing *Poor Richard's Almanack* during a peaceful time in Pennsylvania politics. However, the political scene grew more turbulent during the 1740s and 1750s. Franklin's almanacs changed accordingly. After 1747 they featured a decidedly political bent as Franklin used the publication to distribute his Whig viewpoints. Broadly, Whigs were a political party of England that advocated commercial and industrial development and individual independence. They believed that concentrated governmental power threatened freedom and led to corruption and oppression.

Franklin's adages about tyrants reflected Whig philosophy. He sometimes attacked the French kings Louis XIV and Louis XV as the source of ruination of their country, and he continually emphasized the importance of the common man. In 1734, for example, he wrote, "an innocent Plowman is more worthy than a vicious Prince" (Franklin, *Poor Richard's Almanacks*, p. 20).

The Almanacs in Focus

The contents. Benjamin Franklin published *Poor Richard's Almanack* every year for twenty-five years under the pen name of Richard Saunders.

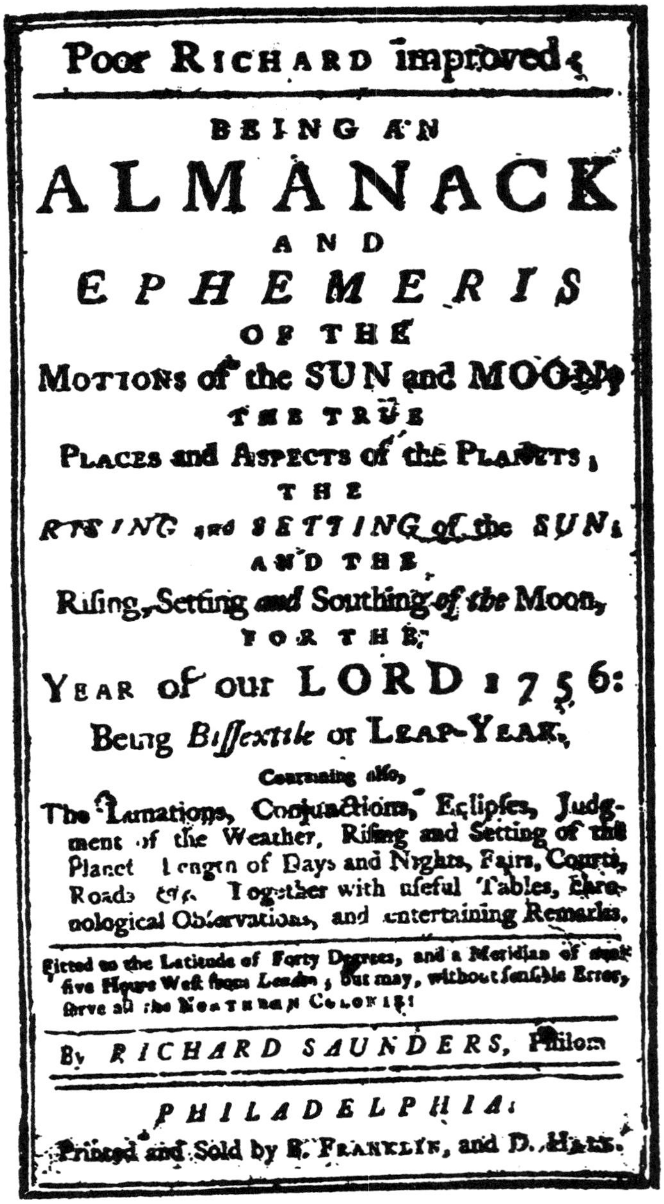

Poor RICHARD improved,

BEING AN

ALMANACK

AND

EPHEMERIS

OF THE

MOTIONS of the SUN and MOON;

THE TRUE

PLACES and ASPECTS of the PLANETS,

THE

RISING and SETTING of the SUN;

AND THE

Rising, Setting and Southing of the Moon,

FOR THE

YEAR of our LORD 1756:

Being Bissextile or LEAP-YEAR,

Containing also,

The Lunations, Conjunctions, Eclipses, Judgment of the Weather, Rising and Setting of the
Planet Length of Days and Nights, Fairs, Courts,
Roads &c. Together with useful Tables, Chronological Observations, and entertaining Remarks.

Fitted to the Latitude of Forty Degrees, and a Meridian of near
five Hours West from London; but may, without sensible Error,
serve all the NORTHERN COLONIES

By RICHARD SAUNDERS, Philom.

PHILADELPHIA:

Printed and Sold by B. FRANKLIN, and D. HALL.

Title page for the 1756 edition of *Poor Richard's Almanack.*

His almanacs contained weather predictions, poems, recipes, tidal forecasts, divinations, scientific information, and advice regarding the making of money through industry. According to the
almanac's introduction, "Richard Saunders" was
a poor farmer who was forced to publish the almanac in order to pacify his wife.

The first issue of *Poor Richard's Almanack* was
published in 1732 for the year 1733. Twenty-
four pages in length, it was an immediate hit. Almanac writers often criticized their competition,
thus drumming up business for themselves and
for almanac sales in general. Franklin, though,
immediately set a humorous tone by entering
into a witty competition with Titan Leeds, a rival almanac publisher. In the introduction to
Poor Richard's Almanack, Franklin—writing as
Saunders—states that he had not previously published an almanac because he feared hurting the
business of his dear friend Titan Leeds. He explains, however, that according to his calculations, Mr. Leeds will die shortly and the problem will cease to exist. Titan Leeds remains alive,
however, which provides material for humorous

banter in following issues. In 1735 Saunders complains that Titan Leeds's ghost is haunting him: "I say, having receiv'd much Abuse from the Ghost of Titan Leeds, who pretends to be still living, and to write Almanacks in spight of me and my Predictions, I cannot help saying, that tho' I take it patiently, I take it very unkindly. And whatever he may pretend, 'tis undoubtedly true that he is really defunct and dead" (*Poor Richard's Almanacks*, pp. 25-6).

Franklin was fond of proverbs, which are short, well-known sayings that gain authority over time, and he included many of these in *Poor Richard's Almanack*. Some of the proverbs and maxims Franklin used are still well known today: "Fish & Visitors stink in 3 days," "God helps them that help themselves," and "Tart Words make no Friends: a spoonful of honey will catch more flies than a Gallon of Vinegar" (*Poor Richard's Almanacks*, pp. 37, 39, 116).

Franklin's almanacs also contained short poems, many of which were funny or didactic. For example, under the month of October 1742, a poem advises readers on how to find true happiness:

On him true happiness shall wait
Who shunning noisy Pomp and State
Those *little* Blessings of the *Great,*
Consults the Golden Mean.
In prosp'rous Gales with Care he steers,
Nor adverse Winds, dejected, fears,
In ev'ry Turn of Fortune bears
A Face and Mind Serene.
(*Poor Richard's Almanacks,* pp. 98-9)

Franklin's zeal for science also prompted him to include scientific information on many occasions. In January 1748 Franklin wrote:

On the 19th of this Month, *Anno* 1493, was born the famous Astronomer Copernicus, to whom we own the Invention, or rather the Revival (it being taught by Pythagoras near 2000 Years before) of that now generally receiv'd System of the World which bears his Name, and supposes the Sun in the Center, this Earth a Planet revolving round it in 365 Days, 6 Hours, etc. and that Day and Night are caused by the Turning of the Earth on its own Axis once round in 24 hours.
(*Poor Richard's Almanacks,* p. 147)

The development of Poor Richard and "The Way to Wealth." Poor Richard was originally a comic character. A poor farmer who fancied himself an astrologer, he had been browbeaten by his wife into publishing an almanac for money. Richard introduces himself in the 1733 issue:

The plain Truth of the Matter is, I am excessive poor, and my Wife, good Woman, is, I tell her, excessive proud; she cannot bear, she says, to sit spinning in Shift of Tow, while I do nothing but gaze at the Stars; and has threatened more than once to burn all my Books and Rattling-Traps (as she calls my Instruments) if I do not make some profitable Use of them for the good of my Family.
(*Poor Richard's Almanacks*, p. 3)

As the years passed, Richard became less of a comic figure and more of a sage. Franklin also changed the tone of the almanac, making it less playful.

A TRUE PROGNOSTICATION, FOR 1739

While Franklin dedicated many pages of *Poor Richard's* to advice and information, humor also played a large role. His predictions, for example, were often made in jest:

Courteous Readers,
    Having consider'd the infinite Abuses arising from the false Prognostications [predictions] published among you, made under the shadow of a Pot of Drink, or so, I have here calculated one of the most sure and unerring that ever was seen....
    Of the diseases this Year.
    This year the Stone-blind shall see but very little; the Deaf shall hear but poorly; and the Dumb shan't speak very plain....
As for old Age, 'twill be incurable this Year, because of the Years past.

(*Poor Richard's Almanacks,* pp. 72-3)

In the twenty-fifth edition of the almanac, published in 1757, Benjamin Franklin wrote a speech that came to be known as "The Way to Wealth." It consisted of adages pertaining to thrift and industry from previous issues. He attributed this speech to a character called Father Abraham, a wise old man at a county auction. Asked for advice about the heavy tax burden and their woeful financial affairs, Father Abraham addresses the people quite seriously: "If you'd have my Advice, I'll give it you in short, for a Word to the Wise is enough, and many Words won't fill a Bushel, as Poor Richard says" (*Poor Richard's Almanacks*, p. 278). Father Abraham then proceeds to present a string of proverbs concerning the value of savings and hard work. The speech quickly became famous. "The Way to Wealth" was considered a "how-to" book for financial success, and colonists who dreamed of becoming rich quickly bought

Pages from the 1756 edition of *Poor Richard's Almanac.*

it. The speech was eventually translated into Russian, Welsh, Chinese, Catalan, Polish, Gaelic, and Bohemian. Along with his **Autobiography** (also covered in *Literature and Its Times*), "The Way to Wealth" became one of Benjamin Franklin's best-known pieces of writing.

Reception. Many almanacs appeared in the colonies over the years. Early colonial almanacs included William Price's *An Almanacke for New-England for the Year 1639,* and others soon followed, such as Nathaniel Ames' *Astronomical Diary and Almanack* (1726-1764) and *Poor Robin's Almanack,* published by Franklin's brother James Franklin in 1728. By the time that Benjamin Franklin printed his first issue of *Poor Richard's Almanack,* there were already five other almanacs in circulation in Philadelphia.

Poor Richard's Almanack outsold them all. The most popular nonreligious publication of its day, it sold second only to the Bible. An average rate of sales for the almanac was approximately one *Poor Richard* for every one hundred colonists. Franklin's initial wealth stemmed from these sales and stands as a symbol of early American capitalism. Franklin noted, "I endeavour'd to make it both entertaining and useful, and it accordingly came to be in such demand, that I reap'd considerable profit from it, vending annually ten thousand" (Franklin, *Writings,* p. 704).

Franklin's almanac outshone his competitors for a number of reasons. First, he printed more information than did other almanacs. Most of his competitors simply printed the phases of the moon, the times of sunrise and sunset, and speculative predictions. Franklin's almanac covered a much wider range of subjects, including proverbs, anecdotes, the times and places of important meetings, scientific tidbits, recipes, political and philosophical discussions, astrological predictions, and fair locations. Most importantly, Franklin's almanac was laced with humor and wit. As one historian notes, "the single greatest reason for the success of *Poor Richard's* was Franklin's ability to spice the prosaic matter of the ordinary almanac with more engaging commentary than his competitors could write" (Miller in Pencak, p. 188).

Sources. The origin of Franklin's pen name, Richard Saunders, has been a subject of some speculation. Some scholars believe that he took the name from an English astrologer named Richard Saunders. Other people point out that,

coincidentally or not, there was also a real person named Richard Saunder who printed an almanac during Franklin's time.

Franklin was a lover of proverbs. As a writer and a statesman, he often resorted to proverbs to augment his opinions. In his hands, these adages became persuasive tools, and he often used them to defeat an opponent's argument. He recited proverbs to support his claims of British injustice against the colonies, to threaten England, and to attack people whom he considered religious hypocrites.

Franklin borrowed these sayings from a variety of sources. He did not draw from other almanacs but rather from a wide range of authors, including François Rabelais, Miguel de Cervantes, Francis Bacon, Geoffrey Chaucer, Alexander Pope, and Lord Michel de Montaigne. According to one scholar, an important source for Franklin's sayings was James Howell's *Lexicon Tetraglotton* (1659-1660), from which Franklin allegedly derived almost two hundred sayings. Other important works include Thomas Fuller's *Gnomologia* (1732), George Herbert's *Outlandish Proverbs* (1640), and Duc de La Rochefoucauld's *Maxims* (1665). A fine writer, Franklin rewrote many proverbs in order to incorporate American elements or make them shorter. For example, *Ray's Collection of English Proverbs* (1678) included the proverb, "God restoreth health, and the physician hath the thanks." Franklin published the saying as "God heals and the doctor takes the fee" (*Poor Richard's Almanacks,* p. xvi).

For More Information

Baida, Peter. *Poor Richard's Legacy.* New York: William Morrow, 1990.

Doren, Carl Van. *Benjamin Franklin.* New York: Viking, 1938.

Franklin, Benjamin. *Poor Richard's Almanacks.* New York: George Macy, 1964.

Franklin, Benjamin. *Benjamin Franklin's Autobiographical Writings.* Edited by Carl Van Doren. New York: Viking, 1945.

Pencak, William. "Politics and Ideology in Poor Richard's Almanack." *The Pennsylvania Magazine of History and Biography* 116, no. 2 (April 1992): 183-211.

Simmons, R. C. *The American Colonies from Settlement to Independence.* New York: David McKay, 1976.

Stowell, Marion B. *Early American Almanacs.* New York: Burt Franklin, 1977.

The Prince

by
Niccolò Machiavelli

THE LITERARY WORK

A political essay in the form of a discourse set in Florence in 1513; first published in 1529.

SYNOPSIS

Intended as a guide for the next leader of Florence, *The Prince* provides an explanation of different kinds of principalities, or territories, ruled by princes. It explains how a successful prince gains and keeps power, and finally exhorts the next leader of Florence to liberate Italy from foreign powers.

orn in 1469, Niccolò Machiavelli entered public life for the first time in 1498. He proceeded to achieve the post of First Secretary of the Republic. He later became Head of Second Chancery, an official who was partly in charge of the war office. While in these positions, Machiavelli was entrusted with several foreign missions. His responsibilities often included traveling on diplomatic errands to foreign states. He never distinguished himself as an outstanding diplomat, but made use of his keen abilities of observation and analysis to learn about power. By traveling to Rome and foreign lands such as France and Germany, Machiavelli gained a political education that very few men of his time were privy to. These experiences proved to be of great value in his later writings.

Events in History at the Time of the Essay

Machiavelli's Italy. The Italy of Machiavelli's day had fallen on political hard times. Plagued by terrible corruption, it consisted of several city-states, each operating as an independent republic. Adding to this chaotic political situation was the fact that Italy was also home to the pope, who controlled his own territory and, because he was the leader of the Catholic Church, exerted an influence far beyond that of a prince of the other Italian city-states.

Florence, Machiavelli's home, was one of these Italian city-states. Florence was the center of some of the greatest artistic achievements the world had ever known, but much like the rest of Italy, its political instability proved to be its downfall. Florence had become a wealthy center of industry, trade, and finance by the early sixteenth century, yet due to its political ineptness, it lacked any sort of capable military force. This combination of economic wealth and military weakness put Florence in an extremely precarious situation since it was surrounded by several hostile city-states, including Milan, Naples, and Venice, as well as the Papal States (areas controlled by the pope).

Embroiled in this tense political atmosphere, the republics constantly shifted alliances as they attempted to secure some sort of balance of power. Under the leadership of Lorenzo de Medici, Florence had made an alliance with Milan to ensure Florence's protection against the powerful city-state of Venice. In 1492 the al-

Portrait of Machiavelli by Santi di Tito.

liance was broken by Lorenzo's son, Piero. This created a situation of instability for Florence that was to be further aggravated by political developments elsewhere in Europe.

Adding to Italy's problems was the fact that two of Europe's major powers, Spain and France, were in the process of consolidating their respective empires. Suddenly, with their newly unified countries strengthened beyond imagination, the French and Spanish each looked toward Italy and found it surprisingly weak. Despite the strength of its individual city-states, a divided Italy was no match for either of these united powers. From 1494 to 1527—most of Machiavelli's life—Italy was repeatedly invaded by foreign powers, enduring almost thirty years of onslaughts from the French alone. Led by three successive kings, the French eventually succeeded in overpowering almost all of Italy. In fact, the only serious opposition to the French invasion came from the Spanish, who at times occupied the south of Italy, which they incorporated into their growing empire.

For a long stretch, Florence remained independent, resisting foreign control. But in 1494 the House of Medici turned control of the city over to the French. Horrified by this development, the Florentine citizens rose up in protest, driving the Medici from power and establishing a republic in their absence. The republic struggled to survive under the enormous foreign and internal pres-

sures. This was the period in which Machiavelli spent important years in public service, attempting at one point to organize a native militia that would free Florence from its reliance on mercenary troops, foreign soldiers who fought for pay. Unfortunately, this militia was no match for the Spanish. After establishing alliances with the pope and Venice, Spain took control of Florence, returning the Medici to power.

It was following the Medici's return to power that Machiavelli started work on *The Prince*. He hoped that the Medici could provide Italy with the greatness of leadership that was required to rescue Florence and the rest of Italy from their political woes. But the Medici were able to produce no such leader, and Italy slipped into further chaos and disarray.

Life's work. Machiavelli lived in one of the most extraordinary eras of history. This period encompassed the remarkable age of exploration, several groundbreaking political events, and the lives of many important historical figures. Yet he managed to stand out as one of the most brilliant minds of that or any era.

It was during Machiavelli's travels that he first conceived the idea of a treatise discussing the science of ruling a state. This idea spawned *How the Duke of Valetinois Killed Vitellozzo Vitellozzi and Oloverotto da Fermo,* which attempted to show a cause and effect relationship between the actions of a certain political leader and the subsequent reaction of the citizens. It was Machiavelli's first attempt at political discourse, which, despite his achievements within the Florentine government, would prove to be his real claim to fame.

Machiavelli spent a great deal of energy on the formation of a Florentine militia, an undertaking that he had been chosen to head. He regarded the task as vital because it would free Florence from reliance on foreign mercenaries. Since mercenaries were primarily fighting for money rather than patriotism, Machiavelli believed that their presence was directly responsible for the insubordination that plagued Florence's military forces at the time. Unfortunately, despite Machiavelli's efforts, invading Spaniards defeated the new militia almost immediately, and the Florentine Republic collapsed.

Following the collapse of the republic, Machiavelli was imprisoned as a suspected enemy of the Medici. Machiavelli was tortured, but later was able to prove his innocence. Moving out of the city, Machiavelli retired to a quiet life. He reflected on the fate of Florence and Italy, attempting to put it all into some sort of historical context. During this time, he wrote his major work, *The Prince,* as well as *The Discourses on the First Ten Books of Titus Livy, The Art of War, Life of Castuccio Castracani,* and *The History of Florence.* He also wrote some literary works, among them *Mandragola,* which is regarded by some critics as the best Italian play of the 1500s.

Despite his tremendous writing output, Machiavelli longed to return to public life. The House of Medici, however, continuously refused his services. When they were overthrown in 1527, Machiavelli thought he would have the chance to work in government again, but his employment was ironically rejected because of suspicions that he had ties to the Medici. Fifty-eight years old at the time, Machiavelli was crushed by the disappointment. He died less than a month later.

Machiavelli's political views. Clearly *The Prince* was born out of Machiavelli's own political beliefs. Machiavelli was a firm believer in the "state," and he considered its survival the top priority. By the "state," it is generally agreed that he was probably referring to Florence. By exerting its strength and influence, the city could possibly unite the whole of Italy, restoring it to the glory of Roman times.

The advice given in *The Prince* is based on the assumption that the freedom and survival of the state supersedes all other concerns. Machiavelli rationalizes the initial cruelty that he advocates in the work, believing it will lead to peace and stability. His reverence for the state led him to conclude that the end, the survival of the state, justifies the means, or methods taken to insure it. This dedication to the state also meant that he favored no particular political dogma or ideol-

ogy, instead placing his trust in realities, like the art of war. Given these beliefs, it becomes easier to understand Machiavelli's desire to serve both the republican government of Florence and the rival Medici government. Ultimately his loyalty was to neither political entity, but rather to Florence itself.

Another of Machiavelli's beliefs concerned the relationship of greatness of a nation to the abilities of its leader. He believed that nations fell into a pattern of gaining power, slipping into an inevitable decline and loss of influence, and then, after the emergence of a great leader, returning to power and strength. He further believed that Florence and Italy, mired in political chaos and forced to endure foreign control during his lifetime, would one day reclaim the glory of ancient Rome. With this in mind, Machiavelli intended *The Prince* as a guide for the next great leader. It was his hope that this future leader would arise to bring Florence and all of Italy back to its former grandeur.

The Essay in Focus

The contents. For purposes of discussion, *The Prince* is often divided into four sections, each dealing with a different subject. The first eleven chapters deal with principalities; section two (chapters 12-14) deals with the military; section three (chapters 15-23) discusses the qualities that a successful prince must possess; and section four (chapters 24-6) deals specifically with the political situation in Italy.

There are, according to Machiavelli, four types of principalities, or princely states:

1. Hereditary principalities. These are principalities traditionally under control of a ruler's family. If governed conservatively, Machiavelli says, these can be controlled with relative ease.
2. Mixed principalities. These arise when a hereditary principality is combined with newly conquered territories. Mixed principalities are more difficult for a ruler to maintain. Machiavelli suggests five methods for such rulers. Among these is the suggestion that, in order to ensure his subjects' loyalty, a ruler must come to a newly acquired territory, install himself as head of its people, and subsequently provide for its protection, allowing no foreign power to enter into that territory.
3. Principalities acquired by a new prince. Machiavelli states that four types of such principalities exist:
   a. The territory that one acquires by force.
   b. The territory that a prince acquires through someone else; for example, as a gift from a king.
   c. The territory acquired through crime or cruelty rather than any sort of admirable greatness.
   d. The territory acquired through the favor of a prince's fellow citizens or the local nobility.
   Machiavelli makes observations about each type of territory. Here, for example, he observes that it is better to have the support of the population than local nobility. He contends that the support of the general populace provides the prince with a greater ability to maintain control. But if that power comes through the nobility, then his job is harder because the nobility invariably long for control themselves.
4. Ecclesiastical (Church)

The second part of The Prince discusses how a principality can prepare itself militarily, specifically in terms of defense or attack. Machiavelli starts out this section by declaring there are four types of armies a prince can employ: mercenary, auxiliary, national, and mixed. Of the four, the first two are described as "useless and dangerous." The problem with mercenaries is that they have no loyalty and are not willing to die for their employer. Machiavelli blames the desperate state of his nation on its reliance on mercenaries, charging that their poor performance allowed Charles VIII of France to easily conquer Italy. Auxiliary troops are those called upon when another more powerful state asks for assistance in an offensive or defensive endeavor. The problem with auxiliary troops is that if they are successful, the prince is almost always indebted to them, and if they fail, the prince is "left in the lurch" (Machiavelli, The Prince, p. 83). Machiavelli contends that native armies are the best fighting forces, surpassing even mixed troops (which combine native, auxiliary, and mercenary troops), because native troops are fighting for their homeland.

In the third part of The Prince, Machiavelli explains how a prince must conduct himself in regard to his friends and subjects, and provides a set of rules for engagement with both groups. He cautions the prince not to try to be viewed as generous, for this leads to the squandering of resources and the need to institute heavy taxation to repair the damage. He contends that the prince will be hated if he places such a burden on the people. Another rule espoused by Machiavelli holds that a few well-publicized acts of cruelty, or harsh punishment, will prove compassionate in the long run and probably prevent further crimes.

Machiavelli further explains that if one cannot be both feared and loved—and one rarely can— it is better for a ruler to be feared than loved, as fear is a stronger and more binding emotion. At the same time, according to another rule, a prince must avoid making himself despised. To accomplish this, he must show extra regard for the property and women of his subjects.

One of the final rules discussed in this section encourages a prince to undertake great works that inspire esteem in the hearts of his subjects. Here Machiavelli provides the example of King Ferdinand I of Spain, who "planned and completed great projects, which have always kept his subjects in a state of suspense and wonder, intent on their outcome" (The Prince, p. 120).

In the last section of The Prince, Machiavelli addresses the political situation that existed in Italy at the time he wrote his treatise. In chapter 24 Machiavelli postulates that the Italian princes have all lost control of their states because they all shared "a common weakness in regard to their military organization" and were unable to balance the allegiance of the people with the loyalty of the nobility (The Prince, p. 128). He discusses whether or not human affairs are governed by fortune. He suggests that, at best, fortune controls half of what men do, while free will dictates the rest. In the final chapter of The Prince, Machiavelli declares that conditions exist "which would make it possible for a prudent and capable man to introduce a new order, bringing honor to himself and prosperity to all and every Italian" (The Prince, p. 134). He urges Lorenzo de' Medici to seize the moment and develop an army to exploit the weaknesses of Italy's foreign oppressors. If he were to succeed, Machiavelli promises, the undying love and devotion of the Italian people would be his.

On cruelty. *The Prince* has been much maligned as a work that advocates cruelty. But steadfastly concerned for the common good, the author distinguishes between well- and ill-used cruelties. He warns, for example, that in conquering and annexing a hereditary state, a prince will not be secure until he kills the entire bloodline of the former ruling family. The general community, however, is to be left alone to practice its familiar customs without interference. There are two concerns—to extinguish the family of the hereditary prince, the people whom the new prince has dispossessed, and to leave the taxes and laws of the community undisturbed. In other words, the prince should not subject the entire community but rather a select few to cruelty. These few unfortunates are victimized because doing so would secure the new prince's position.

Chapter 8 of *The Prince* gives examples of vicious acts of ill-used cruelty. Reaching back to around 300 B.C., the text holds up as an example a tyrant of a city-state in Sicily named Agathocles, who exhibited unacceptable cruelty by putting large numbers of his own citizens to death. Machiavelli regards his behavior as unjustified evil, for it stems not from an interest in forming a republic or a secure kingdom but rather from a thirst for "an absolute power which . . . is called tyranny" (Machiavelli in de Grazia, p. 86).

According to *The Prince,* cruel behavior is to be used only when necessary for the common good. Once such a course of action is decided upon, it should be done quickly and then dropped. A good prince does not persist in such behavior. He does not shy from acting cruelly should such behavior prove necessary, but neither does he resort to it unless he must. It is important to note here that this is not a description of the ideal prince in the view of Machiavelli but rather of the successful prince in his time.

Reaction to *The Prince*. With the possible exception of Plato's *Republic,* there is probably no other political discourse as widely read as Machiavelli's *The Prince,* and very few works have been both so esteemed and criticized. After the release of *The Prince,* Machiavelli was considered by many to be the devil incarnate. In fact, in England, "old Nick," which alluded to Machiavelli's first name, emerged as a nickname for Satan.

Some of this hatred was almost certainly triggered by the contents of *The Prince.* His statements that a prince was better served by being feared than loved, that generosity was a fault, and that the art of war was the highest calling of a leader, all seemed to contradict every moral code the Western world had developed. In fact, the term "Machiavellian," first used by Elizabethan dramatists a few decades after the work was published, has come to symbolize a leader marked by cruelty and ruthlessness.

Machiavelli became a symbol of cruelty and evil, his name and reputation gaining a life of their own, separate from the realities of the words that he had actually written. Taken out of context, twisted, and paraphrased, his ideas were used by numerous political and religious groups to categorize their enemies, most notably in France. There he was blamed for inspiring Catherine de' Medici's infamous Saint Bartholomew's Day Massacre, as well as the Wars of Religion, in which French Protestants (called Huguenots) were slaughtered in the name of the French government and the Roman Catholic Church.

Despite all the criticism *The Prince* has received, however, it has gone down in history as a remarkable and groundbreaking political work. Napoleon Bonaparte considered it the only worthwhile book on politics, and King Henry VIII's advisers urged him to abandon his reading of ancient political discourses, like Plato's *Republic,* and study instead the recently translated English version of *The Prince.* Over the years it would be generalized into a work about how to gain and keep power, although Machiavelli had not intended for his work to be appropriated by all those who sought to consolidate power. He aimed only to provide assistance to the one who would rise to lead Italy by recording his observations and conclusions about the turmoil of his land and times.

For More Information

Barcinou, Edmond. *Machiavelli.* New York: Grove, 1961.

de Grazia, Sebastian. *Machiavelli in Hell.* New York: Vintage, 1994.

Machiavelli, Niccolò. *The Prince.* London: Penguin, 1981.

Morley, John. *Machiavelli.* London: Folcroft, 1969.

Muir, D. Erskine. *Machiavelli and His Times.* New York: E. P. Dutton, 1936.

Pulver, Jeffrey. *Machiavelli, The Man, His Works, & His Times.* London: Herbert Joseph, 1937.

Republic

by
Plato

Plato (428-347 B.C.) was the son of wealthy and powerful Athenian parents. He rejected the political life that had corrupted members of his family and became a student under the famous scholar and philosopher Socrates. The *Republic* was written at a time when Athens was shaking itself off from its defeat by other Greek city-states in the Peloponnesian War, and when it and other city-states were negotiating the best methods of civic organization and rule.

THE LITERARY WORK

A philosophical dialogue set in late fifth-century B.C. Athens; written around 380 B.C.

SYNOPSIS

The *Republic* examines the concept of "justice" in the state and the human soul and provides a detailed description of Plato's vision of the perfect society.

Events in History at the Time the Dialogue Takes Place

Athenian democracy. The established political system out of which Plato wrote the *Republic* was a type of democracy, although Athenian democracy always had an element of aristocratic control about it. The Athenian democracy, which began in 510 B.C., replaced an earlier form of government by individual rulers called *tyrannoi,* or "tyrants," although the Greek word did not at first have a negative connotation. A tyrant was a man who had overthrown a local aristocracy and seized power in the government illegally. The tyrant's power was closely linked to the general populace who had supported him in his overthrow of the former aristocracy. Some of the early tyrants were strong leaders who provided an effective transition government before the eventual democracy. However, the last tyrant of the era became a harsh ruler, and he was ousted in 510 B.C. Some nobles at first attempted to restore the aristocracy, but this was very unpopular with the now democratically inclined populace. It was Cleisthènes, a member of the Alcmaeonid family, who came up with the brilliant idea of bringing the masses of ordinary Athenians into an alliance with his family. Thus was born the Athenian democracy.

Cleisthenes sought to avoid factional disagreements among the Athenian people by breaking up the four regional "tribes" of Athens into ten tribes, with members of each tribe drawn from many different Athenian regions. A strong sense of centralized nationhood was thereby encouraged. He also set up the "Council of 500," manned by fifty men drawn by lot from each of the ten tribes. The council prepared business for the assembly, which included all free adult male citizens. The assembly voted on all matters concerning the city. A program of "ostracism" was also installed; if 6,000 citizens voted to exile a man, he could be banished from the city-state, with his property and other rights intact, for a period of ten years. It was a program designed to ensure that no one person rose to a position of extreme power in the city, whether by wealth or influence, and with a few exceptions, it endured into the time that Plato wrote the *Republic.*

FROM DEMOCRACY TO DICTATORSHIP: THE SOCRATIC METHOD

Socrates: The finest government and the finest kind of man remain for us to discuss, dictatorship and the dictatorial man.

Glaucon: They certainly do remain.

Socrates: Come, my dear friend, what is dictatorship like? That it evolves from democracy is pretty clear.

Glaucon: Obviously.

Socrates: Does it not evolve from democracy in much the same way as democracy does from oligarchy?

Glaucon: How?

Socrates: What they put before them as the good, which was the basis of oligarchy, was wealth, was it not?

Glaucon: Yes.

Socrates: Then their insatiable desire for wealth, and their neglect of other things for money-making was what destroyed it, was it not?

Glaucon: True.

Socrates: Now insatiability for what democracy defines as the good also destroys it.

Glaucon: And what do you say it defines as such?

Socrates: Liberty . . . .

(*Republic,* 562a-c)

There were many different levels of responsibility and rights within the Athenian democracy. Not everyone who lived in the city-state had a voice in what went on. Women, slaves, and foreigners were unable to participate in the democratic process. Early on in the Athenian experiment with democracy, even some of the men who were eligible could not participate in the assembly for practical reasons. Attendance at assembly was an unpaid activity that absorbed a lot of time. Only those with a lot of time and money were able to take part on a regular basis. Although this situation had changed by the time Plato was writing the *Republic*, it does tend to suggest that, at its heart, Athenian democracy was not perceived as the system of utter equality that we sometimes associate with the word "democracy." What's more, the aristocrats did tend to have a dominant role in the city's political life. From 445 to 429 B.C., for example, the Athenian democracy was dominated by Pericles, a great general from the Alcmaeonid family who single-handedly directed the city's lively effort at civic reconstruction and imperial expansion. As one author comments, "so special a position seems to have been possible only in Athens, and there largely because the change to democracy had been so rapid and so thorough that people, used to more authoritarian systems, still looked for a leader" (Bowra, p. 76).

Plato is not tolerant of what he sees as the excesses of democracy; in Book 8 of the *Republic*, Socrates—the central character in the dialogue—sarcastically describes a democracy as a wonderful state in which everyone gets to do what he likes: "In this city ... there is no compulsion to rule, even if you are capable of it, or again to be ruled if you do not want to be, or to be at war when the others are, or at peace unless you desire peace. If some law forbids you to hold office or to go to law, you nevertheless do both if it occurs to you to do so. Is that not a divine and pleasant life for the time being?" (Plato, *Republic*, 557e)

Socrates. The *Republic* is set in the late fifth century B.C., while Socrates, who died in 399 B.C., was still alive. Perhaps the most famous and influential man of his day, Socrates left not a single written word to be remembered by—everything we know about him and his philosophical theories comes from his many students, most notably Plato.

Socrates was born in Athens around 470 B.C., the son of a stonemason. He came into conflict with the Thirty Tyrants, a group of aristocrats installed by the Spartan commander Lysander to oversee the defeated Athens at the conclusion of

Bust of Socrates.

the Peloponnesian War. Yet when these men failed to take control of Athens and democracy returned, Socrates was charged with corrupting youth and failing to worship the old gods of the city. In response to these charges, Socrates chose not to break out of prison, as a friend encouraged him to do, but rather to follow the state's order to poison himself by drinking hemlock. The death of his beloved teacher at the hands of the reinstated democracy in 399 B.C. spurred Plato to try and discover the "just" state by writing the *Republic.*

Socrates is often referred to as "the greatest teacher in European history" (Jaeger, p. 27). He revolutionized Greek society by questioning every traditionally held pattern of thought and by studying the motivations of the individual as a philosophical subject. "Education is more than teaching," one scholar notes, "and Socrates's chief aim was not to impart information but to make the other man think, and thus to make him a better person" (Ehrenberg, p. 381). The late fifth century B.C. is commonly held by modern historians to have been a time when Athenians began to question the political and social traditions that had long guided them; the teachings of Socrates were an important part of this self-examination.

The Thirty Tyrants. In the turmoil surrounding Athens' defeat by Sparta in the Peloponnesian War (431-404 B.C.), the city was badly disorganized. Thirty members of the aristocracy were installed to take charge of the city, a move that was heralded as a return to ancestral laws. The appointments, however, were actually orchestrated by the leaders of Sparta. Plato came from the wealthy and powerful class of landholders in Athens, and his family was well represented among these thirty men; one of his uncles and a cousin were prominent members of the group.

The Thirty Tyrants proved to be a corrupt group. They hired thugs with whips to strike fear into the citizens and keep order in the streets, banished 5,000 of the city-state's residents, and executed more than 1,500 Athenian citizens, mostly rich and powerful men who opposed their policies. The reign of terror was relatively short-lived, however. After about ninety days, the Thirty Tyrants were defeated and exiled, and Athens once again operated under a democratic constitution.

Sparta. The city-state Sparta, the traditional enemy of Athens, figures at different times and in different ways in the *Republic.* Sparta is cited as an example of how things can go wrong in a city

if it is run by its aristocrats or by its military, but also as a model of the ideal city. Sparta was the second largest city-state in Greece and was run in a way almost exactly opposite to the democratic management of Athens. It was led by two hereditary kings who were in charge of the city during times of war, which tended to be often. The city was dominated by its military, which had the leisure to develop its strength because it had groups of other people to tend the land and do most of the labor necessary for running the city. Among these groups were the *helots,* the native people of the area. The helots outnumbered the Spartans by about five to one but were kept in a state of serfdom in the agricultural lands surrounding the city. They were not actually slaves, but they were required to give half or more of their produce to the city-state. Moreover, they were subject to unspeakable abuse by the Spartans, whose soldiers seem to have had an initiation ritual—called the "hiding game"—that involved attacking and killing helots at night. The other large group of people under Spartan rule were the *perioeci,* which means "the people living around here." These people inhabited towns in the vicinity of Sparta and were allowed to be more or less independent except at times of war, when they were forced to serve in the Spartan army.

The single feature of Spartan life for which that city has remained famous is its military might. Sparta built its military prowess in a ruthless manner. Raising the perfect soldier began at birth, when weak-looking babies were killed at the discretion of the state, not of the parents. Beginning at age seven, boys were taken from their parents and housed in military dormitories. Admitted into the army at age twenty, they continued to live in strictly military quarters. They were prevented from residing with their wives unless they had children, though in some cases even this right was refused. "Military training was the central and ongoing part of [a soldier's] life," one historian observes. "All facets of [the soldier's] existence indicated the final goal: the production of the single-minded, simple-living, superbly disciplined soldier" (Robinson, p. 57).

The *Republic*'s perfect city-state bears some likeness to Sparta in several respects. Plato, for example, argues that the ideal form of education is state-sponsored, a notion based in part on the Spartan model. Plato's own city-state, Athens, allowed the family to educate its children, an arrangement that Plato thought made for poor citizens. In addition, Plato's statement that the guardians of the city should not have money echoes the Spartan refusal to provide gold and silver to its citizens, a prohibition that was designed to keep them from trading for foreign luxury goods. It is a mark of how revolutionary the *Republic* was intended to be that Plato, who was writing for an Athenian audience, should invoke Sparta as a model in any way, given the long and ongoing history of war between the two cities.

The Dialogue in Focus

The plot. The *Republic* tries to define justice and to show that justice is better for states and for individual men than injustice. Summing up the author's views, one researcher explains: "Plato taught a conception of justice as a quality of the soul, in virtue of which men set aside the irrational desire to taste every pleasure and to gain a selfish satisfaction out of every object, and accommodated themselves to the discharge of a single function for the general benefit" (Barker, p. 171).

The *Republic* is divided into ten books in which Socrates, the major character of the work, asks questions of his listeners in order to arrive at a definition of the ideal city-state. In the context of his discussion, Socrates describes the three classes of citizens (the guardians, or leaders; the auxiliaries, or soldiers; and the workers, providers of food and clothing) and explores the need for these classes to function together harmoniously. Socrates compares them to the components of the human personality, which must function together well if a person is to succeed in life. In Socrates' view, the ideal man is the philosopher, literally a "lover of wisdom," and guardians of the state should, along with their other preparation, be trained as philosophers so that they might be wise leaders. In a famous analogy, Socrates compares the philosopher to a man who leaves a dark cave and discovers the true world outside; he returns to the cave to illuminate others, who believe that reality consists only of the shadows on the cave wall in front of them. Because he has dared to explore beyond the confines of the average mind, the philosopher becomes able to teach wisdom to the common man.

Examining different types of government, Plato's *Republic* investigates the relative strengths and evils of timocracy (rule by the military), oligarchy (rule by aristocrats), democracy (rule by the masses), and dictatorship (absolute rule by one person). The ideal city as explained in the *Republic* is ruled by the philosopher-king, a completely just man, and managed by the guardians, people of both genders who are intelligent, liberal, and stable.

But the *Republic* is much more than simply a political document; it aims to reorganize the life of every person in the city-state and offers detailed advice on how to carry this out. The work is accordingly wide-ranging, addressing social, economic, political, and religious concerns. Plato develops theories of education, public housing, child-rearing, marriage, labor division, and poetry—all of which are shown to contribute to the happiness of citizens and the effective running of their state.

Gender revolution? In Book 5, Plato writes that women should be allowed to be guardians, the governors of the ideal state under the philosopher-king:

[I]f the male and the female are seen to be different as regards a particular craft or other pursuit we shall say this must be assigned to one or the other. But if they seem to differ in this particular only, that the female bears the children while the male begets them, we shall say that there has been no kind of proof that a woman is different from a man as regards the duties we are talking about, and we shall still believe that our guardians and their wives should follow the same pursuits.

(*Republic*, 454e)

Many historians have seen this statement as an early vote for feminism, but others caution that "Plato's interest is neither in women's rights nor in their preferences as they see them, but rather with production of the common good, and a state

Undated woodcut of Aristotle, Plato's student who commented extensively on the *Republic*.

where all contribute the best they can according to their aptitude" (Annas, p. 181). Just the same, because Athenian women were kept almost completely inside the home—they were not allowed to shop, socialize, or even walk about freely—and were often denied access even to their own husband's social lives, any move toward granting them duties other than bearing and raising children was revolutionary for the time.

Plato's style of family planning. Perhaps the best glimpse into Plato's conception of the role of women in an ideal society comes later in Book 5, where he proposes that "guardian" wives be shared among the ruling class: "All these women shall be wives in common to all the men, and not one of them shall live privately with any man; the children too should be held in common so that no parent shall know which is his own offspring, and no child shall know his parent" (*Republic,* 457d). (The guardian class, it should be noted, is to be small, intelligent, and morally upright; sharing wives and children is not a practice that Plato suggests for all members of the city.) From the age of twenty to forty, women are to breed children for the state; men can continue to father children until they are fifty. Plato writes that only the best men and women should be allowed to bear children and describes how their offspring should be raised communally: "The children of good parents they will take to a rearing pen in the care of nurses living apart in a certain section of the city; the children of inferior parents, or any child of the others born defective, they will hide, as it is fitting, in a secret and unknown place" (*Republic,* 461c). Here, Plato is really recommending that weak babies be killed, a practice that was fairly common even in his day; the Spartans, as noted earlier, practiced this grim version of family planning.

Sources. After Socrates died, Plato went to mainland Italy and Sicily and may have studied with the Pythagorean philosophers living there. These men believed that numbers and ratios were the key to understanding the world. Many scholars have noted the influence of the Pythagorean philosophers on Plato's ideas: "One can easily imagine Plato seeing ... the possibility of giving precise definitions in wholly mathematical terms of such apparently vague and evaluative notions as harmony and disharmony, beauty and ugliness, maybe even justice and injustice, good and evil, and the other things of which Socrates sought definition" (Grube in *Republic,* p. xii).

Of course the most important sources for the *Republic* were the teachings of Socrates, Plato's mentor. His beliefs cannot be studied firsthand because Socrates did not keep any written record of his thoughts. We do know that Plato copied from Socrates the method of learning through dialogue—in which answers to difficult problems are arrived at through a series of logically connected questions. Socrates also influenced Plato's thoughts on the relationship between ethics and politics. Socrates's extraordinary impact on Plato is evident in even a cursory examination of his student's collected works, for Socrates is the main character in most of Plato's dialogues.

The dialogue's impact over the years. In later years, the *Republic* had a varied history. It influenced the Latin writer Cicero in his attempt to work out a just system of government for the Romans. Cicero in turn influenced the early medieval philosopher St. Augustine of Hippo, who tried to do the same for Christian culture. In the Renaissance the *Republic* emerged as a very important text; it influenced Sir Thomas More's *Utopia,* for example. The *Republic* was also embraced by more sinister elements. It has been pointed out that "in our own century a regime like that of Hitler tried to use the *Republic* as some sort of prototype for its own particular type of Brave New World" (Robinson, p. 122).

IMPOSSIBLE DREAM?

What has been said about the State and its government is not a mere dream, and though difficult it is not impossible; but it is only possible when philosophers become kings, or kings philosophers.

(*Republic,* p. 540d)

Events in History at the Time the Dialogue Was Written

The polis. The Greek *polis* is the basic political unit about which Plato writes in the *Republic;* it is commonly referred to by modern historians as the "city-state." But to fifth- and fourth-century B.C. Greeks, as one author points out, it was "not simply a city or a state; it implies active participation, a joint undertaking on the part of its citizens" (Klosko, p. 6). Political life was made more intense and more necessary by the populations of the city-states at the time: when the *Republic* was being written, Athens had a population of only 40,000 active citizens (Athenian males), although this figure climbs to 110-150,000 if Athenian women and children are included, and to 300,000 if foreigners and slaves are counted. Because women, slaves, and foreigners were not allowed to vote, the *polis* was run by a small minority of its population. By the time Plato wrote the *Republic,* a very large percentage of the citizens of Athens were civil servants, earning their living by serving as jurors, or "sitting in the Assembly, in military service, as magistrates" and the like (Klosko, p. 6). But the strongest relationship between citizens and the *polis* was not political or economic, but spiritual: "The *polis* recognized no separation between state and church. Greek religion was state religion; the individual performed religious service by worshipping the gods of his *polis*" (Klosko, p. 6).

Social upheaval. The *Republic* is set during a time of political unrest and general cultural experimentation throughout Greece. The Peloponnesian War (431-404 B.C.), a conflict that pitted Athens against nearby Sparta and her allies, ended in 404 with the defeat of Athens and the widespread decay of all the cities involved in the war. The fall of Athens left a huge power vacuum in Greece that Sparta attempted to fill. Sparta had presented itself as the great liberator of Greek cities from the tyranny of Athens during the war. After the war Sparta became the tyrant. By the time the *Republic* was written, Sparta was more powerful than ever, but the city's power was based on fear rather than respect. Moreover, the shattered Greek city-states were beset with massive interior weaknesses, "incapable not only of leading one another but of following a leader" (Hammond, p. 438). The *Republic* thus appeared at a time when the city-state was put to its crucial test as a political form and its citizens approached a new stage of intellectual freedom and capitalist development.

This fundamental questioning of the political, social, and intellectual status quo enriched Greek culture. It was "an age of bold experiments in politics, philosophy, literature and art" according to one historian; "[I]n the civilization of the fourth century [B.C.] many of the most fruitful ideas in human history came to birth" (Hammond, p. 438). We see the influence of the times in the *Republic*'s recommendation of a radical new view of traditional political and social arrangements such as the family.

The Academy. After the death of Socrates, Plato left Athens for some time and traveled to Sicily

and mainland Italy. Around 385 B.C. Plato founded in Athens what some historians have called the first university. It was at this academy that Plato is said to have written the *Republic*. He spent the rest of his life working there. The Academy was Plato's legacy to the city of Athens; it endured until 529 A.D. The curriculum at the Academy combined the studies of mathematics and geometry with work in ethics, politics, and psychology. Some members of the Academy, including Plato himself, were invited by various Greek and foreign cities to help develop workable civic constitutions. Such invitations put the *Republic* in the context that Plato intended—not as a text of theories with no consequences but as a document intended to be used in political reform. As far as Plato's own efforts are concerned, however, the ideals of the *Republic* did not prove popular in his day, and his career as a political reformer went nowhere.

Aristotle comments on the *Republic*. The most complete response to Plato's work, including the *Republic,* can be found in Aristotle's *Politics.* Aristotle, who studied under Plato at the Academy, was not always the most sympathetic reader of his teacher's work. He registered objections to several of Plato's more radical proposals, including that for a community pool of wives and children for the guardian class: "Each citizen acquires a thousand sons, but these are not one man's sons; any of them is equally the son of any person, and as a result will be equally neglected by everyone" (Aristotle, *Politics,* 1261b32). He argued further that the severing of personal ties among people runs contrary to what is best for the state: "Community of wives and children is prescribed for the Guardian class. It would seem to be far more useful if applied to the agricultural class. For where wives and children are held in common there is less affection, and a lack of strong affection among the ruled is necessary in the interests of obedience and absence of revolt" (Aristotle, *Politics,* 1262a40).

For More Information

Annas, Julia. *Introduction to Plato's Republic.* Oxford: Clarendon Press, 1981.

Aristotle. *The Politics.* Translated by T. A. Sinclair. London: Penguin Books, 1992.

Barker, Ernest. *Greek Political Theory: Plato and His Predecessors.* New York: Methuen, 1960.

Bowra, C. M. *Periclean Athens.* New York: Dial Press, 1971.

Ehrenberg, Victor. *From Solon to Socrates: Greek History and Civilization during the 6th and 5th Centuries B.C.* London: Methuen, 1976.

Hammond, N. G. L. *A History of Greece to 322 B.C.* Oxford: Clarendon Press, 1959.

Jaeger, W. *Paideia.* Volume 2. Oxford University Press, 1944.

Klosko, George. *The Development of Plato's Political Theory.* New York: Methuen, 1986.

Plato. *The Republic.* Translated by G. M. A. Grube. 2nd ed. Indianapolis: Hackett, 1992.

Robinson, T. M. *The Greek Legacy.* Toronto: CBC Merchandising, 1979.

"Rip Van Winkle"

by
Washington Irving

Washington Irving was born in 1783 in New York City, shortly before the end of the American Revolution. He grew up in an era of rapid change for New York and the Hudson River Valley. The region's traditional Dutch culture, which played an important part in Irving's imaginative development, was beginning to fade due to the influence of new settlers from other areas of New England and other forces of modernization. As these changes unfolded Irving felt a sense of loss that he eventually expressed in his work.

THE LITERARY WORK

A short story set in the Catskill Mountains in New York sometime between 1750 and 1799; published in 1819.

SYNOPSIS

A man falls asleep in the woods of colonial New York for twenty years; he awakens to discover that momentous changes have taken place in his absence.

Events in History at the Time the Short Story Takes Place

Dutch heritage in the Catskill Mountain region. In 1609 Henry Hudson, an employee of the Dutch East India Company, explored the river that has since been named for him. The first group of permanent settlers to lay claim to the region that became New York arrived from Holland in 1624. These Dutch settlers called the region New Netherland. Though other Dutch travelers joined the colony, it remained small. Holland was relatively prosperous during the seventeenth century and was one of the few European centers that practiced religious tolerance. Few people living there wanted to leave their homes for an unsettled colony in the New World.

Villages slowly took root along the shores of the Hudson River. These communities resembled the towns of Holland. Buildings were generally constructed in the Dutch style. A typical house stood one or two stories high and featured a steep roof; often the homes were constructed from bricks brought over from Holland. The main entrance typically utilized "dutch" doors that were divided in half horizontally so that either part could be left open or closed. This design proved useful for these sociable people since it allowed them to carry on conversations without the formality of a long visit in the house. Porches were commonplace as well, with benches for people to sit on as they talked with their neighbors. Other common sights of the region included flowers, fruits, vegetables, and farm animals that had been brought from Holland.

The English takeover. The location of New Netherland served as a wedge between English colonies to the north and south. This geographic factor, coupled with England's commercial rivalry with Holland, combined to spur English efforts to gain possession of New Netherland. In

1664 England succeeded in gaining control without bloodshed. When the English navy landed at New Amsterdam (present-day New York City), community members accepted the situation. They knew that their few soldiers were no match for the English and that their fort was too weak to put up serious resistance. The English peacefully extracted a surrender from the colony's Dutch governor, Peter Stuyvesant. Under the terms of the surrender, the Dutch retained full property and inheritance rights in the region.

Dutch language and customs remained strong in the Hudson Valley for many years, particularly in small villages that served as the model for the one inhabited by the fictional Rip Van Winkle. The English made no attempt to impose their language or their king's Catholic religion on the Protestant Dutch settlers. Dutch remained the primary language for many years in some parts of the Hudson Valley, while the Reformed Dutch Church continued as the region's dominant church for generations. The compact size and relative isolation of the Dutch communities and intermarriage among Dutch families further contributed to the enduring influence of Dutch culture.

Pre-revolutionary life in the Hudson Valley. Throughout the seventeenth and eighteenth centuries, New York was primarily rural. The vast majority of the population lived in villages or on small farms, close enough to their neighbors to be in frequent contact. A strong feeling of community existed. Since farming was hard, time-consuming work, social activities often centered around accomplishing some constructive goal: cornhuskings, for example, would make the task of husking the harvested corn a villagewide event. Activities such as fishing and hunting, while of a sometimes recreational nature, were primarily undertaken to provide food for one's family.

Life was slow-paced and peaceful. Inns or taverns were often regarded by the community as places to gather and spend time conversing. They were an important focal point for a town's social life. In New York City in 1772, for example, there was one tavern for every fifty-five inhabitants. The best taverns had rooms for musical parties, political meetings, or dinners; some of the larger ones even served as information centers, supplying newspapers from other cities.

In the small villages of the area, which were often fairly isolated from one another, politics above the local level rarely aroused much immediate concern. As depicted in "Rip Van Winkle," villagers only occasionally saw even an outdated newspaper. Irving captures the atmosphere

at Rip's village inn: "Here they used to sit in the shade through a long, lazy summer's day, talking listlessly over village gossip or telling endless sleepy stories about nothing" (Irving, "Rip Van Winkle," p. 64).

Post-revolutionary changes in the Hudson Valley. Relations between England and its American colonies deteriorated in the mid-eighteenth century. Tensions exploded into the Revolutionary War, which lasted from 1776 to 1783. The United States emerged as a new, independent nation based on the idea of republicanism, a political system in which power is distributed among the citizenry rather than held by a supreme authority such as a king. The success of the new government, therefore, depended on the nature of its citizenry. A republic could survive only if the population consisted of individuals who had a great deal of civic virtue. People were expected to be informed and active participants in the serious business of politics. This attitude is alluded to in Irving's description of Rip's return to his village in "Rip Van Winkle": the first thing the villagers want to know about Rip are his political opinions.

DUTCH PLACE-NAMES IN NEW YORK

The Dutch colonists utilized their native language to refer to places in their new homeland. Many of these terms remain in use today. The name of the Catskill Mountains and one of its streams, for example, comes from the Dutch term *Kaaterskil: kaaters* means "wildcat"; *kil* means "creek." The reference to wild animals serves as a reminder that the Catskill mountain region was quite a wilderness when the early Dutch settlers first arrived.

In the actual history of the nation, friction between New York and the adjoining New England areas existed for many years, with frequent boundary disputes. The situation was worsened by the increasing numbers of New England farmers who moved to the New York area, attracted by the fertile, less rocky soil. After 1783 the influx became a torrent that almost submerged the small Dutch settlements. At that time more people immigrated to New York from New England than from anywhere else in the world. By 1820 people joked that New York was becoming a colony of New England.

The New Englanders, also called Yankees, brought a great deal of change to Dutch New York. Towns became larger and more populous. Yankee woodsmen eventually cleared most of New York's forests, and Yankee businessmen led the expansion of trade and industry in New York. Traditional settlements were stirred into feverish commercial activity. Old Dutch families "resented this invasion by upstarts who ... had no manners and chased dollars too avidly" (Ellis, p. 191).

THE DUTCH PRESENCE IN THE HUDSON VALLEY, 1800

As one approached New York, the Dutch note grew strong and dense ... Communipaw and Bergen, with its little Dutch church, might almost have been villages in Holland. Many of the roofs were high-peaked, with gable-ends and weathercocks, and on holidays the taverns overflowed with merry-makers ... broad-hatted burghers with oxlike frames strolled about their fields or listened, pipe in mouth, to their geese and their swine. Seating themselves on their stoops at the end of the day, they silently smoked, while their [wives] knitted beside them.... One saw on every hand the drowsy ruminant Dutch face.

(Brooks, pp. 32-33)

Folklore in the Catskill Mountains. Indian and Dutch legends surrounding the Hudson River Valley and the Catskill Mountains provided Washington Irving with a rich source of material and played an important part in many of his writings, including "Rip Van Winkle." For example, the Catskill Indians (also called Mohicans) explained that the Catskills were formed from a giant named Onteora, who angered the Great Spirit (Manitou) by carrying out a great deal of destruction and being disrespectful of the land and the people. Manitou punished him by transforming him into a mountain. His eyes became lakes and his tears were transformed into the flowing waters of Lake Creek. Another Indian belief held that day and night, as well as the region's weather, were stored in the Catskill Mountains. Indian legends explained that an old spirit who lived at the highest point of the mountains controlled the weather, forming clouds and new moons every month and creating sunshine, storms, and rain. Other legends told of mischievous spirits in the Catskills who took the shape of animals and played pranks on the Native American hunters who roamed the mountains.

The Dutch created many legends about the region as well. Boat captains sailing on the Hudson often lowered their hats in deference to the Heer, the Dutch goblin who was the Keeper of Donderberg (Thunder) Mountain. The Heer carried a speaking trumpet (a kind of megaphone) that he used to give orders for the creation of sudden gusts of wind or claps of thunder when a storm was rising. Another Dutch legend, which Irving specifically drew on in "Rip Van Winkle," attributed the thunder that came from the mountains to the noise of the late Henry Hudson and his crew bowling.

The Short Story in Focus

The plot. The story opens with a description of the Catskill Mountain region and the pre-revolutionary Dutch village where Rip Van Winkle lives. An easygoing man with a wife and two children, Rip is well-liked throughout his village. He puts a great deal of energy into social and leisure activities such as fishing, hunting, and the village's cornhusking and fence-building events and is always willing to lend a hand to neighbors who need help with odd jobs. The one flaw in his character is his "insuperable aversion to all kinds of profitable labor" ("Rip Van Winkle," p. 61). He is unambitious and lazy and avoids the hard work necessary to keep up his own farm.

Unhappily for him, this passive man is married to an industrious woman who is his complete opposite. His laziness and seeming inability to contribute to his family's well-being upsets her tremendously. She berates and nags him constantly, and is described as a "shrew" who certainly is the dominating force in their marriage. Rip, the "henpecked" husband constantly under assault by his wife, finds life at home utterly miserable.

Rip seeks to escape his unhappy home life on occasion by dropping by an inn where many of the village men frequently gather and talk. Dame Van Winkle sometimes catches him idling his time away at the inn. In such instances, she invariably orders him to leave. His last refuge in these cases is the woods, where he either rambles idly through the countryside or brings along his dog and gun for squirrel or wild pigeon hunting.

One day, Rip wanders into the woods to escape his domineering wife. By the time he stops to rest, he is far into the Catskill Mountains and the sun is beginning to set. He is about to start back for home when he meets a strange man lugging a keg of liquor up the mountain. The man, who is dressed in the fashion of the old Dutch

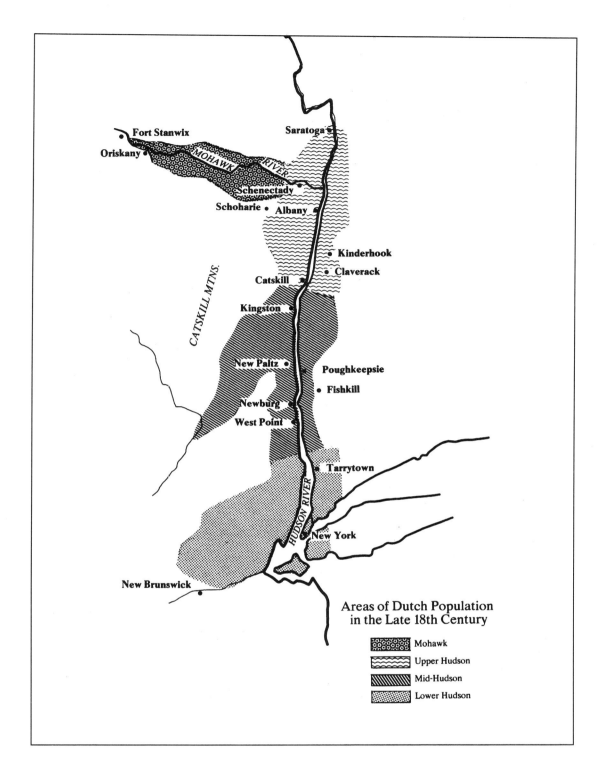

A map showing Dutch settlements along the Hudson River in the late 18th century.

settlers, gestures to Rip to help him; he agrees. After a long hike, they finally make it to a clearing where a number of other odd-looking men dressed similarly to the stranger are congregated. They are playing the game of ninepins (bowling), but the mood is very still and somber. The man whom Rip had helped earlier gestures for him to start serving the ale. Rip starts drinking himself and quickly passes out.

It is morning when Rip awakens. His dog is gone and an old, rusty gun is in the spot where his clean and shiny one had been. Reasoning that the strangers must have stolen his things, he goes looking for them but finds no hint of their whereabouts. Returning to his village, he is surprised to find that he does not recognize anyone. The village seems larger, busier, and more populous, and he is astounded to discover that the village inn has become the Union Hotel and that a political election is taking place.

HUSBAND-WIFE RELATIONSHIPS ON EIGHTEENTH-CENTURY FARMS

Though Dame Van Winkle may be a "shrew," her feelings about her husband's reluctance to contribute to the upkeep of his farm and his family are understandable. Farming entailed a great deal of hard work, and a husband's labor was essential to the success of the farm. Men typically spent their time working in the fields and were responsible for the overall care and concerns of the farm. Women were responsible for domestic tasks in and around the house, such as caring for children, cleaning, cooking, and gardening. If either member proved unwilling or unable to meaningfully contribute, the farm could easily succumb to the many challenges of frontier life.

Amazed, he realizes that he slept for twenty years up in the mountains, oblivious to the changing world around him. He learns that during his absence he became a citizen of a republic rather than a subject of a king. A crowd gathers around him, and he asks after his old acquaintances, most of whom are dead or gone. He discovers that his wife has recently passed away. His reaction to this news suggests that Rip cares less about his freedom from monarchy than his personal freedom from his domineering wife.

Rip proceeds to tell the townspeople the story of what happened to him in the woods. Some dismiss him as a crazy person, but the older, more traditional villagers believe his tale, for according to legend, Henry Hudson and his crew gather in the Catskills every twenty years to check on the river and the region they discovered.

Rip soon finds that his new life is in many ways preferable to his previous one. Old enough now to be idle without being criticized, Rip becomes an admired village elder and spends his time talking and telling stories in front of the new hotel.

Rip Van Winkle and the Yankee invasion. The village Rip left was a small, isolated, sleepy, and tranquil place. The one to which he returns after his twenty-year absence is much larger, louder, and busier. The nature of these changes seems to reflect the influence New Englanders were having on the old Dutch settlements after the Revolutionary War. The negative way Irving depicts these developments shows his attitude toward them, for the village is portrayed as a less attractive place after the passage of the years.

Old New Yorkers tended to resent the continuous influx of New Englanders into the Hudson Valley. A negative stereotype of the Yankees had already developed by the time Irving wrote "Rip Van Winkle." The typical Yankee was tall and thin, with a tendency to be nosy, talkative, cunning, and argumentative.

Certainly, New Englanders held rules and laws in high regard and took politics very seriously. Ambitious and industrious, many New Englanders showed a deep concern for acquiring money and its attendant security. They were regarded as people who had an insatiable desire for change and improvement, of themselves and everyone around them. It was their constant restlessness, their search for something better, that brought them in great numbers to settle in New York and the Hudson Valley.

These characteristics were seen by many of the Dutch New Yorkers as a threat to their stable social order. Traditional Dutch society was much more firmly rooted and conservative, easygoing and tolerant. In his description of Rip Van Winkle's pre-revolutionary village, Irving interprets these qualities as positive ones and implies that the Dutch atmosphere had been peaceful and orderly before the post-revolutionary influx of New Englanders began destroying it. With regretful words, Irving describes "all turnpikes, railroads, and steamboats (as) those abominable inventions by which the usurping Yankees are strengthening themselves in the land, and subduing everything to utility and commonplace" (Myers, p. 410).

In "Rip Van Winkle," Irving brings out the contrast between pre- and post-revolutionary society. The hero, Rip, is the antithesis of the industrious Yankee. He has a definite aversion to any kind of profitable work, preferring to spend his slow-paced days talking, fishing, or hunting. Upon his return to the village, Rip is unconcerned about his new political status or the modern clamor of the elections swirling around him. He is much more affected by news of his own personal freedom from his recently deceased wife. Further, the villagers he meets upon his return have a Yankee quality about them: in place of the old village patriarchs is a thin, mean-looking man who speaks vehemently about political issues. The whole village seems busier, more industrious, more political. "The very character of the people seemed changed. There was a busy, bustling, disputatious tone about it, instead of the accustomed phlegm and drowsy tranquillity" ("Rip Van Winkle," p. 74).

Irving suggests, though, that while the past may be irrevocably gone, it is still important for people to keep a connection to it. Irving concludes the story by describing Rip as an important figure in the town, a patriarch and well-respected storyteller armed with knowledge about the old days before the war.

Sources. Washington Irving grew up in New York City immediately after the end of the Revolutionary War. There were a great number of residents of Dutch origin in the city and throughout the Hudson Valley. A number of Irving's friends during his childhood were Dutch descendants who spoke the Dutch language fluently. Irving had a tremendous interest in history and legend, particularly about the Hudson River Valley, and he spent much of his childhood exploring the region. He was fond of visiting new scenes, and observing strange characters and manners. As he grew up, Irving would ramble around the valley, familiarizing himself with all its places famous in history or fable. He claimed to know every spot where a murder or robbery had been committed, or a ghost had supposedly been seen.

In writing "Rip Van Winkle," Irving drew on his intimate knowledge of the Hudson Valley Dutch and the legends of the region. His descriptions of the Catskill Mountains and Rip's village were based on firsthand observations he had made. Elements of the plot—such as Henry Hudson's appearances in the mountains every twenty years—were drawn from legends he had heard. The main outline of the story, though, seems to come from a German folktale that was published in 1800. According to the tale, a goatherd named

Peter Klaus one day met a young man who silently beckoned for him to follow. He led him to a secluded spot in the Harz Mountains, where twelve knights silently played the game of skittles (a variation of ninepins). Peter came across wine there and drank some of it. Afterwards, he fell into a deep sleep and didn't wake up for twenty years. Irving took this tale, placed it in an American setting, and used it to explore a uniquely American theme—the contrast between pre- and post-revolutionary Hudson Valley society.

ORIGIN OF BOWLING

Under various names (skittles, quills, ninepins, half-bowl), bowling has been played for centuries in many parts of the world. The earliest evidence for the game comes from an Egyptian tomb dating to about 5200 B.C., when stone pins and balls were used. In Germany, records of 300 A.D. indicate that it was performed as part of a religious ritual. Priests there informed their peasant population that the clubs everyone normally carried for self-protection or sport could represent the heathen, the devil, or evil in general. A practice soon emerged wherein a club was stood in a corner. Its owner would then roll a large ball or stone at it. If the stone managed to topple the club, then the individual was cleansed of sin. Over the years various forms of the game developed that featured anywhere from three to fifteen pins. "Ninepins" became the most popular among the Germans and the Dutch, who introduced the game to America.

Events in History at the Time the Short Story Was Written

The growth of American literature. After the Revolutionary War, the desire for a distinctly national literary culture grew in America. Even though the United States had gained its political independence from England, its cultural life was still dominated by British elements. The vast majority of literature in America, for example, continued to be imported from Europe.

With the publication of *The Sketch Book,* a collection of short works that included "Rip Van Winkle," Washington Irving became the first American author to gain both national and international literary acclaim. *The Sketch Book* was originally published in the United States in seven installments between June 1819 and September

1820. Within a month of the first installment, which included "Rip Van Winkle," Irving's work received high praise. In the American *Analectic Magazine* of July 1819, G. C. Verplanck wrote the following: "It will be needless to inform any who have read the book, that it is from the pen of Mr. Irving. His rich, and sometimes extravagant humor, his gay and graceful fancy, his peculiar choice and felicity of original expression, as well as the pure and fine moral feelings which imperceptibly pervade every thought and image ... betray the author in every page...." Before long the *Sketch Book* was the object of praise in England as well. In a February 1820 review that appeared in *Blackwood's Edinburgh Magazine,* John Gibson Lockhard called Irving's work the most graceful American writing he had yet seen and compared it favorably to English work of the time. English writers still set the literary standard, but Irving's *Sketch Book* was the first American work that was regarded as comparable.

Irving was already somewhat well-known for the work he had published ten years earlier in 1809: *A History of New York by Diedrich Knickerbocker.* The book's fictional narrator, Diedrich Knickerbocker, is even referred to in "Rip Van Winkle." *The Sketch Book,* however, became even more popular than the earlier work and firmly established Irving's fame and literary reputation. The book was reprinted ten times between 1828 and 1848, in large part because of the enduring popularity of the "Rip Van Winkle" tale. Over time, the character Rip Van Winkle became one of the most well-known figures in American folklore. Joseph Jefferson staged a popular play about his story, and the French composer Robert Planquette even turned it into an operetta.

The changing world of Washington Irving. The Hudson Valley changed a great deal during Irving's lifetime. Cities and villages experienced tremendous growth. New York's population, for instance, quadrupled between 1800 and 1820. The Northeast also felt the effects of the Industrial Revolution. Power-driven machines began to replace hand-operated tools, a development that permitted the production of greater quantities of goods at faster speeds. Advances in textile machinery led to the building of the first modern factory by Samuel Slater in 1790; other facilities followed. The arrival of the steamboat, perfected by Robert Fulton in the Hudson Valley, and the construction of a number of major turnpikes helped promote the efficient movement of raw materials to factories and finished goods to markets. American inventions such as Eli Whitney's cotton gin in 1793 also contributed to the growth of industry in the Hudson River region. The War of 1812 against Great Britain further fostered the development of native manufacturing since imports were effectively blocked by the British navy during the war.

Although the Hudson Valley remained overwhelmingly rural and agricultural during Irving's lifetime, he was witness to the beginning of an irreversible process of modernization. Many people were excited about America's present and future. The traditional Dutch culture of the region began to fade, however, and Washington Irving was one New Yorker who felt a sense of loss at those developments, a feeling he expressed in "Rip Van Winkle."

For More Information

Brooks, Van Wyck. *The World of Washington Irving.* New York: E. P. Dutton, 1944.

Ellis, David M., James A. Frost, Harold C. Syrett, and Harry J. Carman. *A History of New York State.* Ithaca, NY: Cornell University Press, 1967.

Irving, Washington. "Rip Van Winkle." In *The Legend of Sleepy Hollow & Other Stories.* New York: Lancer Books, 1968.

Kammen, Michael. *Colonial New York: A History.* New York: Charles Scribner's Sons, 1975.

Kenney, Alice P. *Stubborn for Liberty: The Dutch in New York.* Syracuse, N.Y.: Syracuse University Press, 1975.

Myers, Andrew B., ed. *1860-1974: A Century of Commentary on the Works of Washington Irving.* Tarrytown, NY: Sleepy Hollow Restorations, 1976.

Robinson Crusoe

by
Daniel Defoe

A political activist, journalist, merchant, and religious rebel, Daniel Defoe was in a unique position to write about his times. Born the year the Restoration began, Defoe was a middle-class merchant who went bankrupt twice due to bad business deals and shifts in political attitudes. His varied life experiences equipped him to comment on the struggles of the working class and gave him broad insight into the benefits and consequences of England's growing wealth and power.

Events in History at the Time the Novel Takes Place

Restoration England: Emerging world empire. In 1660, the year Daniel Defoe was born, England became a monarchy again after a decade-long experiment with a parliamentary form of government. Charles II was restored to the English throne. His accession brought the royal family of the Stuarts back to power, and his reign marked the emergence of England as a formidable empire. Charles vigorously promoted trade and the shipping industry, and his support soon put England in a position to challenge the Dutch and Spanish—the leading imperial powers of the day—for a share of international markets. Under Charles the shipping tonnage in England soared and small port cities that had been in economic decline, such as Liverpool, began to prosper. London became a wealthy city and a center of world commerce during these years—a marked contrast to previous decades in which the city

> ### THE LITERARY WORK
> A novel set from 1652 to 1694 in Great Britain and South America, on the African coast, and on an island off the coast of South America; published in 1719.
>
> ### SYNOPSIS
> A young man seeking adventure embarks on a series of journeys at sea, gets shipwrecked, and spends twenty-eight years on an isolated South Sea island before returning to civilization.

had been repeatedly ravaged by the plague and the nation had suffered from continual threats of civil war.

England's commercial success was due largely to the expansion of its colonial empire. Like the Spanish, French, and Dutch, the British commissioned and encouraged overseas claims to territory. The British claimed areas in North America, Africa, and the West Indies, and they began exporting goods gathered from overseas locations to European markets. For example, British merchants in the West Indies produced and refined sugar that was shipped to England and Europe to sell or trade for other commodities. In order to produce the sugar at little or no cost, the British exported slaves from Africa to work the fields. These slaves were primarily from Guinea, part of the West African territory claimed by England. The slave trade thus bolstered the British economy, becoming an industry in itself as traders not only supplied British plantation owners with slaves but also sold slaves to others throughout the Caribbean and the Americas.

Slave trade. British trade in Africa started in 1618, when King James I began exporting dyes from Britain's newly acquired colony of Guinea. The Dutch, who also held colonies in Africa, were the first to enter the slave trade. They supplied slaves for the sugar industry in the Caribbean and had a monopoly on such trade until roughly 1672. Eager to increase British holdings in Africa, challenge the Dutch, and enter the lucrative slave trade, King Charles II granted the Royal African Company (RAC) exclusive rights to the land and people of West Africa from Cape Blanco to the Cape of Good Hope for one thousand years. By the 1680s, the RAC was supplying over five thousand slaves a year to the West Indies. It dominated the slave trade until about 1686. Characteristic of the era, both Defoe and his fictional character, Robinson Crusoe, were slave traders who condoned the practice because it benefited the British economy. African slaves were looked upon by these merchants not as human beings but as a commodity to be traded like sugar or dye. In Defoe's eyes, the slave trade was the most useful and profitable business for an Englishman to conduct, and, like Crusoe, he felt little moral conflict in bartering human life.

Rise of the middle class. As British wealth increased, so did the status and prospects of the middle class. It was now possible for those of the lower working class to rise through commercial enterprise to the middle class, and it became a common goal among those in the middle station of life to achieve the ranks of gentility. Like Defoe himself, middle-class men risked what little they had to outfit expeditions and trading voyages overseas. Exchanging a simple but secure life for adventure and possible wealth or bankruptcy, Defoe and many of his contemporaries invested in overseas enterprises. Both Defoe and his fictional character Crusoe suffered the consequences of such high risks. Pirates filled the Atlantic Ocean and Caribbean Sea, making shipping a very dangerous enterprise. In the novel, Crusoe is captured by pirates. In real life, Defoe's cargoes were seized by French sailors in 1692, a development that propelled him into bankruptcy.

Because Defoe had such wide-ranging experiences, he was able to write about the ordinary and extraordinary aspects of middle-class life in his generation. As one of his contemporaries observed, "it is possible to base a study of English society in the early eighteenth century almost entirely on the writings of Daniel Defoe" (Shinagel, p. 17).

Vice, morality, and materialism. The reign of Charles II was characterized not only by commercial enterprise but also by increased materialism and vice. The king's personal life was the subject of controversy—he was known as something of a drinker and a ladies' man. King Charles also promoted trade in spirits and tobacco. The selling of these items accounted for much of the success of the British merchants, but it also furthered practices that were frowned upon by various religions—in particular by the Puritans and Dissenters (Protestants who refused to join the Church of England). These groups preached abstinence and temperance. Defoe, who had a strong religious background, experienced the conflict of material gain versus morality. He derived income by importing brandy from Spain and tobacco from America. Determined to increase his wealth like his fellow merchants, Defoe was a materialist. Still, he saw the ill effects of such a shallow goal as material gain.

In *Robinson Crusoe,* Defoe illustrates the prevailing materialist attitude of England when he describes how Crusoe takes gold from a shipwrecked boat onto his deserted island. Clearly the gold is valueless on an uninhabited island, yet Crusoe cannot help but hoard what he can. After all, he is a merchant, a sea trader who is in business to make money. Through Crusoe's behavior, Defoe illustrates the sometimes illogical but very real preoccupation with material gain characteristic of his age.

Glorious Revolution. In 1688 the Dissenters succeeded in bringing William of Orange to the throne of England. This "Glorious Revolution," as it came to be known, took place without bloodshed and ushered in religious freedom for a time. Under William's religiously tolerant government, Defoe prospered financially and politically. The accession of William brought with it the promise of social reform, such as better legal and economic conditions for women, the poor, and the mentally ill.

Defoe worked closely with King William as a pamphleteer during these years, defending the Glorious Revolution and advocating social reform. The concept of tolerance for people of different religions and nationalities was promoted by Defoe, for it was an idea that contrasted sharply with past and future policies; religious and political persecution had occurred under Charles II and would reappear under William's successors, Queen Anne and George I. In *Robin-*

son Crusoe, Defoe illustrates the idea of tolerance when he shows that African, British, and Spanish men can peacefully coexist on one island. Crusoe's island is the site of cooperation and tolerance among men of different religions and nationalities. Defoe holds up the island as a model upon which his own country, the island nation of England, can rebuild itself. Crusoe's island depicts the peaceful coexistence promised by the Glorious Revolution.

The Novel in Focus

The plot. Defying his father's advice to become a simple country lawyer and seek the "middle state" in life, Robinson Crusoe sets out to have adventures and forge his own path in the world by way of the sea. At age nineteen, he boards a ship to London, firmly resolved to become a great sailor and earn his fortune in the seafaring trade. On his first voyage, though. he narrowly escapes death—an event that makes him question his chosen occupation. But no matter how hard his sense of reason tries to overcome his desire to stay in the business, it fails. Looking back, Crusoe laments his obstinacy:

> ...tho' I had several times loud calls from my Reason and my more composed Judgment to go home, yet I had no Power to do it. I know not what to call this, nor will I urge, that it is a secret over-ruling Decree that hurries us on to be the Instruments of our own Destruction, even tho' it be before us, and we rush upon it with our Eyes open.
>
> (Defoe, Robinson Crusoe, p. 14)

Crusoe boards a second ship bound for the coast of Guinea in Africa, embarking on his most (and he says his only) successful adventure. He becomes both a sailor and a merchant and returns to Great Britain with a considerable amount of gold. The success of this journey inspires him to continue as a "Guiney Trader" (Robinson Crusoe, p. 18). But success is short-lived, for he is captured by pirates on his subsequent trip and enslaved. He serves a Moor captain for nearly two years until the opportunity for escape finally arises. Crusoe steals away in a small boat, throwing a fellow slave overboard and keeping another, Xury, as his own servant. Meeting up with a Portuguese vessel en route to Brazil, Crusoe and Xury accompany the crew to South America. In Brazil, Crusoe becomes a prosperous farmer. He regrets that he has sold Xury because he needs help tending his crops. Crusoe justifies the sale by saying that Xury was willing to go.

Ironically, after several years in South America, Crusoe is "coming into the very Middle Station, or Upper Degree of low life, which my father advised me to before" (Robinson Crusoe, p. 35). Crusoe often speaks of the lucrative slave trade off the coast of Guinea to his neighbors—farmers who all need cheap labor to work their tobacco and sugar plantations—and they soon approach him about outfitting a ship. Crusoe agrees to captain the ship and unknowingly sets sail on a fateful voyage to Africa that will forever change his life.

As on his first voyage, Crusoe encounters a violent windstorm that wrecks his ship. This time all is lost and he is the only one to escape with his life. He lands on a deserted island off the coast of South America and salvages what he can from the ship to provide for his stay there. He scouts the island, builds himself a shelter, and learns to make furniture and tools and to farm. As loneliness settles over him, he begins writing a journal in which he records the minute details of his daily survival. He also begins to talk to God, questioning the circumstances of his predicament and pondering God's existence.

Crusoe's conversations with God become a primary part of the rest of the novel. He begins a religious conversion in which he repents his quest for material gain and his disobedience to his father's advice to seek the middle station in life. Crusoe becomes ill and has what seem to be wild and prophetic dreams. It is unclear to both Crusoe and the reader whether these are dreams, hallucinations, or messages from God. The dreams cause Crusoe to reassess his relationship with God, and he becomes convinced it is his duty to serve God by living a "good" life.

Eventually Crusoe explores the other side of the island. He builds a second home there, where the soil is more fertile and the climate more tropical. He shapes a canoe in case the possibility of escape arises, but Crusoe builds it too large and too far from the water for one man to carry. He then makes himself a second, smaller boat which can take him around the island, although not on the open ocean.

After about fifteen years on the island, Crusoe finds a footprint on the beach that terrifies him. Later he finds human bones scattered in a ritualistic way and realizes cannibals have at some point landed on the island. He debates whether it is right for him to interfere in other peoples' lives, and whether it is proper for him to judge others according to his own Anglo-Christian beliefs. He decides that only God has the authority to pun-

THE
LIFE
AND
STRANGE SURPRIZING
ADVENTURES
OF
ROBINSON CRUSOE,
Of *YORK,* MARINER:

Who lived Eight and Twenty Years,
all alone in an un-inhabited Ifland on the
Coaft of AMERICA, near the Mouth of
the Great River of OROONOQUE;

Having been caft on Shore by Shipwreck, wherein all the Men perifhed but himfelf.

WITH

An Account how he was at laft as ftrangely deliver'd by PYRATES.

Written by Himfelf.

LONDON:
Printed for W. TAYLOR at the *Ship* in *Pater-Nofter-
Row.* MDCCXIX.

Title page of the 1719 edition of *Robinson Crusoe.*

ish and judge and that he will not try to kill the cannibals unless they attack him.

A short time later, a violent storm wrecks a ship directly offshore. Crusoe tries to signal it, but the crew is entirely lost. He manages to salvage the ship's supplies—which at this point he desperately needs—and even takes gold and currency that is valueless on his island. As time passes, Crusoe becomes increasingly desperate for human companionship and conjures ways of escaping. He has spent over twenty years on the island and during that time has not spoken to another living soul. About this time, he has another dream in which he rescues a potential victim of the cannibals. Over a year later, his dream is realized when he rescues Friday, an African who narrowly escapes a band of cannibals.

Crusoe teaches Friday his language and religion as well as survival skills, while Friday becomes Crusoe's servant and companion. Crusoe, like English colonists, views the island as his domain and himself as king. He feels he is "civilizing" his savage companion and cultivating the land, just as the British government felt it was benefiting the colonies it claimed and the natives who peopled them.

Soon the cannibals return with several new victims to be sacrificed, including Friday's father. Crusoe and Friday rescue Friday's father and a Spaniard. The small group, comprised of three different nationalities and religions—Spanish Catholic, African Pagan, English Protestant—works together to save each other and flee the island. In the end, they all escape. Crusoe thanks God for his deliverance and arrives in Great Britain thirty-five years after he departed.

Upon arriving, Crusoe discovers that some of his long-range investments have paid great dividends and that he is a wealthy man. He repays those who helped him along the way, marries, and has three children. After several years, though, true to his nature, he is no longer satisfied with his station in life—the lesson he was supposed to have learned from the shipwreck and his years of isolation—and he once again seeks adventure. He goes abroad in 1694, revisits his island, and lives a life of adventure for the next ten years, which he promises to chronicle in the sequel to *Robinson Crusoe*.

Sources. Defoe based *Robinson Crusoe* on the real-life adventures of Alexander Selkirk, a Scottish sailor who spent four and a half years on a deserted island off the coast of Chile in South America. Selkirk's story was widely publicized after he returned to London in 1711, and it is as-

sumed that Defoe either read of his exploits or interviewed Selkirk personally. But *Robinson Crusoe* is far from a biography of Selkirk; Defoe simply gleaned the basic plot line from the Scotsman's adventure. More than anything, the book is autobiographical, based on Defoe's own personal struggles with his father, religion, career, and politics.

Like his protagonist, Defoe was encouraged by his father to live a simple, middle-class life. He was educated to become a country minister. However, also like Crusoe, he was restless. Attracted to the sea and the world of commerce, Defoe left home for the big city of London at the earliest opportunity. He operated several businesses, invested in overseas trade—including the slave trade—and experienced both success and failure as a businessman. Finally, like Crusoe, he grappled with the question of material gain versus morality. Defoe believed in Puritan ideals, which discouraged smoking and drinking, yet derived income from the sale of tobacco and brandy. Because aspects of the novel bore striking similarities to Defoe's life, many critics feel that *Robinson Crusoe* was a psychological exercise to resolve the various conflicts he felt personally. Calling the novel an allegory of Defoe's life, one critic has commented:

> Crusoe is not Daniel Defoe. And yet, more than any of his books, it is a kind of day-dream in which the author and his hero dissolve into one another.
>
> (Sutherland, p. 29)

Birth of the novel and formal realism. With *Robinson Crusoe,* Defoe is said to have invented a style known as formal realism. The style strove for writing that was true to nature and real life without idealizing people, events, or surroundings. Defoe was not writing for the upper classes or commissioned by a patron, or supporter; members of the middle class were the main buyers of his work. As a result, flowery language or aristocratic, larger-than-life characters did not find their way into his novel. Defoe also used Crusoe's daily journal entries to add to the realism of the story:

> June 27. The Ague again so violent, that I lay a-Bed all Day, and neither eat nor drank. I was ready to perish for Thirst, but so weak, I had not strength to stand up, or to get my self any Water to drink: Pray'd to God again, but was light-headed, and when I was not, I was so ignorant, that I knew not what to say; only I lay and cry'd, Lord look upon me, Lord pity me, Lord have Mercy upon me.
>
> (*Robinson Crusoe*, p. 87)

The details Crusoe records—down to the exact supplies he has, the crops he grows, the tools he makes, and the psychological soul-searching he undergoes—add to the story's realism as well. They lead the reader to believe that Crusoe's adventure actually occurred or could have taken place.

PRESBYTERIAN INFLUENCE ON DEFOE'S STYLE

Defoe's realistic style was heavily influenced by his childhood. Raised by strict Presbyterians to be a preacher, Defoe emulated the schoolmasters and ministers he grew up hearing. He used a direct style of writing, addressing his audience as a commoner or preacher would speak, providing a wealth of facts and figures to back his assertions. Commenting on his simple, journalistic style, Defoe said: "I could give you similes, allegories ... and read you long lectures upon the Roman affairs under the government of their consuls and tribunes [but I prefer] a down-right Plainness ... both in Fact and Style" (Defoe in Shinagel, p. 22). Defoe, who was not university-educated, assumed that his audience had no prior knowledge of a subject, unlike some writers of his day.

Events in History at the Time the Novel Was Written

A new era for England and Defoe. Defoe prospered as long as William of Orange was on the throne, but William died in 1702. When Queen Anne assumed control, Defoe's life changed drastically. Because Defoe was such a well-known propagandist for William and the Dissenters, he was literally a marked man, regarded as an enemy of both Anglicans (members of the Church of England) and Catholics. When Queen Anne, a devout Anglican, renewed the persecution of Dissenters, Defoe was among the first to feel the queen's wrath. He was arrested in 1703 and jailed. The promise of reform, tolerance, and peaceful co-existence ushered in by the Glorious Revolution was broken, and a new phase in British politics and Defoe's life began.

Lord Harley. Defoe's release from jail was secured by Robert Harley, the speaker of the House of Commons. Harley belonged to the Tories, the political party that had gained power along with Queen Anne. In exchange for Harley's help, Defoe went to work for him editing a Tory newspaper, *The Review.* Defoe was called a "turncoat" by many who felt he had abandoned his political and religious views (Earle, p. 19). In his new position, he advocated closing England's Dissenting Academies (Puritan schools) even though he had been educated at such a school and previously took great pride in his educational experience. Furthermore, he spoke out in seeming support of a Jacobite king in 1713. That is, he seemed to support the claim of a Catholic, James VII, to the throne, a position that angered many. He was arrested a second time and again was bailed out by Harley.

Back to the Whigs. In 1714 Queen Anne died and George I came to the British throne. Harley was imprisoned for treason, and Defoe returned to his original political party, the Whigs, who had come back into power. He became a propagandist for the Whigs, just as he had been for the Tories, and began to write his own works of fiction.

Under King George, the newly unified nation of Great Britain prospered, but social reform and cultural development nearly ceased. George was not interested in art and, unlike Queen Anne, who had been an avid patron of the arts, he did not sponsor writers, painters, or performers. The publishing business was born as a result, when, to obtain money, writers sold their works to publishers, who profited by marketing them to the public.

Defoe was in a unique position to benefit from the change. His novels became early products of the new publishing industry, which relied on sales to the growing middle class. Since Defoe wrote for and about members of the middle class, who had become increasingly literate by 1715, his novels met with success. Defoe was also associated with twenty-six different periodicals, even writing one journal (*The Review*) single-handedly. Defoe has often been called the father of modern journalism.

Broken promises. The political climate in England changed dramatically by 1719, the year Defoe's book was published. Wars and bloody conflicts over succession to the throne plagued King William and the rulers that followed. The concepts of social reform promoted by the Glorious Revolution—better representation of minorities in government, social welfare programs, tax breaks for middle-class merchants, and religious tolerance—were replaced with a new emphasis on the individual, a policy of nonresponsibility by the government for social welfare, and religious and political persecution. Though Defoe believed that society could be improved through the betterment of the individual, he also believed in the ideals of the revolution and worked most of his life for social reform.

Defoe, like many in England, experienced a shift in attitude in the decades that followed the Glorious Revolution, and this shift is reflected in *Robinson Crusoe*. Defoe began as an optimist, yet developed a more realistic outlook on life as he grew older. He saw the promises of the revolution shattered and had personally bent his ideals and morals in order to prosper financially and politically. He had gone bankrupt twice, was jailed twice, was sued at least eight times, and would die poor in a building where he had hid in an effort to evade a bill collector. At the end of *Robinson Crusoe,* Defoe paints a picture of harmonious coexistence among three different races and religions, yet at the same time states that to his knowledge this is not yet the case in Great Britain or any other nation. He offers a model of tolerance, probably suspecting that the chance of it being emulated was slim.

There is also the issue of materialism. Robinson Crusoe is punished for his materialist goals by being marooned for twenty-eight years on a deserted island. Yet Defoe ultimately rewards Crusoe by making him a wealthy man once he leaves the island. This ending may partly reflect Defoe's own belief in the rising prosperity of Great Britain and the middle class through foreign trade; this good fortune would continue through the next century.

Reviews. *Robinson Crusoe* was an extremely popular novel when it first appeared in 1719. But it was never the critical success during Defoe's lifetime that it became after his death. Writers of his own time, such as Alexander Pope and Jonathan Swift, criticized Defoe's politics and religious views, his plain, journalistic style, and his lack of attention to detail. Critics also noted that Defoe contradicts himself in the novel several times. For example, he first says Crusoe is naked when he is marooned, but Crusoe later fills his pockets with goods from the ship. Still, Pope acknowledged that "there is something good in all that he [Defoe] has written," and others praised him as "England's watchdog," protecting and voicing the interests of the middle and working classes (Sutherland, p. 6).

For More Information

Defoe, Daniel. *Robinson Crusoe*. Oxford: Oxford University Press, 1972.

Earle, Peter. *The World of Defoe*. New York: Atheneum, 1937.

Keen, Benjamin. *A History of Latin America*. Boston: Houghton Mifflin, 1988.

Shinagel, Michael. *Daniel Defoe and Middle-class Gentility*. Cambridge, Mass.: Harvard University Press, 1968.

Smith, Goldwin. *England: A Short History*. New York: Charles Scribner's Sons, 1971.

Sutherland, James. *Defoe*. London: Longmans, Green, 1965.

Romeo and Juliet

by
William Shakespeare

When William Shakespeare wrote *Romeo and Juliet* in approximately 1595, England had a great deal in common with fourteenth-century Italy, the era in which the play takes place. As in fourteenth-century Italy, Elizabethan England experienced incredible violence and tragedy. In 1592 Great Britain was ravaged by the bubonic plague, a disease that had swept across Italy in 1348. Britain was also deeply enmeshed in a political and religious power struggle that resembled conditions in Italy 250 years before. Both societies, scarred by tragedy, largely adopted the philosophy of the imprisoned Roman statesman and philosopher Boethius (c. 480-524), who asserted that Fortune—both good and bad—is part of life and, along with God, controls human destiny. Further, he insisted that Fortune is random and that adverse fortune is a greater teacher than good fortune.

Events in History at the Time the Play Takes Place

A history of violence. Verona is located near the northern border of Italy on the Po River, east of Venice. It was a very lively city in the fourteenth century. Culturally rich and commercially successful, it boasted a thriving artistic community and a robust business climate centered in international trade that rivaled that of Venice, the wealthiest city-state in Italy. But Verona, like all other regions of the country, was subject to rampant violence and war—a condition that had endured throughout Italy for centuries.

THE LITERARY WORK

A drama set in Verona, Italy, about 1348; first performed around 1595.

SYNOPSIS

A young man and woman from rival families fall in love, leading to tragic results. The "star-crossed lovers" are doomed, but their deaths bring about peace between the Capulets and Montagues.

Since the Etruscan occupation of Italy in the tenth century B.C., the region had suffered from periodic epidemics of violence. Territorial battles between Romans, Etruscans, Gauls, Carthaginians, and a host of others occurred regularly through the founding of Rome in 753 B.C., until the Holy Roman Empire established its dominance after the Second Punic War in 201 B.C. The Roman Empire maintained control of Italy through 400 A.D., when it split into two distinct realms of authority. The governmental faction established its capital in Constantinople and regarded the emperor as its supreme authority. The spiritual faction (often called "Christendom"), centered in Rome, was ruled by the pope. The result of the split was a long-standing and savage power struggle that bred deep-seated hatred between sides. In the absence of a united, central power, city-states emerged and added to the competitive and hostile atmosphere. Territories com-

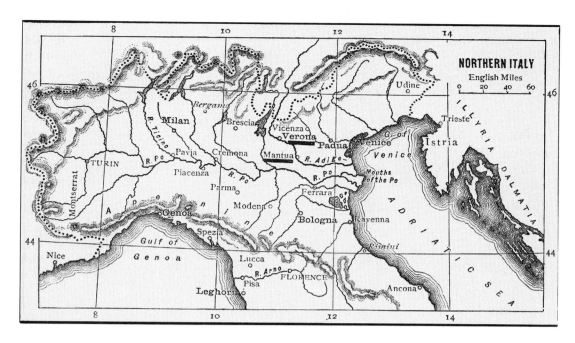

A map of Northern Italy showing the location of Verona and other major cities.

peted for resources, and political leaders clashed with religious leaders over control and influence.

By the fourteenth century, the division between supporters of the emperor and supporters of the pope was firmly established. As in other Italian city-states, a fierce rivalry existed in Verona between both sides. Supporters of the pope, called Guelphs, and partisans of the emperor, called Ghibellines, grappled for control. They also fought deadly battles over the most petty of differences. Blood was spilled over trivial issues such as the proper method of eating garlic and the viability of wearing a feather in the left rather than the right side of the cap. Famed Italian poet Francesco Petrarch lamented this sad state of relations:

> O my own Italy!—though words are vain
> The mortal wounds to close
> Innumerable that thy bosom stain—
> Yet it may soothe my pain
> To sing of Tiber's woes
> And Arno's wrongs, as on Po's saddened shore
> Mournful I wander, and my numbers pour.
> (Durant, p. 45)

The bubonic plague. In 1348 the bubonic plague ravaged Europe. In Italy an estimated one-third of the population died from the disease. The plague sparked a cycle of famine and epidemic that lasted through the end of the century. It contributed to social instability that led to one hundred years of unending warfare and continual upheaval among Italy's citizens. Overcrowding in cities such as Venice, whose population by 1422 approached 200,000, led to fierce competition for few natural resources, further igniting the turmoil that already raged because of political and religious differences. The effects of all this turmoil are significant factors in the play *Romeo and Juliet*.

Boethius. In the sixth century an imprisoned Roman statesman named Boethius wrote *De Consolatione Philosophie* (*The Consolation of Philosophy*), a work in which he attempted, in part, to explain why tragedy is part of life. He proposed that life is governed by both God and Fortune, with Fortune serving as a sort of agent carrying out God's master plan for the universe. He further asserted that good and bad Fortune occur randomly and that:

> You think that Fortune has changed towards you. You are wrong. These are ever her ways; this is her very nature. She has in your case maintained her proper constancy in the very act of changing.
> (Boethius, p. 12)

Boethius was imprisoned and later executed because he fell out of favor with the government. *The*

Consolation of Philosophy, however, was the most popular literary work of the period and regained prominence in the fourteenth century, when it was translated by Geoffrey Chaucer. Its concepts of God, Fate, and Fortune seemed to shed light on the plague and the terrible wars that were destroying hundreds of thousands of innocent lives. The work went so far as to claim that misfortune was a greater teacher than good fortune.

In fourteenth-century Italy, just as in the Elizabethan Age and later, people sought to understand the extent to which human beings controlled their lives. *Romeo and Juliet* reflects fourteenth-century notions of God and Fortune as figures that work together to control the fate of human beings.

THE BENEFIT OF MISFORTUNE

I am convinced that adverse fortune is more beneficial to men than prosperous fortune. When Fortune seems kind, and seems to promise happiness, she lies. On the other hand, when she shows herself unstable and changeable, she is truthful. Good fortune deceives, adverse fortune teaches.

(Boethius, p. 40)

Astrology. Astrology was an influential part of Italian society as well. In the 1300s many people believed that the positions and aspects of heavenly bodies such as stars influenced the course of human events. The concept of astrology was seen as one that seemed to support Boethius's philosophy. Virtually every noble family in Italy had horoscopes drawn for their children upon birth, and most government leaders employed court astrologers to advise them on important issues of state. The newly developing science of astronomy was still closely linked to astrology and further indicated a close relationship between the stars and planets and events on earth. Many believed the conjunction of certain planets gave rise to different religions, and most believed that the stars dictated the outcome of wars.

Throughout *Romeo and Juliet,* references are made to supernatural forces at work, and suggestions are continually put forward that Fate is inextricably linked to the stars. Premonitions abound in the play, and there is evidence of widespread belief—as there was at the time—in unseen forces that control the characters' destinies. At the play's outset we are told that the lovers

are "star-crossed," and soon Juliet foresees Romeo's death:

> O God, I have an ill-divining soul!
> Methinks I see thee, now thou art so low,
> As one dead in the bottom of a tomb.
> Either my eyesight fails, or thou lookest pale.
> (Shakespeare, *Romeo and Juliet,* 4.5.54)

Romeo too foresees his death and links it to a predetermined fate, "hanging in the stars."

> ...my mind misgives
> Some consequence yet hanging in the stars
> Shall bitterly begin his fearful date
> With this night's revels, and expire the term
> Of a despised life clos'd in my breast
> By some vile forfeit of untimely death.
> (*Romeo and Juliet,* 1.4.106-11)

The Play in Focus

The plot. Told in the lyric style of Shakespearian sonnets, *Romeo and Juliet* begins with Romeo brooding over a woman whom he thinks he loves. But when he meets Juliet at a masquerade, he realizes he "ne'er saw true beauty until this night" (*Romeo and Juliet,* 1.5.54). The pair exchange a kiss at the ball and set events in motion. When the lovers discover they are from rival families, they renounce their familial associations and vow their undying love for each other. To them, names seem trivial and "that which we call a rose / By any other name would smell as sweet" (*Romeo and Juliet,* 2.2.43-4). But while the young lovers recognize the folly of their families' feud, they cannot help being dragged into it by an unenlightened society unwilling to make peace.

Juliet is a Capulet and Romeo is a Montague. Romeo is pulled into the feud between the two families when Juliet's cousin, Tybalt, kills Romeo's friend, Mercutio. To avenge his friend's death, Romeo stabs Tybalt and is exiled from Verona by the prince. But Romeo and Juliet have already made plans to marry. Juliet meets Romeo at Friar Laurence's house, and the two are wed in secret. They spend one night together, and then Romeo flees for Mantua, where the two hope they will soon be reunited.

Because Juliet's marriage to Romeo is secret, her father unknowingly arranges for her to marry Count Paris. Juliet frantically seeks help from Friar Laurence to avoid bigamy (the offense of marrying one person while still legally married to another). The friar devises a plan to avert the second wedding. He gives her a sleeping potion

Act 5, scene 3 of Romeo and Juliet: Friar Laurence and Juliet in the Capulets' tomb, with the bodies of Romeo and Paris.

to make it appear that she has died, for he has designed a strategy wherein Juliet can be reunited with Romeo in two days after the effects of the potion dissipate. His plans are foiled, however, when a message informing Romeo of the sleeping potion scheme does not get delivered to him. Instead, Romeo believes the news that Juliet has died. He rides to her tomb and, desperate with grief, kills himself. When Juliet awakens, she finds Romeo dead beside her. Heartbroken, she stabs herself with his dagger and dies at his side. The terrible tragedy convinces the Montagues and Capulets finally to end their feud.

Shakespeare illustrates Boethius's concepts of Fortune by showing how events beyond Romeo or Juliet's control lead to tragic consequences. Friar Laurence blames "unhappy fortune" when Romeo and Juliet are found dead and yet also concludes that "a greater power than we can contradict / Hath thwarted our intents" (*Romeo and Juliet*, 5.3.153-54).

Sources. The story of Romeo and Juliet was based on a long line of tragedies, beginning with *Ephesiaca* by Xenophon, written in the second century A.D. In that version the lovers are called Anthia and Habrocomes: the plot is fundamentally the same as Shakespeare's but with one crucial difference: the lovers are reunited in the end.

The tragic ending and the familial rivalry were introduced by Masuccio Salernitano in *Il Novellino*, written in 1476. Luigi da Porto retold the story in 1530, set it in Verona, and named the lovers Romeo and Giulietta. He based the family conflict on a well-known feud between the Capelletti family of Guelphs and the Montecchi family of Ghibellines.

Though all of these authors and several others wrote previous versions of the tragedy, the only source Shakespeare appears to have used was Arthur Brooke's *The Tragicall Historye of Romeus and Juliet*. Written in 1562, the narrative poem was the first English translation of the story. As was common practice for writers in the Elizabethan Age, Shakespeare began with Brooke's classic model and enhanced it, creating an original work of his own. His version—the first that was produced as a stage play—makes significant modifications to Brooke's poem. He condensed the time-frame of the story from nine months to four days; expanded the roles of several characters, including Mercutio, Paris, and Tybalt; added several humorous minor characters, including Samson, Balthasar, Gregory, and Potpan; killed off Paris; anglicized some of the character's names; and employed a variety of literary styles, including the sonnet form and blank and rhyming

COMPARISONS OF THE STORY OF ROMEO AND JULIET

Author	Title	Storyline
Xenophon	*Ephesiaca*	Anthia and Habrocomes are star-crossed lovers who, instead of dying, are re-united in the end.
Masuccio Salernitano	*Il Novellino*	Lovers die and family rivalry established.
Luigi da Porto	*Novella*	Tragedy is located in Verona, Italy; lovers are named Romeo and Giulietta; story based on feud between Capelletti and Montecchi families.
Shakespeare	*Romeo and Juliet*	Protagonists are named Romeo and Juliet; feuding families are Capulets and Montagues; new plot and character elements added.

verse. These forms were a significant change from Brooke's use of "Poulter's Measure" (alternating lines of twelve and fourteen syllables).

Shakespeare's play more fully develops all of the characters and enhances their personality traits. For example, the nurse in Shakespeare's version is bawdier than her counterpart in Brooke's tale, while Mercutio is more cunningly combative, witty, and mercurial. Hardly mentioned in Brooke's poem, Mercutio becomes a central and pivotal character in Shakespeare's play.

In Shakespeare's more conversational version, Juliet's father becomes a full-bodied, frustrated father who tries to understand his teenage daughter but is exasperated nonetheless.

The influence of Petrarch. Written between 1594 and 1596, *Romeo and Juliet* was one of Shakespeare's early tragedies. Its style is more closely linked to his romantic comedies, such as *A Midsummer Night's Dream,* than to his later dark tragedies, such as *Othello* or *Hamlet.* The play's lyric style reflects the influence of the Italian poet Petrarch, who wrote his romantic, lovelorn sonnets during the fourteenth century. Petrarch did not invent the form, but he made it famous. Using him as a model but modifying the structure, Shakespeare wrote his own collection of sonnets in the early 1590s and incorporated the style into *Romeo and Juliet.*

Shakespeare was influenced by Petrarch in content as well as form. In *Romeo and Juliet,* he echoes Petrarch's lament over the violence and tragedy so prevalent in society. Just as Petrarch

decried "the mortal wounds" inflicted on his country by constant civil war, Shakespeare's Friar Laurence observes how war devastates all concerned.

Puns. Shakespeare's *Romeo and Juliet* employs literary devices traditionally found in comedies or farces. Such devices are especially prevalent in the first half of the play. The drama features a healthy amount of punning and the combat of wits (a favorite style of the Elizabethans), suggesting that the characters have a playful quality and are also given to frequent misunderstandings. Miscommunication is a major theme of the play and is conveyed through constant punning. For example, the play opens with servants carrying on a conversation in which they play on each others' words and misinterpret what the other is saying:

> *Samson:* Gregory, on my word, we'll not carry coals.
> *Gregory:* No, for then we should be colliers.
> *Samson:* I mean, an we be in choler, we'll draw.
> *Gregory:* Ay, while you live, draw your neck out of collar.
> (*Romeo and Juliet,* 1.1.1-4)

The puns on "collier" (a coal miner), "choler" (anger), and "collar" (a band around the neck or hangman's noose) illustrate how easily language can mislead and establishes at the outset the absurdity of wars and feuds based on innocent misunderstandings. Through his use of puns, Shakespeare shows the folly and potential tragic consequences of miscommunication and seems to suggest it has been a major cause of violence throughout history.

Battles of wit, punning, and satire were commonly used in both the Elizabethan Age and in fourteenth-century Italy to make political statements. Because blatant attacks on the church or government were punishable by imprisonment or even death in both eras, wit was used as a covert weapon. The well-known fourteenth-century Italian satirist Dolcibene commented to Holy Roman Emperor Charles IV: "You fight with the sword, the Pope with his bulls, and I with my tongue" (Burckhardt, p. 117). Similarly, Shakespeare commented on British society with his pen, articulating serious messages behind a veil of wit. In *Romeo and Juliet* he slyly condemned the in-fighting between the royal Stuart and Tudor families, a feud that proved deadly during Shakespeare's time. At one point Queen Elizabeth of the Tudor family even had her cousin Queen Mary Stuart executed because she posed a threat to the throne and to the state religion.

Events in History at the Time the Play Was Written

Episodes of extreme violence and bitter clashes of ideologies created a sometimes dark atmosphere in England. In *Romeo and Juliet* Shakespeare illustrated the tragic consequences of feuding and war between rival factions, a message that his Elizabethan audience could surely understand. This relevant quality perhaps explains why *Romeo and Juliet* emerged as one of Shakespeare's most popular plays. It was staged often during his lifetime; only *Hamlet*, it is believed, was produced on more occasions.

England in the Elizabethan Age. Queen Elizabeth I set the tone for the Elizabethan Age, which was both a violent and progressive era in English history. Under Elizabeth, the fifth Tudor monarch, Great Britain achieved prominence as a world power and its citizens brimmed with national pride. In 1588 the Spanish Armada mounted a formidable naval invasion against England but was destroyed with the help of a sudden storm in the English Channel. The incredible defeat of Spain's powerful navy bolstered Elizabeth's popularity and suggested to some of her supporters that her reign was divinely ordained.

But not all citizens supported the queen. Though a thirty-year feud between rival royal bloodlines, the Yorks and Lancasters, had ended in 1485, a new rivalry between the Stuarts and Tudors emerged. Elizabeth, an Anglican Protestant, was challenged by both the Catholic Stuarts and Puritan reformers and was beset by plots to unseat her from the throne. Her cousin Mary

---

ARTHUR BROOKE VS. WILLIAM SHAKESPEARE

Brooke's scene where Juliet's father tries to convince her to marry Paris:

Unless by Wednesday next thou bend as I am bent,
And at our castle called Freetown thou freely do assent
To County Paris' suit, and promise to agree
To whatsoever then shall pass 'twixt him, my wife, and me,
Not only will I give all that I have away
From thee, to those that shall me love, me honour, and obey,
But also to so close and to so hard a gaol
I shall thee wed, for all thy life, that sure thou shalt not fail
A thousand times a day to wish for sudden death,
And curse the day and hour when first thy lungs did give thee breath.

(Arthur Brooke, *Romeus and Juliet,* lines 1973-82)

Shakespeare's version of same scene:

God's bread! It makes me mad.
Day, night, hour, tide, time, work, play,
Alone, in company, till my care hath been
To have her match'd, and having now provided
A gentleman of noble parentage,
Of fair demesnes, youthful, and nobly lien'd,
Stuff'd, as they say, with honorable parts,
Proportion'd as one's thought would wish a man—
And then to have a wretched puling fool,
A whining mammet, in her fortune's tender,
To answer, "I'll not wed, I cannot love,
I am too young; I pray you, pardon me."
But, an you will not wed, I'll pardon you.
Graze where you will, you shall not house with me.
Look to 't, think on 't, I do not jest.
Thursday is near. Lay thy hand on thy heart; advise.
An you be mine, I'll give you to my friend;
An you be not, hang, beg, starve, die in the streets,
For, by my soul, I'll never acknowledge thee,
Nor what is mine shall never do thee good.
Trust to 't, bethink you; I'll not be forsworn.

(*Romeo and Juliet,* 3.5.176-96)

Stuart, Queen of Scots, was beheaded because she posed a threat to Elizabeth. The Earl of Essex, a one-time court favorite, was similarly executed for plotting her overthrow. Because Elizabeth, known as the virgin queen, was unmarried, the question of succession loomed large during her reign and pitted rivals to the throne against one another.

The Danverses and the Longs. Another well-known feud of Shakespeare's time involved the Danvers and Long families of England. Some scholars have speculated that this rivalry might have been yet another source of inspiration for Shakespeare's drama. The animosity between the two families began when Charles and Henry Danvers killed their neighbor Henry Long during a heated dispute. With the aid of the Earl of Southampton, Shakespeare's patron, the Danvers brothers escaped to France to avoid prosecution. When they returned to participate in a plot to overthrow Queen Elizabeth, Charles was beheaded for his earlier crime.

The plague. The bubonic plague struck England in 1592 and destroyed 10 percent of the population. The plague, coupled with revolts in Ireland and Scotland and challenges to the throne by rival political and religious groups, produced tragedy and death on a broad scale. Shakespeare lived in London during this time and was forced to leave the city for at least one year when the epidemic hit and all theaters were closed. Presumably, his knowledge of the deadly impact of the plague, coupled with his understanding of the family rivalries at court, where he often performed, allowed him to comment with authority on similar events that took place in fourteenth-century Italy.

Romance and tragedy. In addition to violence and intrigue, the Elizabethan Age was marked by romance. As a young single woman in a position of great power, Elizabeth was surrounded by suitors. She had an abundance of court favorites who competed for her affection, and rumors about her love life generated speculation and interest throughout Europe. Because of her single status, her patronage of the arts, and her great achievements in office, Elizabeth was highly romanticized by the English, and it was said that she came to regard the country as her spouse. Her beauty (though apparently exaggerated) and political shrewdness were greatly touted. Many named their children after her, and some even constructed their homes in the shape of an "E" in her honor. An avid patron of the arts, Elizabeth was appreciated by artists and playwrights such as Shakespeare, who staged performances at court for her regularly. Her interest in romance, tragedy, comedy, poetry, and history greatly influenced the writing generated during the era.

Boethius and astrology. In the sixteenth century, Queen Elizabeth had Boethius's *Consolation of Philosophy* translated into modern English. This revived interest in his philosophy, which provided an explanation for much of the tragedy England was experiencing at the time. As in fourteenth-century Italy, Boethius's conception of Fortune as a controller of human destiny supported a common belief in astrology in Elizabethan England. Queen Elizabeth herself employed a court astrologer who advised her on matters of state. Shakespeare thus illustrated Elizabethan views that certain elements of life are beyond human control. But he also concluded that hate was a controllable emotion that ultimately caused the tragic events depicted in *Romeo and Juliet*. The Prince of Verona summarizes this view at the play's end:

> Where be these enemies? Capulet, Montague,
> See what a scourge is laid upon your hate,
> That heaven finds means to kill your joys
> with love.
>
> (*Romeo and Juliet*, 5.3.291-93)

For More Information

Boethius. *The Consolation of Philosophy*. Edited by James J. Buchanan. New York: Frederick Ungar, 1962.

Brooke, Arthur. *Romeus and Juliet*. London: Chatto and Windus Duffield, 1908.

Burckhardt, Jacob. *The Civilization of the Renaissance in Italy*. New York: Modern Library, 1954.

Durant, Will. *The Renaissance*. New York: Simon and Schuster, 1953.

Procacci, Giuliano. *History of the Italian People*. New York: Harper & Row, 1968.

Shakespeare, William. *Romeo and Juliet*. Edited by David Bevington. Toronto: Bantam, 1988.

The Scarlet Letter

by
Nathaniel Hawthorne

In "The Custom-House," the introduction to *The Scarlet Letter*, Nathaniel Hawthorne fabricates a story in which he explains that he stumbled upon a worn piece of red cloth in the shape of an *A* while working in Salem's Custom-House, where taxes were collected on imported goods. Accompanying the cloth, he continues, was an old manuscript about a certain Hester Prynne, who, two centuries earlier, had been forced to wear the now-faded *A* in public as punishment for committing the sin of adultery. While in reality Hawthorne found no such document, his novel was influenced by historical manuscripts about Puritan New England and his own ancestors. Hawthorne's family history harked back to the Massachusetts of the 1600s, where Puritan justice could reasonably have passed down such a punishment for adultery.

Events in History at the Time the Novel Takes Place

The Puritans in Massachusetts. In 1630 a wave of Puritans arrived in New England to populate the Massachusetts Bay Colony founded by John Winthrop. These Puritans came to Massachusetts in an effort to avoid the corruption that they thought had been plaguing the Church of England. Yet despite their objections to what was happening in the English church, they did not come to New England simply to escape that state of affairs but rather, as devoted reformers, to provide England with evidence of a model religious society. In order to ensure the success of their mis-

THE LITERARY WORK
A novel set in the New England village of Boston from 1642 to 1649; published in 1850.

SYNOPSIS
The Scarlet Letter focuses on the aftermath of the illicit love affair between the Reverend Arthur Dimmesdale and Hester Prynne. While Hester is publicly convicted for her crime, Dimmesdale, unwilling to admit his role, suffers his guilt in silence.

sion, the Puritans employed a rigid system of discipline that relied heavily on its citizens' reporting on the individual transgressions of one another.

Challenges of the new society. As Puritans began settling in the Boston colony in the 1630s, they faced a multitude of challenges, one of the greatest being the difficulty of taming the terrain in which they now lived. Surrounded by marshlands, the area was not easily arable; consequently, families were allotted very small parcels of land on which to grow crops. Another problem was a severe lack of wood, which made the biting cold of winter a life-threatening danger; the early history of the Boston colony is fraught with stories of Puritans freezing to death and losing fingers and toes to the frost of harsh winters. In addition, the settlers found little feed for their cattle, which also jeopardized their food supply. These problems diminished as settlers expanded inland to areas where wood and grazing land were more abundant.

Furthermore, during much of the 1630s, the settlers lived in almost constant fear of attack by Indians. Two tribes, the Narragansetts and the Pequots, lived in the territory surrounding Boston. Fortunately for the Puritans, the two tribes were constantly at war with each other. Capitalizing on this warfare, the Puritans joined forces with the Narragansetts and another tribe, the Mohegans, to make war on the Pequots in 1637. Approximately 700 Pequot men, women, and children were massacred, and 180 survivors were absorbed by other Indian tribes. The steady arrival of fresh colonists and the decimation of the Indian tribes by smallpox further reduced the threat of Indian violence. As they gradually gained some control over their environment, the leaders of the new Puritan colony established rules to govern their populace.

GOVERNOR JOHN WINTHROP

A wealthy English gentleman whose religious interests prompted him to sail for the New World with a large contingent of Puritans, John Winthrop was elected governor of the colony. Like his character in Hawthorne's *Scarlet Letter,* Winthrop favored a balance of religion and politics. He blamed the emerging individualism of the colonists on the influence of Satan bending "his forces against us ... so that I thinke heere are some persons who never shewed so much wickednesse in England as they have doone heer" (Winthrop in Rutman, p. 22). He had in mind rebels such as the colonist Anne Hutchinson, who took issue with some of his beliefs.

Government and crime. The founders of Massachusetts Bay Colony attempted to base their new government strictly on the Bible. They set up a system of rule by a governor, a deputy governor, and several assistants, who were collectively known as the "magistrates." These officials were able to make whatever decisions they wanted, for during their first decade of power, no written criminal code existed to limit their authority. By 1635 colonists had grown so alarmed at the unrestrained power of the magistrates that they demanded a code of written laws. This code, which was finally adopted in 1641, became known as the Body of Liberties, and it included some one hundred civil and criminal laws. Every offense

listed was connected to the Bible with references to book, chapter, and verse. Accepting this code, the colony would operate by it for most of the period until 1692.

Anne Hutchinson's Heresies. In 1636 Anne Hutchinson and a group of other colonists later known as "Antinomians" (from the Greek words *anti-,* meaning "against," and *nomos,* meaning "law") began to disturb the strict order of the Massachusetts Bay colony by protesting in meetings that the performance of good works, or, to put it in another way, the observance of religious laws, was not a reliable sign of godliness. Hutchinson and her fellow Antinomians believed that true godliness came from a person's inner acquaintance with the Holy Spirit; one's salvation could not be deduced simply from an outward show of good works. Hutchinson also came to believe that a person who had experienced this inner certainty of salvation could communicate directly with God and that she herself had divine revelations. Further angering leaders of the colony, she hinted that the only two ministers worth listening to were her brother-in-law, John Wheelwright, and a clergyman named John Cotton, whose religious ideas had inspired her own, even before she had loyally followed him across the Atlantic from England. In 1638, Hutchinson underwent two trials, the first of which resulted in her excommunication, and the second in her banishment from Massachusetts.

The heroine of *The Scarlet Letter,* Hester Prynne, also confronts and resists the authority of the magistrates; and although her crime and her punishment differ from those of Anne Hutchinson, Hawthorne twice refers to the famous Antinomian in descriptions of Hester, implying a parallel between his fictional rebel and the historical one. Not only were both women publicly punished, but both refused to confess their association with prominent ministers who, for their part, actually found themselves sitting as judges for "crimes" in which they themselves had been involved. For Hutchinson, the partner was John Cotton, the minister whose teachings had in no small way inspired her own religious beliefs. For Prynne, of course, the partner is the reverend Arthur Dimmesdale, her lover and the unacknowledged father of her daughter Pearl. Hutchinson's story unfolded from 1636 to 1638, while Hester's occurs only a few years later, from 1642 to 1649.

Commenting on the Prynne-Hutchinson comparison, one literary historian has observed that Puritan accounts of Anne Hutchinson's defiance, including several sources Hawthorne was familiar with, repeatedly described Hutchinson's heretical interpretations of religious doctrine in sexual terms. Her beliefs were regarded as illegitimate, "bastard" products of some unidentified male influence, and Hutchinson was even supposed to have given birth to real "monstrous" offspring in the aftermath of her trial (Colacurcio in Hawthorne, p. 224-25). In this light, Hester Prynne's hidden relationship with Dimmesdale and the birth of Pearl, a child whom many of Hester's neighbors think of as "demon offspring," suggest Hawthorne's awareness of how significant—and how threatening—Hutchinson's sexuality was in the eyes of the Puritans who condemned her. They associated it with her ability to bear monstrous ideas.

The Novel in Focus

The plot. The novel opens as Hester Prynne is standing on a public scaffold in front of the townspeople of Boston. A convicted adulteress, she must stay there for three hours, clutching the baby that her illicit love affair produced and facing the scorn of the Puritan community. Hester has also been sentenced to wear a scarlet *A* on the front of her dress as a constant reminder of her crime of adultery.

While staring at the crowd from the scaffold, Hester spots her long-lost husband, a doctor who sent her to Boston two years earlier while he stayed behind in Amsterdam. It was assumed that he had been killed in a shipwreck. Having just arrived, he learns why Hester is on the scaffold and vows to discover the identity of the man who has been her lover.

Hester is questioned by the ministers John Wilson and Arthur Dimmesdale, who implore her to reveal the name of her child's father, but she refuses. Returning to her cell, Hester and her baby are extremely agitated, and the jailer sends for a doctor. The doctor turns out to be Hester's husband, Roger Chillingworth. Providing medicine for Hester and her baby, Chillingworth takes partial blame for her predicament. He admits that, because of his age and physical deformities, he was wrong to have married Hester in the first place. Hester confesses that she has wronged him but nevertheless refuses to give Chillingworth her lover's name. She does agree, however, to his request that she conceal the fact that he is her husband.

After her release from prison, Hester moves to a small house on the edge of town, where she lives alone with her daughter, Pearl. As Pearl grows older, her behavior strikes the townspeople and, at times, Hester herself, as strange and unnatural; Pearl is a wild-eyed, impetuous child whose face sometimes takes on an impish, knowing cast that disturbs those around her. But when the townspeople try to have Pearl removed from Hester's care, the anxious mother visits Governor Bellingham's home, hoping to enlist his help. During the visit, Pearl comes into contact with the reverend Arthur Dimmesdale—her father, though she has never been told this. The usually hard-hearted child is tenderly attracted to Dimmesdale, a fact that does not go unnoticed by Roger Chillingworth, who has been acting as Dimmesdale's personal physician.

One night Dimmesdale returns to the scaffold where, years earlier, Hester and Pearl had stood alone. Plagued with guilt, he mounts the stand; Hester and Pearl join him there. Pearl asks that he stand with them again tomorrow in public view, but he refuses. The tension mounts when the three realize that they are being watched by Chillingworth, whose suspicions about Dimmesdale are rapidly being confirmed.

Concerned about Dimmesdale's declining health, and suspicious of what is slowly draining him, Hester plans to reveal to him that Chillingworth, Dimmesdale's physician, is, in fact, her husband. One day she tells Chillingworth that she must reveal his identity to Dimmesdale, and begs him to forgive the man. Chillingworth counters by saying that a higher power than himself is controlling his actions.

Convinced now that Chillingworth will prove to be the end of Dimmesdale, Hester intercepts her lover in the forest and reveals to him that Chillingworth is her husband. She further declares that her husband is intent on ruining Dimmesdale and urges him to escape the doctor's evil eye. Imploring him to go elsewhere to seek a new life, she promises "Thou shalt not go alone!" (*Scarlet Letter,* p. 216).

Excited by thoughts of escaping to Europe with Hester and Pearl, Dimmesdale returns to town light of heart and full of reckless impulses. He is tempted to utter blasphemy and, in one instance, to speak obscenely to a young girl. Frightened by this sudden change in himself, he runs into Mistress Hibbins, who has long been suspected of being a witch. Mockingly, she questions him about his trip through the forest and laughs when he attempts to deny any wrongdoing. Returning to his room, he fears that he may have sold his soul to the devil. Dimmesdale burns the sermon that he

A painting of Hester Prynne by George Henry Broughton.

had intended to give during the ceremonies marking the election of a new governor and, instead, stays up all night to draft another.

During the Election Day celebration, Hester is horrified to learn that Chillingworth has booked passage on the same ship she was planning to take to Europe with Dimmesdale and Pearl. As she laments this turn of events, she warns Pearl not to expect Dimmesdale to acknowledge their presence in public; throughout the novel, there is the suggestion that Pearl knows who her father is, but Hawthorne leaves it ambiguous at this point. Hester warns her daughter only that their friend the minister might not want to recognize them. But after delivering a brilliant sermon, Dimmesdale stumbles out of the church with the procession. He stops at the scaffolding, where he summons Hester and Pearl to join him. Chillingworth follows, a party to the sin because of the emotional torment he has visited on Dimmesdale. Ascending the scaffold, Dimmesdale escapes Chillingworth's evil clutches by admitting to the crowd that he is Pearl's father. Declaring that everyone should now witness the symbol of his sin, he exposes his bare chest to reveal—as witnesses later insist—a scarlet A "imprinted in the flesh" (*The Scarlet Letter*, p. 174) Following this revelation, Dimmesdale collapses and dies in Hester's arms, but not before he has received a kiss from his daughter. Hester and Pearl leave for parts unknown. Years later, Hester returns alone to her old abode on the edge of town and voluntarily begins to wear the old letter A once again.

Sin and guilt in *The Scarlet Letter*. Sparked by Hester Prynne and Arthur Dimmesdale's adulterous affair, the plot of the novel focuses on sin in Puritan society. Hester's sin is easily visible and identifiable by her Puritan community—the existence of the child Pearl is ample evidence of her transgression.

Hester suffers the ridicule of the Puritan community, clutching her newborn baby to her breast in an effort to hide the A. Unlike her lover, however, she has an ability to come to terms with her sin. This strength allows her, even at this stage, to admit the futility of trying to hide one symbol of her sin—the A—with another, the baby.

Hester's public punishment reflects an actual practice of the time. The prevalent theory of the period held that punishing lawbreakers in public would shame them and discourage them from committing future misdeeds. Public punishments included branding—placing a mark on the lawbreaker's hand or cheek or a bright letter on his or her clothing that served as a symbol of the

crime committed, like Hester's A. As early as 1634 a Boston drunkard was sentenced to wear a red D on his neck for a year.

Enduring public scorn, Hester becomes the only "sinner" in the book who manages to remain unrepentant; she retains her dignity despite the public punishment designed to shame her. Unlike the guilt-ridden Dimmesdale, she remains calm about having bucked the rules of society, a fact that may reflect a belief on Hawthorne's part that women, contrary to sexist stereotypes, were more prone than men to rebel against the conventions of society. Such stereotypes may explain the ironic fact that the Puritan community ultimately fails to recognize her unrepentant attitude; they, not Hester, eventually begin ascribing new meanings like "Able" to the scarlet badge that was meant to brand Hester as an adulteress.

Arthur Dimmesdale, the partner in Hester's sin, is a minister, one of the select individuals who in Puritan society goes about daily performing good works that are evidence of his being saved. Where, then, does committing this sin leave him? As one authority points out, Dimmesdale is a victim of his own beliefs, a Puritan "consumed by fear that . . . he did once and does still love Hester more than God, preferring the creature to the creator (Colacurcio, pp. 118-19). For Dimmesdale, no amount of self-punishment or devoted prayer can ease the emotional turmoil that results. He tries to rationalize the matter, arguing that some men do not openly confess their sins so that they may continue to promote God's glory on earth. While this smacks of the hypocrite who advises others to "do as I say, not as I do," it also brings to mind a real viewpoint held in the Puritan communities of New England; true believers fully expected to receive some hypocrites into their churches. Though they sought diligently to detect and discourage hypocrisy, they accepted the possibility of failure because, in outward practice, the hypocrite was often a more enthusiastic Puritan and so set a more striking example than the true saint.

Sources. While there has been much speculation as to Nathaniel Hawthorne's original inspiration for *The Scarlet Letter*, there is no doubt that in one way or another he was heavily influenced by his own Puritan background. Hawthorne's family was one of the oldest in Massachusetts; his great-great-grandfather, William Hathorne, was one of the presiding judges at the Salem witch trials, responsible for the infamous executions of several women. This blight on his family history weighed heavily on Hawthorne—enough so to have affected his depiction of the judgment that takes place in *The Scarlet Letter* and, more generally, his concern with sin and guilt in the novel.

An interesting historical detail about Hawthorne's family history provides another link between the author's ancestry and *The Scarlet Letter*. County records dating from 1681 reveal that two of Hawthorne's relatives on his mother's side were convicted of incest with their brother. The two were given a public whipping and made to stand in public with a band around their foreheads that revealed the nature of their crime for all to see. Meanwhile, their brother and partner in crime, Captain Nicholas Manning, hid in the forest. While scholars have debated as to whether or not Hawthorne knew of this dark moment, the similarities between this episode and Hester's predicament can hardly be dismissed.

Hawthorne immersed himself in a collection of firsthand sources about Puritan New England, including John Winthrop's *Journal,* Thomas Hutchinson's *History of Massachusetts Bay,* and Cotton Mather's *Magnalia Christi Americana.* His novel features actual historical personalities such as Mistress Ann Hibbins, who was hanged for witchcraft on June 19, 1656, seven years after the action in the novel concludes. Given all his research, it seems unlikely that Hawthorne was simply mistaken in his identification of the governor in his novel as Bellingham, who was actually voted out of office in the spring of 1642. Rather, a deliberate, artistic purpose may have prompted this rearrangement of history: Bellingham was voted out of office for taking part in a sexual relationship that offended his real Puritan community, much like Hester's affair offended the fictional Puritan village in which she resided. The fifty-year-old Bellingham, a widower, wanted to remarry a girl of twenty, and on his own authority as governor simply declared himself wed to her. An attempt to put him on trial for this offense proved unsuccessful.

Events in History at the Time the Novel Was Written

Upheavals of the 1840s. In 1848 Zachary Taylor won the presidency of the United States, a development that would oust Hawthorne from his post as supervisor at the Salem Customs-House. The author took this dismissal hard. By the time he was turned out of office on June 8, 1849, he felt a fury that would spill over into his introductory essay, "The Customs-House," which compares his own political party, the Democrats,

to the one that ousted him, the Whigs. Democrats, he contended, knew how to spare opponent party members in office after an election, and when they did strike, their axe was seldom poisoned with the ill-will that he experienced.

Speaking figuratively of Democrats being guillotined out of public office by the triumphant Whigs, "The Customs House" alludes ironically to the tumultuous revolutions that had broken out all over Europe in 1848—in France, Austria, Germany, Belgium, Poland, Bohemia, Ireland, Italy, and Hungary. Like many others in America, Hawthorne recoiled at the European revolutions of 1848-49. Most of Boston, according to the historian George Bancroft, a contemporary of Hawthorne's, was "frightened out of its wits" (Bancroft in Bercovitch, p. 76). At first, Americans had welcomed the revolutions as a hopeful sign that the principles of popular and national sovereignty were overcoming dynastic rule and imperialism in the Old World; but as leadership failed in one country after another, they began to fear that the chaos and destruction enveloping Europe would spread to the United States.

In the eyes of some, America's social fabric faced another threat along with (or worse, in combination with) the spectre of European revolt: 1848 also saw America's first women's rights convention at Seneca Falls, New York. The conventioners passed a Declaration of Sentiments that listed sixteen forms of discrimination against women in American society, stressing mostly the lack of property and voting rights. According to one conservative argument of the day, feminist activism and European radicalism both aimed "to emancipate woman by making her independent of man, thus giving her up to follow her passions and making a rule of adultery" (Bercovitch, p. 78). For those who subscribed to such arguments, proper moral conduct and even American democracy itself depended on women's remaining in their God-ordained places—the home and family. In *The Scarlet Letter,* Hester's thoughts imply something similar, when she reflects that the whole social system would have to be torn down and built anew before women could assume a fair position in it.

Transcendentalism. One of the dominant American philosophical and social movements of the nineteenth century, transcendentalism was centered in the region of New England in which Hawthorne lived. Based on an idealistic philosophy promoted by writers such as Ralph Waldo Emerson, Henry David Thoreau, and Margaret Fuller, this movement emphasized notions of the unity shared by all creatures, the innate goodness of human beings, and the importance of personal insight. The transcendentalists believed in social reform, but felt that it must begin first with the individual. Members of the movement rejected the standard religious practices of the day and promoted freedom of thought or, as Emerson famously called it, "self reliance." For this dependence on inward illumination, traditional Congregationalists—the religious inheritors of the early New England Puritans—sometimes criticized transcendentalism as a movement that recalled Anne Hutchinson and her fellow Antinomians, who put their faith in a person's inner knowledge of the Holy Spirit.

From 1836 to 1855, transcendentalism's influence was at its peak, and Hawthorne, though never a convinced transcendentalist himself, was sympathetic to some of the movement's ideals. He spent some time living at Brook Farm, where many transcendentalists experimented with communal living, and had some of his works published in *The Dial,* a transcendentalist magazine. Its first editor was Margaret Fuller, a woman who supposedly had a child out of wedlock and may have, along with the rebellious Puritan Anne Hutchinson, been a model for the heroine Hester Prynne. Perhaps Hawthorne's involvement with the transcendentalist movement influenced his views on the individual placed in opposition to society, which is one of the primary issues explored in *The Scarlet Letter.* Certainly he questioned the movement's view of innate human goodness, exposing instead a more complex view of human nature that included a focus, through his character Chillingworth, on a human tendency to commit evil.

Public reaction to *The Scarlet Letter.* Upon its publication, *The Scarlet Letter* was almost universally praised by critics, who lauded Hawthorne's ability to portray the deepest passions of his char- acters. E. P. Whipple, a widely read and influential critic of the day, gave Hawthorne abundant praise, writing that the book "bears on every page the evidence of a mind thoroughly alive, watching patiently the movements of morbid hearts when stirred by strange experiences" (Whipple in Mellow, p. 316).

On the other hand, some critics were taken aback by the scandalous subject matter of *The Scarlet Letter.* They felt that the topic of the novel was revolting, an opinion that found its way into reviews of the day. Hawthorne also received quite a bit of backlash at home in Salem. The backlash was attached mainly to the introductory essay, "The Customs House." The veiled critical references in the essay to the politicians of the town did not go unnoticed, and he received quite a bit of negative response from the citizens of Salem. Hawthorne became so upset by their criticism that he made a public "declaration of independence from his birthplace," claiming that "henceforth, it ceases to be a reality in my life. I am a citizen of somewhere else" (Hawthorne in Mellow, p. 317).

For More Information

Bercovitch, Sacvan. *The Office of The Scarlet Letter.* Baltimore: Johns Hopkins University Press, 1991.

Colacurcio, Michael J., ed. *New Essays on The Scarlet Letter.* New York: Cambridge University Press, 1985.

Emerson, Everett. *Puritanism in America 1620-1750.* Boston: Twayne, 1977.

Hawthorne, Nathaniel. *The Scarlet Letter.* New York: Norton, 1988.

Levy, Babette May. *Preaching in the First Half Century of New England History.* New York: Russel and Russel, 1945.

Mellow, James R. *Nathaniel Hawthorne in His Times.* Boston: Houghton Mifflin, 1980.

Rutman, Darrett B. *Winthrop's Boston: A Portrait of a Puritan Town.* New York: W. W. Norton, 1965.

The Scarlet Pimpernel

by
Baroness Emmuska Orczy

Born in Hungary in 1865, Baroness Emmuska Orczy moved to England with her family when she was fifteen. She lived there the rest of her life. In 1905 she published her best-known work, *The Scarlet Pimpernel*. The novel takes place in 1792 during the French Revolution and has a number of important parallels to European life a century later.

Events in History at the Time the Novel Takes Place

The French Revolution. Peasants in eighteenth-century France endured severe economic and political hardships. Most lived on small farms rented from aristocratic landlords. They worked hard but remained extremely poor, for it was difficult to support a family on the meager income they earned. A peasant spent a large percentage of his annual income paying heavy taxes to the royal government, as well as rent to his noble landlord. The peasant class also owed part of each year's harvest to the Catholic Church. The average peasant earned barely enough to meet all these obligations.

Peasants suffered personal indignities as well. They often watched helplessly as their fields were trampled by nobleman hunters or wild boars and deer under royal protection. They were powerless to change the situation because they were not represented in the royal French government.

Not every French aristocrat abused his position of power over the lower class. Some, like the Marquis de La Fayette, even believed in the

need for widespread social reform. The difficult conditions that the peasants had endured for centuries, however, led to an overall feeling of intense bitterness towards the aristocracy.

On July 14, 1789, a mob of citizens of the Parisien lower classes, who held aristocrats largely responsible for their hardships, attacked the Bastille prison in Paris. The capture of this ancient symbol of aristocratic tyranny triggered the beginning of the French Revolution. In the following months, mobs attacked and burned castles across France, often torturing or murdering their wealthy inhabitants. Severe food shortages prompted an angry mob of peasant women to march to the palace of King Louis XVI at Versailles in October 1789. The women secured a promise from the king to have food supplies sent to Paris. They also forced the king to agree to move back to Paris, where they could remain in close contact with him and make sure that he kept his promise to deliver food.

Conflict between the revolutionaries and the nobility became increasingly violent. In July

An illustration of Robespierre guillotining the executioner after having ordered the deaths of hundreds of his enemies.

1791, royal government troops killed more than fifty people who were protesting against the king. This incident became known as the Champs de Mars Massacre. The following year a mob of working-class revolutionaries initiated a bloody battle at the royal Tuileries Palace in Paris. More than 600 of the king's guards were killed in the violent clash. Soon after, King Louis XVI was overthrown, arrested, and imprisoned. With the king in prison and many aristocrats in flight from the violence directed against them, the revolutionaries found that they wielded much greater influence in the French government.

The revolutionaries turned their new power against the remaining nobility. Laws were passed in the summer of 1792 that allowed police to search homes without warrants and to arrest anyone suspected of opposing the Revolution. Once accused, alleged traitors were often sentenced to death on very little evidence. Thousands of aristocrats were executed. At the same time, violent mobs continued to take the law into their own hands. In September 1792, throngs of people marched to five different prisons and murdered anyone they suspected of crimes against the Revolutionary cause. By the end of the five-day long

"September Massacres," about 1,400 prisoners had been slain. The majority of the victims were innocent of any anti-Revolutionary activities.

In December the trial of King Louis XVI, who by this time had been deprived of his royal title and called simply Louis Capet, began. Two months later, he was executed in Paris by means of the guillotine. This terrifying time of escalating violence against the aristocracy is chronicled in *The Scarlet Pimpernel*.

England and Republican France. Many English people initially applauded the efforts of the French revolutionaries to secure more power for themselves. They believed that the French protesters ultimately aimed to establish a system of government similar to that of England. Under such a system, the French king would share more power with the legislature, and a greater proportion of the nation's people would be represented in the government. As the violence in France grew, however, the tide of English opinion began to turn. Anarchy came to be seen as the dominant characteristic of the French Revolution.

Many of the English found the execution of King Louis XVI in January 1793 particularly disturbing. Politicians and religious leaders across the country spoke out against the French king's death. The majority of English people began to agree with the opinions of the prominent legislator Edmund Burke. His *Reflections on the Revolution in France* (1790) warned that the French Revolution was a tremendous threat to traditional English and European civilization. Urging the British to take action, he advocated intervention in the Revolution to stop it from spreading to other countries. Burke feared that the lower classes everywhere might be inspired to seize the wealth and property of the upper classes. The old hierarchy of social classes, which he believed was essential to the well-being of society, seemed in danger of collapsing.

Eventually, English people of all social classes registered shock at the events taking place across the English Channel, a reaction that was captured in *The Scarlet Pimpernel*. Many in the lower classes feared the social chaos that the Revolution seemed to be generating in France, while members of the upper classes felt threatened by the execution of so many of their fellow aristocrats in France. In November 1792, English nobles created the first Association for the Preservation of Liberty and Property against Republicans and Levellers. (A "Leveller" referred to anyone who advocated attacking the wealthy in order to make society more equal, or level.) The group resolved to support law and order, suppress rebellious publications, and prevent the spread of revolution. By 1793 there were about 2,000 such associations in existence.

As disturbing as the events in France seemed to many people, some powerful English political leaders did not want to intervene. Prime Minister William Pitt, for example, believed that taking action against Revolutionary France would be overly expensive. He argued that England itself did not seem to be in immediate danger and had important problems of its own to handle. Given his views, the official government policy under Prime Minister Pitt toward the French Republican government remained one of neutrality. This ceased, however, on February 1, 1793, when France declared war on England as well as several other nations, in anger against these countries' support of the French aristocracy.

THE GUILLOTINE

The guillotine is a constant source of anxiety to the central characters of *The Scarlet Pimpernel*. In 1792, when the story takes place, this beheading machine—which consisted of a heavy blade dropped between two grooved poles—had only recently been invented by Dr. Joseph Ignace Guillotin. This respected French doctor originally regarded his invention as a humane and merciful alternative to other, more torturous means of execution common at the time, such as being burned alive or drawn and quartered. His method of swift mechanical decapitation was introduced in France in 1789 and adopted as France's main means of execution in early 1792. A thief and forger named Nicholas Pelletier became its first victim on April 25, 1792. During the course of the French Revolution, thousands more people were killed by the guillotine's blade. Although Dr. Guillotin's invention rose to the height of its infamy during the French Revolution, it remained the means of execution in France until 1977.

King George III, whose views contrasted with Pitt's, was pleased with this turn of events. He expected a war to "rouse such a spirit in this country that I trust will curb the insolence of those despots [the revolutionaries], and be a means of restoring some degree of order to that unprincipled country, whose aim at present is to destroy the foundations of every civilized state" (Weiner, p. 71). England viewed France's declaration as an opportunity to put a stop to the Revolution that had appalled and threatened so many of them.

French émigrés. About 120,000 people fled France during the Revolution, more than half of them French aristocrats seeking to escape the revolutionary violence directed against them. Within two months of the peasants' attack on the Bastille in 1789, thousands applied for a French passport. The roads became clogged with the carriages of people fleeing the country. Gradually it became difficult for anyone, particularly aristocrats, to get out of France.

The cost of obtaining a French passport rose enormously during this period. Even if a person could afford the tremendous price, applying for a passport to leave the country could be construed as the action of someone who was unhappy with France and a sign that the person might be a traitor. All passport applicants risked attracting the attention of the authorities, who arrested aristocrats on the slightest evidence.

Although a man known as "the Scarlet Pimpernel" did not actually exist, others like him did help many people escape the dangers of revolutionary France. Numerous Swiss citizens, for example, made multiple trips to France to marry French women. The women could then have themselves listed on their passports as Swiss citizens and be safely escorted across the border. This strategy was effective, although one Swiss man was finally arrested as he tried to take his eighteenth bride to Sweden. People also wore disguises to escape. A French aristocrat named Madame de Falaiseau, for example, disguised herself in a peasant's striped skirt, a muslin kerchief, an old cap, and heavy black shoes with coarse stockings. She was then led over the border by a friendly peasant.

Many émigrés fled to England, where they were generally welcomed and treated kindly, as in *The Scarlet Pimpernel*. Still, most found it emotionally difficult to settle in a foreign country. The French émigré Madame de Falaiseau described her feelings upon arriving in England on January 1, 1793, in the following passage: "Separated perhaps for ever from my family, proscribed, a wanderer outlawed from my country, no longer possessing anything, far from all I knew and loved in my childhood, from my days of happiness, I saw around me nothing but distress and no hope for the future at all" (Weiner, p. 45). Many such émigrés were also worried about the safety of those they had been forced to leave behind. It seems likely that a majority of French émigrés shared the feelings of the Comtesse de Tournay in *The Scarlet Pimpernel,* who is described as deeply affected by "fatigue, sorrow and emotion" after her arrival in England (Orczy, *Scarlet Pimpernel,* p. 30).

The Novel in Focus

The plot. The novel opens in September 1792, the third year of the increasingly violent French Revolution. Masses of people gather daily in Paris to watch the grisly spectacle of nobles being beheaded by the guillotine. A number of aristocrats, though, have been able to escape the threat of execution. This has happened largely through the efforts of a mysterious man known only by his signature symbol—a small, red, star-shaped flower called the Scarlet Pimpernel. The French government, angry and embarrassed at its inability to stop the Scarlet Pimpernel, has ordered all guards to be particularly cautious about letting people go through the city gates of Paris. Even so, the Scarlet Pimpernel manages to safely escort the Comtesse de Tournay and her children out of Paris. After sailing across the English Channel to Dover, England, the de Tournay family is brought to the Fisherman's Rest Inn by a loyal associate of the Pimpernel, Sir Andrew Ffoulkes.

The Englishman Sir Percy Blakeney and his French wife Marguerite arrive at the inn soon after this. Sir Percy appears to be an amiable, though somewhat foolish, man. Marguerite, in contrast, is known as one of the most clever women in Europe. The couple is active in fashionable upper-class English social circles, and in public they appear to be very happy together. In reality, however, the marriage is troubled. Sir Percy learned early in their marriage that Marguerite had made accusations against a noble French family in Paris in front of the revolutionaries. Since that time he has become emotionally distant. Marguerite, out of pride, had never explained to him her side of the story. She had naively been deceived into the betrayal and had not realized that her actions would lead to the death of the aristocratic family. Hurt by her husband's coldness, she tends to treat him with sarcasm and scorn.

Marguerite leaves the inn to say goodbye to her brother, Armand. She knows he is a fervent republican, and believes he is returning to France to continue working for the revolutionary cause. He does not tell his sister, however, that he is actually going back to help the Scarlet Pimpernel rescue a count, the Comte de Tournay, from

France. After Armand's departure, Marguerite meets Chauvelin, a French agent who has been sent to England to catch the elusive Scarlet Pimpernel. He asks for her help in his mission, but she refuses. Warning her that she will yet agree to his offer, he leaves for London.

That night, Chauvelin's associates assault and steal secret papers from two of the Pimpernel's loyal followers. This provides Chauvelin with evidence that Marguerite's brother, Armand, is a colleague of the Scarlet Pimpernel and therefore a traitor to Republican France. Chauvelin catches up with Marguerite at a London opera and threatens to have Armand killed for his activities if Marguerite refuses to help him catch the Scarlet Pimpernel. Frightened for her brother, she reluctantly agrees. At a ball that evening, she manages to intercept a note that indicates that the Pimpernel himself will appear in an empty dining room late that night and soon after depart for France. Marguerite passes on the information to Chauvelin. At the scheduled hour, though, he finds only the foolish Sir Percy soundly asleep on a sofa.

Early the next morning, Sir Percy informs his wife that he must leave for a while on business. After his departure, she walks into his private study. She discovers several scholarly books that are not in keeping with his frivolous public personality, a few maps of France, and a gold ring embossed with a pimpernel flower. She realizes her husband is actually the famous Scarlet Pimpernel who has been bravely rescuing French aristocrats. She enlists the aid of Sir Andrew Ffoulkes and learns of her husband's plan to rescue the Comte de Tournay and her brother Armand, whom Chauvelin was pursuing. Armed with knowledge about her husband's intended route, she and Sir Andrew sail across the English Channel to Calais, France, to search for him.

Chauvelin and his men, who have discovered the Pimpernel's true identity as well, are on his trail. Sir Percy and his plan seem doomed, but Marguerite courageously continues to follow him in the hopes of finding a way to save his life. Just as he is about to be captured, a daring plan is devised. He uses a clever disguise to slip through Chauvelin's trap and fulfill his mission. At the end of the novel, Sir Percy looks upon his brave and loyal wife with new respect and admiration. Having finally settled their differences, the couple begin to rebuild a happy relationship.

Views of aristocracy and peasantry. People throughout the world have had differing interpretations of the French Revolution. Many people who have studied the events of the Revolu-

The citizens of Paris storming the Bastille prison in 1789, the event that signaled the beginning of the French Revolution.

tion over the last two centuries have viewed the French aristocrats as selfish, wealthy, and oppressive villains who largely deserved their violent fate. Baroness Orczy's *The Scarlet Pimpernel*, however, reflects a different vision of the Revolution and the social classes involved.

Orczy's novel presents a highly sympathetic view of nobility. The main characters, including the Scarlet Pimpernel himself, are all aristocrats. The tremendous hardships faced by French nobles such as the de Tournay family are highlighted, along with their innocence of any specific crimes. Deep sympathy is expressed for the injustices done to them: "The daily execution of scores of royalists of good family, whose only sin was their aristocratic name, seemed to cry for vengeance to the whole of civilised Europe" (*Scarlet Pimpernel*, p. 20). This viewpoint, which holds that innocent French nobles are being forced to pay for their ancestors' oppression of the people, is repeated throughout the book.

Not all French aristocrats are portrayed as ideal people in the novel, however. The narrator describes the Comtesse de Tournay as a woman possessed of the typical haughty, rigid bearing of her class. After coldly voicing her desire to never meet Marguerite because of her past denunciation of a noble family in France, the countess is

described as being "encased in the plate-armour of her aristocratic prejudices ... rigid and unbending ..." (*Scarlet Pimpernel*, p. 35).

While some members of the nobility are portrayed in an unfavorable light, much sympathy is still shown for them in the story. The lower classes, on the other hand, are frequently described in extremely unflattering terms. The first sentence of the novel, for example, refers to the common people of Paris as "a surging, seething, murmuring crowd, of beings that are human only in name, for to the eye and ear they seem naught but savage creatures, animated by vile passions and by the lust of vengeance and of hate" (*Scarlet Pimpernel*, p. 1). The violent excesses of the lower classes are characterized as horrible and disturbing throughout the story, further evidence that Orczy's novel is a presentation of the French Revolution from the perspective of the nobles of France.

Sources. A number of prominent historical figures in the English government are referred to in the book. Among them are Prime Minister William Pitt and Edmund Burke, who differed sharply in their views on the appropriate English response to the French Revolution.

There are also a number of parallels in *The Scarlet Pimpernel* to the author's life. She was born in 1865 in Hungary to the Baron Felix Orczy and his wife, Emma. At the time, Hungary had a hierarchy of aristocrats and peasant workers that was much like the one in pre-revolutionary France. Her family moved to London in 1880, but Orczy's childhood experiences were as a member of a noble family in a world of frustrated peasants and lower-class workers.

There was a tremendous amount of tension between the upper and lower classes in Hungary, and peasant uprisings against living and working conditions in that country actually contributed to her family's decision to move to London. Like the characters Marguerite and the Comtesse de Tournay in her novel, then, Baroness Orczy was not a native of England.

Other similarities between Orczy's life and the lives portrayed in *The Scarlet Pimpernel* are evident as well. She married Montagu Barstow in 1894, and the couple became very active in aristocratic London social circles. The central characters in Orczy's novel—Sir Percy and his wife Marguerite—enjoy similar status in upper-class London society. Such parallels make it clear that Baroness Orczy drew on some of her own personal experiences to write her story about aristocrats and their adventures during the French Revolution.

Events in History at the Time the Novel Was Written

The rise of the working class. Throughout the nineteenth century, manufacturing industries were boosted by the Industrial Revolution. Manufacturing gradually displaced agriculture as the basis of European economies. New means of mechanical production were invented that allowed goods to be made more quickly and cheaply than ever before. Industrial business owners were thus able to make a great deal of money. For the growing number of workers in their factories, however, hours were long, factory conditions were squalid, and wages were often barely enough for survival. As was the case with the peasants in eighteenth-century France, many people lived in extreme poverty.

As the century continued, workers throughout Europe took sometimes extreme action to improve their situations. In France a movement called the Paris Commune took over Paris for two months in 1871. This rebellion was similar in some ways to the eighteenth-century French Revolution. Among the rebels were working-class people who felt that the French government was

unresponsive to their needs. They demanded better wages and working conditions, and expressed a desire to create a system that was truly representative of their interests. The revolt did not turn out to be a peaceful one. Troops were sent in by the legitimate government, which had moved to Versailles. The soldiers severely beat any captured Communards, or supporters of the rebellious Paris Commune. In return, the Communards burned public buildings and assassinated the Archbishop of Paris. By the time the legitimate government had again regained control of the city, more than 20,000 people had been massacred over the course of a few days. One English reporter wrote, "Paris the beautiful is Paris the ghastly, Paris the battered, Paris the burning, Paris the blood-spattered, now" (Burchell, p. 120). The reporter could have made the same comment about Paris 100 years earlier during the French Revolution. While the Paris Commune ended after only two months, the French staged peaceful protests for better working and living conditions throughout the rest of the century.

Another violent revolution of the lower classes took place in Russia in 1905, the same year *The Scarlet Pimpernel* was published. That year, on January 22, about 1,000 people were killed when Czar Nicholas II's Imperial Guard opened fire on a crowd of protesters. The uprising spread across Russia; over half a million workers went on strike, wild riots erupted, and the homes of wealthy landowners were looted and burned. This revolt subsided within a year, after the Czar agreed to extend greater political and civil liberties to everyone. By the early 1900s, working-class people across Europe possessed at least somewhat greater influence and power than they had enjoyed during previous centuries.

Nationalist movements. During the French Revolution, many revolutionaries were seized by a fierce patriotism that drove them to destroy people who were suspected of being disloyal to Republican France. In the late nineteenth century, this kind of nationalist feeling was a significant force throughout Europe. People of similar ethnic backgrounds came to feel a growing sense of solidarity, while many wars were caused by the desire to increase national power by extending territory. Germany, for example, fought against both Austria, in the Seven Weeks War, and France, in the Franco-Prussian War. Ernest Hasse, who in 1894 founded a nationalist group called the Pan-Germanic League, said, "we want territory even if it be inhabited by foreign peoples, so that we may shape their future in accordance with our needs" (Burchell, p. 106). Such statements illustrate the negative side of the nationalist movement. Just as aristocrats had been victims of the patriotic fervor of the French Revolution, there were also victims of this late nineteenth-century nationalist movement. As feelings of ethnic unity became the focus of fierce pride, many people became intolerant of those who were of different ethnic groups.

THE DREYFUS AFFAIR

One of the major events of late nineteenth-century France was the Dreyfus Affair. In 1894 a Jewish military captain named Alfred Dreyfus was convicted of espionage against France and sentenced to prison. The small amount of evidence against him consisted mainly of a document containing secret military information that he had allegedly intended to send to a German contact. A few years later, evidence turned up that seemed to prove his innocence, but the army refused to re-open the case. The case escalated into a tremendous debate that divided France. While the debate touched on many issues, the depth of French anti-Semitism revealed by the case was particularly striking. There was even an anti-Semitic journal, *La Libre Parole*, that established a fund for the widow of a man who had helped create the case against Dreyfus. Many of the contributors accompanied their donations with letters suggesting that Jewish people be used as test targets for new guns, or that Jews be attacked, blinded, or thrown into the sewers.

Jewish citizens were frequent victims of this kind of thinking; they were commonly seen as outsiders and blamed for taking away jobs and money from "real" citizens. While Jews had faced deep prejudice for centuries, it intensified during this time of growing nationalism. In Poland and Russia, increasingly severe persecution took place in the form of pogroms, organized massacres of Jewish people. Throughout Europe, less violent expressions of prejudice against Jews were also common during this time. In *The Scarlet Pimpernel*, Baroness Orczy drew on the long-standing anti-Semitism in Europe to devise one of the Pimpernel's most successful disguises, that of an old Jewish man. The disguise is successful in the novel because of the hatred that many French people had for Jewish people. Chauvelin's anti-Semitic revulsion overrides any desire he might have had to examine the disguised Percy more closely. Such extreme anti-Semitism was very powerful in the early twentieth century, the period in which Orczy wrote the book.

Reviews. Though she wrote over thirty books, Baroness Orczy is most famous for *The Scarlet Pimpernel*. It was generally praised for its exciting plot; a typical review, which appeared in the *New York Times* on October 14, 1905, describes it as "thrilling." Orczy wrote many sequels to *The Scarlet Pimpernel* in recognition of its popularity. These include *The Elusive Pimpernel* (1908), *The Triumph of the Scarlet Pimpernel* (1922), and *The Way of the Scarlet Pimpernel* (1933). All of these books take place during the French Revolution and feature many of the main characters from the original novel.

For More Information

Burchell, S. C. *Age of Progress*. New York: Time, 1966.

Crossley, Ceri, and Ian Small. *The French Revolution and British Culture*. New York: Oxford University Press, 1989.

Furet, François, and Denis Richet. *French Revolution*. Translated by Stephen Hardman. New York: Macmillan, 1970.

Orczy, Baroness Emmuska. *The Scarlet Pimpernel*. New York: Dodd, Mead, 1964.

Weiner, Margery. *The French Exiles 1789-1815*. New York: William Morrow, 1961.

Siddhartha

by
Hermann Hesse

H ermann Hesse was born in Germany in 1877 to an Indian mother and missionary father. Raised during the Romantic era in Europe—an artistic and cultural movement that emphasized a love of nature and beauty—Hesse felt a natural attraction to Buddhist philosophy because it promoted similar concepts. His personal ties to the East furthered his interest in both Buddhism and its founder, Siddhartha Gautama. Combining his interest in Buddhism with a personal curiosity about the meaning of life, Hesse wrote *Siddhartha,* which loosely traces Siddhartha Gautama's life and teachings and connects his soul-searching journey to that of all human beings.

THE LITERARY WORK

A novel set in India, approximately 500-400 B.C.; published in German in about 1923 and in English in 1951.

SYNOPSIS

A young Brahman of India embarks on a journey of self-discovery and finds the meaning of life.

Events in History at the Time the Novel Takes Place

Ancient India. In the fifth century B.C., India consisted of sixteen major states in the north. The region's southern parts remained largely undeveloped. Kings or chiefs ruled individual states and acquired income through taxation and trade. Typical goods traded during this period included horses, cotton, textiles, gold, iron ore, and pearls. The Brahmans, or religious leaders, held a very high position in each state. Often they had the authority to approve of the ruling class, and on some occasions they were rulers themselves.

In addition to the major states, there were dozens of smaller regions comprised of various tribes organized as oligarchies, each under a single ruling family. The Shakya tribe, of which Siddhartha Gautama was a prince, was one of these oligarchies. It was located in the area called Kapilavastu, at the foot of the Himalayas in northeast India.

Wars of the Ganges Valley. Control of the Ganges Valley became a major issue between the northern Indian states during the sixth and fifth centuries B.C. Wars were continually fought over the rights to the lucrative trade route, especially between the states of Kashi, Kosala, Magadha, and Vrjji. The state of Magadha established dominance in the region by the mid-400s, but infighting continued between tribes and states into the next century. The nation of India was not unified until the establishment of the Mauryan Empire in 325 B.C.

Evolution and philosophy of Buddhism. Buddhism was founded by Siddhartha Gautama in roughly 500 B.C. Known as *Buddha,* meaning the "Illustrious One" or "Enlightened One," Siddhartha promoted concepts of peace and passive behavior in the face of aggression. His teachings maintained that love is stronger than force; through peaceful co-existence and patience, good can conquer evil just as a stream can erode the most formidable mountain over time. Buddhism stresses that people can find enlightenment through love, gratitude, and respect for all life. The philosophy also teaches that "Nirvana," a state of complete inner peace and happiness, can be achieved when people free themselves from material concerns.

THE CASTE SYSTEM

The caste system consists of four classes or "castes" ranging from the Brahmans down to the Shudras.

1. Brahman (uppermost caste): signifies one who possesses magical or divine knowledge (religious leaders).
2. Kshatriya (second-highest caste): signifies one who possesses power or sovereignty (the ruling and landowning class).
3. Vaishya (the third caste): signifies one who owns and cultivates the land (the landowning and/or merchant class).
4. Shudra (the lowest caste): signifies one who works for or serves the upper castes (the peasant or subservient class)

Siddhartha's philosophy, known as the *dharma*, emerged in opposition to the violence, suffering, and inequality he witnessed in Indian society. Siddhartha felt that war, animal sacrifices, and the caste system (which ranked members of Indian society by heredity) all undermined peace and degraded life. The slaughtering of animals for religious or ceremonial rituals, such as the *abhishekha* or *ashvamedha,* was a common practice during the fifth century B.C. These rituals, performed by the Brahmans, involved the killing of horses or other animals to illustrate a king or chief's power. The sacrifices were part of the popular religions of the day, most of which were based on the worship of various deities. Siddhartha, who felt it was wrong to kill any form of life, condemned the animal sacrifices—as well as any type of murder—in his teachings. He specifically denounced the Brahmans, who were supposed to be the spiritual and moral guides of society, for their participation in the killing of animals and sanctioning of war.

Siddhartha also felt that the caste system resulted in suffering and devalued life. The system, some of which remains in place to this day, is directly opposed to Buddhist beliefs in social equality and freedom of choice. Siddhartha, though of the highest Brahman caste himself, taught that all people are born equal and that everyone must fulfill his or her own destiny, which cannot be dictated by another.

Members are born into a caste and can only rise in class through noble death and subsequent reincarnation, marriage, or via economic means (though this is very rare).

Siddhartha Gautama's search for enlightenment. Siddhartha Gautama was born about 563 B.C., a prince of the Shakya clan of Kapilavastu. His father was a king or prince and raised him in an opulent palace at the foot of the Himalaya Mountains. The king tried to shelter his son from the pain and suffering of life by keeping him inside the palace walls until age twenty-nine, but Siddhartha eventually left his comfortable surroundings to experience the outer world.

According to legend, once outside the comfort of his home, Siddhartha had three encounters that profoundly impressed him: he saw an old man, a sick man, and a dead man. He had never seen such men before. From this experience, he realized that life involves aging, sickness, and death. He then saw an old monk dressed in a tattered yellow robe. The monk had cast off all material possessions and lived as a wandering missionary. Deeply impressed by the monk's lack of desire for material possessions, Siddhartha began to think that the path to "Nirvana," or total peace and happiness, could be found through self-denial. He decided to copy the monk and live the life of an ascetic—a person who has no material possessions and denies himself all physical pleasures and luxuries. Siddhartha cut his hair, stripped off his luxurious robes, and went forth into the woods. He abandoned his noble title, his wife, and his son so that he might extinguish his desire for material things and find true enlightenment.

Siddhartha meditated for six years, living as a homeless wanderer on little or no food. He learned to "think, wait, and fast" (Hesse, *Siddhartha,* p. 52), but he did not achieve enlightenment. He had now lived two extremely different lives: one of pure self-indulgence and another of total self-denial. He realized that the truth was not to be found in either extreme.

At the age of thirty-five, Siddhartha abandoned the life of an ascetic and went into town. There, while meditating under a bodhi tree, he gained enlightenment. He discovered that the means by which to alleviate suffering in life and find inner peace is to live according to the Middle Way. The Middle Way shuns overindulgence in earthly pleasures but also avoids extreme self-denial and self-torture.

Karma. The Buddha further realized that life is a cycle of death and rebirth. He believed that a negative cycle, which produced pain and suffering, could only be broken if people lived by the Middle Way and rid themselves of "bad karma." Karma literally means action that affects life. For example, good deeds breed positive or good karma, while evil deeds breed negative or bad karma. The way to rid oneself of pain and suffering, according to the Buddhist theory, is to cleanse one's karma (which could have been dirtied by evil deeds committed in a present or past life) by living a good life and performing positive deeds. Buddhists believe that until one cleanses his or her karma and breaks patterns of negative behavior, he or she is doomed to the cycle of death and rebirth, or "the wheel of life." Only by positive action can one escape future suffering and ultimately attain Nirvana, or release from the wheel of life.

The Eightfold Path to enlightenment. Though Siddhartha preached that all people must find enlightenment themselves and forge their own destinies, he believed his dharma (which means "the law") could point the way toward reaching Nirvana. In the Buddhist version of the Ten Commandments, Siddhartha outlined an eightfold path toward achieving enlightenment. He believed people should:

1) Seek knowledge of the truth
2) Intend to resist evil
3) Say nothing to hurt others
4) Respect life, morality, and property
5) Hold a job that does not injure others
6) Strive to free one's mind of evil
7) Control one's feelings and thoughts
8) Practice proper forms of concentration (such as meditation)

Siddhartha preached the dharma throughout India and slowly developed a large following. He became known throughout the East as the Enlightened One, and people came from far and near to hear him preach and learn his philosophy. He organized his followers into a religious order of monks, nuns, and lay people, and established Buddhist temples for worship and meditation. Buddhism emerged as a major world religion and became the state religion of India during the Mauryan Empire under Ashoka (268-231 B.C.). Siddhartha Gautama died of an unknown illness when he was about eighty years old. Today there are approximately 300 million Buddhists worldwide—most reside in Sri Lanka, Japan, and Southeast Asia, though Buddhism maintains a strong presence in China, Korea, and the West as well.

The Novel in Focus

The plot. Like Siddhartha Gautama, Hermann Hesse's fictional Siddhartha was the son of a wealthy and distinguished Brahman. But while there are some parallels between the two, Hesse's Siddhartha is a different man from the historical Siddhartha Gautama.

Siddhartha

THE MEANING OF *BRAHMAN*

Siddhartha redefined the term *Brahman* to mean "perfect" or "excellent." His definition did not indicate caste but rather held that anyone who strove for and achieved a perfect or an excellent life could become a Brahman.

Hesse's character is recognized from birth as an extraordinary person, "beloved" and "magnificent" (*Siddhartha*, p. 2). Everyone adores Siddhartha, but "Siddhartha himself was not happy" and began "to feel the seeds of discontent within him" (*Siddhartha*, pp. 2-3). He feels that his spiritual life is not fulfilling. He questions the religion he practices and wonders why wise Brahmans such as his father, who live good and noble lives, still are not at peace with themselves and experience pain and suffering. As Siddhartha ponders these questions, he decides that God lies within every person and that "Atman," the inner Self that is God, must be discovered through experience. Siddhartha concludes that if a man could discover the Atman within himself, he would be enlightened and experience inner peace. Thus, Hesse's Siddhartha—like the historical Buddha—sets out on a journey of self-discovery, leaving behind his family and life of privilege.

Siddhartha first becomes a "samana," or ascetic, stripping himself of all material possessions, including his clothes. He lives in the woods and meditates, eating as little as one grain of rice a day. Like the Buddha, he learns to think, wait, and fast, but still he does not find his "Self" or achieve inner peace.

One day, while walking with a companion named Govinda, Siddhartha discusses Gautama, the Illustrious One, whose teachings are becoming legendary throughout India. Govinda desperately wants to join the Buddha and learn from him. But Siddhartha—like Gautama himself—is skeptical of teachers and wisdom not achieved by oneself. Despite his misgivings, Siddhartha accompanies Govinda to where the Illustrious One resides. He is deeply impressed by Gautama's behavior, his knowledge, and his message. He listens to the Buddha preach his philosophy of the Eightfold Path that leads to enlightenment and learns his message thoroughly. But unlike Govinda, he is not moved to join the Buddha. He leaves Govinda and sets forth on the second leg of his pilgrimage.

Siddhartha realizes he has not reached enlightenment because he does not understand himself fully. He decides he must learn about the outside world—the world of appearances and sensuality and materialism—in order to discover a side of himself he has to this point denied. He travels to the city to learn the art of love from Kamala, the most beautiful courtesan in town. But before he can have Kamala and learn her secrets, he must earn money and become respectable in the eyes of urban society. He goes to work for Kamaswami, a wealthy businessman. Kamaswami is convinced that Siddhartha's experience as an ascetic—someone who learned to think, wait, and fast—qualifies Siddhartha for business.

WORDS OF WISDOM

Siddhartha Gautama (like the novel's Siddhartha) believed that enlightenment and wisdom cannot be taught but must be experienced and attained for oneself. Concerning his own upcoming death he wrote: "The word of the Master is ended; we have no Teacher more. But it is not thus that you should regard it. The [teaching] which I have given you, let that be your Teacher when I am gone ... even he [the Buddha] could not attain Enlightenment for others. Buddhas do but point the way" (Siddhartha Gautama in Humphreys, p. 27).

Siddhartha soon becomes prosperous. He buys nice clothes, lives in a house with a beautiful garden, and sees Kamala regularly. His experiences with Kamala lead him to become a master at the art of love at the same time that his work for Kamaswami brings him great wealth. He takes in all sensual pleasures, drinking excessively, gambling away his money, and committing all kinds of sins. "Slowly the soul sickness of the rich crept over him.... The world had caught him; pleasure, covetousness, idleness, and finally also that vice that he had always despised and scorned as the most foolish—acquisitiveness [owning things]" (*Siddhartha*, p. 61). Although he learns a great deal,

Siddhartha realizes that this way of life is not the path to enlightenment. He spends one last night with Kamala (during which time they conceive a son) and departs the city for good, leaving all of his material possessions behind.

Not knowing where to turn or what to do next, Siddhartha wanders into the countryside and contemplates suicide. Disillusioned and desperate, he feels there is nothing left to try, no other paths to travel to gain enlightenment. Like Gautama, he has lived the extremes of poverty and wealth, of extreme self-indulgence and extreme self-denial, but he has not yet gained inner peace or reached Nirvana. Siddhartha considers plunging his aging body into a river and ending his suffering. But just as he reaches his weakest point, something happens. From deep within his soul he hears the holy chant "Om," and it fills his body with peace. He is reborn in that moment and suddenly feels "full of joyous love toward everything" he sees (*Siddhartha*, p. 76).

Siddhartha concludes that life is a journey or pilgrimage, and that material concerns are virtually meaningless. He realizes that total self-denial and overindulgence are equally destructive, but that "it is a good thing to experience everything for oneself" for then a person gains knowledge not just with intellect, but also with eyes, heart, and stomach (*Siddhartha*, p. 80).

Siddhartha begins living the Middle Way. He adopts the simple life of a ferryman, carting travelers across the river at which he experienced his spiritual awakening. His son comes to live with him for a time; when the boy decides to leave, Siddhartha learns all over again about the need to discover enlightenment for oneself.

The issue of self-reliance. Early in the novel, Siddhartha is willing to go with his friend Govinda to find the Buddha and try to learn from him. But Siddhartha tells his friend: "I have become distrustful of teachings and learning ... and I have little faith in words that come to us from teachers" (*Siddhartha*, p. 18). Like the Buddha, Hesse's Siddhartha believes true wisdom cannot be taught. He must instead learn for himself through personal experience.

One day Siddhartha's son—also called Siddhartha—comes to live with him. But because he has been raised in the city, he despises the dull life of a ferryman. Siddhartha tries to pass his knowledge on to his son, but soon the son returns to town to make a life of his own. His son's departure cuts Siddhartha like a deep, painful wound. But then he whispers the word "Om" and eventually the pain subsides. He comes to realize that his son needs to follow his own path; no one can teach anyone else life's lessons. Just as Siddhartha had left his family as a young man, so his son must forge his own way. The cycle must continue. Siddhartha's recognition of this fact signals his understanding of the "unity of all life" (*Siddhartha*, p. 106). All its different elements together create perfection because of their contrast. This is "the music of life," Siddhartha realizes, and "when he did not bind his soul to any one particular voice and absorb it in his Self, but heard them all, the whole, the unity; then the great song of a thousand voices consisted of one word: Om—perfection" (*Siddhartha*, p. 111).

Like Gautama, Siddhartha uses his life experiences to reach enlightenment by himself. From his lifelong pilgrimage he learns that "it is only important to love the world, not to despise it, not for us to hate each other, but to be able to regard the world and ourselves and all beings with love, admiration and respect" (*Siddhartha*, p. 119). This statement describes the basic philosophy of Buddhism.

Sources. The most obvious source material for the novel is the legend of Siddhartha Gautama. But *Siddhartha* is also an example of Hesse's love of the Italian novella, a form he first adopted in 1904. A story with a tight, pointed plot, the novella is an enlarged anecdote. Its tone is often realistic and its subject matter has a psychological element to it. In addition, *Siddhartha* shows Hesse's fascination with the discontented loner— a character type that he wrote about often and felt he was himself.

In Europe Hesse's novel was immediately popular upon its publication around 1923. As with all of Hesse's novels, *Siddhartha* was not published in English until after he won the Nobel Prize in 1946. It was published in English in 1951 but did not become a bestseller until the late 1960s, after Hesse's death in 1962. From the late 1960s to the early 1970s, more than 15 million copies of Hesse's books, including *Siddhartha*, were sold. That total set a record for book sales by a single author in any decade.

Events in History at the Time the Novel Was Written

Turn-of-the-century Germany. As the twentieth century began, Germany was marked by rapid industrialization. From 1895 to 1907, the number of industrial employees doubled and exports of finished goods rose from 33 to 63 percent. National wealth and urban populations soared, as did national pride. But working conditions were poor, and industrial workers lacked full political rights. Germany's social hierarchy was reminiscent of India's caste system in that it regarded industrial workers and minorities as subservient members of society. When the economy slowed or cities became overpopulated, anti-Semitism surfaced. Jews were seen as outsiders and their business skills were resented.

In the late 1800s and early 1900s, the German government became increasingly militaristic and aggressive. The country's navy was second in might only to Great Britain's, and because of their newfound economic and military power, Germany became a powerful force throughout Europe and North Africa. This was perceived as a threat by other European nations who had their own colonies and imperial interests. A general feeling of insecurity pervaded Europe, and as a result, the major powers formed various alliances to strengthen their positions. France, Great Britain, and Russia formed the Triple Entente alliance; on the other side, Germany was linked with Austria-Hungary and, for a time, Italy. World War I erupted after the heir to the Austrian throne, Archduke Francis Ferdinand, was assassinated by Serbian terrorists in 1914. In retaliation, Austria-Hungary moved against Serbia; Russia, a friend of the Serbs, defended the small country. When Austria-Hungary and Russia squared off with one another, their partners in the two alliances supported them and became part of the dispute. The powerful German nation was therefore at the center of the world war, and many scholars feel that German leaders welcomed this chance to take a dominant role in European and world affairs.

In 1918 World War I ended with a German defeat. But it was not long before nationalism and aggression resurfaced in German society. Capitalizing on the nation's desire to regain power after its earlier loss, Adolf Hitler and fellow Nazis instilled strong feelings of anti-Semitism and fierce national pride in the German population. By 1921 Germany's government was denouncing writers such as Hesse, calling him and others "Jew-lovers" because of their antiwar and antiprejudice views.

Hesse's personal life. Hermann Hesse was born in Germany in 1877. His mother was an Indian national, and his German father worked as a missionary to India as well as a publisher of religious books. A headstrong, fiercely independent young man, Hesse grew up a lonely outsider. By age thirteen, he knew he wanted a career in literature and began composing poetry. He had a deep interest in the Romantic movement—an artistic and cultural movement that featured a love for nature and beauty—and wrote in that vein through 1904. By 1923, when he wrote *Siddhartha,* he had developed a more realistic style.

In 1911 Hesse visited India in search of wisdom and enlightenment. He had heard countless stories from his parents about the spiritual nature of society and beauty in the East. As one who had been taught Buddhist concepts in his childhood, Hesse developed a deep interest in the religion and its founder, Siddhartha Gautama. He was sadly disappointed when he visited India, though. Instead of beauty and truth, he found rampant poverty and unprincipled people who sought to make money from Buddhism, selling religious goods for profit. Disillusioned, he returned to Germany.

Hesse became even more disillusioned with society as World War I approached. A long-time believer in Buddhist concepts, Hesse was vehemently opposed to violence. He denounced the war, a position that made him extremely unpopular in German society at large. He became even more unpopular after his 1914 founding of *Viros Voco,* a magazine dedicated to promoting peace and social reform. By 1924 he was so at odds with Germany and its aggressive, racist policies that he moved to Switzerland and became a citizen there.

Much like the Siddhartha of his novel, Hesse at this time had a spiritual awakening. He spoke out publicly for peace and expressed his belief that people should accept the fact that loneliness and suffering are part of life. He further maintained that everyone should design his or her own individual life path. Hesse, like Siddhartha Gautama, believed that there are no absolutes in life and that all paths can lead to enlightenment, provided that one ultimately strives to live a positive existence and devalues material things. *Siddhartha* was Hesse's attempt to help put the world on a path toward enlightenment and respond to the racism and hatred he viewed all around him. Like his main character, he believed that individuals must attain wisdom through personal experience. His novel was a bid to instill in people the desire to achieve that goal so that the world could become a better place.

For More Information

Hesse, Hermann. *Siddhartha.* New York: New Directions, 1951.

Hesse, Hermann. *My Belief: Essays on Life and Art.* New York: Farrar, Straus and Giroux, 1974.

Humphreys, Christmas. *Buddhism.* New York: Barnes & Noble, 1951.

Khosla, Sarla. *The Historical Evolution of the Buddha Legend.* New Delhi, India: Intellectual, 1989.

LuZanne, Celina. *Heritage of Buddha: The Story of Siddhartha Gautama.* New York: Philosophical Library, 1953.

A Tale
of Two Cities

by
Charles Dickens

An English novelist who lived from 1812 to 1870, Charles Dickens was twelve years old when his father was sent to debtor's prison. Almost the entire Dickens family accompanied Dickens' father and took up residence in the Marshalsea Prison. Only young Charles stayed behind. He lived in a small attic room and worked in a shoe-blacking factory. During this time he gained a firsthand understanding of poverty and class politics, subjects that permeate *A Tale of Two Cities*.

THE LITERARY WORK

A novel set in London and Paris between 1757 and 1793; published in 1859.

SYNOPSIS

Release of a prisoner from the Bastille during the French Revolution leads to the death of an innocent Englishman.

Events in History at the Time the Novel Takes Place

French nobles and peasants in the 1700s. In the latter part of the ninth century, nobles assumed supreme power in France. Even the king exercised little more authority than any other noble. Society consisted of two classes—the nobles and the commoners, with the latter class made up of peasants and craftsmen who received protection from and were subject to the authority of the nobles. In the eleventh century, however, the situation began to change as society saw the slow growth of a middle class, or *bourgeoisie*, made up of independent merchants. Their emergence was accompanied by new activity on the part of the commoners, who increasingly staged uprisings or purchased their freedom from the nobles.

As six centuries passed, these trends strengthened in the ranks of the common people. The king, who aligned himself with the growing middle class, came to dominate the nobles. By the

1700s the old noble-commoner social structure had largely dissolved, although certain practices from earlier times had survived. The nobles, for example, had formerly provided the king with free military service and been declared exempt from paying the *taille,* a tax on both estimated income and land. They remained exempt from this tax in the 1700s, even though they no longer provided the king with free military service. Poor members of French society, already angered by such inequities, were also galled by other habits of the nobles—their fancy balls, hunting parties, and comfortable ignorance of the conditions suffered by workers and peasants.

The French Revolution. During the late 1700s, the situation in France deteriorated. Food grew scarcer, prices soared, and the French government faced bankruptcy. Most of the burden of this economic disarray fell on the peasants and the middle class, while the aristocrats continued to enjoy their lavish lifestyles. By the late 1780s, French rebels openly opposed the heavy taxes and high prices they faced. They blamed these economic hardships on the French elite.

In reality, not all aristocrats were tyrants, and some of them even took responsibility for the unfair aspects of French society that their forefathers had created. Dickens acknowledges the existence of such aristocrats by creating one of his main characters in their image. The character, Charles Darnay, leaves France and renounces his aristocratic birthright precisely because he understands the corruption of the aristocracy and the injustices imposed upon the working classes. "We have done wrong, and are reaping the fruits of wrong" (Dickens, *Tale of Two Cities*, p. 113), he declares to an aristocratic French uncle.

King Louis XVI, who sat on the throne when the Revolution began, was not a tyrant, either. He attempted to institute some reforms, and managed to establish local assemblies in five provinces. But he also spent a great deal of money on festivities and other expenses of no benefit to the commoners, and he was unable to settle on a policy of government. His leadership proved inadequate to stay the tides of revolution.

POLITICAL SLOGANS

During the French Revolution, posters with political slogans such as "liberty, equality, and fraternity—or death" were placed all around France. This particular phrase is used by Dickens throughout his novel.

The uprising began in 1789. Angry mobs stormed the Bastille, a fourteenth-century fort in which political prisoners were traditionally held. Even though the Bastille was nearly empty in 1789, the prison symbolized royal oppression, and its seizure signaled a civil uprising in France against aristocratic injustice. It was followed by the adoption of the Declaration of the Rights of Man, which included guarantees such as equal taxation. A new constitution was later adopted that stripped nobles of their titles and reduced them to the status of ordinary French citizens.

The émigrés. The French word *émigré* refers to someone who leaves his or her country for political reasons. It became commonplace for French nobles to flee their country during the Revolution to reside elsewhere. England, as Dickens' novel points out, became the "refuge of many" (*Tale of Two Cities*, p. 115). Leaving behind their families and aristocratic legacies, characters in the novel settle in London, England. The London neighborhood of Soho, a setting in the novel, was in fact a popular neighborhood among foreigners at the time, especially among émigrés from France.

Reign of Terror. The first stage of the French Revolution ended in 1793 with the execution of Louis XVI and his wife, Marie Antoinette. The Reign of Terror followed from 1793 to 1794. During this period France was ruled by the Jacobins, a group of extremist revolutionaries led by Maximilien Robespierre. The Jacobins kept France in fear, executing thousands for opposing the Revolution. Mere suspicion of royalist sympathies was reason enough to be put to death during the Reign of Terror. Although the French revolt against the aristocracy rid the country of oppression by the elite, a new tyranny arose at the hands of the Jacobins. This, then, truly was "the best of times and the worst of times" in French history (*Tale of Two Cities*, p. 1).

Reactions in England during the French Revolution. Across the channel from France, England looked on with concern as the events of the French Revolution unfolded. Although the French Revolution produced no violent reaction

A scene from the 1935 film adaptation of *A Tale of Two Cities.*

in England at that time, the upheaval in France followed closely on the heels of the American Revolution against England in 1776. English citizens during this era had already shown concern for issues of rights, equality, and civil insurrection. The English focused even more closely on these matters after France declared war on England in 1793.

Two streams of thought about the French Revolution developed in England during this time. On the one hand, people voiced concern over matters of class injustice and inequality. But many also voiced a general fear of popular uprisings. Events in France prompted the English to write a number of political tracts and religious sermons that either supported the French struggle for equality or opposed armed insurrection and, in some instances, the notion of equality itself.

Punishment during the eighteenth century. The guillotine was a frequently used form of punishment in revolutionary France. More than 40,000 people were beheaded by the guillotine during the French Revolution (1789-94); 18,000 were executed during the Reign of Terror alone. The guillotine was named after its inventor, a French doctor named Joseph Guillotin. Comprised of a heavy metal blade that slides within

a large wooden frame, the guillotine beheads people through release of the blade from a height of several feet. It was devised as a more humane method of execution because other, more torturous means of punishment took considerably longer to kill their victim.

ENGLISH OPINIONS ON THE FRENCH REVOLUTION

Edmund Burke: "Government, as well as liberty, is good," yet the French Revolution is a "monstrous thing ... a wild attempt to methodize anarchy."

Richard Price: "Tremble all ye oppressors of the world! ... Restore to mankind their rights; and consent to the correction of abuses, before they and you are destroyed together."

(Smith, p. 279)

Other common forms of punishment during the time in which *A Tale of Two Cities* takes place include quartering. Quartering is execution that concludes by dividing the body into four parts. To be more exact, a convicted person would be hanged until near death, then sliced open while still alive. The internal organs might be removed and burnt before the victim's own eyes. Finally, the head was chopped off and the body cut into quarters.

Most forms of punishment in the eighteenth century were meted out in public. Executions were well-attended events, and until 1772 the heads of traitors were often publicly displayed on spikes at the gates of London. Public hangings remained legal in England well into the 1800s.

The Novel in Focus

The plot. Unjustly imprisoned for eighteen years, Doctor Alexandre Manette is released from the Bastille as the novel opens. Manette had been imprisoned for threatening to expose the rape of a French peasant girl and the murder of her brother by two noblemen—the Saint Evrémonde brothers.

Linked to Manette are various other characters in the novel:

> **Lucie Manette:** The daughter of Doctor Manette. A young woman about seventeen years old, Lucie is living in London at the time her father leaves the Bastille.
> **Charles Darnay:** Lucie Manette's future husband. Originally from France, Darnay has changed his name but belongs to the Evrémonde family.
> **Sydney Carton:** A moody, alcoholic man who bears a remarkable likeness to Charles Darnay. He is hopelessly in love with Lucie Manette.
> **Ernest Defarge:** Doctor Manette's servant before his imprisonment, Defarge becomes a leader of the French Revolution. His wine shop serves as a meeting place for French revolutionaries.
> **Thérèse Defarge:** The wife of Ernst Defarge, she is a revolutionary driven to take revenge against all aristocrats.

Doctor Manette suffers from amnesia and poor health due to his lengthy imprisonment. Still in Paris after his release from the Bastille, he falls under the care of Ernst Defarge. With the help of a London banker named Jarvis Lorry, Lucie Manette learns that her father is alive, rescues him from Paris, and returns with him to London. Like so many other French émigrés, Lucie and her father settle in Soho, far from the horrors of the Revolution. Lucie, who had believed since childhood that her father was dead, proves to be a devoted daughter; she commits herself to nursing him back to health.

During the return to England, Lucie befriends Charles Darnay. He is later tried in a London court for suspected treason against England, and Lucie testifies on his behalf. Her love for him first becomes apparent during the trial. She has no idea that Darnay belongs to the Saint Evrémonde family, two of whose members are responsible for her father's long imprisonment.

More trouble with the authorities follows for Charles Darnay. Upon fleeing France, Darnay had renounced his family name and rejected any ties to the aristocracy. He had also instructed his steward to cancel all taxes of his tenants and collect only a minimum rent from the peasants. A few years after his marriage to Lucie Manette, however, an appeal for his return arrives from France. By this time the Bastille has been stormed and the Reign of Terror is approaching. Despite the kindnesses that Darnay had displayed before his departure from France, his former steward has been imprisoned by French revolutionaries and may be beheaded for having acted against the people as a former employee of an aristocrat. Darnay returns to France to testify on behalf of his onetime steward and remains imprisoned for a year. To secure his release, Doctor Manette travels to Paris with Lucie and the banker Jarvis Lorry. Darnay is finally released, only to be immediately imprisoned once again when the revolutionaries have a change of heart.

By an odd twist of fate, Sydney Carton and Charles Darnay closely resemble each other in features and build. Driven by his unrequited love for Lucie Manette and the sense that his own life ought to have a greater purpose, Sydney Carton visits Charles Darnay in prison. Carton drugs the unsuspecting Darnay and exchanges clothing with him. He then has Darnay carried out of the prison to rejoin Lucie. At the close of the novel, Carton dies by the guillotine while Darnay and his family return to London. On his way to the guillotine, Carton utters the now famous passage, "It is a far, far better thing that I do, than I have ever done; it is a far, far better rest that I go to than I have ever known" (*Tale of Two Cities*, p. 352).

What the characters reveal about society. Dickens' novel focuses in large part on the injustices of class society and the consequences that follow. The Marquis de Saint Evrémonde, Darnay's uncle, is portrayed by Dickens as a vicious tyrant and evil aristocrat. On the other hand, by renouncing his birthright and fleeing France, Darnay illustrates that not all aristocrats are evil. In fact, the working-class Defarges are described as far less charitable than Darnay. Ernst and Thérèse Defarge are leaders of the French Revolution. Although both oppose the French aristocracy, Madame Defarge is clearly the more ruthless of the two.

> "Extermination is good doctrine," says Ernest Defarge feebly to his wife, "in general, I say nothing against it ... but one must stop somewhere, the question is, where?"
> "At extermination," responds Madame Defarge. "Tell Wind and Fire where to stop ... but don't tell me."
>
> (Tale of Two Cities, pp. 316-17)

Dickens makes clear by the end of his story that the ruthlessness of the French Revolution spares no one. Defarge was a trusted servant of Manette's in more tranquil times. Neither this nor the fact that Charles Darnay has renounced his aristocratic heritage prevents Thérèse Defarge (with only slight objections from her husband) from pursuing the Manette entourage as enemies of the Revolution.

The wine shop owned by the Defarges serves as a clandestine gathering place for revolutionaries. Although Madame Defarge is outwardly quiet during these gatherings, she is an integral part of the revolutionary plots and schemes. Ever-present in the background, she silently knits an endless tapestry of yarn. This hobby proves to be significant: Thérèse Defarge is secretly encoding in her knitted work a list of those who must be executed as spies or traitors to the Revolution. Madame Defarge and her revolutionary comrades seek vengeance against anyone opposed to their cause. They see themselves as patriotic and regard all aristocrats as bad.

Thérèse Defarge's character closely resembles that of the citoyennes, or female Jacobins. Public executions during the French Revolution were well attended by citoyennes, who shrieked throughout the public trials held during the Reign of Terror. Citoyennes brought their knitting to the executions that followed the trials; they would shout excitedly or knit indifferently throughout the beheadings.

Various characters who use the alias "Jacques" also appear in the novel. These men conceal their own names because they are members of a revolutionary group, or a "Jacquerie." The Jacques are responsible for the legwork and spying in the Revolution. When the Marquis de Saint Evrémonde runs over a small village child with his carriage, fatally injuring the child, a member of this group seeks revenge and kills the Marquis in his sleep. Historically, use of the alias "Jacques"

in France dates back to a 1358 peasant revolt. During that time, nobles, filled with contempt for the rebellious peasants, called individual members Jacques Bonhomme, an ironic name meaning "Jack the good man" (Guilano, p. 610).

Gabelle, Charles Darnay's former servant, experiences injustice in Revolutionary France. Gabelle has committed no crime, and yet he is imprisoned by French revolutionaries and faces impending death. His sole offense is his past work for an aristocrat. Gabelle's unreasonable detention closely parallels the arrest of countless French people under the Law of the Suspected. Passed in 1793, the law permitted the arrest of all former nobles and anyone else who was even suspected of Royalist sympathies. Few people could escape this broad and indiscriminate law.

Sources. From the time of his early childhood, Dickens was familiar with the history of the French Revolution and interested in its more lurid aspects. Thomas Carlyle's 1837 book, *The French Revolution*, provided a key historical source for Dickens. Dickens held Carlyle's work in high regard; when *The French Revolution* was first published, Dickens carried the book around with him everywhere. Dickens refers to Carlyle in the preface to *A Tale of Two Cities*: "It has been one of my hopes to add something to the popular and picturesque means of understanding that terrible time, though no one can hope to add anything to the philosophy of Mr. Carlyle's wonderful book" (*Tale of Two Cities*, p. v).

Louis-Sebastien Mercier's *Le Tableau de Paris* informed Dickens about Parisian high society, while his *Le Nouveau Paris* provided details regarding life during the French Revolution. Dickens also appears to have read Jean-Jacques Rousseau's *Confessions* and Arthur Young's *Travels in France during the Years 1787, 1788, and 1789*. Young's observations of the agricultural problems in rural France before the upheaval, and his commentary on the initial years of the Revolution, seem to have made their way into Dickens' work. Dickens was also strongly influenced in writing *A Tale of Two Cities* by his acting experience in Wilkie Collins' *The Frozen Deep*, a play that contains ideas similar to those articulated in Dickens' novel.

It is believed that the character of Lucie Manette was inspired by Ellen Ternan, an actress with whom Dickens became infatuated at the time of his separation from his wife, Catherine, and their ten children. Much like Sydney Carton's hopeless love for Lucie Manette, Dickens' love for Ellen Ternan remained, to some degree, unfulfilled. Because of Victorian mores and English law, Charles and Catherine Dickens never divorced.

Others presume, however, that the real-life inspiration for the character of Lucie Manette was Dickens' young sister-in-law, Mary. Mary lived in the Dickens home until her untimely death at the age of sixteen. To Dickens, Mary was the image of womanly perfection, much like Lucie Manette.

Events in History at the Time the Novel Was Written

Revolutions of 1848. Charles Dickens lived and wrote in the midst of England's Victorian era. The effect of the French Revolution upon England throughout this era cannot be overstated. Events of the Revolution remained familiar to the Victorian English through historical writings, personal memoirs, letters, and eyewitness accounts. Subsequent events in Europe also kept the discord alive.

Just eleven years prior to Dickens' publication of *A Tale of Two Cities* was the 1848 "Year of Revolutions." Throughout Europe people took to the streets to rebel against unjust laws. The reasons for many of these rebellions—heavy taxation, high prices, and overwork—were notably similar to those that spurred the French Revolution. The year 1848 also saw the publication of the influential *Communist Manifesto* by Karl Marx and Friedrich Engels. In short, notions of revolution and upheaval were prominent in the minds of English men and women in the 1800s.

Dickens' England. By the time *A Tale of Two Cities* was published in 1859, domestic affairs in England were particularly strained. Class politics there in many ways resembled conditions in France before the Revolution. Although the landed aristocracy of England enjoyed power and prosperity, the working classes suffered from crop failures, factory closures, poverty, and disease. The conservative English upper class resisted any challenge to their monopoly of power. Frightened by the widespread disturbances of the French Revolution, English aristocrats feared that equally unpleasant uprisings might erupt in England. They had good reason to be worried.

For years England had faced considerable economic and political challenges. Depressed economic conditions prevailed through much of England, which had become an industrial as well as an agricultural society. The Corn Laws, for example, kept domestic bread prices high because they prevented people from importing as much grain as they wanted from foreigners. In 1839 the people formed an Anti-Corn Law League to oppose such laws. The Anti-Corn Law League argued that the hunger of the 1840s could be made to disappear if the populace followed its advice. Landlords, it contended, should lose their special power in society and politics. As the struggle to survive continued in the early 1840s, people began to speak openly of class warfare and revolution in England. But in 1846 the Corn Laws were repealed.

The willingness of statesmen to accept such reform partially explains why no outbreak of revolution took place in England in 1848. Dickens' novel further encouraged this spirit of reform and helped people recognize that additional measures were needed to prevent future havoc. In the final chapter of *A Tale of Two Cities*, Dickens explicitly warns that conditions that have produced revolution in the past can do so again, and that the English ruling class must not continue to suppress the working classes. "Crush humanity out of shape once more, under similar hammers, and it will twist itself into the same tortured forms. Sow the same seed of rapacious license and oppression over again, and it will surely yield the same fruit according to its kind" (*Tale of Two Cities*, p. 347).

The author appears to have seen his novel not only as a fictional reconstruction of historical events, but as a warning call to his contemporaries. Because Charles Dickens grew up poor and rose through the ranks of fortune, he had a keen eye and a soft heart for the underclass. Although sympathy toward the poor and the exploited was a common theme in Dickens' time, it is clear in *A Tale of Two Cities* that Dickens was also concerned about the brutality and mayhem that may result from revolution. He seems to caution that mob tyranny, which his characters encounter in Paris, can be as frightening as any oppressive ruler.

How the novel was received. Many of Dickens' novels, including *A Tale of Two Cities*, first appeared as monthly serials. *A Tale of Two Cities* was originally written in 1859 in the monthly publication *All the Year Round*. Later that same year, the novel was published in its entirety. As a serial, the story received widespread exposure. Dickens wrote to a friend that in one month alone, 35,000 back issues of the monthly serial containing his story had been sold. Various stage versions of *A Tale of Two Cities* were produced, and these achieved considerable financial suc-

The cover of the June 1859, installment of *A Tale of Two Cities*.

cess. Two versions of the play opened while Dickens was still alive, the first on February 16, 1860, at the Lyceum Theatre in London.

Despite Dickens' overall popularity, *A Tale of Two Cities* received some harsh criticism. It was described as a historically flawed novel that excessively magnified the faults of French aristocrats and so presented an unfair picture of society in France. Singled out as an exaggerated character was the Marquis de Saint Evrémonde. Although critics may have preferred Dickens' other novels, the author himself believed *A Tale of Two Cities* was the finest work he had ever written.

For More Information

Crossley, Ceri, and Ian Small, eds. *The French Revolution and British Culture.* New York: Oxford University Press, 1989.

Dickens, Charles. *A Tale of Two Cities.* Afterword by Stephen Koch. New York: Bantam, 1981.

Guilano, Edward, and Philip Collins, eds. *The Annotated Dickens, Volume II.* New York: Clarkson N. Potter, 1986.

Jackson, T. A. *Charles Dickens: The Progress of a Radical.* New York: International, 1987.

Rudé, George. *The French Revolution.* New York: Weidenfeld & Nicolson, 1988.

Smith, Goldwin. *England: A Short History.* New York: Charles Scribner's Sons, 1971.

The Tempest

by
William Shakespeare

William Shakespeare was twenty-one years old when the English founded their first North American colony at Roanoke in 1585. He moved to London, most likely in 1587, to pursue a career in the theater. There he rose from actor to mender of others' plays to playwright, director, and company co-owner over the course of some twenty-eight years. Meanwhile, England under Queen Elizabeth I (who reigned from 1558 to 1603) and then under King James I (1603-1625) struggled to build an empire. By 1610, when Shakespeare is thought to have begun *The Tempest,* England had founded a colony at Jamestown, Virginia, but the colony's survival still hung in the balance. *The Tempest,* called a tragicomedy, is tied to this early time in English colonial history as well as to a tumultuous period in Italy's past.

Events in History at the Time the Play Takes Place

Italian history. Single-ruler governments, multiruler republics, and the Papal State (the region controlled by the pope) were all present in Italy in the 1400s. In order of importance, Milan, Rome, and Naples became the most powerful single-ruler governments. After 1500, however, Milan and Naples lost power as foreign invasions brought them under the control of first the French and then the Spanish. These setbacks were compounded by divisions within the city-state. In 1499 Milan rebelled against Duke Ludovico Sforza, who fled with his nobles only to

THE LITERARY WORK

A play set on an isolated island sometime between the 1400s and the early 1600s; first performed in 1611.

SYNOPSIS

On an island with his daughter, the deposed Duke of Milan uses his magical powers to punish his brother for seizing his dukedom and to provide a marriage partner for his daughter.

be captured in 1500 by the French. He spent the rest of his life imprisoned in France, reading works by the Italian poet Dante and drawing on his dungeon walls. Meanwhile, Milan remained subject to the rule of outsiders, a state of affairs that would continue for some time. In terms of Italian history, then, *The Tempest,* which features an independent duke of Milan and the king of Naples, most aptly fits into the 1400s, even though the story is set in an indefinite time and was influenced by England's colonial efforts of a later era.

Italian city-states. Not a unified nation but a region of different city-states, Italy was ruled by various leaders who governed and made shifting alliances with one another in struggles for power. The era gave rise to the despot, or one-man ruler, who assumed control over a city-state. If a despot, or *signore,* was strong enough, he might even seize power over a whole region because of the alliances he made with nearby cities. This occurred in Milan, possibly the most heavily populated city on the Italian peninsula.

Milan proved to be one of the most successful of the domains ruled by despots. The duke of Milan held judicial, legislative, and, after 1385, financial control of the city, though he ruled with the aid of a private council and a public council. The duke was also the city's richest citizen, and his home reflected his wealth. In 1499 the Duke of Milan lived in a walled-in castle in the middle of the city that featured moats, sixty-two drawbridges, and about one thousand mercenaries (hired soldiers). Such a fortress was deemed necessary because of the number of citizens who were jockeying for power, scheming to place dukedoms in various hands.

A duke of the 1300s or 1400s operated as an all-powerful leader. His courtiers devoted themselves to carrying out the duke's every wish, and many of the rulers exercised authority at whim. One of the dukes of Milan, for example, is known to have ordered a tailor thrown into prison for a small mistake—he had "spoiled the doublet [jacket] of crimson silk" belonging to one of the duke's courtiers (Martines, p. 228). Such abuses of power are reflected in *The Tempest* when Prospero imprisons the half-monster Caliban, the spirit Ariel, and the prince Ferdinand. His behavior is quite typical of the times.

The Renaissance. A cultural movement known as the Renaissance began in Italy in the 1300s and 1400s and spread to the rest of Europe in the 1500s. At its heart was an educational movement, a revival of the study of the humanities. These liberal arts included classical Greek and Roman grammar, speech, history, literature, and philosophy. Some Christian leaders objected loudly to the movement, arguing that it undermined their religion. They pointed out that the early Greeks and Romans had engaged in the pagan worship of many gods, a fact reflected throughout their works. The champions of humanism, which included some equally fervent Christians, retorted that this was a closed-minded point of view. There had, after all, been moral behavior before Christianity came into the world. Proponents of humanist studies contended that much could be learned from the ancient teachers.

The humanists studied many elements of classical life, including the writings of Homer, Virgil, and other major poets of Greece and Rome. They then attempted to apply classical principles to their own era. Throughout *The Tempest* are de-

tails that hark back to Greek and Roman legend. In Act 3, for example, a harpy (a creature in ancient Greek mythology who served as a minister of the gods sent to punish wrongdoers) confronts Prince Alonso, who helped overthrow Prospero, the rightful Duke of Milan. The harpy chides Alonso for his misdeed and informs him that he is now suffering the consequences for his actions.

In a work of 1401, *Pier Paolo Vergerio de ingenuis moribua,* the humanists cautioned against the danger of losing oneself in study to the exclusion of the outside world. This treatise cited the Greek teacher Aristotle, who warned against letting literature "absorb all the interest of life. . . . For the man who surrenders himself entirely to the attractions of letters or . . . perhaps follows a self-regarding end is useless as a citizen or a prince" (Martines, p. 192).

Several decades later, the Italian writer Niccolò Machiavelli (1469-1527) drafted his great manual for rulers, **The Prince** (also covered in *Literature and Its Times*), which stressed the need for a ruler to always keep a tight grip on his power. This is something that Shakespeare's main character Prospero admits he did not do. In Act I of *The Tempest,* Prospero reveals that he had once been Duke of Milan but had turned over matters of state to his brother, loosening his grip on the kingdom to devote himself to his studies. Consequently, he was overthrown.

The play also promotes a view of man that can be traced back to the humanists. Theirs was a much more hopeful view than the earlier image of man as a fallen creature, doomed by Adam and Eve's disobedience of God in the Garden of Eden. Instead, the Italian humanists saw the human being as a creature formed in the image of God. In the humanist view, people at first had dignity; they lost much of it because of the disobedience of Adam and Eve in the Garden, but the sacrifice of Jesus Christ had regained a state of grace for them. Beginning with this positive outlook, the humanists embraced the notion that man had the right to rule over the rest of creation. Their belief was that the mind, body, and soul of a human being had been equipped to rule the sub-human universe, a line of reasoning that fits the relationship in Shakespeare's play between Prospero and the half-human monster Caliban.

The Play in Focus

The plot. As *The Tempest* opens, a ship is being tossed about at sea by a violent storm. It carries a royal party of passengers: Alonso, the king of

Naples; his son Ferdinand; his brother Sebastian; the present duke of Milan, Antonio; Gonzalo, a courtier; and two servants, the butler Stephano and the jester Trinculo. They are all on their way home from the wedding of Alonso's daughter Claribel to a prince in the African land of Algiers.

The storm-tossed party abandons ship and manages to reach an island inhabited by only two humans—Prospero and his daughter, Miranda. Prospero, the rightful duke of Milan, had, twelve years earlier, been deposed by his brother Antonio and set adrift on the sea with his daughter. In addition, the island houses Ariel, a spirit, and Caliban, a half-monster. Both serve Prospero. Ariel was once imprisoned in a tree trunk by the now-dead witch Sycorax, who was Caliban's mother and once ruled the island. Prospero, who is a magician as well as a duke, managed to free Ariel. Ariel thus does Prospero's bidding. The spirit does so grudgingly, however, for it wishes to be completely free. Prospero promises to release Ariel if his present scheme succeeds. Using magic, he has orchestrated the shipwreck and drawn the survivors to his island, where a set of carefully planned experiences awaits them.

Prospero plans to gain back his dukedom and to exact revenge on his brother Antonio, but he also wants to punish Alonso, the king of Naples, who had helped Antonio seize power in Milan twelve years earlier. In addition, Prospero has designed an encounter between his learned and lovely daughter, Miranda, now of marriageable age, and Alonso's son, Prince Ferdinand, who has become separated from the other survivors during the storm.

The other shipwrecked passengers conclude that Prince Ferdinand must be dead, which leaves King Alonso grief-stricken and encourages a conspiracy against him. Antonio, as treacherous as he was when he deposed his brother in Milan twelve years ago, now conspires to overthrow Alonso from the throne of Naples. Antonio urges Sebastian, the king's brother, to murder the king and seize his throne. The conspirators are stopped, however, by Ariel, who advances the action according to Prospero's plans.

Another conspiracy is in progress as well. Caliban takes steps to recapture from Prospero the island once ruled by his mother. He meets up with two newcomers from the ship, the jester Trinculo and the drunken butler Stephano, and enlists them in his plan to kill Prospero. Caliban's appearance startles the jester and butler, who describe him as a monster. They feed Caliban wine, after which he volunteers to serve them if they will give him more.

Elsewhere on the island Miranda and Ferdinand meet and immediately fall in love. Miranda has not seen another human since her early childhood and has never encountered a young man of her own age. Ferdinand enchants her and is in turn smitten with her. This blossoming relationship pleases Prospero, although he disguises his feelings. He accuses Ferdinand of being a spy and imprisons the young man so he will not have won Miranda's love too easily.

Ariel casts spells over the visitors, leading them to their final convergence. In the last act, Prospero, who has observed most of the action from a distance, reveals himself to the party and confronts his brother Antonio with his past betrayal. King Alonso is reunited with his son Ferdinand and bestows his blessings upon Ferdinand and Miranda. Prospero demands his dukedom back, discards his magic, and sets Ariel free. The island is left to Caliban as the others prepare to return to Milan.

The travelers have been confronted with their true selves during their stay, but little has changed. As Prospero notes, he is about to return to a conniving world in which "every third thought shall be my grave" (Shakespeare, *The Tempest*, 5.1.369). He believes that many people will think about his future death, presumably because of the scheming tendencies of men in quest of power. There is hope, however, in the union of Ferdinand and Miranda, a happy young couple.

Caliban. One of Shakespeare's strangest creations is the monster Caliban. He is portrayed as a creature of earth and water and a savage man-beast. The creature is a stark contrast to Ariel, a spirit of air and fire. Caliban's name seems to derive from a French essay by Montaigne about Brazilian cannibals, a piece that Shakespeare appears to have read. In fact, the man-beast's name is a near-anagram: Caliban/cannibal. He is the offspring of the witch Sycorax and the devil himself, says Prospero. During his stay on the island, Prospero enslaves Caliban because the man-beast attempted to rape Miranda. He is forced to gather firewood and perform other physical labors; otherwise, Prospero will use magic to torture him with physical pangs and cramps. Prospero, the man of books, dominates Caliban, the native subhuman. This power structure fits the humanist idea of the fifteenth and sixteenth centuries, which held that it was man's right to dominate the subhuman universe.

Alec Clunes as Caliban and John Gielgud as Prospero in a 1957 Shakespeare Memorial Theatre production of *The Tempest.*

Moreover, the relationship between Prospero and Caliban fit popular concepts during the time the play was written. In the late 1500s and early 1600s, reports streamed into European countries from colonies in the New World (the Americas) about strange creatures in faraway lands—crocodiles, unicorns, and monsters whose heads grew beneath their shoulders. Readers marveled at the reports. In Shakespeare's play, their disbelief is acknowledged and dismissed by Antonio, who declares, "Travelers ne'er did lie, / though fools at home condemn 'em " (*The Tempest*, 3.3.32-3).

Furthermore, Native Americans from the colonies were sometimes brought back to Europe and put on public display; the famous Indian woman Pocahontas died on such a trip to England. Stephano, the drunken butler in Shakespeare's play, wants to subject Caliban to a similar public display: "If I can recover him," says Stephano, "and keep him tame and get to Naples with him, / he's a present for any emperor [who] shall pay for him . . . and that soundly" (*The Tempest*, 2.2.69-80).

The honest advisor Gonzalo comments on the marvelous natives on Prospero's island—"If in Naples / I should report this now, would they believe me? / If I should say I saw such [islanders]" (*The Tempest*, 3.3.34-6). He continues, however, to present another view of native peoples that was also common in the later 1500s and early 1600s:

> Though they are of monstrous shape, yet note
> Their manners are more gentle, kind, than of
> Our human generation you shall find
> Many, nay, almost any.
> (The Tempest, 3.3.38-41)

Such thoughts reflect the opinion that appeared in Montaigne's essay "Of Cannibals." Translated from French into English by John Florio in 1603, the essay argued that in many ways New World natives were more moral and more humane than the "civilized" peoples of Europe.

In *The Tempest*, Caliban shows a kind of nobleness in his understanding of how civilization is affecting him. Even his defiance of Prospero lends him a human dignity. In addition, he proves useful to the deposed duke. He shows him around the island upon his arrival and provides him with fresh water and food. Efforts by Miranda and Prospero to "civilize" Caliban seem largely in vain, although they manage to teach him how to speak. Even this accomplishment seems of little merit, though. As Caliban himself points out: "You taught me language, and my profit on 't / Is, I know how to curse. The red plague rid you / For learning me your language!" (*The Tempest*, 1.2.363-65).

Both the negative and positive images of the native appear in Caliban. Portrayed as an undisciplined brute, he tries to rape Miranda at one point. At the same time, however, he shows a keen sensitivity to nature and the supernatural. This awareness manifests itself at the end of the drama when he realizes that he has been foolish in worshipping the drunken Stephano and Trinculo. They had intoxicated Caliban with alcohol to make him do their bidding, an act that would be perpetrated again and again in real life by unscrupulous colonizers on American natives.

Sources. Gonzalo's positive view of natives as superior in many ways to Europeans is part of a fantasy that was popular in Shakespeare's time, that of creating a utopia, or ideal society, on earth. In the play, Gonzalo describes a utopia that might exist if he were in charge of colonization of the island on which they have been shipwrecked. His description echoes a portion of Montaigne's "Of Cannibals" essay, the only known source used by Shakespeare in the creation of *The Tempest*:

Montaigne:

It is a nation . . . that hath no kind of traffic, no knowledge of letters, no intelligence of numbers, no name of magistrate, nor of politic superiority; no use of service, or riches, or of poverty; no contracts, no successions, no partitions, no occupation but idle; no respect of kindred . . . no use of wine, corn, or metal.

(Montaigne in Wilson, p. 354)

Shakespeare:

I' th' commonwealth . . .
. . . no kind of traffic
Would I admit; no name of magistrate;
Letters should not be known; riches, poverty
And use of service, none; contract, succession,
Bourn, bound of land, tilth, vineyard, none;
No use of metal, corn, or wine, or oil,
No occupation; all men idle, all. . . .

(The Tempest, 2.1.162-69)

Shakespeare's drama also bears some resemblance to the classic Roman poem the ***Aeneid*** by Virgil (also covered in *Literature and Its Times*). There are parallels between Aeneas's voyage from Carthage to Rome and the voyage in the play of the royal party from Tunis to Naples; also notable is the fact that both *The Tempest* and *The Aeneid* begin with a powerful storm. Other possible sources include popular reports on current events of Shakespeare's day from deposed dukes, such as Prospero Colonna in Remigio Nannini's *Civil Considerations upon Many and Sundry Histories* (1601).

The plight of Rudolf II, the Holy Roman Emperor, may have also influenced Shakespeare. In 1608 Rudolf became so wrapped up in his studies of the supernatural that he neglected to properly govern his domain. He consequently had to surrender control of much of the Holy Roman Empire to his brother Matthias. Rudolf subsequently set out to win back his realm with help from Protestant leaders like King James I of England.

The degree to which these events influenced creation of *The Tempest* remains unknown. There was, however, a clear connection between the playwright and events concerning England's North American colony at Jamestown, Virginia. Investors in Virginia included close friends and patrons of Shakespeare (Sir Thomas Russell and the earl of Southampton) who must have learned of a certain misadventure on the seas—a shipwreck involving a vessel en route to Jamestown in 1609. Three pamphlets, all written in 1610, reported the details: *A Discovery of the Bermudas*, otherwise called the *Ile of Divels*, by Sylvester Jourdan; *A True Declaration of the Estate of the Colonie in Virginia*, possibly by William Strachey; and *A True Reportory of the Wracke, and Redemption of Sir Thomas Gates Knight; upon, and from the Ilands of the Bermudas* by William Strachey.

Events in History at the Time the Play Was Written

Shipwreck at Bermuda. In June 1609 a fleet of nine vessels sailed for England's new colony in Virginia. Altogether there were some 600 passengers, including three leaders of the expedition—the colony's new governor, Sir Thomas Gates; Admiral George Somers; and Captain Christopher Newport—who sailed on the flagship, the *Sea Venture*. At one point, a huge storm descended on the fleet and separated the *Sea Venture* from the others.

The *Sea Venture* landed safely on the Bermuda Islands, where the survivors lived comfortably for nine or ten months. Although the Bermudas were thought to be haunted by evil spirits, the Englishmen found the climate agreeable and the food bountiful. They spent their time building new vessels that they finally sailed to their original destination, Virginia. The other colonists had all arrived in Virginia intact but had not fared so well there. They had endured a starving winter

at Jamestown; only about sixty of four hundred people remained alive when the *Sea Venture* survivors rejoined them.

Initial reports on the expedition blamed this loss of life on the colonists. The reports alleged that the colonists had not worked hard enough and reassured investors that the colony was set in a rich environment. In Shakespeare's play, Prospero demands hard labor from Caliban and Ferdinand, mindful perhaps of the energy needed to ensure survival in a wilderness.

When the initial reports of the disastrous 1609 storm at sea reached England, investors had shaken their heads over what appeared to be the tragic loss of the *Sea Venture*. As a result, there was great jubilation when its captain finally returned safely to London. As noted in the pamphlet *A True Declaration*, the incident was "a tragical Comedy," a disaster with a happy ending (Wilson, p. 352). People marveled that destiny had preserved the lives of the passengers on the flagship.

Respectable magic. In Shakespeare's day, there were still many who believed in the power of magic. These believers felt certain that spirits could be contacted and used for positive or negative purposes. In *The Tempest*, Prospero practices what was known as white, or positive, magic. In contrast, Caliban's mother, the witch Sycorax, used black magic to trap Ariel in the tree trunk. Distinctions between good and evil magic did not matter to everyone, however. Perhaps most importantly, King James I, the reigning monarch in England from 1603 to 1625, feared anything connected with magic. He must have therefore viewed the final act of *The Tempest*, in which Prospero completely discards his magic, with satisfaction.

A certain class of "magicians" in Shakespeare's day were engaged in alchemy. This was a field of study devoted to transforming base metal into gold, discovering a single cure for all illnesses, and prolonging human life. Around the time *The Tempest* was written, alchemy attracted much attention in England and the rest of Europe. There was not a town in Europe nor any court of consequence without its own alchemist. In fact, the court of England featured two doctors who practiced a special form of alchemy. The founder of this realm of study was Paracelsus (1493-1541), who taught that an alchemist ought to try to cure the soul as well as the body. In *The Tempest*, Prospero—with his books, tools, and knowledge of magic—brings to mind the alchemist. His magic is concerned with the soul as well as the body.

Love and marriage. In Shakespeare's play, Miranda is the daughter of the rightful duke of Milan, and Ferdinand is son to the king of Naples. They fall in love at first sight, which delights Prospero, who seems to have engineered the meeting of these two young people for that purpose. Certainly theirs is a political as well as a romantic union; it promises to keep Prospero's family line in power in Italy's city-states.

Such political marriages were common in Shakespeare's day, although they were frequently not so happy as Miranda and Ferdinand's union promises to be. In general, marriages were usually arranged. It was considered the duty of a father to provide a mate for his son or daughter and for children to accept their parents' choice of this mate. Historical cases of such marriages are common. In 1612 England's King James I arranged for his daughter, Princess Elizabeth, to marry Frederick V, a prince of the Holy Roman Empire. Pressured to make this match, King James finally agreed, but as indicated in the official reports, he made his consent "subject to the Princess' pleasure"; evidently she wished to first see Frederick and "be wooed a while" before the match was sealed (Srigley, p. 132). In keeping with the changing attitudes about marriage at the time, her father was inclined to respect her wishes.

Elizabeth finally did marry Frederick on February 14, 1612. *The Tempest,* which had already been performed for King James, was staged again as part of the wedding celebrations. Some say that Shakespeare added to Act 4 of the play for this performance. This addition was a brief entertainment for the newly engaged characters of Ferdinand and Miranda. Creating a play within his play, Shakespeare had spirits on the island perform a masque—a type of dramatic show that drew on Greek or Roman myth and was popular in England in the early 1600s. *The Tempest*'s masque is modeled after masques performed for King James at the royal court.

As indicated by James's willingness to consider his daughter's thoughts on her marriage, Shakespeare lived during an age of transition. Other playwrights of the era were creating dramas featuring plots that conveyed a message about marriage: the wisest parents were those who deferred to the wishes of their children when it came to selecting a mate. This changing point of view explains Prospero's joy when he sees that Miranda has fallen in love with his choice of a mate. The happy union of Ferdinand and Miranda is a striking counterpoint to the marriage of King Alonso's daughter, Claribel, to the king of Tunis, which is mentioned at the beginning of the play. Alonso regrets this arrangement, which was made for political reasons.

Reception. Early reviewers of Shakespeare's *The Tempest* commented at length on Caliban, praising the playwright for creating such an original character. Since Shakespeare wrote the play at the end of his career, critics have also commented on Prospero, drawing comparisons between the playwright and the magician, who discards his magic. But whether or not Shakespeare intended to reveal anything about himself through Prospero has remained a matter of debate. Only recently have reviewers called attention to the play's focus on Britain's emerging role as an empire builder. As essayist Barbara A. Mowat notes, the play is "now put forward as [Shakespeare's] representation, for good or ill, of the colonizing and the colonized" (Mowat in Shakespeare, *The Tempest,* p. 195).

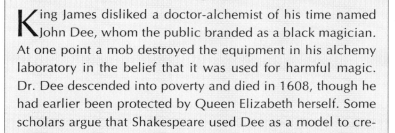

THE ALCHEMIST JOHN DEE

King James disliked a doctor-alchemist of his time named John Dee, whom the public branded as a black magician. At one point a mob destroyed the equipment in his alchemy laboratory in the belief that it was used for harmful magic. Dr. Dee descended into poverty and died in 1608, though he had earlier been protected by Queen Elizabeth herself. Some scholars argue that Shakespeare used Dee as a model to create Prospero.

For More Information

Levi, Peter. *The Life and Times of William Shakespeare.* New York: Henry Holt, 1988.

Martines, Lauro. *Power and Imagination: City-States in Renaissance Italy.* New York: Alfred A. Knopf, 1979.

Rowse, A. L. *The Elizabethans and America.* New York: Harper & Brothers, 1959.

Shakespeare, William. *The Tempest.* New York: Washington Square, 1994.

Srigley, Michael. *Images of Regeneration: A Study of Shakespeare's "The Tempest" and Its Cultural Background.* Stockholm: Uppsala, 1985.

Wilson, Ian. *Shakespeare: The Evidence.* New York: St. Martin's, 1993.

The Three Musketeers

by
Alexandre Dumas

Born in 1802, Alexandre Dumas was the son of Thomas Alexandre Dumas, who took part in the French Revolution of 1789 and rose quickly to the rank of general. General Thomas Alexandre Dumas, a mulatto, campaigned with Napoleon's army in France, Italy, and Egypt. He was a genuine adventurer, as is the main character in *The Three Musketeers*. Unfortunately, General Dumas's military career was cut short, and he died in destitute conditions when his son was four years old. With little formal education, Alexandre Dumas began working at age fifteen as an office boy. He left home for Paris at the age of twenty-one to seek his fortune as a writer.

Events in History at the Time the Novel Takes Place

Soldiers of fortune. During the 1600s, a young Frenchman's best opportunities to improve his circumstances were in the city of Paris. One of the few ways for a young man to change his social station if he was from a poor province such as Gascony (the home of the main character in the novel) was to travel to Paris and join some sort of military outfit as a career soldier.

Peasants of the poor provinces suffered profound poverty and misery. This hardship was partly the result of warring caused by rivalries between nobles and clashes between local feudal lords and King Louis XIII, who had yet to establish full control over his realm. Pillaging and destruction by soldiers were commonplace.

THE LITERARY WORK

A novel set in France during the years 1625-28, under the reign of Louis XIII; published in 1844.

SYNOPSIS

Young, dashing, and clever, d'Artagnan leaves home and goes to Paris, the capital of France, to fulfill his ambition of becoming a musketeer. He and three musketeers subsequently attempt to foil Cardinal Richelieu's schemes to gain control of the country.

The real musketeers. When King Louis XIII first took the throne, there was hardly an army in France. He began to develop one during his reign, however, and his son, King Louis XIV, oversaw completion of the task. This buildup left France with one of the most powerful land forces in Europe. The basic military unit was a regiment, which consisted of about seven hundred men, two-thirds of whom were musketeers. As their name implies, these soldiers wielded the musket, a smoothbore shoulder gun; meanwhile, others in the regiment continued to carry the old-fashioned pike, a long spear.

Over the span of his reign (1610-1643), Louis XIII would see the French military grow to 139 regiments—109 foot regiments, and 30 horse regiments. The national government, though, had not yet taken on the responsibility of training them to fight. Instead, noblemen-officers raised, trained, and equipped their own regiments using government money. In the end, a unit belonged more to the nobleman who outfitted it than to the king—with one notable exception.

Louis XIII's predecessor, King Henry IV, had in 1600 created for himself an elite regiment of personal guards who carried the old carbine rifle. They were to ride horses and to follow him into battle wherever he went. Louis XIII retained this regiment, but in 1622 he replaced their primary weapon, the carbine, with the musket. This personal regiment, which became known as the King's Musketeers, consisted of 100 musket soldiers chosen by the king himself. Known for their jaunty appearance, the King's Musketeers were uniformed in azure cassocks emblazoned with a silver cross. They rode gray horses, which earned them the nickname "Gray Musketeers." It is this regiment that the main character in *The Three Musketeers* strives to join.

Candidates for membership in the King's Musketeers first had to enter another highly respected regiment, known as the French Guards, which admitted cadets who were as young as fourteen. After his basic training, a cadet could become a minor officer or, if he was rich, buy his way to recognition as a major officer. After a few military campaigns, the cadet might be accepted into an elite corps like the King's Musketeers. Many aspired to this path, but few rose through the ranks, and those unfortunate soldiers who were not able to join the elite regiments were often miserable in the regular army. Of the select soldiers that did achieve membership in corps such as the King's Musketeers, some were from the province of Gascony. These Gascons were known for boasting of their bravery, and a few managed to do quite well for themselves in the military. Given these real-life examples, the military advancement of Dumas's main character is entirely believable.

The real d'Artagnan. Dumas's main character, d'Artagnan, is based on an actual young man. The real d'Artagnan was born in the province of Gascony, where he was first known as Charles-Ogier de Batz de Castelmore. Though not poor peasants, his parents were commoners, though for a half century they claimed to be aristocrats. This claim resulted in legal charges being brought against them; they were accused of usurping a noble title.

In 1630 Charles left home for Paris. He probably gained admission into the French Guards that year. There is evidence that within three years he became one of the King's Musketeers. His name appears on a list of King's Musketeers who were presented in a dress parade on March 10, 1633. These facts indicate that the real d'Artagnan was in Paris several years after the action in the novel takes place.

In 1634 Louis XIII took personal charge of the King's Musketeers rather than delegate the task to someone else. According to some royal papers, he himself changed the name of one of his soldiers—Charles de Batz—to d'Artagnan in memory of the soldier's grandfather on his mother's side, who had served under King Henry IV. This explanation is disputed by some scholars, however. It may be that d'Artagnan simply decided to use his mother's family name as his own because she claimed to have noble origins, and he wanted to identify himself with these origins.

The emerging nation. In the early 1600s, France was not yet a single nation in the minds of most of the population. For most people, the realm of France was almost an imaginary idea, except when a visit by the tax collector or the king brought home the reality of its existence. Instead of a centralized state, the country was made up of a conglomerate of separate and locally controlled provinces that often came into conflict with one another. For many people, loyalty to family clan and special interests was often a stronger factor than respect for the authority of the king or the law. Rivalries between the king and local feudal lords, between the French monarchy and other royal houses of Europe, and between Catholics and Protestants threatened the stability of France through much of the 1500s and 1600s.

The centralized and sovereign state of France as we know it today began during the reigns of Louis XIII (1610-1643) and Louis XIV (1643-1715). Playing a large role in its creation was minister of state Cardinal Duc de Richelieu, also known as Armand-Jean du Plessis (1585-1642), who devoted himself to establishing the authority of the king and Catholicism in the country.

Cardinal Richelieu and Louis XIII. When Louis XIII ascended to the throne of France, he was only a nine-year-old boy. Consequently, his mother, Marie de' Medici, assumed the regency and governed in his place. Her rule, driven by personal ambitions, left France greatly weakened in the face of the growing power of the Habsburg rulers of nearby Austria and Spain.

At age sixteen, Louis XIII was finally old enough to govern France himself. He had his

DEFEAT OF THE "NATION" WITHIN THE NATION

1618-48: Thirty Years' War, a conflict with outside nations, sets France against Habsburgs of Vienna and Spain.

1619-24: Rise of Cardinal Richelieu as a ruling force in France, a mainly Catholic realm.

1622: Peace treaty allows Huguenots (French Protestants) to retain strongholds at Montpellier, La Rochelle, and several other French towns.

1625: Protestant uprisings in France are quelled through Treaty of La Rochelle, a truce that proves temporary.

1627: Led by Duke of Buckingham, the English land near La Rochelle at the isle of Ré to aid Protestants, but they are promptly driven off.

1627-28: Richelieu and King Louis XIII conduct a siege against the Protestants at La Rochelle, starving them into defeat.

mother's entourage eliminated by a variety of methods, including assassination, imprisonment, and exile. Cardinal Richelieu, one of Marie de' Medici's ministers, was stripped of his functions. Instead of establishing himself on the throne, though, Louis XIII temporarily turned the reins of power over to Charles d'Albert de Luynes, who had pushed him to oust his mother. For seven years France remained a troubled land, menaced from within by unruly nobles and rebellious Protestants and from without by other European powers.

Finally, Louis XIII appointed the capable Cardinal Richelieu as prime minister. The cardinal pursued his ambitions untiringly, and he never again lost the confidence of the king in matters of importance. He served as France's prime minister from 1624 to 1642. During his tenure, Richelieu strengthened the military (in part through the creation of a fleet of warships), imposed absolute monarchy over the nobles, impeded the spread of Protestant influence, and went to war with Spain and its ally Austria.

The Thirty Years War and the siege of La Rochelle. *The Three Musketeers* is set during the time of the Thirty Years War, which pitted German Protestant princes allied with France, Sweden, England, and Denmark against the Habsburgs of Austria and Spain, who were Catholic, and the Catholic princes of the Holy Roman Empire. Pursuing its own interests, France, primarily a Catholic state, allied itself with Protestant countries in order to counter the domination of the Habsburgs.

At the same time, Cardinal Richelieu pursued his objective of making France a predominately Catholic country. Operating under the auspices of King Louis XIII, he masterminded the successful blockade of La Rochelle, a Protestant stronghold in France. The Protestants of La Rochelle subsequently called on England for help.

Heeding their call, England's Duke of Buckingham (George Villiers) rushed to help the Protestants of La Rochelle. He landed his forces at the nearby isle of Ré in the summer of 1627. Distinguishing themselves for their bravery in the fight, the King's Musketeers joined with other French units to attack the English force, which fled back to England with the French in hot pursuit.

In the fall, after a delay due to illness, the king turned his attention to the Protestants at La Rochelle. Reluctant to take the city by storm, which would have meant spilling the blood of France's own subjects, Richelieu suggested a siege. The town's port was blockaded and trenches were dug on land. The siege lasted fourteen months and starved the townspeople into unconditional surrender. By the time of the town's surrender, its populace had dwindled in number from twenty-seven thousand to eight thousand. After their defeat, the king had his men pass out ten thousand loaves of bread and other supplies to the people, some of whom proceeded to gorge themselves to death.

The king, the queen, and the duke. For many years, history portrayed Louis XIII as a weak, indecisive king who leaned on others and deferred his rule to his prime minister, Richelieu. True, the king was a sickly man who delayed the siege on La Rochelle for several months after his forces had sent the Duke of Buckingham's troops scurrying back home. But recently, many historians have taken issue with the image of Louis XIII as a weak monarch, protesting that he ruled not at the mercy of, but in partnership with, Richelieu. Some have even argued that the king was a highly effective ruler. Certainly, argues one biographer, he was "far from being the do-nothing king ridiculed in Alexandre Dumas's *Three Musketeers*" (Moote, p. 2).

King Louis XIII and his wife Queen Anne had been forced into marriage when they were both only fourteen years old. Their union was a political marriage to strengthen relations between France and Spain, Anne's father being King Phillip III of Spain. Louis and Anne possessed contrary personalities; she seems to have been fun-loving, while Louis was more serious and anxious. There were a few years of closeness, but their marriage grew strained. At one point Louis XIII even suspected her of treason. He believed that she and her friend Marie de Chevreuse knew of a plot against him. This concern supposedly led him to hurl an accusation at her: "You wished my death and to marry my brother" (Louis XIII in Moote, p. 193). Queen Anne retorted that she would have gained too little to soil herself with such a crime. As suggested in *The Three Musketeers*, she and Richelieu were bitter enemies; Richelieu distrusted the queen, who came from the Habsburg family, France's rival in the Thirty Years' War.

England's Duke of Buckingham is known to have contributed to plots against Richelieu and the king. Such plotting began as early as 1626. But there is some uncertainty about the relationship between Queen Anne and the Duke of Buckingham. It is known that the duke visited Queen Anne in 1623 and 1625 and that he professed his love for her. In 1625 he apparently caught her off guard in a garden. According to the queen's own account, he took a liberty during this encounter—meaning he tried either to embrace or to kiss her. Alarmed, she cried out and her attendants came running. Later he returned to her quarters and declared his undying love for her on his knees. How Anne felt about him remains unclear. But she was reported to have remarked that if a virtuous woman could love a man other than her husband, then for her that man would have been the Duke of Buckingham.

The Novel in Focus

The plot. Young d'Artagnan leaves home for Paris in 1625. Armed with a letter of recom-

mendation addressed to the captain of the King's Musketeers, he intends to become one. Once in the capital, he meets the three musketeers who are later to become his faithful companions. He encounters each musketeer separately, though, and due to his reckless cockiness, he ends up challenging each one to a duel. Instead of fighting each other, though, they band together to defend themselves from Cardinal Richelieu's guards, who have come to arrest them for dueling. In this way d'Artagnan proves himself and earns the respect of the three musketeers—Athos, Porthos, and Aramis.

DUELS IN SEVENTEENTH-CENTURY FRANCE

In a vigorous effort to assume control and maintain public order, Richelieu laid down some new rules in France that incensed the nobles. He considered the expenses of the rich exaggerated and so issued an edict against luxury in clothing. He also ordered the destruction of those fortresses not necessary to the defense of France's borders, a blow to feudal lords who saw the symbols of their power suppressed. But the edict they objected to most was the one that forbade dueling.

Duels involved at least four persons, the two duelists and their seconds, or assistants. Often there were more participants, for many duels were fought between groups. In the first decade of the 1600s, four hundred gentlemen died in duels. Richelieu felt that duels were senseless and noted that, since they almost always ended with the death of at least one duelist, they deprived the military of able fighting men. He applied severe penalties to survivors of duels: imprisonment, banishment from the realm, or even, in cases of repeat offenders, public execution. The issue reached a head in 1626 when two noblemen brazenly challenged the edict, choosing to fight in the middle of Paris in broad daylight. Some participants in the duel were caught and condemned to death. The king refused to pardon them, and they were beheaded.

D'Artagnan and the three musketeers become embroiled in the intrigues of the court involving King Louis XIII; Queen Anne; the powerful Duke of Buckingham, the English nobleman; and Cardinal Richelieu. Young d'Artagnan falls in love with Madame Bonacieux, seamstress to the queen, and learns of a problem of some significance that is facing the Queen. The king had given the queen some diamond studs that she later gave to the duke. Cardinal Richelieu, who wishes to compromise the queen in the eyes of the king since she is of the rival House of Habsburg, suggests to Louis that the king give a party, and that he ask the queen to wear her studs. Meanwhile, Richelieu sends an evil woman, Milady (the Lady de Winter), to England to steal the studs from Buckingham so the queen cannot retrieve them before the party. Inspired to protect the queen's honor, d'Artagnan goes to England to foil the cardinal's plot. He succeeds, retrieving the diamond studs and returning them to the queen before the party.

THE DIAMOND STUDS CAPER

The Duke of La Rochefoucauld, who was a child at the time of the episode, described the diamond studs incident in his memoirs. His description differs in several details from the incident as detailed in Dumas's novel. According to the memoirs, Buckingham had a mistress in England who was jealous of his feelings for Queen Anne. The mistress noticed that he had taken to wearing a set of diamond studs and was convinced that they had been given to the duke by the queen. During a subsequent party the mistress was able to cut off the studs with the intention of sending them off to Cardinal Richelieu. The memoirs note, however, that "the Duke noticed his loss ... and believed her capable of giving them to the Cardinal to ruin the Queen. The matter being serious, he immediately gave orders that all English ports be closed" (La Rochefoucauld in Dumas, p. 631). The queen's gift of diamonds could have been used to insinuate that she was not faithful to King Louis and that her first allegiance was not to the French Crown. Buckingham had a jeweler make exact copies which he sent to Anne. She promptly showed them to the king, saving her reputation despite the cardinal's designs. La Rochefoucauld presents his memory of the incident as fact, but there is no evidence to substantiate his account, and it assumes that Anne and the cardinal were enemies as early as 1625, which was not the case.

Despite the cardinal's numerous attempts to capture d'Artagnan and the three musketeers, d'Artagnan makes it back to France in time to keep the queen from being implicated in any intrigue against the king. His return, however, proves too late to save his new love, Madame Bonacieux, from the evil designs of Milady, who

has her imprisoned. A protracted battle between d'Artagnan and the wicked but charming Milady ensues. They become mortal enemies. Before her evil deeds can be exposed, the musketeers are sent off to the siege of La Rochelle.

During the siege, the cardinal entrusts to Milady the mission of assassinating the Duke of Buckingham. As payment, she demands the heads of d'Artagnan and Madame Bonacieux, who had foiled her mission to steal the diamond studs. She manages to poison Madame Bonacieux, then is caught and judged for her crimes. After more adventures, d'Artagnan is finally awarded a commission in the King's Musketeers.

Sources. The idea for the novel came to Dumas while reading fictitious memoirs written by Gatien Courtilz de Sandras (*Mémoires de M. d'Artagnan*). He based the development of his character d'Artagnan on this work. The fictional memoirs often confused the sequence of facts and placed people in events that could not really involve them, "mistakes" that Dumas duplicated in his own novel.

Dumas draws the characters of the three musketeers and Milady from these fictional memoirs as well. Queen Anne, King Louis XIII, Cardinal Richelieu, and the Duke of Buckingham all hark back to historical figures, as does d'Artagnan and the captain of the King's Musketeers. The accuracy of the portrayals of these historical figures, however, varies.

For example, Dumas's portrayal of Tréville, the captain of the King's Musketeers, is a fairly accurate one. The captain in the novel was based on the real Arnaud-Jean du Peyrer (1598-1672), the Count de Troisvilles. Louis XIII, who admired the count's loyalty and courage, made him captain in 1634 (though he was later exiled for opposing Richelieu). On the other hand, Dumas's portrayal of Cardinal Richelieu, although based on the real cardinal, was less accurate. Dumas turns Richelieu into a cruel, calculating villain and shows no regard for his vital role in transforming France into a central European power.

Dumas wrote or co-wrote five other novels the same year that *The Three Musketeers* was published. He also claimed to be the author of more than one thousand books over the course of his lifetime. One of these was *Louis XIV et son siécle,* a historical work that provided him with background for his *Three Musketeers.* He is known to have collaborated with other writers, who usually came to him with rough ideas that he developed into a story. Auguste Maquet, who worked with Dumas on *The Three Musketeers,* may have been the only collaborator who supplied more than ideas. Besides helping to develop the basic plan, Maquet wrote first drafts of scenes that Dumas then expanded or tightened.

Events in History at the Time the Novel Was Written

The adventures of Alexandre Dumas. The character d'Artagnan can be seen as a mirror of Dumas himself. Dumas was born in 1802, thirteen years after the French Revolution began. The country had already witnessed the beheading of King Louis XVI, followed by experiments with various forms of government. The revolutionary leader Napoleon Bonaparte was crowned emperor in 1804, then fell from power in 1814. His rule gave way to the restoration of monarchy in France under King Louis XVIII (who ruled from 1815 to 1824), followed by Charles X (1824-1830). Dumas left his small village of Villers-Cotterets in 1823, in the midst of all these changes. Like his character d'Artagnan, Dumas set out for Paris, a young man with little more than his wits and a letter of recommendation as resources.

In Paris Dumas secured a position as a copy-clerk (someone who took dictation) with the Duc d'Orléans, who became the future constitutional monarch Louis-Phillipe after the Revolution of 1830. Despite a deficient education, Dumas had managed to learn to write rapidly, legibly, and stylishly at a time when such skill was prized, before the typewriter made such talent largely obsolete.

The Revolution of 1830. Louis XVIII, the first to reign when the monarchy was restored in 1815, proved to be a moderate ruler. He governed with an awareness that the Revolution and Napoleon's reign had ended in the need for increased sharing of authority on the part of any French ruler. His successor, though, seemed bent on restoring absolute authority. In 1830 King Charles X issued four new edicts: he censored the press, dissolved the newly elected assembly, downsized the next assembly to 258 members, and issued new election rules that would reduce the number of voters from 100,000 to about 25,000. The population rebelled, seizing Paris in three days and forming a new government with a more responsive king—Louis Phillipe, the Duc d'Orleans.

Dumas's activities during the 1830 Revolution. Like his father, who had taken part in the 1789 revolution, Dumas played a role in the political upheaval of 1830. For a long time Dumas had been a "Républicain," holding high the ideals of the French Revolution and cherishing the groundwork that it had established for a more democratic society. Above all, the Revolution of 1789 had unleashed forces that allowed the middle class to prosper and made it unwilling to relinquish its newfound economic and political power. It was this middle class—the business people, bankers, and other professionals—who backed the toppling of Charles X's government and the rise of Louis Phillipe to power. Dumas also had a personal relationship with Louis Phillipe, having been employed by him in the past.

D'ARTAGNAN'S GASCON HERITAGE

In 1453, the year that marked the end of the Hundred Years' War, d'Artagnan's home province of Gascony was wrested from English control and definitively became part of France. Gascons are by tradition slight of build, courageous, enterprising, and ambitious, but given to boasting and exaggeration. In the novel Dumas exploits these traits and makes them the basis of d'Artagnan's conduct. Reputed to be excellent soldiers, the Gascons were loyal supporters of Henri IV (1553-1610), and their influence was still felt in the court of Louis XIII.

For three days Dumas fought alongside other men against the Royal Army troops that were supporting Charles X. Dumas convinced a general to send him on a mission to capture gunpowder for his revolutionary comrades, then requisitioned the contents of a munitions dump outside Paris. The suspicion was that troops still loyal to Charles X might use the munitions to march on Paris and retake it. Dumas's bravado in this instance was reminiscent of d'Artagnan's behavior in the novel. Dumas bluffed the commander in charge of the gunpowder and succeeded in forcing him to hand over control of the dump.

Rivalry between England and France. Much of *The Three Musketeers* plays on the historic rivalry between England and France. In the years leading up to the publication of the novel, mistrust of the English had again become pronounced because it was thought that they were violating the terms of an agreement to end slavery. It was believed that England was abusing its right to inspect French merchant ships for contraband slaves; the suspicion was that the true intent of the English was to hinder French trade.

The "Pritchard Affair," which involved an English missionary in Tahiti, also turned French public opinion against the English. In 1842 the French annexed the island of Tahiti. A British missionary and consul on the island by the name of Pritchard had much influence over the Queen Pomare, who ruled Tahiti. He advised the queen to expel the French. To secure their position, the French had her deposed and sent Pritchard back to England. This provoked an indignant reaction in England, and the English press spoke of war. Dumas may have consciously capitalized on the anti-English sentiment that this incident provoked in France when he sat down to write *The Three Musketeers*.

Reviews. First written in installments for a major newspaper, *The Three Musketeers* was immensely popular when it appeared; readers waited anxiously for each new installment. *The Three Musketeers* was nevertheless faulted by many reviewers for lack of style and for historical inaccuracies. "We are at no pains to conceal the contempt which we feel for Dumas," said one reviewer, "[but] he is not an artist, and [so] cannot be criticized as such" (Harris, p. 52). Other

critics of the 1800s disagreed, however. They praised Dumas's dialogue, his realistic scenes, and his talent for making history entertaining: "[We] owe more innocent amusement [to Dumas]," one of these critics said, "than to almost any other writer of his generation" (Harris, p. 64). Perhaps the greatest compliment was to his enduring ability to enthrall readers. The novel, said reviewer George Saintsbury in 1878, was as entertaining to him then as it had been twenty years earlier.

For More Information

Belloc, Hilaire. *Richelieu: A Study*. Philadelphia: J. B. Lippincott, 1929.

Dumas, Alexandre. *The Three Musketeers*. Oxford: Oxford University Press, 1991.

Harris, Laurie Lanzen, and Cherie D. Abbey, eds. *Nineteenth-Century Literature Criticism*. Vol. 11. Detroit: Gale Research, 1986.

Kleinman, Ruth. *Anne of Austria: Queen of France*. Columbus: Ohio State University Press, 1985.

Moote, A. Lloyd. *Louis XIII, the Just*. Berkeley: University of California Press, 1989.

Schopp, Claude. *Alexandre Dumas: Genius of Life*. Translated by A. J. Koch. New York: Franklin Watts, 1988.

Tituba of Salem Village

by
Ann Petry

Born in Old Saybrook, Connecticut, in 1908, Ann Petry grew up in one of the small town's only two black families. She moved to the predominantly poor, black community of Harlem, New York, in 1938. *Tituba of Salem Village* is one of the author's many novels that focus on the lives of black people and the racial tensions of American society. Although it chronicles the seventeenth-century Salem witch trials, the novel concerns issues that reappear in twentieth-century America.

Events in History at the Time the Novel Takes Place

Puritanism in colonial Massachusetts. Puritanism was a Protestant sect that had its roots in sixteenth-century England. It originally grew from a desire to "purify" the country's national religious institution, the Church of England. Puritans wanted to eliminate all the church's similarities to Catholicism by simplifying worship, reducing its elaborate administrative hierarchy, and employing clergy with more extensive religious education. Due in part to the slow progress of reform in England, many Puritans were motivated to emigrate to America. There they established a new society in Massachusetts based entirely on their own ideals.

The Puritans held several strong religious convictions. First, they believed in the absolute sovereignty of God. They thought that God was active in the world and that God's forces of good were in constant battle with Satan's forces of evil.

THE LITERARY WORK

A novel set in Salem Village, Massachusetts, about 1692; published in 1964.

SYNOPSIS

A female slave is accused, tried, and convicted of practicing witchcraft in colonial New England.

They further believed that human beings were sinful by nature and completely dependent on divine grace for salvation. Puritan beliefs held that God "elected" some people before birth to be saved, but also condemned others to damnation in hell. There was no way to change one's fate; grace could not be earned by human action. But many believed that their chances of salvation might be revealed by the way that they led their lives. An evil or idle life was seen as a sign of eventual damnation; piety, hard work, and success were signs of grace. This provided the Puritans with a strong incentive to lead virtuous and productive lives.

The Puritans placed high value on seriousness and hard work. They regarded idleness as an awful sin, and viewed dancing, merrymaking, and drunkenness as wicked distractions from productive tasks. When they weren't engaged in work, much of the Puritans' lives centered around the local church. They frequently read the Bible, listened to sermons, and attended prayer meetings. Puritans typically attended two church services, each three hours in length, on Sundays.

Indentured servants. A number of characters in *Tituba of Salem Village*, such as Pim and Mercy Lewis, are indentured servants. In the late seventeenth century, indentured servants made up one of the largest elements of New England society. They were obligated to work for a master for a fixed number of years; most served for between two and seven years. The majority of the region's indentured servants had traveled from England voluntarily, selling their labor in return for passage to America. Others became servants against their will. Involuntary servants included a few groups of convicts shipped by the English government to be sold into servitude; poor white children, orphans, and paupers from London's slums. Some had been kidnapped by unscrupulous merchants.

Indentured servants were usually white and held their positions only temporarily. Their situation was similar to that of slaves in some ways, however. Indentured servants, like slaves, received food and shelter for the length of their servitude. Both classes owed complete obedience to their master, who sometimes indulged his authority to order brutal beatings of both white servants and slaves. Finally, both were often stereotyped as lazy, unruly, dishonest, and inferior people. Like slaves, indentured servants were considered to be among the lowest elements of Puritan society.

Slavery in colonial America. Twenty blacks are known to have been sold to the settlers of Jamestown, Virginia, in 1619. Whether they were indentured servants or slaves remains uncertain. It is known, however, that members of the Puritan community in Massachusetts owned slaves as early as the 1630s, although there was no mass settlement of slaves there. The small number of slaves was due in part to geography of the region. Massachusetts soil did not lend itself to large-scale plantations that demanded massive labor forces. Another reason for the small slave population was the Puritan desire to keep out those who were strangers to their ways. Despite this relatively closed society, some seventeenth-century Massachusetts Puritans did buy slaves to work on their farms or perform various other tasks for them. Even ministers, such as Reverend Samuel Parris, were slaveowners.

Many Puritans believed that blacks were more closely related to animals than to human beings. Some argued about whether they even had souls to save. In addition, Puritans closely associated black, the color of the slaves' skin, with evil. They often referred to Satan as the Black Man. The Puritans associated white, on the other hand, with goodness and virtue. These prejudicial attitudes helped the Puritans rationalize their enslavement of blacks.

Belief in witchcraft. As in other areas of the world at the time, people in Massachusetts believed in the ability of Satan, the major spirit of evil, to assert his power on earth. One way he was thought to do this was through human agents called witches, who allegedly caused a great deal of mischief in the world. Witches promised to honor, worship, and obey Satan by putting a mark, or signature, in his book. In return for her service, the witch received various supernatural powers.

According to those who believed in witchcraft, the witch's main instrument in performing crimes was her own specter or spirit. She could send her invisible specter anywhere to do harm while her physical body remained far from the scene of the crime. Only the victim could see the specter of an attacking witch. In addition, Puritans charged that a witch was often aided by one or more familiars. Familiars were low-ranking evil spirits given to witches by Satan; they typically appeared in the shape of a small animal such as a cat or a bird. A familiar was the witch's constant companion.

The Puritans of Massachusetts believed that witches tormented others by squeezing and pinching articles of their victims' clothing, or by sticking pins into dolls or puppets made to resemble their victims. According to the Puritans, some of the physical symptoms that resulted from these devilish activities included convulsive fits; temporary loss of hearing, speech, or sight; loss of memory or appetite; choking sensations; and terrifying hallucinations. Anyone who had the power to hurt others in such frightening, supernatural ways was considered to be a major enemy of society. Consequently, the punishment for practicing witchcraft was very severe. If a person was convicted of being a witch, the judges often sentenced the person to death. Confession—the accused person's admission that he or she was a witch—sometimes resulted in a reprieve from execution. In Salem, a "witch" who confessed would escape the death penalty. Tituba receives such a reprieve in *Tituba of Salem Village.*

The real-life Tituba. Little is known about the historical Tituba, a woman who did in fact live in Salem during the witch trials of the late seventeenth century. It has been determined that she had originally lived on Barbados, an island of the West Indies, and that she was married to a slave named John Indian. Whether Tituba was black or Indian remains uncertain. Purchased along with her husband, she departed for Salem Village, Massachusetts, to work in the household of the minister Samuel Parris, where she was to care for Parris's children.

It is thought that Tituba spoke about the practice of voodoo, a religious cult of the West Indies, to a few young girls in Salem. The girls also experimented with fortunetelling. Huddling over a makeshift crystal ball, they tried to foretell the occupations of their future sweethearts, as people in various parts of the world often did in those days. In February 1692, two of the girls began acting strangely and complained of pains similar to those described in a popular 1689 book on witchcraft by the Reverend Cotton Mather. The doctor who examined the two girls announced the cause of their behavior: they were bewitched.

Tituba was quickly accused of involvement in witchcraft. She confessed to contact with the devil, but said that she had resisted orders to hurt the children. Much later she explained that her owner, Samuel Parris, had beaten her until she confessed to being a witch and named other residents of Salem as witches. Tituba named the beggarwoman Sarah Good and the poorly regarded Sarah Osborne (sometimes spelled Osburne) as fellow witches.

The three women—Tituba, Sarah Good, and Sarah Osborne—were arrested on March 1, 1692. During her examination by the court, Tituba stuck to her story of dealings with the devil. She remained in prison for months, escaping execution because she had confessed. Charges against her were dropped in 1693 and she was released. Before leaving, she had to repay the cost of her chains, shackles, and other prison expenses because her owner refused to make payment. Tituba was then sold for the price of her prison fees, possibly to a slave trader. Meanwhile, a few other slaves besides Tituba had been named as witches at Salem. Among them was a female slave, the maid of a Mrs. Thatcher, who had been confined along with Tituba in quarters separate from the white "witches" of Salem.

The Salem witch trials. The hysteria over witches erupted at Salem Village while the trials were held at nearby Salem Town. Other witchcraft cases had been investigated earlier in the century; at least eighty-three trials resulted in ex-

Portrait of Cotton Mather (1663-1728).

ecutions in the colonies of Massachusetts and Virginia dating back to 1647. These incidents, however, were small-scale episodes that featured no more than four accused witches at a time. By contrast, the panic at Salem resulted in the jailing of more than 100 colonists before the hysteria ended. Nineteen were convicted and hanged. One more, a man named Giles Corey, was pressed to death by heavy weights, the common English punishment for someone who refused to plead innocent or guilty.

The hysteria began with the two girls who had been examined and pronounced bewitched. At first these two girls, who were the daughter and niece of Samuel Parris, were the only ones to behave oddly. Soon, however, other girls in the village were seized by similar fits. Villagers grew frightened, and a frenzy against witches spread throughout the community. An account by the onlooker John Hale described the villagers' fear that "the witches design was to destroy Salem Village, and to begin at the minister's house, and to destroy the Church of God, and to set up Satan's kingdom" (Hale in Robinson, p. 7).

Public hearings were convened on the cases of the accused witches. To a large extent, each case relied on testimony about specters, or ghostly visions, invisible to all except the bewitched witnesses. Though this spectral evidence was impossible to confirm, the judges accepted such testimony as completely valid. It was on the strength of this evidence that Sarah Good, Sarah Osborne, and Tituba were all convicted of witchcraft and imprisoned.

Judges John Hathorne and Jonathan Corwin questioned Tituba on March 1st, 3rd, and 7th. An excerpt from the examination of March 7th follows:

> Hathorne: Did you never see the devil?
> Tituba: The devil came to me and bid me serve him.
> Hathorne: Who have you seen?
> Tituba: Four women sometimes hurt the children.
> Hathorne: Who were they?
> Tituba: Goody Osburne [Osborne] and Sarah Good and I do not know who the other were. Sarah Good and Osburne would have me hurt the children but I would not...they hurt the children and they lay all upon me and they tell me if I will not hurt the children they will hurt me.
> (Adapted from *Records of Salem Witchcraft*, pp. 44-5)

Judge Hathorne persisted, asking Tituba how the witches traveled. She informed him that they would ride to places on sticks.

ANN PUTNAM V. TITUBA INDIAN

The deposition of Ann Putnam who testifieth and saith that on the 25th of February 1691-92 I saw the [ghostly] apparition of Tituba, Mr. Parish's Indian woman, which did torture me most greviously by pricking and pinching me most dreadfully till the first day of March, being the day of her examination....

(Adapted from *Records of Salem Witchcraft*, p. 49)

Examinations continued as the number of prisoners grew and formal trials followed. Eventually, with the jails overflowing and people openly questioning how valid it was to convict someone based on spectral evidence, the hysteria began to abate. The governor of Massachusetts, Sir William Phipps, granted a reprieve in 1693, freeing those in jail. In 1711 the heirs of alleged witches were voted compensation by the state government. At least one of Tituba's original accusers, Ann Putnam, Jr., later admitted that her stories of being a victim of witchcraft had been made up. Today there is disagreement

among scholars about why she or the other "bewitched" girls behaved as they did.

In Petry's novel, Tituba observes that the "bewitched" girls mostly have their fits in public, when they have an audience. Their fits and accusations garner them more attention than they've ever had before. The girls are even excused from doing any chores. Over the course of the novel, such observations imply a particular interpretation of the whole affair. They suggest that the girls were motivated by self-interest to pretend to be bewitched. Others suggest that the girls' behavior can be traced back to the combined effect of Cotton Mather's 1689 book on witchcraft and local talk about witches. Proponents of this theory contend that the two factors produced such an intense fear of being possessed by the devil that the girls' behavior was affected.

The Novel in Focus

The plot. *Tituba of Salem Village* opens in Barbados, an island in the West Indies, in the late seventeenth century. The slave Tituba and her husband John are sold to a Massachusetts minister named Samuel Parris. Within a day of discovering they have been sold, the couple must sail from their home of many years to Massachusetts. On board the ship, they meet their new master's sickly wife, as well as the minister's daughter, Betsey, and his niece, Abigail. Tituba also meets Pim, a young stowaway who is later caught and sold as an indentured servant to a resident of Salem Village, Massachusetts.

The Reverend's family remains in Boston for the winter while he seeks employment. Living next door to the family is a weaver named Samuel Conklin, who teaches Tituba the art of spinning thread. Finally, Reverend Parris is offered a job as minister of Salem Village, where the family soon moves.

During one winter in Salem Village, Tituba tells some of the village girls vivid stories about Barbados. At one of these gatherings, Betsey Parris falls into a trancelike state from staring at a bowl of water. After this episode, Abigail and the other village girls try to induce this state in her again. They also become interested in fortunetelling after Tituba tells their fortunes with tarot cards brought to the Reverend's house by Mercy Lewis, the indentured servant of the Putnam family.

A few days later, a village vagrant named Sarah Good and her daughter Dorcas arrive at the Reverend's house and beg for food. Upon their de-

The house in which interrogations were conducted during the Salem witch trials.

parture, Dorcas accidentally leaves behind a doll that she calls Patience Mulenhouse, the name of one of the other village children. Abigail throws the doll into the fire, where it seems to writhe with eerie expressions of almost human anguish. Later, Abigail and her companions learn that the Mulenhouse girl has recently burned to death. The coincidence greatly disturbs everyone, and Abigail and Betsey begin having strange fits.

The girls are examined by a doctor, who declares that they must be bewitched. Before long, four other village girls join Betsey and Abigail in their strange behavior. A public fervor develops to find out who is tormenting the girls. A woman named Mary Sibley prepares a "witch cake" at Reverend Parris's house. The purpose of the cake is to attract the witches to the house and reveal their identity. Tituba, Sarah Good, and Sarah Osburne all appear at the house and are accused of being witches.

Reverend Parris intimidates and beats Tituba into confessing that she is a witch. Tituba, Sarah Good, and Sarah Osburne are arrested and put on trial. All three publicly deny being witches. Many witnesses come forward, however, and claim that the women are indeed witches who did them harm. Meanwhile, the "bewitched" girls continue to have fits that instantly disappear when the girls are touched by the alleged witches.

This phenomenon helps convince people of the women's guilt, and the judges sentence Tituba, Sarah Good, and Sarah Osburne to a Boston jail.

As the weeks pass, more and more accused witches from Salem Village crowd into their jail. Eventually, some of the prisoners, including Sarah Good, are put to death. The furor gradually subsides, and the trials come to an end. Governor William Phipps pardons all the prisoners, but they are not allowed to leave prison until the money spent for their upkeep—on necessities such as food and blankets—has been repaid. Reverend Parris refuses to pay Tituba's fees. Having no money of her own, she therefore remains in prison longer than any of the others accused of practicing witchcraft. Eventually, she is bought by Samuel Conklin, the weaver who had taught her to spin thread when she had lived in Boston.

The nature of slavery. *Tituba of Salem Village* describes life in seventeenth-century Massachusetts through the eyes of a female black slave. While the story focuses on the Salem witch trials, it also provides a sense of what it was like to be a slave in those times. Many of Tituba's experiences illustrate the hardships of slavery. When she and her husband are sold by their mistress in Barbados to a Boston minister, they are forced to leave within a day. This short period of time gives them little opportunity to prepare for their journey. Moreover, they have no desire to leave their warm island for an uninviting home in the cold, harsh climate of New England, but they are powerless to stop the move.

The gravest example of the abuses of slavery occurs toward the end of the novel. Reverend Parris has learned of the accusations leveled against Tituba. Angry that she has brought this humiliation to his house, and concerned about his reputation (and the possibility that he might be implicated as some kind of associate of witches), Parris demands a full confession from Tituba. She refuses until the Reverend begins beating her with great force. The beating, which marks the first time she has been hit over the course of the story, affects her very deeply. She finds it both painful and humiliating, "an unspeakable hurt to the spirit, to the soul" (Petry, *Tituba of Salem Village,* p. 194).

Other parts of the novel, however, suggest that relations between blacks and whites were not always so grim and hostile. Tituba seems to have a close relationship with the young Betsey Parris. Betsey turns to Tituba for comfort on many occasions, such as times when the girl is frightened about her sickly mother's bad health. "Sometimes she thrust her small, cold hand into Tituba's hand whispering, 'Don't let her die, Tituba. Don't let her die'" (*Tituba of Salem Village,* p. 176). Tituba also enjoys a positive relationship with Samuel Conklin, the Boston weaver who introduces her to spinning. He visits Tituba in the Boston jail at least once a week, bringing her extra bread and cheese. Even Mary Sibley, the person who first suggested making the witch cake, confesses to Tituba that if she had "known the way the witch cake would turn out, I would have cut off my right hand rather than make it" (*Tituba of Salem Village,* p. 207). None of these relationships changes the fact that Tituba is a black slave, obligated to obey the orders of a white master. Tituba's experiences with these people, however, indicate that not all relationships between blacks and whites in the days of slavery were hostile. There were whites who respected black slaves like Tituba and treated them like human beings.

Sources. *Tituba of Salem Village* is based on accounts of the 1692 witch trials in Salem, Massachusetts. The main characters are people who actually participated in the trials, but there is scant information on their lives and personalities. Petry's novel expands on the little direct evidence that exists. For example, Petry notes that the real Tituba insisted that she loved her

owner's daughter. The novelist subsequently portrays the relationship between the two characters as a close one.

The novel ends with a postscript that contains facts about the trials and how they ended. It claims that the Boston weaver Samuel Conklin purchased Tituba, but historical records suggest that her purchaser, while not known for certain, may have been a slave dealer.

Events in History at the Time the Story Was Written

The Cold War. In 1692 the belief that witches posed a serious threat to the well-being of New England society led to the Salem witch trials. In the 1950s and 1960s, Communists, rather than witches, were seen as dangerous conspirators against America. Across the country, all kinds of institutions—state and local governments, schools and universities, labor unions—tried to purge themselves of real or imagined Communists. Anti-Communist fervor reached a climax in the 1950s with the McCarthy trials. Senator Joseph McCarthy conducted highly publicized investigations into the Communist sympathies of hundreds of people working in the government. Just as in the Salem witch trials, there was little hard evidence against the accused, but mere suspicion of Communist tendencies was usually enough to ruin a person's reputation and gain a conviction.

Congress singled out people suspected of being committed to the Communist cause. In the House of Representatives, members of the House of Un-American Activities committee interrogated and arrested people who were suspected of being Communists. Among them were actors and singers such as the black star Paul Robeson. Like Tituba nearly 400 years earlier, Robeson was swept up in the frenzy of fear that gripped his era.

Congress questioned Robeson, determined to find out whether blacks in America had become dedicated to an international movement to make communism the dominant form of government in the world. The answer was "no," although Communists had made attempts to win blacks over to their cause in the United States. After World War II, members of the Communist Party sought to cultivate a separateness among African Americans that would weaken their commitment to the nation. But the attempt failed miserably. Blacks such as Paul Robeson reiterated their support for the existing United States plan

of government. In 1958 Robeson co-wrote *Here
I Stand,* in which he declared that his first allegiance was to his own community, not to international communism.

For a while, even President Dwight Eisenhower was too intimidated to oppose McCarthy.
In 1954, however, the Eisenhower administration and members of Congress organized a special investigation of McCarthy's charges against
Secretary of the Army Robert Stevens and the
armed services in general. In December 1954 the
Senate voted to condemn McCarthy for conduct
unbecoming a senator. But while McCarthy and
his allies were discredited, America's fear of communism continued in different forms in the
1960s. It was most evident in American attitudes
toward the Soviet Union, the largest Communist
country in the world, and in the reaction of some
officials to the growing civil rights movement.

The civil rights movement. The institution of
slavery lasted in the United States for many years
after the times depicted in *Tituba of Salem Village.*
Even after slavery was abolished in 1865, racism
and prejudice against blacks remained a powerful force. It was openly practiced in the southern states, where segregation provided a legal
foundation for an elaborate system of racial separation. Blacks were required to ride in separate
railroad cars, sit in different waiting rooms, use
their own bathrooms, and entertain themselves
in "blacks only" theaters. They were denied access to many parks, beaches, and picnic areas,
and barred from some hospitals. Isolated acts of
resistance to these laws occurred for many years
before a unified movement devoted to full and
equal civil rights for blacks began to emerge. Not
until 1964, the year that Petry published her
novel, did the efforts of these civil rights champions result in changes to the nation's laws.

J. Edgar Hoover, the head of the Federal Bureau of Investigation (FBI), believed that the civil
rights movement was part of a Communist plot.
He therefore tapped the phones of black leaders
like Martin Luther King, Jr., but in the end he
came up with no indication that they had ties to
Communist organizations. Just as the Puritans
several hundred years earlier had to abandon
their witch-hunt for lack of hard evidence that
the accused were witches, Hoover's opinion that
the civil rights workers were Communists fell
into disrepute.

The civil rights movement reached a high
point in 1963. Blacks and whites held sit-ins and
demonstrations at whites-only facilities through-

out the South. In a series of nonviolent demonstrations by civil rights workers in Birmingham,
Alabama, the police resorted to the use of attack
dogs, tear gas, electric cattle prods, and fire hoses
in brutal efforts to break up the peaceful protests.
Hundreds of people were arrested. Later the same
year, a crowd of 200,000 gathered in Washington, D.C., for the largest civil rights demonstra-
tion in the country's history. The March on
Washington provided dramatic proof of the
growing power of the movement.

The efforts of the protesters paid off early in
1964, when the Senate passed the most com-
prehensive civil rights bill in the nation's history.
Segregation in public places such as stores,
restaurants, and theaters was prohibited, along
with discrimination in employment. Neither the
abandonment of the witch trials in Puritan New
England nor the passage of the Civil Rights Bill
of 1964 ended prejudices in the societies of their
times. But both events acknowledged the nation's
commitment to justice and the rights of the individual.

Reviews. *Tituba of Salem Village* has been widely
praised since its publication in 1964. Admired
elements of the novel include its believable characters and its exciting and informative storyline.
It has been called the finest novel on the subject
of witchcraft ever written for young people. Reviews also cited the novel's relevance to such important issues of modern times as prejudice and
race relations. In the *New York Times Book Review,* for example, the novelist Madeline L'Engle
described *Tituba* as a well-written historical novel
about racial problems at a time when such problems were at the forefront of everybody's mind.

For More Information

Petry, Ann. *Tituba of Salem Village.* New York:
HarperCollins, 1964.

Records of Salem Witchcraft. Vol. 1. New York: Da
Capo, 1864.

Robinson, Enders A. *The Devil Discovered: Salem
Witchcraft 1692.* New York: Hippocrene, 1991.

Ryken, Leland. *Worldly Saints: The Puritans As They
Really Were.* Grand Rapids: Zondervan, 1986.

Starr, Raymond, and Robert Detweiler, eds. *Race,
Prejudice and the Origins of Slavery in America.*
Cambridge, Mass.: Schenkman, 1975.

Walker, Martin. *The Cold War: A History.* New York:
Henry Holt, 1993.

Weisbrot, Robert. *Freedom Bound: A History of
America's Civil Rights Movement.* New York:
Penguin Books, 1991.

Treasure Island

by
Robert Louis Stevenson

Robert Louis Stevenson, whose grandfather and father were lighthouse engineers, felt a fascination for the sea and its promise of travel during his childhood. This fascination did not fade with age. When, as an adult, the author found himself at home due to poor weather, he began writing a sea adventure about a young boy from England who travels to a tropical island. Although Stevenson does not directly date his novel, he does state in its opening pages that Jim "takes up his pen in the year of grace 17—" (Stevenson, *Treasure Island*, p. 11). Later, when reading through the ship's log of the pirate Captain Flint, Jim finds one entry that dates to "June 12, 1745" (*Treasure Island*, p. 45). Since the log covers over twenty years, the novel must take place sometime in the latter half of the eighteenth century, during the reign of King George III (1760-1820).

Events in History at the Time the Novel Takes Place

England in the 1700s. Britain began to emerge as a world power in the eighteenth century. England's American colonies gave the country a strong presence in the New World, and England established a foothold in India and Africa, too. These holdings were connected by a vigorous foreign trade. Sailors and adventurers from around the world set out for the Americas in search of the treasures that this new land promised.

Bristol, the town from which Jim and the oth-

THE LITERARY WORK

An adventure novel set in England and on a West Indies island in the second half of the 1700s; published in 1881.

SYNOPSIS

Young Jim Hawkins travels with pirates aboard a schooner in search of gold. Once the vessel reaches Treasure Island, a pitched battle ensues for possession of the gold.

ers aboard the *Hispaniola* sailed, is a seaport located in western England at the mouth of the Avon River. The town outfitted many "privateers" with ships and men during the 1700s. The term "privateer" referred to a ship privately owned and manned but permitted by the government to attack and capture enemy vessels in wartime. The sailors that manned such ships were also known as privateers.

Piracy in the 1700s. Although piracy reached its height during the 1600s, it remained a concern for sailing vessels at the dawn of the eighteenth century. As the century progressed, the British government legalized certain acts of piracy against the French and Spanish governments. Because the three European nations were competing for property in the Americas, they all took great and sometimes illegal pains to ensure their holdings. The sailors on vessels from these nations attacked foreign ports in the New World as well as foreign ships that sought to trade with the colonies. Financed by merchants on shore, the pirates divided their spoils between their investors and themselves. Contrary to popular belief, most takeovers of targeted ships were accomplished without bloodshed. The firing of cannons, after all, would often ruin the property they planned to seize.

Although they often seemed to disregard the laws of other men, pirates governed themselves in a fairly strict fashion under the "Articles of Agreement":

1. Every man has a vote in affairs of moment....
2. All shall keep their firelocks, pistols and cutlass [sword] clean and fit for service.
3. No women allowed....
4. Desertion of the ship or quitting quarters in battle is punished by death or marooning [abandonment on a deserted shore].

(Woodbury, pp. 90-1)

Stevenson's novel shows an awareness of such rules. Although the mutineers aboard the Hispaniola desert the ship's original captain, they maintain a fairly democratic system among themselves. Dissatisfied with their second elected captain, one sailor states, "I ax your pardon, sir, acknowledging you for to be capting at this present; but I claim my right, and steps outside for a council" (*Treasure Island,* p. 174). Even in mutiny the men observe the pirate tradition of taking a vote.

Schooners. In his letter announcing the purchase of the ship that sails for Treasure Island, the character John Trelawney expresses his awe for the vessel: "You never imagined a sweeter schooner— a child might sail her—two hundred tons; name, *Hispaniola*" (*Treasure Island,* p. 49). For someone without a broad sailing background, such a vessel might prove difficult to imagine.

Originally built for pleasure sailing, schooners began to be used in the eighteenth century for all types of commercial purposes, carrying almost any type of cargo. They served fishermen, slave traders, and private merchants. Because of their speed and dexterity, schooners were also favorites among pirate crews.

A schooner's distinctive features are its two masts which "rake aft," or lean back at an angle (MacGregor, p. 10). The first mast is the foremast, while the one behind it is referred to as the mainmast. They hold three and two sails, respectively. In front of these are triangular sails called the staysail, the jib, and the flying jib.

The Jolly Roger. One of the most obvious symbols associated with pirating is the "Jolly Roger," a black flag inscribed with a skull and crossbones. While pirates have roamed the seas since the earliest days of maritime exploration, the flag did not come into existence until the eighteenth century. Two different and equally plausible stories account for its name. One explanation holds that buccaneers of the seventeenth century typically raised a red flag that had supposedly been dipped in blood to signal to opposing ships that the pirates demanded that they surrender. Known in French as the "joli rouge," the name of the flag was allegedly changed to the Jolly Roger by English buccaneers. The other theory concerns the name's possible origins in the eastern seas. The pirates of this region, who also flew red flags, called themselves "Ali Raja," which meant king of the sea. Proponents of this theory contend that years of English mispronunciation turned this title into Jolly Roger.

The first known account in which a pirate ship utilized a black flag dates back to 1700, when the French pirate Emanuel Wynne raised the flag. By this time, Jolly Roger referred not only to the red flag but to any flag of piracy. When Jim recovers the *Hispaniola* from the pirates in *Treasure Island,* his first order of business is to "strike the Jolly Roger" and throw it overboard (*Treasure Island,* p. 148).

Marooning. On Treasure Island young Jim meets a maroon named Ben Gunn. The practice of marooning was quite common among pirates. When Spain lost Jamaica to the English during the latter half of the seventeenth century, the black slaves who belonged to the Spanish fled to the woods. There they re-established life as they had

An illustration of a schooner, the same type of ship as the *Hispaniola*.

known it in Africa. They were known as Cimaroons or "dwellers in the mountains." The English later abbreviated this title to "maroons."

Eventually the word developed into a term used to designate the practice of abandoning a person on a deserted island. A man who was so punished was typically left on an island in the West Indies that offered little food or drink. He was given a bottle of water, a sea biscuit, and a gun, stripped of his clothing, and left for dead.

The Novel in Focus

The plot. Jim Hawkins leads a fairly quiet existence helping his mother run the Admiral Benbow Inn until old Billy Bones appears. One day the old buccaneer shows up to rent a room. The "captain," as he is called, does not make a very favorable impression on the townspeople, and when Billy's old sea mates show up to harass him, events take a turn for the worse. Perhaps due to the stress of the encounter—or his fondness for rum—Billy dies, leaving behind a locked sea chest. The contents of the chest trigger an incredible adventure for Jim.

Jim and his mother search through the chest to collect money that Bill owes them. The throng of pirates returns, however, and Jim and his mother are forced to flee for their lives. As they

make their escape, Jim grabs an oilskin packet from the chest, unaware that this is the very object that the buccaneers seek.

Wasting no time, Jim shares his secret with Dr. Livesy and Squire John Trelawney. He then discovers that the packet, known as "Flint's Fist," contains a map and a ship's log that provide the location of the buried treasure of Captain Flint, an infamous pirate. The two men, along with Jim, make plans to outfit a vessel and sail in search of the gold.

The squire is an experienced seaman, albeit a talkative one, and he quickly assembles a schooner and crew at the sea town of Bristol. By the time that Jim and the doctor appear, the entire port is abuzz with talk of buried treasure. Captain Smollett, the man hired to run the ship, expresses misgivings about the voyage, hinting that he fears a mutiny. But the doctor quiets the captain's worries, and the *Hispaniola* soon sets sail.

During the voyage, Jim overhears the ship's cook, one-legged Long John Silver, plotting with another sailor to overthrow the ship's officers. Silver, who has sailed previously with Captain Flint, is anxious to seize the great stores of gold. Sly and ambitious, Silver's physical disability barely hinders him. Stevenson describes the pirate as "agile as a monkey even without leg or crutch" (*Treasure Island*, p. 91).

Jim steals away and relays the mutiny plot to the captain, the squire, and the doctor. They conclude that only a few honest hands remain loyal to their cause. At that moment Treasure Island is spotted.

Once on Treasure Island, the mutineers waste no time in exposing their intentions. During their first trip to shore, Long John Silver and his men kill two of the few honest crewmen. Jim nevertheless manages to find an ally on the seemingly deserted island. Ben Gunn, an old sailor who had been marooned on the island three years earlier, encounters Jim in the woods. After receiving promise of a passage back to England, Ben joins forces with Jim and the officers. Just as they form this alliance, the pirates fire their first shots from the cannon of the *Hispaniola.*

For the next two days the fighting ensues, and while the officers are far outnumbered, they manage to adequately defend their position. At one point during the episode, Jim escapes the brawl and secures the ship for his side. Afterward, however, Jim is captured by Long John Silver and his fellow mutineers. The next day the mutineers set out in search of the treasure.

As the pirates make their way toward the supposed treasure, Ben Gunn imitates the singing of the long-dead Flint while maintaining cover behind thick foliage. Unsettled by this "ghostly" voice, the pirates begin to quarrel among themselves. Their bickering reaches a climax when they discover that someone has already dug up the buried gold. Ben, it turns out, had found Flint's treasure some time ago. Just as the other mutineers turn on Silver, the doctor and Gunn spring upon the party. They waylay the pirates and escape with Jim. Long John Silver becomes their captive in the process.

The officers, along with Jim, Ben, and the few remaining loyal hands, quickly load the ship and sail for England. They leave behind not only the mutineers, but also a legacy of blood spilled in the name of treasure. As for Long John Silver, he escapes his captors at a seaport along the way and remains at large.

Long John Silver the hero. Although written in the first person from the point of view of Jim Hawkins, the novel seems to feature the villain, Long John Silver, as its true hero. Silver personifies the legendary traits of pirates, and the novel paints him as a colorful and memorable character. At the end of the novel, Silver remains the only pirate not punished by death or marooning; he in fact escapes.

One of the most interesting aspects of the Long John Silver character is his autobiographical link to his creator. When Stevenson took ill in a Scottish infirmary, his editor, Leslie Stephen, introduced him to another friend staying at the hospital. The man, William Henley, had lost one foot due to tuberculosis, but he had retained his good spirits. He and Stevenson began a friendship that would last a lifetime. The author later stated that the inspiration for the one-legged Long John Silver came from Henley. Stevenson remarked, "it was the sight of your maimed strength and masterfulness that begot John Silver in Treasure Island" (Stevenson in McLynn, p. 201).

The outbreak of the American Civil War in 1861 brought a virtual end to naval traffic in the American waters. This, along with strict measures of punishment, led to the decline of piracy. By the time Stevenson wrote *Treasure Island,* the age of pirates had decidedly come to a close. Ironically, Stevenson was not the only notable author to use these "gentlemen of fortune" (*Treasure Island,* p. 72) as central characters in fictional works. Such notable writers as Washington Irving and Edgar Allan Poe included pirate deeds in their fictional works as well.

Sources. A descendant of lighthouse engineers and architects, Stevenson developed an appreciation for the majesty of the sea at an early age. As a child, his father frequently entertained him with tales of "ships, roadside inns, robbers, old sailors and commercial travelers before the era of steam" (Cooper, p. 10). The direct inspiration for *Treasure Island,* however, remains a subject of some dispute. While autobiographical evidence maintains that Stevenson's father, Thomas, provided most of the fodder for the novel, one account asserts that the author found his source through his stepson Lloyd.

According to the latter story, bad weather played a pivotal part in the eventual creation of *Treasure Island.* Confined to the house by the miserable weather of Braemar, Scotland, young Lloyd Osbourne showed his stepfather a map of an island he had drawn to amuse himself. Stevenson seized upon the notion of a boy's travel adventure. He immediately started his novel. Within fifteen days the first fifteen chapters of the book, originally entitled *The Sea Cook,* had been completed. Although Stevenson denied using the boy's map as a source, Lloyd later claimed as an adult that, "Had it not been for me, and my childish box of paints, there would have been no such book as *Treasure Island*" (McLynn, p. 198).

Stevenson's fictional island appears to combine the traits of a number of actual places. Scholars debate whether its primary basis comes from a highland view of Edinburgh, Scotland, or from the Isle of Pines near Cuba. Most likely a bit of each locale is used to provide details of the island's description. Stevenson also based much of his scenery on Charles Kingsley's descriptions of the Caribbean islands in his book *At Last.* From this work Stevenson also took the "Dead Man's Chest," the name of the song repeated by the pirates throughout *Treasure Island.*

The author based the character Israel Hands, the gunner for the mutineers, on a London man named Israel Hand who worked for the famous pirate Blackbeard. The real Israel Hand suffered a crippling gunshot wound during a battle in which Blackbeard was killed. Hand then traveled back to England, where he became a beggar and a well-known figure on the London streets.

STEAM-POWERED VESSELS

By 1854 most naval and merchant captains had abandoned sailing schooners for steam-powered ships. For those raised on the seas, the emergence of a naval generation with little or no knowledge of sails was disconcerting. Nevertheless, the French harnessed this relatively new power, and the British soon followed suit.

Events in History at the Time the Novel Was Written

Stevenson's Scotland. Robert Louis Stevenson was born in Edinburgh, Scotland, in 1850. Although he lived all over the world, in places ranging from San Francisco, California, to the South Pacific island of Samoa, Stevenson's primary home would remain his native Scotland. There he attended Edinburgh University, where he originally intended to follow in his father's footsteps and acquire a degree in engineering. Each summer his father sent him to various Scottish sea towns in order to learn the marine construction trade. Stevenson, though, found that writing about the local surroundings interested him more than details of marine construction. "The awareness of tides and currents and swells, of rocks and sandbars and headlands, that these journeys gave him . . . is reflected again and again in his novels and stories" (Daiches, p. 22). When Stevenson returned to the university, he switched

his area of study to law, then finally became a full-time fiction writer.

Stevenson's illnesses. As a young boy and throughout his adult years, Robert Louis Stevenson spent many hours bedridden from illnesses. One of the few comforts he found during long periods of recovery was his childhood nurse Alison Cunningham, also known as Cummie. Cummie entertained her charge with a strong imagination that sparked his own. Using cutout figures from a local stationery shop, she dazzled the boy with creative tales of adventure. Stevenson later remarked, "It's you that gave me a passion for the drama, Cummie" (Stevenson in Daiches, p. 12).

This desire for escape from illness and frailty is reflected in Stevenson's work. His stories show a relish for physical labor and the outdoors. Even the one-legged Long John Silver does not suffer any great impediments to his physical capabilities.

Stevenson's travels. Stevenson's poor health kept him moving all over the world in search of a climate that would prove beneficial to his condition. A chronology of his travels follows:

    1878: France
    1879: California, United States
    1880: England
    1881: Davos, Switzerland
    1882: South of France
    1883-85: France
    1887: New York, United States
    1888: South Seas, Hawaii
    1890: Samoa (dies here in 1894)

Other than his primary years in Scotland, Stevenson did not spend more than four years in any one locale. Although this constant movement did not necessarily help his health problems, it did contribute to his writing. A walking tour through the Cévennes mountains in France, for example, prompted the author to write *Travels with a Donkey,* a book that discusses this expedition.

Foreign trade in the 1800s. Robert Louis Stevenson was born during a rare period of peace for Great Britain. The British navy, therefore, focused most of its efforts in the 1850s on the protection of trade markets. Although Britain's policies had contributed to the conditions that incited piracy in the preceding century, the British found themselves working to protect their merchants from foreign pirates 100 years later.

Britain's increased trade, as well as the establishment of a fixed trade route between England and its colony India, spurred the growth of a

British naval presence in the Mediterranean Sea. For many years, Britain had been battling the Barbary pirates in this area. Although this group had been suppressed by the early 1850s, as late as 1851 British warships engaged in regular patrols to discourage local acts of piracy.

On the eastern seas, people manning British naval posts battled Chinese pirates near the borders of India. The destruction of sixty-four junk boats at the hands of Captain Hay in 1850 suppressed the Chinese pirate attacks. This group of ruffians was not brought under full control, though, until the last quarter of the 1800s. It seems, then, that while most history books mention the close of the 1700s as the time when British citizens stopped practicing piracy, Britain continued to battle foreign pirates well into the nineteenth century.

Reception of *Treasure Island*. Like many novels during this period, *Treasure Island* was not published as a complete manuscript. It first appeared in the journal *Young Folks* as a story written by Captain George North, a pseudonym, or pen name, used by the author. It met with immediate success. The American author Jack London predicted, "*Treasure Island* will be a classic to go down with ***Robinson Crusoe*** (also covered in *Literature and Its Times*), *Through the Looking Glass,* and *The Jungle Books*" (London in McLynn, p. 203). Still valued after more than a hundred years, the novel has borne out his prediction.

For More Information

Bartlett, C. J. *Great Britain and Sea Power.* Oxford: Clarendon, 1963.

Cooper, Lettice. *Robert Louis Stevenson.* London: Home and Van Thal, 1949.

Daiches, David. *Robert Louis Stevenson and His World.* London: Thames and Hudson, 1973.

Mac Gregor, David R. *Schooners in Four Centuries.* Annapolis: Naval Institute Press, 1982.

McLynn, Frank. *Robert Louis Stevenson.* New York: Random House, 1993.

Stevenson, Robert Louis. *Treasure Island.* New York: Signet Classics, 1965.

Woodbury, George. *The Great Days of Piracy in the West Indies.* New York: W. W. Norton, 1951.

A Vindication of the Rights of Woman

by
Mary Wollstonecraft

A woman with a tumultuous career, Mary Wollstonecraft was a single parent, writer, teacher, mistress, wife to a philosopher, and mother of a famous novelist. Her life reflected the social and political uncertainties of her day. Born into a middle-class London family, Wollstonecraft endured a harsh upbringing. The decline of her family's fortunes resulted in their eventual descent into the lower classes. The work for which she is most remembered, *A Vindication of the Rights of Woman*, was the product of personal experience and the turbulent events and ideas of the late 1700s.

Events in History at the Time of the Essay

Romanticism. The movement that served as a backdrop for Wollstonecraft's work is referred to as "Romanticism," a European cultural trend that took place roughly from 1770 to 1848. Romanticism was a reaction to the focus on reason and skepticism in the movement known as the Enlightenment. In contrast, Romantics focused on emotions, personal reactions, nature, and the imagination. Excited by the revolutions in America and France as well as wars of independence elsewhere, members of the movement championed new attitudes and standards of behavior in society. Proponents aimed to inspire social progress.

The writer—especially the poet—frequently appears in Romantic literature and philosophy as a figure of social and political salvation, a being

THE LITERARY WORK
A political essay written in England in 1792.

SYNOPSIS
Written after the onset of the French Revolution, Wollstonecraft's essay focuses on the real and potential roles of women in society and the family in an effort to inspire a gradual, nonviolent revolution that would begin in the home.

of a higher order whose passion and imagination have the power to transform the world. Leading Romantic writers, who were primarily men, included the poets William Wordsworth, John Keats, and Lord Byron.

Female writers were also very active during this period, however. They began the long struggle for gender equality through their writing. Mary Wollstonecraft's philosophy, as presented in *A Vindication of the Rights of Woman,* was in many ways the model that other women of the period followed in their own work. Like her, they attempted to effect social progress. Above all, female Romantic writers took the community (generally the family) as their most important subject. Their works, as one authority noted, "insisted on the equal value and rational capacities of women" (Mellor, p. 210).

Wollstonecraft's life. Wollstonecraft's father was an ambitious man who lived beyond his resources to such an extent that at one time Mary was forced to support the entire family. She worked as a governess and educator to the children of nobility and thus gained insight into the ways of the upper classes and the roles that wealthy women were forced to adopt. She also was the friend and confidante to some of the most influential men of her day, including the painter Henri Fuseli, the poet and engraver William Blake, and the philosopher William Godwin. She believed that an educated person was an individual of greater value than those who inherited aristocratic status.

Flouting social convention, Wollstonecraft had a variety of passionate relationships with men to whom she was not married. The man she eventually married, William Godwin, had been her friend and lover for some time before she became pregnant and they wed. Her pregnancy would lead to her death. The child of their marriage, Mary Wollstonecraft Godwin, is better known today as Mary Shelley, author of the novel **Frankenstein** (also covered in *Literature and Its Times*).

Newington Green. When Wollstonecraft, along with sisters Eliza and Everina and best friend Fanny Blood, set up a school in Newington Green (a northern suburb of London) in 1784, she became acquainted with Richard Price. Price was a famous man in those days—a philosopher, a Presbyterian minister, and a liberal political theorist who was a close friend of Benjamin Franklin. Price had supported the American Revolution wholeheartedly and would later claim that the French Revolution should be a model for English political reform. Price's greatest desire seemed to be for an end to the excesses of the monarchy and a broadening of the civil rights of ordinary people.

Price and many other people in the small settlement of Newington Green were "Rational Dissenters"; they believed, optimistically, in the ability of the individual, including (to some degree) women, to change society. Critical thinkers, they maintained that majority interests and happiness should govern political decisions and that all taxpayers should be able to play a role in the government. They were also religious dissenters who refused to join the Church of England and dismissed the concepts of hell and original sin (which holds that because Adam, the first man, sinned, all members of humankind come into the world marked as sinners).

Wollstonecraft often went to hear Dr. Price preach at the Presbyterian church in Newington

An engraving of Mary Wollstonecraft.

Green. She remained an Anglican throughout her life and did not totally adopt Price's political and religious ideals, but he and the other Dissenters in the village certainly influenced her later social criticism. While she never officially became a Dissenter, her time in Newington Green taught Wollstonecraft to look at social and political institutions carefully and critically.

Joseph Johnson. Johnson was Wollstonecraft's publisher in London and would prove to be the most important influence in her life. Like Price, Johnson was a Rational Dissenter, and his printing shop became the center of Dissenter circles. In 1787 Wollstonecraft arrived in London fresh from a humiliating dismissal, because of a personality conflict and her radical social ideas, from Lady Kingsborough's household in Ireland. She went straight to Johnson, who had recently published her tract on the education of women, *Thoughts on the Education of Daughters*. He immediately offered to set her up in her own house; she was to pay rent by writing for him. She worked primarily on the editorial staff of the *Analytical Review*, a journal that featured book reviews and commented on social issues. Through Johnson, Wollstonecraft met the most demanding young intellectuals of the time, male and female, and spent her days doing what she had always wanted to do—write. She wrote not only

LANDMARK DATES IN WOLLSTONECRAFT'S LIFE

1759: Born to a middle-class family outside of London
1784: Helps sister Eliza flee her husband and infant; opens a school north of London
1785: Best friend Fanny Blood dies in Portugal from childbirth
1786: Serves as governess to children of Lord and Lady Kingsborough
1787: *Thoughts on the Education of Daughters* published
1789: French Revolution begins
1790: *Vindication of the Rights of Men* published
1792: *Vindication of the Rights of Woman* published; France declares war on England
1793-94: Has affair with Gilbert Imlay; bears daughter Fanny Imlay
1797: Marries William Godwin; dies in childbirth

book reviews but also translations of important new works from Germany, France, and Italy. Wollstonecraft thus became immersed in the atmosphere of change and inquiry that was sweeping across Europe.

Impact of the French Revolution in England. "Liberty, equality, fraternity" was the motto of the French revolutionaries who in 1789 unseated kings and priests and eventually sent most of the French nobility, including King Louis XVI and Marie Antoinette, to the guillotine. The revolutionaries then engaged in "the Terror," a bloodthirsty period of mayhem in which thousands of people lost their lives.

Debate about the merits of the French Revolution grew more heated as events unfolded, and Wollstonecraft was soon one of the more well-known commentators on the issue. Johnson ran two editions of her 1790 essay, *A Vindication of the Rights of Men,* in which she replied to the comments of famous politician and essayist Edmund Burke. Burke was shocked by the London Dissenters, who extolled the virtues of the French Revolution and voiced the hope that its values of liberty and radical equality would catch on in England. Arguing against this hope, Burke reasoned in his *Reflections on the Revolution in France* that the French Revolution was actually a very dangerous and potentially horrifying event. Wollstonecraft dashed off a reply to Burke that confronted him with a wide range of ills in English society, such as its habits of placing power in the hands of ignorant nobles, of impressing (kidnapping) sailors to serve in the Royal Navy, and of respecting inherited wealth more than individual worth and intellect. Her

essay was described as hotheaded and poorly organized, but *A Vindication of the Rights of Men* made her famous anyway.

Developments in France prompted Wollstonecraft to follow up the essay with a book on the rights of women. Abandoning church-controlled education, France planned to replace it with a system better suited to a democratic society. On September 10, 1791, its legislators heard a proposal that called for free education but made no mention of education for women. Despite its efforts to establish a freer, more equal society, the French Revolution seemed to be showing no concern for improving the position of women. This shocked Wollstonecraft, who wrote her book in an effort to influence events in France as well as to stir up the state of society in England

The Essay in Focus

The contents. *A Vindication of the Rights of Woman* is divided into thirteen chapters, along with a dedication and an introduction. The dedication is to "M. Tallyrand-Périgord, Late Bishop of Autun," the French minister of education who proposed a national system of education for males only. Wollstonecraft had believed that the post-Revolutionary French nation would honor its claims of equality among citizens, so she was appalled to discover that women were to be excluded from any political reforms that would guarantee equal rights. *A Vindication of the Rights of Woman* was penned in an indignant spirit of protest, which seems to have both given the piece much of its wonderful passion and strength and caused it to be less than perfectly organized and reasoned in certain places.

Addressed in the *Vindication* are several major themes: the justice of educating women in the same way that men are educated; the importance of treating women with dignity and training them to be attentive and intelligent mothers; and the hateful characteristics of women who have been subjected to an environment that demands so little of them. Although Wollstonecraft's attention does turn to lesser issues, such as the hypocrisy of valuing modesty in women at the expense of other more useful and fulfilling characteristics, the desirability of physical exercise for both sexes, and the useless frippery of women's fashion, *A Vindication of the Rights of Woman* time and again returns to the overriding concern of educating women to be more useful and happier members of society.

Wollstonecraft's tack in *A Vindication of the Rights of Woman* is to show how much better life would be for *men* if women were to be treated with more equality. She contends "that the most salutary effects tending to improve mankind might be expected from a REVOLUTION in female manners" (*Vindication*, p. 192). Women behave in foolish, coquettish, and even vicious ways, she contends, because they have not been taught other ways to secure the things they have been bred to desire: fashion, leisure, wealth. The effect on the families of such women is horrible, states Wollstonecraft:

> [These women] spend many of the first years of their lives in acquiring a smattering of accomplishments; meanwhile, strength of body and mind are sacrificed to libertine notions of beauty.... Can they govern a family with judgment, or take care of the poor babes whom they bring into the world?
>
> (*Vindication*, p. 10)

Although Wollstonecraft argues that, at the core, men and women are equal and that a woman should be allowed to pursue any avenue of thought or career that appeals to her individual capabilities or interests, she also understands that most women will go on to be wives and mothers. It is to these women that *A Vindication of the Rights of Woman* is addressed.

Families, as Wollstonecraft sees them, are too often at risk of providing only poisonous and unhappy environments for parents and children. She lays the blame for this situation squarely on the weak characters of women and the selfish shortsightedness of the men who have encouraged them to be that way. In Wollstonecraft's

ideal family, reason would be the principle by which a household organized itself. Mother and father, both educated and in respectful friendship with each other, would employ reason in their domestic duties, teaching their children to do likewise. Families would thus be knit together by love and a sense of responsibility, rather than by the forceful application of a haphazard discipline.

THE OPPOSITION

The writings of Jean Jacques Rousseau (1712-1778), the famous French philosopher, inspired later members of the Romantic movement. At one point, Wollstonecraft was very impressed with Rousseau's social theories, but that changed after she read of his views on female education and the perfect wife. His work on child-rearing, *Emile,* spoke of the best ways in which to educate boys and girls for their future roles in society. Girls, wrote Rousseau, are to be trained as the obedient companions and attentive caregivers for men:

> The education of women should always be relative to men. To please, to be useful to us, to make us love and esteem them, to educate us when young, and take care of us when grown up, to advise, to console us, to render our lives easy and agreeable: these are the duties of women at all times, and what they should be taught in their infancy.
>
> (Rousseau in Wollstonecraft, *Vindication*, pp. 79–80)

Although *A Vindication of the Rights of Woman* has rightly been identified as the earliest source of modern English feminism, it is immediately apparent that its author has little liking for or sympathy with most women of her time. Throughout the essay, she adopts a superior tone that one critic has identified with that of a preachy older sister:

> Her own life-style of economic, intellectual and social independence ... all achieved with difficulty, industry and self-restraint, led Mary Wollstonecraft to believe that she had reached a superior status from which she could give advice to her less self-reliant sisters.
>
> (Lorch, p. 89)

Education. According to Wollstonecraft, the most important method of effecting a "revolution in female manners" is through education. She herself was educated in the day schools of a small town called Beverley, where her family lived for a few years. The experience left her less than elated: "I object to many females being shut up together in nurseries, schools, or convents" (*Vindication*, p. 128). The unhealthiness of being cooped up together also applies to boys, who were most often sent to boarding schools far from home: "At boarding-schools of every description, the relaxation of the junior boys is mischief; and of the senior, vice" (*Vindication*, p. 159).

Wollstonecraft proposed a system of national education, a combination of day school and home schooling. Girls and boys would be taught together, something which would lead to earlier and happier marriages between people who respected each other. Moreover, education should be open to all classes:

> Boys and girls, the rich and poor, should meet together. And to prevent any of the distinctions of vanity, they should be dressed alike, and all obliged to submit to the same discipline, or leave the school
>
> (*Vindication*, p. 168)

WILLIAM BLAKE'S "MARY"

William Blake, the great poet and engraver, was a friend and admirer of Wollstonecraft. After her death, he memorialized her in a poem:

> Some said she was proud, some call'd her a whore,
> And some, when she passed by, shut to the door....
> 'O, why was I born with a different face?
> Why was I not born like this envious race?
> Why did Heaven adorn me with bountiful hand,
> And then set me down in an envious land?'
>
> (William Blake, "Mary," in Sunstein, frontispiece)

In Wollstonecraft's day, girls' education consisted primarily of subjects that might make them desirable as wives. Little Mary Wollstonecraft learned basic arithmetic and literature, but also music and dancing, with just a smattering of French or perhaps Italian. This was the standard curriculum for girls of the middle and upper classes. Recognizing how limiting such studies were, the essay proposed an ideal national education system in which all children learn botany, mechanics, astronomy, reading, writing, arithmetic, natural history, natural philosophy, gymnastics, religion, history, politics, and whatever else would be useful and instructive for them to know.

The education options of English girls of the 1700s were few not only in terms of subject matter, but also in the realm of institutions. If English girls were to receive any further education than the rather paltry offerings open to them in most schools, they had to undertake such studies at home. Such instances of home schooling were rare, for it was commonly held that educating girls was a waste of time because they lacked the ability to reason. One prominent woman of the time, Mrs. Anna Barbauld, a Dissenter whose father taught her modern and classical languages at home, summed up the prevailing attitude: "Women must often be content to know that a thing is so, without understanding the proof.... They cannot investigate; they can remember" (Barbauld in Sunstein, p. 23). Intellectual pursuits that seemed immodest, such as botany (which, presumably, entailed drawing and labeling a plant's reproductive parts) and portraiture (which entailed staring at people), were to be avoided. If a girl could emerge from her school days as a charming and modest woman, then her education was deemed a success.

Marriage and the family. Marriage was one of the few options that women had at the time in which Wollstonecraft was writing. Hardly any "career" choices were open to them, other than being a governess, teacher, or companion to a wealthy woman. Having at one time or another filled all three of these positions, Wollstonecraft was also one of the first English women to make her living through her pen. Wollstonecraft herself was involved in two marriages—only one of which was legal. Before her official marriage to the English philosopher William Godwin (March 29, 1797), she had been involved with an American man, Gilbert Imlay, in a relationship both regarded as a marriage, though it was never legalized as such. Her relationship with Imlay began in Paris in 1793, the year after the publication of *A Vindication of the Rights of Woman*; readers of that work may be struck by the difference between the strength of her pronouncements on marriage and motherhood and the very sad and vulnerable single mother who struggled in 1795 to detach herself emotionally from her unsuccessful relationship with Imlay.

Wollstonecraft acknowledges in *A Vindication of the Rights of Woman* that the majority of women will marry and that they can be of most use socially as educated and talented domestic authorities. Marriage, she maintains, should be a matter of friendship and equality, without the distracting and destructive force of passion or sexual tensions. Passion quickly passes, and if it has been the basis for marriage, then the whole family is in jeopardy:

> Personal attachment is a very happy foundation for friendship; yet, when even two virtuous young people marry, it would, perhaps, be happy if some circumstances checked their passion.... In that case they would ... try to render the whole of life respectable, by forming a plan to regulate a friendship which only death ought to dissolve.
>
> (*Vindication*, p. 93)

Perhaps because of her own unhappy treatment at the hands of a cold mother, Wollstonecraft associated the presence and passing of sexual passion in a marriage with the neglect of children. She even goes so far as to speculate that the sexually neglected wife makes the best mother, for she will lavish all the attention that her husband refuses upon her children. It is, perhaps, wise to remember that marriage turned out to be a disaster for many of the women that Wollstonecraft loved: her sister Eliza fled her home and her newborn infant, claiming abuse at the hands of her husband, and her best friend Fanny Blood pined away for years, waiting for her beloved to ask her to marry him. When he finally did, she died shortly thereafter in childbirth.

Sources. The Dissenters exerted an important influence on Wollstonecraft. She was exposed as well to other English women writers who argued for the improved education of females and for their basic equality in the home and in society. For example, in the anonymous tract "Woman Not Inferior to Man" (1739), written perhaps by Lady Mary Wortley Montagu, it was argued that denying education to women turned them into the slaves of men. Catherine Macaulay's *Letters on Education* (1790), one of the books that Wollstonecraft reviewed for the *Analytical Review,* influenced her ideas about physical as well as mental training for women.

Wollstonecraft's friend Thomas Paine, himself the author of **Common Sense** (also covered in *Literature and Its Times*) and a work entitled *The Rights of Man,* may have been the person who told her about the Marquis de Condorcet, a French writer. Condorcet was an outspoken advocate of equal rights for French women, and England had not yet produced his counterpart.

William Godwin, husband of Mary Wollstonecraft.

His 1790 *Essai sur l'admission des femmes au droit de cité* (On the granting of civil rights to women) supported the idea of letting women property owners vote, and pointed out that France was behaving inconsistently in permitting a country to be governed by a female ruler but failing to allow women of that country to be citizens.

Reviews. As a treatise on education, *A Vindication of the Rights of Woman* was fairly well received; few critics, however, seemed to notice its revolutionary potential. After Wollstonecraft's death, William Godwin published his *Memoirs of the Author of Vindication of the Rights of Woman* (1798). Although this work was written with the best of intentions, it met with the worst of results. Among other details, Godwin made public his wife's illicit relationship with Gilbert Imlay, her suicide attempts in the aftermath of its breakup, and the fact that Godwin and Wollstonecraft had lived together before being married. Wollstonecraft had been calling herself "Mrs. Imlay" ever since she returned to England from Europe in 1795, but when she married Godwin it became public knowledge that she and Imlay had never actually been married. The social scandal that resulted in the aftermath of Godwin's book weakened the impact of Wollstonecraft's writings. As one biographer reported, *European Magazine* in April 1798 portrayed her as a disgusting example to delicate ladies:

> The latter part of her life was blemished with actions which must consign her name to posterity as one whose example if followed would be attended by the most pernicious [harmful] consequences to society.
>
> (Nixon, p. 253)

Wollstonecraft and Godwin suffered at the hands of cruel reviews. But a friend, Mary Hays, tried to keep alive the message about women's rights that Wollstonecraft wanted to convey. Shortly after Wollstonecraft's death, Hays published *Appeal to the Men of Great Britain in Behalf of the Women* (1798). Her work met with the same response as Wollstonecraft's, probably because of her personal pursuit of relationships with men who were not interested in her. Contemporary women writers were careful to distance themselves from the two disgraced Marys, and for a long time British feminism took a much quieter and more gradual approach to women's rights.

It was not until the Education Act of 1870 that the schooling of girls finally became compulsory in England. The legislation passed almost eighty years after Wollstonecraft had written her urgently worded essay calling for new public policy on the schooling of the English female.

For More Information

Lorch, Jennifer. *Mary Wollstonecraft: The Making of a Radical Feminist.* New York: Berg, 1990.

Mellor, Anne K. *Romanticism and Gender.* New York: Routledge, 1993.

Nixon, Edna. *Mary Wollstonecraft: Her Life and Times.* London: J. M. Dent & Sons, 1971.

Sunstein, Emily W. *A Different Face: The Life of Mary Wollstonecraft.* New York: Harper & Row, 1975.

Wollstonecraft, Mary. *A Vindication of the Rights of Woman.* Edited by Carol H. Poston. New York: W. W. Norton, 1988.

Wuthering Heights

by
Emily Brontë

Growing up in the isolated moors of northern England, young Emily Brontë and her siblings relied on their environment for entertainment and exploration. They also invented complex fantasy worlds, complete with imaginary histories. In the late 1840s Emily and her sisters Charlotte and Anne drew on their experiences to pen novels that focused on the relationships and particular qualities of their native home.

THE LITERARY WORK

A novel set in Yorkshire, England, between 1771 and 1803; published in 1848.

SYNOPSIS

A dual love story involving two neighboring families spans two generations.

Events in History at the Time the Novel Takes Place

The Romantic period. For much of the 1700s, European society elevated reason and the intellect above feelings. Around the 1750s, however, people began to show renewed interest in earlier medieval romances, which focused on the emotions and exploits of individuals as well as strange and mysterious aspects of life. This interest in medieval romance grew, fanned in part by France's Revolutionary War of 1789, an event that inspired a sense of rebirth and renewal as well as a freer political atmosphere throughout Europe.

By the 1790s a new trend in English literature was evident. This was commonly called the Romantic movement, named after the interest in medieval romances that had first sparked it. *Wuthering Heights* was one of the principal works of this era. Brontë's novel dealt with such key concerns of the movement as nature, individuals and their feelings, and the mystical or supernatural.

Landed gentry. The landed gentry of England fell just below royalty in social rank. Unlike the family of the king or queen, however, the future of such a family was not assured. From the sixteenth to the nineteenth centuries, holding on to the land owned by a family was the only way to ensure a comfortable existence for future generations. Property served as the sole means through which to safeguard the family name, money, and social position.

A country house owned by one of these aristocratic families was commonly known as a "seat." This seat referred not only to the structure and land itself, but more importantly, to the family history and ancestral traditions associated with the residence. In almost all cases, the family property included a burial ground and place of worship. The properties described in *Wuthering Heights* included similar features. For instance, at one point in the novel the housekeeper Ellen Dean remarks that the place of Mrs. Catherine Linton's burial, "to the surprise of the villagers, was neither in the chapel, under the carved monument of the Lintons, nor yet by the tombs of her own relations, outside" (Brontë, *Wuthering Heights,* p. 130). Since the notion of joining loved ones in eternal rest was an all important aspect of family unity, Catherine's separate burial served to emphasize her independent nature.

Generally, five variables ensured the continuation of the family seat. These were:

1. The building itself
2. The land
3. Family heirlooms within the structure
4. Family name
5. Hereditary title (such as "earl" or "duke")

Nearly all seats passed from father to firstborn male, but if none existed, the next closest male relative stood to inherit the property. Some families passed property through what was known as a "strict settlement" device. Developed in 1650 and practiced until 1880, this act virtually tied the hands of heirs by transferring control of the property to a trustee. In his will, a fa-

---

WALKING FOR MENTAL RECREATION

The sole recreation mentioned in *Wuthering Heights* involves rambling walks taken through the moors. During the nineteenth century, walking became associated with the intellectual pursuits of such individuals as parsons, schoolmasters, and the learned aristocracy. It was not done for physical exercise but instead for its mental and emotional rewards.

---

ther could place his holdings in the keeping of a trustee who would preserve the seat for a son, safeguard a daughter's pension, and provide adequate financial support for any future offspring. In Wuthering Heights the owner of Thrushcross Grange attempts to implement this strict settlement procedure before his death, for he wants to ensure that his daughter, Cathy, receives her inheritance. But he fails to alter his will before his death. The land thus passes first to her husband. After he dies, ownership of the land passes to his father Heathcliff. This series of events leaves the daughter penniless while her father-in-law, Heathcliff, ends up with Thrushcross Grange and the area of Wuthering Heights.

Marriage. Incest between nuclear family members was forbidden under laws passed by King Henry VIII back in the sixteenth century. By the

eighteenth century English society favored marriages between close, but not direct, blood ties. A union between first cousins was regarded as ideal since it preserved both family landholdings and social connections. The most typical arrangement in a marriage between cousins featured a woman who married her father's brother's son. This kind of union kept the seat of the bride's family under their control. In *Wuthering Heights,* however, Cathy marries her father's *sister's* son. When her father dies, his landholding passes to her husband and then to her father-in-law. Possession of the seat is lost to her father's family as a result.

Servants. Although servants who signed contracts for wage labor were often utilized by landholding families of the era, the most effective way to ensure adequate help was to establish a sense of "family loyalty" among the servants. Since most families were tied to their land, servants sometimes remained in the same household with one family for their entire lives. Because such homes usually employed a staff of between thirty and forty persons, a hierarchy divided the house into "upper" and "lower" servants. Lower servants were staff members supervised by the upper servants. Male upper servant positions included steward, kitchen and stable clerk, valet, butler, gardener, and groom. In *Wuthering Heights,* Heathcliff's servant Joseph served as both valet and steward. Female upper servant positions included lady's woman (a personal servant who assisted the lady of the house in everything from getting dressed to organizing her social calendar), housekeeper, cook, and nurse. The housekeeper's position could be enlarged to include supervision of maids, control of the kitchen, and care of the children, as is the case with the character of Ellen in *Wuthering Heights.* The rise in servants' wages often made this type of combined duty necessary, and in households such as the one depicted in *Wuthering Heights,* where the family was not given to entertaining, a staff of smaller size made more economic sense.

Mourning. Mourning was a practice wherein people wore dark, somber clothing after a death for a period of time appropriate to one's relation with the deceased. An older female member of the family typically kept track of deaths. After a family member passed away, it was her responsibility to inform the household as to how long the mourning period for that person would last. This ritual served three purposes—it publicly indicated one's affection for the deceased; it maintained harmony with living relatives; and it aided the bereaved in coping with their own grief. This practice is referred to at one point in *Wuthering Heights,* when the servant Ellen is "bid to get mourning" for the daughter in the house, whose mother has died (*Wuthering Heights,* p. 153). This is a social as well as personal request.

The following table indicates the appropriate periods of mourning in the 1700s. As is evident, social expectations of the time dictated that even some rather distant family relations be honored with a period of mourning.

12 months:	Death of husband or wife
6 months:	Death of parents or parents-in-law
3 months:	Death of sibling, uncle, or aunt
6 weeks:	Death of sister-in-law
3 weeks:	Death of aunt who remarried or cousin
1 week:	Death of second cousin or husband of stepmother's sister

The Novel in Focus

The plot. *Wuthering Heights* combines first-person and third-person narration. The opening of the novel uses a first-person point of view, telling the story from the perspective of Lockwood, a renter at Thrushcross Grange. Lockwood is in fact a virtual stranger in the isolated moors. The reader initially finds him calling at the nearby estate, Wuthering Heights, in an effort to meet his only neighbor and landlord, Heathcliff. Forced by a snowfall to stay the night in the unfamiliar house, Lockwood reads from a diary belonging to a woman named Catherine Earnshaw. Strange dreams and ghostly figures accompany his sleep. Upon returning home, Lockwood falls ill. During his convalescence he asks his housekeeper, Ellen Dean, to shed light on the mysterious family at the Heights. Dean obliges, for she has served on the property since birth and knows the details of Heathcliff and his household. The housekeeper proceeds to relate the family's history, beginning with the events of the year 1771. Brontë uses this third-person narration for most of her text.

The housekeeper's history of Wuthering Heights begins with Mr. and Mrs. Earnshaw, who occupy the seat with their two children, Hindley and Catherine, ages fourteen and six, respectively. To the shock and horror of his family, Mr. Earnshaw returns one evening from a business trip with an orphan child, whom he adopts and names Heathcliff. Catherine finds in Heathcliff a constant companion and playmate, but his unknown lineage relegates him to an inferior status

in the household. Within five years of the boy's arrival, both parents die and their son Hindley becomes master of the Heights. Hindley, who always resented Heathcliff's presence, creates misery for the adopted boy. Catherine falls victim to her brother's tyranny as well, but she and Heathcliff find comfort in each other.

One day Catherine and Heathcliff escape from the house and trek four miles to Thrushcross Grange, where they encounter the Linton family. Heathcliff is turned away, but Catherine, who had injured an ankle, stays for five weeks. During this time she becomes fast friends with the Linton children, Edgar and Isabella. When she returns to Wuthering Heights, she has matured and exhibits a new interest in propriety. This change both intimidates and angers Heathcliff. A gap develops between Catherine and Heathcliff that Hindley widens at every possible turn. After his wife, Frances, dies in childbirth, Hindley grows even more unpleasant. Taking no comfort in Hareton, his healthy baby boy, Hindley turns to alcohol.

CURRER, ELLIS, AND ACTON BELL

Emily was by no means the only author in her family. Her sisters Charlotte and Anne received literary recognition for the novels *Jane Eyre* (also covered in *Literature and Its Times*) and *Agnes Grey,* respectively. Due to the male bias of the Victorian Age, however, each girl wrote under a pseudonym. Charlotte published as Currer Bell, Anne as Acton Bell, and Emily as Ellis Bell. One publisher, convinced that all three novels were composed by the same author, demanded to meet all three women at once. Although Emily would not attend, Charlotte and Anne traveled to London to allay his suspicions.

Although Catherine still loves her former playmate, as the years progress she realizes that her social position requires a marriage to Edgar Linton. Heathcliff overhears Catherine voice her intention to wed Edgar but remains unaware of her love for him. Brokenhearted, he disappears. Three years later, Edgar and Catherine marry and settle down at Thrushcross Grange, living in apparent harmony until Heathcliff's return.

When Heathcliff returns he is a grown man with a sum of money. He takes up residence at Wuthering Heights with the hated Hindley and waits for an opportunity to exact revenge for Hindley's earlier mistreatment of him. To the great distress of Edgar, Heathcliff also visits frequently at the Grange for the pleasure of Catherine's company. Edgar's sister, Isabella, unexpectedly reveals her own affection for the unwelcome caller, and soon she and Heathcliff elope. Edgar, in anger, refuses to recognize Isabella and bans Heathcliff from the house. Nevertheless, Heathcliff manages to return and finds Catherine in poor health. She bears a daughter, Cathy, then passes away.

Though grief-stricken by his wife's death, Edgar takes comfort in the baby and his life with her. When little Cathy is thirteen, Edgar is called away to tend to his dying sister, Isabella. She, it turns out, left Heathcliff early in their marriage to live alone and raise her sickly son, Linton Heathcliff. Upon her death, Edgar returns with the boy to Thrushcross Grange, but the boy's father, Heathcliff, soon demands his son's presence at Wuthering Heights. Heathcliff is now the owner of Wuthering Heights, for Hindley died the same year as Catherine, and he had mortgaged his property to Heathcliff.

BRONTË ON DEATH

Emily Brontë felt a great "closeness to the dead, greater sometimes than her closeness to the living," and she was convinced "that the dead do not leave the earth" (Chitham, pp. 200, 207).

Heathcliff and Edgar reject each other's company. In a chance meeting, however, Cathy and Linton make each other's acquaintance. Cathy, who is a free spirit like her mother, frequently disobeys her father and visits Linton. Heathcliff's desire to hurt his old rival Edgar is so great that he holds Cathy prisoner and forces her to marry his son, Linton. Within a week, Cathy escapes to say one final good-bye to her dying father. Her new husband dies three months later.

Cathy grows bitter after Linton's death and she refuses to have anything to do with the household at the Heights. She eventually befriends Hindley's son Hareton, however, and their friendship blossoms into love after Heathcliff's death. The close of the novel promises their eventual marriage.

The supernatural relationship between Heathcliff and Catherine. Heathcliff obviously never fully recovers from Catherine's death. Upon hear-

ing of her death, he cries, "I pray one prayer—I repeat it till my tongue stiffens—Catherine Earnshaw, may you not rest, as long as I am living! You said I killed you—haunt me then!" (*Wuthering Heights,* p. 129). Unable to withstand her mortal absence, he entreats her spirit to remain on earth with him. Lockwood overhears him begging to the wind "[Catherine] do come. Oh, do—once more!" (*Wuthering Heights,* p. 23). This love, which crosses the boundary between earthly and heavenly realms, incorporates aspects of Christian mysticism.

During the nineteenth century, Christian mysticism gained a rather large following. It was a movement based on the belief that a developing self-consciousness is vital to religious growth. Mysticism focuses primarily on the "immediate contact real or supposed between the human soul and the soul of the world" (Elliott-Binns, p. 289). Relative contemporaries of Emily Brontë such as the writers William Blake, William Wordsworth, and Samuel Taylor Coleridge explored these mystical feelings throughout their poems. They express seemingly supernatural experiences—visions, for example—that foster a greater self-awareness.

The characters in *Wuthering Heights,* however, are unable to achieve harmony between their mystical feelings and human duties in the earthly world. The author instead describes a doctrine of suffering on earth. There was a feeling among some Christian mystics that a balance between the human self and the divine was not possible because one's presence on earth was an exile from God. Brontë's work depicts this perceived disharmony between the natural and supernatural. Before his death, the character Heathcliff senses "a strange change approaching" that seems to fuse his mortal soul with that of the deceased Catherine (*Wuthering Heights,* p. 245). He finds solace in the prospect of his own death and eats nothing for four days to hasten the process. His most welcome rest occurs when he leaves his life on earth and lies beside his Catherine in the grave.

Sources. Although the majority of the novel's characters owe their creation entirely to Brontë's imagination, a brief period of employment as a governess provided the author with the opportunity to view many inspirational structures in the Yorkshire area that served as models for the estates of Wuthering Heights and Thrushcross Grange. A building called High Withins, located in Haworth Moor, provided the setting for Wuthering Heights, although some of the fic-

High Sunderland Hall, in Halifax, West Yorkshire. Brontë used some of the features of this structure in creating the Wuthering Heights house.

tional house's features also come from High Sunderland Hall in Halifax. Another local building, Ponden Hall, offered the inspiration for Thrushcross Grange. Not all of Emily's sources, however, came from architectural structures.

Brontë's mother died in 1821, when Emily was only three years old. This aspect of the author's life may help explain why so many children featured in *Wuthering Heights* grow up without their mothers. After the death of Brontë's mother, a housemaid named Tabitha Akroyd became a maternal figure. Akroyd was a country woman whose strong Yorkshire dialect resurfaces through the speeches of the old servant Joseph in the novel, while the friendship that she provided comes across in the character of Ellen Dean. In real life, "Tabby cooked and cleaned and ruled the [Brontë] children with a rough though loving hand" (Bentley, p. 27). The character Ellen owes much of her personality to this inspiration.

As for the characters of Heathcliff and Catherine, the basis for their personalities was perhaps planted by "Tabby" as well. She used to entertain the Brontë children with tales of a long dead minister, Mr. Grimshaw, who adopted several orphan children and took them into his parsonage. These tales, coupled with the author's imagination, may have helped shape the hero and heroine of her novel.

Events in History at the Time the Novel Was Written

The Victorian Age (1837-1901). Nineteenth-century England was an age of expansionism. While Western civilization had previously looked to Paris as a trendsetter, by the second half of the 1800s London had assumed that role. Its population grew in sixty years from 2 million to 6.5 million, a jump due in large part to the Industrial Revolution, which triggered a shift from agricultural communities to factory-oriented towns. Emily Brontë and her sisters grew up in the waning years of England's rural age.

Yorkshire. Emily Brontë, who was fairly isolated from the outside world, based all her writing on experiences in her native Haworth, Yorkshire, located in northern England. It is this landscape that she draws upon for the setting of *Wuthering Heights*. During Queen Victoria's reign (1837-1901), the regional architecture offered buildings made of a coarse-grained rock called gritstone. The cottages sat beneath low, gabled roofs and held rows of narrow windows. Like Thrushcross Grange, many of these buildings lay nestled deep in V-shaped hollows. Surrounding the properties were the Yorkshire moors. These marshy wastelands provided hours of exploration not only for the Brontë children, but for

Haworth Moor in Yorkshire, believed to be the inspiration for the location of *Wuthering Heights*.

Emily Brontë's characters as well. One Brontë biographer described the landscape as "sombre, sweeping slopes of black rock, rough pale grass and tough heather . . . scoured by strong Atlantic winds which drive clouds turbulently across the grey sky" (Bentley, pp. 21-2), and added that no

---

ILLNESS IN THE NOVEL

Emily Brontë lost two older sisters, Maria and Elizabeth, to tuberculosis after they stayed at a negligent boarding school. They died at the ages of twelve and ten, respectively. The effect of these deaths on young Emily can be seen in the manner by which Edgar and Linton die in *Wuthering Heights*. Both take ill with ailments that linger for months before finally killing them. Because of poor heating, nourishment, and medical care, such early deaths were not uncommon in the English moor land.

---

author of the English language so aptly detailed these surroundings as Emily Brontë in *Wuthering Heights*.

The region was often buffeted by fierce weather as well. The ferocious storms that Brontë

witnessed during her childhood instilled in her an addiction to the tumultuous weather. This fascination with the tempestuous weather of the area found its way into her novels. Heathcliff and Catherine, for instance, both brave violent storms in *Wuthering Heights*.

Folklore. Tabby Akroyd, the maid who became a maternal figure to Emily Brontë, was a Christian woman of religious conviction. But she was equally partial to the country lore of the Yorkshire community. When she entered the Brontë household in 1824 at the age of fifty-six, she carried with her memories and tales reaching back into the 1780s. That period was an age when villagers believed in a variety of fairies, ghosts, and apparitions. Yorkshire residents, in fact, warned visitors of apparitions such as the ghost of Holy Trinity Church or the headless woman who accosted horsemen at White Cross. In Brontë's novel, Lockwood has a dream in which Catherine pays him a ghostly visit, a scene inspired to some degree by these childhood stories told by Tabby.

Other pieces of folklore find their way into the novel as well. Throughout the course of her novel, for instance, Emily Brontë describes several deathbed watches. In one scene, Edgar maintains a night-long vigil at the side of Catherine's body after her death. This prompts Ellen to remark, "I don't know if it be a peculiarity in me, but I am seldom otherwise than happy while watching in the chamber of death" (*Wuthering Heights,* p. 127). She finds comfort in the "repose that neither earth nor hell can break" (*Wuthering Heights,* p. 127). According to Yorkshire custom, the corpse had to be laid out and watched constantly until the time of its burial. This served to ensure the peaceful sleep that Ellen discusses.

There were rituals to observe in attending funerals as well. Brontë makes the point that "Isabella was not asked" to accompany Catherine's body to the grave. The term "bidding" describes this invitation. One or two local women would tell neighbors, friends, and relatives of the recent death and ask them to attend the funeral. It was an honor to be "bid," and failing to extend the honor usually indicated or caused a family dispute. In *Wuthering Heights,* Isabella's absence demonstrates Edgar's anger toward her. Apparently such funeral practices continued well beyond the time of the novel's publication and Emily Brontë's death.

Religion. The daughter of a minister, Brontë experienced the impact of religion on a daily basis. Although her father was a loving man, in 1824 the six-year-old Emily was sent to join her sisters at the Clergy Daughter's Boarding School at Cowen Bridge. There the Reverend Carus Wilson preached a devout, evangelical lifestyle that struck fear in the hearts of his pupils. The reverend told the small children frequent tales of death and hell and doled out liberal doses of punishment. Living conditions were also poor, for the school was cold and the nourishment given to the children was substandard. Brontë perhaps recalled these early experiences when she wrote *Wuthering Heights,* for at one point the character Joseph recalls his experiences in a harsh religious climate that was steeped in the fear of God.

Reception of the novel. Unlike Charlotte Brontë's *Jane Eyre,* published in the same year as *Wuthering Heights,* Emily Brontë's novel did not meet with critical success. It contained several printer's errors, and most reviewers found her work to be "the product of a dogged, brutal and morose mind" (Bentley, p. 96). Though the subject remains open to debate, most scholars agree that this professional disappointment accelerated Emily Brontë's death from tuberculosis in December 1848. Two years later, her book appeared in a second edition that included a preface by her sister Charlotte. The moving words penned by Emily's sister perhaps aided this edition, for it was well received and has since been regarded as a masterful tale of passion and revenge.

For More Information

Bentley, Phyllis. *The Brontës.* London: Thames & Hudson, 1969.

Brontë, Emily. *Wuthering Heights.* New York: W. W. Norton, 1990.

Chitham, Edward. *A Life of Emily Brontë.* Oxford: Blackwell, 1987.

Elliott-Binns, L. E. *Religion in the Victorian Era.* London: Lutterworth Press, 1953.

Mingay, G. E. *The Gentry.* New York: Longman Group, 1976.

Nicholson, John. *Folk Lore of East Yorkshire.* London: Simpkin, Marshall, Hamilton, Kent, 1890.

Wallace, Anne D. *Walking, Literature, and English Culture.* Oxford: Clarendon Press, 1993.

"Young Goodman Brown"

by
Nathaniel Hawthorne

Nathaniel Hawthorne's great-great-grandfather, William Hathorne, immigrated to the Massachusetts Bay Colony in 1630. He settled in Salem, the colony's oldest town, and became one of Salem's most prominent townsmen. An Indian fighter and a judge, Hathorne in one instance ordered that a burglar's ear be cut off and his forehead branded with the letter *B*—both common punishments at that time. During Salem's 1691-1692 witchcraft frenzy, in which many townspeople were accused of being witches, his son, John Hathorne, interrogated suspects such as Martha Corey, who was later hanged as a witch. Corey would become a character in "Young Goodman Brown." The fact that Hawthorne's ancestors had pursued such "evildoers" on behalf of the Puritan faith troubled him. Although there is no evidence for this claim, some have suggested that his ancestors' actions bothered him so much that he changed the spelling of his last name to distance himself from them.

Events in History at the Time the Short Story Takes Place

The Puritan colonies. The Puritan religion grew out of the religious void that existed in England in the late 1500s when King Henry VIII severed ties between England and the Catholic pope. The purpose and structure of organized religion became subjects of serious debate. One result of this debate was Puritanism, which has been simply defined as "a belief that the Church of England should be purged of its hierarchy and of the

THE LITERARY WORK

A short story set in Salem Village, in the Massachusetts Bay Colony, about 1690; first published in 1835 in the *New England Magazine;* subsequently published in 1846 in *Mosses from an Old Manse,* Hawthorne's fourth collection of short stories.

SYNOPSIS

A young man appears to attend a witches' Sabbath presided over by the devil, who reveals to the man the secret evil of humankind.

traditions and ceremonies inherited from Rome" (Morgan, p. 7). Puritanism stripped organized religion of the ceremonial trappings as well as the hierarchy of authority that existed in the Catholic Church. The Puritan Church was a spare, ascetic religious body that placed responsibility for salvation on the individual rather than on religious leaders. As their numbers grew and they became increasingly disheartened by the perceived corruption and sin present in their country, English Puritans sought ways to "purify" the Protestant Church of England (Anglican Church) as well. Puritan ministers spoke of traveling to a new place to establish a "pure" church, thereby avoiding the vengeance that they believed was an inevitable result of God's displeasure with sinful England.

Beginning in 1620 Puritan settlers began to establish colonies in New England—spreading from Massachusetts to Connecticut, Maine, and New Hampshire. These early colonists attempted to devote their lives to performing God's work, establishing not a democracy but a theocracy, a society governed by religious laws and values. These Puritan immigrants believed that hard work, a strict interpretation of the Bible, and devotion to biblical ideas and values would enable them to recreate God's first earthly paradise, the Garden of Eden. Over time, however, the Puritan settlers grew more worldly; acquisition of material wealth became a preoccupation of the Puritans. In this respect, Puritan theology presents a paradox: while viewed as a distraction from performing God's work, material riches were also seen as evidence of God's grace, a sign that the wealthy person was among the "elect," those whom God had predestined to go to heaven after death.

Puritan beliefs and the Half-Way Covenant. Puritans believed that due to Adam's original sin—disobeying God in the Garden of Eden—human beings were impure creatures, incapable of bettering their status in the eyes of God. However, the Puritans also believed that God was loving and had predestined some of his fallen creatures for salvation.

Those fortunate enough to have been predestined for salvation would supposedly pass through several stages on earth. A key stage was sanctification, in which the person became spiritually awakened and felt reborn—in effect, underwent a conversion from sinner to saint. Full membership in the church was restricted to those who could convince others that they had passed through this stage. A candidate for full membership would be questioned by officers of the church. If satisfied with the answers, they might then ask the candidate for a public confession, a description of his or her born-again experience. Finally the candidate would be voted into full membership. In other words, he or she would become a saint.

Around the 1650s, in the second generation of Puritans who came to America, far fewer than before stepped forward to claim full membership in the church. They had been baptized, but this indicated only that there was a likelihood that they would become saints, not that the transition from sinner to saint was a certainty. Their parents, sorely disappointed at how few of the second generation were becoming full members, worried about the survival of their churches. A question arose. The second generation were now adults with children of their own. Were third-generation children entitled to be baptized into the faith if their parents had not yet become full members? In 1662 some leaders responded "yes," and the Half-Way Covenant came into being. The covenant gave these adults and children of the later generations half-way membership in the church in exchange for their leading Christian lives.

In Hawthorne's short story, his main character, Young Goodman Brown, is a third-generation Puritan. Whether Brown is a full or a half-way member of the church is unclear. He, however, presumes that his fate is already sealed—he will be saved. After all, God had made a covenant with his grandfather and his grandfather's seed, or offspring. If Brown sins for one night, he reasons, it is of little consequence. But Puritan religion taught that there were no guarantees; even full members could not bank on salvation for certain. In fact, Brown's line of reasoning was in itself regarded as a sin.

At the end of the story, Brown becomes preoccupied with his thoughts. Soul-searching and self-examination were common in Puritan society as individuals tried to fathom their own true nature and destiny. Therefore, Brown's behavior here would not have been altogether unusual. He, however, moves through life gloomily, apparently plagued by thoughts not only of himself but also of the evil in all humankind, and this distinguishes him from most of the other Puritans in Salem. They were, to be sure, a serious group, but their beliefs did not stop them from sometimes acting gay and lighthearted, as Brown's wife, Faith, does in the story.

The Salem witchcraft trials and spectral evidence. In 1691 the colonists in Salem suffered a number of blows, including a harsh winter, steep taxes by the British colonial government, and an outbreak of smallpox. Bloody encounters with nearby Indian tribes had also become part of the colony's recent history. It seemed obvious to some members of the community that all of this trouble could have only one cause: the devil. The Bible, which had warned them of the devil's evil intentions, had also warned them of witches, humans who do the devil's work.

In 1692 the Reverend Samuel Parris served as the pastor of Salem Village Church. For reasons that have never been entirely clear, Parris's niece and daughter began to behave strangely, running through the house, shrieking, and displaying unprecedented defiance of adult authority. Parris called the village physician, who quickly diagnosed that the girls had been possessed by demons. The odd behavior of the Parris girls soon surfaced in other Salem young people. They charged that several individuals in the village had "bewitched" them.

In Salem Village the penalty for witchcraft was death. A special court of Oyer and Terminer (to hear and determine) was assembled to hear the cases against those accused of witchcraft. Among the judges was John Hathorne, Nathaniel Hawthorne's great-grandfather. Like other court examiners, Hathorne relied upon hearsay, forced confessions, and "spectral evidence" to convict thirty-one people of witchcraft.

Spectral evidence, which played the most vital role in the Salem witchcraft trials, was evidence that appeared only to the alleged victims of witchcraft. During the trials, accusers often claimed to see an apparition of the accused. They blamed these apparitions for the witchcraft that was causing such turmoil in Salem. This spectral evidence was seen as important because of the prevailing belief that these apparitions were prompted by Satan, who had made a pact with the person whose image he had assumed. It was believed that any specters who looked like one of the defendants must be acting with his or her permission; through the power of the devil, people's specters were enacting their evil wishes.

One of the remarkable facts of the Salem witch trials is that no one who confessed was hanged. Only those accused persons who persistently denied committing the crime of witchcraft were executed. Fifty-five accused people confessed and received reprieves, while twenty men and women who refused to admit wrongdoing were executed.

The admission of spectral evidence as a determining factor in convicting the accused seems to have been an aspect of the trials that greatly interested Hawthorne. In his story, Young Goodman Brown sees what may be specters of townspeople—Goodwife Cloyse, Goodwife Corey, and his own bride, Faith. Their appearances in "Young Goodman Brown" resemble the specters cited as evidence in the witchcraft trials.

The decline of spectral evidence. The Salem witch hysteria of 1691-92 finally died down because the use of spectral evidence to convict an accused witch fell into disrepute. It was not that fear of the devil flagged in Puritan society. On the contrary, people began to contend that the devil might as easily appear in the shape of an innocent victim who had never conspired with him as in the shape of a guilty one. Opinion gradually changed, and it came to be thought that

such evidence could no longer be trusted. Perhaps more important to understanding the short story than any other fact is a decision reached in 1692 by a group of Boston churchman. It was possible, they agreed, for a demon to take the shape of an innocent man or woman, in which case the demon and not the innocent person was committing the crime. In other words, a victim thought to have been hurt by, for example, old Goody Cloyse might have seen an evil spirit who had assumed her shape while she was sleeping harmlessly and peacefully in her bed.

In Hawthorne's story, not only spectral evidence but visible evidence in general is held to be untrustworthy. The story places full members of the Puritan faith at the witch-meeting in the forest, suggesting that outward signs of goodness—such as regular attendance at church services—are not a true indication of a person's inner nature. Hawthorne distrusted organized religion in both early Puritan and his own times, a view that surfaces in "Young Goodman Brown."

Puritans and the devil. The Puritans believed that the American colonies existed on lands that had once belonged to the devil. They further believed that they had disturbed the devil by settling in his territories, a belief discussed by the famous Puritan minister Cotton Mather in his book *Wonders of the Invisible World* (1693). The Puritans therefore lived in constant fear of the devil's wrath. They attributed Indian attacks, famine, and sickness to the devil, who they believed was launching reprisals for their invasion of his domain. Guided by Mather's book, they regarded the so-called witches of Salem as another part of the devil's plot. The devil, warned Mather, aimed to use witchcraft to uproot the Christian faith and restore devil worship to the area; a witch, he recalled, had informed them of this forty years earlier, before they had executed her.

The Puritans thought that the wilderness surrounding their colonies had achieved its "wildness" because it was the retreat of the devil. It was from this wilderness that the Indians, who the Puritans believed were servants of the devil, launched their attacks on the villages. It is appropriate, then, that the wilderness featured in "Young Goodman Brown" becomes the meeting ground for the villagers who are devoted to the devil.

This fear in the Puritan community that some of its members were in league with the devil was aggravated by the Salem witch trials. The testimony of some individuals was particularly troubling. For instance, one woman accused of witchcraft, a slave named Tituba, gave testimony that

An artist's rendering of a witch trial.

she had seen the devil's book and had observed marks made in it by nine members of the village. The Puritans believed that marks in the devil's book signified a pact made with him by members of their community. Such testimony heightened an already existing anxiety.

The Short Story in Focus

The plot. "Young Goodman Brown" tells the story of a young man of the colonial middle class who has a prearranged meeting in the forest with a mysterious stranger. Told in third person by a nameless narrator, the story begins at sunset when Brown, who does not heed his young wife's pleas to the contrary, leaves his home to venture off into the forest. Before long Brown seems to have second thoughts about keeping his mysterious appointment, but he encounters an old man who appears to resemble Brown's father. The stranger persuades Brown to continue through the forest.

After walking a while with the old stranger, Brown again wants to turn back. An old woman whom Brown recognizes as Goody Cloyse, a "very pious and exemplary dame, who had taught him his catechism in youth," then appears walking along the forest path (Hawthorne, "Young Goodman Brown," p. 137). The woman addresses Brown's companion as "the Devil" and

appears to be familiar with him; this familiarity causes Brown great distress. After the woman leaves, Brown hears the voices of the minister and deacon of his village discussing the meeting in the forest to which they are traveling. This incident disturbs Brown as well.

Finally, Brown hears the rolling sound of voices emanating out of a black mass of cloud. The voices belong to a great many people in his village, including his new wife, Faith. As he listens to the voices of the cloud screaming and laughing, he hears his wife pleading for something unknown and sees her pink ribbon float down out of the cloud, then catch on a branch in the forest. This seems to drive Brown to madness, and he races wildly through the forest, finally arriving at an eerily lit clearing populated by Salem villagers and Indian priests. In the clearing "a figure," possibly the devil, stands at a stone altar. The figure offers "communion" to Brown in order that Brown may accept and surrender to the evil that resides in the hearts of all people. In addition, there is to be another new initiate at the ceremony—Brown's wife. Brown cries for her to look heavenward and resist the offer.

The next morning Brown returns to the village. The narrator wonders whether Brown actually attended a witch-meeting or whether it was all a dream. From that night on, though, Young

CHARACTERS AND THEIR SOURCES

In the Story	Real-life Source
Goody Cloyse	Sarah Cloyse—convicted of witchcraft, but later reprieved
Goody Corey	Martha Corey—hanged for witchcraft in 1692
Martha Carrier	Martha Carrier—hanged for witchcraft in 1692
Deacon Gookin	Daniel Gookin—Superintendent of the Indians and the author of a book on the native peoples of Massachusetts
Brown's grandfather	William Hathorne, Nathaniel Hawthorne's great-great-grandfather and an original Puritan settler
Brown's father	John Hathorne—Nathaniel Hawthorne's great-grandfather, a fanatical Puritan who examined suspects at the Salem witch trials

Goodman Brown recoils from the villagers and often shrinks away from Faith, his own wife.

Dreams in "Young Goodman Brown." The question of the reality of the events related in the story has divided critics. There are three possible interpretations of the events: Brown met real people in the forest; he met specters; or the whole incident was simply a dream. In any case, critics agree that something of consequence happened to Brown in the forest and that the tale reflects a respect for dreams that existed in Puritan society.

Dreams are mentioned throughout the story, implying that they contain some elements of truth. When Brown leaves his wife Faith to begin his trip, she tells him, "A lone woman is troubled with such dreams and such thoughts, that she's afraid of herself sometimes" ("Young Goodman Brown," p. 133). Brown's reaction to Faith's words also alludes to dreams: "Methought, as she spoke, there was trouble in her face, as if a dream had warned her what work is to be done tonight" ("Young Goodman Brown," p. 134). Both characters take dreams seriously.

Brown's actions at the end of the story show that he believes that the things he saw the night before really happened. He avoids the blessing of the minister and asks, regarding the town deacon, "What God doth the wizard pray to?" ("Young Goodman Brown," p. 147). He also looks sternly upon his wife. But despite Brown's own belief in what he saw, the next passage asks, "Had Goodman Brown fallen asleep in the forest and only dreamed a wild dream of a witch-meeting?" ("Young Goodman Brown," p. 147). The question recalls the three possibilities—that the meeting was a real event, a dream, or an assembly of specters—and highlights the unreliable nature of spectral evidence. Just as judges relied on spectral

evidence to convict persons of witchcraft, Brown relies on his perhaps unreal forest experience in his subsequent assessment of society around him. The result is an attitude of gloomy aloofness, a posture that he keeps for the remainder of his life.

Sources. Some characters in Hawthorne's story are based on historical Salem villagers who were associated with witchcraft, while others are simply members of the Salem community or characters based on Hawthorne's Puritan ancestors.

Many primary sources on the period in which "Young Goodman Brown" was set were available to Hawthorne. Principal sources included *Cases of Conscience concerning Evil Spirits Personating Man* (1693) by Increase Mather and *Wonders of the Invisible World* (1693) and *Magnali Christi Americana* (1702) by Cotton Mather. Hawthorne is known to have steeped himself in records and writings of the times.

Events in History at the Time the Short Story Was Written

The Second Great Awakening. The United States experienced a renewal of religious activity in the early 1800s, described by many historians as a "back-to-basics" reaction to developments in American society. With national expansion pushing the frontier westward, proponents of various religions and sects traveled extensively through the new lands in an attempt to recruit new members. Their actions led to a growth in religious activity that became known as the Second Great Awakening.

The nation was primarily Protestant, but within that broad religious spectrum various systems of belief found room to grow. Among these were the Congregationalists, early churches that grew out of the Puritan doctrine. Having estab-

A depiction of a revival meeting.

lished themselves firmly in New England, they were to remain dominant there until the late 1800s. The Dutch Reformed Church, whose seat was in New York, was nearly as old as the Congregationalist faith, but it did not fare so well in the competition for membership during the revivals of the Second Great Awakening.

As the movement gained momentum, revival meetings were held in rural areas, towns, and urban areas as ministers sought to increase the membership of their organizations. Visiting ministers tried to determine the ability of growing communities to support additional churches. If they deemed that sufficient support existed, another church would be established in the area. The passion and persuasive power of the revival meetings may have influenced Hawthorne's description of the witch-meeting in his short story. His mistrust of the religious fervor of his own times was combined with his guilt concerning his ancestors' participation in the Salem witch trials. Both find expression in "Young Goodman Brown."

The critics and Hawthorne. When "Young Goodman Brown" was published, critics did not quite know what to make of it. Some focused their attention on the mystical aspects of the story. For example, a reviewer commenting in the *American Review* said that "as a tale of the supernatural it certainly is more exquisitely man-

aged than anything we have seen in American Literature, at least" (Harris, p. 293). The famous author Herman Melville, Hawthorne's close friend, wrote of "Young Goodman Brown" that its title was deceptively simple but the tale itself a triumph in depth.

THE HAWTHORNE CURSE

After one Puritan woman, Rebekah Nurse, was sentenced to death for witchcraft, she delivered a curse upon her judge John Hathorne and upon his children's children. One historian explained how it affected the family: "This was the curse that lingered in the family memory like a black blot in the blood, and was ever after used to explain any ill luck that befell the house" (Woodbury, p. 2).

While the story exposes the hypocrisy of the early Puritan colonists, it is so cleverly constructed that it also attacks the new wave of religious enthusiasm in Hawthorne's lifetime. The devil's gathering, for instance, bears some similarity to a backcountry Congregationalist revival. The story's main character also experiences an inability to fit into his society that paralleled Hawthorne's inability to find his place in the mainstream society of his time. It is the incorporation of various ideas like these that makes Hawthorne's short story such a hauntingly successful work.

For More Information

Harris, Laurie Lanzen, ed. *Nineteenth-Century Literature Criticism.* Vol. 2. Detroit: Gale Research, 1982.

Hawthorne, Nathaniel. "Young Goodman Brown." In *Selected Tales and Sketches.* New York: Penguin, 1987.

Hudson, Winthrop S. *Religion in America.* New York: Charles Scribner's Sons, 1981.

Morgan, Edmund S. *The Puritan Dilemma: The Story of John Winthrop.* Boston: Little, Brown, 1958.

Rosenthal, Bernard. *Salem Story: Reading the Witch Trials of 1692.* Cambridge: Cambridge University Press, 1993.

Woodbury, George E. *Nathaniel Hawthorne.* New York: Chelsea House, 1980.

Index

A

Aaron, Hank **4**:*145, 148*

Abernathy, Ralph **5**:*89 (illus.)*

Abolitionists/Abolition of slavery
    John Brown's raid on Harper's Ferry **2**:*188–94*
    changing little for freed slaves **5**:*19–20*
    controversy and disagreement with, in North
      2:*9, 315, 404*
    as core political issue by mid-19th century
      2:*88, 242*
    early efforts **2**:*22–24*
    Emancipation Proclamation (1862) **2**:*59, 60*
      (sidebar), *135, 308, 309*
    Liberia **2**:*404*
    proposals for land for freed slaves **2**:*41*
    and Underground Railroad **2**:*16, 60, 62, 189,*
      238, 406–7
    women's role in **2**:*23–24*
    (*See also* African Americans; Jim Crow laws;
      Reconstruction)

Abortion **5**:*51, 136*

Abraham Lincoln: The Prairie Years, Sandburg, Carl
  2:*1–7*

Achebe, Chinua, *Things Fall Apart* **2**:*360–65*

Acheson, Dean **5**:*101*

Achilles **1**:*169–70*

Across Five Aprils, Hunt, Irene **2**:*8–14*

Adam and Eve **1**:*301–2*

Adams, John **1**:*29, 72, 94*

Adams, John Quincy **1**:*209*

Adams, Richard, *Watership Down* **5**:*346–51*

Addison, Joseph **1**:*307*

Adoption of children, by African Americans **4**:*33*

Adultery/infidelity **5**:*273, 287*
    in *Anna Karenina* **2**:*34–40*

    in *Ethan Frome* **2**:*125–29*
    in *Madame Bovary* **2**:*209–15*
    in *Medea* **1**:*238–41*
    in *Scarlet Letter* **1**:*351–57*

Adventures of Don Quixote, The, Cervantes Saavedra,
  Miguel de **1**:*1–7*

Adventures of Huckleberry Finn, The, Twain, Mark
  2:*15–21*

Advertising
    fostering consumer culture **3**:*26*
    targeting teenagers **4**:*392*
    WWII-related ads excluding minorities **4**:*197*

Advise and Consent **5**:*4*

Aegean Sea **1**:*60 (map)*

Aeneas. *See Aeneid, The*

Aeneid, The, Virgil **1**:*8–13*
    parallels to *Beowulf* **1**:*49*
    parallels to Shakespeare's *The Tempest* **1**:*383*

Affirmative action **5**:*181, 183–84, 342*

AFL (American Federation of Labor) **3**:*44*

Africa and Africans
    in 16th-century England **1**:*299*
    Algeria **3**:*212*
    apartheid in South Africa **1**:*63;* **3**:*86*
    Belgian Congo **2**:*145–46, 150–51*
    Ethiopia **4**:*67*
    Gambia **5**:*298*
    Ghana **4**:*314*
    impact of WWI **3**:*292–93*
    independence movements **4**:*314*
    ivory trade **2**:*147*
    Kenya **3**:*290–96*
    Liberia **2**:*404*
    Maasai **3**:*295*
    Medea as Egyptian "woman of color" **1**:*240*
    (sidebar)

Moors   1:297, 299
natives as "squatters"   3:293–94
Nigeria   2:360–62, 364–65; 3:84; 4:314
oral tradition and griots   5:298–300, 301–2
post-WWI economic problems   3:293
racism of colonial powers   2:360–65; 3:291
Rhodesia   4:165–66
slave trade   1:37, 39, 103, 274, 299, 337–38;
   2:361
Tanzania   3:290
(*See also* Colonialism, imperialism, and
   interventionism)
African American men
   "humiliations, emasculation" faced by   4:53–54;
      5:146, 328–29
   physicians in Georgia   3:154–55, 156–57
   relationship of class, race, and manhood
      4:313–14
   as soldiers in Vietnam War   5:102–3
African American women
   accused of black male-bashing   3:87; 5:121
   African-style clothing and hairdos   4:56; 5:145,
      300
   and black feminism   2:64; 3:86–87; 4:56
   cosmetics for   4:50, 56
   devaluation of   3:80–82; 4:54; 5:115–16
   differences with white women in civil rights and
      feminist movements   3:354–55; 5:92–93, 117
   employment in South   3:418–19
   as heads of families   3:355, 375, 423
   as "mammies"   3:392
   race- and gender-based limitations upon
      5:115–16
   sexual abuse of   2:49, 60, 169, 406; 4:54; 5:117
   as single heads of households   2:65; 3:80, 423;
      4:2; 5:68, 117, 328–29
African Americans in 19th century
   churches as cornerstones of community   5:189
   exodus from South to West   3:249–50
   gospel songs and black spirituals   2:398, 402,
      407; 4:258
   mixed race offspring and color prejudice   5:21
   (*See also* Civil War; Jim Crow laws; Segregation;
      Slavery in America; Slaves)
African Americans in 20th century
   adopting white society's values   4:52
   adoption of children   4:33
   in black ghettos. See Ghettos
   class/social stratification among   4:2–3, 30
   communism and   1:398–99; 3:164, 238–39
   community, kinship, and closeness   2:341–42;
      3:383–84, 394; 4:52
   crime, some turning to   4:145
   crime, victims of   4:31; 5:340–41
   during Great Depression   3:154, 236–37
   education   4:3; 5:342
   employment opportunities and limitations
      4:311; 5:341 (*sidebar*)
   family life   3:80, 84–86, 353–55, 375, 422–23;
      4:33; 5:68, 145–46, 329–30

Harlem Renaissance   3:159–65, 256, 321,
   384–85, 421; 4:204 (*sidebar*), 207
Hollywood's stereotypical images of   2:142;
   4:50, 369
middle class, rise of   3:252, 255, 387–88; 4:2,
   51
mixed race offspring and color prejudice   2:49;
   3:17–18, 81, 83, 387–88; 4:3, 50, 51–52; 5:130
oral tradition   5:298–300, 301–2
poverty of many   3:37; 4:5 (*sidebar*), 145; 5:329
race colonies   3:383
religion's importance to   3:372
riot following assassination of King (1968)
   5:112 (*sidebar*)
riots in central Los Angeles (1992)   5:340
riots in Watts (1965)   5:340
(*See also* Great Migration; Jim Crow laws;
   Segregation)
African Americans' civil rights/reform/power
   movements
   activism for FEPC (Fair Employment Practices
      Commission)   3:42
   anti-integrationist   5:15
   assassinations of leaders   4:54; 5:112 (*sidebar*)
   autobiographies as genre   4:205; 5:304
   Black arts movement   4:207
   black feminism   2:64; 3:86–87
   "Black is Beautiful" slogan   4:54, 56
   Black Muslims and Nation of Islam   3:238, 325;
      4:56, 248–50; 5:12–13, 69, 110–11, 302
   black nationalism, separatism, and Pan-
      Africanism   3:160, 238, 325; 4:56, 211,
      311–12
   Black Panther Party   4:54, 56, 207
   Black Power movement   2:97–98; 3:43, 325;
      4:56, 207; 5:143–44
   CORE (Congress of Racial Equality)   3:42; 4:376
   efforts of 1940s and '50s   4:28–29, 255
   emphasizing African heritage   5:300–302
   fostered by Harlem Renaissance   3:163–64, 256
   King's approach, compared to Malcolm X's
      4:250; 5:13, 15, 111
   militancy and Malcolm X   2:98; 3:324–25; 4:54,
      249–50; 5:69–70, 110, 111
   in Missouri   4:28–29
   NAACP   2:342, 415; 3:250, 320, 396; 4:195,
      255, 310; 5:88, 120 (*sidebar*)
   Niagara Movement (1905)   3:250, 320
   OAAU (Organization of Afro-American Unity)
      5:16–17
   pacifist versus outspoken, sometimes violent
      protest   4:205, 207
   passive resistance and nonviolence   5:11–12,
      108, 189, 192
   SCLC (Southern Christian Leadership
      Conference)   5:189
   seeking African roots   3:86; 5:145
   self-empowerment philosophies   3:325
   SNCC (Student Nonviolent Coordinating
      Committee)   4:56; 5:300

UNIA (United Negro Improvement Association)
　3:*160*; 4:*211*
　urban blacks' involvement in　5:*143*
　WPC (Women's Political Council)　5:*88*
African Americans, literary works concerning
　Adventures of Huckleberry Finn, The　2:*15–21*
　"Ain't I a Woman?"　2:*22–27*
　Almos' a Man　4:*1–6*
　Autobiography of Malcolm X, The　5:*11–18*
　Bear, The　2:*47–53*
　Beloved　2:*59–65*
　Benito Cereno　1:*37–43*
　Betsey Brown　4:*28–34*
　Black Boy　3:*36–43*
　Bluest Eye, The　4:*49–57*
　Color Purple, The　3:*80–87*
　Confessions of Nat Turner, The　2:*93–98*
　Cry, the Beloved Country　4:*94–100*
　Fences　4:*144–50*
　Fire Next Time, The　5:*107–14*
　*for colored girls who have considered suicide / when
　　the rainbow is enuf*　5:*115–21*
　Gathering of Old Men, A　5:*129–34*
　Gone with the Wind　2:*137–44*
　Hero Ain't Nothin' but a Sandwich, A　5:*143–48*
　His Own Where　5:*149–55*
　Home to Harlem　3:*159–65*
　"I Have a Dream"　5:*185–93*
　I Know Why the Caged Bird Sings　4:*201–8*
　Incidents in the Life of a Slave Girl　2:*168–73*
　Invisible Man　4:*209–15*
　John Brown's Final Speech　2:*188–94*
　Leaves of Grass　2:*197*
　Manchild in the Promised Land　4:*247–53*
　Member of the Wedding, The　4:*254–59*
　Narrative of the Life of Frederick Douglass
　　2:*236–41*
　Native Son　3:*236–42*
　Not without Laughter　3:*249–56*
　Raisin in the Sun, A　4:*309–15*
　Roots　5:*298–305*
　Souls of Black Folk, The　2:*340–46*
　Sounder　3:*370–76*
　Sweet Whispers, Brother Rush　5:*328–32*
　Their Eyes Were Watching God　3:*383–89*
　Tituba of Salem Village　1:*393–99*
　Uncle Remus　2:*397–402*
　Uncle Tom's Cabin　2:*403–9*
　Understand This　5:*339–45*
　Up From Slavery　2:*410–15*
　Worn Path, A　3:*418–24*
African Methodist Episcopal Church　3:*83*
Age of Reason　1:*268–69, 272*
Agee, James, *Death in the Family, A*　3:*100–105*
Agnosticism　3:*265*
AIDS (Acquired Immune Deficiency Syndrome)
　5:*9*
Aiken, Conrad　3:*414*
AIM (American Indian Movement)　2:*79 (sidebar)*;
　5:*246–47*

"Ain't I a Woman?" Truth, Sojourner　2:*22–27*
Air pollution　4:*9*
Alaska　3:*52–56, 261 (sidebar)*
Albania　2:*101*
Albee, Edward, *Zoo Story, The*　4:*397–402*
Alchemy　1:*384, 385 (sidebar)*
Alcohol and alcoholism
　among American Indians　1:*220*; 4:*83, 189
　　(sidebar)*; 5:*361*
　among Irish　3:*220, 398, 400*
　among war wives　4:*317*
　among Welsh　3:*65–66*
　Anti-Saloon League and temperance movements
　　2:*25 (sidebar), 85–86*; 3:*69, 75, 147, 401*
　Prohibition　3:*22–23*
　saloons as social halls　3:*219, 398, 400*
　as woman's issue　2:*25 (sidebar)*; 3:*219*
　(*See also* Prohibition)
Alcott, Louisa May, *Little Women*　2:*202–8*
Aldrin, Edwin E. ("Buzz") Jr.　5:*82, 292, 295 (illus.)*
Aleichem, Sholom　3:*123*
Alexander the Great, Czar of Russia　1:*169
　(sidebar)*
Alexander II, Czar of Russia　3:*57, 120*
Alexander III, Czar of Russia　3:*120*
Alger, Horatio, *Ragged Dick*　2:*301–7*
Ali, Muhammad　5:*70 (sidebar), 72 (illus.), 307–8*
Alianza, La　4:*175–76, 321*
Alice's Adventures in Wonderland, Carroll, Lewis
　2:*28–33*
All Creatures Great and Small, Herriott, James
　3:*1–7*
All Quiet on the Western Front, Remarque, Erich
　Maria　3:*8–14*
Allegory, *Animal Farm*, Orwell, George　4:*14–20*
Allen, Ethan　3:*98 (sidebar)*
Allende, Isabel, *House of the Spirits, The*　5:*163–70*
Allende, Salvador　5:*164–65, 166 (illus.), 168–69*
Almanacs, *Poor Richard's Almanac*, Franklin,
　Benjamin　1:*309–15*
Almos' a Man, Wright, Richard　4:*1–6*
Amadis of Gaul　1:*6*
Amazons　1:*58–59, 61–62, 258, 259–60*
America. *See* Colonial America; United States
American Childhood, An, Dillard, Annie　4:*7–13*
American Communist Party
　popularity of, during Great Depression　3:*45*
　standing against racism　3:*40*
　(*See also* Communism)
American Dream
　achievement as impossible for black men　4:*313*
　achieving through hard work and frugality
　　2:*302, 305*; 4:*111*
　achieving through salesmanship in 1950s
　　4:*111*
　Ben Franklin as embodiment of　1:*26–27, 309*
　in colonial times　1:*97*
　Dreiser's preoccupation with　2:*331–32*
　merit rather than rank determining success
　　1:*72*

American Indians in 16th century, decimated by smallpox   **5**:*214*

American Indians in 17th century, displayed in Renaissance Europe   **1**:*383*

American Indians in 18th century
   as allies of British in Revolutionary War   **1**:*108*
   as allies of French in French and Indian War **1**:*204–5*
   decimated by smallpox   **1**:*220, 352*
   enslaved   **1**:*103;* **2**:*175*
   French and Indian War (Seven Years' War) **1**:*93, 123, 204–6*
   land/natural resources as considered by   **1**:*220;* **2**:*78, 178*
   legends and Folk, Thelore   **1**:*332*
   Paxton Boys massacre   **1**:*220–21*
   pressure of westward expansion of American colonists   **1**:*108, 204, 220–21*
   Puritans' view of   **1**:*102, 422*
   Uncas   **1**:*207 (sidebar), 208*
   "walking purchase" of land from   **1**:*220 (sidebar)*

American Indians in 19th century
   art   **2**:*348–49, 351–52*
   Battle of Wounded Knee   **2**:*69, 78*
   BIA (Bureau of Indian Affairs)   **5**:*246*
   Black Hills War (1876)   **2**:*67–68, 77*
   buffalo, Great Plains tribes' dependency on **2**:*66–67, 75*
   Crazy Horse   **2**:*348 (illus.)*
   and Dawes Act (1887)   **2**:*68, 179;* **4**:*186*
   decimated by smallpox   **2**:*347*
   defended by Bret Harte   **2**:*287*
   family and family life   **2**:*347*
   Ghost Dance   **2**:*69, 77–78*
   holy men   **2**:*71–72*
   horse culture of Plains tribes   **5**:*364 (sidebar)*
   missions/missionaries and   **2**:*161–62, 392 (sidebar)*
   national guilt felt by whites   **2**:*79*
   Ongpatonga   **1**:*209 (illus.)*
   parallels to Anglo-Saxons after Norman Conquest **1**:*257*
   peyote religion   **4**:*188*
   religion of   **2**:*71–72, 78*
   Removal Act (1830)   **1**:*208–10;* **2**:*316, 317 (sidebar)*
   reservations policies of U.S. gov't.   **1**:*224;* **2**:*67, 68, 73, 76, 79, 179, 316, 317 (sidebar), 351;* **4**:*186–87*
   Sand Creek Massacre   **2**:*77*
   "second parents" among Sioux   **2**:*347*
   spirituality of   **2**:*72, 161;* **5**:*246*
   Sun Dance   **2**:*349 (sidebar);* **4**:*187–88*
   "Trail of Tears"   **5**:*29–30*
   treaties and U.S. gov't.'s failure to enforce **2**:*75–76, 162*

American Indians in 20th century
   AIM (American Indian Movement)   **2**:*79 (sidebar);* **5**:*246–47*
   alcoholism   **1**:*220;* **4**:*83, 189 (sidebar);* **5**:*361*
   BIA (Bureau of Indian Affairs)   **5**:*246*
   Catholic Church   **5**:*244, 361–62*
   citizenship status   **4**:*80*
   Civil Rights Act of 1964 affecting   **2**:*351 (sidebar)*
   cultural mixture of American Southwest **4**:*320–21*
   Indian Reorganization Act (1934)   **2**:*73;* **4**:*186*
   matrilineal cultures   **4**:*82 (sidebar)*
   military service   **4**:*80, 185–87;* **5**:*362–63*
   mission school of Anglican Church   **5**:*195*
   Navajo Night Chant   **4**:*188*
   poverty of   **5**:*360–61*
   prestige factor of Indian ancestry   **5**:*30*
   Red Power and rights movements   **2**:*79 (sidebar), 179, 351*
   relocation program (1952)   **4**:*186–87*
   self-determination policies (1961 and 1970) **2**:*351;* **4**:*190–91*
   storytelling, powers of   **4**:*83 (sidebar), 85, 188, 189, 192*
   and tribal rights (1934)   **2**:*73*

American Indians, literary works concerning
   Bear, The (Chickasaw)   **2**:*47–53*
   Black Elk Speaks (Oglala Sioux)   **2**:*66–73*
   Bury My Heart at Wounded Knee (Western tribes) **2**:*74–80*
   Ceremony (Laguna Pueblo)   **4**:*79–86*
   Drums Along the Mohawk (Iroquois)   **1**:*108*
   House Made of Dawn (Navajo, Jemez Pueblo, and WWII veterans)   **4**:*185–92*
   I Heard the Owl Call My Name (Kwakiutl) **5**:*194–200*
   "I Will Fight No More Forever" (Nez Percé) **2**:*160–67*
   Ishi, Last of His Tribe (Yahi)   **2**:*174–80*
   Last of the Mohicans, The (Delaware and Iroquois) **1**:*204–10*
   Leaves of Grass (America's Indian heritage) **2**:*195–201*
   Light in the Forest, The (Delaware)   **1**:*219–24*
   Love Medicine (Chippewa)   **5**:*243–50*
   Story Catcher, The (Oglala Sioux)   **2**:*347–52*
   Tempest, The (Europeans' explorations of New World)   **1**:*383*
   Yellow Raft in Blue Water, A (Cree)   **5**:*360–66*

American Indians by tribe
   Arawak (Taino)   **5**:*214*
   Cherokee   **5**:*29–30*
   Cheyenne   **2**:*75, 79*
   Chippewa   **5**:*243–50*
   Chiricahua Apache   **2**:*74–75*
   Cree   **5**:*361 (sidebar), 362 (illus.), 364 (sidebar)*
   Delaware (Lenape)   **1**:*206, 219–20*
   Iroquois   **1**:*108, 110, 205–6*
   Jemez Pueblo   **4**:*187, 189–90, 191*
   Kiowa   **4**:*186, 187–88*
   Kwakiutl (Canada)   **5**:*194–200*
   Laguna Pueblo   **4**:*79–86*

métis   **5**:*244*
Modoc   **2**:*79*
Mohegan   **1**:*352*
Narragansett   **1**:*352*
Navajo   **2**:*79*; **4**:*80, 186, 188*; **5**:*360*
Nez Percé   **2**:*75, 79, 160–67*
Pequot   **1**:*352*
Pueblo   **4**:*47*
Sioux   **2**:*66–67, 347–50*; **5**:*360*
Ute   **2**:*79*
Yahi   **2**:*174, 175, 177*
Zuni Pueblo   **4**:*186*
American Revolution
    Continental Congress   **1**:*125*
    Declaration of Independence   **1**:*93–100*
    in *Drums Along the Mohawk*   **1**:*107–14*
    influence of *Common Sense*   **1**:*71–77, 94*
    influence of "Give Me Liberty or Give Me Death"
      speech   **1**:*122–28*
Amistad mutiny   **1**:*43*
Anaya, Rudolfo A.
    Bless Me, Ultima   **4**:*42–48*
    Heart of Aztlán   **4**:*171–76*
Anderson, Robert, *I Never Sang for My Father*
    5:*201–7*
Anderson, Sherwood, on *Babbitt*   **3**:*27*
André, Major John   **1**:*213 (sidebar)*
Angelou, Maya, *I Know Why the Caged Bird Sings*
    4:*201–8*
Angels in America, Kushner, Tony   **5**:*1–10*
Anglican Church (Church of England)   **1**:*78, 123,*
    129, 232, 233 (sidebar), 306, 351, 393
    Dissenters   **1**:*129, 338, 342, 407, 411*; **3**:*265*
Anglo-Saxon England   **1**:*44–45, 153, 181*
    Norman Conquest of   **1**:*181, 250–51, 290*
Animal Farm, Orwell, George   **4**:*14–20*
    politically motivated rejection by publishers
      5:*252–53*
Animals, stories concerning
    All Creatures Great and Small   **3**:*1–7* ·
    Bless the Beasts and Children   **5**:*34–38*
    Call of the Wild, The   **3** *51–56*
    Day No Pigs Would Die, A   **3**:*94–99*
    Red Pony, The   **3**:*334–37*
    Sounder   **3**:*370–76*
    Watership Down   **5**:*346–51*
Anna Karenina, Tolstoy, Leo   **2**:*34–40*
Anne, Queen of England   **1**:*130–31, 342*
Anne, Queen of France   **1**:*389*
Annesley, Brian   **1**:*201*
Anonymous, *Beowulf*   **1**:*44–50*
Anthropology
    comparative   **5**:*42*
    interest in Polynesian peoples' origins   **4**:*221–27*
    researchers' interest in American Indians   **2**:*72,*
      179
Antigone, Sophocles   **1**:*14–21*
Antinomians   **1**:*352, 357*
Anti-Semitism
    in accusations of fix of 1919 World Series   **4**:*261*

of African Americans   **4**:*376–77*
of Argentina's "dirty war"   **5**:*210*
in Brooklyn   **3**:*402*
of Charles Lindbergh   **4**:*373*
contributing to generation gap   **5**:*203*
diminishing in 1950s and '60s   **5**:*203*
and Dreyfus affair   **1**:*91–92, 364 (sidebar)*
in England   **1**:*182–83*; **2**:*264–65*
of Father Charles Coughlin   **4**:*373*
in Germany   **1**:*370*; **4**:*157–59*
holocaust denial   **4**:*40*
in Italy   **1**:*243–44, 246*
Kristallnacht   **4**:*159, 162–63*
and moneylending   **1**:*182–83*; **2**:*264*
and nationalism   **1**:*364*
origins of "ghetto"   **1**:*244, 249*
Pale of Settlement   **3**:*119–20, 121*
pogroms   **1**:*364*; **3**:*120–21*
in Poland   **1**:*364*
in Russia   **1**:*364*; **3**:*119–21*
in Soviet Union   **3**:*124–25*; **5**:*122*
in U.S. of 1940s   **4**:*236–37, 373*
in U.S. military   **4**:*36–37*
in Wharton's works   **3**:*170*
(*See also* Holocaust)
Antiwar literature
    All Quiet on the Western Front   **3**:*8–14*
    Catch-22   **4**:*66–72*
    Fallen Angels   **5**:*101–6*
    Farewell to Arms, A   **3**:*112–18*
    Red Badge of Courage, The   **2**:*308–13*
    Slaughterhouse Five   **4**:*343–48*
    Waste Land, The   **3**:*411–17*
Appalachian Trail   **5**:*278–79*
Arabs, anti-Zionism   **4**:*107*
Archery   **1**:*253*
Argentina   **5**:*208–11, 212–13*
Aristotle
    commenting upon *Republic*   **1**:*328*
    influence in 16th century   **1**:*233*
    influence on Jefferson   **1**:*100*
    woodcut of   **1**:*326 (illus.)*
Armenia   **3**:*338–43*; **4**:*199*
Arms control   **4**:*71*; **5**:*126, 225, 239, 252 (sidebar)*
    prohibiting military use of space   **5**:*239*
Armstrong, Neil A.   **5**:*82, 292*
Armstrong, William H., *Sounder*   **3**:*370–76*
Army. *See* Military
Arnold, Benedict   **1**:*213 (sidebar)*
Arnold, Thomas   **2**:*373–74*
Art
    African   **4**:*56*
    artists benefitting from New Deal's WPA   **3**:*391,*
      424
    as barrier against chaos and loss of faith   **3**:*117*
    Black arts movement   **4**:*207*
    Carnegie Institute of Pittsburgh   **4**:*9*
    first International Exhibition for   **4**:*8 (sidebar)*
    French atelier system of teaching   **3**:*266*
    Modernism   **3**:*411*; **5**:*42*

Paris as western capital of   3:265–66
patrons for artists   1:88
Primitivism   3:385 (sidebar)
(See also Literature)
Arthur, King of Celtic England   1:288, 290
in Once and Future King, The   1:288–94
Asians. See Chinese and Chinese Americans;
Japanese and Japanese Americans
Asimov, Isaac, Foundation   5:122–28
Astrology   1:346, 350
ASWPL (Association of Southern Women for the
Prevention of Lynching)   3:391–92
Athena   1:282, 283
Athens. See under Greece in ancient times
Atom bomb
creating "atomic anxiety"   4:255; 5:126
decision to use   4:178–79
Hiroshima and Nagasaki as targets   4:179–82,
180 (illus.), 181 (sidebar)
Manhattan Project   4:71, 81–82, 316; 5:123
Soviets' capability   4:183; 5:96, 126
test site at Bikini atoll   5:124 (illus.)
UN attempts to regulate   5:96
(See also Nuclear weapons)
Atomic energy. See Nuclear energy
Atwood, Margaret, Handmaid's Tale, The   5:135–42
Austen, Jane, Pride and Prejudice   2:295–300
Austria-Hungary   3:11 (sidebar)
Autobiography
American Childhood, An, Dillard, Annie   4:7–13
Autobiography of Benjamin Franklin, The   1:22–29
Autobiography of Malcolm X, The, X, Malcolm and
Haley, Alex   5:11–18
Barrio Boy, Galarza, Ernesto   3:28–35
Black Boy, Wright, Richard   3:36–43
Bound for Glory, Guthrie, Woody   3:44–50
Diary of a Young Girl, The, Frank, Anne
4:116–23
Endless Steppe, The: Growing Up in Siberia,
Hautzig, Esther   4:131–36
Farewell to Manzanar, Houston, Jeanne W. and
James D. Houston   4:137–43
Hiroshima Diary, Hachiya, Michihiko   4:177–84
Hunger of Memory, Rodriquez, Richard
5:178–84
I Know Why the Caged Bird Sings, Angelou, Maya
4:201–8
Incidents in the Life of a Slave Girl, The, Jacobs,
Harriet   2:168–73
Manchild in the Promised Land, Brown, Claude
4:247–53
Narrative of the Life of Frederick Douglass,
Douglass, Frederick   2:16, 236–41
Out of Africa, Dinesen, Isak   3:290–96
So Far from the Bamboo Grove, Watkins, Yoko K.
4:349–55
Up From Slavery, Washington, Booker T.
2:410–15
Woman Warrior, The, Kingston, Maxine Hong
5:352–59

Autobiography of Benjamin Franklin, The, Franklin,
Benjamin   1:22–29
Autobiography of Malcolm X, The, X, Malcolm and
Haley, Alex   5:11–18
Autobiography of Miss Jane Pittman, The (a novel),
Gaines, Ernest J.   5:19–26
Aviation
breaking sound barrier   5:293–94
golden age of   3:211–12
Lindbergh and   3:367
Right Stuff, The   5:291–97
and UFOs (unidentified flying objects)
4:347–48; 5:59 (illus.)
(See also Space Age; War weaponry)
Awakening, The, Chopin, Kate   3:15–20
Azerbaijan   3:343
Aztlán   4:173, 174–75, 176

B

Ba'al Shem Tov   4:87
Babbitt, Lewis, Sinclair   3:21–27
Babe Ruth   4:262, 265
Babi Yar massacre   4:120
Baby boom   1:224; 2:325–26; 4:38, 74, 240
Backswording   2:375
Baer, Dov   4:89
Bakke, Allan   5:181
Baldwin, James, Fire Next Time, The   5:107–14
Baptists   5:19, 188
Baraka, Amiri (Leroi Jones)   4:207
Barbed wire   3:113, 260
Barn Burning, Faulkner, William   2:41–46
Barrio Boy, Galarza, Ernesto   3:28–35
Baseball
Aaron, Hank   4:145, 148
Babe Ruth   4:262, 265
changing strategies of play   4:261–62
creation of two-league system   4:261
growing popularity leading to scouts   3:284
history of scandals   4:260–61, 265
Jackie Robinson   4:146
minor leagues and decrease in college-educated
players   4:261
Negro League   4:145, 148
Pittsburgh Pirates   4:10
segregation in   4:146, 147
White ("Black") Sox fix of 1919 World Series
3:149–50; 4:260–61
(See also Shoeless Joe)
Bay of Pigs fiasco   5:226
Bean Trees, The, Kingsolver, Barbara   5:27–33
Bear, The, Faulkner, William   2:47–53
Beat movement   4:75
(See also Counterculture)
Beauty: A Retelling of the Story of Beauty and the Beast,
McKinley, Robin   1:30–36
Becker, Charles   3:149
Becket, Thomas   1:146
Begin, Menachem   4:103, 105, 107

Behavior modification and conditioning   5:156–57
Behaviorism   5:45
Behn, Aphra   3:361–62
Belaúnde, Fernando   5:334
Belgium   2:146–47, 150–51; 3:9; 4:254, 357, 359
Bell, Clive   3:356
Bell Jar, The, Plath, Sylvia   4:21–27
Bellamy, Edward   2:423
Belle of Amherst, The, Luce, William   2:54–58
Belle Glade, Florida   3:383–84
Bellecourt, Clyde   5:247 (illus.)
Belleforest, François de   1:139, 141 (sidebar)
Beloved, Morrison, Toni   2:59–65
Benito Cereno, Melville, Herman   1:37–43
Beowulf, Anonymous   1:44–50
    influence upon Tolkien   1:153
Bergson, Henri   3:213
Betsey Brown, Shange, Ntozake   4:28–34
Bible, source for Milton's *Paradise Lost*   1:301
Bierce, Ambrose
    as character in *The Old Gringo*   3:279, 280, 281
    Occurrence at Owl Creek Bridge, An   2:255–60
Bilingual education   4:45; 5:172, 179–81, 183, 217
Billy Budd, Melville, Herman   1:51–56
Biloxi Blues, Simon, Neil   4:35–41
Biography (and autobiography)
    Abraham Lincoln: The Prairie Years, Sandburg,
        Carl   2:1–7
    American Childhood, An, Dillard, Annie   4:7–13
    Autobiography of Benjamin Franklin, The, Franklin,
        Benjamin   1:22–29
    Autobiography of Malcolm X, The, Malcolm X as
        told to Alex Haley   5:11–18
    Barrio Boy, Galarza, Ernesto   3:28–35
    Belle of Amherst, The (Emily Dickinson), Luce,
        William   2:54–58
    Black Boy, Wright, Richard   3:36–43
    Black Elk Speaks, Neihardt, John G.   2:66–73
    Bound for Glory, Guthrie, Woody   3:44–50
    Diary of a Young Girl, The, Frank, Anne   4:116–23
    Endless Steppe, The: Growing Up in Siberia,
        Hautzig, Esther   4:131–36
    Farewell to Manzanar, Houston, Jeanne W. and
        James D. Houston   4:137–43
    Hiroshima Diary, Hachiya, Michihiko   4:177–84
    Hunger of Memory, Rodriquez, Richard
        5:178–84
    I Know Why the Caged Bird Sings, Angelou, Maya
        4:201–8
    Incidents in the Life of a Slave Girl, Jacobs, Harriet
        2:168–73
    Manchild in the Promised Land, Brown, Claude
        4:247–53
    Narrative of the Life of Frederick Douglass,
        Douglass, Frederick   2:16, 236–41
    Out of Africa, Dinesen, Isak   3:290–96
    Up From Slavery, Washington, Booker T.
        2:410–15
    Woman Warrior, The, Kingston, Maxine Hong
        5:352–59

Black Boy, Wright, Richard   3:36–43
Black Death. *See* Bubonic plague (Black Death)
Black Elk Speaks, Neihardt, John G.   2:66–73
Black feminism   2:64; 3:86–87
Black Muslims and Nation of Islam   3:238, 325;
    4:56, 248–50; 5:12–13, 69, 110–11, 302
Black Panther Party   4:54, 56, 207
Black Power movement   2:97–98; 3:43, 325; 4:56,
    207; 5:143–44
Blacks. *See* African Americans
Blair, Eric Arthur. *See* Orwell, George
Blake, William   1:410 (sidebar), 416; 2:92
Bless the Beasts and Children, Swarthout, Glendon
    5:34–38
Bless Me, Ultima, Anaya, Rudolfo A.   4:42–48
Bligh, Cap't. William   1:273–74, 276–77;
    4:64–65
Blindness. *See* Disabled persons
Blixen, Karen. *See* Dinesen, Isak
Bloomsbury Group   3:356, 358–59
Blue Ridge Mountains   5:278
Blues, the   3:254 (sidebar); 4:258
Bluest Eye, The, Morrison, Toni   4:49–57
Boethius   1:344, 345–46, 350
Boleyn, Anne   1:149, 150, 231
Bolt, Robert, *Man for All Seasons, A*   1:231–37
Booth, John Wilkes   2:191
Bosnia   2:37–39
Boston   3:43
Bound for Glory, Guthrie, Woody   3:44–50
Bouquet, Col. Henry   1:221
Bowling   1:335 (sidebar)
Boxer Rebellion in China (1900)   3:205; 5:354
Boxing   5:68–69
Bracero Program (1942–1964)   3:34; 4:44
Bradbury, Ray
    Dandelion Wine   3:88–93
    Fahrenheit 451   5:95–100
Braddock, Gen'l. Edward   1:205
Bradford, Richard, *Red Sky at Morning*   4:316–22
Brahmans   1:365, 367 (sidebar)
Brave New World, Huxley, Aldous   5:39–45, 141,
    157, 252
Britain. *See* England
Brontë, Charlotte, *Jane Eyre*   1:415 (sidebar);
    2:181–87
Brontë, Emily, *Wuthering Heights*   1:413–19
Bronze Age of ancient Greece   1:14, 258, 280, 283
    (sidebar)
Brook Farm (utopian community)   1:357; 2:418
Brooke, Arthur   1:347, 349 (sidebar)
Brooklyn, New York   3:397–98; 4:88; 5:149–51
Brotherhood of Sleeping Car Porters   3:42
Brown, Claude, *Manchild in the Promised Land*
    4:247–53
Brown, Clifford   4:376
Brown, Dee, *Bury My Heart at Wounded Knee*
    2:74–80
Brown, John   2:89 (sidebar), 172
    Final Speech   2:188–94

Brown v. Board of Education   3:375; 4:29–30, 314; 5:90, 108, 180, 181

Brutus (Marcus Junius Brutus)   1:190, 191, 192–93

Bubonic plague (Black Death)   1:159, 160, 344, 345, 350

Buck, Pearl S., *Good Earth, The*   3:131–37

Buckingham, Duke of (George Villiers)   1:388, 389

Buddhism   1:365–69; 3:186–87; 5:48

Buffalo Bill (William F. Cody)   2:68, 177

Buffalo (bison)   2:66, 67, 75; 5:34–35

Bull from the Sea, The, Renault, Mary   1:57–63

Bunche, Ralph   4:255; 5:54

Burial customs
  among Canadian Kwakiutl   5:197
  in ancient Greece   1:18–19
  catacombs in Sicily   2:82
  mourning traditions in Victorian England
    1:414–15

Burke, Edmund   1:52–53, 359, 362, 373 (sidebar), 408

Burns, Olive Ann, *Cold Sassy Tree*   3:75–79

Bury My Heart at Wounded Knee, Brown, Dee
  2:74–80

Byron, George Gordon Noel (Lord Byron)   1:115, 116, 119, 120; 2:110

C

Caen, Herb   3:226

Caesar, Julius   1:12, 13

Caine Mutiny, The, Wouk, Herman   4:58–65

Cajuns   4:365; 5:21, 130

California
  Clear Lake   4:340–41
  farming and migrant workers   3:29–30, 49, 140–42, 269–71, 275, 335, 337; 4:297 (sidebar)
  gold rushes   2:174–75, 195, 249–50, 281–84
  Sacramento   3:30
  Salinas Valley   3:334–35
  South Central Los Angeles   5:339–42
  Spanish mission system   2:392, 394, 395
  timeline: colonization to independence   2:392
    (sidebar)
  (See also San Francisco)

Call of the Wild, The, London, Jack   3:51–56

Calvin, John, and Calvinism   2:54, 55; 3:377–78; 4:10, 304

Canada, Kwakiutl of British Columbia   5:194–200

Canals
  Panama   3:231–32, 270
  Suez   3:184; 4:107
  U.S. system of   2:230

Canterbury Tales, The, Chaucer, Geoffrey   1:64–70
  Shakespeare influenced by   1:262

Capital punishment   4:379–80; 5:131

Capitalism
  in America's Gilded Age   2:20, 306, 328
  ethics and regulation, lack of   4:9
  failures of, enhancing appeal of communism
    3:208, 210

Hellman's attack on excesses of   3:207, 210
  Steinbeck's warning about   3:144
  versus socialism and Marxism   3:321; 4:18–19
  (See also Industrialization)

Capone, Alphonse   3:366

Capote, Truman
  as basis for character in *To Kill a Mockingbird*
    3:395
  Christmas Memory, A   3:68–74

Caribbean islands
  Dominican Republic   5:220
  Haiti (formerly Saint-Domingue)   5:116–17
  Puerto Rico   3:277; 4:385–86, 388–89, 401; 5:214–21
  slavery in   1:39
  (See also Cuba)

Carlyle, Thomas   1:375; 2:92

Carmichael, Stokely   2:98; 3:325; 4:55 (illus.), 56; 5:145 (illus.)

Carnegie, Andrew   2:306; 4:8, 9

Carranza, Venustiana   3:279

Carrie, King, Stephen   5:46–52

Carroll, Lewis, *Alice's Adventures in Wonderland*
  2:28–33

Carson, Rachel, *Silent Spring*   4:337–42

Carthage   1:10, 12

Carver, George Washington   3:418

Cask of Amontillado, The, Poe, Edgar Allan   2:81–86

Castro, Fidel   2:273; 4:279; 5:225

Catch-22, Heller, Joseph   4:66–72; 5:318 (sidebar)

Catcher in the Rye, Salinger, J. D.   4:73–78; 5:318
  (sidebar)

Catesby, Robert   1:229 (sidebar)

Cather, Willa, *O Pioneers!*   3:257–63

Catholicism and Catholic Church
  among American Indians   5:244, 361–62, 365–66
  anti-Semitism of   2:264
  comparison to Anglican Church   1:233 (sidebar)
  conflict with English Protestants   1:131, 132, 229, 305–6
  control of education in France   2:210
  criticisms by
    Cervantes   1:6–7
    Chaucer   1:65
    Dante   1:174–75; 3:111
    Joyce   3:111
  Crusades   1:182, 291
  cult of Our Lady of Fatima   5:365–66
  decline in Scotland   4:304–5
  equivocation doctrine   1:230
  Inquisition   1:2, 3
  in Ireland   1:269; 3:107–8, 109–10, 305–7
  Jesuits   3:307–8
  in medieval England and Europe   1:49–50, 65
  Merton, Thomas   5:280–81
  monasticism   3:186–87; 5:280
  opposition to contraception   4:304 (sidebar)
  parochial schools   5:62–63
  Penitentes   4:318 (sidebar)

perpetuation of machismo sentiment   5:173
pilgrimages   1:64–70, 145–46
popes   1:174, 176, 296, 344, 345
Reformation   1:231
Trappist monks   5:280
(*See also* Protestantism)
Cattle ranching
on Great Plains   2:321–22
and leather trade on California missions   2:392
on reservations   4:79
(*See also* Farming)
Celts
Britons (Gauls)   1:196–97
Scotland   1:187
Censorship and banning of literary works
in 14th- and 15th-century Europe   1:349
Adventures of Don Quixote, The   1:4
blacklisting by McCarthyites   3:178; 4:72;
   5:96
Brave New World   5:45
Catcher in the Rye   4:78; 5:62
in Communist China   5:98
Flowers for Algernon   4:156
Hero Ain't Nothin' but a Sandwich, A   5:148
His Own Where   5:154
by Nazis   3:13; 5:99
One Day in the Life of Ivan Denisovich   4:285
by Smith Act (1940)   5:97
by Soviet dictatorship   4:286; 5:96
Central America
Guatemala and refugees   5:27–29
Panama Canal   3:231–32, 270
(*See also* Mexico)
Central Intelligence Agency (CIA)   4:293
Ceremonies and celebrations
Chinese New Year   5:75, 76 (illus.)
Christmas
   A Doll's House   2:111–17
   Child's Christmas in Wales, A   3:63–67
   Christmas Memory, A   3:68–74
   Worn Path, A   3:418–24
Indian healing ceremonies   4:82–83; 5:249
Kwakiutl Candlefish   5:196 (sidebar)
Kwakiutl *hamatsa* (Cannibal Dance)   5:196–97
Kwakiutl potlatch   5:198 (illus.), 199
(*See also* Burial customs)
Ceremony, Silko, Leslie Marmon   4:79–86
Cervantes Saavedra, Miguel de
Adventures of Don Quixote, The   1:1–7
in Battle of Lepanto   1:296 (sidebar)
Chagall, Marc   3:123
Chamberlain, Neville   4:357, 359
Chambers, Whittaker   5:96
Chaplin, Charlie   3:101
Charles I of England   1:299, 303, 304 (illus.), 305,
   306
Charles II of England   1:129, 130, 306, 337, 338
Charles X of France   1:391
Chateaubriand, François René de   1:165
Chaucer, Geoffrey, *Canterbury Tales, The*   1:64–70

Chávez, César   3:33 (illus.), 34; 4:47, 175, 300–302,
   301 (illus.),409
Chekhov, Anton, *Cherry Orchard, The*   3:57–62
Chennault, Claire   3:190
Chernobyl disaster   5:286, 287 (illus.)
Cherry Orchard, The, Chekhov, Anton   3:57–62
Chesapeake Bay   4:216–17, 219
Chiang Kai-shek   3:189, 190 (illus.)
Chicago
in 1920s   3:89–90
barrios of   5:174
black activism   3:238
ethnic makeup   3:176
and King's northern civil rights campaign
   5:174
in late 19th century   2:327–28, 330 (illus.)
meat-packing industry   2:328 (sidebar)
South Side and Black Belt   3:237–38; 4:309–11
streetcars   2:328
suburbs of   5:261–62
Chicanos
affirmative action programs   5:181, 183–84
César Chávez   3:33 (illus.), 34; 4:47, 175,
   300–302, 409
discrimination   5:178
   zoot suit riots of 1940s   4:295–97, 403–10
education dropout rates and reform efforts
   5:179
family life   4:45
folk healing (*curanderos*)   4:45
immigration to U.S. from Mexico   3:282;
   4:44–48
life in New Mexico   4:45
literary Renaissance of 1960s and '70s
   5:172–73
Luna (land) and Marez (sea)   4:47
mestizo (mixed-race) heritage   5:172
myth of Aztlán   4:174
origin of term   5:171
pachuco zoot-suit culture of 1950s   4:173,
   295–97, 403
post-WWII community   5:178–79
rights movement   4:47–48, 300–302; 5:171–72,
   179
   Brown Berets   4:176
   Chicanas   3:202; 5:174
   Community Service Organization (CSO)
      4:300
   El Teatro Campesino   4:409; 5:172
   G.I. Forum   4:300
   impact of military service on   4:44
   La Alianza   4:175–76, 321
   La Raza Unida   4:176
   League of United Latin American Citizens
      (LULAC)   4:300
   Mexican American Legal Defense and
      Education Fund (MALDEF)   5:179
   table grape boycott   4:175, 301 (illus.), 409
   United Farm Workers   4:175, 300–302, 409;
      5:171

Richard Rodriguez's autobiography   5:178–84
Rubén Salazar   4:410
Vietnam War protesters   4:409–10
WWII military service   4:44
(*See also* Latinos)
Child abuse
Fetal Alcohol Syndrome   5:361
relationship to poverty   5:329 (sidebar)
and suicide   5:288, 289–90
Child labor   2:103–4, 335 (sidebar); 3:76 (sidebar), 77 (illus.), 285
Childbearing
abortion   5:51, 136
midwifery   4:218
by unwed couples   5:267
in vitro   5:42–43
(*See also* Family and family life)
Childhood's End, Clarke, Arthur   5:53–60
Childress, Alice, *Hero Ain't Nothin' but a Sandwich, A*   5:143–48
Child's Christmas in Wales, A, Thomas, Dylan   3:63–67
Chile   5:163–70
Chin, Frank, *Donald Duk*   5:74–80
China
Boxer Rebellion (1900)   3:205; 5:354
civil strife (1911–49)   3:189–90; 5:229, 254
communist victory in civil war (1949)   5:254, 354–55
communists' land reform   5:355
communists' purge of opponents   5:254–55
Confucius   3:193 (sidebar)
divorce in   2:370, 371; 3:132, 193; 5:230
dynasties and alien invaders   3:189
footbinding of girls   3:135; 5:230 (sidebar)
Guomindang   4:126 (sidebar); 5:230, 254
Hong Kong conceded to Great Britain   5:354
Japanese invasion (1930s–40s)   3:189–90; 4:59; 5:229–30
marriages as business deals   3:192–93
missionaries   3:133
Nixon's visit (1972)   5:358
opium addiction   3:134 (sidebar)
Opium Wars (1839–42 and 1856–60)   5:354
peasant farmers   3:131–32
prostitution in   3:135
Republican era (1912–49)   5:229–30, 354
superstition and syncretism   3:133, 190–91
Taiping Rebellion (1851–64)   5:354
and Taiwan   3:190; 5:254
women in   2:366–67, 368 (sidebar), 370–71; 3:132–33, 134–35; 5:352, 355
Chinese and Chinese Americans
assimilation of second generation   5:231–32, 234–35
Chinese New Year festival   5:75, 76 (illus.)
defended by Bret Harte   2:287
immigration in 19th century   2:367–68, 370 (sidebar), 371; 4:124–27
immigration in 20th century   2:368; 4:125, 127, 129
as miners in Old West   2:367–68, 369 (illus.)
as "model minority"   3:194
in New York's Chinatown   4:126
racism and prejudice against   2:175, 287, 367–68, 370 (sidebar), 371; 3:30; 4:124–27, 194, 330; 5:230–31
in San Francisco's Chinatown   3:226; 5:74–75, 77–79
tongs   4:129
Chinese and Chinese Americans, literary works concerning
Donald Duk   5:74–80
Eat a Bowl of Tea   4:124–30
Joy Luck Club, The   5:229–35
Kitchen God's Wife, The   3:189–95
Thousand Pieces of Gold, McCunn, Ruthanne Lum   2:366–71
Woman Warrior, The   5:352–59
Chivalry   1:2, 66, 291
Chocolate War, The, Cormier, Robert   5:61–66
Chopin, Kate, *Awakening, The*   3:15–20
Chorus in Greek drama   1:10
Chosen, The, Potok, Chaim   4:87–93
Christian, Fletcher   1:273, 274
Christianity
among pioneers of midwest   3:259
Baldwin on "racist hypocrisy" of   5:112
clergymen extolling WWI   3:10
missionaries   2:118–19, 147, 161–62, 361–62; 3:133, 280; 5:195
suicide as sin   4:22
(*See also* Catholicism and Catholic Church; Protestantism; Puritanism)
Christmas Memory, A, Capote, Truman   3:68–74
Chu, Luis, *Eat a Bowl of Tea*   4:124–30
Churchill, Winston   1:237; 5:53, 95
Speech on the Evacuation at Dunkirk   4:356–63
CIA (Central Intelligence Agency)
experiments with drugs   4:293–94
role in Cuba's Bay of Pigs "invasion"   5:226
Cicero   1:327
Cicotte, Eddie   3:149; 4:260
Ciénaga massacre (Colombia)   2:270
Cinema. *See* Hollywood and motion picture industry
CIO (Congress of Industrial Organizations)   3:44
Cisneros, Sandra, *House on Mango Street, The*   5:171–77
Citizenship
in ancient Athens   1:241
for Chinese immigrants   5:231
for Puerto Ricans   5:215
City-states
of ancient Greece   1:286, 327–28
of Italy   1:379–80
Civil Disobedience, Thoreau, Henry David   2:87–92
Civil rights movements
affirmative action   5:181, 183–84, 342
American Indians   4:190–91; 5:246–47

assassination of King   4:54; 5:112 (sidebar)
Chicano. See Chicanos
Civil Rights Acts of 1957, '64, and '65   2:97;
    3:354, 375; 4:148; 5:91
FBI & J. Edgar Hoover's theory of communist
    inspiration of   1:399
focus on South, then North   2:13; 5:25
fostering literary efforts
        autobiographies   4:205; 5:304
        ethnic and cultural explorations   4:92–93,
            207; 5:15, 62, 145, 217, 300–302
        women's studies programs   5:117
Freedom Rides   5:88–90
gay rights movement   4:241
judicial opposition in 1980s to   5:1–2
in Louisiana   5:25
March on Washington (1963)   5:110, 186–88
origins and growth of   2:97; 3:42–43; 4:28–29,
    155–56, 255, 314–15; 5 185, 192, 300
        Alabama as testing ground   2:220–21; 3:73,
            395–96; 4:314–15; 5:11, 88–90, 185–86
race riots in "long hot summer" of 1966
    2:97–98; 4:207
students' free speech movement   5:311
TV's role in creating public support for   5:108
women's involvement in   5:92–93
(See also African Americans' civil
    rights/reform/power movements)
Civil War
    blockade runners   2:138–39
    causes of   2:130–31
    Chancellorsville   2:309
    demise of plantations and wilderness   2:49, 53
    desertion from armies   2:10–11, 312
    draft of mostly poor and lower classes   2:256,
        309
    and Emancipation Proclamation (1862)   2:59,
        60 (sidebar), 135, 308, 309
    families torn by conflicting loyalties   2:10
    in Georgia   2:139, 140 (illus.)
    Gettysburg   2:131–32
    glorification vs. reality of battle   2:257, 258,
        308, 309 (sidebar), 312, 313
    and industrialization of meat-packing   3:175
    John Brown's raid at Harper's Ferry contributing
        to   2:190
    major battles of   2:131 (sidebar)
    Northerners' point of view   2:11, 22
    overview of   2:308–10
    railroads' importance   2:255, 256 (illus.)
    Shiloh   2:257
    in southern Illinois   2:9–10
    Southerners' point of view   2:11, 22
    spies   2:255–56
    Union Army leadership troubles and poor morale
        2:308–10
    Vicksburg   2:217
    western migration and Mexican War contributing
        to   2:88, 89, 395, 405
    Walt Whitman, impact on   2:195–96

(See also Reconstruction)
Clairvoyance   5:239
Clark, Walter Van Tilburg, Ox-Bow Incident, The
    2:288–94
Clarke, Arthur, Childhood's End   5:53–60
Clay, Cassius. See Ali, Muhammad
Clemens, Samuel. See Twain, Mark
Cleopatra   1:190
Clipper ships   2:391
Clothing
    for slaves   2:237
    (See also Fashions)
Coal mining   3:63, 64
Cody, William F. (Buffalo Bill)   2:68, 177
Cohn, Roy   5:2–4
Cold Sassy Tree, Burns, Olive Ann   3:75–79
Cold War
    arms race   5:252 (sidebar)
    Berlin Wall   5:238, 293
    Cuban missile crisis and Bay of Pigs   4:135;
        5:225, 226, 238–39, 293
    and "domino" theory   2:13–14
    FBI investigations   4:129; 5:127
    fear of Communist China and Chinese
        immigrants   4:129
    fear of nuclear war   4:12, 13 (illus.); 5:53, 59,
        225
    fear of "radicalism"   1:399; 4:236
    fear of "socialized" medicine   4:12
    fear of Soviet strength   4:110; 5:225, 292
    fostering American interventions in third world
        1:223
    as indirect, hostile competition of ideologies
        5:225, 254, 292
    iron curtain for Eastern Europe   5:95–96
    Kennedy's olive branch with militancy
        5:224–26
    and McCarthyism   1:84, 398; 3:208, 209 (illus.);
        4:71, 110, 398; 5:2, 3 (illus.), 96, 97, 127
    NATO (North Atlantic Treaty Organization)
        5:124, 224, 292
    and "Red Scare"   1:84–86; 3:105; 4:71–72; 5:2,
        127
    reflected in United Nations   5:254
    trade as weapon in   5:126
    Truman Doctrine (1947–49)   4:110; 5:123–24
    Truman's loyalty program for federal employees
        4:72, 236
    U.S. support for oppressive Latin American
        military dictatorships   5:27–28
    U.S.-Soviet competition for global influence
        5:95–96
    U.S.-Soviet competition in space   5:53
    (See also Communism)
Coleridge, Samuel Taylor   1:116, 416
Colombia, South America   2:268–70, 272–73
Colonial America
    American Revolution   1:122–27
    Boston Tea Party   1:125
    class and economic stratification   1:97, 102, 108

democracy and revolutionary fervor   1:71–72, 74, 76–77, 93–94, 96–97, 108
Dutch in New Netherland (New York)   1:211, 212, 330–32, 333 (illus.), 335 (sidebar), 336
French and Indian War (Seven Years' War)   1:93, 123, 204–6
indentured servants   1:394
materialism   1:102, 105, 311
militias and Continental Army   1:110 (sidebar)
money, credit, and inflation   1:103–4
New England area   1:78–80
New York area   1:107–8, 110, 112 (illus.)
population and economic growth   1:310
reactions to Stamp/Tea/Townshend/Intolerable/Molasses Acts   1:93, 94 (sidebar), 102, 123–25
regional conflicts   1:211–12
rhetoric in   1:123
smuggling   1:102–3
towns and cities   1:102
westward expansion   1:102, 103, 107, 204
Yankee stereotype   1:217
(See also American Indians; American Revolution; Slavery in America; United States)
Colonialism, imperialism, and interventionism
American
bolstered by social Darwinism   3:234–35
Chile   5:164–65
Cuba   3:231, 278; 4:135; 5:225, 226, 238–39, 293
Domican Republic   5:220
El Salvador   3:282
Guam   3:277
Guatemala   5:27–28
Latin America   3:231, 277–78, 280–81
Liberia   2:404
Monroe Doctrine (1823) and "big stick" corollary (1904)   3:277
Nicaragua   3:282
Panama Canal   3:231–32
Philippines   3:101, 278
Puerto Rico   3:277; 4:385–86; 5:215
Spanish-American War (1898)   3:101, 278
Belgian   2:145–46, 150–51
British   2:118–19
in America. See Colonial America
bolstered by overseas commerce   1:337
criticized by H. G. Wells   3:406, 410
and decolonization of late 1940s   4:165
East Africa   3:290–91
end of   5:107
fostering sense of superiority   2:154
India   2:182–84, 276–77; 3:181–82, 297–98
Ireland. See Ireland
Nigeria and Igbo people   2:362, 364; 3:84
Palestine   4:102–5
Rhodesia   4:165–66
Tasmania   3:406
viewed as "bettering" and "civilizing" native peoples   1:118; 2:146; 3:84
Wales   1:149
West Indies   2:183–84
in China   3:205
Dutch   1:338
French
Algeria   3:211–13
Indochina (Vietnam)   5:101, 306
Saint-Domingue (Haiti)   5:116–17
German   3:290
Italian   4:67
Japanese   4:58–59, 92, 177–78, 349–54
missionaries   2:118–19, 147, 161–62, 183, 361–62; 3:133, 280
segregation of rulers and ruled   3:182
Spanish
Colombia   2:268
Mexico   5:172
Puerto Rico   5:214–15
Color Purple, The, Walker, Alice   3:80–87
Comiskey, Charles   3:149; 5:314, 316
Common Sense, Paine, Thomas   1:71–77
effectiveness of   1:94
Communal movements
Communards and Paris Commune   1:363
Shakerism   3:95, 99
Twin Oaks colony   5:279
Communism
and anti-Bolshevik reactions of 1920s   3:21–22, 44
appeal of, to blacks   3:164, 238–39
in China   3:136, 194
communists as targets of Holocaust   4:160, 267
contrast with capitalism   4:166
global disillusion with, following revelations of Stalin's purges   4:166
Great Depression enhancing appeal of   3:39–40, 45, 129, 208–10
influence on Jack London   3:52
labor organizers accused of   3:144
landowners as "capitalist" enemies of   4:282
and Marxism   3:59, 179, 321; 4:18–19
opposition to racism and prejudice   3:40; 4:211
as theory   4:166
use of folksongs   3:47, 50
(See also Cold War; Soviet Union)
Communist Manifesto   1:376
Computers   5:97, 127
Comstock Lode (Nevada silver mines)   2:288–89, 290 (sidebar)
Comte, Auguste   3:213
Confessions of Nat Turner, The, Styron, William   2:93–98
Confucius   3:193 (sidebar)
Congregationalists   1:357, 424–25
Connell, Richard, *Most Dangerous Game, The*   3:231–35
Conrad, Joseph, *Heart of Darkness*   2:145–51
Conroy, Pat, *Prince of Tides, The*   5:285–90
Conservatism

fundamentalism and New/Religious Right
5:137–39

pro-business policies of Reagan presidency   5:1

Contender, The, Lipsyte, Robert   5:67–73

Copernicus, Nicolaus   1:24, 94, 305

Corcoran, Thomas "Tommy the Cork" Gardiner
3:402

CORE (Congress of Racial Equality)   3:42; 4:376

Corey, Giles   1:83 (sidebar), 395

Corinth   1:238, 241

Cormier, Robert, *Chocolate War, The*   5:61–66

Cossacks   3:233

Cotton

causing soil exhaustion   3:390

crop failures from boll weevil   4:2

as "King" Cotton   2:15, 22, 44 (illus.), 168, 403

North-South contention over trade in   3:203–4

plummeting of prices for farmers in 1920s and
'30s   3:153, 390, 391

for typhus prevention, advantages of clothing and
bedding of   1:115

Cotton, John   1:352

Coughlin, Father Charles   4:373

Count of Monte-Cristo, The, Dumas, Alexandre
2:99–104

Counterculture (beatniks, hippies, and protesters)

in 1950s   4:75, 289, 293, 399–400

in 1960s   5:37, 64 (sidebar), 83, 158, 237, 272,
279, 308–10, 323–25

Coxey, Jacob S. and Coxey's Army   3:51–52

Crane, Stephen, *Red Badge of Courage, The*
2:308–13

Craven, Margaret, *I Heard the Owl Call My Name*
5:194–200

Creationism   2:30

Creoles   3:15–18; 4:365; 5:21, 130

Creon   1:15, 17, 18, 19

Crime

blacks and Latinos as victims of   4:31;
5:340–41

blacks turning to   4:145

and capital punishment   4:379–80; 5:131

by Chinese American tongs   4:129

and creation of police detectives   2:153–54

drug-related   4:250–51

during Reconstruction, violence and unequal
justice for freed slaves   5:20–21

gang truce in Los Angeles   5:341

by gangs, juvenile delinquents   4:251, 386,
387–89

gangsters (*tsotsi*) of South Africa   4:97

outlaws on American western frontier
1:256–57

outlaws in medieval England   1:252–53

and Pinkerton's National Detective Agency
3:225–26

Prohibition fostering corruption, bootlegging, and
gangsterism   3:69, 147–48, 366–67, 401

in slums, ghettos   5:13, 67–68, 112, 146, 150,
339–42

(*See also* Law enforcement; Lynching)

Cromwell, Oliver   1:299, 306

Crucible, The, Miller, Arthur   1:78–86

Crusades   1:182, 291

Cry, the Beloved Country, Paton, Alan   4:94–100

Cuba

American interventions of 1898 and 1901
3:231, 278

Bay of Pigs and missile crisis   4:135; 5:225,
226, 238–39, 293

personalismo   4:275

religion   4:274–75

Revolution of 1950s   2:273

role of luck   4:275–76

Cultural conflict. *See* Ethnic and cultural conflicts

Cyprus   1:296

Cyrano de Bergerac, Rostand, Edmond   1:87–92

Cyrano de Bergerac, Savinien de   1:87, 88
(sidebar), 89–90

D

Daisy Miller, James, Henry   2:105–10

Daly, Carroll John   3:227

Damnation. *See* Sin and damnation

Dana, Richard Henry, Jr., *Two Years before the Mast*
2:391–96

Dance   4:387

Dandelion Wine, Bradbury, Ray   3:88–93

Dante Alighieri

Divine Comedy   1:175 (sidebar), 178

Inferno   1:174–80

influence on Joyce   3:111

Daoism (also Taoism)   5:237

D'Artagnan (Charles-Ogier de Batz de Castelmore)
1:387

Darwin, Charles   2:29, 119

Darwin, Erasmus   1:116

Darwinism. *See* Evolution

Dawes Act (1887)   2:68, 179; 4:186

Dawn, Wiesel, Elie   4:101–8

Day No Pigs Would Die, A, Peck, Robert Newton
3:94–99

DDT   4:338–39

De Beauvoir, Simone   4:167

De Gaulle, Charles   3:214

De Tocqueville, Alexis   2:106

Deafness. *See* Disabled persons

Dean, James   4:392, 400

Dean, John   5:159 (illus.)

Death in the Family, A, Agee, James   3:100–105

Death of a Salesman, Miller, Arthur   4:109–15

Debs, Eugene V.   3:54, 175

Declaration of Independence, The, Jefferson, Thomas
1:93–100

comparison to language in *Common Sense*   1:76

evoked in King's "I Have Dream" speech   5:191

evoked in Lincoln's Gettysburg Address
2:134–35

Declaration of the Rights of Man (French Revolution) 1:*372*

Declaration of Sentiments (for women's rights) 2:*24, 55, 204*; 3:*16*

Dee, John 1:*385* (sidebar)

Defoe, Daniel 1:*131, 268, 342*
  Robinson Crusoe 1:*337–43*

Delamere, Hugh Cholmondeley, Baron 3:*295*

Delaware (Lenape) Indians 1:*206, 219–20*

Democracy
  in 19th-century America 2:*87–88, 89–91*
  in ancient Greece 1:*18, 321, 322*
  before and after publication of *Common Sense* 1:*74*
  individualism and egalitarianism contributing to 2:*302*
  influence of Declaration of Independence upon 1:*100*
  Kennedy's call for defense of freedom 5:*226–27*
  at King Arthur's round table 1:*292*
  rise of common people as political force in France 1:*164, 165*
  role of printing press in promoting 1:*162* (sidebar)
  Whitman as poet of 2:*196*
  (See also Suffrage)

Denmark 1:*136–38, 141*

Depression, The Great 2:*45*

Detective fiction. *See* Mystery and detective stories

Developmental disabilities. *See* Disabled persons

Devil (Satan)
  comparative conceptions of 5:*57* (sidebar)
  in Dante's *Inferno* 1:*177, 179* (illus.)
  Lucifer in Milton's *Paradise Lost* 1:*301–3, 305*
  Puritans' belief in 1:*79–81, 102, 393, 394*

Devil and Tom Walker, The, Irving, Washington 1:*101–6*

DeWitt, John 4:*138*

Diary of a Young Girl, The, Frank, Anne 4:*116–23*

Diaspora 4:*101*

Díaz, Porfirio 3:*28, 29, 197, 278*

Dickens, Charles 2:*92, 375*
  Oliver Twist 2:*261–67*
  Tale of Two Cities, A 1:*371–78*

Dickinson, Emily 2:*54–58*

Dictatorship
  of Argentina's military rulers 5:*208–11, 212–13*
  of Chile's military junta 5:*169*
  in Communist China 5:*254–55*
  and "divine right" of Charles I of England 1:*303*
  of Japan's prewar military 4:*178, 183*
  opposition to, in *Twenty-Thousand Leagues under the Sea* 2:*387*
  Orwell's attacks upon 5:*254* (sidebar)
  of Peru's military junta 5:*333–34*
  warnings against 1:*18*
  (See also Fascism; Hitler, Adolf; Soviet Union; Stalin, Josef)

Diem, Ngo Dinh 5:*102*

Diet
  of concentration camp inmates 4:*268*
  of poor farmers 3:*371*
  of Siberian work camp inmates 4:*283–84*
  of slaves 2:*237*

Dillard, Annie
  American Childhood, An 4:*7–13*
  Pilgrim at Tinker Creek 5:*278–84*

Dinesen, Isak, *Out of Africa* 3:*290–96*

Disabled persons
  in almshouses in 18th-century America 2:*216, 219* (sidebar)
  Clubfooted 3:*264*
  education for 2:*216–17, 221–22*
  Independent Living movement 2:*123*
  overcoming pity 2:*218–19*
  views of, in 1970s 2:*123*
  views of, in Victorian Age 2:*119–20*
  (See also Mental and emotional disabilities)

Diseases
  AIDS 5:*9*
  atomic radiation sickness 4:*181*
  bronchitis 2:*335*
  bubonic plague (Black Death) 1:*159, 160, 344, 345, 350*
  cancer 2:*335*; 4:*340*
  cholera 2:*103*
  "fainting" 3:*420*
  "hysteria" 2:*425*
  leprosy 2:*362*
  measles 1:*220*
  "nerves" (stress, depression) 2:*278–79*
  neurofibromatosis 2:*122*
  polio 4:*9–10*
  postcombat syndrome 4:*80* (sidebar)
  postpartum depression 2:*425*
  Proteus syndrome 2:*122*
  puerperal fever 3:*285*
  rabies 3:*387, 406*
  radioactive poisoning 4:*85*
  respiratory 2:*335*; 3:*2, 76, 219, 223*
  resulting from depression 5:*273*
  scarlet fever 2:*206* (sidebar)
  sickle cell anemia 2:*362* (sidebar)
  smallpox 1:*220, 352*; 2:*347*; 5:*214*
  trench foot and trench fever 3:*9, 115* (sidebar)
  tuberculosis 2:*335*; 3:*2, 219, 223*
  typhoid, typhus 2:*185* (sidebar); 3:*2*
  venereal 4:*37*
  (See also Alcohol and alcoholism; Drug/substance abuse; Medicine; Mental and emotional disabilities)

Dissenters. *See* Anglican Church

Divine Comedy. *See* Inferno

Divorce
  in 1800s 2:*126, 127, 158, 212, 355–56*
  among Issei couples 4:*332*
  in China 2:*370, 371*; 3:*132, 193*; 5:*230*
  in czarist Russia 2:*37, 39*

Doyle's support for reform   2:*158*
in early 20th-century America   3:*167–68, 272, 368*
for Jews   3:*427, 429 (sidebar)*
legalization spurred by Protestantism   2:*113*
and remarriage   4:*242*
soaring rate of, in late 20th century   2:*65;* 4:*241–42;* 5:*36, 138, 267, 273, 286–88*
Dix, Dorothy   3:*17*
Doctorow, E. L., *Ragtime*   3:*319–25*
Doctors. *See* Diseases; Medicine
Documents
    Declaration of Independence (American Revolution)   1:*93–100*
    Declaration of the Rights of Man (French Revolution)   1:*372*
    Declaration of Sentiments (for women's rights in America)   2:*24, 55 204;* 3:*16*
    (*See also* Essays; Narratives; Speeches)
Dodgson, Charles Lutwidge. *See* Carroll, Lewis
Doll's House, A, Ibsen, Henrik   2:*111–17*
Dominican Republic   5:*220*
Don Quixote. *See Adventures of Don Quixote, The*
Donald Duk, Chin, Frank   5:*74–80*
Doolittle, James "Jimmy"   4:*68*
Dorris, Michael, *Yellow Raft in Blue Water, A*   5:*360–66*
Douglas, Stephen A.   2:*2, 242*
Douglass, Frederick
    influence upon Toni Morrison   2:*63*
    Narrative of the Life of Frederick Douglass   2:*236–41*
    on *Uncle Tom's Cabin*   2:*409*
Doyle, Arthur Conan, *Hound of the Baskervilles*   2:*152–59*
Drama. *See* Plays; Theater
Dreiser, Theodore, *Sister Carrie*   2:*327–33*
Dreyfus, Alfred   1:*91–92, 364 (sidebar)*
Drug/substance abuse
    among African Americans   4:*250–51*
    among American Indians   4:*83*
    attitudes of 1950s   5:*99 (sidebar)*
    among beatniks   4:*75*
    dealers' self-concept as respectable and superior   5:*341–42*
    experiments by CIA   4:*293–94*
    fines and prison required by Boggs Act (1951)   5:*99 (sidebar)*
    LSD   4:*288, 289, 292, 293–94;* 5:*82–83, 324–25*
    morphine addiction   3:*218–19, 223*
    Narcotics Control Act (1956)   4:*250*
    opium addiction in China   3:*134 (sidebar)*
    opium products   3:*379*
    in prep schools   4:*74*
    psychedelic   5:*82–83*
    by Puerto Ricans   5:*217*
    risk of AIDS   5:*342*
    suspicions of conspiracy by white officials to allow in ghettos   5:*144*
    unequal, unjust penalties for dealing   5:*342*

aomng youth of 1950s   4:*173*
(*See also* Alcohol and alcoholism)
Drums Along the Mohawk, Edmonds, Walter D.   1:*107–14*
Drury, Allen   5:*4*
Du Bois, W. E. B.
    advocating education for "talented tenth"   3:*250, 385*
    advocating no toleration of segregation or inequality   3:*320*
    compared to Booker T. Washington   2:*345 (sidebar);* 3:*250, 320, 385*
    criticism of *Up from Slavery*   2:*415*
    Souls of Black Folk, The   2:*340–46;* 3:*162–63*
Du Maurier, Daphne, *Rebecca*   3:*326–33*
Dubliners, Joyce, James   3:*106–11*
Dueling   1:*389 (sidebar)*
Dumas, Alexandre
    Count of Monte-Cristo, The   2:*99–104*
    Three Musketeers, The   1:*386–92*
Duncan, King of Scotland   1:*225*
Dune, Herbert, Frank   5:*81–87*
Dunkirk evacuation   4:*356, 359–63*
Dust Bowl, The   3:*34, 46, 138–40;* 4:*297*
Dutch in New Netherland (New York)   1:*211, 212, 330–32, 333 (illus.), 335 (sidebar), 336*
Dutch Reformed Church   1:*331, 425*
Dystopian literature
    Brave New World as   5:*141, 252*
    described   5:*100, 141, 252*
    Handmaid's Tale, The as   5:*141*
    Nineteen Eighty-Four as   5:*100, 141*

E

Earthquakes, in Chile   5:*168 (sidebar)*
Eat a Bowl of Tea, Chu, Luis   4:*124–30*
Eatonville, Florida   3:*383*
Edmonds, Walter D., *Drums Along the Mohawk*   1:*107–14*
Education
    in 19th-century America   2:*42–43, 204–5*
    for African Americans
        in blacks-only schools   2:*413;* 3:*371, 375*
        and *Brown v. Board of Education*   3:*375;* 4:*29–30, 314;* 5:*90, 108, 180, 181*
        demand for more control by   5:*144*
        dropout rates of   5:*342*
        forbidden use of libraries   3:*40, 371*
        freed slaves   2:*411–12, 413, 414*
        improvements in   3:*375, 420*
        integrated   3:*43, 396;* 4:*29–30, 31 (illus.), 314;* 5:*116, 131–32, 181*
        in "Movable School"   3:*380*
        negative effects of segregation on   4:*33*
    of American Indian children   5:*244, 246, 361–62*
    bilingual   4:*45;* 5:*172, 179–81, 183, 217*
    of black South Africans   4:*97*
    creating generation gap   5:*182, 198, 244, 246*

criticality for Jews   3:425
for disabled persons   2:216–17, 221–22;
   4:151–52
by governesses in Victorian Age   2:182, 183
   (sidebar), 378–80
increases in school attendance during Depression
   3:153–54
in Japanese schools in 1930s California   4:333
and *Lau v. Nichols*   5:180
of migrant farm workers' children   3:144
   (sidebar)
minority studies programs
   African American history   5:147–48
   in Black English or Ebonics   5:145, 154, 342
   increasing college enrollments   5:217
   Puerto Rican history and culture   5:217
   women's studies   5:117
at prep schools   4:74
promoted by G.I. Bill   3:92; 4:73
schools handling contentious issues   5:311–12
in small communities   4:217
in Southern mill towns   3:78; 4:256
in Southern rural towns during Depression
   3:352
textbook content reviewed by Religious Right
   5:138
through Americorps program   5:340
University of California v. Bakke   5:181
Education, of men
   apprenticeship system   2:262
   in boarding schools   4:240
   boys' street gangs   3:400–401
   in colonial America   1:23, 123
   in czarist Russia   3:58
   English schools   2:372–77; 3:346
   fagging   2:375
   G.I. Bill (1944)   3:92; 4:73
   hunting as rite of passage   2:48
   importance for achieving middle-class status
      2:303
   in New Netherland   1:212–13
   in private/prep schools   4:325–27; 5:62–63
   reforms in 19th-century England   3:265
   scientific, in France   2:386
   in skills of knighthood   1:182 (sidebar), 290–91
   in traditional Jewish communities of Eastern
      Europe   3:425–26
   Wollstonecraft on   1:410
Education, of women
   in 17th-century England (Tudor era)   1:232–33,
      236
   in 17th-century France   1:30
   in 18th-century France   1:32
   in 18th-century New Netherland   1:212–13
   in 19th-century America vs. Europe   2:106
   in 19th-century England   1:412; 2:30, 181–82,
      297, 422–23
   in 19th-century France   1:408; 2:210, 245
   in 19th-century New England   2:55, 56
      (sidebar), 203

in 19th-century South   2:42
in 20th-century America   1:35
in 20th-century Scotland   4:303–4
Ben Franklin on   1:24 (sidebar)
blacks on athletic scholarships   4:149
college and increased opportunities for   5:174
Jewish   3:427, 430
skepticism for   1:236
in Victorian Age   1:412; 2:30, 181–82, 422–23
Wollstonecraft on   1:409–10; 2:297
Edward I of England   1:244, 291
Egypt, Six-Day War with Israel   4:107
Eichmann, Adolf   4:107 (sidebar), 269, 270, 272,
   273; 5:210
Eisenhower, Dwight D.   4:398; 5:53, 91
Eleanor of Aquitaine   1:250
Elephant Man, The, Pomerance, Bernard   2:118–24
Eliezer, Israel Ben   4:87
Eliot, T.S.   5:42
   Waste Land, The   3:411–17
Elizabeth I of England
   bolstering national pride   1:349
   Catholic faction's opposition to   1:149, 349
   conspiracy of Earl of Essex   1:194, 349
   courtiers   1:263
   proving effectiveness of female monarch   1:233,
      236
   rivalry with, execution of Mary, Queen of Scots
      1:141, 149, 150, 349
   succession of crown to James of Scotland
      1:201
   unification and commercial strengthening of
      England   1:150, 201, 263
   as virgin queen   1:201, 261, 262–63, 350
Elizabethan Age
   belief in supernatural   1:4, 141, 142 (sidebar),
      194–95, 227–28, 262, 346, 350
   bubonic plague   1:344, 350
   concepts of sin and damnation   1:143
   education of women in Tudor era   1:232–33,
      236
   family life and obligations   1:203
   foreign influence/corruption   1:150
   growth of American colonies   1:149
   kinship ties   1:141, 145
   popularity of history plays   1:150
   popularity of revenge tragedies   1:142
   popularity of satire and puns   1:349
   treatment of insane   1:203
   wars with Spain   1:1–2
Ellison, Ralph, *Invisible Man*   4:209–15
Emancipation
   Emancipation Proclamation (1862)   2:59, 60
      (sidebar), 135, 308, 309
   life little changed for freed slaves   5:19–20
   (*See also* Abolitionists/Abolition of slavery)
Embrey, Sue Kunitomi   4:143
Emerson, Ralph Waldo
   influence on Dickinson   2:57
   on John Brown   2:193

as model for Prof. Bhaer in *Little Women*   **2**:*207*
opposition to war with Mexico   **2**:*89*
Self-Reliance   **2**:*314–20*
support for abolition   **2**:*315, 316*
support for American Indians   **2**:*316, 317*
support for Thoreau   **2**:*417*
as transcendentalist   **1**:*356*; **2**:*92, 314*
on *Two Years before the Mast*   **2**:*396*
Endless Steppe, The: Growing Up in Siberia, Hautzig,
   Esther   **4**:*131–36*
Engels, Friedrich   **1**:*376*
England in medieval times
   Anglo-Saxons   **1**:*44–45, 153, 181*
   Celts, Britons, and Arthurian legends   **1**:*196–97,
      288, 289 (illus.), 290*
   expulsion of Jews   **1**:*244, 246, 248*
   feudalism   **1**:*65–66, 153*
   Magna Carta   **1**:*255*
   Norman Conquest   **1**:*181, 251–53*
   relations with Scotland   **1**:*145, 149–50*
   Romans   **1**:*288*
   royal forests   **1**:*251–52*
   Saxon invaders and Wales   **1**:*288*
   wars with France   **1**:*159, 160*
England in 16th century
   Henry VIII   **1**:*149, 150, 231, 232, 234 (illus.)*
   (*See also* Elizabeth I; Elizabethan Age)
England in 17th century
   civil war, execution of King Charles I, and
      Restoration   **1**:*129, 303, 305–6*
   class consciousness   **1**:*338*
   foreign influences upon   **1**:*150*
   Glorious Revolution and William of Orange
      1:*130, 338–39, 342–43*
   growth of tolerance   **1**:*299–300*
   Gunpowder Plot   **1**:*229*
   slave trading by   **1**:*337–38*; **2**:*361*
   wars with France   **1**:*130–31, 305*
   wars with Spain   **1**:*87, 201*
England in 18th century
   British Royal Navy   **1**:*273–79*
   class consciousness   **1**:*342*
   Dissenters and Test Act   **1**:*129, 338, 342, 407,
      411*
   French and Indian War   **1**:*93, 123*
   historic rivalry with France   **1**:*391–92*
   London vs. country living   **2**:*296–97*
   as power in foreign trade   **1**:*400, 401*
   publishing industry's growth   **1**:*342*
   reactions to French Revolution   **1**:*359–60,
      372–73, 373 (sidebar), 376, 408*
   Tories vs. Whigs   **1**:*129–31, 305–6, 311, 337, 342*
   wars with France   **1**:*51–52, 93, 123, 204–6,
      220–21*
   wars with Spain   **1**:*130–31*
England in 19th century
   apprenticeship system   **2**:*262*
   British Royal Navy   **1**:*51–56, 404–5*
   class consciousness   **1**:*376, 413–14*; **2**:*152–53,
      157, 277–78, 296–97*
   and *nouveaux riches*   **3**:*327*
   War of 1812   **1**:*53*
   (*See also* Victorian Age; Victorian women)
England in 20th century
   birthrate/population decline   **3**:*347*; **5**:*348*
   British Library   **3**:*360*
   British Royal Navy   **4**:*229*
   classes, and fading of social hierarchies   **3**:*312,
      315–16, 326–27*; **5**:*347–48*
   consumerism, materialism, conspicuous
      consumption   **1**:*237*; **3**:*344–45, 348*
   as cultural superpower in 1950s   **4**:*307*
      (sidebar)
   despair, decay, and decline   **2**:*275–76*;
      3:*344–45, 348*; **5**:*39–40*
   fascism in 1930s   **4**:*304*
   General Strike of 1926   **5**:*40*
   London "season"   **3**:*312*
   nationalism and socialism   **4**:*231*
   post-WWII decline and recovery   **3**:*66*; **4**:*229,
      231*; **5**:*256–57*
   Scotland   **4**:*305*
   Wales   **3**:*63–64, 66*
   in WWI   **3**:*9, 11 (sidebar)*
   Yorkshire   **3**:*1–3*
Enlightenment, The (Age of Reason)
   American   **2**:*416*
   and American "moral sense"   **1**:*94, 96*
   backlash as Romantic movement   **1**:*106*
   as belief in reason, science, and "progress":
      perfectibility of humankind and its institutions
      1:*24–25, 268*; **2**:*416*
   decline of religious influence and increase of
      materialism   **1**:*102, 311*
   early scientific discoveries fostering   **1**:*24–25,
      94, 96*
   failures of, fostering fierce satires   **1**:*272*
   Franklin's common sense approach to
      experimentation   **1**:*25–26*
   influence on Patrick Henry   **1**:*123*
   Jewish (*Haskalah*)   **3**:*120, 426*; **4**:*88*
   "natural rights" theories of John Locke   **1**:*100*
   treatment of disabled persons   **2**:*119–20*
Entailment   **2**:*296 (sidebar)*
Entertainment
   carnival season of Italy and France   **2**:*81–82*
   circuses and freak shows   **2**:*33, 120, 329*
   dancing   **3**:*23*
   drive-in restaurants of 1950s   **4**:*392*
      (sidebar)
   illicit wartime amusements   **4**:*37, 38*
   as industry   **2**:*329*
   jazz clubs   **3**:*161*
   lotteries   **4**:*235–36*
   minstrel shows   **2**:*16–17, 21, 398*
   ouija board   **5**:*56*
   practical jokes   **1**:*212*
   pubs in England   **3**:*3*
   radio   **3**:*154, 364–65*; **4**:*386, 391*
   standardization of, in 1920s   **3**:*101*

tale-telling and storytelling   1:49, 66–68, 70;
  2:397; 3:421; 4:83 (sidebar), 85
taverns   1:331; 3:219, 398, 400
theaters and concert halls   2:329
for troops of WWII   4:38, 68–69
of working and middle classes   2:303–4
(See also Games and sports; Hollywood and
  motion picture industry; Television)
Environment
  air pollution   4:9
  Chernobyl disaster   5:286, 287 (illus.)
  concerns reflected in Dune   5:85–86
  conservation of buffalo   5:34–35
  destruction of wilderness   2:49, 53
  first Earth Day (April 22, 1970)   5:279 (sidebar)
  nuclear waste disposal   5:286
  pesticides ("biocides") and DDT   4:337–42;
    5:347, 351
  rabbit population in England   5:347
  Walden movement and Twin Oaks colony
    5:279
Epic poems   1:49, 153, 172, 173, 282 (sidebar), 285
  (See also Poetry)
Equal Rights Amendment (ERA)   3:79; 5:51, 136,
  358–59
"Equality" in America
  Emancipation Proclamation (1862)   2:59, 60
    (sidebar), 135, 308, 309
  on eve of Revolution   1:99
  individualism and egalitarian ideals of late 19th
    century   2:302
  (See also African Americans' civil
    rights/reform/power movements; Civil rights
    movements; Segregation; Women's rights
    movement)
Equivocation doctrine   1:230
Erasmus, Desiderius   1:2, 6
Erdrich, Louise, Love Medicine   5:243–50
Escapism
  fantasies of African American youths   4:4
    (sidebar)
  as response to despair   5:40
  and Thurber's Walter Mitty   3:364, 369
Espionage
  Civil War spies   2:255–56
  Cold War spies   4:71–72
  Rosenbergs executed for   4:72, 380, 381 (illus.);
    5:2, 127
Esquivel, Laura, Like Water for Chocolate
  3:196–202
Essays
  Civil Disobedience, Thoreau, Henry David
    2:87–92
  Common Sense, Paine, Thomas   1:71–77, 94
  Fire Next Time, The, Baldwin, James   5:107–14
  Modest Proposal, A, Swift, Jonathan   1:266–72
  Pilgrim at Tinker Creek, Dillard, Annie
    5:278–84
  Prince, The, Machiavelli, Niccolò   1:316–20
  Republic, Plato   1:321–29

Room of One's Own, A, Woolf, Virginia
    3:356–63
  Self-Reliance, Emerson, Ralph Waldo   2:314–20
  Silent Spring, Carson, Rachel   4:337–42
  Souls of Black Folk, The, Du Bois, W. E. B.
    2:340–46
  Vindication of the Rights of Woman, A,
    Wollstonecraft, Mary   1:406–12
  Walden, Thoreau, Henry David   2:416–21
Essex (Robert Devereaux, Earl of Essex)   1:194,
  248, 349
Ethan Frome, Wharton, Edith   2:125–29
Ethiopia   4:67
Ethnicities. See African Americans; American
  Indians; Chinese and Chinese Americans; Japanese
  and Japanese Americans; Jews; Latinos; Puerto Rico
  and Puerto Ricans)
Ethnic and cultural conflicts
  American Indian versus white. See American
    Indians
  Anglo-Saxon English versus Norman   1:181
  Asian versus white. See under Racism and
    prejudice
  Christian versus modern-day secular in U.S.
    3:102; 5:138
  Christian versus warrior, in England   1:49–50
  Dutch versus English in New Netherland
    1:330–32, 334–35
  Eastern (Muslim, Hindu) versus Western
    3:303
  Latino versus white. See Chicanos; Latinos
  male-dominated versus ancient matriarchal
    1:61–62
  rural versus urban in U.S.   3:101–2, 140–41
  Scottish Highlanders versus English   1:187
  Southern versus Southwestern U.S.   4:320–21
  Southern versus Yankee in U.S.   2:217–18
  (See also Multiculturalism; Racism and prejudice)
Ethnology   2:232–33
Eugenics   3:272; 4:152; 5:41–42
Euripides, Medea   1:238–41
Europe, appeal of, to American upper class
  2:105–6
Europe, James Reese   3:162 (sidebar), 163 (illus.)
Everything That Rises Must Converge, O'Connor,
  Flannery   5:88–94
Evolution
  as Darwin's theory of (Darwinism)   1:293; 2:29,
    121
  fostering belief in progress and man's capacity to
    reform   2:195; 3:378
  fostering doubt of man's divine nature   3:378
  interest of H. G. Wells in   3:404–5
  opposed by religious-minded   3:102, 404; 5:138
  and Scopes Trial   3:102 (sidebar)
  as social Darwinism ("survival of the fittest")
    contributing to racism   2:341
    impact on views of poor and disabled
      2:217, 306, 312; 3:207, 410
  H. G. Wells' criticism of   3:410

white superiority, Manifest Destiny, and
    "white man's burden"   **2**:*119, 147, 341;*
    3:*170, 172, 182 (sidebar)*
Extrasensory perception (ESP)   **5**:*47, 239*

F

Fabre, Jean Henri Casimer   **5**:*282*
Facism
    depression of 1930s enhancing appeal of   **3**:*129*
    (*See also* Nazis)
Fahrenheit 451, Bradbury, Ray   **5**:*95–100*
Fairfield, John   **2**:*189*
Fallen Angels, Myers, Walter Dean   **5**:*101–6*
Falwell, Jerry   **5**:*137–38, 140 (illus.)*
Family and family life
    in 19th-century New England   **2**:*54, 126–27*
    in 20th-century England   **3**:*347*
    of African Americans   **3**:*80, 84–86, 353–55,*
        375, 422–23; **4**:*33;* **5**:*68, 145–46, 329–30*
    for Truman Capote   **3**:*72*
    in Celtic society   **1**:*197*
    changing roles within   **5**:*139*
    Chicano   **4**:*45*
    in China   **3**:*131–32, 192–93*
    in colonial America   **1**:*207–8, 217, 221, 334*
    in Elizabethan/Jacobean England   **1**:*141, 150,*
        203
    of gang members, and gangs as substitutes for
        5:*266–67*
    intergenerational conflicts
        among African Americans   **3**:*255;* **4**:*252*
        among American Indians   **5**:*244, 246*
        among Canadian Kwakiutl   **5**:*198*
        among Chicanos   **5**:*182*
        among Chinese Americans   **5**:*358*
        over marriage to person of differing ethnicity
            5:*203–4, 232*
        over WWII   **4**:*327*
    of Mexican Americans   **4**:*172–73*
    pro-family movement of religious right
        5:*138–39*
    role of black female servants in   **4**:*257–58*
    in sharecropper families   **3**:*370–71, 373, 375*
    single-female heads of households   **2**:*65;* **3**:*80,*
        423; **4**:*2;* **5**:*68, 117, 136, 138, 267, 328–29*
    in slave families   **2**:*60, 169, 237–38, 405, 406,*
        410; **4**:*204–5*
    in South   **3**:*78, 80*
    in stepfamilies   **5**:*36*
    in Dylan Thomas's work   **3**:*65*
    (*See also* Divorce; Love and marriage)
Family and family life: literary works depicting
    Beloved   **2**:*59–65*
    Betsey Brown   **4**:*28–34*
    Bless Me, Ultima   **4**:*42–48*
    Bluest Eye, The   **4**:*49–57*
    Cold Sassy Tree   **3**:*75–79*
    Color Purple, The   **3**:*80–87*
    Dandelion Wine   **3**:*88–93*

Death in the Family, A   **3**:*100–105*
Death of a Salesman   **4**:*109–15*
Doll's House, A   **2**:*111–17*
Ethan Frome   **2**:*125–29*
Fences   **4**:*144–50*
Fiddler on the Roof   **3**:*119–24*
Gone with the Wind   **2**:*137–44*
Good Earth, The   **3**:*131–37*
Hamlet   **1**:*136–43*
Heart of Aztlán   **4**:*171–76*
Hero Ain't Nothin' but a Sandwich, A   **5**:*143–48*
His Own Where   **5**:*149–55*
Human Comedy, The   **4**:*193–200*
I Never Sang for My Father   **5**:*201–7*
In Nueva York   **5**:*214–21*
Jacob Have I Loved   **4**:*216–20*
King Lear   **1**:*196–203*
Like Water for Chocolate   **3**:*196–202*
Little Foxes, The   **3**:*203–10*
Little Women   **2**:*202–8*
Long Day's Journey into Night   **3**:*218–24*
Love Medicine   **5**:*243–50*
Man without a Face, The   **4**:*240–46*
Member of the Wedding, The   **4**:*254–59*
Not without Laughter   **3**:*249–56*
Ordinary People   **5**:*259–64*
Pocho   **4**:*295–302*
Prince of Tides, The   **5**:*285–90*
Raisin in the Sun, A   **4**:*309–15*
Red Sky at Morning   **4**:*316–22*
Roll of Thunder, Hear My Cry   **3**:*350–55*
Runner, The   **5**:*306–13*
Seventeen Syllables   **4**:*330–36*
Sons and Lovers   **2**:*334–39*
Sounder   **3**:*370–76*
Sweet Whispers, Brother Rush   **5**:*328–32*
Tree Grows in Brooklyn, A   **3**:*397–403*
Yellow Raft in Blue Water, A   **5**:*360–66*
    (*See also* Autobiography)
Fantasy
    Alice's Adventures in Wonderland   **2**:*28–33*
    Beauty: A Retelling of the Story of Beauty and the
        Beast   **1**:*30–36*
    Devil and Tom Walker, The   **1**:*101–6*
    Handmaid's Tale, The   **5**:*135–42*
    Hobbit, The   **1**:*152–58*
    Rip Van Winkle   **1**:*330–36*
    Secret Life of Walter Mitty, The   **3**:*364–69*
    (*See also* Folklore and fairy tales; Science fiction)
Fard, W. D.   **5**:*12–13, 110*
Farewell to Arms, A, Hemingway, Ernest   **3**:*112–18*
Farewell to Manzanar, Houston, Jeanne W. and
    James D. Houston   **4**:*137–43*
Farley, James Aloysius   **3**:*402*
Farming
    Bracero Program (1942–1964)   **3**:*34;* **4**:*44*
    in California   **3**:*269–71, 275, 334–35*
    chemicalization of, in 1950s   **4**:*203*
    by Cherokee   **5**:*29*
    in Chile   **5**:*163–64, 165*

Dust Bowl of 1930s   3:34, 46, 138–40; 4:297
in England   2:353–54, 358; 3:2, 5–6
families displaced by large corporations   3:92, 269
hard times in 1920s   3:25, 94–95
Homestead Act (1870)   2:322–23; 3:244, 257
mechanization of, in 1930s and '40s   4:203 (sidebar)
in Mexico's *ejidos* system   3:282
in Mexico's hacienda system   3:29, 278, 282
migrant workers and discrimination   3:29–30, 49, 140–42, 269–71, 275, 335, 337; 4:297 (sidebar)
in New England   1:102, 217; 2:125
nurture versus exploitation debate   3:262
racism against Japanese farmers   4:331
skyrocketing production and surpluses of 1960s   4:338
social stratification of owners versus workers   3:336
in South Africa   4:94
Spreckels sugar interests   3:269, 270 (sidebar), 319
tenant farming and sharecropping   2:42, 411; 3:80, 249, 370–71
in Texas of 1900s   3:244
training in, of and by blacks in "Movable School"   3:380
under Soviet Five-Year Plans   4:132
unions for farm workers   3:34, 49–50, 141, 275; 4:175–76
United Farm Workers   4:175, 300–302, 409
and use of pesticides ("biocides")   4:337–42
working conditions, long hours   3:244 (sidebar)
(*See also* Cattle ranching; Cotton)
Fascism
characteristics of   4:304, 306–7
described   1:293–94
neo-fascists   4:40
origins in Italy   4:66
and *Ox-Bow Incident*   2:293
Fashions
African-style clothing and hairdos   4:56; 5:145, 300
American Indian style   5:247
cosmetics for African American women   4:50, 56
global popularity of American   1:223
as symbols of generational conflict   5:271–72
women's
daring styles of 1920s   3:23
"New Look" of 1940s and '50s   4:22
restrictiveness in Victorian era   3:420
as status symbol   2:246, 247 (sidebar)
in youth culture of 1950s   4:172, 392
"zoot suits"   4:173, 403, 404–5, 408–9
(*See also* Clothing)
Fate
in ancient Greece   1:169
in Middle Ages   1:160

portents in Elizabethan era   1:194–95
Faulkner, William
Barn Burning   2:41–46
Bear, The   2:47–53
FDR. *See* Roosevelt, Franklin Delano
Federal Writers' Project   3:237
Felsch, Oscar "Happy"   3:149
Feltre, Fra Bernardino de   1:244
Feminine Mystique, The, and Betty Friedan   1:62; 2:58; 3:430; 4:11 (sidebar), 167, 241, 394; 5:51 (illus.), 136
Feminism. *See* Women's rights movement (and feminism)
Fences, Wilson, August   4:144–50
Fencing   1:141
FEPC (Fair Employment Practices Commission)   3:42
Feudalism   1:65–66, 159–61, 187, 290
Fiddler on the Roof, Stein, Joseph   3:119–24
Film. *See* Hollywood and motion picture industry
Fire Next Time, The, Baldwin, James   5:107–14
First Inaugural Address, Roosevelt, Franklin D.   3:125–30
Fishing
aquaculture   5:285–86
crabs and oysters   4:216–17, 219
game fish   4:274, 275 (sidebar), 279 (sidebar)
by Kwakiutl of British Columbia   5:195
shrimping   5:285–86
Fitzgerald, F. Scott, *Great Gatsby, The*   3:146–52
Flaubert, Gustave, *Madame Bovary*   2:209–15
Fleming, Alexander   3:365–66
Florence, Italy   1:174–76, 316–18
Florida
Belle Glade   3:383–84
Eatonville   3:383
Flowers for Algernon, Keyes, Daniel   4:151–56
Folklore and fairy tales   1:31–32, 36, 106
adapted to American themes   1:335
African   2:63, 64
American Indian   1:332
of American South   2:48–49
Beauty: A Retelling of the Story of Beauty and the Beast, McKinley, Robin   1:30–36
Dutch   1:332
efforts to collect in late 19th century   2:397
Germanic   1:105, 106
impact of Disney fairy tales on socialization of girls   1:36
Merry Adventures of Robin Hood, The, Pyle, Howard   1:250–57
mixed with Judeo-Christian beliefs   1:50, 138
origins of *Beowulf* in   1:49
as social commentary and criticism   1:31–32, 36
Uncle Remus, Harris, Joel Chandler   2:397–402
in Yorkshire, England   1:418–19
(*See also* Myth)
Football   4:145–46, 147; 5:63
for colored girls who have considered suicide / when the rainbow is enuf, Shange, Ntozake   5:115–21

Ford, Henry and Ford Motor Company   3:23, 77, 88, 101; 5:43 (illus.), 44–45
Fordism   5:46
Forster, E. M.   3:356
    Passage to India, A   3:297–304
Fort William Henry Massacre   1:205
Foundation, Asimov, Isaac   5:122–28
France in 15th century   1:159–61
France in 16th century, invasion of Italy   1:317
France in 17th century
    dueling   1:389 (sidebar)
    Gascons   1:386, 391
    musketeers   1:386, 387
    wars and civil turmoil   1:87–89, 305, 386–89
    women's position in   1:30
France in 18th century
    class hatred   1:358–60, 361, 371–72
    love and marriage   1:31
    wars with England   1:51–52, 93, 123, 130–31, 204–6, 220–21, 360
    women's position in   1:408, 409
France in 18th century: French Revolution
    American Revolution's contributions to 2:223–24
    echoes in *Frankenstein*   1:116
    emigrés fleeing   1:360–61, 372
    English reactions to   1:359–60, 372–73, 373 (sidebar), 376, 408
    guillotine   1:360 (sidebar), 373
    Jacobins   1:372
    origins of   1:51, 358–60, 371–72; 2:223–24, 295
    Paris Commune and Communards   1:363
    Reign of Terror   1:372; 2:102, 224
    storming of Bastille   1:358, 362 (illus.), 372; 2:224
    women ignored in proposals for education reform   1:408
France in 19th century
    bourgeoisie   2:209–10
    censorship in   2:383
    class hatred   2:224
    Dreyfus affair   1:91–92, 364 (sidebar)
    historic rivalry with England   1:391–92
    Industrial Age in   2:103–4
    landmark historical dates   1:160 (sidebar)
    Louis Napoleon and end of republic (1848) 2:228–29
    Napoleonic era and wars   2:99–100, 224, 227 (sidebar), 245, 295–96
    Paris as capital of Western art   3:265–66
    Republican government of 1870s   1:91
    Restoration of monarchy after Napoleon (1816) 2:100–101, 224
    Revolution of 1830   1:163–65, 391; 2:100
    Revolution of 1832   2:224–25
    wars with England   1:123, 130–31, 159, 160, 204–6, 220–21, 305, 360
    White Terror (1815)   2:102
    women, education and rights   1:32; 2:210, 245
France in 20th century

African colonies   3:211–13
    as nonracist haven for Richard Wright   4:4
    in WWI   3:9, 11 (sidebar)
Franco, Francisco   4:67
Frank, Anne, *Diary of a Young Girl, The*   4:116–23
Frankenstein, Shelley, Mary   1:115–21
Franklin, Benjamin
    Autobiography of Benjamin Franklin, The 1:22–29
    as embodiment of American Dream   1:26–27, 309
    Poor Richard's Almanac   1:309–15
Freedom Rides   5:88–90
Freemasons (Masons)   2:82
French and Indian War (Seven Years' War)   1:93, 123, 204–6, 220–21
Freud, Sigmund   2:336; 5:260, 261
    and psychoanalysis   4:168 (sidebar); 5:42, 260–61, 263
Frick, Henry Clay   4:8
Friedan, Betty   1:62; 2:58; 3:430; 4:11 (sidebar), 167, 241, 394; 5:51 (illus.), 136
Friedrich, Richter, Hans Peter   4:157–64
Fuchs, Klaus   4:72
Fuentes, Carlos, *Old Gringo, The*   3:277–83
Fugitive Slave Acts (1793 and 1850)   1:42; 2:16, 62, 170, 189, 410
Fujimori, Alberto   5:334
Fuller, Edward   3:149
Fuller, Margaret   1:356, 357
Fundamentalism and New/Religious Right 5:137–39

G

G.I. Bill (1944)   3:92; 4:73
Gaelic League   3:109, 308–9
Gaines, Ernest J.
    Autobiography of Miss Jane Pittman, The   5:19–26
    Gathering of Old Men, A   5:129–34
Galarza, Ernesto, *Barrio Boy*   3:28–35
Galileo   1:305
Games and sports
    archery and quarterstaff fencing   1:253
    backswording   2:375
    bowling   1:335 (sidebar)
    boxing   5:68–69
    "chicken"   4:172
    fencing   1:141
    football   4:145–46, 147; 5:63
    frog-jumping contests   2:251–52
    gambling in mining camps   2:250, 282–83
    hero-worship of players   4:262
    horseracing in England   3:345–46
    hunting   2:47–48; 3:232
    hurling   3:109, 309
    involving animals   1:212
    jingling matches   2:375
    mahjong   5:232 (sidebar)
    racism continuing into 1980s   4:149

rodeo   5:362, 364 (sidebar)
rugby in England   2:374–75
running feats of Jemez Pueblo   4:191
tournaments of knights' skills   1:291
values inculcated in students   5:63
(See also Baseball; Entertainment)
Gandhi, (Mahatma) Mohandas Karamchand   2:92;
   3:298–300, 302; 5:192
Gandil, Arnold "Chick"   3:149; 4:260; 5:314, 315
García Márquez, Gabriel, One Hundred Years of
   Solitude   2:268–74
Garden of Eden   1:301–2
Garnet, Father Henry   1:230
Garrison, William Lloyd   2:23, 89 (sidebar), 242
Garvey, Marcus   3:160, 163; 4:211, 312
Gathering of Old Men, A, Gaines, Ernest J.
   5:129–34
Gay rights movement   4:241
Geller, Uri   5:48
Gematriya   4:89
General literature, Poor Richard's Almanac, Franklin,
   Benjamin   1:309–15
Geoffrey of Monmouth   1:290
George I of England   1:131, 266, 342
George II of England   1:130, 269, 270 (illus.)
George III of England   1:93, 95 (illus.), 97
Germany
   Berlin Wall   5:238, 293
   early 20th century   1:370
   education in post-WWII period ignoring Third
      Reich   4:163
   fascism in   1:293–94
   Tripartite Pact (Japan, Germany, Italy; 1940)
      4:59
   WWI   1:277–78; 3:8, 11 (sidebar)
   (See also Hitler; Nazis)
Gettysburg Address, Lincoln, Abraham   2:130–36
   influence on white South Africans of 20th
      century   4:99
Ghana   4:314
Ghettos
   black   4:30–31; 5:71–72, 143, 149–51
      Bedford-Stuyvesant   5:149–51
      crime in   5:13, 67–68, 112, 146, 150,
         339–42
      drugs, suspicions of conspiracy by white
         officials to allow   5:144
      South Central Los Angeles   5:339–42
   Brooklyn   3:397–98; 4:88
   Jewish   1:244, 249; 4:118
   schools in, as overcrowded and inadequate
      5:151–52
Ghibellines   1:174, 175, 345
Ghosts. See Supernatural
Gibson, William, Miracle Worker, The   2:216–22
Gilded Age (late 19th-century America)   2:20, 306,
   328, 331
Gilman, Charlotte Perkins   3:168–69
   Yellow Wallpaper, The   2:422–28

Ginsberg, Allen   4:75; 5:83, 84 (illus.), 324
"Give Me Liberty or Give Me Death," Henry, Patrick
   1:122–28
Glenn, John   5:292, 296
Glover, Goodwife (Goody)   1:79
Goddard, Robert   5:54
Godwin, William   1:115, 119, 407, 411 (illus.),
   411–12
Gold rushes and silver strikes
   in Black Hills of Dakota   2:67–68
   boom towns   2:289
   in California   2:174–75, 195, 249–50, 281–84
   on Cherokee land in Oklahoma   5:29
   Chinese immigration for   4:124; 5:74, 352
   Klondike   3:52–56, 261 (sidebar)
   miners subject to robbers   1:256
   in Nevada   2:288–89, 290 (sidebar)
   in Nez Percé territory   2:162
   (See also Mining industry)
Golden Notebook, The, Lessing, Doris   4:165–70
Golding, William, Lord of the Flies   4:228–34
Goldman, Emma   3:321
Gone with the Wind, Mitchell, Margaret   2:137–44
Good Earth, The, Buck, Pearl S.   3:131–37
Good, Sarah   1:79, 395, 396
Good versus evil. See Sin and damnation
Gorbachev, Mikhail   5:8
Gothic horror stories and romances   2:81, 85, 185;
   3:338
   Jane Eyre   1:415 (sidebar), 419; 2:181–87
   Rebecca   3:326–33
Gouzenko, Igor   4:72
Governesses in Victorian Age   2:182, 183 (sidebar),
   378–80
Gowrie Conspiracy   1:229
Grady, Henry   2:399
Graetz, Heinrich   4:89
Grant, Duncan   3:356
Grant, Ulysses S.   2:217
Grapes of Wrath, The, Steinbeck, John   3:138–45
"Graying" of America   5:202–4
Great Awakenings
   in American colonies   1:73, 106, 122
   in early 19th-century America   1:424–25
Great Britain. See England
"Great Chain of Being"   1:201, 203
Great Depression, The (1930s)
   in agriculture   3:32, 34, 138–40, 153, 247,
      350–51
   causes of   3:125, 138
   comparisons to hard times of Reconstruction
      2:143–44
   Coxey's Army   3:51–52
   Dust Bowl   3:34, 46, 138–40; 4:297
   in England   5:39–40
   enhancing appeal of communism   3:39–40, 45,
      129, 208–10
   hobo tradition   3:46, 270
   homelessness   3:126, 140, 142

impact on African Americans   3:*154*, *236–37*
impact on South   3:*68–69*
New Deal programs
Farm Relief Act (Agricultural Adjustment Act) (1933)   3:*247*
Federal Writers' Project   3:*237*
FERA (Federal Emergency Relief Administration)   1:*113*
FLSA (Fair Labor Standards Act) (1938)   3:*49*
FSA (Farm Security Administration) (1937)   3:*142*
NLRA (National Labor Relations Act) (1933)   3:*128*
NRA (National Recovery Act) (1933)   3:*390–91*
purposes of   3:*45, 142*
questionable effectiveness   3:*69, 128*
Social Security System   3:*49, 128*
WPA (Works Progress Administration)   3:*128, 391, 423–24*; 4:*44*
Okies   3:*140*
plight of sharecroppers and tenant farmers   3:*105, 350–51*
rural Southern education   3:*352*
soup kitchens   3:*45 (illus.)*
stock market crash and bank failures   3:*125–26, 208*
teamwork, as preoccupation of Steinbeck   3:*337*
widespread unemployment and poverty   3:*68, 126, 350*
WWII helping to end   2:*45*; 3:*424*
Great Gatsby, The, Fitzgerald, F. Scott   3:*146–52*
Great Goddess (ancient Greece)   1:*59, 61–62*
Great Migration (1915–1960)
affecting Harlem Renaissance   3:*159–65, 256, 321, 384, 421*
blacks and issue of union membership   3:*39*; 4:*210*
causing increase of single female-headed families   3:*80, 423*; 4:*2*
estimates of numbers of   4:*2, 50, 203*
exacerbating racial tensions in Northern cities   2:*6*
housing discrimination in North   3:*39, 159*; 4:*30–31*
increasing with WWI   3:*236, 384*
increasing with WWII   4:*51*
making race a national question   4:*209–10*
offering hope, then disillusion   3:*39, 80, 159, 236*; 4:*50–51*
to Pittsburgh's steel and coal industries   4:*144*
reasons for   4:*202–3*
sharecroppers fleeing economic and racial oppression   3:*351*
targeting Chicago and New York City   4:*309*
transforming African Americans' sense of identity   4:*210*

two phases of   4:*309*
Great War, The. *See* World War I
Greece, invasion of Turkey (1920)   3:*340*
Greece in ancient times
Athens
citizenship law   1:*241*
Parthenon   1:*240*
Pericles   1:*17, 18, 240, 241, 322*
Plato   1:*321–22, 328*
Socrates   1:*240, 322, 323 (illus.), 324, 327*
Sophists   1:*19, 240*
Theseus   1:*57, 61 (sidebar), 258, 259*
Bronze Age   1:*14, 258, 280, 283 (sidebar)*
burial rites   1:*18–19*
civic/human laws versus divine   1:*17, 20*
and concept of barbarians   1:*173*
Corinth   1:*238, 241*
"Dark Ages"   1:*167, 172, 283 (sidebar), 286*
Mycenaean Age   1:*57–59, 167, 258, 281–82, 283 (sidebar)*
Peloponnesian War   1:*241, 324, 328*
position of women in   1:*17, 20, 58–59, 230–40, 259*
ritual sacrifice   1:*283*
Sparta   1:*324–25, 328*
suicide as honorable   4:*22*
Thebes   1:*14*
Thirty Tyrants   1:*322, 324, 325 (sidebar)*
Trojan War   1:*8, 14, 166–69, 281, 283 (sidebar)*
Greek myths
basis of *Aeneid* in   1:*9*
basis of *Antigone* in   1:*14*
basis of *Medea* in   1:*238*
basis of *Midsummer Night's Dream* in   1:*259 (sidebar)*
Great Goddess and Amazons   1:*58–59, 61–62, 258, 259–60*
Ovid's *Metamorphoses* as source of   1:*262*
as sources of ideas for humanists   1:*380*
as sources for Milton's *Paradise Lost*   1:*301*
Zeus   1:*9, 59, 61, 170, 282, 283, 301*
Green Mountain Boys   3:*98 (sidebar)*
Greene, Bette, *Summer of My German Soldier*   4:*371–77*
Griffes   3:*18*
Grissom, Gus   5:*296*
Guatemala and refugees   5:*27–29*
Guelphs   1:*174, 175, 345*
Guest, Judith, *Ordinary People*   5:*259–64*
Guillotine   1:*360 (sidebar), 373*
Guillotine, Dr. Joseph Ignace   1:*360*
Gulliver's Travels
Swift, Jonathan   1:*129–35*
War of the Worlds compared to   3:*410*
Gunpowder Plot   1:*229*
Guthrie, Woody
Bound for Glory   3:*44–50*
on songs of New Deal era   3:*128 (sidebar)*
Gypsies

in England   3:3
as victims of holocaust   4:119, 160, 267

H

Hachiya, Michihiko, *Hiroshima Diary*   4:177–84
Hades   1:283, 285
Haiti (formerly Saint-Domingue)   5:116–17
Haley, Alex
    Autobiography of Malcolm X, The (with Malcolm X)   5:11–18
    Roots   5:298–305
Hall, James Norman, *Mutiny on the Bounty*   1:273–79
Hamer, Fanny Lou   3:354
Hamilton, Virginia, *Sweet Whispers, Brother Rush*   5:328–32
Hamlet, Shakespeare, William   1:136–43
Hammett, Dashiell
    influence upon Hellman   3:210
    Maltese Falcon, The   3:225–30
Handmaid's Tale, The, Atwood, Margaret   5:135–42
Hansberry, Lorraine, *Raisin in the Sun, A*   4:309–15
Harding, Warren G.   3:22 (illus.)
Hardy, Thomas, *Tess of the D'Urbervilles*   2:353–59
Harlem, New York   4:247–48; 5:67–68
Harlem Renaissance   3:159–65, 256, 321, 384–85, 421; 4:204 (sidebar), 207
Harrington, Michael   5:266 (sidebar)
Harris, Joel Chandler, *Uncle Remus*   2:397–402
Hart, Leo   3:144 (sidebar)
Harte, Bret, *Outcasts of Poker Flat, The*   2:281–87
Harwood, Richard   4:40
Hasidim   3:425, 426; 4:87–90
Hate groups
    Knights of the White Camellia   5:21 (sidebar)
    (*See also* Ku Klux Klan)
Hathorne, John   1:83 (sidebar), 396, 420, 422, 424 (sidebar), 425 (sidebar)
Hathorne, William   1:420, 424 (sidebar)
Hautzig, Esther, *Endless Steppe, The: Growing Up in Siberia*   4:131–36
Hawthorne, Nathaniel
    Scarlet Letter, The   1:351–57
    Young Goodman Brown   1:420–26
Haya de la Torre, Raul   5:333, 334
Hays, Mary   1:412
Health issues
    Medicaid   5:68
    overcrowding of hospitals in ghettos   5:150
    scientific improvements in Victorian Age   1:115; 2:119
    (*See also* Disabled persons; Diseases; Drug/substance abuse; Mental and emotional disabilities)
Heart of Aztlán, Anaya, Rudolfo A.   4:171–76
Heart of Darkness, Conrad, Joseph   2:145–51
Heart Is a Lonely Hunter, The, McCullers, Carson   3:153–58
Hebrides   1:226

Hector   1:170
Heinlein, Robert A., *Stranger in a Strange Land*   5:321–27
Heinz, Henry   4:8
Heisenberg, Werner   5:283
Helen of Troy   1:8, 166, 168 (illus.), 281
Hell. *See* Devil (Satan); *Inferno*; *Paradise Lost*; Sin and damnation
Heller, Joseph, *Catch-22*   4:66–72
Hellman, Lillian, *Little Foxes, The*   3:203–10
Hemingway, Ernest
    Farewell to Arms, A   3:112–18
    Old Man and the Sea, The   4:274–80
Henry II of England   1:250, 251, 254–55
Henry IV of England   1:144
Henry IV, Part I, Shakespeare, William   1:144–51
Henry, Patrick
    as "American, not Virginian"   1:96–97
    "Give Me Liberty or Give Me Death" speech   1:122–28
Henry V of England   1:146
Henry VIII of England   1:149, 150, 231, 232, 234 (illus.)
Herbert, Frank, *Dune*   5:81–87
Hero Ain't Nothin' but a Sandwich, A, Childress, Alice   5:143–48
Herodotus   1:286
Herriott, James, *All Creatures Great and Small*   3:1–7
Herzl, Theodore   4:102
Hesse, Hermann, *Siddhartha*   1:365–70
Heyerdahl, Thor, *Kon-Tiki*   4:221–27
Hidalgos   1:2–3
Highlanders of Scotland   1:187
Hinduism   3:300, 302
Hine, Lewis   3:285
Hinton, S. E., *Outsiders, The*   5:265–70
Hippies. *See* Counterculture
Hippolyta and Amazons   1:58–59, 61–62, 258, 259–60
Hirohito, Emperor of Japan   4:178, 183
Hiroshima Diary, Hachiya, Michihiko   4:177–84
Hirsch, Samson Raphael   4:90 (sidebar)
His Own Where, Jordan, June   5:149–55
Hispanics. *See* Chicanos; Latinos
Hiss, Alger   4:110; 5:96
Histories
    Bury My Heart at Wounded Knee, Brown, Dee   2:74–80
    Two Years before the Mast, Dana, Richard Henry, Jr.   2:391–96
Hitler, Adolf   1:113–14, 294; 3:210; 4:157–58, 305 (illus.), 356–57; 5:122–23
Hobbit, The, Tolkien, J.R.R.   1:152–58
Holinshed, Raphael   1:148, 227
Holland   4:116–19
Holland, Isabelle, *Man without a Face, The*   4:240–46
Hollywood and motion picture industry
    Caucasian ideal of beauty reinforced by   4:50

development of   3:3, 89, 101
end of golden age of (1920s–45)   4:75–76
ethnic stereotypes used by   2:142; 4:50, 369
female as sex object   4:393
late 1940s attempts to address real issues
    4:75–76
patriotic films for WWII   4:325
reflecting and influencing teenagers and
    generation gap   4:392, 394
as target of witch hunts for "Reds"   4:236
"thrillers" as new genre   3:329
(See also Television)
Holocaust
adding to urgency of Zionist appeal   4:102
beginnings within Germany (1933–38)
    3:401–3; 4:267
collusion of some Jews in   4:269–70, 272–73
concentration camps   4:160–61, 194, 267–73
delayed U.S. acceptance of proof   3:403
denial by anti-Semites and neo-fascists   4:40
described   4:119–20
estimates of number of victims   4:194
extension outside German borders (1939)
    3:403; 4:267
as "final solution"   4:267
Israel exacting justice for atrocities   4:107
    (sidebar)
Jews in Siberia "spared"   4:134
Kristallnacht   4:159, 162–63
liberation of Buchenwald   4:269, 272
made easier by Nazis' deceptions and some Jews'
    willingness to be deceived   4:272, 273
Nazi "scapegoating" of Jews (1933–39)
    4:159–60
in occupied Holland   4:117–18
reactions of Germans to   4:194
subsequent pressure upon Jewish women to bear
    children   3:430
Vrba-Wetzler report and warnings to Hungarian
    Jews   4:269, 272
war crimes trials   4:272–73
(See also Diary of a Young Girl, The; Friedrich;
    Night)
Holy Grail legends   4:264–65
Holy League   1:296
Holy Roman Empire   1:87, 174, 176, 344, 345
Home to Harlem, McKay, Claude   3:159–65
Homelessness
of deinstitutionalized mental patients   4:289
during The Great Depression of 1930s   3:126,
    140, 142
in South Africa   4:97
of Vietnam veterans   5:106
Homer
Iliad   1:166–73
Odyssey   1:280–87
Homosexuality
in Angels in America   5:1–10
in Biloxi Blues   4:38
in Catcher in the Rye   4:74

growth of gay subculture   4:241, 245–46
and lesbianism   3:327–28, 357, 362
in Man without a Face, The   4:244
in military   4:38, 39–40
and Mormonism   5:4–5
as reported by Kinsey   4:398 (sidebar); 5:324
seen as pathological deviance   4:77
targeted by Nazis in Holocaust   4:119, 160
targeted by New/Religious Right   5:136, 137–38
Hood, Robin   1:188, 255 (sidebar)
(See also Merry Adventures of Robin Hood)
Hoover, Herbert   3:126–27
Hoover, J. Edgar   1:84 (sidebar), 399
Horror fiction
Carrie   5:46–52
Frankenstein   1:115–21
Psycho   5:46–47
Hound of the Baskervilles, Doyle, Arthur Conan
    2:152–59
House Made of Dawn, Momaday, N. Scott
    4:185–92
House of Mirth, The, Wharton, Edith   3:166–73
House of Stairs, Sleator, William   5:156–62
House of the Spirits, The, Allende, Isabel   5:163–70
House on Mango Street, The, Cisneros, Sandra
    5:171–77
Housing
adobes   4:318
in barrios   5:174
in black ghettos. See Ghettos
discrimination against African Americans   2:13;
    3:39, 237; 4:30–31, 310; 5:13
in middle-class suburbs   5:261–62
postwar prosperity, G.I. Bill, and home
    ownership   4:73
and racial violence   4:310 (sidebar)
racist restrictions ruled illegal   4:201
rent control ordinances   4:384, 400
rent supplements   5:68
shacks of sharecropper families   3:371
in slum tenements of New York   3:397–98;
    4:384–85, 401; 5:67–68, 149–50
in South Africa   4:95, 96–97
streetcars' impact on   4:366
"white flight" to suburbs   4:384, 385
Houston, Jeanne W. and James D. Houston, Farewell
    to Manzanar   4:137–43
Howe, Samuel Gridley   2:217
Huerta, Dolores   4:47
Huerta, Victoriano   3:278–79
Hughes, Langston   3:164
Not without Laughter   3:249–56
Hughes, Thomas, Tom Brown's Schooldays
    2:372–77
Hugo, Victor
Hunchback of Notre Dame, The   1:159–65
on John Brown   2:193
Les Misérables   2:223–29
Human Comedy, The, Saroyan, William   4:193–200
Humanism   1:2, 142, 233, 380, 381

Hunchback of Notre Dame, The, Hugo, Victor
  1:*159–65*
Hundred Years' War   1:*159, 160*
Hungary   4:*166*
Hunger of Memory, Rodriguez, Richard   5:*178–84*
Hunt, Irene, *Across Five Aprils*   2:*8–14*
Hurston, Zora Neale, *Their Eyes Were Watching God*
  3:*383–89*
Hutchinson, Anne   1:*352 (sidebar), 352–53*
Huxley, Aldous, *Brave New World*   5:*39–45*
Huxley, Thomas Henry   3:*265, 404*; 5:*324–25*
Hydrogen bomb   4:*183*

I

"I Have a Dream," King, Martin Luther, Jr.
  5:*185–93*
I Heard the Owl Call My Name, Craven, Margaret
  5:*194–200*
I Know Why the Caged Bird Sings, Angelou, Maya
  4:*201–8*
I Never Sang for My Father, Anderson, Robert
  5:*201–7*
"I Will Fight No More Forever," Chief Joseph
  2:*160–67*
Ibsen, Henrik   3:*406*
    Doll's House, A   2:*111–17*
Idaho   2:*367*
Igbo of Africa, late 19th century   2:*360–62*
Iliad, Homer   1:*9, 166–73*
Illinois. *See* Chicago
Imagining Argentina, Thornton, Laurence   5:*208–13*
Imagism   3:*413–14*
Imlay, Gilbert   1:*410*
Immigration in 19th century
    Chinese   2:*367–68, 370 (sidebar), 371*;
      4:*124–27*; 5:*74*
    Chinese Exclusion Acts (1882 and 1902)
      2:*368*; 4:*125*; 5:*74, 231*
    Geary Act (1892)   2:*368*; 4:*125*
    Irish   3:*107, 398–99*
    Jewish   3:*121*
    to steel mills   4:*8*
    Swedish   3:*243–44, 259–60*
    urbanization with   2:*302, 327*; 3:*166*
    to Western homesteads   3:*258–61*
Immigration in 20th century
    America as "salad bowl" rather than melting pot
      5:*176*
    anti-immigrant bigotry and fears   3:*233, 402*;
      4:*330–31*; 5:*180*
    Armenian   4:*199*
    California Alien Land Act (1913)   4:*331*
    Chinese   2:*368*; 4:*125, 127, 129*; 5:*229, 352–54*
    Chinese Exclusion Act and Geary Acts (1904,
      1922, 1924)   2:*368*; 5:*231*
    feelings of shame and inferiority among children
      of   5:*78–79*
    generational conflicts between children and
      parents   4:*385*; 5:*78–79, 182, 358*

Guatemalan political refugees   5:*28–29*
Immigration Acts (1924, 1965, 1980)   4:*331*;
    5:*28, 75 (sidebar)*
Irish   3:*401–2*
Japanese   3:*30*; 4:*137, 143, 330–31*
Japanese "picture brides"   4:*331–32*
Jewish   3:*121*; 4:*92, 102–3, 104 (illus.), 106*
Literacy Test (1917)   3:*233*
Mexican   3:*29–30*; 4:*44–48*
National Origins Act (1924)   3:*233*
of Puerto Ricans   4:*385*; 5:*215–16*
restrictions of 1920s enhancing opportunity for
    blacks   4:*203*
Russian   3:*233*
Sanctuary Movement   5:*29*
urbanization with   3:*101, 102*
War Brides Act (1945)   4:*124, 127*; 5:*231*
Imperialism. *See* Colonialism, imperialism, and
  interventionism
Impressment of sailors by Royal Navy   1:*52*
In medias res   2:*62*
In Nueva York, Mohr, Nicholasa   5:*214–21*
Inaugural Address
    Kennedy, John F.   5:*222–28*
    Roosevelt, Franklin D.   3:*125–30*
Incest   4:*52*
Incidents in the Life of a Slave Girl, Jacobs, Harriet
  2:*168–73*
    influence upon Toni Morrison   2:*63*
Independent Living Movement   2:*123*
Indeterminacy, principle of   5:*283*
India
    500s to 300s b.c.   1:*365*
    Amritsar massacre   3:*298*
    Buddhism   1:*365–69*; 3:*186–87*; 5:*48*
    caste system   1:*366*; 3:*182, 184*
    civil service   3:*185*
    infrastructure   3:*184–85*
    map of   3:*183 (illus.)*
    nationalism   3:*298–300*
    religions   1:*366*; 3:*300–301, 302*
    under British rule   2:*182–84, 276–77*; 3:*181–82,
      297–98*
Indians. *See* American Indians
Individualism
    and classical liberalism   3:*268*
    criticism of "cult" of   5:*2 (sidebar)*
    decline in, during 1950s era of conformity
      4:*382*; 5:*323–24*
    and egalitarian ideals in 19th-century America
      2:*302*
    machine age as debasing   5:*41, 46*
    Teddy Roosevelt popularizing "Old West" myth
      of   5:*206*
    of Thoreau   2:*88–89*
Industrialization
    allowing growth of middle class   2:*118, 153*
    democracy and capitalism, shift toward
      2:*334–35*
    in France   2:*103–4, 245–46*

leading to Romantic movement   **1**:*106, 115–16*
leading to worker/owner class distinctions
   2:*303*
reaction of Luddites   **1**:*119–20, 120 (illus.)*
social and economic improvement and upheaval
   1:*106*; **2**:*417*
stimulants of   **1**:*115, 336, 417*
women's increasing opportunities for jobs
   2:*423*
working conditions and attempts to improve
   3:*174–75, 178–79*
working conditions and worker's revolts   **1**:*363*;
   2:*328, 329, 404*
(*See also* Capitalism; Labor unions; Urbanization)
Inferno, Dante Alighieri   **1**:*174–80*
Inheritance, by entailment   **2**:*296 (sidebar)*
Integration
   Baldwin on moral standards of   **5**:*113*
   Brown v. Board of Education   **3**:*375*; **4**:*29–30,*
      314; **5**:*90, 108, 180, 181*
   opposition of Malcolm X to   **5**:*15*
   of schools   **3**:*43, 396*; **4**:*29–30, 31 (illus.), 314*;
      5:*116, 131–32, 181*
   slow pace of   **4**:*33–34*
   of University of Mississippi   **5**:*19*
Internment of Japanese Americans (1942–44)
   4:*138–43, 195, 335–36*
Interventionism. *See* Colonialism, imperialism, and
   interventionism
Invisible Man, Ellison, Ralph   **4**:*209–15*
Ionesco, Eugène   **4**:*400*
Ireland
   Absentees   **1**:*266, 269 (sidebar), 269*
   Catholicism in   **1**:*269*; **3**:*107–8, 109–10, 305–7*
   concessions by James I   **1**:*131*
   cultural revival   **3**:*108–9, 308–9*
   English subjugation of   **1**:*131–32, 267*; **3**:*106–7,*
      305–6
   famine and emigration in mid-19th century
      2:*302*
   Home Rule movement   **3**:*109, 307*
   Irishness as depicted in *Kim*   **3**:*187*
   misgovernment and economic decline in 18th
      century   **1**:*266–69*
   Parnell, Charles   **3**:*109–10*
   Potato Famine of 1845   **3**:*107*
   Protestants and Patriots   **1**:*267*
   (*See also* England)
Irish Americans
   growing acceptance of   **3**:*401–2*
   sense of community   **3**:*400–401*
   stereotypes of heavy drinking   **3**:*220, 398, 400*
Irving, Washington
   Devil and Tom Walker, The   **1**:*101–6*
   Legend of Sleepy Hollow, The   **1**:*211–18*
   Rip Van Winkle   **1**:*330–36*
   The Sketch Book   **1**:*335–36*
   on slavery   **1**:*103*
Ishi, Last of His Tribe, Kroeber, Theodora   **2**:*174–80*
Islam   **1**:*296*; **3**:*300*

and Nation of Islam   **3**:*238, 325*; **4**:*56, 248–50*;
   5:*12–13, 69, 110–11, 302*
Israel
   Biblical history of   **4**:*101*
   as British mandate of Palestine   **4**:*102–3, 105*
   conflicts with Arabs   **4**:*106–8*
   Hasidic opposition to   **4**:*88*
   immigration to
      denied by Soviet government   **3**:*124*
      from Europe of 1880s   **3**:*121*
   Six-Day War (1967)   **4**:*93*
   War of Independence (1948–49)   **4**:*106*
   Women's Equal Rights Law (1951)   **3**:*430*
Italy
   in 16th century   **1**:*316*
   in ancient times   **1**:*9*
   fascism in   **1**:*293–94*
   Florence   **1**:*174–76, 316–18*
   Jews in   **1**:*246, 248–49*
   map of   **1**:*345 (illus.)*
   Milan   **1**:*379–80*
   Mussolini, Benito   **2**:*293–94*
   Venice   **1**:*242–46, 295–97*
   Verona   **1**:*344–45*
   in and after WWI   **3**:*11 (sidebar), 113–14*; **4**:*66*
   in WWII   **4**:*66–67*
Ithaca   **1**:*281*
Ivanhoe, Scott, Sir Walter   **1**:*181–88*

J

Jackson, Andrew   **1**:*209–10*
Jackson, Shirley, *Lottery, The*   **4**:*235–39*
Jackson, "Shoeless" Joe   **3**:*149*; **4**:*265*; **5**:*314, 316*
Jacob Have I Loved, Paterson, Katherine   **4**:*216–20*
Jacobs, Harriet, *Incidents in the Life of a Slave Girl*
   2:*168–73*
James, Henry
   Daisy Miller   **2**:*105–10*
   on *Dr Jekyll and Mr. Hyde*   **3**:*382*
   Turn of the Screw, The   **2**:*378–83*
James I of England (James IV of Scotland)
   belief in supernatural and witchcraft   **1**:*228,*
      384, 385
   concessions to Irish   **1**:*131*
   daughter's marriage subject to her own approval
      1:*385*
   increase of political and religious factions
      1:*299*
   parallels to life of Hamlet   **1**:*141*
   subject of regicidal conspiracies   **1**:*229, 230*
   succession to throne of England   **1**:*141, 149,*
      150, 201
   support for theater and arts   **1**:*299*
James II of England   **1**:*130*
Jamestown, Virginia   **1**:*379, 384, 394*
Jane Eyre, Brontë, Charlotte   **1**:*415 (sidebar), 419*;
   2:*181–87*
Japan
   in 19th century   **4**:*177*

countries conquered during WWII   5:123
  (sidebar)
dictatorship of prewar military   4:178, 183
Emperor Hirohito   4:178, 183
frosty relations with Korea   4:353–54
furor over textbooks' coverage of WWII   4:354
Hiroshima as first atom bomb target   4:179–82
imperialism of   4:58–59
invasion of China (1930s and '40s)   3:189–90;
  5:229–30
invasion and occupation of Korea (1894-95,
  1904-05, 1910-45)   4:59, 177, 349–54
Korean laborers in   4:353
Nagasaki as second atom bomb target   4:180
  (illus.), 181 (sidebar)
rapprochement with South Korea   4:354
Russo-Japanese War (1904–05)   4:59
WWII   4:58–61
Japanese and Japanese Americans
  as farm workers   3:30
  immigration   3:30; 4:137, 143, 330–31
  Issei and Nisei   4:137
Japanese and Japanese Americans, works concerning
  Farewell to Manzanar   4:137–43
  Hiroshima Diary   4:177–84
  Seventeen Syllables   4:330–36
  So Far from the Bamboo Grove   4:349–55
Jara, Victor   5:164, 168
Jason   1:238–39
Jazz   3:162 (sidebar); 4:258
Jefferson, Thomas
  Declaration of Independence, The   1:93–100
  on Patrick Henry   1:127
Jerusalem   1:182
Jesuits   3:307–8
Jews
  in America   3:430
  assimilation, threat of   3:120, 123, 430; 4:88, 90
    (sidebar), 91
  British offer of homeland in Africa   3:291
  criticality of education for   3:425
  Diaspora   4:101
  divorce   3:427, 429 (sidebar)
  education of women   3:427, 430
  in England   1:182–83, 185; 2:264–65
  expulsion or conversion to Christianity   1:244,
    246; 2:264
  Gematriya   4:89
  in ghettos   1:244, 249; 4:118
  Hasidim   3:425, 426; 4:87–90; 5:283 (sidebar)
  immigrating to America and Israel   3:121
  immigration in 20th century   3:121; 4:92,
    102–4, 106
  in Italy   1:243, 246, 248–49
  Jewish Enlightenment (*Haskalah*)   3:120, 426;
    4:88
  Levantines   1:248
  Marranos   1:248, 249
  marriage-bed custom   3:428 (sidebar)
  Mitnagdim   3:426

and moneylending   1:182–83; 2:264
Orthodox   4:93
of Poland   4:131–32
revival of American   4:91–92, 93
role and rights of women   3:427–30
suicide and   3:428; 4:22
traditional marriage   3:119
Zionism   3:121; 4:88, 101–2
(*See also* Anti-Semitism; Holocaust)
Jews, literary works concerning
  Biloxi Blues   4:35–41
  Chosen, The   4:87–93
  Dawn   4:101–8
  Diary of a Young Girl, The   4:116–23
  Endless Steppe, The: Growing Up in Siberia
    4:131–36
  Fiddler on the Roof   3:119–24
  Friedrich   4:157–64
  Night   4:267–73
  Summer of My German Soldier   4:371–77
  A Tree Grows in Brooklyn   3:402
  Yentl, the Yeshiva Boy   3:425–31
Jim Crow laws
  African American responses to   2:413
  challenges to, by black soldiers of WWI   3:252
  coming under fire in 1930s and '40s   2:53
  described   3:81, 351; 5:90
  federal authorities ignoring   4:1
  origins of term   2:21, 341; 3:351
  upheld by *Plessy v. Ferguson*   2:21, 341,
    399–400, 413; 3:351, 375, 419; 4:1; 5:90, 107–8
John Brown's Final Speech, Brown, John   2:188–94
John I of England   1:251
Johnson, Lyndon Baines   3:324; 4:347, 375; 5:68,
  102
Johnson, Samuel   1:307
Jolly Roger (pirates' flag)   1:401
Jones, Leroi (Amiri Baraka)   4:207
Jonson, Ben   1:150, 300
Jordan, June, *His Own Where*   5:149–55
Joseph, Chief of Wallowa Nez Percé, "I Will Fight
  No More Forever"   2:160–67
Joy Luck Club, The, Tan, Amy   5:229–35
Joyce, James   5:42
  Dubliners   3:106–11
  Portrait of the Artist as a Young Man, A
    3:305–11
Julius Caesar   1:169 (sidebar), 189–91
Julius Caesar, Shakespeare, William   1:189–95
Jung, Carl Gustav   3:329
Jungle, The, Sinclair, Upton   3:174–80
Jupiter   1:191

K

Kansas-Nebraska Act (1854)   1:42; 2:5 (sidebar),
  172, 193
Karma   1:367
Kasztner, Rezso   4:269–70, 272–73
Katherine of Aragon   1:231

Keats, John 1:*406*
Keller, Helen 2:*220 (illus.)*
  (*See also Miracle Worker, The*)
Kelly, Charles T. and Kelly's Army 3:*51–52*
Kennedy, John F.
  appeal to, by King for civil rights 5:*186*
  Bay of Pigs and Cuban Missile Crisis 4:*135*;
    5:*225, 226, 238–39, 293*
  environmental concerns 4:*338, 341 (sidebar)*
  expanding U.S. role in Vietnam 4:*375*
  Inaugural Address 5:*222–28*
  intervention on behalf of civil rights protesters in
    Alabama 5:*12*
  moon walk goal launching space race 5:*81,
    292, 293 (sidebar), 321–22*
  opposing Nixon for president 5:*321–22*
  President's Panel on Mental Retardation 4:*152*
  sending "advisors" to Vietnam 5:*158, 307*
Kennedy, Joseph P. 3:*402*
Kennedy, Robert 5:*90*
Kentucky
  in Civil War 2:*60 (sidebar)*
  slavery in 2:*59–60*
Kenya 3:*290–96*
Kerensky, Alexander 3:*232*
Kerouac, Jack 4:*75*
Kesey, Ken, *One Flew over the Cuckoo's Nest*
  4:*288–94*
Keyes, Daniel, *Flowers for Algernon* 4:*151–56*
Keynes, John Maynard 3:*356*
Kherdian, David, *Road from Home, The* 3:*338–43*
Khrushchev, Nikita 4:*135, 166, 286, 398, 399
  (illus.)*; 5:*225*
Kim, Kipling, Rudyard 3:*181–88*
King, Dr. Martin Luther, Jr. 5:*14 (illus.), 89 (illus.),
  109 (illus.)*
  appeal to Kennedy for help in civil rights
    movement 5:*12, 186*
  assassination of 4:*54*; 5:*112 (sidebar)*
  criticism of, by Malcolm X 4:*250*; 5:*13, 15, 111*
  education and pastorate 5:*108*
  influenced by Ghandi and passive resistance
    2:*92*; 5:*108, 189, 192*
  influenced by Thoreau 2:*92*
  organization of Montgomery bus boycott 5:*11,
    88, 108*
  protesting residential segregation 2:*12 (illus.),
    13, 97*
  speech: "I Have a Dream" 5:*185–93*
King Lear, Shakespeare, William 1:*196–203*
King, Rodney 5:*340*
King, Stephen, *Carrie* 5:*46–52*
Kingsolver, Barbara, *Bean Trees, The* 5:*27–33*
Kingston, Maxine Hong, *Woman Warrior, The*
  5:*352–59*
Kinsella, W. P., *Shoeless Joe* 5:*314–20*
Kinsey, Alfred Charles and Kinsey Report 4:*75,
  241, 398–99 (sidebar)*; 5:*324*
Kipling, Rudyard, *Kim* 3:*181–88*
Kitchen God's Wife, The, Tan, Amy 3:*189–95*

Klondike 3:*52–56, 261 (sidebar)*
Knights and knighthood 1:*182 (sidebar), 290–91*
Knights of the White Camellia 5:*21 (sidebar)*
Knowles, John, *Separate Peace, A* 4:*323–29*
Knox, John 4:*304*
Kon-Tiki, Heyerdahl, Thor 4:*221–27*
Korea
  frosty relations with Japan 4:*353–54*
  invasion by Japan (1894–95 and 1904–05)
    4:*59, 177*
  occupation by Japan (1910–45) 4:*349–50*
  reprisals against fleeing Japanese (1944–45)
    4:*350, 352 (sidebar)*
Korean War 1:*223*; 3:*73*; 4:*92*
Kristallnacht 4:*159, 162–63*
Kroeber, Theodora, *Ishi, Last of His Tribe* 2:*174–80*
Ku Klux Klan
  birth of, in 1865–66 2:*141 (sidebar), 412*;
    3:*102*; 5:*21*
  law enforcement officers enlisting in 4:*4, 202*
  lynchings and violence against blacks 2:*141
    (sidebar), 143 (sidebar), 412*; 3:*419*; 5:*25, 130*
  re-emergence during
    1920s xenophobic, anti-Bolshevik era 2:*143
      (sidebar)*; 3:*22*; 4:*201–2*
    1940s 4:*201–2*
    1960s civil rights era 5:*21 (sidebar), 25*
Kushner, Tony, *Angels in America* 5:*1–10*

L

Labor unions
  accused of being "red" (communist or socialist)
    3:*144*
  AFL (American Federation of Labor) 3:*44*
  African Americans excluded, then included
    2:*341*; 3:*250*; 4:*210–11*
  Agricultural Labor Relations Act (1975) 4:*48*
  anti-labor and anti-Bolshevik reactions of 1920s
    3:*21–22*
  attempts to limit power of, Taft-Hartley Act
    (1947) 4:*172, 173 (sidebar)*
  Brotherhoood of Sleeping Car Porters 3:*42*
  Carnegie Steel and Homestead Strike (1892)
    3:*321*
  CIO (Congress of Industrial Organizations)
    3:*44*
  "closed" and "union" shops 4:*173 (sidebar)*
  conflicts with management 2:*328, 336 (sidebar)*
  and Debs, Eugene V. 3:*54*
  for farm workers 3:*34, 49–50, 141, 275*
  growth of 2:*328, 336 (sidebar), 341*; 3:*176
    (sidebar)*
  leaders cooperating with business owners
    4:*172*
  leaders' corruption 4:*145*
  and Mexican Americans 4:*172, 175–76*
  National Labor Relations Act (1933) 3:*128*
  opposition to 3:*44, 141, 155 (sidebar), 208*
  Pinkerton's detectives hired to thwart 3:*225*

STFU (Southern Tenant Farmers' Union)   3:208
strikes and violence   3:176 (sidebar), 179; 4:109
table grape boycott   4:175
Language. See Linguistic considerations
Lasch, Christopher   4:111
Last of the Mohicans, The, Cooper, James Fenimore
   1:204–10
Latinos
   Chicanos. See Chicanos
   concepts of machismo and marianismo   3:201;
      4:278–79, 299; 5:167, 173–74, 337
   curanderos   3:199; 4:45
   decline of paternal authority   4:172–73
   enlisting in military for WWII   4:44
   help to Dust Bowl migrants   4:297 (sidebar)
   life in barrios   4:172 (sidebar)
   men admired for adultery   5:337
   mestizo or mixed-race heritage   5:172, 334
   Puerto Rico and Puerto Ricans   3:277;
      4:385–86, 388–89, 401; 5:214–21
   the Virgin de Guadalupe and La Malinche
      5:173
   women's roles   4:299; 5:167–68, 173–74
   in WWII   4:295, 406
   (See also Cuba; Mexico)
Latinos, literary works concerning
   Barrio Boy   3:28–35
   Bless Me, Ultima   4:42–48
   Heart of Aztlán   4:171–76
   House of the Spirits, The   5:163–70
   House on Mango Street, The   5:171–77
   Hunger of Memory   5:178–84
   Imagining Argentina   5:208–13
   In Nueva York   5:214–21
   Like Water for Chocolate   3:196–202
   Old Gringo, The   3:277–83
   Old Man and the Sea, The   4:274–80
   One Hundred Years of Solitude   2:268–74
   Pocho   4:295–302
   Time of the Hero, The   5:333–38
Laudanum   3:379
Laurents, Arthur, et al., West Side Story   4:384–90
Law
   American jury system   4:378–79
   capital punishment   4:379–80; 5:131
   conviction, then successful appeal in Sleepy
      Lagoon murder case   4:405
   judicial opposition in 1980s to civil rights
      legislation   5:1–2
   Jury Selection and Service Act   4:379
   lawyers' apprenticeships and circuit riding   2:1–2
   legal challenges to internment of Japanese
      4:140–41
   legal challenges to restrictive housing covenants
      4:310
   as legislation. See under individual topics, e. g. Civil
      rights movements; Great Depression; Labor
      unions; Segregation
   weakness of Prohibition as legislation   3:22–23,
      69
Law enforcement
   absence on American frontier   2:323
   absence on rural California farms   3:274
   attacking civil rights protesters   5:23 (illus.)
   at Democratic National Convention of 1968
      5:271
   officers enlisting in Ku Klux Klan   4:4, 202
   prisons   3:371, 374 (illus.)
   slave patrols   2:190 (sidebar)
   (See also Crime; Vigilantism)
Lawrence, D. H.
   Rocking-Horse Winner, The   3:344–49
   Sons and Lovers   2:334–39
Leary, Timothy   5:82–83, 324
Leaves of Grass, Whitman, Walt   2:195–201
Lee, Ann   3:95
Lee, Harper, To Kill a Mockingbird   3:390–96
Left Hand of Darkness, The, LeGuin, Ursula
   5:236–42
Legend of Sleepy Hollow, The, Irving, Washington
   1:211–18
Legends. See Myth
Legislation. See under individual topics, e. g. Civil
   rights movements; Great Depression; Labor unions;
   Segregation
LeGuin, Ursula, Left Hand of Darkness, The
   5:236–42
Lenape (Delaware) Indians   1:206, 219–20
Lenin, Vladimir   4:14, 15 (illus.)
Leopold, King of Belgium   2:146–47, 150–51
Lepanto, Battle of   1:296
Lesbianism
   and bisexuality of Woolf   3:357
   hints in Rebecca and concern for du Maurier
      3:327–28
Lessing, Doris, Golden Notebook, The   4:165–70
Leuchter, Fred. A.   4:40
Levantine Jews   1:248
Levellers   1:359
Lewis, C. S.   1:158
Lewis, John L.   3:155 (sidebar)
Lewis, Oscar   5:266
Lewis, Sinclair, Babbitt   3:21–27
Liberalism, classical
   and individualism   3:268
   targeted by New Right   5:136
Liberia   2:404
Liddell, Alice   2:29 (illus.)
Light in the Forest, The, Richter, Conrad   1:219–24
Like Water for Chocolate, Esquivel, Laura
   3:196–202
Lincoln, Abraham
   biography of   2:1–7
   Emancipation Proclamation (1862)   2:59, 60
      (sidebar), 135, 308, 309
   Gettysburg Address   2:130–36
   influence on white South Africans of 20th
      century   4:99
   quote from Declaration of Independence   1:99
   on race   2:3, 5

Walt Whitman on   2:196 (sidebar)
Lindbergh, Charles   3:367; 4:373
Lindner, Robert   4:77–78
Linguistic considerations
    alliteration   5:223
    Black English, or Ebonics   5:145, 154, 342
    Churchill's rhetoric   4:361–62
    colloquial prose of Lardner   4:262 (sidebar)
    Dutch place-names in New York   1:331
        (sidebar)
    English accents   3:4–5, 313–14
    English as melding of French and Old English
        1:183 (sidebar)
    ethnic idioms, street slang, and group
        identification   4:249 (sidebar), 386
    ethnic/racist slurs   4:32, 386
    fading/loss of native or immigrants' languages
        4:85, 142
    Gaelic League   3:109, 308–9
    ghetto street slang   5:17
    Kennedy's rhetoric   5:186
    King's rhetoric   5:223–24
    metaphor   5:186
    Mycenaean alphabet   1:172 (sidebar)
    "naming", power of   5:176
    non-Greek-speakers as barbarians   1:173
        (sidebar)
    oratory, rhetoric of speeches   5:186, 223
    Phoenician alphabet   1:286–87
    plain, simple language of common men
        1:72–73, 76, 163, 342
    pronouns, inclusive   5:186
    puns in Shakespeare   1:348–49
    puns in Victorian Age   2:30
    repetition   5:186
    rhyme   5:223
    rhythm   5:223
    Roman names   1:190
    Roosevelt's (Franklin Delano) rhetoric   3:127
    Southern dialect
        in Cold Sassy Tree   3:79
        in Color Purple, The   3:87
        in Gathering of Old Men, A   5:133
        in Huckleberry Finn   2:17
        in Uncle Remus   2:397, 398–99
    Southwestern dialects   4:321 (sidebar)
    suppression of native languages by colonialists
        4:350
    Western dialect in Notorious Jumping Frog   2:252
    Yiddish   3:120
Linguistic considerations: etymological
    "acid and acid heads"   5:83
    barrios   4:44
    "bindlestiffs"   3:269–70, 275
    "blackamoor"   4:54
    "blacklisting"   3:178; 4:72
    "Catch-22"   4:70 (sidebar)
    "Chinaman's chance"   2:368
    "colored", "Negro", "African American" and
        "black"   5:120 (sidebar)

    "coolies"   4:124
    "democracy", Paine's redefinition of   1:74
    "dry" years and "Drys"   3:69, 75
    "Dust Bowl"   3:46
    "flappers"   3:147
    "flipping" trains   3:46
    "freaking out"   5:83
    "gas him"   5:37 (sidebar)
    "ghetto"   1:244
    "greasers"   5:266
    "Hoovervilles"   3:126
    "Jim Crow"   2:21, 341
    "lost generation" (post-WWI)   3:13, 112,
        116–17
    "mashers"   2:331
    "moonshine"   3:69
    "no man's land"   3:9, 113
    "octoroons"   3:18
    "Okies"   3:46
    "pachuco"   4:173, 296
    "quadroons"   3:17–18
    "revolution," Paine's redefinition of   1:74
    "runrummers"   3:147
    "Say it ain't so, Joe"   3:150
    "Simon Legree"   2:409
    "skid row"   3:46
    "speakeasies"   3:69, 147
    "Tenderloin"   4:37
    "trench foot"   3:9
    "trips and bad trips"   5:83
    "Uncle Tom"   2:409
    "wage slavery"   3:179
    "Walter Mitty"   3:369
Lipsyte, Robert, Contender, The   5:67–73
Literature
    for adolescents and young adults, as genre
        5:61–62, 265–66, 268–70, 331
    allegory and fable   4:16 (sidebar), 19
    almanacs (Poor Richard's Almanac)   1:309–15
    bildungsroman   3:264, 311; 4:47
    calendarios de las señoritas (Mexican magazines for
        women)   3:196–97
    choreopoems   5:117–18
    crime stories and "Newgate Novels"   2:83, 267
    detective fiction   2:325; 3:226–27
    development in 17th-century French salons
        1:88
    "dime" novels with romance, adventure, and
        violence   2:306; 3:226–27
    dystopian   5:100, 141, 252
    of Enlightenment   2:211 (sidebar)
    for ethnic groups, minorities   5:62
    future history   5:127
    Gothic horror stories and romances   2:81, 85,
        185; 3:338
    horror fiction   5:46–47
    Imagism   3:413–14
    Latin American   2:273
    "magical" realism   2:271, 273; 3:196, 202; 4:48;
        5:169, 213, 330

novels, birth of   **1**:*341–42*
pornographic   **3**:*381*
printing and publishing, impact of advances in
   1:*160, 162 (sidebar)*; **2**:*234, 306, 419*
pulp magazines   **2**:*325*; **3**:*226–27*
realism. *See* Realism
repetition as literary device   **4**:*70*
romance novels of 1980s   **5**:*331*
romances   **2**:*210*
of Romantic era. *See* Romantic movement
satirical. *See* Satire
science fiction. *See* Science fiction
slave narratives. *See* Slave narratives
Southern renaissance in   **3**:*421*
stream of consciousness technique   **3**:*111, 358*
thrillers, psychological   **3**:*328–29*
utopian   **5**:*251–52*
westerns   **2**:*321, 325*
Wilder's view of importance of   **3**:*288*
writers
   benefitting from New Deal's Federal Writers'
      Project   **3**:*237*
   patrons for   **1**:*88*
   prejudice against women as   **2**:*186, 203,
      212, 424–25*; **5**:*282 (sidebar)*
   (*See also* Biography (and autobiography);
      Censorship and banning of literary works;
      Documents; Essays; Narratives; Novels; Plays;
      Short stories; Speeches)
Little Foxes, The, Hellman, Lillian   **3**:*203–10*
Little Prince, The, Saint-Exupéry, Antoine de
   3:*210–17*
Little Women, Alcott, Louisa May   **2**:*202–8*
Locke, Alain   **3**:*256, 389*
Locke, John   **1**:*100*
London, England   **1**:*417*
London, Jack, *Call of the Wild, The*   **3**:*51–56*
Long Day's Journey into Night, O'Neill, Eugene
   3:*218–24*
López, Dr. Roderigo   **1**:*248*
Lord of the Flies, Golding, William   **4**:*228–34*
"Lost generation" (post-WWI)   **3**:*13, 112, 116–17*
Lotteries   **4**:*235–36*
Lottery, The, Jackson, Shirley   **4**:*235–39*
Louis Napoleon   **2**:*228–29*
Louis Phillippe of France   **1**:*164*
Louis XI of France   **1**:*160*
Louis XIII of France   **1**:*386, 387, 388*
Louis XIV of France   **1**:*31, 87, 88, 130, 386, 387*;
   3:*212*
Louis XVI of France   **1**:*51, 358, 359, 372*
Louis XVIII of France   **1**:*391*
Louisiana   **3**:*15–18*; **4**:*365–66*; **5**:*21, 22, 25, 130,
   131–32*
L'Ouverture, Toussaint   **5**:*116–17*
Love and marriage
   in 18th-century France   **1**:*31*
   according to Thurber   **3**:*367–68*
   adultery/infidelity   **5**:*273, 287*
   in ancient Greece   **1**:*285*

children of immigrants marrying Caucasians
   5:*232*
in China and Chinese culture   **3**:*132, 192–93,
   194*; **4**:*128*
in colonial America   **1**:*24*
debutantes' "coming out"   **3**:*326–27*
in early 17th-century England   **1**:*263–64, 385*
for Emily Dickinson   **2**:*55–56, 57*
for England's landed gentry   **1**:*414*; **2**:*296,
   354–55*; **3**:*326–27*
happiness versus duty in   **3**:*271–72*
Japanese "picture brides"   **4**:*331–32*
polygamy   **5**:*4*
problems of adjustment to retirement   **5**:*203,
   273*
sexual dimension of, in 19th century   **2**:*212,
   423*
or spinsterhood   **2**:*297*
for traditional Jews   **3**:*119, 123*
for underage teens   **5**:*151*
in Victorian Age   **2**:*116, 336*
War Brides Act (1945)   **4**:*124, 127*; **5**:*231*
Wollstonecraft on   **1**:*410–11*
for women of 1970s   **2**:*58*
(*See also* Divorce; Family and family life)
Love and marriage, works emphasizing
   Anna Karenina   **2**:*34–40*
   *Beauty: A Retelling of the Story of Beauty and the
      Beast*   **1**:*30–36*
   Color Purple, The   **3**:*80–87*
   Daisy Miller   **2**:*105–10*
   Doll's House, A   **2**:*111–17*
   Ethan Frome   **2**:*125–29*
   Farewell to Arms, A   **3**:*112–18*
   Gone with the Wind   **2**:*137–44*
   Handmaid's Tale, The   **5**:*135–42*
   His Own Where   **5**:*149–55*
   House of Mirth, The   **3**:*166–73*
   Jane Eyre   **2**:*181–87*
   Kitchen God's Wife, The   **3**:*189–95*
   Like Water for Chocolate   **3**:*196–202*
   Love Medicine   **5**:*243–50*
   Madame Bovary   **2**:*209–15*
   Merchant of Venice, The   **1**:*247*
   Othello   **1**:*297*
   Pride and Prejudice   **2**:*295–300*
   Romeo and Juliet   **1**:*346*
   Scarlet Letter   **1**:*351–57*
   Seventeen Syllables   **4**:*330–36*
   Sons and Lovers   **2**:*334–39*
   Tess of the D'Urbervilles   **2**:*353–59*
   Wuthering Heights   **1**:*413–19*
Love Medicine, Erdrich, Louise   **5**:*243–50*
Lower classes   **1**:*363, 366 (sidebar), 366*
LSD (lysergic acid diethylamide)   **4**:*288, 289, 292,
   293–94*; **5**:*82–83, 324–25*
Luce, William, *Belle of Amherst, The*   **2**:*54–58*
Lucifer. *See* Devil (Satan)
Luddite movement   **1**:*119–20, 120 (illus.)*
Luther, Martin   **1**:*231–32, 232 (illus.)*; **2**:*113*

Luxembourg   **4**:*254–55*
Lynching
   advocation of, by racist propaganda   **2**:*400*
   anti-lynching crusader Ida B. Wells-Barnett
     3:*83, 238*
   ASWPL (Association of Southern Women for the
     Prevention of Lynching)   **3**:*391–92*; **5**:*133*
   of black soldiers during WWII   **4**:*197*
   "defense of white womanhood" excuse   **5**:*133*
   Dyer Antilynching Bill   **3**:*392*
   economic aspect of excuses for   **3**:*83, 391*
   estimates of deaths from   **2**:*341*; **3**:*37, 83, 238,*
     419; **4**:*202*; **5**:*131*
   FDR's reason for refusal to sign Dyer
     Antilynching Bill   **3**:*154, 392*; **4**:*202*
   horrific cruelties of   **2**:*412*; **3**:*274, 391*
   increasing with desperation of Great Depression
     (1930s)   **3**:*45*
   by Ku Klux Klan   **2**:*141 (sidebar), 143 (sidebar),*
     412; **3**:*419*; **5**:*130–31*
   in Northern states   **3**:*238*
   perpetrators generally escaping punishment
     3:*274*
   police joining mobs   **4**:*4, 202*
   to prevent exercise of voting rights   **2**:*412*; **3**:*419*
   sexual aspect of excuses for   **3**:*83, 238, 273*
   as Southern phenomenon   **3**:*238*
   of whites   **3**:*273–74*

M

MacArthur, Douglas   **4**:*80–81, 350*
Macbeth, Shakespeare, William   **1**:*225–30*
McCarthy, Joseph and McCarthyism   **1**:*84, 398*;
   3:*208, 209 (illus.)*; **4**:*71, 110, 398*; **5**:*2, 3 (illus.), 96,*
   97, 127
McCullers, Carson
   Heart Is a Lonely Hunter, The   **3**:*153–58*
   Member of the Wedding, The   **4**:*254–59*
McCunn, Ruthanne Lum, *Thousand Pieces of Gold*
   2:*366–71*
Machiavelli, Niccolò, *Prince, The*   **1**:*316–20*
McKay, Claude, *Home to Harlem*   **3**:*159–65*
McKinley, Robin, *Beauty: A Retelling of the Story of*
   Beauty and the Beast   **1**:*30–36*
McMullin, Fred   **3**:*149*
Madame Bovary, Flaubert, Gustave   **2**:*209–15*
Madero, Francisco   **3**:*29, 197, 278*
"Magical" realism   **2**:*271, 273*; **3**:*196, 202*; **4**:*48*;
   5:*169, 213, 330*
Magna Carta   **1**:*255*
Maimon, Solomon   **4**:*88*
Malamud, Bernard, *Natural, The*   **4**:*260–66*
Malcolm II of Scotland   **1**:*225*
Malcolm III of Scotland   **1**:*226*
Mallory, Thomas   **1**:*290, 293*
Maltese Falcon, The, Hammett, Dashiell   **3**:*225–30*
Man for All Seasons, A, Bolt, Robert   **1**:*231–37*
Man without a Face, The, Holland, Isabelle
   4:*240–46*

Manchild in the Promised Land, Brown, Claude
   4:*247–53*
Manchuria   **4**:*59, 178, 350*; **5**:*230*
Manhattan Project   **4**:*71, 81–82, 316*
Manifest Destiny   **2**:*76 (sidebar)*; **3**:*234*
Manorial system   **1**:*251*
Mao Zedong   **3**:*136, 189*; **5**:*254*
Mark Antony   **1**:*13, 189, 191*
Marooning   **1**:*401–2*
Marranos   **1**:*248, 249*
Marsh, Ngaio   **3**:*329*
Marshall Plan   **5**:*123–24, 224, 292*
Martinez, Vilma   **5**:*179*
Marx, Karl   **1**:*376*; **3**:*232*
Marxism
   concept of capitalists versus proletariat   **3**:*321*
   concepts of "wage slavery" and "estranged labor"
     3:*179*; **4**:*18–19*
   in Czarist Russia   **3**:*59*
   (*See also* Communism)
Mary Stuart, Queen of Scots   **1**:*141, 149–50, 349*
Masons (Freemasons)   **2**:*82*
Mather, Cotton
   associated with Puritan excess   **1**:*213*
   comparison to J. Edgar Hoover   **1**:*84 (sidebar)*
   excerpt from *Bonifacius*   **1**:*28*
   impact of *Memorable Providences*   **1**:*79, 80, 396*
   impact of *The Wonders of the Invisible World*
     1:*80 (illus.), 80, 422, 424*
Mather, Increase   **1**:*424*
Matlovich, Leonard Jr.   **4**:*39*
Maugham, W. Somerset, *Of Human Bondage*
   3:*264–68*
Maupassant, Guy de, *Necklace, The*   **2**:*244–48*
Meat-packing industry   **3**:*175*
Medea, Euripides   **1**:*238–41*
Media
   black press airing grievances of black soldiers in
     WWII   **4**:*195*
   contributing to anti-Japanese hysteria of WWII
     4:*138, 140, 141, 194*
   creating crime-ridden image of Central Park
     4:*401*
   decrying racial violence   **4**:*310 (sidebar)*
   fanning 1940s hysteria over zoot suiters and
     "Mexican goon squads"   **4**:*296, 404, 405*
   FDR's popularity with and concealment of
     disability   **3**:*127*
   misrepresentation of "black power"   **4**:*56*
   misrepresentation of Malcolm X   **5**:*16*
   muckraking journalists   **3**:*176, 320*
   "New Journalism"   **5**:*293*
   overlooking violence against minorities and
     homeless   **4**:*401*
   patriotic emphasis during WWII   **4**:*371*
   role in consolidation of Japanese culture in
     California   **4**:*332*
   use of, for propaganda   **4**:*66–67*
   and "yellow journalism"   **3**:*279*
   (*See also* Television)

Medici, House of   1:*316, 317, 318*
Medici, Marie de'   1:*387*
Medicine
    ambulances of WWI   3:*114*
    Chinese   3:*194 (sidebar)*
    Chippewa "love medicine"   5:*249*
    homeopathy   3:*68–69*
    Indian remedies   3:*68–69*; 5:*249*
    Latino *curanderos*   3:*199*; 4:*45*
    as male dominated   4:*218*
    midwifery   4:*218*
    Navajo Night Chant   4:*188*
    opium products   3:*379*
    penicillin   3:*366*
    polio vaccines   4:*10*
    "socialized", 1950s fear of   4:*12*
    (*See also* Diseases)
Mediterranean
    Albania   2:*101*
    in ancient times   1:*9*
    Egypt   4:*107*
    Ethiopia   4:*67*
    Palestine   4:*102–3, 105*; 5:*54*
    Peloponnesian War   1:*241, 324, 328*
    Sicily   4:*67*
    Suez Canal   3:*184*; 4:*107*
    (*See also* Greece in ancient times; Israel; Italy;
        Turkey)
Melanesia   4:*222*
Melville, Herman   2:*92*
    Benito Cereno   1:*37–43*
    Billy Budd   1:*51–56*
    Moby Dick   2:*230–35*
    praise for *Young Goodman Brown*   1:*425*
Member of the Wedding, The, McCullers, Carson
    4:*254–59*
Mencken, H. L.
    on *Babbitt*   3:*25, 27*
    influence on Sinclair Lewis   3:*26–27*
    on Scopes Trial   3:*102 (sidebar)*
    on Southern culture   3:*40 (sidebar)*
Mendel, Gregor   2:*217*
Mendelssohn, Moses   4:*88*
Menelaus   1:*281*
Mental and emotional disabilities
    association with pressure to conform   4:*74*
    asylums/institutions
        abuses in   3:*244–45*
        and deinstitutionalization   4:*289*
        as fashionable "resorts"   3:*413*
        hospitalization in   3:*272*; 4:*77*
    changing attitudes in 1950s and '60s   4:*151–56*
    connectedness of mental health and human
        relationships   4:*153*
    developments in psychology   3:*329, 378*; 4:*77*
    education for children   4:*151–52*
    effects of childhood abuse   5:*289–90*
    eugenic sterilization of retarded   3:*272*; 4:*152*;
        5:*41, 42*
    Fetal Alcohol Syndrome   5:*361*

"frontier madness"   3:*259*
history of   4:*288–89*
National Association for Retarded Children
    (NARC)   4:*151*
in Shakespeare's time   1:*139 (sidebar), 203*
stigma of   5:*262–63*
targeted by Nazis in Holocaust   4:*119*
treatments for
    electroconvulsive therapy (ECT)   4:*24*
        (sidebar), 289–90
    lobotomy   4:*290*
    methods of 1940s and '50s   4:*289–90*
    pyschosurgery   4:*290*
    "rest cure"   2:*425–26*
    tranquilizing drugs   4:*289*
in Victorian Age   2:*119–20, 184, 185–86,*
    278–79
writers suffering from
    T. S. Eliot's wife   3:*412–13*
    Gilman   2:*427*
    Plath   4:*21–26*
    Woolf   3:*358*
of WWII veterans   4:*80 (sidebar), 325*
Merchant of Venice, Shakespeare, William
    1:*242–49*
    parallels to *Ivanhoe*   1:*187*
Meredith, James   5:*19*
Merry Adventures of Robin Hood, The, Pyle, Howard
    1:*250–57*
Merton, Thomas   5:*280–81*
Metamorphoses, Ovid   1:*262*
Methodism   2:*357–58*
Mexican Americans. *See* Chicanos; Latinos
Mexican War   2:*88, 89, 242*; 5:*172*
Mexico
    Bracero Program (1942–1964)   3:*34*; 4:*44*
    close ties to U.S.   3:*282*
    dictatorship of Díaz (1876–1910)   3:*28–30*
    ejidos system   3:*282*
    hacienda system   3:*29, 278, 282*
    immigration to U.S. from   3:*282*; 4:*44–48*
    mining industry   3:*28*
    PRI and one-party democracy   3:*282*
    Revolution (1910–20)   3:*29, 278–79*; 4:*295,*
        296 (sidebar)
    women in   3:*197–98, 200–202*
Micronesia   4:*222*
Middle Ages
    as depicted in *Beowulf*   1:*44–50*
    as depicted in Chaucer   1:*64–70*
    importance of kings and kinship   1:*153*
Middle class, rise of
    African Americans in 20th century   3:*252, 255,*
        387–88; 4:*2, 51*
    in American East   2:*303, 306*
    bourgeoisie of France   2:*209–10, 245–46*
    in England   1:*66, 72, 338, 342, 371*; 2:*118, 153,*
        354; 3:*312*
    importance of proper manners   2:*297*
    moving to suburbs   4:*73*

replacing aristocray of Old South 4:364–65

Midsummer Night's Dream, A, Shakespeare, William 1:258–65

Midwifery 4:218

Migrant farm workers 3:29–30, 34, 49, 140–42, 143 (sidebar), 269–71, 275, 335, 337; 4:297 (sidebar)
  braceros 3:34; 4:44

Milan, Italy 1:379–80

Military
  African Americans in 3:160, 424
  American Indians in 4:80, 185–87; 5:362–63
  anti-Semitism in 4:36–37
  Army training camps 4:36
  authority and mutiny 4:63–64
  British "batmen" 3:348
  Claire Chennault and American Volunteer Group 3:190
  desertion during Civil War 2:10–11, 312
  desertion in Vietnam 2:13 (sidebar)
  and "Flying Tigers" 3:190
  homosexuals in 4:38, 39–40
  illicit wartime amusements 4:37, 38
  Latinos in 4:44
  racial discrimination in 3:41–42; 4:195, 197, 212
  reservists and regulars 4:63 (sidebar)
  United Service Organizations (USO) 4:38
  (*See also* War)

Military draft
  of American Indians for WWII 4:80
  of blacks for Vietnam 5:102–3
  of Chicanos for Vietnam 4:176
  of Chinese Americans for WWII 4:127
  of disadvantaged for Vietnam (Project 100,000) 5:102–3, 158, 307
  dodging and avoiding 2:256, 309; 4:324, 327
  induction process 4:35–36
  of Nisei for WWII 4 140 (sidebar)
  of poor/lower classes for Civil War 2:256, 309
  of Puerto Ricans for WWI 5:215
  as target of blacks' protest 4:213
  for WWII in 1940 4:35, 324–25

Mill, John Stuart 2:182 (sidebar)

Miller, Arthur
  Crucible, The 1:78–85
  Death of a Salesman 4:109–15
  importance in American theater 1:85

Mills, C. Wright 4:74

Milton, John, *Paradise Lost* 1:301–8

Minh, Ho Chi 5:101

Mining industry
  accidents and disease 2:335
  child labor 2:335 (sidebar)
  in Chile 5:163, 164
  Chinese in 2:367; 5:352
  coal 3:63, 64; 4:9; 5:39–40
  in Mexico 3:28
  (*See also* Gold rushes and silver strikes; *Thousand Pieces of Gold*)

Minotaur 1:259

Minstrel shows 2:16–17, 21

Miracle Worker, The, Gibson, William 2:216–22

Les Misérables, Hugo, Victor 2:223–29

Missionaries 2:118–19, 147, 161–62, 361–62; 3:133, 280; 5:195

Mississippi River 2:16, 17

Missouri Compromise (1820) 2:5 (sidebar), 15–16, 22

Mitchell, Margaret, *Gone with the Wind* 2:137–44

Mitnagdim 3:426

Moby Dick, Melville, Herman 2:230–35

Modernism 3:411; 5:42

Modest Proposal, A, Swift, Jonathan 1:266–72

Mohammed, Sufi Abdul 4:211

Mohr, Nicholasa, *In Nueva York* 5:214–21

Momaday, N. Scott, *House Made of Dawn* 4:185–92

Monasticism 3:186–87
  Trappist monks 5:280

Money
  in colonial America 1:103–4, 310
  "Wood's Coins" in Ireland 1:268

Moneylending (usury) 1:103–4, 182–83, 243 (sidebar), 243, 247

Monro, Lt. Col. George 1:205

Monroe, James 1:209

Moors 1:297, 299; 3:212, 213

More, Sir Thomas 1:232, 233, 237

Mormonism 5:4

Morrison, Toni
  Beloved 2:59–65
  Bluest Eye, The 4:49–57

Mortimer family 1:144, 145

Most Dangerous Game, The, Connell, Richard 3:231–35

Motion pictures. *See* Hollywood and motion picture industry

Mott, Lucretia Coffin 2:24, 55; 3:16

Moynihan, Daniel
  Moynihan Report (1965) 3:355, 375
  on Project 100,000 5:103

Muhammad, Elijah 3:239 (*illus.*); 4:249; 5:13, 69, 110–11

Mulattos 3:18

Multiculturalism
  America as "salad bowl" rather than melting pot 5:176
  encouraging autobiographies 3:32, 34
  ethnic studies programs
    African American history 5:147–48
    in Black English, or Ebonics 5:145, 154, 342
    increasing college enrollments 5:217
    Puerto Rican history and culture 5:217
  and women's studies 5:117
  (*See also* African Americans; American Indians; Chinese and Chinese Americans; Japanese and Japanese Americans; Jews; Latinos; Puerto Rico and Puerto Ricans)

Murphy, Charles F.   3:*148, 399*
Music
    blues   3:*254 (sidebar)*; 4:*258*
    Chinese opera   5:*75*
    and dance   4:*387*
    effectiveness in theatrical productions   4:*258*
    folksongs of 1930s and 1940s   3:*47, 128*
    gospel songs and black spirituals   2:*398, 402, 407*; 4:*258*
    importance to slaves   2:*398*
    jazz   3:*162 (sidebar)*; 4:*258*
    New Chilean Song   5:*164*
    ragtime   3:*321 (sidebar)*
    reflecting generation gap   4:*386*
    rock 'n' roll   4:*172, 386, 391–92*
    Smith, Bessie   3:*253 (illus.)*
    Welsh regard for   3:*65*
Musicals
    for colored girls who have considered suicide / when the rainbow is enuf, Shange, Ntozake   5:*115–21*
    golden age on Broadway   4:*387*
    West Side Story, Laurents, Arthur, *et al.*   4:*384–90*
Musketeers   1:*386, 387*
Muslim Turks   1:*296*
Mussolini, Benito   2:*293–94*; 4:*66–67, 305 (illus.)*
Mutiny
    aboard *Amistad*   1:*43*
    aboard HMS *Bounty*   1:*273–79, 276 (illus.)*
    aboard USS *Somers*   1:*56*
    in *Benito Cereno*   1:*37–43*
    in *Billy Budd*   1:*51–56*
    in *Caine Mutiny, The*   4:*58–65*
    at Spithead and Nore   1:*53*
Mutiny on the Bounty, Nordhoff, Charles and James Norman Hall   1:*273–79*
Mycenaean Age of ancient Greece   1:*57–59, 167, 258, 281–82, 283 (sidebar)*
Myers, Walter Dean, *Fallen Angels*   5:*101–6*
Mystery and detective stories
    Hound of the Baskervilles   2:*152–59*
    Jane Eyre   1:*415 (sidebar), 419*; 2:*181–87*
    Maltese Falcon, The   3:*225–30*
    rise of   2:*325*; 3:*226–27*
Mysticism   1:*416*
    Hasidic Jews   3:*425, 426*
Myth
    Arthurian   1:*288, 290*
    Chinese   5:*77 (sidebar), 358*
    and comparative anthropology   5:*42*
    creation of   1:*152*
    disguising contemporary social criticism   1:*15, 63*
    founding of Rome   1:*10 (sidebar)*
    Holy Grail legends   4:*264–65*
    Irish   3:*109*
    Mexican and Aztlán   4:*173, 174–75, 176*
    Norse   1:*50, 152, 153, 156*
    (*See also* Folklore and fairy tales; Greek myth)

N

NAACP (National Association for the Advancement of Colored People)   2:*342, 415*; 3:*250, 320, 396*; 4:*195, 255, 310*; 5:*88, 120 (sidebar)*
Nairobi   3:*293*
"Naming", power of   5:*176*
Napoleon Bonaparte   1:*163, 391*; 2:*99–100, 224, 225 (sidebar), 295–96*
Napoleonic code   4:*365*
Narrative of the Life of Frederick Douglass, Douglass, Frederick   2:*236–41*
    inspiring resistance on part of slaves   2:*16*
Narratives
    Black Elk Speaks, Neihardt, John G.   2:*66–73*
    Bury My Heart at Wounded Knee, Brown, Dee   2:*74–80*
    Kon-Tiki, Heyerdahl, Thor   4:*221–27*
    Two Years before the Mast, Dana, Richard Henry, Jr.   2:*391–96*
    (*See also* Slave narratives)
NASA (National Aeronautics and Space Administration)   5:*81, 291*
Nation of Islam   3:*238, 325*; 4:*56, 248–50*; 5:*12–13, 69, 110–11, 302*
National Labor Relations Act (1933)   3:*128*
National Organization of Women (NOW)   1:*62*; 4:*22, 394*; 5:*136, 237*
Nationalism
    and anti-Semitism   1:*364*
    as aspect of fascism   4:*304*
    of Black Muslims and Nation of Islam   3:*238, 325*; 4:*56, 248–50*; 5:*12–13, 69, 110–11, 302*
    of black separatists   3:*160*
    caused by economic hardship   1:*113*
    ethnic movements   1:*363–64*
    extremes of   1:*292, 293–94*
    in *Hound of the Baskervilles*   2:*157*
    under Young Turks   3:*339*
Native Americans. *See* American Indians
Native Son, Wright, Richard   3:*236–42*
NATO (North Atlantic Treaty Organization)   5:*124, 224, 292*
Natural, The, Malamud, Bernard   4:*260–66*
Naturalism   1:*293*
Nature
    celebration of   1:*413, 416*
    (*See also* Romantic movement)
Nazis
    achieving dictatorship   4:*158*
    anti-Semitism fostering emigration of Jews   4:*102*
    condemnation of *All Quiet on the Western Front*   3:*13*
    countries conquered by   5:*123 (sidebar)*
    escaping to Argentina   5:*210*
    execution of Remarque's sister   3:*14*
    Great Depression enhancing appeal of fascism   3:*129*
    nationalism of   1:*294*

neo-nazis   **4**:*163–64*

   plans for extermination of Jews and
     "undesirables"   **3**:*124*

   rabid racism and belief in Aryan superiority
     4:*158, 193*; **5**:*42*

   remilitarization of Germany   **4**:*356–57*

   rise of and consolidation of power   **4**:*157, 158,*
     356–57

   (*See also* Holocaust; World War II)

Nebraska   **3**:*257–58, 260*

Necklace, The, Maupassant, Guy de   **2**:*244–48*

Neihardt, John G., *Black Elk Speaks*   **2**:*66–73*

Neruda, Pablo   **5**:*164, 168*

New Deal. *See under* Great Depression, The

New England

   agricultural decline   **2**:*125–26*

   Boston   **3**:*43*

   Boston Tea Party   **1**:*125*

   Massachusetts   **1**:*78–80, 355, 395–97*

"New Journalism"   **5**:*293*

New Mexico

   Chicano life in   **4**:*45, 171*

   Gallup   **4**:*83*

   Laguna Pueblo   **4**:*79–80, 85*

   Los Alamos   **4**:*81, 316–17*

   Manhattan Project   **4**:*71, 81–82, 316–17*

   Sagrado   **4**:*318*

   Tierra Amarilla   **4**:*174*

   Trinity Site detonation of atom bomb   **4**:*81–82*

   Walatowa (Jemez Pueblo)   **4**:*187*

   WWII village life   **4**:*318–21*

New Netherland (New York)   **1**:*211, 212*

New Orleans   **3**:*15*

New York

   Brooklyn   **3**:*397–98*; **4**:*88*; **5**:*149–51*

   Chinatown   **4**:*126*

   Dutch in (New Netherland)   **1**:*211, 212,*
     330–32, 333 (illus.), 335 (sidebar), 336

   Hudson Valley   **1**:*330–32, 333 (illus.), 334–35,*
     336

   in late 18th century   **1**:*107–8, 110*

   Mohawk Valley   **1**:*108, 110, 112 (illus.)*

   New York City   **2**:*301–7, 313*; **3**:*146–47*

     Central Park   **4**:*401*

     "garbage riots" (1969)   **5**:*220 (sidebar)*

     Harlem   **4**:*247–48*; **5**:*67–68*

     Harlem and Harlem Renaissance   **3**:*159–65,*
       256, 321, 384–85, 421; **4**:*204 (sidebar), 207*

     Harlem Renaissance   **3**:*159–65, 256, 384–85,*
       421

     Manhattan's West Side   **4**:*384–89, 400–401*

     Puerto Ricans   **4**:*385–86, 388–89, 401*;
       5:*214–21*

     Spanish Harlem (*El Barrio*)   **5**:*214, 216–17*

     Tweed Ring   **2**:*306–7*

   Tammany Hall   **3**:*148–49, 398–99*

Newspapers

   origins of   **1**:*268*

   "yellow journalism"   **3**:*279*

Newton, Huey P.   **4**:*54*

Newton, Sir Isaac   **1**:*24, 94*

Niagara Movement (1905)   **3**:*250, 320*

Nicholas II, Czar of Russia   **3**:*121, 232*

Nietzsche, Friedrich   **3**:*54*

Nigeria   **2**:*360–62, 364–65*; **3**:*84*; **4**:*314*

Night, Wiesel, Elie   **4**:*267–73*

Nineteen Eighty-Four, Orwell, George   **5**:*251–58*

   as dystopian   **5**:*100*

Nirvana   **1**:*366, 367*

Nixon, Richard

   "kitchen debate" with Khrushchev   **4**:*398, 399*
     (illus.); **5**:*321–22*

   loss to Kennedy attributed to poor appearance on
     TV   **5**:*223*

   use of anti-communism for campaign   **5**:*96*

   visit to Communist China   **5**:*358*

   Watergate scandal   **3**:*99*; **5**:*158–59, 263, 317*

Nonfiction

   almanacs (*Poor Richard's Almanac*)   **1**:*309–15*

   Kon-Tiki, Heyerdahl, Thor

   Right Stuff, The, Wolfe, Tom   **5**:*291–97*

   Two Years before the Mast, Dana, Richard Henry,
     Jr.   **2**:*391–96*

   (*See also* Biography (and autobiography);
     Documents; Essays; Slave narratives; Speeches)

Noon Wine, Porter, Katherine Anne   **3**:*243–48*

Nordhoff, Charles, *Mutiny on the Bounty*   **1**:*273–79*

Norman Conquest of Anglo-Saxon England   **1**:*181,*
   250–51, 290

Norse myths   **1**:*50, 152, 153, 156*

North Carolina   **2**:*168*

North Dakota   **5**:*244*

Norway   **1**:*137–38*; **2**:*111–13*

Not without Laughter, Hughes, Langston   **3**:*249–56*

Notorious Jumping Frog of Calaveras County, The,
   Twain, Mark   **2**:*249–54*

Notre Dame cathedral   **1**:*161, 162 (illus.), 163, 164*
   (sidebar)

Novellas

   Awakening, The, Chopin, Kate   **3**:*15–20*

   Daisy Miller, James, Henry   **2**:*105–10*

   Heart of Darkness, The, Conrad, Joseph
     2:*145–51*

   Of Mice and Men, Steinbeck, John   **3**:*269–76*

   Turn of the Screw, The, James, Henry   **2**:*378–83*

Novels

   birth of   **1**:*341–42*

   Across Five Aprils, Hunt, Irene   **2**:*8–14*

   Adventures of Don Quixote, The, Cervantes
     Saavedra, Miguel de   **1**:*1–7*

   Adventures of Huckleberry Finn, The, Twain, Mark
     2:*15–21*

   Alice's Adventures in Wonderland, Carroll, Lewis
     2:*28–33*

   All Creatures Great and Small, Herriott, James
     3:*1–7*

   All Quiet on the Western Front, Remarque, Erich
     Maria   **3**:*8–14*

   Animal Farm, Orwell, George   **4**:*14–20*

   Anna Karenina, Tolstoy, Leo   **2**:*34–40*

Autobiography of Miss Jane Pittman, The, Gaines, Ernest J.   **5**:*19–26*

Babbitt, Lewis, Sinclair   **3**:*21–27*

Bean Trees, The, Kingsolver, Barbara   **5**:*27–33*

Beauty: A Retelling of the Story of Beauty and the Beast, McKinley, Robin   **1**:*30–36*

Bell Jar, The, Plath, Sylvia   **4**:*21–27*

Beloved, Morrison, Toni   **2**:*59–65*

Benito Cereno, Melville, Herman   **1**:*37–43*

Betsey Brown, Shange, Ntozake   **4**:*28–34*

Billy Budd, Melville, Herman   **1**:*51–56*

Bless the Beasts and Children, Swarthout, Glendon   **5**:*34–38*

Bless Me, Ultima, Anaya, Rudolfo A.   **4**:*42–48*

Bluest Eye, The, Morrison, Toni   **4**:*49–57*

Brave New World, Huxley, Aldous   **5**:*39–45*

Bull from the Sea, The, Renault, Mary   **1**:*57–63*

Caine Mutiny, The, Wouk, Herman   **4**:*58–65*

Call of the Wild, The, London, Jack   **3**:*51–56*

Carrie, King, Stephen   **5**:*46–52*

Catch-22, Heller, Joseph   **4**:*66–72*

Catcher in the Rye, Salinger, J. D.   **4**:*73–78*

Ceremony, Silko, Leslie Marmon   **4**:*79–86*

Childhood's End, Clarke, Arthur   **5**:*53–60*

Chocolate War, The, Cormier, Robert   **5**:*61–66*

Chosen, The, Potok, Chaim   **4**:*87–93*

Cold Sassy Tree, Burns, Olive Ann   **3**:*75–79*

Color Purple, The, Walker, Alice   **3**:*80–87*

Confessions of Nat Turner, The, Styron, William   **2**:*93–98*

Contender, The, Lipsyte, Robert   **5**:*67–73*

Count of Monte-Cristo, The, Dumas, Alexandre   **2**:*99–104*

Cry, the Beloved Country, Paton, Alan   **4**:*94–100*

Dandelion Wine, Bradbury, Ray   **3**:*88–93*

Dawn, Wiesel, Elie   **4**:*101–8*

Day No Pigs Would Die, A, Peck, Robert Newton   **3**:*94–99*

Death in the Family, A, Agee, James   **3**:*100–105*

Donald Duk, Chin, Frank   **5**:*74–80*

Drums Along the Mohawk, Edmonds, Walter D.   **1**:*107–14*

Dune, Herbert, Frank   **5**:*81–87*

Eat a Bowl of Tea, Chu, Luis   **4**:*124–30*

Ethan Frome, Wharton, Edith   **2**:*125–29*

Fahrenheit 451, Bradbury, Ray   **5**:*95–100*

Fallen Angels, Myers, Walter Dean   **5**:*101–6*

Farewell to Arms, A, Hemingway, Ernest   **3**:*112–18*

Flowers for Algernon, Keyes, Daniel   **4**:*151–56*

Foundation, Asimov, Isaac   **5**:*122–28*

Frankenstein, Shelley, Mary   **1**:*115–21*

Friedrich, Richter, Hans Peter   **4**:*157–64*

Gathering of Old Men, A, Gaines, Ernest J.   **5**:*129–34*

Golden Notebook, The, Lessing, Doris   **4**:*165–70*

Gone with the Wind, Mitchell, Margaret   **2**:*137–44*

Good Earth, The, Buck, Pearl S.   **3**:*131–37*

Grapes of Wrath, The, Steinbeck, John   **3**:*138–45*

Great Gatsby, The, Fitzgerald, F. Scott   **3**:*146–52*

Gulliver's Travels, Swift, Jonathan   **1**:*129–35*

Handmaid's Tale, The, Atwood, Margaret   **5**:*135–42*

Heart of Aztlán, Anaya, Rudolfo A.   **4**:*171–76*

Heart Is a Lonely Hunter, The, McCullers, Carson   **3**:*153–58*

Hero Ain't Nothin' but a Sandwich, A, Childress, Alice   **5**:*143–48*

His Own Where, Jordan, June   **5**:*149–55*

Hobbit, The, Tolkien, J.R.R.   **1**:*152–58*

Home to Harlem, McKay, Claude   **3**:*159–65*

Hound of the Baskervilles, Doyle, Arthur Conan   **2**:*152–59*

House Made of Dawn, Momaday, N. Scott   **4**:*185–92*

House of Mirth, The, Wharton, Edith   **3**:*166–73*

House of Stairs, Sleator, William   **5**:*156–62*

House of the Spirits, The, Allende, Isabel   **5**:*163–70*

House on Mango Street, The, Cisneros, Sandra   **5**:*171–77*

Human Comedy, The, Saroyan, William   **4**:*193–200*

Hunchback of Notre Dame, The, Hugo, Victor   **1**:*159–65*

I Heard the Owl Call My Name, Craven, Margaret   **5**:*194–200*

Imagining Argentina, Thornton, Laurence   **5**:*208–13*

In Nueva York, Mohr, Nicholasa   **5**:*214–21*

Invisible Man, Ellison, Ralph   **4**:*209–15*

Ishi, Last of His Tribe, Kroeber, Theodora   **2**:*174–80*

Ivanhoe, Scott, Sir Walter   **1**:*181–88*

Jacob Have I Loved, Paterson, Katherine   **4**:*216–20*

Jane Eyre, Brontë, Charlotte   **2**:*181–87*

Joy Luck Club, The, Tan, Amy   **5**:*229–35*

Jungle, The, Sinclair, Upton   **3**:*174–80*

Kim, Kipling, Rudyard   **3**:*181–88*

Kitchen God's Wife, The, Tan, Amy   **3**:*189–95*

Last of the Mohicans, The, Cooper, James Fenimore   **1**:*204–10*

Left Hand of Darkness, The, LeGuin, Ursula   **5**:*236–42*

Light in the Forest, The, Richter, Conrad   **1**:*219–24*

Like Water for Chocolate, Esquivel, Laura   **3**:*196–202*

Little Prince, The, Saint-Exupéry, Antoine de   **3**:*210–17*

Little Women, Alcott, Louisa May   **2**:*202–8*

Lord of the Flies, Golding, William   **4**:*228–34*

Love Medicine, Erdrich, Louise   **5**:*243–50*

Madame Bovary, Flaubert, Gustave   **2**:*209–15*

Maltese Falcon, The, Hammett, Dashiell   **3**:*225–30*

Man without a Face, The, Holland, Isabelle   **4**:*240–46*

Merry Adventures of Robin Hood, The, Pyle, Howard   **1**:250–57

Les Misérables, Hugo, Victor   **2**:223–29

Moby Dick, Melville, Herman   **2**:230–35

Mutiny on the Bounty, Nordhoff, Charles and James Norman Hall   **1**:273–79

Native Son, Wright, Richard   **3**:236–42

Natural, The, Malamud, Bernard   **4**:260–66

Night, Wiesel, Elie   **4**:267–73

Nineteen Eighty-Four, Orwell, George   **5**:251–58

Not without Laughter, Hughes, Langston   **3**:249–56

O Pioneers!, Cather, Willa   **3**:257–63

Of Human Bondage, Maugham, W. Somerset   **3**:264–68

Old Gringo, The, Fuentes, Carlos   **3**:277–83

Old Man and the Sea, The, Hemingway, Ernest   **4**:274–80

Oliver Twist, Dickens, Charles   **2**:261–67

One Day in the Life of Ivan Denisovich, Solzhenitsyn, Alexander   **4**:281–87

One Flew over the Cuckoo's Nest, Kesey, Ken   **4**:288–94

One Hundred Years of Solitude, García Márquez, Gabriel   **2**:268–74

Ordinary People, Guest, Judith   **5**:259–64

Outsiders, The, Hinton, S. E.   **5**:265–70

Ox-Bow Incident, The, Clark, Walter Van Tilburg   **2**:288–94

Passage to India, A, Forster, E.M.   **3**:297–304

Pigman, The, Zindel, Paul   **5**:271–77

Pocho, Villarreal, José Antonio   **4**:295–302

Portrait of the Artist as a Young Man, A, Joyce, James   **3**:305–11

Pride and Prejudice, Austen, Jane   **2**:295–300

Prime of Miss Jean Brodie, The, Spark, Muriel   **4**:303–8

Prince of Tides, The, Conroy, Pat   **5**:285–90

Ragged Dick, Alger, Horatio   **2**:301–7

Ragtime, Doctorow, E. L.   **3**:319–25

Rebecca, du Maurier, Daphne   **3**:326–33

Red Badge of Courage, The, Crane, Stephen   **2**:308–13

Red Pony, The, Steinbeck, John   **3**:334–37

Red Sky at Morning, Bradford, Richard   **4**:316–22

Road from Home, The, Kherdian, David   **3**:338–43

Robinson Crusoe, Defoe, Daniel   **1**:337–43

Roll of Thunder, Hear My Cry, Taylor, Mildred   **3**:350–55

Roots, Haley, Alex   **5**:298–305

Runner, The, Voigt, Cynthia   **5**:306–13

Scarlet Letter, The, Hawthorne, Nathaniel   **1**:351–57

Scarlet Pimpernel, The, Orczy, Baroness Emmuska   **1**:358–64

Separate Peace, A, Knowles, John   **4**:323–29

Shane, Schaefer, Jack   **2**:321–26

Shoeless Joe, Kinsella, W. P.   **5**:314–20

Siddhartha, Hesse, Hermann   **1**:365–70

Sister Carrie, Dreiser, Theodore   **2**:327–33

Slaughterhouse Five, Vonnegut, Kurt, Jr.   **4**:343–48

Sons and Lovers, Lawrence, D. H.   **2**:334–39

Sounder, Armstrong, William H.   **3**:370–76

Story Catcher, The, Sandoz, Mari   **2**:347–52

Strange Case of Dr. Jekyll and Mr. Hyde, The, Stevenson, Robert Louis   **3**:377–82

Stranger in a Strange Land, Heinlein, Robert A.   **5**:321–27

Summer of My German Soldier, Greene, Bette   **4**:371–77

Sweet Whispers, Brother Rush, Hamilton, Virginia   **5**:328–32

Tale of Two Cities, A, Dickens, Charles   **1**:371–78

Tess of the D'Urbervilles, Hardy, Thomas   **2**:353–59

Their Eyes Were Watching God, Hurston, Zora Neale   **3**:383–89

Things Fall Apart, Achebe, Chinua   **2**:360–65

Thousand Pieces of Gold, McCunn, Ruthanne Lum   **2**:366–71

Three Musketeers, The, Dumas, Alexandre   **1**:386–92

Time of the Hero, The, Vargas Llosa, Mario   **5**:333–38

Tituba of Salem Village, Petry, Ann   **1**:393–99

To Kill a Mockingbird, Lee, Harper   **3**:390–96

Tom Brown's Schooldays, Hughes, Thomas   **2**:372–77

Treasure Island, Stevenson, Robert Louis   **1**:400–405

Tree Grows in Brooklyn, A, Smith, Betty   **3**:397–403

Twenty-Thousand Leagues under the Sea, Verne, Jules   **2**:384–90

Uncle Tom's Cabin, Stowe, Harriet Beecher   **2**:403–9

Understand This, Tervalon, Jervey   **5**:339–45

War of the Worlds, The, Wells, H.G.   **3**:404–10

Watership Down, Adams, Richard   **5**:346–51

Wuthering Heights, Brontë, Emily   **1**:413–19

Yellow Raft in Blue Water, A, Dorris, Michael   **5**:360–66

NOW (National Organization of Women)   **1**:62; **4**:22, 394; **5**:136, 237

Nuclear energy   **5**:124, 127, 286
  Chernobyl disaster   **5**:286, 287 (illus.)

Nuclear weapons
  and arms control   **4**:71; **5**:126, 225, 239, 252 (sidebar)
  arms race   **5**:252 (sidebar)
  hydrogen bomb   **4**:183
  (*See also* Atom bomb)

O

O Pioneers!, Cather, Willa   **3**:257–63

Oates, Joyce Carol, *Where Are You Going, Where*

Have You Been? **4**:*391–96*
Occurrence at Owl Creek Bridge, An, Bierce, Ambrose **2**:*255–60*; **3**:*281*
O'Connor, Flannery, *Everything That Rises Must Converge* **5**:*88–94*
Octavian (Octavius Caesar) **1**:*12 (sidebar), 13*
Octoroons **3**:*18*
Odria, Manuel **5**:*333–34*
Odyssey, Homer **1**:*280–87*
    Odysseus and the Sirens **1**:*284 (illus.)*
    parallels to *Ivanhoe* **1**:*187*
Oedipus complex (Freud) **2**:*336–37*
Of Human Bondage, Maugham, W. Somerset **3**:*264–68*
Of Mice and Men, Steinbeck, John **3**:*269–76*
Ohio River, and Underground Railroad **2**:*16, 60*
Oil booms of 1920s **3**:*45–46*
"Okies" **3**:*46, 47, 49*
Oklahoma **5**:*29, 269*
Old age. *See* Senior citizens
Old Gringo, The, Fuentes, Carlos **3**:*277–83*
Old Man and the Sea, The, Hemingway, Ernest **4**:*274–80*
Oliver Twist, Dickens, Charles **2**:*261–67*
Olympians **1**:*301*
Once and Future King, The, White, T.H. **1**:*288–94*
One Day in the Life of Ivan Denisovich, Solzhenitsyn, Alexander **4**:*281–87*
One Flew over the Cuckoo's Nest, Kesey, Ken **4**:*288–94*; **5**:*318 (sidebar)*
One Hundred Years of Solitude, García Márquez, Gabriel **2**:*268–74*
O'Neill, Eugene, *Long Day's Journey into Night* **3**:*218–24*
Ongpatonga **1**:*209 (illus.)*
Open Window, The, Saki **2**:*275–80*
Oppenheimer, Robert **4**:*316*
Orczy, Baroness Emmuska, *Scarlet Pimpernel, The* **1**:*358–64*
Ordinary People, Guest, Judith **5**:*259–64*
Orwell, George
    Animal Farm **4**:*14–20*
    Nineteen Eighty-Four **5**:*251–58*
Osborne, Sarah **1**:*79, 395, 396*
Othello, Shakespeare, William **1**:*295–300*
Ottoman Turks **1**:*295–96*; **3**:*338–40*
Our Town, Wilder, Thornton **3**:*284–89*
Out of Africa, Dinesen, Isak **3**:*290–96*
Outcasts of Poker Flat, The, Harte, Bret **2**:*281–87*
Outsiders, The, Hinton, S. E. **5**:*265–70*
Ovid, *Metamorphoses* **1**:*262*
Ox-Bow Incident, The, Clark, Walter Van Tilburg **2**:*288–94*

P

Pabel, Reinhold **4**:*373 (sidebar)*
Pacificism **1**:*23 (sidebar), 142, 365, 369, 370*
Paine, Thomas
    Common Sense **1**:*71–77, 94*
    opposition to slavery **1**:*72 (sidebar)*
    The Rights of Man **1**:*52*
Pakistan **3**:*300, 301*
Palestine **4**:*102–3, 105*; **5**:*54*
    (*See also* Israel)
Pamphlets
    Common Sense, Paine, Thomas **1**:*71–77*
    Modest Proposal, A, Swift, Jonathan **1**:*266–72*
    popularity in England **1**:*268*
    popularity and limitations in colonies **1**:*72–73, 122*
    by Swift **1**:*132*
Panama Canal **3**:*231–32, 270*
Pankhurst, Emmeline **2**:*335–36*; **3**:*359*
Paradise Lost, Milton, John **1**:*301–8*
    influence on Herman Melville **1**:*54*
    popularity in America **1**:*307*
Paranormal phenomena **2**:*383 (sidebar)*; **5**:*47–48, 56, 239*
Paredes, Américo **5**:*172*
Paris, France
    as capital of western art **3**:*265–66*
    Notre Dame cathedral **1**:*161, 162 (illus.), 163, 164 (sidebar)*
Paris (Trojan prince) **1**:*8, 166, 281*
Parks, Rosa **3**:*73*; **5**:*11, 88, 185*
Parnell, Charles **3**:*109–10*
Parody **1**:*4*
Parris, Rev. Samuel **1**:*79, 83 (sidebar), 394, 395, 421*
Parthenon **1**:*240*
Passage to India, A, Forster, E.M. **3**:*297–304*
Pastoral novels **1**:*6*
Paterson, Katherine, *Jacob Have I Loved* **4**:*216–20*
Paton, Alan, *Cry, the Beloved Country* **4**:*94–100*
Paxton Boys massacre **1**:*220–21*
Peck, Robert Newton, *Day No Pigs Would Die, A* **3**:*94–99*
Peloponnesian War **1**:*241, 324, 328*
Pennsylvania **1**:*22, 71–72, 310*
    Pittsburgh **4**:*7–9, 144, 149*
Percy family **1**:*144–45, 149*
Pericles of ancient Athens **1**:*17, 18, 240, 241, 322*
Perón, Juan and Eva **5**:*208–9, 210*
Persephone **1**:*283*
Peru **4**:*221, 222*; **5**:*333–38*
Pesticides ("biocides") **4**:*337–42*; **5**:*347, 351*
Petrarch **1**:*345, 348*
Petry, Ann, *Tituba of Salem Village* **1**:*393–99*
Philadelphia, Pennsylvania **1**:*71–72, 310*
Philippines **3**:*101*
    Bataan Death March **4**:*81*
Phillips, Wendell **2**:*89 (sidebar)*
Phoenician alphabet **1**:*286–87*
"Phrenology" **2**:*211*
Pigman, The, Zindel, Paul **5**:*271–77*
Pilgrim at Tinker Creek, Dillard, Annie **5**:*278–84*
Pilgrimages **1**:*64–70, 145–46, 182*
Pinkerton's National Detective Agency **3**:*225–26*
Pinochet, August **5**:*169 (illus.)*

Piracy   **1**:*400–402, 405*
Pittsburgh, Pennsylvania   **4**:*7–9*
Plath, Sylvia, *Bell Jar, The*   **4**:*21–27*
Plato
    Academy   **1**:*328*
    complaining of Homer   **1**:*285, 286 (sidebar)*
    Republic   **1**:*321–29*
Plays
    Angels in America, Kushner, Tony   **5**:*1–10*
    Antigone, Sophocles   **1**:*14–21*
    Belle of Amherst, The, Luce, William   **2**:*54–58*
    Biloxi Blues, Simon, Neil   **4**:*35–41*
    Cherry Orchard, The, Chekhov, Anton   **3**:*57–62*
    Crucible, The, Miller, Arthur   **1**:*78–86*
    Cyrano de Bergerac, Rostand, Edmond   **1**:*87–92*
    Death of a Salesman, Miller, Arthur   **4**:*109–15*
    Doll's House, A, Ibsen, Henrik   **2**:*111–17*
    Elephant Man, The, Pomerance, Bernard
        2:*118–24*
    Fences, Wilson, August   **4**:*144–50*
    Fiddler on the Roof, Stein, Joseph   **3**:*119–24*
    *for colored girls who have considered suicide / when
        the rainbow is enuf*, Shange, Ntozake   **5**:*115–21*
    Hamlet, Shakespeare, William   **1**:*136–43*
    Henry IV, Part I, Shakespeare, William   **1**:*144–51*
    I Never Sang for My Father, Anderson, Robert
        5:*201–7*
    Julius Caesar, Shakespeare, William   **1**:*189–95*
    King Lear, Shakespeare, William   **1**:*196–203*
    Little Foxes, The, Hellman, Lillian   **3**:*203–10*
    Long Day's Journey into Night, O'Neill, Eugene
        3:*218–24*
    Macbeth, Shakespeare, William   **1**:*225–30*
    Man for All Seasons, A, Bolt, Robert   **1**:*231–37*
    Medea, Euripides   **1**:*238–41*
    Member of the Wedding, The, McCullers, Carson
        4:*254–59*
    Merchant of Venice, The Shakespeare, William
        1:*242–49*
    Midsummer Night's Dream, A, Shakespeare,
        William   **1**:*258–65*
    Miracle Worker, The, Gibson, William   **2**:*216–22*
    Othello, Shakespeare, William   **1**:*295–300*
    Our Town, Wilder, Thornton   **3**:*284–89*
    Pygmalion, Shaw, George Bernard   **3**:*312–18*
    Raisin in the Sun, A, Hansberry, Lorraine
        4:*309–15*
    Romeo and Juliet, Shakespeare, William
        1:*344–50*
    Streetcar Named Desire, A, Williams, Tennesse
        4:*364–70*
    Tempest, The, Shakespeare, William   **1**:*379–85*
    Twelve Angry Men, Rose, Reginald (screenplay)
        4:*378–83*
    West Side Story, Laurents, Arthur, *et al.*
        4:*384–90*
    Zoo Story, The, Albee, Edward   **4**:*397–402*
    Zoot Suit, Valdez, Luis   **4**:*403–10*
Plays, descriptions by type
    choreopoems   **5**:*115, 117–18, 120–21*

    histories   **1**:*150*
    morality plays   **1**:*148*
    revenge tragedies   **1**:*142*
Plessy v. Ferguson (Supreme Court ruling allowing
    segregation)   **2**:*21, 399–400, 413*; **3**:*351, 375,
    419*; **4**:*1*; **5**:*90, 107–8*
Plutarch   **1**:*193–94*
Pocho, Villarreal, José Antonio   **4**:*295–302*
Poe, Edgar Allan, *Cask of Amontillado, The*   **2**:*81–86*
Poetry
    Welsh regard for   **3**:*64*
    Aeneid, The, Virgil   **1**:*8–13*
    Beowulf, Anonymous   **1**:*44–50*
    Canterbury Tales, The, Chaucer, Geoffrey
        1:*64–70*
    haiku   **4**:*333, 334*
    Iliad, Homer   **1**:*166–73*
    Inferno, Dante Alighieri   **1**:*174–80*
    Leaves of Grass, Whitman, Walt   **2**:*195–201*
    Odyssey, Homer   **1**:*280–87*
    Paradise Lost, Milton, John   **1**:*301–8*
    Waste Land, The, Eliot, T.S.   **3**:*411–17*
Poetry, types of
    blank verse   **1**:*303 (sidebar)*
    choreopoems   **5**:*117–18*
    epic poems   **1**:*49, 153, 172, 173, 282 (sidebar),
        285*
Pogroms
    against Armenians   **3**:*342*
    against Jews   **1**:*364*
Poland
    of 1800s   **2**:*384–85*
    "capitalists" deported from, by Soviets
        4:*131–32*
    Nazi invasion of   **3**:*214*; **4**:*193*
    Stalin/Hitler partition agreement   **4**:*17, 131*
"Polis" or Greek city-state   **1**:*286, 327–28*
Political parties in America
    American Communist Party   **3**:*40*
    Democratic, as party of Irish Americans
        3:*401–2*
    Democratic South becoming Republican   **3**:*79*
    Republicans of Progressive era   **3**:*286*
    Socialist Labor Party   **3**:*174–75*
    ward bosses   **3**:*398*
    Whigs, Democrats, and Republicans   **2**:*2, 87*
Politics in America
    campaigning in mid-19th century   **2**:*2*
    Chinese American influence on   **4**:*126–27*
    during Reconstruction, African Americans in
        2:*412*
    enactment of income tax   **3**:*285, 320*
    enactment of referenda provisions   **3**:*285*
    first recall act   **3**:*319*
    Irish American neighborhoods   **3**:*398–99*
    New York's Tammany Hall   **3**:*148–49, 398–99*
    politicians' invocation of Lincoln   **2**:*7*
    Teapot Dome scandal   **3**:*25*
    televised debates costing Nixon 1960 presidential
        election   **5**:*223*

Polynesia 4:222

Pomerance, Bernard, *Elephant Man, The* 2:118–24

Poor Richard's Almanac, Franklin, Benjamin 1:309–15

Poorhouses, almshouses in 18th-century America 2:216, 219 (*sidebar*)

Pope, Alexander 1:343

Pope Boniface VIII 1:176, 177

Popes
competing for control of Tuscany 1:174
conflicts with Holy Roman Emperors 1:174, 176, 344, 345
fathering children 1:296

Pornography, prevalence in Victorian Age 3:381

Porter, Katherine Anne, *Noon Wine* 3:243–48

Portrait of the Artist as a Young Man, A, Joyce, James 3:305–11
as example of bildungsroman 3:264, 311

"Positivism" 3:213

Post-traumatic stress disorder 5:106

Potlatch ceremony of Kwakiutl 5:198 (*illus.*), 199

Potok, Chaim, *Chosen, The* 4:87–93

Pound, Ezra 3:413–14, 416; 5:42

Poverty
of African American families 3:37; 4:5 (*sidebar*), 145; 5:329
of American Indians 5:360–61
and child abuse 5:329 (*sidebar*)
as deserved, in Hinduism 3:300
of Great Depression years 3:68, 126, 350
and Johnson's War on Poverty 3:324; 5:68, 150, 266
linked to emotional depression and pessimism 5:266 (*sidebar*)
of Puerto Ricans 5:215–16
and Reagan's welfare cuts 5:1, 329
in South Central Los Angeles 5:339–42
studies of, in 1960s 5:266

Poynings Law 1:267

Prairie Years, The. See Abraham Lincoln: The Prairie Years

Predestination 4:304

Prejudice. *See* Racism and prejudice

Premarital sex 5:324

Presbyterianism 4:10, 304

Presley, Elvis 4:172, 386

Pride and Prejudice, Austen, Jane 2:295–300

Prime of Miss Jean Brodie, The, Spark, Muriel 4:303–8

Primitivism 3:385 (*sidebar*)

Prince, The, Machiavelli, Niccolò 1:316–20
influence in early 16th century 1:233
influence upon Shakespeare 1:200, 380

Prince of Tides, The, Conroy, Pat 5:285–90

Printing and publishing
advances in 1:160, 162 (*sidebar*); 2:234, 306, 419
muckraking magazines 3:176
paperback books 2:325
pulp magazines 2:325; 3:226–27

Prisons 3:371, 374 (*illus.*)

Privateers 1:400

Proctor, John 1:81 (*sidebar*), 83 (*sidebar*)

Progress, belief in
Stephen Crane's objections to 2:313
destroyed by WWI 3:412
fostered by Enlightenment (Age of Reason) 1:24–25, 268; 2:416
reality belying 3:217, 227
science and technology ("positivism") as 19th century's evidence for 2:416; 3:213
Second Great Awakening contributing to 2:417–18
tempered by Victorians' doubt 3:314
and utopian philosophies of 19th century 2:195
H. G. Wells's objections to 3:409
(*See also* Evolution; Science/technology)

Prohibition
disillusionment with 3:69, 227, 401
fostering corruption, bootlegging, and gangsterism 3:69, 147–48, 366–67, 401
restrictions retained in South 4:207 (*sidebar*)
in San Francisco 3:226
support by Anti-Saloon League and temperance movements 2:25 (*sidebar*), 85–86; 3:69, 75, 147, 401
support from rural, anti-urban areas 3:69–70
Volstead Act 3:147, 151, 401
weaknesses of, as legislation 3:22–23, 69
(*See also* Alcohol and alcoholism)

Project 100,000, draft of disadvantaged for Vietnam 5:102–3, 158, 307

Propaganda
as aspect of fascism 4:304; 5:253
pro-war, from Hollywood 4:325
use by British 5:252, 257
use of media for 4:66–67
use by Soviets 5:252

Prosser, Gabriel 1:39, 42; 2:94

Prostitution
in China 3:135
of female Chinese immigrants 2:366–67
near military installations 4:37
serving gold miners of California 2:283–84
women driven to, by lack of work
America of 1880s 2:328–29
France of 1800s 2:228
Victorian England 2:264, 355
women kept as, for repayment of debts (Victorian London) 2:264

Protest movements. *See* Civil rights movements; Counterculture

Protestantism
African Methodist Episcopal Church 3:83
all-black churches 3:250, 252
Anglican Church (Church of England) 1:78, 123, 129, 232, 233 (*sidebar*), 306, 351, 393
and anti-Catholic prejudice and policies 1:74, 132, 230, 269

Baptists **5**:*19, 188*

Christian Socialist movement **2**:*377*

clergymen denouncing women's rights activists
2:*25*

creationism **2**:*30*

decline of influence in late 18th century **1**:*102*

decline of influence in late 19th century **2**:*329*

Dutch Reformed Church **1**:*331, 425*

establishment of distinct denominations in
colonial America **1**:*106*

fundamentalists and New/Religious Right
5:*137–39*

Great Awakening in American colonies **1**:*73,*
106, 122, 424–25

in Ireland **1**:*267, 269*

Methodism **2**:*357–58*

Presbyterianism **4**:*10, 304*

as protest against abuses of Catholic Church
1:*231*

Quakerism **1**:*23;* **2**:*22, 25, 88–89*

as Reformation of Catholic Church **1**:*231;*
2:*113*

revival meetings **1**:*425;* **2**:*315–16*

Second Great Awakening in America **1**:*424–25;*
2:*23, 315–16, 404, 417–18*

segregation of churches **5**:*189*

Shakerism **3**:*95–99*

spread of, spurring legalization of divorce **2**:*113*

television evangelists **5**:*31–32*

Unitarianism **2**:*54, 315*

(*See also* Puritanism)

Psychology

behavior modification and conditioning
5:*156–57*

changing views of mental illness **4**:*289*

conceptions of intelligence **4**:*152–53*

conflicting theories of nature of mankind
4:*233–34*

connectedness of mental health and human
relationships **4**:*153*

development of **3**:*329, 378;* **4**:*77*

ethical considerations of experimentation **4**:*153*

insistence on domesticity and dependence for
women **4**:*167*

as means of rehabilitation of nonconformists
4:*399*

and paranormal phenomena **2**:*383 (sidebar);*
5:*47–48, 56, 239*

psychiatry **4**:*289 (sidebar)*

psychoanalysis **4**:*168 (sidebar);* **5**:*42, 260–61,*
262

PTSD (post-traumatic stress disorder) **5**:*106*

theories of absent father **4**:*244–45*

theories of community collusion in evil **4**:*238*

twins and struggle for identity **4**:*219*

(*See also* Mental and emotional disabilities;
Suicide)

Ptolemy **1**:*305*

Puerto Rico and Puerto Ricans **3**:*277;* **4**:*385–86,*
388–89, 401; **5**:*214–21*

Punishments

in 19th-century America **2**:*17*

in 19th-century France **2**:*225, 228*

aboard ships of Royal Navy **1**:*273–74, 275 (illus.)*

branding **1**:*420*

capital **4**:*379–80;* **5**:*131*

collective, in British colonies **2**:*362*

of drug users, racial inequality of **4**:*250*

dueling **1**:*389 (sidebar)*

in Elizabethan England **1**:*198 (sidebar)*

of English schoolboys **2**:*373–74*

feuds **2**:*17 (sidebar)*

flogging **2**:*394, 395*

guillotining **1**:*373*

hazing on ship **2**:*394*

inequality of, for blacks **5**:*16*

marooning **1**:*401–2*

prisons **3**:*371, 374 (illus.)*

public hanging **1**:*374*

quartering **1**:*373–74*

of seamen **2**:*394, 395*

in Southern prisons and road/chain gangs
3:*371, 374 (illus.)*

in Soviet Union, Siberian exile and forced labor
4:*132, 282*

tarring and feathering **2**:*17 (sidebar)*

Puns

in Shakespeare **1**:*348–49*

in Victorian Age **2**:*30*

Puritanism

and Antinomians **1**:*352, 357*

austerity and discipline **1**:*78, 101, 393–94*

belief in witchcraft and Satan **1**:*79–81, 394,*
395–96, 421–23

Calvinism **2**:*54, 55;* **3**:*377–78;* **4**:*304*

concept of conversion **2**:*55 (sidebar)*

and Congregationalists **1**:*357, 424–25*

Defoe influenced by **1**:*338*

doctrines of **1**:*23, 101–2, 352, 393–94*

Franklin influenced by **1**:*311*

good works and redemption **1**:*23, 101–2, 352*

Half-Way Covenant **1**:*421*

hardships faced by colonists in New England
1:*351*

immigration to New England **1**:*421*

intolerance **1**:*102, 394*

Milton influenced by **1**:*307*

as "purifiers" of Church of England **1**:*299, 420*

Putnam, Ann **1**:*79, 83 (sidebar), 396*

Pygmalion, Shaw, George Bernard **3**:*312–18*

Pyle, Howard, *Merry Adventures of Robin Hood, The*
1:*250–57*

Pyramus and Thisbe **1**:*259 (sidebar)*

Q

Quadroons **3**:*17–18*

Quakerism **1**:*23;* **2**:*22, 25, 88–89*

Quarterstaff fencing **1**:*253*

Quixote. *See Adventures of Don Quixote, The*

R

Rabbits   5:336–37, 348 (*illus.*)

Racism and prejudice
American Communist Party's stand against
   3:40; 4:211
in American jury system before 1969   4:379
   (*sidebar*)
of Aryans, neo-Nazis, and neo-fascists   4:40, 50;
   5:42
in concept of "white man's burden"   2:147;
   3:170, 172, 182 (*sidebar*)
eliminating through claiming of identity   5:176
of eugenics movement   5:42
FEPC (Fair Employment Practices Commission)
   to investigate   3:42
(*See also* Holocaust)

Racism and prejudice, against
African Americans
   among immigrants   4:52
   antiblack propaganda   2:400
   Baldwin's condemnation of   5:111, 113
   in Caucasian standards of beauty   4:49–50
   combated by Du Bois   2:343–46
   covert   4:314
   creating self-hatred   4:53–54; 5:116
   economic   4:30–31, 33
   exacerbated by economic competition   2:43
   housing discrimination   2:13; 3:39, 237;
      4:30–31
   by Ku Klux Klan   2:141 (*sidebar*), 143
      (*sidebar*), 412; 3:419; 5:25, 130
   by labor unions   2:341
   in legal and prison systems   3:371
   Lincoln on   2:3, 5
   in minstrel shows   2:16–17, 21, 398
   in New South   2:399–400; 3:36–37, 41, 203,
      320
   in professional sports   4:149
   race riots of early 19th century   2:6, 404;
      3:160, 252, 321; 4:310
   race riots of 1940s   4:197, 201, 213, 247,
      248 (*illus.*)
   "science" of ethnology contributing to
      2:232–33
   Scottsboro case   3:39, 239
   sexual taboos   3:391
   social Darwinism contributing to   2:341
   soldiers in WWII   4:212–13
   stereotyping justifying slavery   1:39, 41, 42,
      394; 2:403, 404
   as viewed by Styron   2:97
   by white supremacists   3:352
   (*See also* Lynching; Segregation; Slavery)
African blacks   1:63; 2:360–65; 3:291; 4:94–100
American Indians. *See* American Indians
Anglos   4:320
Armenians   4:200
Chinese   2:175, 287, 367–68, 370 (*sidebar*), 371;
   3:30; 4:124–27, 194, 330; 5:230–31
Germans during WWII   4:375
immigrants in general   4:194
Irish   3:220, 221 (*sidebar*)
Japanese   3:30; 4:137, 138–43, 194, 195,
   330–31
Jews. *See* Anti-Semitism
Latinos
   deportations of braceros in 1930s   4:44
   mestizos or *criollos*   5:334–36
   in Southwest   4:320
   zoot suit riots of 1940s   4:295–97, 403–10
lower castes in India   1:366; 2:183; 3:182, 184,
   300
migrant farm workers   3:29–30, 34, 49, 140–42,
   143 (*sidebar*), 269–71, 275, 335, 337; 4:297
   (*sidebar*)
Moors   1:297, 299, 300
Poles   4:369
users of sign language   2:217

Radio
Dylan Thomas's broadcasts   3:66–67
FDR taking advantage of   3:127
new teenage audience of 1950s   4:386, 391
popularity of   3:3, 45
"thrillers" produced on   3:329

Ragged Dick, Alger, Horatio   2:301–7

Ragtime, Doctorow, E. L.   3:319–25

Railroads
in England   2:353, 354, 358
in France   2:209–10
in India   3:184–85

Railroads in U.S.
California population boom and   2:175, 195
Chinese workers on   4:124, 125; 5:75–77, 78
   (*illus.*)
contributing to western migration   2:327
federal and state funding for expansion of
   2:230
hobo tradition of 1930s   3:46
importance in Civil War   2:255, 256 (*illus.*)
importance to travelers   2:175
luxury travel in Pullman cars   2:306
raising farm incomes   2:417
refrigerated cars for transport of perishables
   2:328; 3:175
Thoreau's disapproval of   2:416

Raisin in the Sun, A, Hansberry, Lorraine   4:309–15

Randolph, A. Philip   3:42, 159–60; 4:255; 5:186,
   188

Realism
Bierce on   2:259–60
of Crane   2:312
described   2:259
of Dreiser   2:327, 331
of Joyce, as "slice of life"   3:111
levels of   1:4, 6 (*sidebar*)
in literature for young adults   5:265–66, 276
"magical"   2:271, 273; 3:196, 202; 4:48; 5:169,
   213, 330
of *Les Misérables*   2:229

versus stereotypes 1:42
  Whitman's impact on 2:200
Rebecca, du Maurier, Daphne 3:326–33
Reconnaissance planes 5:96
Reconstruction
  African Americans in politics 2:412
  Black Codes 2:412; 5:21
  carpetbaggers and scalawags 2:141
  civil rights granted, then ignored 2:21, 340–41, 412
  demise of plantations and wilderness 2:49, 53
  economy of South 2:41–42
  education of freed slaves 2:411–12, 413, 414
  end of 2:412–13
  Force Acts (1871 and 1872) 2:412
  Freedman's Bureau 2:411
  in Georgia 2:139–40
  Ku Klux Klan 2:141 (sidebar), 143 (sidebar), 412
  lack of training or means of survival for freed slaves 2:59, 411
  sharecropping and tenant farming 2:42, 411
  violence and unequal justice for freed slaves 5:20–21
  white backlash following 2:340–41, 412–13
  (See also Jim Crow laws; Segregation)
Red Badge of Courage, The, Crane, Stephen 2:308–13
Red Pony, The, Steinbeck, John 3:334–37
Red Power movement 2:79 (sidebar)
"Red Scare" 1:84–86; 3:105; 4:71–72; 5:2, 127
  (See also Cold War)
Red Sky at Morning, Bradford, Richard 4:316–22
Reform movements of 19th century
  child labor laws 2:103–4
  encouraged by belief in progress 2:195, 196
  multifaceted nature of 2:23
  as response to rapid change of Industrial Revolution 2:417
  settlement houses 3:397–98
  strengthened by Romantic movement 2:316
  temperance movement 2:25 (sidebar), 85; 3:147
  utopian societies of 1840s 2:418
  women's involvement in 2:423
Reform movements of 20th century
  against child labor 3:76 (sidebar), 77 (illus.)
  during Progressive Era 3:75–76
  Independent Living Movement 2:123
  Pure Food and Drug Act (1906) 3:179
  temperance movement 3:69, 75, 147
  (See also Civil rights movements; Prohibition)
Reformation 1:231; 2:113
Refugees 5:28–29
Reincarnation 3:300
Reisman, David 4:75, 111, 382
Religion
  and agnosticism 3:265
  of American Indians 2:71–72, 78, 178; 4:188
    healing ceremonies for returning war veterans 5:363

in ancient Greece 1:15–16, 169
  ancient sacrificial rites 4:238
  Buddhism 1:365–69; 3:186–87; 5:48
  in China 3:133, 190, 193
  Chippewa *manitou* 5:246, 249 (sidebar)
  comparative conceptions of 5:57 (sidebar)
  conflicts with Darwinists 3:102, 404
  conflicts with non-believers in 20th century 3:102
  cults 5:83–84
  Daoism (also Taoism) 5:237
  Eastern, in America 5:237
  freedom of, in America 1:73–74
  "Great Chain of Being" 1:201, 203
  Hinduism 3:300, 302
  in India 1:366; 3:300–301
  Islam 1:296; 3:300
  miracles and paranormal phenomena 5:48
  monasticism 3:186–87
  moral sense directed toward political issues 1:96
  Mormonism 5:4
  Nation of Islam 3:238, 325; 4:56, 248–50; 5:12–13, 69, 110–11, 302
  of Nez Percé 2:161
  People's Temple and Jim Jones 5:84
  pilgrimages 1:64
  of Pueblo Indians 4:79
  rationalistic versus mystical/emotional 1:425; 3:426
  reincarnation 3:300
  vs. science in Victorian Age 2:29–30, 121–22
  syncretism 3:190–91; 4:44 (sidebar)
  transcendentalism 1:356–57; 2:54, 92, 314, 316–19, 416, 418–19
  Unification Church 5:83
  Zen Buddhism 4:334
  (See also Christianity; Greek myth; Jews; Sin and damnation)
Remarque, Erich Maria, *All Quiet on the Western Front* 3:8–14
Renaissance 1:2, 380
Renan, Ernest 3:213
Renault, Mary, *Bull from the Sea, The* 1:57–63
Republic, Plato 1:321–29
Republican Party of 1830s 2:2
"Resurrection men" 1:120–21
Retirement, problems of adjustment to 5:203, 273
Revival meetings 1:425
Revolution, French. *See* France in 18th century: French Revolution
Revolutions of 1848 1:376
Rhetoric
  of Churchill's speeches 4:361–62
  in colonial America 1:123
  of Kennedy's speeches 5:223
  of King's oratory 5:186
Rhodesia 4:165–66
Richard I of England (the Lion-Hearted) 1:181–82, 184 (illus.), 188, 251

Richard II of England   **1**:*144*
Richelieu, Cardinal Duc de   **1**:*387–89*
Richter, Conrad, *Light in the Forest, The*   **1**:*219–24*
Richter, Hans Peter, *Friedrich*   **4**:*157–64*
Riegner, Gerhardt,   **3**:*403*
Right Stuff, The, Wolfe, Tom   **5**:*291–97*
Riis, Jacob   **3**:*169 (sidebar), 285, 320*
Rip Van Winkle, Irving, Washington   **1**:*330–36*
Risberg, Charles "Swede"   **3**:*149*
Road from Home, The, Kherdian, David   **3**:*338–43*
Roberts, Oral   **5**:*31–32*
Robeson, Paul   **1**:*389–90*
Robespierre, Maximilien   **1**:*359 (illus.), 372*
Robinson Crusoe, Defoe, Daniel   **1**:*337–43*
Rock 'n' roll   **4**:*172, 386, 391–92*
Rockefeller, John D.   **2**:*306*
Rocking-Horse Winner, The, Lawrence, D.H.
    3:*344–49*
Rodeo   **5**:*362, 364 (sidebar)*
Rodriguez, Richard, *Hunger of Memory*   **5**:*178–84*
Roll of Thunder, Hear My Cry, Taylor, Mildred
    3:*350–55*
Romantic movement
    Darwin's influence on   **1**:*116*
    disapproval of Industrial Revolution   **1**:*115–16,*
        120
    emphasizing emotion, imagination, mystery,
        individuality, and nationalism   **1**:*106, 115,*
        118–19, 217, 406
    favoring plain speech of common people   **1**:*163*
    influence on Dumas   **2**:*104*
    influence on Emerson   **2**:*316–17, 319*
    influence of French Revolution   **1**:*116*
    influence on Hermann Hesse   **1**:*365, 370*
    interest in medieval romance   **1**:*413*
    interest in past   **2**:*104*
    as reaction against rationality of Enlightenment
        1:*106, 217, 406*
    reflections in Emily Brontë's works   **1**:*413*
    reflections in Jane Austen's works   **2**:*300*
    and transcendentalism   **1**:*356–57;* **2**:*54, 92, 314,*
        316–19, 416, 418–19
Rome, Italy
    in ancient times   **1**:*9, 12–13, 189–92*
    civil war, republic, and dictatorship   **1**:*190*
    mythical founding of   **1**:*10 (sidebar)*
    religious holidays   **1**:*191–92*
Romeo and Juliet, Shakespeare, William   **1**:*344–50*
    as model for *West Side Story*   **4**:*384*
Room of One's Own, A, Woolf, Virginia   **3**:*356–63*
Roosevelt, Eleanor   **3**:*154, 392, 395, 424;* **4**:*297*
Roosevelt, Franklin Delano
    authorizing internment of Japanese Americans
        4:*138*
    First Inaugural Address   **3**:*125–30*
    invocation of Lincoln   **2**:*7*
    New Deal   **1**:*113;* **3**:*45, 69, 128, 141*
    political appointments of Irish Americans
        3:*401–2*
    political support from Sandburg   **2**:*7*
    reason for refusal to sign Dyer Antilynching Bill
        3:*154, 392*
    support for equal rights   **4**:*255*
Roosevelt, Theodore
    as big game hunter   **3**:*232 (sidebar)*
    "big stick" corollary to Monroe Doctrine   **3**:*277*
    coining term "muckrakers"   **3**:*176*
    expansionism of   **3**:*101, 231*
    popularizing "Old West" myth of individualism
        5:*206*
    as Progressive reformer   **3**:*284–85*
    support for preservation of buffalo   **5**:*34*
    support for trade union movement   **3**:*420*
    as trust buster   **3**:*167*
Roots, Haley, Alex   **5**:*298–305*
Rose, Reginald, *Twelve Angry Men* (screenplay)
    4:*378–83*
Rosenberg, Julius and Ethel   **4**:*72, 380, 381 (illus.);*
    5:*2, 127*
Rostand, Edmond, *Cyrano de Bergerac*   **1**:*87–92*
Rotarians   **5**:*202*
Rothstein, Arnold   **3**:*149–50;* **4**:*261;* **5**:*315, 316*
    (illus.)
Rousseau, Jean-Jacques   **1**:*409 (sidebar)*
Runner, The, Voigt, Cynthia   **5**:*306–13*
Rush, Benjamin   **4**:*289*
Russia, czarist
    anti-Semitism and pogroms   **1**:*364;* **3**:*119–21*
    Bolshevik Revolution   **4**:*14, 16*
    Bolsheviks and Mensheviks   **4**:*14*
    Cossacks   **3**:*233*
    decline of nobility   **2**:*35–36;* **3**:*57*
    education reform   **3**:*58*
    emancipation of serfs   **2**:*34*
    industrialization   **4**:*14*
    intelligentsia   **3**:*58*
    land ownership   **3**:*57–58, 60*
    local government   **2**:*35*
    marriage and divorce   **2**:*37, 39*
    oppression of Poland   **2**:*384–85*
    peasants and intelligentsia   **4**:*14*
    revolution of 1905   **1**:*363;* **3**:*59, 232*
    Russo-Japanese War (1904–05)   **4**:*59*
    Russo-Turkish war   **2**:*37–39*
    as threat to British-controlled Punjab   **3**:*184,*
        185
    women's rights movement   **2**:*37, 39*
    WWI   **3**:*8, 11 (sidebar)*
    (See also Soviet Union)
Rustin, Bayard   **5**:*188*

S

Sacatras   **3**:*18*
Sackville-West, Vita   **3**:*361–62*
Sailboats   **2**:*395*
Saint-Domingue (Haiti)   **5**:*116–17*
Saint-Exupéry, Antoine de, *Little Prince, The*
    3:*210–17*
Saki, *Open Window, The*   **2**:*275–80*

Salazar, Rubén   **4**:*47, 410*
Salem, Massachusetts   **1**:*78–80, 355, 395–97*
Salinas Valley, California   **3**:*334–35*
Salinger, J. D.
   Catcher in the Rye   **4**:*73–78*
   as reclusive   **5**:*319*
Salk, Jonas Edward   **4**:*10*
San Francisco
   in 1920s   **3**:*226*
   Chinatown   **3**:*226*; **5**:*74–75, 77–79*
   prejudice against Chinese   **2**:*367–68*
   vigilantes   **2**:*286–87*
Sand, George (Amantine-Aurore-Lucile Dupin)
   2:*212*; **3**:*406*
Sandburg, Carl
   Abraham Lincoln: The Prairie Years   **2**:*1–7*
   on *Call of the Wild*   **3**:*56*
Sandoz, Mari, *Story Catcher, The*   **2**:*347–52*
Saroyan, William, *Human Comedy, The*   **4**:*193–200*
Satan. *See* Devil (Satan)
Satire
   Adventures of Don Quixote, The   **1**:*4, 6–7*
   Devil and Tom Walker, The   **1**:*101–6*
   Gulliver's Travels   **1**:*129–35*
   Modest Proposal, A   **1**:*266–72*
   use in Shakespeare's time   **1**:*349*
Saxo Grammaticus   **1**:*136, 139, 141 (sidebar)*
Scarlet Letter, The, Hawthorne, Nathaniel   **1**:*351–57*
Scarlet Pimpernel, The, Orczy, Baroness Emmuska
   1:*358–64*
Schaefer, Jack, *Shane*   **2**:*321–26*
Schlafly, Phyllis   **5**:*136–37, 138 (illus.)*
Schooners   **1**:*401*
Science fiction   **2**:*388–89*; **4**:*347*; **5**:*54–56, 126*
   (sidebar)
   Brave New World   **5**:*39–45*
   Childhood's End   **5**:*53–60*
   Dune   **5**:*81–87*
   episodes in *Slaughterhouse Five*   **4**:*347*
   Fahrenheit 451   **5**:*95–100*
   Foundation   **5**:*122–28*
   House of Stairs   **5**:*156–62*
   Left Hand of Darkness, The   **5**:*236–42*
   Nineteen Eighty-Four   **5**:*251–58*
   and purported UFOs   **4**:*347–48*; **5**:*59 (illus.)*
   as "speculative fiction"   **5**:*141*
   Stranger in a Strange Land   **5**:*321–27*
   Jules Verne as father of   **2**:*388–89*
   War of the Worlds, The   **3**:*404–10*
   H. G. Wells as father of   **2**:*389*
   women writers of   **5**:*239*
   (See also Fantasy)
Science/technology
   American Enlightenment   **2**:*416*
   anthropology   **2**:*72, 179*; **4**:*221–27*; **5**:*42*
   assembly line production and mass production
      3:*89, 100–101, 102*
   automobile   **2**:*128 (sidebar)*; **3**:*23, 77, 88–89,*
      94, 101; **5**:*40 (illus.)*
   aviation   **3**:*211–12, 367*; **5**:*96, 293–94*

behaviorism   **5**:*45*
civilian applications of war technology   **4**:*236*
computers   **5**:*97, 127*
contraceptives   **2**:*211*; **5**:*272, 324*
cotton gin   **2**:*403*
drugs and pharmaceuticals   **3**:*379*
electricity   **3**:*89*
in Elizabethan Age   **1**:*142 (sidebar), 200*
in Enlightenment   **1**:*24–26, 268–69, 272*
"ethnology"   **2**:*232–33*
eugenics   **3**:*272*; **4**:*152*; **5**:*41–42*
explorations   **1**:*118 (sidebar)*
explosives   **5**:*76*
extrasensory perception (ESP)   **5**:*47, 239*
on farms   **3**:*5–6*
in Franklin's day   **1**:*24–26*
Galileo, Copernicus, and Newton   **1**:*24, 94, 305*
indoor plumbing   **3**:*77*
Industrial Revolution   **1**:*115, 336*; **2**:*119*
influence on H. G. Wells   **3**:*404–5*
innoculations against disease   **3**:*378, 406*
jet engine   **4**:*71*
motion pictures   **3**:*3, 89, 101*
nuclear energy   **5**:*124, 127, 286*
Pasteur's discoveries   **3**:*285, 406*
penicillin   **3**:*366*
pesticides ("biocides") and DDT   **4**:*337–42*
"phrenology"   **2**:*211*
physics and principle of indeterminacy   **5**:*283*
printing and publishing   **1**:*160, 162 (sidebar)*;
   2:*234, 306, 419*
professionalization and specialization of   **2**:*119*
psychiatry   **4**:*289 (sidebar)*
psychoanalysis   **4**:*168 (sidebar)*; **5**:*42, 260–61,*
   263
psychokinesis and telekinesis   **5**:*47–48*
radio   **3**:*3, 45, 89*
religion and   **2**:*29–30, 121–22*
and "resurrection men"   **1**:*120–21*
in Romantic period   **1**:*116*
satellites in space   **5**:*54*
space exploration   **5**:*53, 54, 81–82*
steam threshing machine   **2**:*354*
steamships   **2**:*391, 394–95*
submarines   **2**:*385–86*
telecommunications   **5**:*54*
telephone   **2**:*128 (sidebar)*; **3**:*77*
tractors   **3**:*6, 92*
(See also Evolution; Progress, belief in;
   Psychology; Railroads; Television; War
   weaponry)
Scopes Trial   **3**:*102 (sidebar)*
Scotland
   Calvinism in   **3**:*377*; **4**:*304*
   education of women in 1930s   **4**:*303–4*
   Gowrie Conspiracy   **1**:*229*
   Hebrides   **1**:*226*
   Highlanders   **1**:*187*
   as Presbyterians   **4**:*10, 304*
   status of women in 11th century   **1**:*226*

in time of *Macbeth* (11th century)   1:225–26
troubled relations with England   1:145, 150, 181, 187, 201
Scott, Sir Walter
    emulated by Cooper   1:208
    friend of Washington Irving   1:105
    influencing Hugo   1:165
    Ivanhoe   1:181–88
Scottsboro case   3:39, 239
Seale, Bobby   4:54
Second Great Awakening   1:424–25; 2:23, 404, 417–18
Secret Life of Walter Mitty, The, Thurber, James   3:364–69
Secular humanism   5:138
Segregation
    acceptance for time being by Booker T. Washington   2:341, 342, 343, 344, 345, 410, 413, 414; 3:162, 250, 320, 385
    of churches   5:189
    documentation of negative effects   4:32–33
    in New Orleans   3:17–18; 5:22
    protest by (multiracial) high school football team   4:29
    in public facilities   3:38 (illus.), 42 (illus.); 4:29 (illus.)
    in public transportation   5:88–90, 185–86
    in schools for disabled   2:221 (sidebar)
    in South   1:399; 2:97; 3:419; 4:28–29, 373–74; 5:22
    in Supreme Court rulings
        overturned for residential housing, interstate bus travel   4:201
        overturned for schools in *Brown v. Board of Education*   3:375; 4:29–30, 314; 5:90, 108, 180, 181
        sanctioned by *Plessy v. Ferguson*   2:21, 399–400, 413; 3:351, 375, 419; 4:1; 5:90, 107–8
    of U.S. military during WWII   3:41–42; 4:195, 197, 374 (sidebar)
    (*See also* African Americans' civil rights/reform/power movements; Integration; Jim Crow laws)
Self-Reliance, Emerson, Ralph Waldo   2:314–20
Senior citizens
    loneliness, depression, serious illness, and suicide   5:273, 275 (illus.)
    problems of adjustment to retirement   5:203, 273
Separate Peace, A, Knowles, John   4:323–29
Serbia   3:8, 11 (sidebar)
Serling, Rod   4:379
Seventeen Syllables, Yamamoto, Hisaye   4:330–36
Sex education
    for mentally handicapped   4:152
    programs of 1960s   5:153 (sidebar)
    social purity movement of late 19th century   2:423
Sexual dimension of life

in 19th century   2:212, 423
    abuse of African American women   4:54
    abuse of female slaves   2:49, 60, 169, 406
    adultery/infidelity   5:273, 287
    AIDS   5:9
    Catholic and Presbyterian views on   4:304 (sidebar)
    changing mores   5:272–73
    contraceptives   2:211; 5:272, 324
    effects of childhood abuse   5:289–90
    "free love" movement of 1960s   5:272
    Freud's arguments against repression   3:23
    harassment of women in workplace   1:35
    hypocrisy of public attitudes   4:75
    impotence   4:128
    incest   4:52
    interracial taboos, miscegenation   3:391
    Kinsey Report   4:75, 241, 398–99 (sidebar); 5:324
    rape   4:395; 5:117, 136, 141
    sexual revolution of 1960s and '70s   5:151
    treatment in literature as shocking   4:74
    Victorians' repression of   2:334, 336, 338–39, 355; 3:18, 380–81
    (*See also* Homosexuality; Love and marriage; Prostitution)
Shakerism   3:95–99
Shakespeare, William
    Hamlet   1:136–43
    Henry IV, Part I   1:144–51
    Julius Caesar   1:189–95
    King Lear   1:196–203
    Macbeth   1:225–30
    Merchant of Venice, The   1:242–49
    Midsummer Night's Dream, A   1:258–65
    Othello   1:295–300
    Romeo and Juliet   1:344–50
    Tempest, The   1:379–85
Shane, Schaefer, Jack   2:321–26
Shange, Ntozake
    Betsey Brown   4:28–34
    for colored girls who have considered suicide / when the rainbow is enuf   5:115–21
Sharecropping and tenant farming   2:42, 411; 3:80, 104, 105, 249, 350–51, 370–71, 418; 4:2
    STFU (Southern Tenant Farmers' Union)   3:208
Shaw, George Bernard, *Pygmalion*   3:312–18
Shelley, Mary
    daughter of Mary Wollstonecraft   1:115, 116, 407
    Frankenstein   1:115–21
Shelley, Percy Bysshe   1:115, 116, 119
Shepard, Alan   5:292, 296
Sherman, William Tecumseh   2:139, 140 (illus.), 165 (sidebar)
Shipping industry
    of early 19th century   2:391–92, 393, 394–95
    longshoremen   3:161 (sidebar)
Ships
    privateers   1:400

sailboats   2:395
schooners   1:401
steam-powered   1:404 (sidebar); 2:394–95
Shoeless Joe, Kinsella, W. P.   5:314–20
Short stories
    Almos' a Man, Wright, Richard   4:1–6
    Barn Burning, Faulkner, William   2:41–46
    Bear, The, Faulkner, William   2:47–53
    Cask of Amontillado, The, Poe, Edgar Allan
        2:81–86
    Child's Christmas in Wales, A, Thomas, Dylan
        3:63–67
    Christmas Memory, A, Capote, Truman   3:68–74
    Devil and Tom Walker, The, Irving, Washington
        1:101–6
    Dubliners, Joyce, James   3:106–11
    Everything That Rises Must Converge, O'Connor,
        Flannery   5:88–94
    Legend of Sleepy Hollow, The, Irving, Washington
        1:211–18
    Lottery, The, Jackson, Shirley   4:235–39
    Most Dangerous Game, The, Connell, Richard
        3:231–35
    Necklace, The, Maupassant, Guy de   2:244–48
    Noon Wine, Porter, Katherine Anne   3:243–48
    Notorious Jumping Frog of Calaveras County, The,
        Twain, Mark   2:249–54
    Occurrence at Owl Creek Bridge, An, Bierce,
        Ambrose   2:255–60
    Open Window, The, Saki   2:275–80
    Outcasts of Poker Flat, The, Harte, Bret
        2:281–87
    Rip Van Winkle, Irving, Washington   1:330–36
    Rocking-Horse Winner, The, Lawrence, D.H.
        3:344–49
    Secret Life of Walter Mitty, The, Thurber, James
        3:364–69
    Seventeen Syllables, Yamamoto, Hisaye
        4:330–36
    Where Are You Going, Where Have You Been?,
        Oates, Joyce Carol   4:391–96
    Worn Path, A, Welty, Eudora   3:418–24
    Yellow Wallpaper, The, Gilman, Charlotte Perkins
        2:422–28
    Yentl, the Yeshiva Boy, Singer, Isaac Bashevis
        3:425–31
    Young Goodman Brown, Hawthorne, Nathaniel
        1:420–26
Siberia   4:133–35
Sicily   4:67
Siddartha Gautama   1:365–68
Siddhartha, Hesse, Hermann   1:365–70
Silent Spring, Carson, Rachel   4:337–42; 5:35
Silko, Leslie Marmon, *Ceremony*   4:79–86
Silver. *See* Gold rushes and silver strikes
Simon, Neil, *Biloxi Blues*   4:35–41
Sin and damnation
    beliefs of Calvinists   3:377; 4:304
    beliefs of Puritans   1:23, 393, 421
    beliefs in Shakespeare's time   1:143
    depictions in morality plays   1:148
    and guilt in *The Scarlet Letter*   1:351, 355–56
    in *Paradise Lost*   1:301, 306
    and predestination   4:304
    in *Young Goodman Brown*   1:420–26
Sinclair, Upton, *Jungle, The*   3:174–80, 320
Singer, Isaac Bashevis, *Yentl, the Yeshiva Boy*
    3:425–31
Sister Carrie, Dreiser, Theodore   2:327–33
Skinner, B. F.   5:156, 279
Slaughterhouse Five, Vonnegut, Kurt, Jr.   4:343–48
Slave narratives
    described   2:171; 4:205
    Douglass, Frederick (*Narrative of the Life of
        Frederick Douglass*)   2:236–41
    Jacobs, Harriet (*Incidents in the Life of a Slave Girl*)
        2:168–73
    by Northrup, Solomon   2:410
    Roots as   5:305
Slave trade
    auction block   1:40 (illus.)
    diagram of slave ship   1:38 (illus.)
    English involvement in/prohibition of
        1:274–75, 299, 337–38; 2:361
    impelled by need for labor   1:103
    missionaries' attempts to atone for   2:361–62
    overview   1:37, 103
    traders despised   1:103
Slavery in America
    of American Indians by forced indenture
        2:175
    causing rift between North and South   2:88,
        172, 188, 403–4
    of Chinese prostitutes   2:366–67
    in colonial America   1:394; 2:93, 175
    Compromise of 1850   2:404–5
    as depicted in *Tituba of Salem Village*   1:397–98
    extent of, in Old South   2:188, 405, 410
    Fugitive Slave Acts (1793 and 1850)   1:42;
        2:16, 62, 170, 189, 404–5, 410
    Kansas-Nebraska Act (1854)   1:42; 2:5
        (sidebar), 172, 193
    in Kentucky   2:59–60
    Kongo kingdom and   2:145
    legacy of, in late 20th century   2:65
    in Maryland   2:236–37
    Missouri Compromise (1820)   2:5 (sidebar),
        15–16, 22
    Nat Turner's Rebellion   2:169–70
    in North Carolina   2:168
    opposition of
        Patrick Henry   1:126 (sidebar)
        Thomas Paine   1:72 (sidebar)
        Henry David Thoreau   1:88, 89 (sidebar)
    racist justifications of   1:39, 41, 42, 394; 2:403,
        404
    references to, deleted from Declaration of
        Independence   1:98
    reliance upon, for harvesting of cotton   2:15,
        22, 44 (illus.), 59, 168, 403

slave codes and patrols   **1**:*103*; **2**:*189, 190 (sidebar)*
  as soul-corrupting for whites   **2**:*52, 408*
  Southern states avoiding mention in state constitutions   **1**:*99 (sidebar)*
  and Underground Railroad   **2**:*16, 60, 62, 189, 238, 406–7*
  whites' feelings of guilt at   **2**:*52, 53*
  (*See also* Abolitionists/Abolition of slavery; African Americans)
Slavery in North America
  among Canadian Kwakiutl   **5**:*194–95*
  brought by Spaniards to Puerto Rico   **5**:*214*
Slaves
  Amistad mutiny   **1**:*43*
  arson by   **2**:*189*
  cimaroons   **1**:*401–2*
  communities and culture   **2**:*407*
  escapes, rebellions, and resistance   **1**:*39, 43, 401–2*; **2**:*60, 93, 94–95, 169–70, 188–89, 406–7*
  family life   **2**:*60, 169, 237–38, 405, 406, 410*; **3**:*423*; **4**:*204–5*
  female, sexual abuse of   **2**:*49, 60, 169, 406*
  food and clothing   **2**:*237*
  freed before Emancipation Proclamation   **2**:*93–94, 168–69, 238*
  ill-prepared for freedom   **2**:*411*
  literacy   **2**:*16, 24–25*
  living and working conditions   **2**:*189 (sidebar), 237, 405, 410*
  loyalty of some to white masters during Civil War   **2**:*410–11*
  music   **2**:*398, 407*
  punishment   **2**:*240–42, 405, 410*
  religion   **2**:*407*; **3**:*83*
  social distinctions between   **3**:*387*
  use of cunning and manipulative behavior   **2**:*401*
Sleator, William, *House of Stairs*   **5**:*156–62*
Smith, Bessie   **3**:*253 (illus.)*
Smith, Betty, *Tree Grows in Brooklyn, A*   **3**:*397–403*
Smith, Henry Nash   **3**:*226*
Smith, Joseph Jr.   **5**:*4*
Smoking. *See* Tobacco
So Far from the Bamboo Grove, Watkins, Yoko K.   **4**:*349–55*
Social Darwinism. *See under* Evolution
Social Security System   **3**:*128*
Socialism
  American, birth of   **3**:*174–75*
  labor unions accused of   **3**:*144*
  opposed by fascism   **4**:*66*
  popular among European immigrants   **3**:*321*
  utopian   **5**:*251–52*
Socrates   **1**:*240, 322–24, 327*
Solzhenitsyn, Alexander, *One Day in the Life of Ivan Denisovich*   **4**:*281–87*
Sons and Lovers, Lawrence, D. H.   **2**:*334–39*
  as example of bildungsroman   **3**:*264*
Sophists   **1**:*19, 240*

Sophocles, *Antigone*   **1**:*14–21*
Souls of Black Folk, The, Du Bois, W. E. B.   **2**:*340–46*; **3**:*320*
Sounder, Armstrong, William H.   **3**:*370–76*
South, The
  of 1980s   **3**:*78–79*
  anti-Yankee bias   **3**:*76*
  Christmas traditions   **3**:*69*
  folklore in   **2**:*48–49*
  homeopathy and Indian remedies   **3**:*68–69*
  hunting in   **2**:*47–48*
  Illinois' ties to   **2**:*8–9*
  industrialization/decline of agriculture and aristocracy   **3**:*76, 203*; **4**:*364–65, 368*; **5**:*91, 129–30*
  and "King" Cotton   **2**:*15, 22, 44 (illus.), 168, 403*
  mixed race offspring   **2**:*49*; **3**:*17–18, 81, 83*
  "New"   **3**:*72–73, 203*
  plantation life   **2**:*137–38*
  religious influences   **3**:*76–77*
  segregation in   **1**:*399*; **2**:*97*; **3**:*419*; **4**:*28–29, 373–74*; **5**:*22*
  social stratification in rural areas and small towns   **3**:*393*
  storytelling tradition   **3**:*421*
  textile mills and mill towns   **3**:*76, 153, 203–4*; **4**:*256*
  womanhood, ideal of   **3**:*19, 392–93*; **4**:*366–67*
  (*See also* Civil War; Jim Crow laws; Reconstruction)
South Africa, racism and apartheid   **1**:*63*; **3**:*86*; **4**:*94–100*
South America
  Argentina   **5**:*208–11, 212–13*
  Chile   **5**:*163–70*
  Colombia   **2**:*268–70, 272–73*
  Peru   **4**:*221, 222*; **5**:*333–38*
South Carolina   **5**:*285–86*
South Pacific
  climate   **4**:*231 (sidebar)*
  island fighting and major sea battles (1942–45)   **4**:*60–61*
  island peoples' origins   **4**:*221–22*
  Japanese conquests in WWII   **4**:*178*
  Philippines   **3**:*101*; **4**:*81*
Southey, Robert   **1**:*121*
Soviet Union
  anti-Semitism   **3**:*124–25*; **5**:*122*
  anti-Zionism   **4**:*107–8*
  atomic bomb capability   **4**:*183*; **5**:*96, 126*
  centralized planning and control of means of production   **5**:*124*
  de-Stalinization   **4**:*285–86*
  European conquests and sphere of influence   **5**:*123 (sidebar), 224, 253–54*
  Five-Year Plans and forced labor   **4**:*16, 132*
  forced collectivization of agriculture   **4**:*281–85*
  Gorbachev and "perestroika"   **5**:*8*
  gulag system of labor camp prisons   **4**:*282–85*; **5**:*239 (sidebar)*

invasion of Armenia   3:340
invasion of Poland   3:340; 4:131
propaganda   5:252
reprisals against Japanese in Korea and
   Manchuria   4:350
seen as "controlling" international communism
   4:166
Siberia   4:133–35
Sputniks and space program   5:81, 291, 292,
   293, 294, 321
Stalin/Hitler non-aggression pact (1939)   3:210,
   214; 4:17
Stalin's reign of terror and purges   4:16–17, 166
suppression of Hungarian uprising (1956)
   4:166
totalitarianism   4:16
Ukraine, Babi Yar massacre   4:120
(*See also* Russia)
Space Age
   Dillard's musings   5:279–80, 281 (*sidebar*)
   manned space flight highlights   5:294 (*sidebar*)
   moon landing   5:81–82
   NASA (National Aeronautics and Space
      Administration)   5:81, 291
   Right Stuff, The   5:291–97
   satellites for communications   5:54
   treaty prohibiting military use of space   5:239
   U.S.-Soviet competition in space race   5:53, 81,
      321–22
   (*See also* Aviation; War weaponry)
Spain
   Civil War   4:67
   decline of empire   1:1–3
   fascism in   1:293–94; 4:67
   Inquisition   1:2–3
   invasion of Italy   1:317
   wars with England and France   1:1–2, 87, 88,
      130–31, 201, 305
Spanish-American War (1898)   3:101, 278
Spark, Muriel, *Prime of Miss Jean Brodie, The*
   4:303–8
Sparta   1:324–25, 328
Speech on the Evacuation at Dunkirk, Churchill,
   Winston   4:356–63
Speeches
   "Ain't I a Woman?", Truth, Sojourner   2:22–27
   John Brown's Final Speech, Brown, John
      2:188–94
   First Inaugural Address, Roosevelt, Franklin D.
      3:125–30
   Gettysburg Address, Lincoln, Abraham   2:130–36
   "Give Me Liberty or Give Me Death", Henry,
      Patrick   1:122–28
   "I Have a Dream", King, Martin Luther, Jr.
      5:185–93
   "I Will Fight No More Forever", Joseph, Chief
      2:160–67
   Inaugural Address, Kennedy, John F.   5:222–28
   On the Evacuation at Dunkirk, Churchill,
      Winston   4:356–63

Spencer, Herbert   2:341
Spinsterhood, in early 19th-century England
   2:297
Spock, Benjamin   4:21–22
Sports. *See* Entertainment; Games and sports
Spreckels, Claus and sugar interests   3:269, 270
   (*sidebar*), 319
Sputnik   5:81, 291, 292, 293, 294, 321
Stalin, Josef
   banning books depicting life in West   5:96
   British outrage at   4:17
   Five-Year Plans for economic development
      4:16, 282
   forced collectivization of agriculture   4:281–82;
      5:122
   as Marxist Party member   4:14, 15 (*illus.*)
   non-aggression pact with Hitler   3:210, 213–14;
      4:17
   oppression or extermination of Jews   3:123–24
   political prisoners exiled to Siberian gulags
      4:282–85; 5:239 (*sidebar*)
   purges of opponents   4:16–17; 5:122, 254
   (*See also* Soviet Union)
Stanley, Henry Morton   2:146
Stanton, Elizabeth Cady   2:24, 55; 3:16
Steamships   1:404 (*sidebar*); 2:391, 394–95
Stein, Joseph, *Fiddler on the Roof*   3:119–24
Steinbeck, John
   Grapes of Wrath, The   3:138–45
   Of Mice and Men   3:269–76
   Red Pony, The   3:334–37
Stevenson, Robert Louis
   on *Pride and Prejudice*   2:300
   Strange Case of Dr. Jekyll and Mr. Hyde, The
      3:377–82
   on *Tess of the D'Urbervilles*   2:359
   Treasure Island   1:400–405
STFU (Southern Tenant Farmers' Union)   3:208
Stock market
   1929 crash and bank failures   3:125–26, 208
   speculation fever of 1920s   3:146
   speculations in trusts and railroads of 1900
      3:167 (*sidebar*)
   (*See also* Great Depression)
Stoicism   1:192–93
Stoneham, C. A.   3:149
Story Catcher, The, Sandoz, Mari   2:347–52
Stowe, Harriet Beecher
   relationship with Harriet Jacobs   2:172
   Uncle Tom's Cabin   2:403–9
Strachey, Lytton   3:356
Strange Case of Dr. Jekyll and Mr. Hyde, The,
   Stevenson, Robert Louis   3:377–82
Stranger in a Strange Land, Heinlein, Robert A.
   5:321–27
"Stream of consciousness" writing   3:111, 358
Streetcar Named Desire, A, Williams, Tennesse
   4:364–70
Streetcars   2:328; 3:25; 4:366
Stuyvesant, Peter   1:331

Styron, William, *Confessions of Nat Turner, The* 2:93–98
Submarines 2:385–86
Suburbia 4:73
Suez Canal 3:184; 4:107
Suffrage (right to vote)
  for African Americans 4:148
    granted by 14th and 15th Amendments 5:21
    Jim Crow laws restricting 3:37, 352, 419; 4:1; 5:22
    Mississippi Plan (1890) preventing 5:22
    protected by Civil Rights and Voting Rights Acts (1957 and 1965) 5:22, 186
  for American Indians 4:80
  expansion by elimination of property qualifications 2:302
  hindered for freed blacks 2:341
  Nationality Act (1940) 4:80
  for women. *See* Women's suffrage
Suicide
  by American Indians 4:83
  attempts by Shange 5:120
  effects of childhood abuse 5:288, 289–90
  of interned Japanese Americans 4:140
  of Japanese girls in Korea (1944–45) 4:350, 353
  of Jim Jones and 911 members of People's Temple 5:84
  by kamikazi pilots 4:61 (sidebar), 62 (illus.)
  in *Madame Bovary* 2:211–12
  by men 4:23, 114 (sidebar)
  of prep school students 4:74
  as response to depression 5:259–60
  of Sylvia Plath 4:22–26
  of teenagers 5:259–60, 261
  by Vietnam War veterans 5:106
  by white males 5:273
Sullivan, Joseph 3:149
Summer of My German Soldier, Greene, Bette 4:371–77
Sumner, William 3:207
Sun Yat-Sen, Dr. 4:126; 5:229
Supernatural
  alchemy 1:384, 385 (sidebar)
  astrology 1:346, 350
  belief in, by American Indians 4:83
  belief in *curanderismo* 4:45
  belief in, in China 3:133
  belief in, in Elizabethan/Jacobean era 1:194–95, 227–28, 262, 346, 350
  belief in, in Victorian England 1:418–19; 2:185, 383
  in *Beloved* 2:63
  in *Beowulf* 1:46–48, 49
  brujas (witches) 4:46
  dreams related to 1:424
  in *Hamlet* 1:138, 141, 142 (sidebar)
  in *The Hobbit* 1:153
  in *Julius Caesar* 1:195

  in *Legend of Sleepy Hollow, The* 1:213, 215, 217
  and "mysteriousness" of African and African American culture 5:330
  and mysticism 1:416
  and paranormal phenomena 2:383 (sidebar); 5:47–48, 56, 239
  in *Romeo and Juliet* 1:346, 350
  superstitions associated with Chinese New Year 5:75, 76 (illus.)
  in *Tempest, The* 1:381, 383
  in *Turn of the Screw, The* 2:381
  (*See also* Witchcraft)
Swarthout, Glendon, *Bless the Beasts and Children* 5:34–38
Sweden, immigration to U.S. 3:243–44, 259–60
Sweet Whispers, Brother Rush, Hamilton, Virginia 5:328–32
Swift, Jonathan
  criticism of *Robinson Crusoe* 1:343
  Gulliver's Travels 1:129–35
  Modest Proposal, A 1:266–72
Syncretism 3:190–91; 4:44 (sidebar)

T

Tahiti, 1:274, 278, 392
Taine, Hippolyte 3:213
Taiwan 3:190; 5:254
Tale of Two Cities, A, Dickens, Charles 1:371–78
Tammany Hall, New York 3:148–49, 398–99
Tan, Amy
  Joy Luck Club, The 5:229–35
  Kitchen God's Wife, The 3:189–95
Tasmania 3:406
Taverns 1:331
Taylor, Mildred, *Roll of Thunder, Hear My Cry* 3:350–55
Teapot Dome scandal 3:25
Technology. *See* Science/technology
Teilhard de Chardin, Pierre 5:93
Telecommunications 5:54
Telekinesis 5:47–48
Telepathy 5:239
Television
  as babysitter 5:36–37
  Bonanza creating sense of family security 5:203 (sidebar)
  debates costing Nixon 1960 presidential election 5:223
  development of 3:92; 5:96–97
  golden age of TV drama 4:379
  impact on conduct of Vietnam War and antiwar sentiment 5:37
  impact on public support for civil rights protesters 5:108
  interconnectedness versus loneliness of viewers 4:398
  spreading conformity 4:236
  violent content of programming 5:62

westerns **5**:*201–2*
(*See also* Media)
Television evangelists **5**:*31–32, 137–38, 140 (illus.)*
Temperance movement **2**:*25 (sidebar), 85–86;*
3:*69, 75, 147*
Tempest, The, Shakespeare, William **1**:*379–85*
Templars **1**:*182, 185 (sidebar)*
Tenant farming and sharecropping **2**:*42, 411;*
3:*80, 104, 105, 249, 350–51, 370–71, 418;* **4**:*2*
Terrorism
Arab against Israel **4**:*106*
by Argentine military junta **5**:*209–10, 212–13*
by Chilean military junta **5**:*169*
by Guatemalan military **5**:*28*
of Herut Party in Israel **4**:*107*
of Irgun in British Mandatory Palestine **4**:*103*
(*See also* Ku Klux Klan)
Tervalon, Jervey, *Understand This* **5**:*339–45*
Tess of the D'Urbervilles, Hardy, Thomas **2**:*353–59*
Theater
Chinese opera **5**:*75*
in early 1900s in America **3**:*220–21*
El Teatro Campesino **4**:*409;* **5**:*172*
Elizabethan **1**:*261–62, 263*
golden age of television drama **3**:*92;* **4**:*236,*
379
importance in ancient Greece **1**:*19–20, 240*
innovations of Wilder **3**:*287–88*
musicals **4**:*387*
in postmodern era **2**:*123*
realism in **1**:*92*
supported by James I **1**:*299*
Teatro Rodante Puertorriqueño **5**:*216*
and Theater of the Absurd **4**:*400*
(*See also* Plays)
Thebes (in ancient Greece) **1**:*14*
Their Eyes Were Watching God, Hurston, Zora Neale
3:*383–89*
Theseus **1**:*57, 61 (sidebar), 258, 259*
Things Fall Apart, Achebe, Chinua **2**:*360–65*
Thirty Years War **1**:*87, 88, 388 (sidebar), 388*
Thisbe **1**:*259 (sidebar)*
Thomas, Dylan, *Child's Christmas in Wales, A*
3:*63–67*
Thoreau, Henry David
Civil Disobedience **2**:*87–92*
influence on Dickinson **2**:*57*
influence on King **5**:*192*
on John Brown **2**:*193*
as transcendentalist **1**:*356;* **2**:*92, 416*
Walden **2**:*416–21*
Thornton, Laurence, *Imagining Argentina* **5**:*208–13*
Thousand Pieces of Gold, McCunn, Ruthanne Lum
2:*366–71*
Three Musketeers, The, Dumas, Alexandre
1:*386–92*
Thucydides **1**:*14*
Thurber, James, *Secret Life of Walter Mitty, The*
3:*364–69*
Tijerina, Lopez Reies **4**:*175, 176, 321*

Time of the Hero, The, Vargas Llosa, Mario
5:*333–38*
Titans **1**:*301*
Tituba (in real life) **1**:*79, 83 (sidebar), 394–96,*
422–23
Tituba of Salem Village, Petry, Ann **1**:*393–99*
To Kill a Mockingbird, Lee, Harper **3**:*390–96*
Tobacco
cigars **3**:*65*
rise during 1920s in popularity of smoking
3:*89*
snuff **3**:*71 (sidebar)*
for women **3**:*19, 23, 167, 168 (illus.)*
Tolkien, J.R.R., *Hobbit, The* **1**:*152–58*
Tolstoy, Leo
Anna Karenina **2**:*34–40*
on *Uncle Tom's Cabin* **2**:*409*
Tom Brown's Schooldays, Hughes, Thomas
2:*372–77*
Totalitarianism. *See* Dictatorship
Tournaments **1**:*291*
Towns and cities, growth of. *See* Urbanization
Transcendentalism **1**:*356–57;* **2**:*54, 92, 314,*
316–19, 416, 418–19
Transportation
Appalachian Trail **5**:*278–79*
automobiles **2**:*128 (sidebar);* **3**:*23, 77, 88–89,*
94, 101; **5**:*40 (illus.)*
aviation **3**:*211–12*
canals **2**:*230;* **3**:*184, 231–32, 270;* **4**:*107*
public, segregation of **5**:*88–90, 185–86*
roads and highways **3**:*77, 91*
Blue Ridge Parkway **5**:*278*
creating suburbs **5**:*262*
National System of Interstate and Defense
Highways (1956) **3**:*73*
Route 66 **3**:*140*
sled dogs **3**:*52–56*
streetcars **2**:*328;* **3**:*25;* **4**:*366*
(*See also* Railroads in U.S.)
Treasure Island, Stevenson, Robert Louis
1:*400–405*
Tree Grows in Brooklyn, A, Smith, Betty **3**:*397–403*
Trojan War **1**:*8, 14, 166–69, 281, 283 (sidebar)*
Trotsky, Leon **4**:*16;* **5**:*254*
Truman Doctrine (1947–49) **4**:*110;* **5**:*123–24*
Truman, Harry S **4**:*72, 173 (sidebar);* **5**:*96, 123*
Truth, Sojourner, "Ain't I a Woman?" **2**:*22–27*
Tubman, Harriet **2**:*189*
Turkey
Ali Pasha **2**:*101*
genocide of Armenians **3**:*338–43;* **4**:*199*
"guest" workers from, in Europe **4**:*163–64*
under Ottoman Turks **1**:*295–96;* **3**:*338–40*
WWI and British occupation of former holdings
4:*102*
and Young Turks **3**:*339, 340, 342*
Turn of the Screw, The, James, Henry **2**:*378–83*
Turner, Nat **2**:*93–94, 95, 169–70, 188*
(*See also Confessions of Nat Turner, The*)

Tuskegee Institute   **2**:*413, 414*

Twain, Mark
   Adventures of Huckleberry Finn, The   **2**:*15–21*
   Notorious Jumping Frog of Calaveras County, The
   2:*249–54*

Twelve Angry Men, Rose, Reginald (screenplay)
   4:*378–83*

Twenty-Thousand Leagues under the Sea, Verne, Jules
   2:*384–90*

Twinship   **4**:*219*

Two Years before the Mast, Dana, Richard Henry, Jr.
   2:*391–96*

Tyler, Wat (Peasant's Revolt of 1381)   **1**:*65*

U

UFOs (unidentified flying objects)   **4**:*347–48;* **5**:*59*
   (illus.)

Ukraine, Babi Yar massacre   **4**:*120*

Uncas   **1**:*207* (sidebar), *208*

Uncle Remus, Harris, Joel Chandler   **2**:*397–402*

Uncle Tom's Cabin, Stowe, Harriet Beecher   **2**:*403–9*
   aggravating North-South rift over slavery   **2**:*172*

Underground Railroad   **2**:*16, 60, 62, 189, 238,*
   406–7

Understand This, Tervalon, Jervey   **5**:*339–45*

UNIA (United Negro Improvement Association)
   3:*160;* **4**:*211*

Unions. *See* Labor unions

Unitarianism   **2**:*54, 315*

United Nations   **4**:*103, 107–8*
   birth of   **5**:*53–54*
   Cold War reflected in   **5**:*254*
   "Convention Relating to Status of Refugees"
      5:*28–29*
   and Declaration of Women's Rights (1967)
      5:*174*

United Service Organizations (USO)   **4**:*38*

United States in 19th century
   American Enlightenment   **2**:*416*
   American literature, birth of   **1**:*210, 211, 217,*
      218, 335–36; **2**:*419*
   American literature, maturation of   **2**:*109,*
      234–35
   appeal of European travel to middle- to upper-
      class Americans   **2**:*105–6*
   belief in progress   **2**:*195, 196, 313, 416*
   canal system   **2**:*230*
   conservatism and commerce   **2**:*199, 306, 312,*
      328, 331
   democracy, growth of   **2**:*87–88, 89–91*
   depressions in later years   **3**:*51, 169*
   dissent, protest, and civil disobedience   **2**:*87,*
      89, 90, 312
   economic growth   **2**:*195, 230, 416*
   Gilded Age   **2**:*20, 199, 306, 312, 328, 331*
   Jackson administration   **2**:*314–15*
   Mexican War   **2**:*88, 89, 242*
   rural New England   **2**:*125–26*
   War of 1812   **1**:*53;* **2**:*416*

whaling industry   **2**:*230, 232–34*
   (*See also* Civil War; Railroads in U.S.;
      Reconstruction; Slavery in America; West, The;
      Western migration)

United States in 20th century: Progressive Era
   (1900–1919)
   as era of reform   **3**:*75–76, 284–85*
   labor unions, support for   **3**:*420*
   muckraking journalists   **3**:*176, 320*
   multifaceted agenda of   **3**:*285, 319–20*
   postwar return to (probusiness) normalcy
      3:*21*
   reformers as elitist   **3**:*319*
   reforming zeal carried to other countries   **3**:*280*
   trust busters and Teddy Roosevelt   **3**:*167*
   women's roles changing   **3**:*271–72, 280*
      (sidebar)
   Woodrow Wilson   **3**:*279–80, 319*
   World War I (1917–18). *See* World War I

United States in 20th century: Roaring Twenties
   (1920–1929)
   assembly line/mass production   **3**:*89, 100–101,*
      102
   boomtowns   **3**:*25*
   buying on credit   **3**:*89*
   car culture   **3**:*23*
   consumer/mass culture, advertising   **3**:*26, 89,*
      100–101, 102
   gangsters and St. Valentine's Day Massacre
      3:*366–67*
   hard times for farmers   **3**:*94–95, 138–40*
   machine age as degrading individualism and
      culture   **5**:*41*
   modern morals and changing status of women
      3:*23, 228–29*
   postwar economic boom   **3**:*146*
   Prohibition. *See* Prohibition
   race riots (1919)   **2**:*6, 404;* **3**:*160, 252, 321;*
      4:*310*
   San Francisco's corruption   **3**:*226*
   stock market speculation fever   **3**:*146*
   Teapot Dome scandal   **3**:*25*
   and United Fruit Company in South America
      2:*269–70*

United States in 20th century: Thirties (1930–1940).
   See Great Depression, The

United States in 20th century: World War II
   (1941–45). *See* World War II

United States in 20th century: 1946–1959
   age of big government   **4**:*110*
   baby boom   **1**:*224;* **2**:*325–26;* **4**:*38, 74, 240*
   beatniks, counterculture, hippies, and protesters
      4:*75, 289, 293, 399–400*
   Cold War. *See* Cold War
   consumerism, credit buying, and conformity
      3:*2, 91;* **4**:*73–74, 110–11, 236, 328, 397–401;*
      5:*322–23*
   disillusion, dehumanization, and dystopian
      literature   **5**:*252*
   divorce rate increase   **4**:*38*

global commercial and cultural influence
1:223; 3:92

"heroes" as powerful and nonconformist   4:262,
292, 381–82

inflation and anxiety   4:109–10

mass culture and influence of television   4:111,
379, 398

postwar boom, prosperity   4:109–10, 328

teenage culture   4:391–93, 394–95

War Brides Act   4:124, 127; 5:231

white male economic dominance   4:397

women and cult of domesticity   4:237, 240–41

women as sex objects   4:393

United States in 20th century: 1960s
appeal of Eastern religions   5:237, 281

civil rights protests. *See* Civil rights movements

counterculture, hippies, and protesters   5:37,
64 (*sidebar*), 83, 158, 237, 272, 279, 308–10,
323–25

cults, iconoclasm, rebels as heros   5:83–84, 318
(*sidebar*), 323–24

decade of tumult   5:309 (*sidebar*)

environment, concern for   4:337–42; 5:85–86,
279

feminism. *See* Women's rights movement (and
feminism)

"free love" movement   5:272

"graying" of America   5:202–4

Johnson's Great Society and War on Poverty
3:324; 5:68, 150, 266

riots   2:97–98; 3:324; 4:207; 5:112 (*sidebar*),
340

self-fulfillment and human potential movement
5:204, 287–88

(*See also* Vietnam War)

United States in 20th century: 1970s–1980s
antibusing incidents   3:324

disillusion with government after Nixon and
Watergate   3:99; 5:158–59, 263, 317

environment, concern for   5:279 (*sidebar*)

feminism. *See* Women's rights movement (and
feminism)

judicial opposition to civil rights legislation
5:1–2

"me" generation and self-help movements
5:263, 287–88

official apology and monetary compensation to
Japanese Americans for WWII internment
4:143, 195

probusiness conservatism (Reagan presidency)
5:1

recession, unemployment, and welfare cuts
5:1, 329

rise of New Right and religious fundamentalists
5:136–39

sexual revolution   5:151

(*See also* Vietnam War)

U.S. Army. *See* Military

United States Military. *See* Military

U.S.S.R. *See* Soviet Union

Up From Slavery, Washington, Booker T.   2:410–15

Urbanization
in 19th-century America   2:125, 195, 301–4

of 19th-century England   1:106, 217, 417;
2:118, 353, 354, 358

in 19th-century France   2:103–4, 209

in 20th-century America   3:25, 73, 88–89;
4:171–72

in 20th-century South   5:91

in 20th-century South Africa   4:95

by American Indians in 20th century   4:186

in Chile   5:164

cities viewed as hotbeds of sin   3:69

of colonial America   1:102

department stores made possible by   2:303

with immigration   2:302, 327; 3:101, 102, 166

and Mexican Americans   4:171

promoting individualism   2:302

replacing rural, agrarian society   2:312, 327;
5:91

rise of crime and police detectives   2:153–54

(*See also* Ghettos; Housing)

USS *Somers*   1:56

Usury (moneylending)   1:103–4, 182–83, 243, 247

Utopian societies
depicted in literature   5:251–52

in novel *Looking Backward* (1888)   2:423

of 1840s   2:418

Shakers   3:95–99

Twin Oaks colony   5:279

Walden movement   5:279

V

Valdez, Luis   5:172
Zoot Suit   4:403–10

Van Dine, S. S.   3:227

Vargas Llosa, Mario   5:211 (*sidebar*)
Time of the Hero, The   5:333–38

Veblen, Thorstein   3:169

Venice, Italy   1:242–46, 295–97

Verne, Jules
Twenty-Thousand Leagues under the Sea
2:384–90

H. G. Wells compared to   3:410

Verona, Italy   1:344–45

Verrall, Richard   4:40

Vesey, Denmark   2:94–95

Veterinarians   3:1

Victor Emmanuel III, King of Italy   4:66, 67

Victoria, Queen of England   2:28, 335

Victorian Age
agricultural depression   2:353

charity   2:264

circuses and freak shows   2:33, 120, 329

class divisions and social stratification
2:152–53, 157, 358

crime in London   2:262–64

debt, bankruptcy, and poorhouses   2:211–12,
261–62, 266

divorce   2:158, 355–56
education, progress in   1:412; 2:334
England as world's leading economic power
   2:334
foreign competition and economic depression
   2:152
humor and puns   2:30
hypocrisy of   3:381
imperialism   2:118–19
landed gentry's decline   2:354–55
London as center of   1:417; 2:20, 196
love and marriage in   2:106, 116, 336
men's roles in   2:107–8, 336
mining industry   2:335
mourning traditions   1:414–15
police, reorganization of   2:153–54
pride plus anxiety   3:405–6, 408–9
public school system   2:372–77
science vs. religion   2:29–30; 3:404
sexual repression   2:334, 336, 338–39, 355;
   3:18, 380–81
urbanization with industrialization   1:417;
   2:118, 353, 354, 358
work ethic and circumscribed codes of
   behavior/decorum   2:20, 108, 196, 378–79;
   3:381
Yorkshire   1:417–18
(*See also* Colonialism, imperialism, and
   interventionism)
Victorian women
American stereotype of   2:107
divorce   2:158, 355–56
dowries for   2:246
education of   1:412; 2:30, 181–82, 422–23
emancipation of, opponents and proponents
   1:356; 3:167
employment
   denial of meaningful work   2:426, 427
   as governesses   2:182, 183 (sidebar), 378–80
   limited opportunities for   2:203, 355
   need to supplement husband's income
      3:168–69
   in prostitution   2:228, 264, 328–29, 355
evolution and the "Woman Question"
   2:423–24
fashion and home furnishings for status   2:246,
   247 (sidebar); 3:420
fashionable clothing as restricting   3:420
as "feminine"   2:204, 206–7
as "helpless"   3:19
as "hysterical"   2:425
ignorant preferred to educated, by men   2:380
as innocent and chaste   2:422–25
lack of rights   2:356
marriage and domestic roles for   2:106–7, 108,
   116, 202, 303, 336; 3:167
as "maternal"   2:212, 404
prejudice against as writers   1:415 (sidebar);
   2:56, 186, 203, 212, 424–25
shopping and department stores   2:303

social calls   3:321–23
as spinsters in England   2:297
supposed moral superiority of   2:106; 3:16, 18,
   167, 228
view of themselves as "interesting"   2:106
Vidocq, François-Eugène   3:226
Vietnam War
American Indian soldiers in   5:362–63
anti-Vietnam war movements   3:98, 324
arising from Cold War's "domino theory"
   4:347, 375; 5:101–2, 158
arising from French hopes to recolonize
   Indochina   5:306–7
atrocities, compared to those inflicted upon
   American Indians   2:79
black soldiers in   5:102–3
combat against jungle guerillas   5:103
draft of disadvantaged for (Project 100,000)
   5:102–3, 158, 307
fall of South Vietnam to communist North
   5:307
Johnson's escalation of involvement   5:158, 307
Kennedy's sending of "advisors"   5:158, 307
protested by
   antiwar forces in U.S.   2:13–14; 4:347;
      5:105–6, 158, 307–8
   blacks   4:207; 5:103 (sidebar)
   Chicanos   4:409–10
   students at Kent State University   5:158
   women and mothers   5:308
   young men subject to draft   5:307–8
   young people   5:271
return of POWs   4:376
seen as West's failure to contain communism
   4:135
U.S. forces withdrawn from   4:375–76
U.S. soldiers questioning purposes of   5:104–5
U.S. soldiers' reasons for enlisting   5:307
   (sidebar)
veterans' postwar experience   5:105–6
Vietnam Memorial   5:105 (illus.), 106, 312
as world's first "television" war   5:3–7, 37
Vigilantism
in frontier West   1:256–57; 2:323–24
in rural California   3:273–74
in San Francisco of 1850s   2:286–87
tarring and feathering by mobs   2:17 (sidebar)
(*See also* Ku Klux Klan; Lynching)
Vikings   1:49, 138, 226
Villa, Pancho (Doroteo Arango)   3:197, 279
Villarreal, José Antonio   5:172
   Pocho   4:295–302
Vindication of the Rights of Woman, A, Wollstonecraft,
   Mary   1:406–12; 2:297
Viracocha people   4:221, 222
Virgil
   Aeneid, The   1:8–13
   as character in Dante's *Inferno*   1:176–77,
      178–79
Virginia   1:379, 384, 394; 5:278–84

Voigt, Cynthia, *Runner, The*   **5**:*306–13*
Vonnegut, Kurt, Jr., *Slaughterhouse Five*   **4**:*343–48*

W

Walden, Thoreau, Henry David   **2**:*416–21*
Wales   **1**:*288*; **3**:*63–64, 66*
Walker, Alice, *Color Purple, The*   **3**:*80–87*
Walpole, Robert   **1**:*266, 269*
War
    and antiwar sentiment. *See* Antiwar literature
    Arab-Israeli Six-Day War (1967)   **4**:*93*
    Cold War   **1**:*84, 223, 388–89*
    England's civil war   **1**:*303, 305–6*
    England's wars with France   **1**:*51–52, 93, 123,*
      130–31, 159, 160, 204–6, 220–21, 305
    England's wars with Spain   **1**:*1–2, 87, 88,*
      130–31, 201, 306
    French and Indian War (Seven Years' War)
      1:*93, 123, 204–6, 220–21*
    glorification vs. reality of battle   **2**:*257, 258,*
      308, 309 (sidebar), 312, 313; **3**:*9–11, 12–13;*
      4:*69–70*
    Korean   **1**:*223*; **3**:*73*; **4**:*92*
    Mexican   **2**:*88, 89, 242*; **5**:*172*
    Napoleonic   **2**:*99–100, 295–96*
    Peloponnesian   **1**:*241, 324, 328*
    Revolutions of 1848   **1**:*376*
    Russo-Turkish   **2**:*37–39*
    Spanish-American (1898)   **3**:*101, 278*
    Thirty Years   **1**:*87, 88, 388 (sidebar), 388*
    Trojan   **1**:*8, 14, 166–69, 281 (illus.), 281, 283*
      (sidebar)
    Vietnam. *See* Vietnam War
    War of 1812   **1**:*53*; **2**:*416*
    (*See also* American Revolution; Antiwar literature;
      Civil War; France in 18th century: French
      Revolution; Military; World War I; World War
      II)
War on Poverty   **3**:*324*; **5**:*68, 150, 266*
War weaponry
    aircraft
      bombers   **4**:*67–68*
      dive-bombers   **4**:*359*
      fighter bombers   **4**:*67*
      fighters   **4**:*361*
      helicopters   **4**:*71*
      jets   **4**:*71*
    aircraft carriers   **4**:*59*
    atomic/nuclear   **4**:*71*
      arms control proposals   **4**:*71*; **5**:*126, 225,*
        239, 252 (sidebar)
      hydrogen bomb   **4**:*183*; **5**:*126*
      Manhattan Project   **4**:*71, 81–82, 316*
      missiles   **5**:*124*
      (*See also* Atom bomb)
    barbed wire used as   **3**:*113*
    in *Beowulf*   **1**:*46 (illus.)*
    field artillery   **3**:*113*
    incendiary bombs   **4**:*179*

    landing craft   **4**:*60*
    machine gun   **3**:*9, 113*
    minesweepers   **4**:*61*
    rockets   **5**:*54, 96*
    submarines   **1**:*277–78*
    technological enhancements during WWI
      3:*113*
    technology causing anxiety   **3**:*406*; **4**:*255*
War of the Worlds, The, Wells, H.G.   **3**:*404–10*
    Orson Welles' October 1938 broadcast of
      3:*154, 365, 408 (sidebar)*
Warren, Mary   **1**:*81 (sidebar), 83 (sidebar)*
Washington, Booker T.
    advocating (temporary) acceptance of segregation
      2:*341, 342, 343, 344, 345, 410, 413, 414*; **3**:*162,*
      250, 320, 385
    autobiography: *Up From Slavery*   **2**:*410–15*
    compared to Du Bois   **2**:*345 (sidebar)*; **3**:*162,*
      250, 320, 385
Waste Land, The, Eliot, T.S.   **3**:*357, 411–17*
Watergate scandal   **3**:*99*; **5**:*158–59, 263, 317*
Watership Down, Adams, Richard   **5**:*346–51*
Watkins, Yoko K., *So Far from the Bamboo Grove*
    4:*349–55*
Watson, John Boradus   **5**:*45*
Weaver, George "Buck"   **3**:*149*
Weizmann, Chaim   **4**:*102, 103*
Weld, Theodore D.   **2**:*242*
Welles, Orson   **3**:*365, 408*
Wells Fargo   **2**:*293*
Wells, H. G.
    influenced by science and Darwinism   **3**:*404–5*
    on *Portrait of the Artist as a Young Man*   **3**:*309*
      (sidebar), 311
    rejection of Christianity   **3**:*404*
    War of the Worlds, The   **3**:*404–10*
Wells-Barnett, Ida B.   **3**:*83, 420*
Welty, Eudora, *Worn Path, A*   **3**:*418–24*
West, The
    California gold rush   **2**:*174–75, 195, 249–50,*
      281–84
    Chinese prostitutes   **2**:*366–67*
    gunfighters   **2**:*323–24*
    homesteaders   **2**:*127 (sidebar), 128, 322–23;*
      3:*244, 257, 259, 260–61*
    humor, practical jokes, and tall tales   **2**:*250–51*
    Nebraska   **3**:*257–58, 260*
    racism against Chinese   **2**:*175, 287, 367–68,*
      370 (sidebar), 371
    ranching and cattle barons on Great Plains
      2:*321–22*
    Teddy Roosevelt popularizing "Old West" myth
      of individualism   **5**:*206*
    settling and demise of frontier   **2**:*312*
    Wells Fargo   **2**:*293*
    women on frontier   **2**:*323*
West Side Story, Laurents, Arthur, *et al.*   **4**:*384–90*
Western migration
    beginning in colonial times   **1**:*102, 103, 107*
    California gold rush   **2**:*174–75, 195, 249–50*

Donner Party   2:282 (*sidebar*)
encouraged by Homestead Act (1870)
   2:322–23; 3:244, 257
encouraged by U.S. gov't.   2:314
end of western frontier   2:68
hardship and survivalism   3:259–60
increasing job opportunities for women in East
   2:423
land speculators   3:258
and Manifest Destiny   2:76 (*sidebar*); 3:234
and Mexican War   2:88, 395
to Nebraska   3:257–58
Nevada silver strikes   2:288–89, 290 (*sidebar*)
pressures upon American Indians   2:67, 74
railroads   2:175, 195
single women absent from   2:56, 250
(*See also* Gold rushes and silver strikes)
Weston, Jessie L.   3:415
Wet-nurses   2:211
Whaling industry   2:230, 232–34
Wharton, Edith
   Ethan Frome   2:125–29
   House of Mirth, The   3:166–73
Where Are You Going, Where Have You Been?, Oates,
   Joyce Carol   4:391–96
"White man's burden" and white supremacy
   2:119, 147, 341; 3:170, 172, 182 (*sidebar*)
Whitman, Walt
   on imperialism   3:300 (*sidebar*)
   Leaves of Grass   2:195–201
Whyte, William   4:75, 382
Wiesel, Elie
   Dawn   4:101–8
   Night   4:267–73
Wiesenthal, Simon   4:273
Wight, James Alfred. *See* Herriott, James
Wilder, Thornton, *Our Town*   3:284–89
Wilhelm II, Kaiser (Germany)   3:8
Wilkins, Roy   5:186, 188
William the Conqueror   1:250, 290
William of Orange   1:130
Williams, Claude "Lefty"   3:149; 4:260, 261; 5:316
Williams, Paulette Linda. *See* Shange, Ntozake
Williams, Tennesse, *Streetcar Named Desire, A*
   4:364–70
Williamson, Joel   3:387
Wilson, August, *Fences*   4:144–50
Wilson, Edmund
   praise for *Animal Farm*   4:19–20
   praise for *The Waste Land*   3:417
Wilson, Woodrow   3:279–80, 319
Winthrop, Gov. John   1:78, 352 (*sidebar*)
Witchcraft
   belief in, in medieval Scotland   1:227–28
   belief in, by Latinos (*brujas*)   4:46
   belief in, by Puritans   1:79–81, 102, 393, 394
   in *The Crucible*   1:78–86
   in *The Devil and Tom Walker*   1:101–6
   interest of James I in   1:228
   in *Macbeth*   1:227–28

spectral evidence of   1:421–22
   in *Tituba of Salem Village*   1:394–97
   witch trials   1:79, 83, 85 (*illus.*), 355, 395–96,
      397 (*illus.*), 423 (*illus.*)
   in *Young Goodman Brown*   1:420–26
   (*See also* Supernatural)
Wolfe, Tom, *Right Stuff, The*   5:291–97
Wollstonecraft, Mary
   as first English feminist   3:359
   mother of Mary Shelley   1:115, 116, 407
   similarities to, in Elizabeth Bennet   2:297
   tribute by William Blake   1:410 (*sidebar*)
   Vindication of the Rights of Woman, A   1:406–12
Woman Warrior, The, Kingston, Maxine Hong
   5:352–59
Women, (*See also* Education of women; Love and
   marriage)
Women in ancient times
   as "Great Goddesses" and Amazons   1:58–59,
      61–62, 258, 259–60
   in Greece   1:17, 20, 58–59, 259, 327
   names in Rome   1:190 (*sidebar*)
   Plato on leadership roles for   1:325, 327
   as rulers in Celtic England   1:197
   as spoils of war   1:8, 169, 170–71
Women in medieval times
   as depicted by Chaucer   1:69
   in Scotland   1:226
Women in 15th century, in salons of Paris   1:31,
   88–89
Women in 16th century
   prejudice against, as leaders   1:236
   in Tudor and Elizabethan England   1:232–33,
      236, 263–64
Women in 17th century, targeted in witchhunts
   1:80
Women in 18th century
   on colonial farms   1:334
   defiance of convention   1:406, 407, 409
   urging education and rights for   1:406, 408–11
   as wet-nurses   2:211
Women in 19th century
   American Southern ideal of, 2.138, 3.19m
      3:392–93
   Chinese   2:366–67, 368 (*sidebar*), 370–71
   in France   2:212, 244, 247
   involvement in abolition of slavery   2:23–24
   involvement in reform movements   2:423
   isolation of farms and homesteads   2:127
      (*sidebar*), 128; 3:259, 260–61
   in prostitution   2:228, 264, 283–84, 328–29,
      355; 4:37
   teaching freed slaves   2:411–12
   as wet-nurses   2:211
   (*See also* Victorian women)
Women in 20th century
   Chinese   3:132–33, 134–35, 191–93; 4:128
   dangers of childbirth   3:285–86
   as domestic, passive, and "feminine"   1:33–34,
      35–36; 2:326; 4:22, 74, 167, 237, 240–41

emancipation of
    negative portrayals in detective fiction of
        1920s   3:228–29
    new freedoms of 1920s   3:147
    opponents and proponents   3:167
    single mothers of 1950s as "irrational"
        4:169 (sidebar)
employment for   2:326; 3:271; 5:138
    as chorus girls   2:329
    as midwives   4:218
    as repugnant to Religious Right   5:137
    in wartime and afterwards   4:21–22, 74,
        166–67, 196 (illus.), 197–98
fashions for. See Fashions
importance of marriage   3:168
Jewish   3:427–30
in Maoist thought   3:136
Mexican   3:197–98, 200–202
participation in Progressive Era's reform
    movements   3:75, 76
protesting Vietnam War   5:308
rural life
    isolation of   3:271
    for sharecropper families   3:370–71
    on Texas frontier   3:246
as sexual goddesses, sex objects   4:74, 393
as single heads of households   2:65; 3:80, 423;
    4:2; 5:68, 117, 136, 138, 267, 328–29
subject to sexual double standard   4:38, 74, 395
and suicide   4:22–26
(See also African American women)
Women's rights movement (and feminism)
    abortion and Roe v. Wade   5:51, 136
    advocating self-determination   5:138–39
    antifeminist backlash   5:136
    authors active in
        Gilman   2:424
        Le Guin's take on   5:237–38
        Morrison   2:64
        Renault's sympathy with   1:62
        Woolf   3:330–32
    battered wives shelters   5:136
    and black feminism   2:64; 3:86–87, 354–55;
        5:92–93, 117
    in Britain   3:359
    Chicana women's movement   3:202
    in czarist Russia   2:37, 39
    educated women at core of   5:135
    hiatus between 1918 and 1960s   5:135–36
    legislation affecting
        Civil Rights Act (1964), Title VII   1:35;
            5:136
        Equal Pay Act (1963)   1:35; 5:237
        Equal Rights Amendment (ERA)   3:79; 5:51
            (illus.), 136, 358–59
        Higher Education Act (1972), Title IX
            5:136
    in Mexico   3:201–2
    National Organization of Women (NOW)
        1:62; 4:22, 394; 5:136, 237
    in Norway   2:112–13
    origins in
        19th century   2:22, 24, 25, 27, 55, 204, 423;
            3:16
        abolitionist movement   2:24, 204
        civil rights movement of 20th century   1:35;
            2:58
        discontent of women in 1950s   4:167–70;
            5:136
        EEOC's refusal to enforce Title VII   5:237
        Friedan's Feminine Mystique   1:62; 2:58;
            3:430; 4:11 (sidebar), 167, 241, 394; 5: 136
        gender discrimination in workplace   1:35;
            5:136
        myths of women's selfless inclination to serve
            and nurture   5:136, 288
        objections to sexual double standard   4:38,
            74, 395
        oppression and discrimination   2:23–24,
            355–56, 380, 422, 423–26
        sexual harassment in workplace   1:35
        women's subordination to men   4:169,
            170
    rape crisis centers   5:136
    role of women's clubs   2:336; 3:16–17, 287
        (sidebar)
    in Victorian England   2:335
    women's studies programs resulting   5:117
Women's rights and roles, discussion pertaining to
    Antigone   1:14–21
    Canterbury Tales, The   1:68–69
    Ethan Frome   2:126–27, 128–29
    Left Hand of Darkness, The   5:237–38, 239–40,
        242
    Lottery, The   4:237
    Macbeth   1:226
    Maltese Falcon, The   3:228–29
    Midsummer Night's Dream, A   1:259–60, 261–64
    Noon Wine   3:246–47
    Odyssey   1:282, 285
    Of Mice and Men   3:271–72
    Passage to India, A   3:301–2
    Sweet Whispers, Brother Rush   5:329
    Turn of the Screw, The   2:378–83
    Worn Path, A   3:420–21
Women's rights and roles, literary works
emphasizing
    "Ain't I a Woman?"   2:22–27
    Anna Karenina   2:34–40
    Awakening, The   3:15–20
    Beauty: A Retelling of the Story of Beauty and the
        Beast   1:30–36
    Bell Jar, The   4:21–27
    Belle of Amherst, The   2:54–58
    Beloved   2:59–65
    Bluest Eye, The   4:49–57
    Carrie   5:46–52
    Color Purple, The   3:80–87
    Daisy Miller   2:105–10
    Doll's House, A   2:111–17

*For Colored Girls Who Have Considered Suicide
   When the Rainbow Is Enuf*   **5:**115–21
Golden Notebook, The   **4:**165–70
Gone with the Wind   **2:**137–44
Handmaid's Tale, The   **5:**135–42
House of Mirth, The   **3:**166–73
House of the Spirits, The   **5:**163–70
House on Mango Street, The   **5:**171–77
I Know Why the Caged Bird Sings   **4:**201–8
Incidents in the Life of a Slave Girl   **2:**168–73
Jacob Have I Loved   **4:**216–20
Jane Eyre   **1:**415; **2:**181–87
Joy Luck Club, The   **5:**229–35
Kitchen God's Wife, The   **3:**189–95
Like Water for Chocolate   **3:**196–202
Little Women   **2:**202–8
Madame Bovary   **2:**209–15
Medea   **1:**238–41
Member of the Wedding, The   **4:**254–59
O Pioneers!   **3:**257–63
Out of Africa   **3:**290–96
Pride and Prejudice   **2:**295–300
Prime of Miss Jean Brodie, The   **4:**303–8
Pygmalion   **3:**312–18
Rebecca   **3:**326–33
Room of One's Own, A   **3:**356–63
Scarlet Letter, The   **1:**351–57
Seventeen Syllables   **4:**330–36
Sister Carrie   **2:**327–33
Streetcar Named Desire, A   **4:**364–70
Sweet Whispers, Brother Rush (portions of)
   5:329
Tess of the D'Urbervilles   **2:**353–59
Their Eyes Were Watching God   **3:**383–89
Thousand Pieces of Gold   **2:**366–71
Turn of the Screw, The   **2:**378–83
Vindication of the Rights of Woman, A   **1:**406–12;
   2:297
Where Are You Going, Where Have You Been?
   4:391–96
Woman Warrior, The   **5:**352–59
Wuthering Heights   **1:**413–19
Yellow Raft in Blue Water, A   **5:**360–66
Yellow Wallpaper, The   **2:**422–28
Yentl, the Yeshiva Boy   **3:**425–31
Women's suffrage
   achieved in 1919 and 1930 in Britain   **3:**359
   achieved in 1920 in U.S.   **3:**76, 287
   agitation for change   **2:**335–36; **3:**16
   in California by 1911   **3:**271
   in Chile in 1952   **5:**167
   defeated in many states of U.S.   **3:**286–87
   denounced in Victorian Age   **2:**335
   expanding by 1890   **2:**424
   in Kansas (1861), although limited   **2:**424
   ratification denied in Alabama   **3:**392
   in Wyoming in 1869   **2:**323
Woodstock Music and Art Fair (1969)   **5:**65
   (illus.), 324
Woolf, Virginia   **5:**42

Room of One's Own, A   **3:**356–63
Wordsworth, William   **1:**416
World War I
   Africa, impact on   **3:**292–93
   ambulance service   **3:**114
   British occupation of former Ottoman Empire
      4:102
   casualties of   **3:**11 (sidebar)
   causes and outbreak   **1:**157–58; **3:**8–9, 112–13,
      411
   Italy's role in   **3:**113–14
   losses, destruction   **1:**157–58; **3:**11 (sidebar),
      411–12
   "lost generation"   **3:**13, 112, 116–17
   navies' roles in   **1:**277–78
   older generations supporting   **3:**9–11, 12–13
   Ottoman slaughter of Armenians   **3:**339–40
   postwar issues
      disillusionment and despair   **3:**227, 412
      German reparations, inflation, and
         unemployment   **4:**157
      global expansion   **1:**223; **3:**21, 88
   proving H. G. Wells's fiction as prophetic   **3:**406
   racial issues
      African Americans as employees and soldiers
         3:160, 252; **4:**144, 145, 212–13
      segregation of U.S. military   **4:**212–13
   reasons for joining   **1:**278
   Russian defeats, civil war, revolution (1917)
      3:232–33
   sacrifices on German home front   **3:**11
   technological enhancements of weaponry   **3:**113
   Treaty of Berlin (1921)   **3:**88
   trench warfare   **3:**9, 113, 115 (sidebar)
World War II
   American mobilization for   **2:**45; **3:**424; **4:**325
   America's prewar isolationism   **4:**323, 362
   aviation
      bomber crews   **4:**68–70
      Lindbergh's contributions to   **3:**367
   causes of   **1:**113–14; **4:**157, 356–57
   chronology
      Nazi precursor conquests in Europe
         (1935–366)   **1:**113–14; **3:**213, 214; **4:**357
      British "appeasements" of Hitler (1936–39)
         4:356, 357, 362
      Rome-Berlin Axis (1936)   **4:**67
      Stalin/Hitler nonaggression pact (1939)
         3:210, 214; **4:**357
      Poland partitioned by Germany and Soviet
         Union (1939)   **4:**131
      France and England declare war on Germany
         (1939)   **3:**214
      French unpreparedness (1939)   **3:**213–14
      Tripartite Pact (Japan, Germany, Italy; 1940)
         4:59
      standoff at Maginot Line   **4:**357
      "blitzkrieg"; Germany invades Belgium,
         Luxembourg, and France   **4:**254–55, 357,
         359

first American peacetime draft (1940) **4**:*35, 324–25*

Italy helps Nazis (1940)   **4**:*67*

German occupation of Holland (1940) **4**:*116–19*

Dunkirk, evacuation of (May 1940)   **4**:*356, 359–63*

German invasion of Russia, (1941)   **3**:*124;* **4**:*131*

Pearl Harbor (1941)   **4**:*59, 178, 323*

Lend-Lease (1941–45)   **4**:*228–29, 363*

Pacific theater (1942–45)   **4**:*60–61, 80–81, 178*

Philippines' Bataan Death March   **4**:*81*

Aleutian islands, battles for (1942–43) **4**:*254*

Allies establish North African base (1942–44) **3**:*214*

emergence of De Gaulle (1943)   **3**:*214*

Allied invasion of Sicily (1943)   **4**:*67*

Italy declares war on Germany (1943)   **4**:*67*

kamikazi missions (1944)   **4**:*61 (sidebar), 62 (illus.)*

liberation of France (1944)   **3**:*214*

Battle of the Bulge (Dec. '44)   **4**:*343*

Yalta Conference (Feb. '45)   **4**:*344*

Dresden, firebombing by Allies (Feb. '45) **4**:*343–44*

founding of United Nations   **5**:*54*

atomic bombing of Japan (Aug. '45) **4**:*178–82, 180 (illus.), 181 (sidebar)*

Nuremberg war crimes trials of former Nazis **4**:*272–73*

conquests by dictatorships   **5**:*123 (sidebar), 224, 253–54*

on home front

for American South, industrialization and economic recovery from Depression   **2**:*53;* **3**:*72–73*

cynicism and opportunism   **4**:*371*

families of servicemen   **4**:*317–18*

German prisoners of war   **4**:*371–73*

intergenerational conflict   **4**:*327*

media's partiotic emphasis on war issues **4**:*371*

persecution and internment of Japanese Americans (1942–44)   **4**:*137–43, 194–95, 335–36*

race riots of 1940s   **4**:*197, 201, 213, 247, 248 (illus.), 295–97, 403–10*

racism   **4**:*199, 200*

rationing and inflation   **3**:*424;* **5**:*256–57*

women at work   **4**:*21–22, 74, 166–67, 196 (illus.), 197–98*

importance of Churchill's rhetoric and determination   **4**:*361–62*

Palestine   **4**:*102–5*

postwar issues

baby boom   **1**:*224;* **2**:*325–26;* **4**:*38, 74, 240*

Britain   **4**:*229, 231;* **5**:*256–57*

emphasis on home and materialism **2**:*325–26*

Marshall Plan   **5**:*123–24, 224, 292* (*See also* Cold War)

psychological casualties and postcombat syndrome   **4**:*80 (sidebar), 325*

racial issues

African Americans as employees and soldiers **3**:*424*

American Indians in   **4**:*80–81*

Chicano rights movement watershed   **4**:*44*

Latinos in   **4**:*295, 406*

segregation of U.S. military   **3**:*41–42;* **4**:*195, 197, 374 (sidebar)*

(*See also* Holocaust)

reservists and regulars   **4**:*63 (sidebar)* (*See also* Nazis)

Worn Path, A, Welty, Eudora   **3**:*418–24*

Wouk, Herman, *Caine Mutiny, The*   **4**:*58–65*

WPA (Works Progress Administration)   **3**:*128, 391, 423–24;* **4**:*44*

Wright, Richard

Almos' a Man   **4**:*1–6*

on anti-Semitism of his youth   **4**:*376*

Black Boy   **3**:*36–43*

as critic of Hurston   **3**:*385, 389*

Native Son   **3**:*236–42*

on *The Heart Is a Lonely Hunter*   **3**:*157*

Wuthering Heights, Brontë, Emily   **1**:*413–19*

Wyoming, women's suffrage in 1869   **2**:*323*

X

X, Malcolm   **2**:*98;* **3**:*324–25;* **4**:*54, 249–50;* **5**:*69–70, 111*

with Alex Haley, *Autobiography of Malcolm X, The* **5**:*11–18*

Y

Yamamoto, Hisaye, *Seventeen Syllables*   **4**:*330–36*

Yankees   **1**:*217, 332, 334, 335;* **2**:*8–9, 137*

Yeager, Chuck   **5**:*293*

Yellow Raft in Blue Water, A, Dorris, Michael **5**:*360–66*

Yellow Wallpaper, The, Gilman, Charlotte Perkins **2**:*422–28*

Yentl, the Yeshiva Boy, Singer, Isaac Bashevis **3**:*425–31*

Yorkshire, England   **1**:*417–18;* **3**:*1–3, 5–6*

Young Goodman Brown, Hawthorne, Nathaniel **1**:*420–26*

Young Turks   **3**:*339, 340, 342*

Youth

adolescence in hiding from Holocaust   **4**:*121–22*

antiestablishment rebellion   **5**:*272*

and dance   **4**:*387*

distinctive *pachuco* culture of 1950s   **4**:*173, 296*

distinctive teenage culture of 1950s   **4**:*172, 391–93, 394–95*

facing conflict and violence   5:268–69
gang membership   4:251, 386, 387–89; 5:216
gang truce in Los Angeles   5:341
and generation gap   4:386, 394; 5:198
juvenile delinquency   4:251, 386, 387–89; 5:37
literature for adolescents, as genre   5:61–62,
    265–66, 268–70
moral laxity of war years   4:37
peer pressure and negativity   5:65–66, 71–72,
    217
protesting against Vietnam War   5:271
psychotherapy for   5:260–61
students' free speech movement   5:311
suicide by teenagers   5:259–60, 261
television as babysitter   5:36–37
television as too violent   5:62

Yukon territory and Klondike River   3:52–56, 261
    (sidebar)

Z

Zapata, Emiliano   3:197, 198 (illus.)
Zen Buddhism   4:334
Zeus   1:9, 59, 61, 170, 282, 283, 301
Zindel, Paul, *Pigman, The*   5:271–77
Zionism   3:121; 4:88, 101–2
    and Arabic anti-Zionism   4:107
    and Soviet anti-Zionism   4:107–8
Zoo Story, The, Albee, Edward   4:397–402
Zoot Suit, Valdez, Luis   4:403–10
Zundel, Ernst   4:40